United Nations Legislative Series

NATIONAL LEGISLATION AND TREATIES RELATING TO THE LAW OF THE SEA

Série législative des Nations Unies

LÉGISLATION NATIONALE ET TRAITÉS CONCERNANT LE DROIT DE LA MER

UNITED NATIONS   New York, 1976   NATIONS UNIES

ST/LEG/SER.B/18

UNITED NATIONS PUBLICATION

Sales No. E/F.76.V.2

Price: $ U.S. 20.00
(or equivalent in other currencies)

PUBLICATION DES NATIONS UNIES

Numéro de vente : E/F.76.V.2

Prix : $ E.-U. 20,00
(ou l'équivalent en monnaie du pays)

GENERAL TABLE OF CONTENTS

TABLE DES MATIERES GENERALE

INTRODUCTION

In two notes dated 8 March 1973 and 29 May 1974, the Secretary-General requested Governments to provide the texts of legislation or treaties recently adopted or concluded, so as to bring up to date the information previously transmitted and contained in the volumes on the law of the sea printed in the *United Nations Legislative Series*[1]. This was done in order to provide as complete and up-to-date information as possible for the participants in the Third United Nations Conference on the Law of the Sea.

The present volume contains the texts received from Governments in reply to the above-mentioned notes from the Secretary-General. While the notes anticipated that the texts would, in general, be those adopted since 1972, it was stated that texts of an earlier date might also be supplied if they had not been included in earlier volumes in the *Legislative Series*. The present volume also contains relevant material transmitted, without reference to the Secretary-General's notes, by several Governments requesting that it be circulated.[2]

The present volume, like the 1974 volume,[3] is arranged in two parts. Part One reproduces the texts of national legislation and other acts of national regulation. Part Two comprises treaty provisions. Each Part is divided into four Divisions, as follows:

Division I. The territorial Sea and the Contiguous Zone;
Division II. The Continental Shelf;

---

[1] The volumes previously published are as follows:
(a) *Laws and Regulations on the Régime of the High Seas,* Volume I (Continental Shelf, Contiguous Zones, Supervision of Foreign Vessels on the High Seas) (ST/LEG/SER.B/1, United Nations publication, Sales No. 1951.V.2);
(b) *Laws and Regulations on the Régime of the High Seas,* Volume II (Laws relating to Jurisdiction over Crimes Committed Abroad or on the High Seas) (ST/LEG/SER.B/2, United Nations publication, Sales No. 1952.V.1);
(c) *Laws concerning the Nationality of Ships* (ST/LEG/SER.B/5 and Add.1, United Nations publications, Sales No. 1956.V.1);
(d) *Laws and Regulations on the Régime of the Territorial Sea* (ST/LEG/SER.B/6, United Nations publication, Sales No. 1957.V.2);
(e) *Supplement to Laws and Regulations on the Régime of the High Seas* (volumes I and II) and *Laws concerning the Nationality of Ships* (ST/LEG/SER.B/8, United Nations publication, Sales No. 59.V.2);
(f) *National Legislation and Treaties relating to the Territorial Sea, the Contiguous Zone, the Continental Shelf, the High Seas and to Fishing and Conservation of the Living Resources of the Sea* (ST/LEG/SER.B/15, United Nations publication, Sales No. E/F.70.V.9); and
(g) *National Legislation and Treaties relating to the Law of the Sea* (ST/LEG/SER.B/16, United Nations publication, Sales No. E/F.74.V.2).

[2] It should be noted that most of the texts received from Governments printed in the present volume were contained in preliminary issues of the volume circulated in 1974 and 1975, in mimeograph form, for the convenience of participants in the Third United Nations Conference on the Law of the Sea.

[3] See *supra* p. vii, note 1 *(g)*.

Division III.   The High Seas;

Division IV.   Fishing and Conservation of the Living Resources of the Sea.

The material contained in Part One, Division I, is further divided into subdivisions and chapters. In Part One the texts are arranged as far as possible chronologically under the name of the State concerned; the texts of laws and similar enactments normally precede the texts of decrees and regulations. The names of the States are given in English and follow the English alphabetical order. In Part Two a distinction is made between multilateral and bilateral treaties which are arranged separately in chronological order in each Division. It should be noted that the inclusion of a particular treaty in the present volume does not necessarily mean that the treaty in question is in force at the time of editing. For treaties in force, information is provided, as available, as to their publication in the *United Nations Treaty Series,* or registration with the Secretariat.

Charts and maps are not reproduced for technical reasons.

In accordance with the practice followed in the *United Nations Legislative Series,* texts received in English or French are given in the original language. Texts received in other languages are given in English. A footnote to the title of the text indicates when the text reproduced is a translation made by the Secretariat of the United Nations.

INTRODUCTION

Par deux notes en date du 8 mars 1973 et du 29 mai 1974, le Secrétaire général a prié les gouvernements de lui faire parvenir le texte des dispositions législatives qu'ils avaient adoptées ou des traités qu'ils avaient conclus récemment afin de mettre à jour les renseignements communiqués antérieurement et contenus dans les volumes de la *Série législative des Nations Unies* relatifs au droit de la mer[1]. Cette demande a été formulée en vue de mettre à

---

[1] Les volumes déjà publiés sont les suivants :

a) Laws and Regulations on the Régime of the High Seas, vol. I (Plateau continental, zones contiguës, surveillance des navires étrangers en haute mer) [ST/LEG/SER.B/1, publication des Nations Unies, numéro de vente : 1951.V.2];

b) Laws and Regulations on the Régime of the High Seas, vol. II (Lois relatives à la compétence juridictionnelle en matière d'infractions pénales commises à l'étranger ou en haute mer) [ST/LEG/SER.B/2, publication des Nations Unies, numéro de vente : 1952.V.1];

c) Laws concerning the Nationality of Ships (ST/LEG/SER.B/5 and Add.1, publication des Nations Unies, numéro de vente : 1957.V.1);

d) Laws and Regulations on the Régime of the Territorial Sea (ST/LEG/SER.B/6, publication des Nations Unies, numéro de vente : 1957.V.2);

e) Supplement to Laws and Regulations on the Régime of the High Seas (vol. I et II) et *Laws concerning the Nationality of Ships* (ST/LEG/SER.B/8, publication des Nations Unies, numéro de vente : 59.V.2);

f) National Legislation and Treaties relating to the Territorial Sea, the Contiguous Zone, the Continental Shelf, the High Seas and to Fishing and Conservation of the Living Resources of the Sea (ST/LEG/SER.B/15, publication des Nations Unies, numéro de vente : E/F.70.V.9); et

g) National Legislation and Treaties relating to the Law of the Sea (ST/LEG/SER.B/16, publication des Nations Unies, numéro de vente : E/F.74.V.2).

la disposition des participants à la troisième Conférence des Nations Unies sur le droit de la mer des renseignements aussi complets et aussi à jour que possible.

Le présent volume contient les textes adressés par les gouvernements en réponse aux deux notes du Secrétaire général susmentionnées. Ces notes prévoyaient que les textes seraient en général ceux adoptés depuis 1972, mais il était toutefois précisé que les gouvernements pouvaient communiquer des textes antérieurs à cette date dans la mesure où ils n'avaient pas été publiés dans les volumes précédents de la *Série législative*. Le présent volume contient également la documentation pertinente communiquée, indépendamment des notes du Secrétaire général, par plusieurs gouvernements qui ont demandé qu'elle soit diffusée[1].

Comme le volume de 1974[2], le présent volume comprend deux parties. La première partie reproduit le texte des dispositions législatives nationales et autres mesures de réglementation prises par les pays. La deuxième partie contient des dispositions de traités. Chaque partie comprend quatre sections :

Section I.   La mer territoriale et la zone contiguë;
Section II.   Le plateau continental;
Section III. La haute mer;
Section IV.   Pêche et conservation des ressources biologiques de la mer

La section I de la première partie est subdivisée en sous-sections et chapitres. Dans la mesure du possible, les textes qui figurent dans la première partie sont présentés dans l'ordre chronologique sous le nom de l'Etat intéressé; les lois et autres textes législatifs précèdent en principe les décrets ou règlements. Le nom des Etats est donné en anglais et selon l'ordre alphabétique anglais. Dans la deuxième partie, on fait une distinction entre les traités multilatéraux et les traités bilatéraux qui, dans chaque section, sont classés à part et selon l'ordre chronologique. Il convient de noter que le fait qu'un traité figure dans le présent volume ne signifie pas nécessairement qu'il soit en vigueur au moment de la publication. Pour les traités en vigueur, des renseignements sont donnés en ce qui concerne leur publication dans le *Recueil des Traités* des Nations Unies ou leur enregistrement au Secrétariat.

Les cartes ne sont pas reproduites pour des raisons d'ordre technique.

Conformément à la pratique suivie pour la *Série législative des Nations Unies*, les textes reçus en anglais ou en français sont publiés dans la langue originale. Les textes reçus en d'autres langues sont publiés en anglais. Une note placée après le titre indique, le cas échéant, que le texte reproduit est une traduction établie par le Secrétariat de l'Organisation des Nations Unies.

---

[1] Il convient de noter que la plupart des textes adressés par les gouvernements qui sont reproduits dans le présent volume figuraient dans l'édition préliminaire de ce volume publiée en 1974 et 1975 sous forme miméographiée pour la commodité des participants à la troisième Conférence des Nations Unies sur le droit de la mer.

[2] Voir ci-dessus p. viii, note 1, *g*.

SUBJECT INDEX AND TABLE OF CONTENTS[1]
INDEX ANALYTIQUE ET TABLE DES MATIERES DETAILLEE[2]

Part I. National Legislation
Première partie. Législation nationale

DIVISION I. THE TERRITORIAL SEA AND THE CONTIGUOUS ZONE
SECTION I. LA MER TERRITORIALE ET LA ZONE CONTIGUE

SUBDIVISION A. THE TERRITORIAL SEA
SOUS-SECTION A. LA MER TERRITORIALE

CHAPTER I. STATUS, BREADTH AND DELIMITATION
OF THE TERRITORIAL SEA
CHAPITRE I. STATUT, LARGEUR ET DELIMITATION
DE LA MER TERRITORIALE

---

[1] A title in square brackets indicates that the text concerned is either reproduced in another division, subdivision or chapter of this volume or not included therein. In each case, a foot-note at the page indicated gives, as appropriate, a cross reference to the division, subdivision or chapter in which the text is actually reproduced or a short explanation of the text.

[2] Un titre entre crochets indique, ou bien que le texte en question est reproduit dans une autre section, sous-section ou chapitre de ce volume, ou bien qu'il n'est pas reproduit dans le volume. Dans chaque cas, une note à la page correspondante indique la section, la sous-section ou le chapitre où le texte est effectivement reproduit ou donne des renseignements sur le texte.

CHAPTER II.   NAVIGATION THROUGH THE TERRITORIAL SEA AND SAFETY OF SHIPS THERE

CHAPITRE II.   NAVIGATION ET SECURITE DES NAVIRES DANS LA MER TERRITORIALE

CHAPTER III. SECURITY OF THE COASTAL STATE
CHAPITRE III. SECURITE DE L'ETAT RIVERAIN

CHAPTER IV. CUSTOMS, FISCAL AND SANITARY MATTERS
CHAPITRE IV. QUESTIONS DOUANIERES, FISCALES ET SANITAIRES

CHAPTER VI. STATUS OF FOREIGN WARSHIPS IN THE TERRITORIAL SEA
CHAPITRE VI. STATUT DES NAVIRES DE GUERRE ETRANGERS DANS LA MER TERRITORIALE

CHAPTER VII.   POLLUTION OF THE TERRITORIAL SEA

CHAPITRE VII.   POLLUTION DE LA MER TERRITORIALE

DIVISION II.   THE CONTINENTAL SHELF
SECTION II.   LE PLATEAU CONTINENTAL

DIVISION III.   THE HIGH SEAS

SECTION III.   LA HAUTE MER

DIVISION IV.   FISHING AND CONSERVATION OF THE LIVING RESOURCES OF THE SEA

SECTION IV.   PECHE ET CONSERVATION DES RESSOURCES BIOLOGIQUES DE LA MER

Part II.   Treaties

Deuxième partie.   Traités

DIVISION I.   THE TERRITORIAL SEA AND THE CONTIGUOUS ZONE

SECTION I.   LA MER TERRITORIALE ET LA ZONE CONTIGUE

SUBDIVISION A.   MULTILATERAL TREATIES

SOUS-SECTION A.   TRAITES MULTILATERAUX

SUBDIVISION B.   BILATERAL TREATIES

SOUS-SECTION B.   TRAITES BILATERAUX

DIVISION II. THE CONTINENTAL SHELF

SECTION II. LE PLATEAU CONTINENTAL

SUBDIVISION A. MULTILATERAL TREATIES

SOUS-SECTION A. TRAITES MULTILATERAUX

SUBDIVISION B. BILATERAL TREATIES

SOUS-SECTION B. TRAITES BILATERAUX

DIVISION III. THE HIGH SEAS

SECTION III. LA HAUTE MER

SUBDIVISION A. MULTILATERAL TREATIES

SOUS-SECTION A. TRAITES MULTILATERAUX

SUBDIVISION B. BILATERAL TREATIES

SOUS-SECTION B. TRAITES BILATERAUX

DIVISION IV. FISHING AND CONSERVATION OF THE LIVING RESOURCES OF THE SEA

SECTION IV. PECHE ET CONSERVATION DES RESSOURCES BIOLOGIQUES DE LA MER

SUBDIVISION A. MULTILATERAL TREATIES

SOUS-SECTION A. TRAITES MULTILATERAUX

SUBDIVISION B.   BILATERAL TREATIES

SOUS-SECTION B.   TRAITES BILATERAUX

Part I
NATIONAL LEGISLATION

Division I

THE TERRITORIAL SEA AND THE CONTIGUOUS ZONE

Subdivision A. The Territorial Sea

Chapter I

STATUS, BREADTH AND DELIMITATION OF THE TERRITORIAL SEA

1. DAHOMEY

CODE DE LA MARINE MARCHANDE DU 18 JUIN 1968[1]

TITRE II. – LA NAVIGATION MARITIME

Chapitre V. – Pêche réservée

Article 8. La pêche dans les eaux territoriales est réservée aux navires dahoméens et, sous réserve de réciprocité, aux navires d'autres Etats ou à certaines catégories d'entre eux.

Article 9. Les dispositions de l'article 8 ne portent pas atteinte au droit de libre circulation reconnu aux bateaux de pêche étrangers naviguant ou mouillant dans la zone de pêche réservée des eaux territoriales dahoméennes, à condition que ces navires se conforment aux règles spéciales de police qui pourraient être édictées en application de l'article 10 du présent Code.

Chapitre VI. – Police de la navigation maritime

Article 10. La police de la navigation dans les eaux maritimes est réglementée par l'autorité maritime. Cela ne fait pas obstacle à l'établissement dans les ports et rades de règlements particuliers d'utilisation par les autorités qui en assurent la gestion. Ces règlements sont cependant soumis à l'approbation de l'autorité maritime.

Les limites des ports et rades sont fixées par décret.

---

[1] Ordonnance No 68-38/P.R./M.T.P.T.P.T. du 18 juin 1968, modifiée par ordonnance No 69-39/P.R./M.A.E. du 9 décembre 1969. Transmis par la Mission permanente du Dahomey auprès de l'Organisation des Nations Unies par note en date du 25 octobre 1974.

TITRE III. – STATUT DU NAVIRE

Chapitre premier. – Définition du navire de mer

Article 11. Est considéré comme navire de mer tout engin flottant qui effectue à titre principal une navigation maritime, soit par ses propres moyens, soit en remorque.

La qualité de navire de mer est constatée par l'immatriculation de l'engin par les soins de l'autorité maritime.

Chapitre II. – Dahoméisation des navires

Article 12. La dahoméisation est l'acte administratif qui confère au navire le droit de porter le pavillon de la République du Dahomey avec les privilèges qui s'y rattachent.

Article 13. Tout navire dahoméen qui prend la mer doit avoir à bord un acte de dahoméisation délivré par l'autorité maritime au nom du Chef de l'Etat.

Article 14. Les navires d'Etat et les navires armés pour le compte de la République du Dahomey recoivent une lettre de nationalité qui leur confère le droit de porter le pavillon national.

Article 15. L'autorité administrative peut dispenser de l'acte de dahoméisation certains navires de moins de 10 tonneaux de jauge brute.

Article 16. Pour recevoir l'acte de dahoméisation, les navires doivent appartenir pour moitié au moins à des nationaux dahoméens ou à des nationaux d'un autre Etat avec lequel auront été passés des accords de réciprocité.

Si le navire appartient à une société, celle-ci doit avoir son siège social au Dahomey et avoir un conseil d'administration ou de surveillance dont le Président, le Président directeur général s'il y en a un, le gérant et la majorité des membres soient de nationalité dahoméenne ou de la nationalité d'un autre Etat avec lequel auront été passés des accords de réciprocité.

Si la société est une société de personnes ou une société à responsabilité limitée, il faut, en outre, que la moitié du capital au moins appartienne à l'Etat dahoméen ou à un autre Etat avec lequel auront été passés des accords de réciprocité, à des collectivités publiques ou à des nationaux dahoméens ou d'un autre Etat avec lequel auront été passés des accords de réciprocité. Des dérogations à ces conditions pourront être accordées par décret en faveur des Etats limitrophes ne possédant pas de frontière maritime, des collectivités publiques des sociétés et des nationaux de ces Etats.

Chapitre IV. – Immatriculation des navires – publication – radiation

Article 22. Les navires sont immatriculés à Cotonou par les soins de l'autorité maritime.

Seuls peuvent être immatriculés les navires ayant obtenu un acte de dahoméisation ou ceux dont les propriétaires ont déposé une demande non contestée en ce sens et ceux régulièrement dispensés de l'acte de dahoméisation en application de l'article 15 du présent Code.

Article 23. L'immatriculation originelle d'un navire et toute nouvelle immatriculation au nom d'un nouveau propriétaire fait l'objet d'une publication au *Journal officiel* de la République du Dahomey.

Cette publication mentionne les noms, tonnage et port d'immatriculation du navire, les noms, domiciles ou sièges sociaux du vendeur ou constructeur et de l'acquéreur, la date de la mutation de propriété.

Sauf opposition dûment notifiée dans un délai de deux mois à compter de cette publication, le changement de propriété est considéré comme inattaquable et définitif.

Article 24. L'immatriculation donne lieu à la perception d'une taxe dont le montant et l'imputation sont fixés par arrêté.

Article 25. L'autorité maritime détermine les règles et conditions à remplir pour obtenir l'immatriculation des navires et fixe les modalités de leur radiation des matricules.

Chapitre V. – Pavillon et signalement extérieur permanent des navires

Article 26. Les navires dahoméens arborent à la poupe ou à la corne d'artimon le pavillon national.

Les capitaines de ces navires sont tenus d'arborer le pavillon national à l'entrée et à la sortie des ports et sur toute réquisition d'un bâtiment de guerre quelle que soit sa nationalité.

Dans les ports et rades, le pavillon national est arboré les dimanches, jours fériés et fêtes légales et sur ordre de l'autorité maritime.

Le petit et le grand pavois comportent des pavillons nationaux hissés en tête de chaque mât.

Article 27. Hors le pavillon national, aucun pavillon, marque ou guidon ne peut être utilisé sans accord préalable de l'autorité maritime. En particulier, tout pavillon ou marque de Compagnie de navigation doit faire l'objet d'une décision de l'autorité maritime qui en approuve les dispositions.

. . .

Article 29. Tout navire doit porter un signalement extérieur permanent qui permette de l'identifier.

Ce signalement est réglementé par l'autorité maritime en fonction des caractéristiques des navires et du genre de navigation pratiqué.

. . .

*TITRE V[1]. – LE DOMAINE PUBLIC MARITIME
ET LES EAUX TERRITORIALES*

Chapitre premier. – Le domaine public maritime

Article 178.   Le domaine public maritime est la partie du domaine public formée par la mer et les espaces qu'elle baigne soit temporairement, soit d'une manière continue.

Article 179.   Le domaine public maritime comprend :

1° Les eaux intérieures, à savoir celles qui sont situées en deçà de la ligne à partir de laquelle est mesurée l'étendue de la mer territoriale et les eaux des ports et rades;

2° Le rivage de la mer, c'est-à-dire la partie des côtes alternativement couverte et découverte par la mer;

3° Les constructions ou ouvrages publics d'utilité maritime situés dans les zones ci-dessus.

Article 180.   Les modalités de délimitation du domaine public maritime sont réglementées par décret.

Article 181.   La circulation est libre sur le domaine public maritime sous réserve de l'observation des règlements de police en vigueur.

Article 182.   Le domaine public maritime est inaliénable, insaisissable et imprescriptible.

Les conditions dans lesquelles il peut être occupé ou concédé, les règles applicables aux extractions du domaine public maritime et aux travaux effectués sur le domaine public maritime, les mesures d'ordre et de police qui s'y rattachent sont fixées par décret, sous réserve des dispositions prévues à l'article 190, paragraphe 7, du présent Code.

Chapitre II. – Les eaux territoriales et contiguës

Article 183.   Les eaux territoriales s'étendent jusqu'à une distance de 12 milles marins à compter de la laisse de la plus basse mer.

Pour les golfes, rades ou estuaires, des décrets fixent, en tant que de besoin, la ligne à partir de laquelle la distance de douze milles est comptée.

Article 184.   Il peut être créé par décret une zone contiguë aux eaux territoriales.

Article 185.   Outre la pêche ainsi que prévu au titre II, chapitre V, du présent Code, la République du Dahomey se réserve tous droits d'exploitation de la mer et du sous-sol marin dans les eaux territoriales de l'Etat et dans la zone contiguë qui pourrait être déterminée en application de l'article 184 du présent Code, conformément aux usages internationaux.

. . .

---

[1] Dans sa note du 25 octobre 1974, le représentant permanent du Dahomey appelle l'attention du Secrétaire général sur le titre V de ce code qui est en train d'être révisé en vue de tenir compte de la décision du Dahomey d'étendre sa mer territoriale à 200 milles nautiques.

TITRE VI. – LES ACTIVITES MARITIMES

. . .

Chapitre II. – La pêche maritime et ses activités annexes

Article 189. La pêche maritime consiste dans la capture par des moyens appropriés de tout animal vivant en mer ou dans la partie maritime des fleuves et lagunes.

Section première. – Réglementation administrative de la pêche maritime

Article 190. Des arrêtés de l'autorité maritime préparés en liaison avec l'Organisme chargé des recherches en matière de pêche maritime déterminent en tant que de besoin :

1° Les zones et époques où la pêche est interdite soit entièrement, soit pour certaines espèces;

2° Les filets, engins, instruments, procédés et modes de pêche prohibés soit entièrement, soit dans certaines conditions;

3° Les dispositions de nature à prévenir la destruction du frai et à assurer la conservation des fonds de pêche et en particulier celles concernant la taille marchande des diverses espèces pêchées;

4° Les interdictions relatives à la pêche, à la mise en vente, à l'achat, au transport, au colportage ou à l'emploi du frai, des poissons, crustacés, coquillages et autres animaux marins qui n'atteignent pas les dimensions prescrites;

5° Les appâts ou substances dont l'emploi est interdit en dehors de celles prévues à l'article 191 du présent Code;

6° Les mesures d'ordre et de police propres à assurer la conservation de la pêche ainsi qu'à en régler l'exercice;

7° Les conditions d'établissement et d'exploitation des pêcheries, viviers, parcs à huîtres, moules ou autres animaux marins situés en mer où sur le domaine public maritime, sous réserve que le montant et l'imputation des taxes à percevoir lors de l'octroi, de la cession ou du renouvellement de ces autorisations soient fixés par décret.

Article 191. Il est interdit de faire usage pour la pêche soit de dynamite, soit de tout autre explosif, soit de substances ou d'appâts pouvant enivrer ou détruire les poissons, crustacés et coquillages.

. . .

TITRE VII. – LE REGIME DISCIPLINAIRE ET PENAL

Chapitre premier. – Dispositions générales

Article 194. Sont soumis aux dispositions du présent titre :

1° Les personnes, de quelque nationalité qu'elles soient, embarquées à bord des navires battant pavillon dahoméen soit comme membres de l'équipage pendant la durée de leur embarquement, soit comme passagers ou pilotes pendant la durée de leur présence à bord.

Cependant, les militaires et marins des Forces Armées du Dahomey demeurent justiciables des tribunaux militaires pour tout crime ou délit commis pendant leur présence à bord des navires.

2° Les personnes qui, bien que non embarquées à bord d'un navire battant pavillon dahoméen ont commis une des infractions prévues au présent titre.

Article 195. Pour l'application des dispositions contenues dans le présent titre :

— L'expression "capitaine" désigne le capitaine ou patron ou à défaut, la personne qui exerce, régulièrement, en fait, le commandement du navire;

— L'expression "officier" désigne le second, les lieutenants, le chef mécanicien, les officiers mécaniciens, les radioélectriciens, les commissaires, les médecins, les élèves officiers et, d'une façon générale, toutes personnes portées comme officiers sur le rôle d'équipage;

— L'expression "maître" désigne les maître d'équipage, maîtres-charpentiers, maîtres d'hôtel ou assimilés, les premiers chauffeurs ou assimilés, les graisseurs, les radiotélégraphistes n'ayant pas rang d'officier et, d'une façon générale, toutes personnes portées comme maîtres ou chefs de service sur le rôle d'équipage;

— L'expression "homme d'équipage" désigne toutes les autres personnes de l'équipage inscrites sur le rôle;

— L'expression "passager" désigne les passagers proprement dits ainsi que toutes les personnes qui se trouvent en fait à bord du navire en vue d'effectuer le voyage et sans faire partie de l'équipage;

— L'expression "autorité maritime" continue à désigner l'autorité définie au titre 1er du présent Code;

— L'expression "bord" désigne le navire, ses embarcations et ses divers moyens de communication avec la terre.

Article 196. En ce qui concerne les crimes et délits prévus par le présent titre, les délais de prescription de l'action publique, de l'exécution de la peine et de l'action civile sont fixés conformément au droit commun.

En ce qui concerne les fautes contre la discipline, les délais dans lesquels l'action doit être intentée, la punition prononcée et la peine exécutée sont ceux prévus pour les contraventions de simple police.

Les délais prévus aux paragraphes précédents ne commencent à courir qu'à partir du jour où, après l'infraction commise, le navire a touché un port du Dahomey.

Article 197. Aucune poursuite ne peut être exercée en application des dispositions du présent titre lorsque la personne inculpée a été jugée définitivement à l'étranger pour les mêmes faits, sous réserve, en cas de condamnation, qu'elle ait subi ou prescrit sa peine ou obtenu sa grâce.

Article 198. Les dispositions du droit commun concernant les circonstances atténuantes sont applicables aux crimes et délits prévus par le présent Code. Il en est de même des dispositions relatives au sursis et à la récidive, sauf stipulation contraire.

Article 199. Il sera, lors de l'armement de chaque navire, ouvert un livre spécial appelé "livre de discipline" qui sera coté et paraphé par l'autorité maritime pour être conservé à bord.

Article 200. Le capitaine ou l'autorité maritime, selon le cas, mentionne au livre de discipline la date, la nature et les circonstances de toute faute ou infraction commise à bord, qu'il s'agisse d'une "faute de discipline", d'un délit ou d'un crime. Il y consigne également les résultats des enquêtes effectuées, les punitions infligées et les mesures spéciales ordonnées.

Le livre de discipline doit être présenté au visa de l'autorité maritime toutes les fois qu'une faute de discipline, un délit ou un crime a été commis à bord.

Pour les navires de moins de cent tonneaux de jauge brute, la tenue du livre de discipline peut être rendue facultative par décision de l'autorité maritime.

Article 201. Il est tenu en outre par l'autorité maritime un livre spécial dit "livre de punitions" qui mentionne les punitions infligées, les enquêtes ouvertes pour crimes ou délits et les suites qui y ont été données.

Article 202. Les punitions ou sanctions infligées sont, avec l'indication des fautes ou infractions qui les ont provoquées, inscrites à la diligence de l'autorité maritime à l'article matriculaire du marin intéressé.

Article 203. L'autorité maritime peut, en cas de nécessité, demander l'intervention de la force publique à l'autorité compétente, soit pour procéder à l'arrestation des délinquants, soit pour procéder à la saisie des navires, embarcations, engins, installations, appâts ou produits de la pêche qui ont été l'objet d'un crime ou délit.

Article 204. Lorsqu'il s'agit des faits prévus par la présente loi et ses textes d'application et imputables à une ou plusieurs personnes appartenant à l'équipage d'un navire étranger, l'autorité maritime peut, sans préjudice des mesures de droit commun, arrêter le navire jusqu'au dépôt à la Caisse des Dépôts et Consignations ou d'un organisme en tenant lieu, d'un cautionnement destiné à garantir l'exécution des condamnations dont elle fixe le montant.

En cas de condamnation définitive et non exécutée, le cautionnement est acquis au budget du Dahomey déduction faite des frais et des réparations civiles.

Article 205. Le droit commun est applicable aux infractions, aux règles de compétence, de procédure, d'instruction ou autres non prévues ou non précisées par le présent Code.

Il est cependant précisé que quiconque, propriétaire, armateur ou autre personne, étant à terre ou à bord, incite par parole ou par écrit le capitaine, un homme d'équipage ou l'équipage et les passagers d'un navire à commettre l'un des crimes ou délits prévus par le présent titre, ou se fait le complice de ce crime ou délit, est puni de la même peine que celle prévue pour les auteurs du crime ou délit commis, sauf dispositions contraires prévues par le présent Code.

La peine applicable aux auteurs du crime ou délit peut être réduite par la juridiction répressive, s'il apparaît que ceux-ci ont agi à l'instigation de l'une des personnes susvisées.

. . .

Chapitre III. – Des délits et crimes maritimes

. . .

Section II. – Des délits et crimes concernant la police de la navigation

Article 239. Toute personne, même étrangère, embarquée sur un navire dahoméen ou étranger, qui, dans les eaux maritimes et jusqu'à la limite des eaux territoriales, ne se conforme pas aux règlements ou aux ordres émanant de l'autorité maritime et relatifs, soit à la police des eaux et rades, soit à la police de la navigation maritime, soit à la sécurité de la navigation, est punie d'un emprisonnement de dix jours à six mois et d'une amende de 25 000 à 250 000 francs, ou de l'une de ces deux peines seulement.

La même peine est encourue par toute personne embarquée sur un navire dahoméen qui, hors des eaux territoriales du Dahomey, ne se conforme pas aux ordres régulièrement donnés par l'une des autorités visées au chapitre 1er du titre I du présent Code ou par le commandant d'un navire de guerre de la République du Dahomey.

Si les infractions au présent article sont commises en temps de guerre, la peine peut être triplée.

Article 240. Tout capitaine requis par l'autorité compétente, qui, sans motif légitime, refuse de se charger du dossier de l'enquête ou des pièces à conviction, ou d'assurer le transport d'un prévenu, ou qui ne livre pas le prévenu ou le dossier confié à ses soins à l'autorité maritime désignée pour les recevoir, est puni d'une amende de 25 000 à 250 000 francs sans préjudice, s'il y a lieu, en cas d'évasion ou de complicité d'évasion, de l'application aux personnes embarquées, au capitaine et au prévenu, des dispositions des articles 237 à 243 du Code pénal.

Article 241. Est puni d'une amende de 25 000 à 250 000 francs, tout capitaine ou armateur qui, sans motif légitime, refuse de déférer à la réquisition de l'autorité maritime pour rapatrier des nationaux dahoméens au Dahomey.

Article 242. Tout capitaine qui, en mer, n'obéit pas à l'appel d'un navire de guerre de la République du Dahomey et le contraint à faire usage de la force est puni d'un emprisonnement de trois mois à deux ans et d'une amende de 25 000 à 250 000 francs, ou de l'une de ces deux peines seulement.

Article 243. Tout capitaine ou armateur qui enfreint les obligations qui incombent à l'armement concernant soit les soins à donner aux marins malades ou blessés, soit le rapatriement et la conduite de ces marins ainsi qu'il est prévu au chapitre V du titre IV du présent Code, est puni d'un emprisonnement de dix jours à deux mois et d'une amende de 25 000 à 250 000 francs, ou de l'une de ces deux peines seulement.

La même peine est encourue par le capitaine qui, ayant laissé à terre, avant qu'il ait atteint son lieu de destination un passager malade ou blessé, ne donne pas avis de cette mesure à l'autorité diplomatique ou consulaire du pays auquel appartient le passager débarqué, ou à défaut, à l'autorité locale.

Article 244. Est puni d'une amende de 25 000 à 250 000 francs, pour chaque infraction constatée, tout propriétaire ou armateur qui ne se conforme pas aux prescriptions du présent Code relatives à la réglementation du travail, de la nourriture et du couchage, des congés et repos, des salaires minima à bord des navires, et aux prescriptions des règlements pris pour leur application.

Est puni de la même peine sans préjudice des mesures disciplinaires prévues par l'article 213, tout capitaine qui commet personnellement, ou d'accord avec l'armateur ou propriétaire du navire, les infractions prévues par le paragraphe précédent. Toutefois, la peine prononcée contre le capitaine peut être réduite du quart de celle prononcée contre le propriétaire ou l'armateur s'il est prouvé que le capitaine a reçu un ordre écrit ou verbal de cet armateur ou propriétaire.

Les peines prévues aux deux paragraphes précédents peuvent être portées au double en cas de récidive. Il y a récidive lorsque le contrevenant a subi, dans les douze mois qui précèdent, une condamnation pour les faits réprimés par le présent article.

Article 245. Toute personne qui, sur un navire dahoméen, exerce sans l'autorisation de l'autorité maritime et hors le cas de force majeure soit le commandement du navire, soit toute autre fonction, sans satisfaire aux conditions exigées par les règlements maritimes, est punie d'un emprisonnement de dix jours à un an et d'une amende de 25 000 à 250 000 francs, ou de l'une de ces deux peines seulement.

Est punie de la même peine toute personne qui, sans une commission régulière de pilote, aura entrepris ou tenté d'entreprendre la conduite d'un navire en qualité de pilote commissionné.

Article 246. Est puni d'une amende de 25 000 à 250 000 francs tout armateur ou propriétaire qui ne se conforme pas aux règlements relatifs à l'immatriculation des navires.

Article 247. Tout propriétaire ou armateur qui ne se conforme pas aux règlements relatifs à la dahoméisation des navires ou se rend coupable d'une dahoméisation frauduleuse est puni d'un emprisonnement de dix jours à six mois et d'une amende de 100 000 à 5 000 000 de francs, ou de l'une de ces deux peines seulement.

...

Section IV. – De la piraterie

Article 271. Seront poursuivis et jugés comme pirates :

1° Tout individu faisant partie de l'équipage d'un navire armé militairement et naviguant sans avoir été muni pour le voyage d'un passeport, rôle d'équipage, commissions ou autres actes constatant la légitimité de l'expédition;

2° Tout capitaine d'un navire armé militairement et porteur de commissions délivrées par deux ou plusieurs puissances ou Etats différents;

3° Tout individu faisant partie de l'équipage d'un navire battant pavillon du Dahomey, lequel commettrait à main armée des actes de déprédation ou de violence soit envers des navires dahoméens ou des navires d'une puissance avec laquelle le Dahomey ne serait pas en état de guerre, soit envers les équipages ou chargements de ces navires;

4° Tout individu faisant partie de l'équipage d'un navire étranger, lequel, hors l'état de guerre et sans être pourvu de lettres de marque ou de commissions régulières, commettrait les actes visés à l'alinéa précédent envers des navires dahoméens, leurs équipages ou chargements;

5° Le capitaine et les officiers de tout navire quelconque qui auraient commis des actes d'hostilité sous un pavillon autre que celui de l'Etat dont ledit navire aurait commission;

6° Tout Dahoméen qui, ayant obtenu, même avec l'autorisation du Gouvernement, commission d'une puissance étrangère pour commander un navire armé militairement, commettrait des actes d'hostilité envers des navires dahoméens, leurs équipages ou leurs chargements;

7° Tout individu faisant partie de l'équipage d'un navire dahoméen qui tenterait de s'emparer dudit navire par fraude ou violence envers le capitaine;

8° Tout individu faisant partie de l'équipage d'un navire dahoméen qui le livrerait à des pirates ou à l'ennemi.

Article 272. Quiconque aura été déclaré coupable du crime de piraterie sera puni de la peine de mort, des travaux forcés ou de la réclusion.

Les mêmes peines sont applicables aux passagers qui participeraient aux actes visés à l'article 271 du présent Code ou en seraient les auteurs

La vente des navires capturés pour cause de piraterie sera, en outre, ordonnée par le Tribunal au profit de l'Etat.

. . .

Chapitre IV. – Des infractions en matière de pêche maritime

Section première. – Des délits concernant la réglementation administrative des pêches maritimes et des activités annexes

Article 283. Est puni d'une amende de 20 000 à 1 000 000 de francs et d'un emprisonnement de dix jours à six mois, ou de l'une de ces deux peines seulement, quiconque contrevient aux dispositions prévues aux articles 190 et 191 du présent Code.

Lorsqu'il s'agit d'établissements de pêcheries, viviers, parcs à huîtres, moules, coquillages ou autres animaux marins, l'autorité maritime peut ordonner en outre l'enlèvement ou la destruction immédiate, aux frais des contrevenants, des installations construites sans autorisation.

Article 284. L'autorité maritime procède à la saisie et à la mise en vente immédiate au profit de l'Etat des produits de la pêche des contrevenants aux dispositions de l'article précédent.

Article 285. En cas de récidive dans les deux ans à l'une quelconque des infractions réprimées par l'article 283, le contrevenant peut être condamné au double de la peine d'amende.

En outre, les embarcations, navires, installations et engins utilisés sont saisis par l'autorité maritime et le Tribunal peut prononcer leur confiscation et leur mise en vente au profit de l'Etat.

Article 286. Est puni d'une amende de 20 000 à 1 000 000 de francs et d'un emprisonnement de dix jours à six mois, ou de l'une de ces deux peines seulement, quiconque contrevient aux dispositions réglementaires édictées en application de l'article 192 du présent Code.

L'autorité maritime peut, en outre ordonner soit la destruction, soit la mise en vente au profit de l'Etat des produits ou lots qui ne répondent pas aux normes fixées.

En cas de récidive dans les deux ans, le contrevenant peut être condamné au double de la peine d'amende prévue à l'alinéa 1 du présent article.

Article 287. Les sanctions prévues par les articles 283 à 286 du présent Code sont infligées :

1° Au capitaine ou patron lorsque l'infraction est commise par un navire. Cependant, l'armateur est seul responsable des condamnations civiles. Il est en outre solidairement responsable du paiement des amendes pénales prononcées;

2° A la personne qui dirige, en fait, l'établissement ou l'exploitation lorsqu'il s'agit d'infractions relatives soit au commerce, transport, colportage ou emploi des produits de la pêche qui n'atteignent pas les dimensions prescrites, soit à l'installation de pêcheries, viviers, parcs à huîtres, moules, coquillages ou autres animaux marins, soit aux mesures d'hygiène et de salubrité prescrites pour l'élevage, le transport, la vente et le commerce des produits de la pêche;

Cette même personne est en outre seule responsable des condamnations civiles;

3° Aux délinquants eux-mêmes dans les autres cas, sans préjudice toujours des condamnations civiles.

Article 288. Tout capitaine et membre d'équipage d'un navire étranger surpris en pêche dans les eaux territoriales ou la zone contiguë aux eaux territoriales dont l'exploitation peut être réservée aux Dahoméens, sous reserve des accords de réciprocité, est puni d'une amende de 200 000 à 4 000 000 de francs et d'un emprisonnement de dix jours à six mois ou de l'une de ces deux peines seulement.

En cas de récidive dans les deux ans, la confiscation du navire, des engins et des produits de la pêche est obligatoirement prononcée par le Tribunal au profit de l'Etat.

L'armateur est solidairement responsable du paiement des amendes prononcées.

Article 289. Les délits en matière de pêche maritime sont recherchés et constatés :

1° Par les représentants qualifiés de l'autorité maritime;

2° Par les officiers de police judiciaire;

3° Par les officiers et officiers mariniers commandant les bâtiments ou embarcations de la République du Dahomey, les gendarmes, les officiers et maîtres de port et les autres agents spécialement habilités à cet effet.

Ils donnent lieu à l'établissement de procès-verbaux.

Article 290. Les procès-verbaux établis par les agents énumérés à l'article précédent font foi jusqu'à preuve du contraire. Ils ne sont pas soumis à l'affirmation.

Les procès-verbaux sont transmis directement par leurs auteurs à l'autorité maritime qui saisit le Procureur de la République près le Tribunal dont relève sa résidence.

A défaut de procès-verbaux ou en cas d'insuffisance de ces actes, les infractions peuvent être prouvées par témoins.

Article 291. Le Ministère public ne peut engager les poursuites qu'au vu des conclusions de l'autorité maritime ou à l'expiration d'un délai de quinze jours après qu'il aura réclamé ces conclusions par lettre recommandée.

L'autorité maritime doit, si elle le demande, être entendue par le Tribunal.

Article 292. La partie lésée a le droit de se porter partie civile devant le Tribunal, conformément aux textes en vigueur.

Toutefois, elle ne peut donner citation directement au prévenu et doit saisir le juge d'instruction.

Article 293. Pour tous les délits de pêche, l'autorité maritime peut transiger avec les délinquants dès lors qu'ils ne sont pas considérés comme récidivistes.

Le montant de la transaction, qui ne peut être opérée qu'avant jugement, est au minimum celui du montant de la peine d'amende encourue par le délinquant.

. . .

TITRE VIII. – DISPOSITIONS DIVERSES

Article 299. Sont abrogées toutes dispositions contraires à la présente ordonnance, qui sera exécutée comme loi de l'Etat.

2. ECUADOR

(a) CIVIL CODE AS AMENDED BY DECREE NO. 256-CLP
OF 27 FEBRUARY 1970[1]

. . .

Book II, Title III − National Property

628.   The adjacent sea, to a distance of 200 nautical miles measured from the low-water mark, at the most salient points of the continental Ecuadorian coast and the outer-most islands of the Colón Archipelago, according to the baseline to be indicated by Executive Decree,[2] shall constitute the territorial sea and be part of the national domain.

The adjacent sea between the baseline referred to in the preceding paragraph and the low-water mark shall constitute internal waters and be part of the national domain.

If maritime police and defence zones more extensive than those specified in the preceding paragraphs are determined under relevant international treaties, the provisions of such treaties shall prevail.

The different zones of the territorial sea that shall be subject to the régime of free maritime navigation or of innocent passage for foreign ships shall be established by Executive Decree.

The bed and subsoil of the adjacent sea also form part of the public domain.

629.   The air space corresponding to the territory of the State, including the territorial sea as defined in the preceding article, shall also be part of the national domain.

Regulations governing the free air transit zone above the territorial sea shall be made by the Executive.

. . .

(b) SUPREME DECREE NO. 959-A OF 28 JUNE 1971 PRESCRIBING STRAIGHT BASELINES FOR THE MEASUREMENT OF THE TERRITORIAL SEA[3]

Whereas article 628 of the Civil Code[4] in force provides that the Ecuadorian territorial sea shall be measured in both the continental territory of the Republic of the Colón Archipelago (Galapagos Islands), from the straight baselines which will be determined for this purpose by Executive Decree; and

---

[1] Spanish text provided by the Permanent Mission of Ecuador to the United Nations in a note verbale of 16 October 1973. Translation by the Secretariat of the United Nations.

[2] See Supreme Decree No. 939-A of 28 June 1971, reproduced *infra (b)*.

[3] *Registro Oficial* No. 265 of 13 July 1973, pp. 1-2. Translation by the Secretariat of the United Nations.

[4] Reproduced *supra (a)*.

Whereas a Commission composed of representatives of the Ministry of Foreign Affairs, the Navy and the Military Geographic Institute has studied the plotting of such lines and determined their course; and

Whereas such study has been approved by the Ministry of Foreign Affairs and the Ministry of National Defence on the grounds that it is in the national interest and fully conforms to the rules of international law which are in force on the matter.

It is hereby decreed·

Article 1. The straight baselines from which the breadth of the territorial sea of the Republic shall be measured shall be constituted by the following traverses:

I. On the continent

(a) The line shall start from the point of intersection of the maritime frontier with Colombia, with the straight line Punta Manglares (Colombia)–Punta Galera (Ecuador);

(b) From this point a straight line passing through Punta Galera and meeting the northernmost point of Isla de la Plata;

(c) From this point a straight line to Puntilla de Santa Elena;

(d) A straight line from Puntilla de Santa Elena in the direction of Cabo Blanco (Peru) to the intersection with the geographic parallel constituting the maritime frontier with Peru.

II. In the Colón Archipelago (Galapagos Islands)

(a) From Islote Darwin a straight line to the north-eastern tip of Isla Pinta.

(b) A straight line to the northernmost point of Isla Genovesa;

(c) A straight line passing through Punta Valdizan, Isla San Cristobal, and intersecting the northern extension of the straight line joining the south-eastern tip of Isla Española to Punta Pitt, Isla San Cristobal;

(d) A straight line from this intersection to the south-eastern tip of Isla Española:

(e) A straight line to Punta Sur, Isla Santa Maria;

(f) A straight line passing through the south-eastern tip of Isla Isabela, near Punta Esex, and intersecting the southern extension of the line joining the outermost projecting point of the western coast of Isla Fernandina, approximately in its middle, with the western tip of the southern sector of Isla Isabela, in the vicinity of Punta Cristobal;

(g) From this point of intersection a line passing through the western tip of the southern sector of Isla Isabela, in the vicinity of Punta Cristobal, to the outermost projecting point on the western coast of Isla Fernandina, approximately in its middle; and

(h) A straight line to Isla Darwin.

Article 2. The sea areas lying between the lines described in article 1 (I) and the coast line on the Continent, and within the lines described in article 1 (II), in the Colon Archipelago, shall constitute internal waters.

3. FRANCE

a) LOI No 71-1060 DU 24 DECEMBRE 1971 RELATIVE A LA DELIMITATION
DES EAUX TERRITORIALES FRANCAISES[1]

Art. 1er. Les eaux territoriales françaises s'étendent jusqu'à une limite
fixée à 12 milles marins à partir des lignes de base.

Les lignes de base sont la laisse de basse mer ainsi que les lignes de base
droites et les lignes de fermeture des baies qui sont déterminées par décret.

La souveraineté de l'Etat français s'étend à l'espace aérien ainsi qu'au lit
et au sous-sol de la mer dans la limite des eaux territoriales.

Art. 2. Sauf convention particulière, la largeur des eaux territoriales ne
s'étend pas au-delà d'une ligne médiane dont tous les points sont équidistants
des points les plus proches des lignes de base des côtes françaises et des côtes
des pays étrangers qui font face aux côtes françaises ou qui leur sont
limitrophes.

Art. 3. Lorsque la distance entre les lignes de base des côtes françaises et
celles des côtes d'un Etat étranger qui leur font face est égale ou inférieure à
24 milles ou ne permet plus l'existence d'une zone de haute mer suffisante
pour la navigation, des dispositions pourront être prises en vue d'assurer la
libre navigation maritime et aérienne, dans le respect des conventions
internationales et, s'il y a lieu, après accord avec les Etats intéressés.

Art. 4. Les dispositions de la présente loi ne portent pas atteinte à
l'exercice des droits de pêche accordés à certains navires étrangers dans les
conditions prévues par les accords internationaux et le droit interne français.

Art. 5. La présente loi est applicable aux territoires d'outre-mer.

b) DECRET DU 29 JUIN 1971 DEFINISSANT LES LIGNES DE BASE DROITES
SERVANT A LA DETERMINATION DES LIGNES DE BASE A PARTIR
DESQUELLES EST MESUREE LA LARGEUR DES EAUX TERRITORIALES AU
LARGE DE LA GUYANE FRANCAISE[2]

Le Premier Ministre

. . .

Vu le décret No 67-451 du 7 juin 1967[3] portant extension de la zone de
pêche interdite aux navires étrangers, et notamment ses articles 2 et 5;

Vu le décret No 70-1183 du 11 décembre 1970[4] relatif à l'extension au
département de la Guyane française du décret No 67-451 du 7 juin 1967,

Décrète :

Art. 1er. Les lignes de base droites servant à la détermination des lignes
de base à partir desquelles est mesurée la largeur des eaux territoriales au large

---

[1] *Journal officiel,* 30 décembre 1971.
[2] *Journal officiel,* 7 juillet 1971.
[3] Reproduit dans ST/LEG/SER.B/15, p. 636.
[4] Reproduit partiellement dans ST/LEG/SER.B/16, p. 301.

de la Guyane française sont celles joignant les points A, B, C, D, E et F ainsi définis :

Point A. – L'îlot le plus à l'ouest des Roches Blanches (latitude 5° 26'6 N., longitude 52° 56'7 O.).

Point B. – Le feu de l'île Royale (latitude 5° 17'2 N., longitude 52° 35'6 O.).

Point C. – Le feu de l'Enfant perdu (latitude 5° 02'55 N., longitude 52° 21'37 O.).

Point D. – Le sommet de l'îlot Le Père (latitude 4° 55'7 N., longitude 52° 12'3 O.).

Point E. – Le sommet de l'îlot Grand Connétable (latitude 4° 49'5 N., longitude 51° 56'3 O.).

Point F. – (latitude 4° 34' N., longitude 51° 46'3 O.)

. . .

4. GERMAN DEMOCRATIC REPUBLIC

(a) EXCERPT FROM THE CONSTITUTION OF THE GERMAN DEMOCRATIC REPUBLIC OF 6 APRIL 1968 AS MODIFIED BY THE LAW OF 7 OCTOBER 1974[1]

. . .

Article 7. (1) The State organs ensure the territorial integrity of the German Democratic Republic and the inviolability of its national frontiers, inclusive of its air space and its territorial waters, and the protection and exploitation of its continental shelf.

. . .

Article 12. (1) Mineral resources: mines, power stations, barrages and large bodies of water, the natural resources of the continental shelf, the industrial enterprises, banks and insurance companies, nationally owned farms, traffic routes, the means of transport of the railways, ocean shipping and civil aviation and post and telecommunications installations are nationally owned property. Private ownership thereof is inadmissible.

(b) *EXCERPT FROM THE REGULATION*[2] BY THE NATIONAL DEFENCE COUNCIL OF THE GERMAN DEMOCRATIC REPUBLIC ON THE PROHIBITION OF ACCESS TO CERTAIN AREAS–CLOSED AREA ORDER OF 21 JUNE 1963

. . .

Prohibited areas in inland sea-waters and in territorial waters

Article 16. For the purpose of the defence of the German Democratic Republic, certain areas within the inland sea-waters and territorial waters of

---

[1] German text provided by the Permanent Mission of the German Democratic Republic to the United Nations in a note verbale of 19 December 1974. Translation by the Secretariat of the United Nations.

[2] *Legal Gazette of the German Democratic Republic,* part I, 1963, p. 93. German text provided by the Permanent Mission of the German Democratic Republic to the United Nations in a note verbale of 19 December 1974. Translation by the Secretariat of the United Nations.

the German Democratic Republic may be declared closed areas either temporarily or, whose such areas are of negligible significance for the peaceful passage of foreign ships, permanently.

Article 17. (1) Proposals for the establishment of closed areas in inland sea-waters and in territorial waters shall be submitted to the Commander-in-Chief of the People's Navy.

(2) The Commander-in-Chief of the People's Navy shall determine such closed areas with the prior agreement of the heads of the competent State and economic organs.

(3) The establishment of permanently closed areas in inland sea-waters and in territorial waters shall require the prior approval of the Minister of Defence.

Article 18. (1) The marking of closed areas in the inland sea-waters and territorial waters shall be the responsibility of the Commander-in-Chief of the People's Navy and shall be carried out by the People's Navy.

(2) The co-ordinates of such closed areas shall be published by the Nautical Hydrography Department in *Nautische Mitteilungen für Seefahrer.*

(3) Prior to the establishment of such closed areas, the Minister for Foreign Affairs shall be consulted, through the Minister of Defence, as a rule not less than 14 days before the closure.

Article 19. Any declaration of sea-areas outside the territorial waters of the German Democratic Republic as danger zones because of exercises by the armed forces of the German Democratic Republic shall be made in conformity with the rules of international law and with due regard for the interests of international shipping and international air traffic.

. . .

(c) EXCERPT FROM THE REGULATION[1] ON ORDER IN THE FRONTIER AREAS AND TERRITORIAL WATERS OF THE GERMAN DEMOCRATIC REPUBLIC—FRONTIER ORDER—OF 15 JUNE 1972

. . .

Section IV

Regulations concerning order in the frontier area along the coast and in the territorial waters of the German Democratic Republic.

Article 29. The national frontier of the German Democratic Republic at sea (sea-frontier) is the line which separates the territorial waters from the high seas.[2]

---

[1] Legal Gazette of the German Democratic Republic, part II, 1972, p. 483. German text provided by the Permanent Mission of the German Democratic Republic to the United Nations in a note verbale of 19 December 1974. Translation by the Secretariat of the United Nations.

[2] The breadth of the territorial waters of the German Democratic Republic is three nautical miles.

Article 30. (1) The baseline from which the breadth of the territorial waters is measured is established in conformity with the geographical features of the coast with reference to the course of the coastline and in conformity with the principle of the straight baseline (annex 1).

(2) The inland sea-waters of the German Democratic Republic include:

(a) The waters of harbours as far as the line drawn through the permanent harbour installations situated furthest out to sea;

(b) The waters of bays whose coasts belong wholly to the German Democratic Republic, as far as a straight line drawn through the natural projections of the coast which are not more than 24 nautical miles distant from each other;

(c) The waters of lagoons and haffs whose coasts belong wholly to the German Democratic Republic

. . .

Article 37. (1) The stay and anchoring of foreign merchant ships and fishing and pleasure vessels in the territorial waters, inland sea-waters and established roadsteads of the German Democratic Republic (hereinafter called "waters of the German Democratic Republic") is permissible only when customary as part of normal navigation or when made necessary by reason of *force majeure* or distress;

(2) Entry into the harbours of the German Democratic Republic may take place only by the approaches and established navigation routes published in *Nautische Mitteilungen für Seefahrer.*

Article 38. (1) The right to peaceful passage through the territorial waters shall be guaranteed, provided that such passage does not endanger peace, sercurity and order and that the existing legal provisions of the German Democratic Republic are not violated.

(2) Passage means crossing the territorial waters without entering the inland seawaters and without putting into or out from the inland seawaters from or to the high seas.

(3) The passage and stay of foreign warships in the waters and harbours of the German Democratic Republic is permissible only with the authorization and consent of the Government of the German Democratic Republic or its authorized organs and is subject to observance of the special regulations for such passage and stay.[1]

Article 39. No ship, boat and passenger traffic may cross the sea-frontier of the German Democratic Republio except through the established frontier crossing points or check points.

. . .

Article 57. (1) The competent defence and security organs shall be entitled, in the waters of the German Democratic Republic:

(a) To require any ship to show its national or State flag;

---

[1] Regulation of 11 August 1965 on the stay of foreign warships in the waters of the German Democratic Republic. *Infra* Chapter VI, 1.

(b) To demand to know the reason for entry into the waters of the German Democratic Republic;

(c) To give instructions as to course and speed;

(d) To stop any ship and to check the ship's papers, and cargo manifest, to check the passengers and crew and to examine the cargo and the holds;

(e) To arrest persons on board a foreign ship passing through territorial waters if the said persons have, in the course of transit, committed an offence in violation of order in the territorial waters or if the captain of the foreign ship requests assistance.

(2) The customs authorities of the German Democratic Republic shall have the rights referred to in paragraph 1 *(c)* and *(d)* above.

Article 58. (1) The defence and security organs shall be entitled, in the waters of the German Democratic Republic, to stop any ship and bring it into port, if the ship:

(a) Does not comply with the instructions given under article 57, paragraph 1 *(a)* to *(c)*, or resists the measures provided for in article 57, paragraph 1 *(d)* and *(e)*;

(b) Undertakes the loading or unloading of cargo in areas other than those designated for that purpose;

(c) Embarks or disembarks passengers in violation of the relevant regulations;

(d) Establishes contact with the coast or islands of the German Democratic Republic or with other craft for illegal purposes;

(e) Carries on fishing activities or exploitation of the sea in any other manner in violation of the relevant regulations;

(f) Violates the customs of foreign exchange control regulations;

(g) Enters waters which use closed to shipping;

(h) Leaves port without the authorization of the customs or port authorities and does not comply with the order to stop;

(i) Violates the rules of peaceful passage.

(2) The customs authorities of the German Democratic Republic shall have the same right if the ship:

(a) Does not comply with the instructions given under article 67, paragraph 1 *(c)*, or resists the measures provided for in article 57, paragraph 1 *(d)*;

(b) Commits the acts described in paragraph 1 *(b)* to *(d)* *(f)* and *(h)*.

Article 59. Foreign ships which have violated laws of the German Democratic Republic may be pursued, stopped and brought into port. The pursuit may be continued on the high seas (hot pursuit) if it was commenced within the waters of the German Democratic Republic and has not been interrupted. The pursuit shall cease when the foreign ship enters the territorial waters of its own or of a third State.

Article 60. (1) A protocol relating to the measures referred to in article 57, paragraph 1 *(d)* and *(e)*, article 58 and article 59, signed by both parties, in two copies in the German language, shall be prepared in every case. The captain of the ship may include his reservations in the protocol or may record them in any language in a separate appendix.

(2) These provisions shall not apply to the operations of the authorities operating at frontier crossing points.

Article 61. The provisions of articles 57 to 60 shall not apply to foreign warships.

. . .

ANNEX 1[1]

The baseline of the territorial waters of the German Democratic Republic shall be determined by the course of the coastline and of the connecting lines between the co-ordinates of the following points:

1.	Frontier with the Polish People's Republic	Latitude 53° 55' 46" Longitude 14° 13' 42"
2.	Peenemünder Haken	Latitude 54° 10' 06" Longitude 13° 48' 56"
3.	Greifswalder Oie	Latitude 54° 15' 00" Longitude 15° 35' 43"
4.	Nordperd	Latitude 54° 20' 33" Longitude 13° 46' 06"
5.	Kollicker Ort along the coastline to	Latitude 54° 33' 49" Longitude 13° 40' 51"
6.	Ranzow	Latitude 54° 35' 11" Longitude 13° 38' 21"
7.	Kap Arkona	Latitude 54° 41' 12" Longitude 13° 25' 45"
8.	Rehbergort	Latitude 54° 38' 42" Longitude 13° 13' 27"
9.	Dornbusch (Insel Hiddensee)	Latitude 54° 36' 28" Longitude 13° 08' 05"
10	Bernsteininsel	Latitude 54° 29' 27" Longitude 12° 32' 06"
11.	Darsser Ort along the coastline to	Latitude 54° 29' 00" Longitude 12° 30' 48"
12.	Halbinsel Wustrow	Latitude 54° 05' 40" Longitude 11° 33' 13"
13.	Gross-Klütz-Höved along the coastline to	Latitude 54° 00' 58" Longitude 11° 10' 50"
14.	Frontier between the German Democratic Republic and the Federal Republic of Germany . .	Latitude 53° 57' 30" Longitude 10° 54' 18"

---

[1] *Supra* Article 30, paragraph 1.

5. GHANA

TERRITORIAL WATERS AND CONTINENTAL SHELF DECREE, 1973[1]

In pursuance of the National Redemption Council (Establishment) Proclamation, 1972, this Decree is hereby made:

1. *Extent of territorial waters*

(1) It is hereby declared that the territorial waters of the Republic shall extend to the limits of thirty nautical miles from low-water mark.

(2) The National Redemption Council may, if satisfied that it is in the public interest so to do, by legislative instrument declare any part of the sea touching or adjoining the coast, and seaward of the outer limits of the territorial waters of the Republic to be an area over which the Government shall exercise any right of protection.

2. *Fishing conservation zone*

Where the National Redemption Council is satisfied that it is in the public interest so to do, it may by legislative instrument declare any area of the sea touching or adjoining the coast, and within a distance of one hundred nautical miles from the outer limits of the territorial waters of the Republic, to be a fishing conservation zone; and may in the same or any other instrument specify the measures which shall be taken for the conservation of the resources of any such area.

3. *Vesting of continental shelf*

It is hereby declared that the continental shelf is vested in the National Redemption Council on behalf of the Republic in trust for the people of Ghana.

4. *Regulations*

(1) The National Redemption Council may by legislative instrument make regulations for giving full effect to the provisions of this Decree.

(2) Regulations made under this section may prescribe a penalty for an infringement thereof of a fine not exceeding ₵100,000 or a term of imprisonment not exceeding fifteen years or both and may also require the forfeiture of anything used in the commission of the offence.

(3) Where an offence under any regulations made under this section is committed by a body of persons—

(a) Where the body of persons is a body corporate, every director and officer of the body corporate shall be deemed to be guilty of the offence; and

(b) Where the body corporate is a firm, every partner of the firm shall be deemed to be guilty of the offence:

Provided that a person shall not be deemed to be guilty of an offence by virtue of this subsection if he proves that the act constituting the offence was

---

[1] N.R.C.D. 165; 16 March 1973. Text provided by the Permanent Representative of Ghana to the United Nations in a note verbale of 5 July 1973.

committed by a person other than himself and without his knowledge or connivance and that he exercised all due diligence to prevent the commission of the offence having regard to all the circumstances.

5. *Interpretation*

For the purposes of this Decree and any other enactment—"continental shelf" includes—

(a) The sea-bed and subsoil of the submarine areas to a depth of one hundred fathoms contiguous to the coast and seaward of the area of land beneath the territorial waters of the Republic; and

(b) Such further parts lying beyond the said depth of one hundred fathoms of the sea-bed and subsoil of the submarine areas whose natural resources are capable of exploitation; and

(c) All the natural resources of the areas specified in this defintion including minerals and other inorganic and organic matter;

"territorial waters" shall have the meaning assigned to it by section 1 of this Decree.

6. *Repeals*

The Territorial Waters and Continental Shelf Act, 1963 (Act 175)[1] and the Territorial Waters and Continental Shelf Act, 1963 (Amendment) Decree, 1968 (N.L.C.D. 309) are hereby repealed.

6. GUINEA-BISSAU

DFCISION No 14/74 EN DATE DU 31 DECEMBRE 1974, DU CONSEIL D'ETAT RELATIVE A LA DELIMITATION DES EAUX TERRITORIALES DE L'ETAT DE GUINEE-BISSAU[2]

Article premier. La mer territoriale de la République de Guinée-Bissau s'étend sur 150 milles marins à partir des principales lignes de base définies par les points suivants :
- Baie de Varela (12° 12′ N., 16° 29′,6 O.)
- à Caió (11° 50′,7 N., 16° 20′,2 O.);
- Sud-ouest de l'île de Unhocomo (11° 16′,4 N., 16° 29′ O.) au sud-ouest de l'île de Orango (11° 1′,5 N., 16° 11′ O.);
- Est de l'île de Joâo Vieira (11° 2′,7 N., 15° 36′,5 O.) au sud-ouest de l'île de Canhabaque (10° 54′ N., 15° 6′,3 O.).

Paragraphe unique. Les points limites de comptage de la mer territoriale de la République de Guinée-Bissau sont les suivants :

- Au nord — 12° 20′, 2 N., 16° 43′, 2 W.
- Au sud — 10° 35′,8 N., 15° 4′ W.

---

[1] Reproduced in part in ST/LEG/SER.B/15, pp 85, 360 and 637.

[2] Texte communiqué par lettre en date du 31 décembre 1974 du représentant permanent auprès de l'Organisation des Nations Unies.

Article 2. La pêche à l'intérieur des eaux territoriales de la République de Guinée-Bissau est formellement interdite à tout navire étranger qui ne soit pas autorisé à cela par une convention signée par le pays du pavillon respectif.

Article 3. La violation aux dispositions de l'article 2 est punie d'une amende de 100 à 200 contos. En cas de récidive, l'amende sera le double de ces montants.

Article 4. L'agent de l'autorité qui aura vérifié l'infraction conduira le navire et son équipage au port national le plus proche et informera les autorités.

Article 5. Par détermination des autorités maritimes, on procédera immédiatement à la vente du poisson (s'il y en a), versant le produit de cette vente, en cas de condamnation, dans les coffres de l'Etat.

Article 6. Outre la condamnation au paiement de l'amende prévue par l'article 3, le tribunal qui a jugé la violation ordonnera la confiscation des instruments de pêche utilisés au cours de cette violation.

7. IRAQ

INFORMATION CONCERNING THE SOVEREIGNTY OVER IRAQ'S TERRITORIAL WATERS AND ITS CONTINENTAL SHELF[1]

In 1968, an official spokesman in the Iraqi Ministry of Foreign Affairs issued the following Statement:

" 'In a joint communique issued in Teheran and Kuwait on January 13th, 1968, after the official visit of His Highness The Ruler of Kuwait to Iran, it was stated that both sides have agreed on a final solution regarding the continental shelves pertaining to both States. Since the Government of the Republic of Iraq did not participate in the negotiations held between the Iranian and the Kuwaiti Governments, and in view of Iraq's rights in the area and the interjacence of its territorial waters and continental shelf with those of the neighbouring countries, the Government of the Republic of Iraq declares that it shall maintain its full sovereignty over Iraq's territorial waters, and the air-space above it, its continental shelf and the subsoil thereof, and affirms that all works and installations, already undertaken or which may be undertaken in future in the said area are subject to Iraqi sovereignty. While the Iraqi Government declares this affirmation of Iraq's rights, it wishes to emphasize its full adherence to the rules and principles of international law, but at the same time it will not recognize any communique, declaration, legislation, or plan of any neighbouring State which infringes upon Iraq's territorial waters and continental shelf in contravention with Iraq's sovereign rights.' "

---

[1] Text provided by the Deputy Permanent Representative of Iraq to the United Nations in a note verbale of 15 May 1973.

8. ISRAEL

TERRITORIAL WATERS LAW, 1956[1]

1. In the definition of "territorial waters" in section I of the Interpretation Ordinance (New Version),[2] the words "three nautical miles" shall be replaced by the words "six nautical miles".

2. Wherever it is said in any law that a part of the open sea adjoining the coast of the State is included in the territory of the State or that any law or a power under any law applies to such a part, and the extent of that part is not fixed or is fixed at less than six nautical miles from low water mark or from some other point on the coast, such extent shall be six nautical miles as aforesaid.

9. LIBYAN ARAB REPUBLIC

INFORMATION CONCERNING THE JURISDICTION OF THE GULF OF SURT[3]

"The Libyan Arab Republic makes the following announcement:

"The Gulf of Surt located within the territory of the Libyan Arab Republic and surrounded by land boundaries on its East, South, and West sides, and extending North offshore to latitude 32 degrees and 30 minutes, constitutes an integral part of the territory of the Libyan Arab Republic and is under its complete sovereignty.

"As the Gulf penetrates Libyan territory and forms a part thereof, it constitutes internal waters, beyond which the territorial waters of the Libyan Arab Republic start.

"Through history and without any dispute, the Libyan Arab Republic has exercised its sovereignty over the Gulf. Because of the Gulf's geographical location commanding a view of the Southern part of the country, it is, therefore, crucial to the security of the Libyan Arab Republic. Consequently, complete surveillance over its area is necessary to insure the security and safety of the State.

"In view of the aforementioned facts, the Libyan Arab Republic declares that the Gulf of Surt, defined within the borders stated above, is under its complete national sovereignty and jurisdiction in regard to legislative, judicial, administrative and other aspects related to ships and persons that may be present within its limits.

"Private and public foreign ships are not allowed to enter the Gulf without prior permission from the authorities of the Libyan Arab Republic and in accordance with the regulations established by it in this regard.

---

[1] *Laws of the State of Israel,* vol. XI, 5717 1956/57, p. 3. English text provided by the Permanent Representative of Israel to the United Nations in a note verbale of 29 February 1973.

[2] Reproduced in part in ST/LEG/SER.B/6, pp. 26-27.

[3] Provided by the Permanent Representative of the Libyan Arab Republic to the United Nations in a note verbale of 19 October 1973.

"The Libyan Arab Republic reserves the soverign rights over the Gulf for its nationals. In general, the Libyan Arab Republic exercises complete rights of sovereignty over the Gulf of Surt as it does over any part of the territory of the State."

10. MADAGASCAR

ORDONNANCE No 73-060 DU 28 SEPTEMBRE 1973 FIXANT LES LIMITES DE LA MER TERRITORIALE ET DU PLATEAU CONTINENTAL DE LA REPUBLIQUE MALGACHE[1]

Le général de division Gabriel Ramanantsoa, chef du Gouvernement,

— Vu la loi constitutionnelle du 7 novembre 1972;

— Vu l'ordonnance No. 60-047 du 25 juin 1960 modifiée et complétée par l'ordonnance No 62-012 du 10 août 1962 et la loi No 66-007 du 5 juillet 1966 portant Code maritime[2] et notamment l'article 1-2-01;

— Vu la loi No 70-016 du 15 juillet 1970 portant réglementation maritime des installations et autres dispositifs sur le plateau continental[3];

— Vu le décret No 63-131 du 27 février 1963 fixant la limite de la mer territoriale de la République malgache[4];

— Vu la décision No 63-CSI/D du 12 septembre 1973 du Conseil supérieur des Institutions;

— En Conseil des Ministres, le 31 août 1973,

Ordonne

Article 1er. La mer territoriale de la République malgache s'étend jusqu'à une limite fixée à cinquante (50) milles marins à partir des lignes de base.

Article 2. Le "plateau continental" de la République malgache (zone économique exclusive) s'étend jusqu'à une limite fixée à cent (100) milles marins au-delà de sa mer territoriale.

Toutefois, et sauf convention particulière, le plateau continental malgache ne s'étend pas au-delà d'une ligne médiane dont tous les points sont équidistants des points les plus proches des lignes de base des côtes malgaches et des côtes des Etats qui lui font face.

L'expression "plateau continental" désigne le lit de la mer et le sous-sol des régions sous-marines adjacentes aux côtes malgaches situés au-delà de la mer territoriale de la République malgache.

Article 3. Les lignes de base à partir desquelles est mesurée la largeur de la mer territoriale sont fixées par décret.

---

[1] Texte transmis par le Chargé d'Affaires a.i. de la Mission permanente de Madagascar auprès de l'Organisation des Nations Unies par lettre en date du 19 février 1974.

[2] Reproduite partiellement dans ST/LEG/SER.B/15, p. 164-165 et 248.

[3] Reproduite partiellement dans ST/LEG/SER.B/16, p. 152-154.

[4] Reproduit partiellement dans ST/LEG/SER.B/15, p. 98-100.

Article 4. Toutes dispositions contraires à celles de la présente ordonnance sont abrogées, et notamment :

— Le 2ème alinéa de l'article 1-2-01 de l'annexe 2 de la loi No 66-007 du 5 juillet 1966 portant Code maritime;
— L'article 1er du décret No 63-131 du 27 février 1963.

. . .

11. MALDIVES

CONSTITUTION OF THE REPUBLIC,[1]
ARTICLE 1, AMENDMENT CONCERNING THE TERRITORIAL LIMITS

. . . The political territory of Maldives extends over the islands situated within 12 miles of the territorial waters measured from the outside reef adjoining the Ocean in every Atoll in Maldives, and over the seas, air and everywhere connected with these islands.

12. MEXICO

GENERAL ACT OF 31 DECEMBER 1941 ON NATIONAL PROPERTY,[2]
AS AMENDED IN 1969[3]

. . .

Article 18. Property subject to public use consists of:

I. . . .

II. The territorial sea to a distance of 12 nautical miles (22,224 metres), in accordance with the provisions of the Political Constitution of the United Mexican States, the laws derived from it, and international law. Except as provided in the following subparagraph, the breadth of the territorial sea shall be measured from the low-water mark on the coast of the mainland and on the shore of islands forming part of the national territory.

Where there are deep bays and inlets in the coast, or where there is a fringe of islands immediately adjacent to the coast, the method of straight baselines joining the points farthest out to sea may be employed in drawing

---

[1] Amendment approved by Citizen's Special Majlis on 15 April 1975. English text of amendment provided by the Under-Secretary, Department of External Affairs of the Republic of Maldives, in a letter dated 31 August 1975. For original text of article 1, see ST/LEG/SER.B/16, p. 16.

[2] The relevant provision (quoted as article 17) of the 1941 Act as amended in 1967 is reproduced in ST/LEG/SER.B/15, p. 101

[3] Amended by the Decree of 12 December 1969, published in *Diario Oficial* of 26 December 1969 and in force since 27 December 1969. This Decree amends article 18, paragraph II (first and second subparagraphs) of the General Act on National Property. Translation by the Secretariat of the United Nations

According to section 3 of the Transitional Provisions of the 1969 amending decree, this amendment would not affect agreements concluded or to be concluded pursuant to transitional article 3 of the Act of 13 December 1966 on the Exclusive Fishing Zone, reproduced in ST/LEG/SER.B/15, p. 649.

the baseline from which the breadth of the territorial sea is measured. Such baselines must not depart appreciably from the general direction of the coast, and the areas of the sea lying landward from these lines must be sufficiently closely linked to the land domain to be subject to the régime of internal waters. The lines shall be drawn to the elevations which emerge at low tide, when these support lighthouses or installations which remain constantly above water level or when they lie wholly or partly at a distance from the coast of the mainland or from an island which does not exceed the breadth of the territorial sea. Permanent installations farther out to sea forming an integral part of the port system shall be considered part of the coast for the purposes of delimiting the territorial sea.

. . .

13. MONACO

ORDONNANCE SOUVERAINE No 5.094 DU 14 FEVRIER 1973
PORTANT DELIMITATION DES EAUX TERRITORIALES MONEGASQUES[1]

. . .

Les eaux territoriales monégasques s'étendent jusqu'à une limite fixée à 12 milles marins à partir de la ligne de base formée par la laisse de basse mer longeant la côte.

Notre Secrétaire d'Etat, notre Directeur des Services judiciaires et notre Ministre d'Etat sont chargés, chacun en ce qui le concerne, de la promulgation et de l'exécution de la présente Ordonnance.

14. MOROCCO

DAHIR PORTANT LOI No 1.73.211 DU 2 MARS 1973 FIXANT LA LIMITE DES
EAUX TERRITORIALES ET DE LA ZONE DE PECHE EXCLUSIVE MAROCAINES[2]

Article premier. Les eaux territoriales marocaines s'étendent jusqu'à une limite fixée à 12 milles marins à partir des lignes de base.

Les lignes de base sont la laisse de basse mer ainsi que les lignes de bases droites et les lignes de fermeture de baies qui sont déterminées par décret.

La souveraineté de l'Etat marocain s'étend à l'espace aérien ainsi qu'au lit et au sous-sol de la mer dans la limite des eaux territoriales.

Article 2. Sauf convention particulière, la largeur des eaux territoriales ne s'étend pas au-delà d'une ligne médiane dont tous les points sont équidistants des points les plus proches des lignes de base des côtes marocaines et des côtes des pays étrangers qui font face aux côtes marocaines ou qui leur sont limitrophes.

Article 3. Lorsque la distance entre les lignes de base des côtes marocaines et celles d'un Etat étranger qui leur font face est égale ou

[1] *Journal de Monaco*, No 6 022 du 23 février 1973, p. 144.

[2] Texte fourni par la Mission permanente du Royaume du Maroc auprès de l'Organisation des Nations Unies par note en date du 25 mars 1973.

inférieure à 24 milles marins ou ne permet plus l'existence d'un couloir de haute mer suffisant pour la libre navigation maritime ou aérienne, le droit de transit par les eaux territoriales marocaines et celui de les survoler sont accordés selon les conditions stipulées par les conventions internationales auxquelles le Maroc est partie et conformément au principe du "passage inoffensif" tel qu'il est reconnu et défini par le droit international.

Article 4. Une zone de pêche exclusive marocaine est instituée sur une étendue de 70 milles marins à partir des lignes de base définies dans l'article premier et selon les mêmes critères de délimitation que ceux mentionnés pour les eaux territoriales dans l'article 2.

Article 5. La souveraineté de l'Etat marocain s'étend à toutes les ressources biologiques de la colonne d'eau de cette zone.

L'exercice des droits de pêche est exclusivement réservé dans cette zone aux bateaux battant pavillon marocain ou exploités par des personnes physiques ou morales marocaines.

Ces dispositions ne font pas obstacle aux principes de coopération internationale auxquels le Maroc souscrit, sans préjudice pour ses droits de souveraineté et dans le respect de ses intérêts nationaux.

Article 6. Toute recherche ou exploration scientifique ou archéologique entreprise par un Etat étranger ou par les ressortissants d'un Etat étranger dans la zone de pêche exclusive est soumise à l'autorisation préalable du Gouvernement marocain.

. . .

15. PHILIPPINES

CONSTITUTION OF THE REPUBLIC[1]

Article 1

The national territory

Section 1. The national territory comprises the Philippine archipelago, with all the islands and waters embraced therein, and all the other territories belonging to the Philippines by historic right or legal title, including the territorial sea, the air space, the subsoil, the sea-bed, the insular shelves, and the other submarine areas over which the Philippines has sovereignty or jurisdiction. The waters around, between, and connecting the islands of the archipelago, irrespective of their breadth and dimensions, form part of the internal waters of the Philippines.

. . .

---

[1] Entered into force on 17 January 1973. Text provided by the Permanent Representative of the Philippines to the United Nations in a note verbale of 27 April 1973.

16. TANZANIA

PROCLAMATION BY THE PRESIDENT OF 24 AUGUST 1973 ON THE EXTENT
OF THE TERRITORIAL WATERS OF THE UNITED REPUBLIC OF TANZANIA[1]

Whereas the Law of Nations recognizes that the sovereign power of a
State extends to a belt of sea adjacent to its coasts:

And whereas, in the absence of uniformity in international practice
relating to the extent of the territorial waters of states, it is necessary that a
declaration be made of the extent of the territorial waters of the United
Republic of Tanzania:

Now therefore, I, Julius Kambarage Nyerere, President of the United
Republic of Tanzania, in exercise of the powers vested in me by the Interim
Constitution of Tanzania 1965, and other written laws of the United
Republic do hereby declare and proclaim that, notwithstanding any rule of
law or any practice which may have been observed hitherto in relation to the
United Republic of Tanzania or the territorial waters of the United Republic
of Tanzania, the territorial waters of the United Republic of Tanzania extend
across the sea a distance of fifty nautical miles measured from the appropriate
base lines along the coasts and adjacent islands, as marked on charts
numbered 1 to 4 issued by the Surveys Division of the Ministry of Lands,
Settlement and Water Development, Dar es Salaam, on 30th March, 1967 and
registered with the Secretary-General of the United Nations:

Provided that in respect of the island of Pemba where the distance
between the base line measured on Pemba and the mainland of Kenya is less
than one hundred nautical miles, the territorial waters of the United Republic
of Tanzania extend up to the median line every point of which is equidistant
from the nearest point on the base-line between Pemba and the mainland of
Kenya as marked on the aforesaid charts.

The Proclamation made by me on the tenth day of July, 1963 **and**
published as Government Notice numbered 353 of 1963 and the Proclamation made by me on the thirtieth day of March, 1967[2] and published as
Government Notice No. 137 of 1967 are hereby revoked.

17. TOGO

(a) RENSEIGNEMENTS CONCERNANT LA LEGISLATION
SUR LE DROIT DE LA MER[3]

"Le Togo n'a pas encore défini une législation complète sur la question
de la délimitation et du contrôle de la mer territoriale, des zones contiguës et
du plateau continental ainsi que de l'exploitation des ressources de la mer, du
fond de la mer et de son sous-sol au-delà des eaux intérieures togolaises;

---

[1] Government Notice No. 209. Supplement No. 48 to the *Gazette of the United
Republic of Tanzania,* Vol. LIV, No. 36; 7 September 1973.

[2] Reproduced in ST/LEG/SER.B/15, p. 127.

[3] Transmis par la Mission permanente du Togo auprès de l'Organisation des Nations
Unies par note en date du 23 mai 1973.

cependant, la loi No 64-14 du 11 juillet 1964[1] portant réglementation de la pêche donne des indications à ce sujet.

. . .

"Aujourd'hui, la question du droit de la mer est d'actualité et la tendance du Togo est à l'extension de la largeur de la mer territoriale et de la zone exclusive de pêche, de manière que la souveraineté nationale couvre toutes les ressources de la mer adjacente à la mer territoriale jusqu'à la limite d'une "zone économique" à définir et incluant au moins le plateau continental. Cette zone économique exclusive ne s'étendra pas au-delà de 200 milles marins; le Togo y aura des droits souverains sur les ressources biologiques et non biologiques du fond de la mer et de son sous-sol; toutefois, les Etats étrangers jouiront dans cette zone des libertés de navigation et de survol, du droit de pose des câbles sous-marins et des pipe-lines."

(b) [LOI No 64-14 DU 11 JUILLET 1964 PORTANT REGLEMENTATION DE LA PECHE, article 4] [1]

18. TONGA

(a) ROYAL PROCLAMATION OF 11 JUNE 1887 DEFINING THE BOUNDARIES OF THE KINGDOM [2]

Whereas it seems expedient to Us that We should limit and define the extent and boundaries of Our Kingdom, We do hereby erect as Our Kingdom of Tonga all islands, rocks, reefs, foreshores and waters lying between the fifteenth and twenty-third and a half degrees of south latitude and between the one hundred and seventy-third and the one hundred and seventy-seventh degrees of west longitude from the Meridian of Greenwich.

(b) ROYAL PROCLAMATION OF 15 JUNE 1972 RELATING TO THE ISLANDS OF TELEKI TOKELAU AND TELEKI TONGA [3]

Whereas the Reefs known as North Minerva Reef and South Minerva Reef have long served as fishing grounds for the Tongan people and have long been regarded as belonging to the Kingdom of Tonga; *and whereas* the Kingdom of

---

[1] *Infra* Division IV, 13.

[2] *Government Gazette,* vol. II, No. 55, 24 August 1887. Text sent to the Secretary-General of the United Nations by the Prime Minister and Minister for Foreign Affairs of Tonga, in a letter dated 21 June 1971, requesting that it be brought to the attention of the Chairman of the Committee on the Peaceful Uses of the Sea-Bed and the Ocean Floor beyond the Limits of National Jurisdiction with the following note:

"[The Proclamation] has been acquiesced in by all countries, including the Powers to whom it was communicated in 1887, as indicating, by reference to the co-ordinates therein designated, the legal extent of the national jurisdiction of the Kingdom within which legislation of the Kingdom is expressed to operate, without prejudice to the Government of Tonga's postion on the legal status of the sea and the sea-bed beyond the limits of national jurisdiction."

[3] *Government Gazette Extraordinary* No. 7, 15 June 1972. Text transmitted to the Secretary-General of the United Nations by the Acting Prime Minister and Minister for Foreign Affairs of Tonga, in a letter dated 25 June 1974.

Tonga has now created on these Reefs islands known as Teleki Tokelau and Teleki Tonga; *and whereas* it is expedient that we should now confirm the rights of the Kingdom of Tonga to these islands; *therefore* we do hereby *affirm* and *proclaim* that the islands of Teleki Tokelau and Teleki Tonga and all islands, rocks, reefs, foreshores and waters lying within a radius of twelve miles thereof are part of our Kingdom of Tonga.

19. WESTERN SAMOA

TERRITORIAL SEA ACT 1971[1]

. . .

2. Interpretation—In this Act, unless the context otherwise requires,—

"Bay" means an indentation of the coast such that its area is not less than that of the semi-circle whose diameter is a line drawn across the mouth of the indentation; and for the purposes of this defintion the area of an indentation shall be taken to be the area bounded by low-water mark around the shore of the indentation and the straight line joining the low-water marks of its natural entrance points; and where, because of the presence of islands, an indentation has more than one mouth the length of the diameter of the semi-circle referred to shall be the sum of the lengths of the straight lines drawn across each of the mouths; and in calculating the area of an indentation the area of any islands lying within it shall be treated as part of the area of the indentation:

"Island" means a naturally formed area of land which is surrounded by and is above water at mean high-water spring tides:

"Government" means the Government of Western Samoa:

"Low-water mark" has the meaning assigned thereto by section 8 of this Act:

"Low-tide elevation" means a naturally formed area of land which is surrounded by and is above water at mean low-water spring tides but is submerged at mean high-water spring tides:

"Nautical mile" means the international nautical mile of 6,080 feet:

"Western Samoa" means the Independent State of Western Samoa.

3. The territorial sea—The territorial sea of Wester Samoa comprises those areas of the sea having, as their inner limits, the baseline described in section 5 and 6 of this Act and, as their outer limits, a line measured seaward from that baseline, every point of which is distant twelve nautical miles from the nearest point of the baseline.

4. Internal waters—The internal waters of Western Samoa include any areas of the sea that are on the landward side of the baseline of the territorial sea of Western Samoa.

---

[1] Act No. 3 of 15 July 1971. Text transmitted through the Chargé d'Affaires a.i. of New Zealand to the United Nations in a note verbale of 9 July 1974.

5. Baseline of the territorial sea—

(1) Except as otherwise provided in section 6 of this Act, the baseline from which the breadth of the territorial sea of Western Samoa is measured shall be the low-water mark along the coast of Western Samoa, including the coast of all islands.

(2) For the purposes of this section, a low-tide elevation which lies wholly or partly within the breadth of sea which would be territorial sea if all low-tide elevations were disregarded for the purpose of the measurement of the breadth thereof shall be treated as an island.

6. Baseline of the territorial sea adjacent to a bay—In the case of the sea adjacent to a bay, the baseline from which the breadth of the territorial sea is measured shall—

(a) If the bay has only one mouth and the distance between the low-water marks of the natural entrance points of the bay does not exceed twenty-four nautical miles, be a straight line joining the said low-water marks;

(b) If, because of the presence of islands, the bay has more than one mouth and the distances between the low-water marks of the natural entrance points of each mouth added together do not exceed twenty-four nautical miles, be a series of straight lines across each of the mouths so as to join the said low-water marks;

(c) If neither paragraph (a) nor paragraph (b) of this section applies, be a straight line twenty-four nautical miles in length drawn from low-water mark to low-water mark within the bay in such a manner as to enclose the maximum area of water that is possible with a line of that length.

7. Bed of territorial sea and internal waters vested in Western Samoa—

(1) For the purposes of this section, the term "high-water mark" means the line of median high tide between the spring and neap tides.

(2) Subject to the grant of any estate or interest therein (whether by or pursuant to the provisions of any enactment or otherwise, and whether made before or after the commencement of this Act), the sea bed and subsoil of submarine areas bounded on the landward side by the high-water mark along the coast of Western Samoa including the coast of all islands, and on the seaward side by the outer limits of the territorial sea of Western Samoa shall be deemed to be and always to have been public land vested in Western Samoa.

8. Official charts—

(1) For the purposes of this Act, the low-water mark in any specified area shall be the line of low water at mean low-water spring tides as depicted on the largest scale nautical chart of that area produced by any authority and for the time being held and used by the Government.

(2) In any proceedings in any Court, a certificate purporting to be signed by the Director of Lands or by a Harbour-master of the Marine Department that any specified nautical chart of any area is the largest scale nautical chart of that area produced by any authority and for the time being held and used by the Government shall be admissible as evidence of the matters stated in the certificate.

(3) Every person signing any such certificate shall, in the absence of proof to the contrary, be presumed to be duly authorized to sign it.

9. Permanent harbour works—For the purposes of this Act, permanent harbour works which form an integral part of a harbour system shall be treated as forming part of the coast.

. . .

————————————

Chapter II

NAVIGATION THROUGH THE TERRITORIAL SEA
AND SAFETY OF SHIPS THERE[1]

1. ARGENTINA

(a) [ACT NO. 20,489 OF 23 MAY 1973 REGULATING SCIENTIFIC AND TECH-
NICAL RESEARCH ACTIVITIES CONDUCTED BY FOREIGNERS AND INTER-
NATIONAL ORGANIZATIONS, Articles 1-7 and 9][2]

(b) [DECREE NO. 4,915 OF 23 MAY 1973 REGULATING SCIENTIFIC AND
TECHNICAL RESEARCH ACTIVITIES CONDUCTED BY FOREIGNERS AND
INTERNATIONAL ORGANIZATIONS, Articles 1-4, 6 and 7][3]

2. ECUADOR

(a) [CIVIL CODE AS AMENDED BY DECREE NO. 256-CLP OF 27 FEBRUARY
1970, Articles 628 and 629][4]

(b) REGULATIONS OF 17 FEBRUARY 1973 FOR THE GRANTING OF PERMITS
TO FOREIGN VESSELS TO VISIT THE TERRITORIAL SEA OF ECUADOR, ITS
COASTS OR ISLANDS FOR THE PURPOSE OF TOURISM OR SCIENTIFIC
RESEARCH, Articles 1-6, 8-12[5]

Article 1. Any foreign vessel intending to visit the territorial sea, its
coasts or islands for the purpose of tourism or scientific research must obtain
the appropriate written authorization from the Ministry of National Defence.

Article 2. In order to obtain the authorization referred to in article 1,
the operators, owners or captains of the vessel shall submit a written
application, not less than 60 days before the date set for the expedition,
either directly to the Ministry of National Defence or through any
Ecuadorian embassy abroad, attaching thereto the data, requisite information
and documents referred to in the articles below.

Article 3. When the expedition is being undertaken solely for the
purpose of tourism, the application referred to in the preceding article shall
be accompanied by the following documents and data:

1. Characteristics of the vessel;

---

[1] On navigation see also *infra* Chapter IX as well as Division II, where a number of
laws and regulations refer to the protection of navigation in connexion with the
exploitation of natural resources on the sea-bed and the subsoil thereof.

[2] *Infra* Division II, 1 *(a)*.

[3] *Ibid.,* 1 *(b)*.

[4] *Supra* Chapter I, 2 *(a)*.

[5] Spanish text provided by the Permanent Mission of Ecuador to the United Nations
in a note verbale of 16 October 1973. Translation by the Secretariat of the United
Nations.

2. Itineraries and description of activities to be carried out;
3. Names of national and foreign sponsors of the voyage, with their postal addresses, duly authenticated;
4. Place and date of embarkation and disembarkation;
5. An undertaking that if the Ministry deems necessary, an Ecuadorian tourist guide, to be paid by the Company, will be taken on board at a specified Ecuadorian port;
6. An express undertaking to observe the rules for the preservation of national parks and protected natural species, and to compensate for any damages caused thereto.

Article 4. When the purpose of the expedition is to carry out scientific research, the application shall be accompanied by the following documents and requisite information, in addition to those listed in article 3:

1. A list of the names of the scientific personnel participating;
2. The names of representatives or authorized agents in Ecuador, with their postal addresses, duly authenticated;
3. Details of the research to be carried out in the following fields: oceanography, physics, chemistry, biology, geophysics, meteorology and hydrology;
4. An undertaking to put in at the first Ecuadorian port and to take on board there, at the expense of the expedition, an official or functionary of the Naval Institute of Oceanography;
5. The use to be made of the results of the research;
6. An undertaking to make available through diplomatic channels, the complete results and conclusions of the studies carried out, indicating the date on which the undertaking is to be put into effect;
7. An undertaking to collaborate with Ecuadorian technical personnel in scientific work of interest to the Naval Institute of Oceanography;
8. In specific cases where the vessel is to carry out geophysical research involving underwater seismographic exploration, the granting of concessions of carboniferous materials shall be the responsibility of the Ministry of Natural Resources and Tourism, in accordance with the Supreme Decree published in *Registro Oficial* No. 400 of 31 May 1970. The General Naval Command, through the said Ministry, shall require natural or juridical persons to furnish the following information within six months from the completion of the survey works:

— Method of seismographic exploration used;
— Number of sheet-pilings and sheets;
— Shot recording method used;
— Filter system from initiation to final reproduction of the recordings;
— "Deconvolution" procedure used and manner in which it was carried out, specifying whether it was done before or after "backing up";
— A base map showing the location of shot points;
— Copies of the cross-sections and longitudinal sections of the seismic recordings—showing density or variable, galvanometric or combined

areas—duly corrected and processed at appropriate vertical and horizontal scales;

— A copy of the bathymetric chart.

Article 5. Following receipt of the application by the Ministry, and subject to the favourable opinion of the General Naval Command and verification that the application contains all the requisite information referred to in article 4, the Ministry shall issue the resolution granting or refusing the authorization.

Article 6. If the resolution authorizes the expedition, it shall stipulate the express conditions under which the authorization is granted; if it refuses the authorization, it shall indicate the reasons or the grounds for such refusal.

. . .

Article 8. If the Ministry or the General Naval Command considers, upon examination of the relevant documents, that the expedition is inadvisable or inconsistent with the national interests, the authorization may be postponed or refused without there being any obligation to explain the reasons for such action.

Article 9. After the authorization has been granted, if supervening circumstances so necessitate, or if the recipient fails to comply with one or more of the requirements or conditions stipulated for the expedition in the relevant resolution, the Ministry may, by means of a new resolution, cancel the authorization, allowing the captain of the vessel a reasonable period in which to leave the territorial waters.

Article 10. Although an application for the authorization of the expedition may have been submitted through the proper channels, no vessel may enter the territorial waters of Ecuador before the appropriate permit has been obtained.

Article 11. On the commencement of the expedition within Ecuadorian territorial waters, the captain of the vessel shall deliver the authorizing Ministerial Resolution to the official or agent responsible for tourism and shall be provided in return with:

(a) The orders and provisions of the General Naval Command;

(b) The provisions of the Naval Institute of Oceanography concerning the tasks to be carried out and verified.

Article 12. Upon completion of the expedition, the captain shall receive the appropriate authorization to sail from the competent Harbour Master.

. . .

3. FRANCE

[LOI No 71-1060 DU 24 DECEMBRE 1971 RELATIVE A LA DELIMITATION DES EAUX TERRITORIALES FRANCAISES, article 3][1]

---

[1] *Supra* Chapter I, 3 *(a)*.

4. GERMANY, FEDERAL REPUBLIC OF

(a) ACT OF 26 JULY 1957 ON COASTAL SHIPPING[1]

The Bundestag has adopted the following Act:

Article 1

Coastal shipping, within the meaning of this Act, shall be deemed to be carried on by any person taking on board passengers or goods at any place in the area of application of this Act and transporting them for remuneration, using sea routes, to any point of destination in the said area. For purposes of delimiting sea routes, the provisions of the Third Executive Order relating to the Flag Rights Act, dated 3 August 1951 (*Bundesgesetzblatt* II, p. 155) shall apply as appropriate.

Article 2

(1) Coastal shipping may be carried on only:

1. With sea-going ships flying the federal flag in accordance with the Flag Rights Act, dated 8 February 1951 (*Bundesgesetzblatt* I, p. 79);

2. With inland ships which are entered in a register in the area of application of this Act and which possess the documents prescribed for sea voyages under article 6 of the Inland Ship Inspection Order, dated 18 July 1956 (*Bundesgesetzblatt* II, p. 769).

(2) If a vessel with which coastal shipping may be carried on in accordance with paragraph (1) is unavailable or is available only on much more unfavourable terms at the place where the transport is to begin, the waterways and shipping administration competent for the locality may on request authorize the transport to be made with a sea-going ship flying a foreign flag. A certificate in writing attesting to such authorization must be issued. The certificate must be carried on board.

Article 3

(1) Any person carrying on coastal shipping as master of a ship not authorized for coastal shipping under article 2, paragraph (1), and not possessing the authorization prescribed in article 2, paragraph (2), shall be guilty of a disciplinary offence.

(2) A disciplinary offence or an attempt to commit a disciplinary offence shall be punishable by a fine of up to 10,000 marks.

(3) The administrative authority within the meaning of article 73 of the Act on Disciplinary Offences shall be the waterways and shipping adminis-

---

[1] *BGBl* 1957, part II, p. 738. For the entry into force and the status of previous legislation, see article 6. The texts of this Act and of the Regulations of 3 May 1971 governing maritime shipping routes, *infra*, 4 *(b)*, were transmitted by the Permanent Representative of the Federal Republic of Germany to the United Nations in a note verbale dated 4 March 1975. Translation by the Secretariat of the United Nations.

tration. The Federal Minister of Transport shall exercise the functions of the supreme administrative authority under article 66, paragraph (2), of the Act on Disciplinary Offences.

Article 4

In accordance with article 13, paragraph (1), of the Third Transference Act, dated 4 January 1952 (*Bundesgesetzblatt* I, p. 1), this Act shall also be valid in *Land* Berlin.

Article 5

This Act shall not be valid in the Saarland.

Article 6

(1) This Act shall enter into force on 1 October 1957, except that in *Land* Berlin it shall enter into force with regard to article 3, paragraph (2), only on the day following the promulgation of the Acceptance Act in the Official Gazette of *Land* Berlin.

(2) At the same time the following shall cease to have effect:

1. The Act on Coastal Shipping, dated 22 May 1881 (*Reichsgesetzblatt*, p. 97);

2. The Ordinance concerning the Authorization of Foreign-Flag Ships to Engage in German Coastal Cargo Shipping, dated 29 December 1881 (*Reichsgesetzblatt*, p. 275);

3. The Ordinance concerning the Authorization of Ships Flying the Flag of the Netherlands to Engage in German Coastal Cargo Shipping, dated 1 June 1886 (*Reichsgesetzblatt*, p. 179).

(b) REGULATIONS OF 3 MAY 1971 BY THE MINISTRY OF TRANSPORT GOVERNING MARITIME SHIPPING ROUTES[1], AS AMENDED Articles 3, 4, 40-42[2]

SECTION ONE. GENERAL PROVISIONS[3]

. . .

Article 3

Basic rules governing conduct in traffic

(1) Every participant in traffic must so conduct himself that safety and ease of movement of traffic is ensured and that no one else is harmed,

---

[1] *BGBl* 1971, part I, p. 641. Entered into force on 1 November 1971 in accordance with article 67 (1). A few provisions not reproduced in this volume entered into force at a later date in accordance with article 67 (2)-(3). Translation of the Regulations and amendments thereto by the Secretariat of the United Nations.

[2] By Ordinance No. 1 of 7 July 1972, *BGBl*, part I, p. 1169.

[3] As provided in article 1, the Regulations apply to maritime shipping routes, namely "water areas lying between the coastline at mean high water or the seaward boundary of inland waterways and the seaward boundary of the territorial sea." In terms of article 1 (3) the provisions in these rules shall prevail over a conflicting rule of the International Regulations for Preventing Collisions at Sea (Annex B to the Final Act of the International Conference on Safety of Life at Sea, 1960).

endangered or more seriously hampered or inconvenienced than is unavoidable under the circumstances. In particular, he must observe such rules governing precautions as are required by the custom of seamen or by the special circumstances of the case.

(2) All necessary measures for averting an imminent danger must be taken, with due regard to the special circumstances, even when the taking of such measures necessitates some deviation from the provisions of this Ordinance.

(3) A person whose ability to handle a vessel is impaired by reason of some bodily or mental defect or the use of alcoholic beverages or other intoxicants shall not be permitted to handle a vessel.

Article 4

Responsibility

(1) The master of the vessel shall be responsible for the observance of the provisions of this Ordinance concerning conduct in traffic and concerning the equipping of vessels with devices for the carrying and showing of visual signals.

(2) The pilot shall also bear responsibility; he must so advise the master of the vessel or the latter's representatives as to enable them to observe the provisions of this Ordinance.

(3) In the case of pushing and towing units, without prejudice to the provision contained in paragraph (1), the master of the unit shall be responsible for its safe handling. The term "master of the unit" means the master of the tugboat or the pusher craft; the masters of the vessels concerned may also, before the beginning of the passage, designate another vessel master as master of the unit.

(4) Where no vessel master has been designated and several persons are entitled to handle a vessel, they shall decide before the beginning of the passage who is to be the responsible vessel master.

(5) The provisions of this article shall not affect any responsibility of any other person which arises out of this Ordinance or other provisions.

. . .

SECTION FIVE. TRAFFIC AT REST

. . .

Article 40

Anchoring, docking, mooring and passing involving vessels which are transporting especially dangerous goods[1]

(1) Vessels which are transporting especially dangerous goods may anchor or moor only in the roadsteads and moorings designated by notice by

---

[1] As defined in article 2 (16) of these Regulations, "especially dangerous goods" means: cargo totalling more than 100 kg and belonging to classes I *(a)* and I *(b)* of annex I of the Ordinance on Dangerous Sea Freight, dated 4 January 1960 *(Bundesgesetzblatt* II, p. 9), last amended by the Ordinance of 14 June 1966 *(Bundesgesetzblatt,* II, p. 429), and cargo carried by tankers and belonging to classes I *(d)* and III *(a)* (1), (2), (3) and (5) of annex I of the Ordinance on Dangerous Sea Freight, as well as other liquids with flash points of up to 55°C.

the river and shipping police authority, and only if they observe the requirements which have been designated by notice.

(2) Where several vessels transporting especially dangerous goods are simultaneously lying within the area of the roadstead or mooring, they must be kept at an adequate distance from one another, having due regard to the local conditions.

(3) Where vessels are transporting especially dangerous goods, other vessels, except tugboats, maintenance vessels, tank-cleaning vessels and vessels participating in the transfer of cargo, must keep at an adequate safe distance from them, with special regard to the flight of sparks. Such vessels may enter the area of the roadstead or mooring only when the smokestacks and exhaust pipes have been equipped with devices which prevent the flight of sparks.

(4) Where a moored tanker has not been degassed after the unloading of especially dangerous goods, or other inflammable liquids or of gases, no vessels may lie alongside it during the process of filling the tanks with ballast water, and only the required tank-cleaning vessels may lie alongside it during the degassing process.

(5) Moored vessels which are transporting especially dangerous goods and vessels lying in their vicinity must be capable at all times of being immediately warped away.

Article 41

Transfer of unusually dangerous goods

(1) The transfer of unusually dangerous goods shall be permitted only at the roadsteads and moorings designated for the purpose by notice by the river and shipping police authority and only when the designated requirements are satisfied. The transfer must be reported in advance in good time to the competent river and shipping police authority.

(2) During the transfer, a vessel transporting especially dangerous goods may have no more than one vessel participating in the transfer lying alongside it on each side at any time.

(3) Vessels not participating in transfer must maintain an adequate safe distance from the vessels participating in the transfer which are transporting especially dangerous goods; otherwise they must leave the anchorage or mooring.

(4) After completion of the transfer the vessel must leave the roadstead or mooring without delay.

(5) All other provisions relating to the handling of dangerous goods shall remain unaffected.

SECTION SIX.   OTHER PROVISIONS

Article 42

Conduct in the case of casualty or loss of objects

(1) Where a vessel is in danger of sinking, it must, in so far as possible, be moved so far away from the fairway that shipping is not impaired. After a

collision this shall also be the obligation of the master of any vessel involved which has remained seaworthy.

(2) Where the condition of the maritime shipping route necessary for navigation or the safety and ease of movement of traffic is impaired by vessels, floating installations or unusual floating objects which are drifting helplessly, have run aground, have become stranded or have sunk in the maritime shipping route or by other drifting or grounded objects, the water traffic and shipping office competent for the locality (in the Kiel Canal, the Kiel-Holtenau Canal Office) must be notified without delay.

(3) The location of a sunken vessel must be provisionally marked without delay by the master of the vessel. After a collision this shall also be the obligation of the master of any vessel involved which has remained seaworthy. He may not continue on his way until he has obtained permission therefor from the water traffic and shipping office competent for the locality (in the Kiel Canal, the Kiel-Holtenau Canal Office.)

(4) A grounded vessel may use its engine to free itself except where this is not possible without damaging the maritime shipping route, including the banks, river structures and shipping installations, or where shipping is endangered. If the vessel is in the Kiel Canal and cannot free itself by its own power, it must shut down its engine and, in so far as possible, free the fairway for passing vessels.

(5) In the event of fires and other occurrences endangering the safety and ease of movement of traffic that take place on board vessels, floating installations and unusual floating objects, the water traffic and shipping office competent for the locality (in the Kiel Canal, the Kiel-Holtenau Canal Office) must be notified thereof without delay.

. . .

5. GHANA

[MINERALS (OFFSHORE) REGULATIONS 1963, AS AMENDED IN 1968, Regulations 11, 16 (2) and 19 (2)][1]

6. TOGO

[LOI No 64-14 DU 11 JUILLET 1964 PORTANT REGLEMENTATION DE LA PECHE, article 8][2]

---

[1] *Infra* Chapter IX, 4 *(b)*.

[2] *Infra* Division IV, 13.

7. UNITED KINGDOM OF GREAT BRITAIN AND NORTHERN IRELAND

(a) PROTECTION OF WRECKS ACT 1973, Sections 1-3[1]

1. *Protection of sites of historic wrecks*

(1) If the Secretary of State is satisfied with respect to any site in United Kingdom waters that—

(a) It is, or may prove to be, the site of a vessel lying wrecked on or in the sea-bed; and

(b) On account of the historical, archaeological or artistic importance of the vessel, or of any objects contained or formerly contained in it which may be lying on the sea-bed in or near the wreck, the site ought to be protected from unauthorized interference,

he may by order designate an area round the site as a restricted area.

(2) An order[2] under this section shall identify the site where the vessel lies or formerly lay, or is supposed to lie or have lain, and—

(a) The restricted area shall be all within such distance of the site (so identified) as is specified in the order, but excluding any area above high water mark of ordinary spring tides; and

(b) The distance specified for the purposes of paragraph *(a)* above shall be whatever the Secretary of State thinks appropriate to ensure protection for the wreck.

(3) Subject to section 3 (3) below, a person commits an offence if, in a restricted area, he does any of the following things otherwise than under the authority of a licence granted by the Secretary of State—

(a) He tampers with, damages or removes any part of a vessel lying wrecked on or in the sea-bed, or any object formerly contained in such a vessel; or

(b) He carries out diving or salvage operations directed to the exploration of any wreck or to removing objects from it or from the sea-bed or uses equipment constructed or adapted for any purpose of diving or salvage operations; or

(c) He deposits, so as to fall and lie abandoned on the sea-bed, anything which, if it were to fall on the site of a wreck (whether it so falls or not), would wholly or partly obliterate the site or obstruct access to it, or damage any part of the wreck;

and also commits an offence if he causes or permits any of those things to be done by others in a restricted area, otherwise than under the authority of such a licence.

. . .

2. *Prohibition on approaching dangerous wrecks*

(1) If the Secretary of State is satisfied with respect to a vessel lying wrecked in the United Kingdom waters that—

---

[1] 1973 Chapter 33; 18 July 1973.

[2] See the Protection of Wrecks (Designation) Order 1973, cited *infra (b)*.

(a) Because of anything contained in it, the vessel is in a condition which makes it a potential danger to life or property; and

(b) On that account it ought to be protected from unauthorized interference,

he may by order designate an area round the vessel as a prohibited area.

(2) An order under this section shall identify the vessel and the place where it is lying and—

(a) The prohibited area shall be all within such distance of the vessel as is specified by the order, excluding any area above high water mark of ordinary spring tides; and

(b) The distance specified for the purposes of paragraph *(a)* above shall be whatever the Secretary of State thinks appropriate to ensure that unauthorized persons are kept from the vessel.

(3) Subject to section 3 (3) below, a person commits an offence if, without authority in writing granted by the Secretary of State, he enters a prohibited area, whether on the surface or under water.

3. *Supplementary provisions*

(1) In this Act—

"United Kingdom waters" means any part of the sea within the seaward limits of United Kingdom territorial waters and includes any part of a river within the ebb and flow of ordinary spring tides;

"the sea" includes any estuary or arm of the sea; and references to the sea-bed include any area submerged at high water of ordinary spring tides.

. . .

(3) Nothing is to be regarded as constituting an offence under this Act where it is done by a person—

(a) In the course of any action taken by him for the sole purpose of dealing with an emergency of any description; or

(b) In exercising, or seeing to the exercise of, functions conferred by or under an enactment (local or other) on him or a body for which he acts; or

(c) Out of necessity due to stress of weather or navigational hazards.

(4) A person guilty of an offence under section 1 or section 2 above shall be liable on summary conviction to a fine of not more than £400, or on conviction on indictment to a fine; and proceedings for such an offence may be taken, and the offence may for all incidental purposes be treated as having been committed, at any place in the United Kingdom where he is for the time being.

. . .

(b) [PROTECTION OF WRECKS (DESIGNATION) ORDER 1973][1]

---

[1] Dated 3 September 1973. *Statutory Instruments,* 1973 No. 1531. This Order designated as a restricted area for the purposes of the Protection of Wrecks Act 1973, *supra (a),* an area in Cattewater, Plymouth around the site of a wreck of historical and archaeological importance.

Chapter III

SECURITY OF THE COASTAL STATE

1. ARGENTINA

(a) [ACT NO. 20,489 OF 23 MAY 1973 REGULATING SCIENTIFIC AND TECH-
NICAL RESEARCH ACTIVITIES CONDUCTED BY FOREIGNERS AND INTER-
NATIONAL ORGANIZATIONS, Articles 1-7 and 9] [1]

(b) [DECREE NO. 4,915 OF 23 MAY 1973 REGULATING SCIENTIFIC AND
TECHNICAL RESEARCH ACTIVITIES CONDUCTED BY FOREIGNERS AND
INTERNATIONAL ORGANIZATIONS, Articles 1-4, 6 and 7] [2]

---

[1] *Infra* Division II, 1 *(a)*.
[2] *Infra* Division II, 1 *(b)*.

Chapter IV

CUSTOMS, FISCAL AND SANITARY MATTERS

1. DENMARK

(a) CUSTOMS ACT OF 1972[1]

Chapter 1

The Customs territory

Article 1. 1. The Customs territory shall comprise the land area of Denmark, the inner territorial waters and the outer territorial sea within a distance of four nautical miles (7,408 m) from the coastline or from such straight base-lines as are or may be established, as well as the air space over the territory thus defined.

2. The Customs territory shall not include the Faroe Islands or Greenland.

. . .

Chapter 8

Customs inspection and Customs clearance

. . .

Article 71. 1. Ships and aircraft within the Customs territory and other means of transport operating between the Customs territory and points abroad, as well as means of transport carrying uncleared goods, shall be subject to inspection by the Customs. The Customs shall have the right to undertake everywhere in the said means of transport such searches as are necessary for carrying out the inspection.

2. Ships under way shall stop at the request of the Customs.

3. Aircraft arriving in or departing from the Customs territory may land at and take off from only those airports which are approved by the Customs (Customs airports). The Minister of Finance may dispense specific categories of aircraft from this requirement in accordance with conditions laid down in detail.

4. The operators of means of transport shall be obliged to provide orally and in writing such information concerning the means of transport, the crew, the passengers, the cargo, etc., as may be necessary for carrying out the inspection and to show and open or uncover all means of access to the cargo, hold and store-rooms.

---

[1] Act No. 519 of 13 December 1972. Danish text provided by the Ministry of Foreign Affairs of Denmark in a note verbale of 4 January 1974. Translation by the Secretariat of the United Nations.

5. Operators of means of transport shall report to the Customs upon arrival in and before departure from the Customs territory. The Minister of Finance may exempt operators of certain categories of means of transport from this reporting requirement in accordance with conditions laid down in detail.

6. Goods may be unloaded or loaded and passengers disembarked or taken on board only at ports approved by the Customs. The Customs, may, however, when special circumstances so require, allow unloading and loading to take place elsewhere.

7. The Customs shall specify where passengers entering the Customs territory may be disembarked.

. . .

Chapter 10

Other provisions

. . .

Article 110. 1. The regulations concerning Customs inspection and Customs clearance established in or pursuant to this Act may be applied outside the Customs territory only to such extent as may be determined by international agreement. The Minister of Finance shall make known the scope of such extensions.

Article 111. 1. Within the framework of the provisions of this Act, the Minister of Finance may conclude agreements with foreign States on co-operation in the prevention of smuggling and may take such measures as are necessary for the implementation of such agreements.

2. The Minister of Finance may decide that Customs supervision staff of a foreign State with which an agreement is concluded on common supervision to combat illicit import or export of goods shall, in the performance of their duties in those parts of the Danish Customs territory which are covered by the agreement, have the same powers and enjoy the same protection of the law as Danish Customs supervision staff.

. . .

Chapter 11

Penal and other provisions

Article 117. 1. Any person shall be punishable by a fine who:

(i) fails to declare to the Customs goods which are introduced into the Customs territory or carried from a free port to the other part of the Customs territory, where such declaration is required under this Act or under regulations issued pursuant thereto;

(ii) removes goods which are under Customs seal;

. . .

2. If the act is committed for the purpose of avoiding payment of duty or taxes, it shall be punished, in the same manner as smuggling, by fine,

detention or imprisonment for up to two years, unless a more severe penalty is provided for in article 289 of the Civil Penal Code.

3. Any person who sells or otherwise assigns, who buys or otherwise acquires or receives, or who transports or keeps goods smuggled into the Customs territory, even though he knows or suspects, or should suspect, that the goods are smuggled, shall be punishable in the same manner as provided for in paragraph 2.

4. Contravention of paragraphs 1 to 3 of this article or of article 289 of the Civil Penal Code shall render the offender liable to payment of the amount of duty or tax due on goods concerned.

Article 118. 1. If, in means of transport which have arrived at the Customs territory, dutiable or taxable goods are found which are not listed in the cargo documents and which are not duly declared to the Customs, such goods shall be treated as goods which their owner has attempted to smuggle in, unless the said owner can demonstrate the unlikelihood of an attempt at smuggling having been made.

2. If a vessel of under 120 tons net is encountered within the Customs territory with highly dutiable goods on board on which the duty or tax amounts to 500 kr or more, an attempt at smuggling shall be considered to have taken place, unless the extreme unlikelihood of vessels being operated for the purpose of smuggling is established.

Article 119. 1. The use of a Danish vessel for the smuggling of alcoholic liquors for gain into the foreign States which have ratified the Convention for the suppression of the contraband traffic in alcoholic liquors[1], signed at Helsingfors on 19 August 1925, shall render the owner of the vessel and the shipping agent, if any, on the one hand, and the charterer and master on the other liable to punishment if they were aware or should have been aware that the vessel was being used for smuggling under article 117 of this Act or under article 289 of the Civil Penal Code. The trans-shipment of goods outside the Customs territories of the above-mentioned States under circumstances which make it extremely likely that the intention was to smuggle the goods into the Customs territory of one of them shall also be regarded as smuggling. The vessel shall be liable for any fine which may be incurred.

. . .

Article 127. 1. Means of transport that have been used for the smuggling or attempted smuggling or highly dutiable goods or for the transport of such smuggled goods within the Customs territory may be attached by the Customs or by the police on the Customs' behalf until such time as the amount of the duty tax or fine and any costs, payable by the owner, operator, crew or others serving on the means of transport has been paid, or security for payment has been furnished. If payment is not made within two months of the final disposition of the case, satisfaction may be sought against the means of transport.

. . .

---

[1] League of Nations, *Treaty Series*, vol. XLII, No. 1033.

(b) MINISTRY OF FINANCE NOTICE NO. 578 OF 22 DECEMBER 1972
CONCERNING CLEARANCE[1]

Pursuant to articles 1, 15, 70-94, 97, 105, 108, 110, 111 and 123 of the Customs Act[2] and articles 8 and 9 of the Danish Statistics Act (cf. Legislative Notice No. 15 of 12 January 1972) and article 1 of the Act on administration of the European Economic Community regulations concerning marketing schemes for agricultural and other products, the following regulations are laid down concerning the inspection and Customs clearance of means of transport, persons and goods within the Customs territory:

Chapter 1

The customs territory

Article 1. 1. The Customs territory shall comprise the land areas of Denmark, the inner territorial waters and the outer territorial sea within a distance of four nautical miles (7,408 m) from the coastline or from the straight baselines established by Order No. 437 of 21 December 1966 on the delimitation of the territorial waters[3], as well as the air space over the areas thus defined.

2. The Customs territory shall not include the Faroe Islands or Greenland.

Article 2. 1. Within the areas and to the extent provided for in article 9 of the Convention of 19 August 1925 for the suppression of the contraband traffic in alcoholic liquors (Helsingfors Convention)[4] and its Final Protocol, the provisions of the Customs Act and of this Notice concerning the transport of goods by sea, etc., as well as the penal provisions established in connexion therewith, shall apply to ships whose home port is in a State which has ratified the Convention.

I. CUSTOMS CLEARANCE OF MEANS OF TRANSPORT AND PERSONS

Chapter 2

Ships

Article 3. 1. Ships shall be understood in this Notice to mean ships, boats and vessels of all kinds.

Article 4. 1. Ships which are within the Customs territory shall be subject to Customs inspection.

2. Ships which are under way shall stop at the request of the Customs. An order by the Customs to stop shall be given orally or by means of the stop signal: "Stop your ship immediately".

---

[1] Danish text provided by the Ministry of Foreign Affairs of Denmark in a note verbale of 4 January 1974. Translation by the Secretariat of the United Nations.

[2] Reproduced in part *supra (a)*.

[3] Reproduced in ST/LEG/SER.B/15, pp. 71-76.

[4] League of Nations *Treaty Series,* vol. XLII, No. 1033.

3. The master of the ship shall be obliged to furnish such information as may be necessary for the inspection concerning the ship, its cargo, etc., and, in confirmation of the information furnished, to produce the ship's papers and cargo documents, etc., and to show and open or uncover all means of access to the cargo, hold and store-rooms.

4. The Customs shall have the right to undertake everywhere in the ship the search (rummaging) required for the inspection.

5. Paragraphs 1 to 4 shall apply as appropriate whenever Swedish Customs supervision staff carry out Customs supervision duties within the Customs territory in accordance with the Convention of 28 October 1935 between Denmark and Sweden for common supervision in order to prevent the smuggling of alcoholic liquors. Swedish Customs supervision staff shall enjoy hereunder the same protection of the law as is afforded to Danish Customs supervision staff.

Article 5. 1. When a ship is within the Customs territory or when, while sailing between points in the Customs territory, it passes through foreign or international waters, the Customs may require that uncleared goods be placed under Customs seal. If a seal cannot be applied satisfactorily, a Customs guard may be placed on board the ship at the latter's expense.

2. Ships within the Customs territory may not carry uncleared provisions, etc., unless they have commenced a voyage the final destination of which is a place of call outside the Customs territory. The vessels referred to in article 88, paragraphs 6 and 7, may, however, carry uncleared provisions which have been taken on board in accordance with the rules established for those vessels.

3. Foreign pleasure craft sailing exclusively between points in their country of registry and points in the customs territory, as well as Danish pleasure craft, may carry uncleared provisions, etc., only in so far as they can be imported free of duty under the regulations concerning the exemption from duty of baggage, etc.

Article 6. 1. The loading and unloading of goods and the disembarkation and taking on board of passengers shall be subject to Customs inspection and may take place only at ports approved for the purpose by the Customs. The Customs may, however, when special circumstances so require, allow unloading and loading to take place at other places.

2. The Customs shall specify where passengers entering the Customs territory may be disembarked.

. . .

Article 7.

. . .

2. The master of a ship shall, as soon as possible after its arrival, orally inform the Customs from where the vessel has come and what cargo it carries.

3. The unloading and loading of goods, the disembarkation and taking on board of passengers and the disembarkation of crew members shall be

announced orally in advance to the Customs and may not be commenced until the permission of the Customs has been received.

4. Passenger ships on scheduled services and ferry boats arriving according to a time-table communicated to the Customs in advance shall be exempted from the provisions of paragraphs 1 to 3. The Customs may, however, regulate the disembarkation and taking on board of passengers and may, in special circumstances, prohibit the loading or unloading of goods until the ship has been searched.

. . .

Article 12. The master of a ship shall be liable for any duty or taxes on goods, including residual cargo and supplies of provisions, which are loaded, unloaded or consumed within the Customs territory in contravention of the regulations laid down in this Notice.

. . .

2. PAKISTAN

CUSTOMS ACT, 1969[1]

Section 164: Power to stop and search conveyances

(1) Where the appropriate officer has reason to believe that within the territories of Pakistan (including territorial waters) any conveyance has been, is being, or is about to be, used in the smuggling of any goods or in the carriage of any smuggled goods, he may at any time stop any such conveyance or, in the case of an aircraft, compel it to land, and:—

(a) Rummage and search any part of the conveyance;

(b) Examine and search any goods thereon; and

(c) Break open the lock of any door, fisture package for making search.

(2) Where in the circumstances referred to in sub-section (1):—

(a) It becomes necessary to stop any vessel or compel any aircraft to land it shall be lawful for any vessel or aircraft in the service of the Government while flying her proper flag or bearing flag marks and any authority authorized in this behalf by the Central Government to summon such vessel to stop or the aircraft to land, by means of an international signal, code or other recognized means, and thereupon such vessel shall forthwith stop or such aircraft shall forthwith land, and if it fails to do, so chase may be given thereto by any vessel or aircraft as aforesaid and if after a gun is fired as a signal the vessel fails to stop or the aircraft fails to stop or the aircraft fails to land, it may be fired upon;

(b) It becomes necessary to stop any conveyance other than a vessel or aircraft, the appropriate officer may use or cause to be used all lawful means for stopping it or preventing its escape including, if all other means fail, firing upon it.

. . .

---

[1] Text provided by the Permanent Representative of Pakistan to the United Nations in a note verbale of 8 October 1974.

Chapter V

CRIMINAL AND CIVIL JURISDICTION OVER FOREIGN SHIPS IN THE TERRITORIAL SEA[1]

---

[1] No text concerning criminal and civil jurisdiction over foreign ships in the territorial sea was received during the period covered by this volume.

Chapter VI

STATUS OF FOREIGN WARSHIPS IN THE TERRITORIAL SEA

1. GERMAN DEMOCRATIC REPUBLIC

REGULATION OF 11 AUGUST 1965 ON THE STAY OF FOREIGN WARSHIPS
IN THE WATERS OF THE GERMAN DEMOCRATIC REPUBLIC[1]

In pursuance of article 8 of the ordinance of 19 March 1964 concerning the defence of the frontier of the German Democratic Republic (GB.1.II, p. 255), with a view to the uniform regulation of the stay of foreign warships in the waters of the German Democratic Republic it is hereby ordered as follows:

1. (1) The stay of foreign warships in the territorial waters, inland sea-waters and established roadsteads of the German Democratic Republic (hereinafter called "waters of the German Democratic Republic") is permissible only if duly authorized.

(2) The provisions of paragraph 1 shall also apply to the passage of foreign warships through the waters of the German Democratic Republic.

2. With regard to the stay of foreign warships in the waters of the German Democratic Republic, a distinction shall be drawn between:

(a) Visits
Official visits, conducive to the development of friendly relations between States;
Unofficial visits, usually by training and research ships; and

(b) Cases of distress at sea

3. (1) An application for authorization in accordance with article 1 must be submitted to the Ministry of Foreign Affairs of the German Democratic Republic not less than 30 days before the intended stay or intended passage.

(2) The following particulars must accompany the application;

(a) Purpose of the visit;

(b) Length of stay;

(c) Number, classes and names of the ships;

(d) Principal measurements (displacement, length, beam, draught);

(e) Name and rank of the commanding officer of the ship or ships;

(f) Port of call.

---

[1] GB1.II, p. 638. In force as of 11 August 1965, in conformity with article 20. German text provided by the Permanent Mission of the German Democratic Republic to the United Nations in a note verbale of 19 December 1974. Translation by the Secretariat of the United Nations.

4. The provisions of articles 1 and 3 shall not apply to:

(a) Warships carrying or escorting a Head of State or Government. Such warships must be notified to the Ministry of Foreign Affairs of the German Democratic Republic 10 days before the intended visit;

(b) Warships in distress or forced by damage at sea to enter the waters of the German Democratic Republic.

In such cases, the warships concerned must comply with the instructions given by a ship or of the vessel of the People's Navy or of the Coast guard.

5. Not more than three foreign warships of a State may stay in the waters of the German Democratic Republic for a period not exceeding seven days, unless otherwise agreed.

6. Foreign submarines shall be permitted to stay in the waters of the German Democratic Republic only on condition that they remain on the surface.

7. During their stay in the waters of the German Democratic Republic, foreign warships shall not be permitted to enter areas closed to shipping, as announced in *Nautische Mitteilungen für Seefahrer.*

8. The ceremonial with which foreign warships entering the waters of the German Democratic Republic for a visit are received, and all related formalities, shall be settled in accordance with the relevant laws and regulations of the German Democratic Republic.

9. (1) A liaison officer shall be appointed by the officer of the People's Navy (hereinafter referred to as the senior local officer) to receive foreign warships entering the waters of the German Democratic Republic for a visit. It shall be his duty, in particular, to inform the commanding officer of the ship or ships of the existing rules and instructions.

(2) The commanding officer of a visiting foreign warship or warships shall be required to supply the liaison officer with the particulars called for in the annex to these regulations, unless they have already been transmitted previously.

10. During the stay in a port of the German Democratic Republic, unarmed cutters or dinghies of the foreign warship may move about only with the authorization of the competent senior local officer and in accordance with the relevant harbour regulations.

11. (1) Shore leave for the crew shall require the approval of the senior local officer.

The following particulars must be supplied:

(a) Number of persons taking shore leave (ratings, petty officers, officers);

(b) Commencement of the shore leave;

(c) End of the shore leave.

(2) While on shore leave, members of the crew must observe the rules for the wearing of uniforms applicable to them.

(3) Members of the crew shall be forbidden to carry weapons while on shore leave. The foregoing shall not apply to officers who wear a sword or poniards as part of their uniform.

12. The conditions under which persons not belonging to the crew may board or leave a foreign warship shall be laid down by the senior local officer with the agreement of the commanding officer of the ship or ships.

13. During the stay in the waters of the German Democratic Republic, the crews of foreign warships shall not perform in particular, the following activities:

(a) Research work, measurements and surveys;

(b) Production of photographs and the like, drawings, sketches, descriptions of harbour areas, installations and military equipment;

(c) Movement of armed cutters or dinghies or boat manoeuvres with an armed crew and disembarkation of landing parties;

(d) Firing practice with any kind of weapons (except gun salutes);

(e) Searchlight exercises;

(f) Laving and clearing of mines;

(g) Exercises in the use of chemicals;

(h) Underwater explosions;

(i) Take-off or landing of aircraft, launching of balloons, etc.;

(k) Work with direction-finding apparatus and other radio and hydro-acoustic devices (except for navigational safety when the ship is in motion);

(l) The taking of any kind of fish or other aquatic fauna;

(m) Pollution of the waters by oil or other substances.

14. At the request of the commanding officer of the foreign warship or warships, the senior local officer may grant authorization for:

(a) The use of the radio equipment for radio communication with the ship's own country;

(b) Underwater work for inspection or repair of the ship;

(c) The landing of armed or unarmed troops, not in marching order, to take part in parades, funeral ceremonies or marches.

15. During their stay in the waters of the German Democratic Republic, foreign warships shall be exempt from all charges (including customs duties) except for services rendered.

16. (1) In the event of violation or non-observance of the laws, regulations or instructions of the German Democratic Republic by foreign warships or members of their crews, the senior local officer shall notify the commanding officer of the ship or ships of the violation.

(2) Foreign warships which disregard such a notification may be required to leave the waters of the German Democratic Republic.

(3) In exceptional circumstances, foreign warships may at any time be ordered to leave the waters of the German Democratic Republic within a specified period.

17. The provisions of articles 3, 4, 5, 6, 7, 13, 15 and 16 shall apply *mutatis mutandis* to passage through the waters of the German Democratic Republic.

18. This regulation shall also apply to the naval auxiliary vessels and armed ships of the fisheries protection service of a State.

19. This regulation shall be published annually in the first issue of the *Nautische Mitteilungen für Seefahrer.*

20. This regulation shall enter into force on its publication.

Chapter VII

POLLUTION OF THE TERRITORIAL SEA

1. CANADA

(a) [OIL POLLUTION PREVENTION REGULATIONS OF 21 SEPTEMBER 1971, AS AMENDED IN 1973][1]

(b) [NON-CANADIAN SHIPS COMPLIANCE CERTIFICATE REGULATIONS OF 6 MARCH 1973][2]

2. DENMARK

(a) [ACT NO. 285 OF 7 JUNE 1972 CONCERNING THE EXPLOITATION OF STONE, GRAVEL AND OTHER NATURAL DEPOSITS IN THE GROUND IN THE TERRITORIAL SEA, Article 1 (2)][3]

(b) [EXECUTIVE ORDER NO. 141 OF 13 MARCH 1974 CONCERNING PIPELINE INSTALLATIONS IN THE AREA OF THE DANISH CONTINENTAL SHELF FOR THE TRANSPORT OF HYDROCARBONS][4]

3. FINLAND

(a) [ACT NO. 668 OF 22 SEPTEMBER 1972 FOR THE PREVENTION OF OIL DAMAGE CAUSED BY SHIPS, Articles 1-6, 8, 10, 13-20 and 25][5]

(b) [ORDER NO. 710 OF 26 OCTOBER 1972 FOR THE PREVENTION OF OIL DAMAGE CAUSED BY SHIPS, Articles 1-4, 7 and 12][6]

4. FRANCE

[LOI No 64-1331 DU 26 DECEMBRE 1964 REPRIMANT LA POLLUTION DES EAUX DE LA MER PAR LES HYDROCARBURES, MODIFIEE PAR LA LOI No 73-477 DU 16 MAI 1973, articles 1-3, 3 *bis*, 5 et 6][7]

---

[1] *Infra* Division III, 1 *(a)*.

[2] *Ibid.*, 1 *(b)*.

[3] *Infra,* Chapter IX, 3.

[4] *Infra,* Division II, 4.

[5] *Infra,* Division III, 2 *(a)*.

[6] *Ibid.*, 2 *(b)*.

[7] *Infra* Division III, 3.

5. GERMANY, FEDERAL REPUBLIC OF

(a) FEDERAL WATER ACT OF 27 JULY 1957,[1] AS AMENDED UP TO 1970[2]

The following Act has been enacted by the Bundestag, with the consent of the Bundesrat:

INTRODUCTION

Article 1. Matters to which this Act applies

(1) This Act shall apply to the following waters

1. Water which permanently or temporarily stands or flows in beds or which flows from natural springs (surface waters);
1a. The sea between the coast line at medium flood water level or the seaward limitation of the surface waters and the seaward limitation of the coastal sea (coastal waters);
2. Underground water.

(2) The *Länder* may exclude from the provisions of this Act small waters which are economically of minor importance as well as springs which have been declared to be healing mineral springs. This provision shall not, however, apply to article 22.

(3) The *Länder* shall determine the seaward limitation of those surface waters which are not inland waterways of the Federation.

PART I. GENERAL PROVISIONS RELATING TO WATERS

Article 2. Basic principle

(1) Waters may not be used without a permit *(Erlaubnis)* (art. 7) or a licence *(Bewilligung)* (art. 8) issued by the authorities, subject however to any provisions to the contrary contained in this Act or in the regulations issued by a *Land* in accordance with the provisions of this Act.

(2) The grant of a permit or a licence does not confer a title to a supply of water in any specific quantity or quality. Notwithstanding article 11, they shall not affect any claims under private law to a supply of water of any specific quantity or quality.

Article 3. Uses of water

(1) For the purpose of this Act uses of water are defined as

1. The withdrawal or diversion of water from surface waters;
2. The impounding or draw-down of surface waters;
3. The withdrawal of solid matter from surface waters, so far as this has any effect on the condition of such waters or their flow;

---

[1] *BGBl* 1957, part I, p. 1110. In force as of 1 March 1960 in accordance with article 45. English text provided by the Permanent Representative of the Federal Republic of Germany to the United Nations in a note verbale dated 4 March 1975.

[2] Amended in 1959, 1964, 1967, 1968 and 1970. For the latest amendment see BGBl 1970, part I, p. 805.

4. The introduction or discharge of matter into surface waters;

4a. Introduction and discharge of substances into coastal waters, if such substances

   (a) Were introduced or discharged from the main land or from plants which have been established or moored in coastal waters not only temporarily; or

   (b) Were brought into coastal waters to be disposed of there;

5. The discharge of matter into underground water;

6. The withdrawal, bringing or drawing-off to the surface, or the diversion of underground water.

(2) The following shall also be deemed to constitute uses of water

1. The impounding, draw-down or diversion of underground water by means of installations designed for, or suitable for, such purposes;

2. Any measures which are likely to cause, either permanently or to a not merely insignificant degree, harmful changes in the physical, chemical or biological constitution of water.

(3) Any measures which serve to maintain or improve surface waters shall not be deemed to constitute uses thereof.

Article 4. *Conditions of use*

(1) A permit or a licence may be granted subject to the imposition of conditions. Conditions may also be imposed in order to prevent or make good any effects which are detrimental to other persons.

(2) Further, conditions may be imposed with the following particular objects

1. The institution of measures for the observation or ascertainment of the condition of the water before use and of the extent of any damage done or harmful effects caused by their use;

2. Prescribing the appointment of responsible agents of the enterprise;

3. Requiring the enterpriser to make appropriate contributions towards the cost of measures taken, or to be taken, by a public corporation in order to prevent or make good any damage to the common weal arising out of the use of the water.

Article 5. *Reservation*

Permits or licences are granted subject to the reservation that at a subsequent date

1. Additional requirements may be made as to the constitution of any matter which is to be introduced or discharged into waters;

2. Measures may be ordered for the observation of the use of water and the result arising therefrom;

3. Measures may be ordered to ensure the economical use of water, which is called for by the actual state of the supply.

Where the water is used by virtue of a licence, any measures taken under 2 or 3 must be economically justified and compatible with the respective use.

Article 6. Refusal

The grant of a permit or a licence shall be refused in a case where the proposed use is likely to lead to injury to the common weal and, in particular, where it would endanger the public water supply, and where such injury or danger cannot be prevented or made good by the imposition of conditions or by action taken by a corporation under public law (No. 3 of para. 2 of art. 4).

Article 7. Permit

The grant of a permit confers authority to use any water for a specific purpose, in a definite way and to a definite extent; a permit may be granted for a limited period only, and it may be withdrawn.

Article 8. Licence

(1) The grant of a licence confers authority to use waters in a definite way and to a definite extent. It does not confer on the licensee the right to make use of objects which belong to another person or to use land and installations which are in the possession of another person.

(2) A licence may be granted only if

1. The enterpriser cannot be expected to carry out his project without his legal position being assured; and
2. The use of water is for a specific purpose which is pursued in accordance with a definite plan.

(3) If the use of the water is likely to have a detrimental effect on the rights of another person, and if the person concerned raises objections, then the licence shall be granted only if the detrimental effects are prevented or made good by the imposition of conditions. Should this not be possible, the licence may nevertheless be granted on the ground that it operates for the common weal, but in such a case the person concerned shall be granted compensation.

(4) The *Länder* may specify other cases in which persons are entitled to raise objections on the grounds that they are detrimentally affected. In such cases para. 3 shall apply correspondingly. The *Länder* may nevertheless lay down that a licence may also be granted in a case where the benefit which may be expected to arise from the use of the water greatly exceeds the disadvantage which is likely to accrue to the person concerned.

(5) A licence shall be granted for a definite, and an appropriate, period; in special cases such period of time may exceed thirty years.

(6) If there is any change in the ownership of installations for the use of water, the licence shall be transferred at the same time. If the licence is attached to real property and a change of ownership occurs, the licence shall be transferred to the legal successor at the same time, provided that nothing to the contrary is stipulated in the licence.

. . .

Article 11. Exclusion of claims

(1) The person concerned (paras. 3 and 4 of art. 8) cannot make any claim against the holder of a licence in respect of the detrimental effects

arising from the exercise of that licence the object of which is the removal of the disturbance, the refraining to make use of the water, the establishment of protective arrangements or the award of damages. Nothing herein contained shall however preclude claims for damages from being made in respect of any detrimental effects arising from the fact that the licensee has not complied with conditions imposed on him.

(2) The first sentence of paragraph 1 shall not apply in the case of claims based on a contract.

Article 12. Limitation and withdrawal of licence

(1) If the continued unrestricted use of the water is likely to cause considerable injury to the common weal, and in particular to the public water supply, the licence may be limited or withdrawn; in such a case compensation shall be awarded, unless action can be taken under article 5 without payment of compensation.

(2) Apart from the provisions contained in article 5, a licence cannot be limited or withdrawn without the award of compensation, unless the enterpriser

1. Obtained the licence on the basis of evidence which was incorrect or incomplete on material points, and was aware of the incorrectness or incompleteness;
2. Did not begin to use the water within the appropriate period laid down, or did not use it for a consecutive period of three years;
3. Has changed the purpose for which the water is used so that it no longer conforms to the plan (No. 2 of para. 2 of art. 8);
4. Notwithstanding a warning that the licence may be withdrawn, repeatedly uses the water considerably in excess of the limits of his licence, or has not complied with conditions which have been imposed.

. . .

Article 22. Liability for changes in the constitution of water

(1) Any person who introduces or discharges any matter into waters or takes any action which results in their physical, chemical or biological constitution being changed shall be liable to make good damage caused to any other person as a result of his action. If several persons were responsible for the action, they shall be jointly and severally liable for any damage.

(2) If any material from any installation which is designed to manufacture, process, store, mature, transport or conduct elsewhere such material, reaches any waters without being knowingly put or discharged into them, the owner of the installation shall be liable to make good any damage caused thereby to another person; sentence 2 of paragraph 1 shall apply correspondingly. Liability to make good damage shall not, however, arise if such damage has been caused by an Act of God.

(3) If a claim for damages cannot be made under article 11, the person concerned shall be compensated under paragraph 2 of article 10. Such a claim may be admitted even after the expiration of the period of thirty years.

PART II. REGULATIONS FOR SURFACE WATERS

. . .

Section 2. Preservation of the purity of waters

Article 26. Introduction, storage and transport of materials

(1) Solid matter shall not be introduced into waters for the purpose of getting rid of it. Muddy matter shall not be deemed to be solid matter.

(2) If materials are stored near waters, they shall be placed in such a way that there is no pollution of the water and that the quality of the water which flows away is not otherwise detrimentally affected. The same shall apply to the conveyance of liquids or gases through pipes. This is without prejudice to any existing provisions which are more far-reaching.

Article 27. Orders for the preservation of the purity of waters

(1) Where the physical, chemical or biological constitution of surface waters or part thereof is harmfully affected to a considerable degree by the introduction of materials—either alone or in conjunction with the withdrawal of water or by other measures—orders for the preservation of purity of waters may be issued in the form of statutory regulations or administrative regulations. This shall also apply where such injurious effects are to be anticipated. Such orders may prescribe in particular

1. To what minimum standards the constitution of water shall conform;
2. What amount of water may be withdrawn altogether depending upon the available flow of water;
3. That certain materials shall not be introduced;
4. That certain materials which are introduced shall satisfy certain minimum requirements;
5. What other effects shall be prevented, by which the quality of the water might be detrimentally affected.

. . .

PART III. PROVISIONS GOVERNING COASTAL WATERS

Article 32a. Utilizations not subject to permits

The *Länder* may determine that a permit or a licence is not required

1. For the introduction of substances for the purposes of fishery;
2. For the discharge of ground, spring and rain-water;
3. For the introduction and discharge of any other substances if the properties of a coastal water are not, or only to an inconsiderable extent, impaired thereby.

Article 32b. Conservation

Along coastal waters, substances must only be stored or deposited in such way as not to cause any concern about a pollution of the water or any other disadvantageous alteration of its properties. The same shall apply to the conveyance of liquids and gases by means of pipe lines.

. . .

PART VI. PENALTIES AND FINES

Article 38. Harmful pollution of waters

(1) Any person who deliberately

1. And without authority or by failure to comply with a condition, introduces or discharges any matter into waters, thus causing harmful pollution of such waters or some other detrimental change in its qualities;

2. Stores materials or conveys liquids or gases through pipes in such a way that harmful pollution of the waters or some other detrimental change in the properties of the water is caused,

shall be liable to imprisonment for a term not exceeding two years and to a fine, or to either of those penalties.

(2) A person who commits such an offence through negligence shall be liable to imprisonment for a term not exceeding six months or to a fine.

Article 39. Causing danger to life or health

(1) Any person who deliberately commits any of the offences specified in article 38 and thereby endangers the life or the health of others shall be liable to imprisonment for a term not exceeding five years and to a fine or to either of these penalties.

(2) Any person who commits such an act through negligence shall be liable to imprisonment for a term not exceeding three years or to a fine.

. . .

b) WASTE DISPOSAL ACT OF 7 JUNE 1972[1]

The Bundestag, with the consent of the Bundesrat, has adopted the following Act:

Article 1

Definition of terms and sphere of application

(1) For the purpose of this Act, the term "wastes" means movable objects, which the possessor wishes to dispose of or the orderly disposal of which is necessary for the safeguarding of the general welfare.

(2) For the purposes of this Act, waste disposal is deemed to include the collection, transport, handling, storage and dumping of wastes.

---

[1] *BGBl* 1972, part I, p. 873. In force as of 8 June 1972, the day following its promulgation, in accordance with article 34. Text provided by the Permanent Representative of the Federal Republic of Germany to the United Nations in a note verbale dated 4 March 1975. Translation by the Secretariat of the United Nations.

(3) The provisions of this Act shall not apply with respect to:

1. Substances to be disposed of under the Act on the Disposal of Animal Carcasses, dated 1 February 1939 (*Reichsgesetzblatt* I, p. 187), under the Meat Inspection Act, in the wording of the Announcement of 29 October 1940 (*Reichsgesetzblatt* I, p. 1463), last amended by the Act Amending the Executive Act concerning the EEC Guidelines on Fresh Meat, dated 14 December 1970 (*Bundesgesetzblatt* I, p. 1711), under the Communicable Animal Diseases Act, in the wording of the Announcement of 27 February 1969 (*Bundesgesetzblatt* I, p. 158), under the Plant Protection Act, dated 10 May 1968 (*Bundesgesetzblatt* I, p. 352), last amended by the Act Amending the Plant Protection Act, dated 27 July 1971 (*Bundesgesetzblatt* I, p. 1161), and under the administrative orders issued in pursuance of the aforesaid Acts;

2. Nuclear fuels and other radioactive substances within the meaning of the Nuclear Materials Act, dated 23 December 1959 (*Bundesgesetzblatt* I, p. 814), last amended by the Expenditure Authorizations Amending Act, dated 23 June 1970 (*Bundesgesetzblatt* I, p. 805), and of the administrative orders issued in pursuance of the Nuclear Materials Act;

3. Wastes produced in connexion with the prospecting, extraction, preparation and further processing of minerals at plants which are within the jurisdiction of the mining inspection authorities;

4. Gaseous substances which are not confined in containers;

5. Waste water which is discharged into bodies of water or waste-water treatment facilities;

6. Used oil, provided that it is not hauled away in accordance with article 3, paragraph (1), of the Used-Oil Act, dated 23 December 1968 (*Bundesgesetzblatt* I, p. 1419).

Article 2

Basic principle

Wastes must be disposed of in such a way that the general welfare is not adversely affected and especially so that:

1. Human health is not endangered, nor human well-being adversely affected;

2. Domestic animals, birds, wild animals and fish are not endangered;

3. Bodies of water, the soil and useful plants suffer no harmful effects;

4. No harmful impact on the environment is caused by air pollution or noise;

5. The interests of nature protection and landscape maintenance and the interests of town planning are safeguarded; and

6. Public safety and order are not endangered or disturbed in any other way.

The purposes and requirements of land management and land use planning must be taken into account.

Article 3

Obligation to dispose of wastes

(1) Persons in possession of wastes must deliver them to those responsible for waste disposal.

(2) The public-law corporations competent to do so under *Land* law shall dispose of the wastes which are found in their area of competence. They may employ third parties in order to fulfil this obligation.

(3) The corporations referred to in paragraph (2) may, with the consent of the competent authority, exclude from disposal such wastes as cannot, because of their nature or quantity, be disposed of together with household wastes.

(4) In the cases covered by paragraph (3), the person in possession of the wastes shall be required to dispose of them. Paragraph (2), second sentence, shall apply as appropriate.

(5) The operator of a waste-disposal facility may be required by the competent authority to make the waste-disposal facility available for joint use to any person responsible for the disposal of wastes under paragraph (2) or (4) above in return for appropriate compensation, provided that the said person cannot otherwise properly dispose of the wastes or can do so only at considerably higher cost and provided that such joint use is reasonable for the operator. Where compensation cannot be agreed upon, it shall be determined by the competent authority.

(6) Upon application by the operator of a waste-disposal facility who can dispose of wastes more economically than a corporation referred to in paragraph (2), the competent authority may assign to him the responsibility for the disposal of such wastes, provided that this is not contrary to overriding considerations of the public interest. Such assignment may be made subject to the reservation that the applicant should dispose of all wastes found in the area of competence of the said corporation in return for reimbursement of expenses if the corporation cannot remove the remaining wastes or can do so only at disproportionately high cost; this provision shall not apply if the applicant states that he cannot reasonably undertake such disposal.

(7) The holder of a mining franchise or the operator of a mineral extraction enterprise and the owner, occupant or other person authorized to dispose of land for mining operations may be required by the competent authority, within reasonable limits, to permit the disposal of wastes in open diggings at his installation or on his land, to permit access to the said installation or land and also, where absolutely necessary, to make available the operational installations or facilities or portions thereof. The expenses incurred thereby shall be reimbursed to him by the person responsible for disposal. The competent authority shall define the extent of such obligation. The priority of mineral extraction over waste disposal must not be prejudiced. The person required to permit waste disposal shall not be liable for any damages caused thereby.

Article 4

Procedure for waste disposal

(1) Wastes may be processed, stored and dumped only at facilities or installations authorized for that purpose (hereinafter referred to as "waste-disposal facilities").

(2) In so far as animal carcasses, parts of animal carcasses or products of animal origin are excluded from disposal because of their nature and quantity in accordance with article 3, paragraph (3), they shall be utilized at animal-carcass disposal facilities if their characteristics make them suitable for that purpose. The Act on the Disposal of Animal Carcasses shall apply as appropriate. Article 1, paragraph (3), item 1, shall not be affected by this provision.

(3) The competent authority may, in individual cases and subject to revocation, permit exceptions to be made where the general welfare is not adversely affected thereby.

(4) Where the need arises and where there is no reason to fear that the general welfare will be adversely affected, the *Land* governments may, by administrative order, permit the disposal of specific wastes or specific quantities of wastes at places other than disposal facilities and prescribe the prerequisites for and the manner and method of disposal.

Article 5

Wrecked automobiles and old tires

The provisions relating to waste-disposal facilities shall apply to permanent facilities used for storing and processing wrecked automobiles or old tires.

Article 6

Waste-disposal plans

(1) The *Länder* shall draw up plans for waste disposal within their territory in accordance with criteria extending beyond the local level. Appropriate locations for waste-disposal facilities must be specified in such waste-disposal plans. Special consideration must be given to the wastes referred to in article 3, paragraph (3). The plans may further prescribe what carrier is to be engaged and what waste-disposal facility must be used by the persons responsible for disposal. The specifications in the waste-disposal plans may be delcared to be binding on the persons responsible for disposal.

(2) The *Länder* shall determine the procedure for drawing up the plans.

Article 7

Zoning

(1) The construction and operation of permanent waste-disposal facilities and any substantial changes in such facilities or in their operation shall require a zoning decision by the competent authority.

(2) Instead of holding zoning proceedings, the competent authority may upon petition issue a permit for the construction and operation of small-scale waste-disposal facilities or for substantial changes in such facilities or in their operation, provided that no objections are made.

(3) In the case of waste-disposal facilities which are facilities within the meaning of article 16 of the Trade Regulations, the zoning and hearing authority shall be the authority whose permit, under article 16 of the Trade Regulations, is replaced by the zoning decision.

. . .

Article 11

Obligation to give notification; supervision

(1) Waste disposal shall be subject to supervision by the competent authority. The said authority may extend its supervision to include waste-disposal facilities which have been shut down where such extension is necessary to safeguard the general welfare.

(2) Any person operating a facility falling within the scope of article 16 or 24 of the Trade Regulations must notify the competent authority of the nature, composition and amount of the wastes received by the facility and any substantial change therein.

(3) The competent authority may require persons possessing wastes which are not disposed of together with household wastes to provide proof of the nature, amount and disposal of such wastes, to keep record-books and to retain and preserve documentary evidence. Record-books and documentary evidence must be produced for examination to the competent authority upon request. Detailed provisions concerning the establishment, maintenance and production of record-books and the retention of documentary evidence, as well as the time-limits for preserving them, shall be prescribed by the Federal Minister of Interior, with the approval of the Bundesrat, by means of an administrative order.

(4) Persons in possession of wastes and those responsible for disposing of wastes must provide information to the designated representative of the supervisory authority concerning the operation, facilities, installations and all other matters subject to supervision. In order to determine whether they are in compliance with their obligations under this Act, such persons must permit entry into premises and, in so far as is necessary to prevent an immediate threat to public safety or order, into their homes; the fundamental right of inviolability of the home (article 13 of the Basic Law) shall be limited to this extent. Those responsible for waste·disposal must further permit access to waste-disposal facilities, make available such workers, tools and documents as are necessary for purposes of supervision and also, when so ordered by the competent authority, allow the condition and operation of the waste-disposal facility to be inspected at their own expense.

(5) A person having the obligation to provide information may refuse to answer questions to which the answer might expose him or one of the defendants specified in article 383, paragraph (1), items 1 to 3, of the Code

of Civil Procedure to a risk of criminal prosecution or to a proceeding under the Act on Disciplinary Offences.

. . .

Article 16

Criminal offences

(1) Any person who:

1. Contrary to article 4, paragraph (1), processes, stores or dumps wastes containing or capable of producing poisonous substances or pathogenic agents of communicable diseases;

2. Contrary to article 4, paragraph (1), processes, stores or dumps wastes in the vicinity of food-stuffs in such a manner that the latter may become contaminated; or

3. Contrary to article 7, sets up or operates a waste-disposal facility or effects substantial changes in a facility or the operation thereof, thereby endangering the life or health of other persons, shall be liable to a penalty of imprisonment for a period not exceeding five years and/or a fine.

(2) If the person concerned has behaved negligently, he shall be liable to a penalty of imprisonment for a period not exceeding three years or a fine.

. . .

(c) [REGULATIONS OF 3 MAY 1971 BY THE MINISTER OF TRANSPORT GOVERNING MARITIME SHIPPING ROUTES, AS AMENDED, Articles 41-42] [1]

6. GHANA

[MINERALS (OFFSHORE) REGULATIONS 1963, AS AMENDED IN 1968, Regulations 10, 11 and 16 (2)] [2]

7. IRELAND

[OIL POLLUTION OF THE SEA ACT, 1956] [3]

8. MEXICO

[FEDERAL ACT OF 10 MAY 1972 ON FISHERIES DEVELOPMENT, Article 79] [4]

---

[1] *Supra,* Chapter II, 4 *(b)*.
[2] *Infra* Chapter IX, 4 *(b)*.
[3] *Infra* Division III, 6 *(a)*.
[4] *Infra* Division IV, 9 *(b)*.

9. MONACO

a) LOI No 954 DU 19 AVRIL 1974 CONCERNANT LA LUTTE CONTRE LA POLLUTION DE L'EAU ET DE L'AIR[1]

Article premier. Sont interdits, hors des limites et dans les conditions déterminées par les Ordonnances souveraines prévues par l'article 3 ci-après, tous faits, tels que l'immersion, le déversement, le jet ou le rejet direct ou indirect, dans les eaux de la mer intérieure et de la mer territoriale ou dans les eaux superficielles ou souterraines, de matières, d'objets ou de substances quelconques, lorsque ces faits sont de nature à avoir un ou plusieurs des effets suivants :

— Provoquer, accroître ou maintenir la dégradation de ces eaux ;
— Compromettre la faune et la flore marines dans leur rôle naturel ou leur rôle d'auto-épuration ;
— Nuire à la santé publique ;
— Mettre en cause le développement économique ou touristique.

Article 2. Sont interdits, hors les limites et dans les conditions déterminées par les Ordonnances souveraines prévues par l'article 3 ci-après, tous faits, tels que l'émission dans l'atmosphère, quelle qu'en soit la source, de fumées, suies, poussières, gaz et tous autres produits ou matières, lorsque ces faits sont, en raison de leurs caractéristiques propres, de nature à avoir un ou plusieurs des effets suivants :

— Provoquer, accroître ou maintenir la pollution de l'air ;
— Nuire à la sécurité ou à la santé publique ou incommoder, de façon sensible, la population ;
— Porter atteinte à la bonne conservation des immeubles ou au caractère du site ;
— Mettre en cause le développement économique et touristique.

Article 3. Des ordonnances souveraines, prises après avis de la Commission technique pour la lutte contre la pollution et pour la sauvegarde de la sécurité, de l'hygiène, de la salubrité et de la tranquillité publiques ainsi qu'après consultation, le cas échéant, du Comité supérieur de la santé publique, fixeront les conditions d'application de la présente loi.

Elles préciseront notamment :

a) Le délai au terme duquel s'appliquera l'interdiction des faits prévus par les articles 1 et 2 et qui sont nés antérieurement à la publication de la présente loi; ce délai ne pourra toutefois être prévu que pour les faits qui seront la conséquence directe et nécessaire d'une activité économique;

b) Les conditions auxquelles sont assujetties ou dans lesquelles peuvent être interdites l'importation, la fabrication, la diffusion, la mise en vente et l'utilisation d'appareils ou de produits pouvant donner naissance à des pollutions;

c) Les dispositions auxquelles seront subordonnées la construction et la mise en fonctionnement d'ouvrages, l'installation et la mise en service

---

[1] *Journal de Monaco* du 26 avril 1974, p. 304-306.

d'appareillages ainsi que l'ouverture ou l'exploitation d'établissements qui peuvent être la source de pollutions;

d) Les conditions dans lesquelles seront effectués les contrôles des caractéristiques physiques, chimiques, biologiques et bactériologiques des eaux et de l'air, ainsi que les prélèvements et analyses d'échantillons.

Article 4. Au cas où la sécurité ou la salubrité publiques seraient mises en péril par suite des effets de phénomènes polluants ou au cas d'urgence, des arrêtés ministériels, réglementaires ou individuels, pourront ordonner l'exécution immédiate de toutes mesures destinées à faire cesser les troubles et à réparer les dégradations lorsqu'un retard dans l'exécution entraînerait une atteinte irrémédiable au milieu ambiant.

Article 5. Les fonctionnaires ainsi que les agents assermentés de l'Etat, de la commune ou d'un établissement public chargés d'effectuer les contrôles ou prélèvements prescrits pour l'application de la présente loi seront spécialement habilités à cet effet par arrêté ministériel; ils constateront les infractions concurremment avec les officiers et agents de police judiciaire.

Article 6. Ceux qui auront enfreint les dispositions de la présente loi ou celles des ordonnances souveraines et arrêtés ministériels pris pour son application seront passibles d'un emprisonnement de un à cinq jours et de l'amende prévue au chiffre 3 de l'article 29 du Code pénal ou de l'une de ces deux peines seulement.

Si toutefois les infractions aux dispositions susvisées sont commises en raison du fonctionnement d'un ouvrage, de l'exploitation d'un établissement industriel ou commercial ou de l'utilisation d'un appareillage de même nature, leurs auteurs seront passibles d'un emprisonnement de six jours à un mois et de l'amende prévue au chiffre 1 de l'article 26 du Code pénal ou de l'une de ces deux peines seulement.

Lorsque, dans tous les cas, les infractions auront provoqué des dommages irrémédiables au milieu ambiant, leurs auteurs encourront un emprisonnement de un à six mois et l'amende prévue au chiffre 2 de l'article 26 du Code pénal ou l'une de ces deux peines seulement.

Le tribunal ordonnera, s'il y a lieu et dans le délai qu'il fixera, d'exécuter tous travaux et aménagements ou de prendre toutes mesures nécessaires pour qu'il soit satisfait aux dispositions légales.

Article 7. Ceux qui n'exécuteront pas les travaux et aménagements à réaliser ou ne prendront pas les mesures ordonnées en application de l'article précédent seront passibles d'un emprisonnement de trois mois à un an et de l'amende prévue au chiffre 3 de l'article 26 du Code pénal.

Sur réquisition du procureur général et après audition de l'agent qualifié représentant le Ministre d'Etat, le tribunal pourra, en outre et jusqu'à ce que soient exécutés les travaux et aménagements ou prises les mesures utiles :

— Soit prononcer une astreinte dont il fixera le taux,
— Soit interdire d'utiliser les ouvrages et appareils ou d'exploiter les établissements qui sont la source de phénomènes polluants,

— Soit prononcer les interdictions visées ci-dessus et autoriser l'Administration à faire exécuter les travaux et aménagements ou prendre les mesures nécessaires aux frais des contrevenants.

Le tribunal pourra également les obliger à verser, pendant toute la durée des interdictions visées aux deux alinéas précédents, les rémunérations, salaires ou indemnités de toute nature qu'ils payaient jusqu'alors aux travailleurs ainsi que les cotisations sociales y afférentes.

Article 8. Seront punis d'un emprisonnement de six mois à trois ans et de l'amende prévue au chiffre 4 de l'article 26 du Code pénal ceux qui, malgré les interdictions visées à l'article précédent, auront utilisé les ouvrages et installations ou exploité les établissements en cause ou qui se seront opposés ou auront tenté de s'opposer aux travaux, aménagements ou mesures que l'administration aura été autorisée à faire exécuter ou prendre.

Article 9. Ceux qui auront mis ou tenté de mettre un obstacle à l'exercice des fonctions des agents visés à l'article 5 seront punis d'un emprisonnement de six mois à trois ans et de l'amende prévue au chiffre 4 de l'article 26 du Code pénal.

Article 10. La loi n° 232 du 8 avril 1937 ainsi que toutes dispositions contraires à la présente loi sont abrogées.

b) ORDONNANCE SOUVERAINE No 4.884 DU 7 MARS 1972 RELATIVE A LA LUTTE CONTRE LA POLLUTION DES EAUX[1]

Article premier. Les dispositions de la présente Ordonnance ont pour objet la lutte contre la pollution des eaux. Elles s'appliquent au déversement et au rejet direct ou indirect de matières ou objets de toute nature dans les cours d'eau traversant la Principauté ainsi que dans les eaux intérieures ou la mer territoriale de Monaco, et, plus généralement, à tout fait susceptible de provoquer ou d'accroître la dégradation des eaux en modifiant leurs caractéristiques physiques, chimiques, biologiques ou bactériologiques.

Article 2. Est interdit le déversement ou le rejet de matières ou objets de toute nature susceptible de porter atteinte à la santé publique ainsi qu'à la faune et la flore marines et de mettre en cause le développement touristique de la Principauté.

Article 3. Les prélèvements et déversements d'eau de mer par des installations nouvelles sont subordonnés à une approbation préalable du projet technique des dispositifs d'épuration correspondant auxdites installations et à une autorisation de mise en service délivrée par l'Administration après érection effective des dispositifs d'épuration conformes au projet technique préalablement approuvé.

Article 4. Des ordonnances souveraines prises après avis de la Commission pour la lutte contre la pollution et pour la sauvegarde de la sécurité, de l'hygiène, de la salubrité et de la tranquillité publique déterminent les conditions dans lesquelles peuvent être réglementées la mise en vente et la diffusion de certains produits susceptibles de donner satisfaction à des

---

[1] *Journal de Monaco* No 5.972, du 10 mars 1972, p. 185.

déversements qui ont fait l'objet d'une interdiction ou d'une réglementation en vertu des articles 1 et 2 ci-dessus.

Article 5. Les infractions aux prescriptions de la présente Ordonnance et des textes pris pour son application sont constatées par les officiers et agents de police judiciaire ainsi que par tous les fonctionnaires et agents de l'Etat ou de la commune, assermentés à cet effet.

Article 6. Notre Secrétaire d'Etat, notre Directeur des services judiciaires et notre Ministre d'Etat sont chargés, chacun en ce qui le concerne, de la promulgation et de l'exécution de la présente Ordonnance.

c) ORDONNANCE SOUVERAINE No 4.885 DU 7 MARS 1972 INTERDISANT LE DEVERSEMENT DE CERTAINS PRODUITS DANS LES COURS D'EAU TRAVERSANT LA PRINCIPAUTE AINSI QUE DANS LES EAUX INTERIEURES OU LA MER TERRITORIALE DE MONACO ET REGLEMENTANT LA MISE EN VENTE ET LA DIFFUSION DE CERTAINS DETERGENTS DANS LES PRODUITS DE LAVAGE ET DE NETTOYAGE[1]

. . .

Vu notre ordonnance No 4.884, du 7 mars 1972, relative à la lutte contre la pollution des eaux[2] ;

. . .

Article premier. Le déversement dans les cours d'eau de la Principauté, ainsi que dans les eaux intérieures ou dans la mer territoriale de Monaco, de tout produit détergent appartenant à l'une des catégories suivantes :

— Détergents anioniques,

— Détergents cationiques,

— Détergents ampholytes,

— Détergents non ioniques,

est interdit lorsque la biodégradabilité de ces produits n'atteint pas 80 p. 100.

Article 2. Ne peuvent être mis en vente ni diffusés les produits de lavage ou de nettoyage contenant des détergents de l'une ou de plusieurs des catégories visées à l'article 1 ci-dessus, dont la biodégradabilité n'atteint pas 80 p. 100 pour chacune des catégories.

Article 3. Un arrêté ministériel déterminera :

— Les modalités de mesure de biodégradabilité de chacune des 4 catégories de détergents définies à l'article 1 ci-dessus qui peuvent être contenues dans les produits de lavage ou de nettoyage,

— La liste des laboratoires agréés pour procéder à ces mesures.

Article 4. Notre Secrétaire d'Etat, notre Directeur des services judiciaires et notre Ministre d'Etat sont chargés, chacun en ce qui le concerne, de la promulgation et de l'exécution de la présente ordonnance.

---

[1] *Ibid.*, p. 185 et 186.
[2] *Supra, b.*

10. NORWAY

[ACT NO. 46 OF 16 JUNE 1972 CONCERNING MEASURES TO BE ADOPTED IN
PURSUANCE OF THE INTERNATIONAL CONVENTION OF 29 NOVEMBER
1969 RELATING TO INTERVENTION ON THE HIGH SEAS IN CASES OF OIL
POLLUTION CASUALTIES, Sections 1 and 2][1]

11. OMAN

MARINE POLLUTION CONTROL LAW[2]

Chapter I

General provisions

Article 1.1. It is the declared policy of His Majesty the Sultan and the
Government of the Sultanate to prevent, abate and eliminate all forms of
pollution of the waters which are adjacent to the territory of the Sultanate of
Oman so as to preserve the ecology of the area.

Article 1.2. The terms used in this Law and any regulations promulgated
hereunder shall have the following meaning unless otherwise specified:

"Discharge" includes, but is not limited in its meaning to, any spilling,
leaking, pumping, pouring, emitting, emptying, throwing or dumping.

"Minister" means the Minister of Communications and Public Services or
any person or persons appointed by the Minister, including a pollution
control officer as defined herein, to administer and enforce this Law and any
regulations promulgated hereunder; provided, however, that no person or
persons so appointed shall have the authority to promulgate regulations
hereunder or to authorize the sinking or destruction of a vessel or the
destruction of a place on land pursuant to Article 5.7 of this Law.

"Occupier" in relation to any place on land means the person actually
occupying the place on land, the person in charge of the place on land, or the
owner of the place on land; and, in relation to road vehicle, means the person
in charge of or the owner of the vehicle and not the occupier or owner of the
place on land on which the vehicle stands.

"Oil" means oil or liquid hydrocarbon of any kind and without limiting
the generality of the foregoing, includes petroleum of any description, crude
oil, furnace oil, lubricating oil, diesel oil, sludge and oil refuse.

"Oil Transmission Apparatus" includes but is not limited to any pipe or
pipeline used to carry oil from one place or vessel to another, any pumping
or other equipment or storage facilities necessary to utilize such pipes or
pipelines and any other devices such as those commonly used in the operation

---

[1] *Infra,* Division III, 9.

[2] Text provided by the Permanent Representative of Oman to the United Nations in
a note verbale of 2 December 1974. In accordance with the information provided in this
note, the Law was to enter into force on 1 January 1975.

of single-buoy mooring systems for loading or off-loading oil or any facility for storing, pumping or transferring oil in a deep-water port facility.

"Oily Mixture" means any mixture with an oil content of 100 parts or more in 1,000,000 parts of the mixture.

"Owner" in relation to a vessel means the person registered as the owner of the vessel, the person having for the time being either by law or by contract the rights of the owner of the vessel as regards the possession and use thereof, including, but not limited to a charterer of the vessel, and the master of the vessel; and in relation to an oil transmission apparatus, means the owner or the person in charge of the apparatus.

"Place on Land" means anything resting on or anchored to the bed or shore of the sea or of any waters within the pollution-free zone or situated on the mainland of the Sultanate and includes any storage tank or facilities or drilling platforms or rigs, and anything afloat other than a vessel if it is so resting or anchored.

"Pollutant" means (i) oil or oily mixture; (ii) any substance of a dangerous or noxious nature such as sewage, refuse, waste or garbage, which, if added to any waters would degrade or alter or form part of a process of degradation or alteration of the quality of those waters to any extent that is detrimental to their use by man or by any animal, fish or plant that is useful to man; provided, however, that such discharges which do not originate from a commercial or industrial source shall not be deemed to be pollutants unless the Minister shall provide otherwise by regulations promulgated hereunder; (iii) any water which contains such a substance in such quantity or concentration, or that has been so treated, processed or changed, by heat or other means, from a natural state that it would, if added to any waters, degrade, alter or form part of a process of degradation or alteration of the quality of those waters to an extent that is detrimental to their use by man or by any animal, fish or plant that is useful to man; and (iv) any substance which may be designated by the Minister to be a pollutant pursuant to any regulations promulgated hereunder.

"Pollution Control Officer" means any person or persons appointed by the Minister of Communications and Public Services to carry out those specific duties relating to the enforcement of this Law and any regulations promulgated hereunder.

"Pollutant Reception Facilities" means such facilities which the Minister may authorize to be constructed or maintained for purposes of receiving the discharge or deposit of any ballast or any pollutant.

"Pollution-Free Zone" means that body of water encompassing the Territorial Sea of the Sultanate and those waters extending 38 nautical miles seaward, measured from the outer limits of the Territorial Sea of the Sultanate; provided, however, where the coast of another state is opposite or adjacent to the coast of the Sultanate, the outer limits of the pollution-free zone shall not extend beyond such limits as may have been agreed to with such other states or, if there is no such agreement, the median line every point of which is equidistant from the nearest points on the baselines from which the breadth of the Territorial Sea of the Sultanate and the territorial sea of such other state is measured.

"Vessel" means any ship or boat used in navigation including floating barges whether automotive or towed.

Chapter II

Application of law

Article 2.1. (a) It shall be unlawful for any person to discharge a pollutant into the pollution-free zone from a vessel, a place on land, or an oil transmission apparatus, and each such discharge or, in the case of a continuous discharge, each day the unlawful discharge continues, shall be deemed a separate violation.

(b) Any person who violates this Article shall be liable upon being found guilty to a fine not exceeding 5,000 Rials Omani for each violation. The amount of the fine to be imposed pursuant to this Article shall be determined on the basis, *inter alia,* of the degree of culpability of the wrongdoer.

Article 2.2. (a) It shall be unlawful for any vessel to discharge a pollutant into the pollution-free zone, and each discharge or, in the case of a continuous discharge, each day the unlawful discharge continues, shall be deemed a separate violation.

(b) Any vessel which violates this Article shall be liable upon being found guilty to a fine which shall not exceed the aggregate amount of .05 Rials Omani for each ton of the vessel's tonnage, but in no event shall such fine exceed 25,000 Rials Omani for each violation. Each of the owners of the vessel, as defined herein, shall be jointly and severally liable for the payment of any such fine imposed on the vessel pursuant to this Article.

Article 2.3. (a) It shall be unlawful for any owner of a vessel or owner or occupier of a place on land or oil transmission apparatus to fail to comply with and carry out all of their obligations under: (i) Chapter Six of this Law relating to the payment of any costs incurred or damages suffered as a result of an unlawful discharge of a pollutant; (ii) Chapter Four of this Law relating to reporting, record-keeping and insurance requirements; or (iii) any regulations promulgated hereunder.

(b) Any person who violates this Article shall be liable upon being found guilty to a fine not exceeding 2,000 Rials Omani. The amount of the fine to be imposed pursuant to this Article shall be determined on the basis, *inter alia,* of the degree of culpability of the wrongdoer.

Article 2.4. (a) It shall be unlawful for any vessel registered in the Sultanate to discharge a pollutant into any waters beyond the pollution-free zone, and each such discharge or, in the case of a continuous discharge, each day the unlawful discharge continues, shall be deemed a separate violation.

(b) Any vessel which violates this Article shall be liable upon being found guilty to a fine which shall not exceed the aggregate amount of .05 Rials Omani for each ton of the vessel's tonnage, but in no event shall such fine exceed 25,000 Rials Omani for each violation. Each of the owners of the vessel, as defined herein, shall be jointly and severally liable for the payment of any such fine imposed on the vessel pursuant to this Article.

Article 2.5. In addition to the penalties imposed by Articles 2.1 *(b)* and 2.3 *(b)* of this Law, if a master of a vessel has violated Article 2.1 *(a)* or 2.3 *(a)* of this Law, or if any vessel or vessels of which he is master has or have violated Article 2.2 *(a)* or 2.4 *(a)* of this Law, or any combination of such violations, more than three times, such master shall be liable upon being found guilty to an additional fine of not less than 3,000 Rials Omani or imprisonment for a period not exceeding six months, or both.

Article 2.6. For purposes of prosecuting a vessel for violation of Article 2.2 *(a)* or 2.4 *(a)* of this Law, it shall be presumed that the unlawful discharge of a pollutant was committed by the master of the vessel or any other person on board the vessel who appears to be in charge of the vessel whether or not such person has been or can be identified and such discharge shall be deemed to be the act of the vessel.

Article 2.7. A written notice stating that Article 2.1 *(a)*, 2.3 *(a)* or 2.5, of this Law, as the case may be, has been violated and that a fine in a specified amount has been imposed shall be delivered by hand, or, if that is impracticable, by mail, to the person against whom the fine is to be imposed.

Article 2.8. A written notice stating that Article 2.2 *(a)* or 2.4 *(a)* of this Law, as the case may be, has been violated and that a fine in a specified amount has been imposed upon a vessel shall either be delivered by hand to the master of such vessel, or affixed or posted on a conspicuous part of such vessel and, unless payment of such fine or security for the payment thereof is delivered to the Minister or his representative within twenty-four hours of the delivery or affixing of such written notice, a pollution control officer may seize the vessel in accordance with Article 5.8 of this Law.

Article 2.9. If any owner of a vessel or owner or occupier of a place on land or oil transmission apparatus violates the provisions of this Law or any regulations promulgated hereunder, such owner or occupier shall, in addition to any sanction imposed pursuant to Article 2.1 *(b)* or 2.3 *(b)* of this Law and any civil liability accruing under Chapter VI of this Law, be subject, on the basis of the Minister's recommendation subsequent to the third offence, to the temporary or permanent forfeiture of any or all rights granted to such owner or occupier pursuant to any permit, registration or authorization by or from, or any agreement with, the Government of the Sultanate; provided the ministry, department or agency of the Government of the Sultanate which issued any such permit or authorization or which maintains such registration or is a party to or responsible for such agreement, concurs with the recommendation.

Article 2.10. In the event that a determination is made pursuant to Article 5.1 of this Law that there has been a violation of any of the provisions of this Chapter II or that any sanctions may be imposed upon any person or vessel pursuant to this Chapter II such person or vessel shall have the right to appeal such determination to the Committee for the Settlement of Maritime Disputes on or before the 45th day after notice of such violation or sanctions has been served by hand upon or mailed to such person or vessel. If the determination is affirmed by the Committee, the person or vessel shall have a final right of recourse to the Council of Ministers. The decision of the Council shall be final.

Article 2.11. In the event that a determination is made pursuant to Article 5.1 of this Law to impose a fine for the violation of any one or more of Articles 2.1 *(a)*, 2.3 *(a)* or 2.5 of this Law, such fine shall be paid on or before the 45th day after the notice thereof has been served by hand upon or mailed to the person upon whom the fine has been imposed unless, prior to such date, such determination has been appealed pursuant to Article 2.10 of this Law. In the event that, in any such appeal, the determination to impose a fine is affirmed, in whole or in part, the amount of the fine so affirmed shall be paid to the Minister or his representative on or before the seventh day after the decision on appeal has become final.

Chapter III

Special defences

Article 3.1. Where a person or a vessel is charged with an offence under Article 2.1 *(a)*, 2.2 *(a)* or 2.4 *(a)* of this Law, respectively, it shall be a defence to prove that the pollutant in question was discharged for the purpose of:

(a) Saving life;

(b) Securing the safety of any vessel; or

(c) Preventing serious damage to any vessel, its cargo, any place on land or any oil transmission apparatus;

provided, however, that a defence under this Article shall not be available if the Minister is satisfied that the discharge of a pollutant was not necessary for the purpose alleged in the defence or was not a reasonable step to take in the circumstances.

Article 3.2. Where a person or vessel is charged with an offence under Article 2.1 *(a)*, 2.2 *(a)* or 2.4 *(a)* of this Law, respectively, it shall also be a defence to prove that the pollutant in question was discharged:

(a) As a direct consequence of accidental damage to the vessel, place on land or oil transmission apparatus, as the case may be, when the accident did not occur as a result of negligence on the part of the person asserting the defence; or

(b) By reason of leakage which was not due to negligence on the part of the person asserting the defence;

provided, however, that as soon as practicable after the damage occurred or the leak was discovered, all reasonable steps were taken to prevent, or (if it could not be prevented) to stop or reduce the discharge of the pollutant, and that the events were immediately reported to the Minister in accordance with Articles 4.4 and 4.5 of this Law.

Article 3.3. Where an owner or occupier of a place on land or an oil transmission apparatus is charged with an offence under Article 2.1 *(a)* of this Law, it shall be a defence to prove that the discharge was caused by the act of a person who was in that place without the permission (express or implied) of the owner or occupier, as the case may be.

Article 3.4. Where a discharge of a pollutant occurs or is intensified as a direct result of actions taken by or at the direction of a pollution control officer pursuant to Article 5.7 of this Law, to prevent, reduce or stop pollution, then no offence shall be charged under Article 2.1 *(a)*, 2.2 *(a)*, 2.4 *(a)* or 2.5 of this Law for such discharge or such intensification of a discharge, as the case may be.

Article 3.5. Where a discharge of a pollutant occurs at a pollutant reception facility or any other place selected by the Minister to receive the discharge of any ballast or any pollutant and at such times and in such manner as the Minister may prescribe, then such a discharge shall not constitute an offence under Article 2.1 *(a)*, 2.2 *(a)*, 2.4 *(a)* or 2.5 of this Law.

Chapter IV

Record-keeping, reporting and insurance requirements

Article 4.1. Every vessel registered in the Sultanate shall maintain an oil record book within which the owner, master or other person in charge of the vessel shall record the name, number and capacity of the cargo and fuel tanks in the vessel. In addition, such person shall record in the oil record book the date, hour and specific geographical position of the vessel at the time of each of the following events:

(a) The carrying out of the loading, delivery or other transfer of oil cargo, indicating the specific type of oil involved;

(b) The ballasting of oil cargo or fuel tanks, the discharging of ballast from, and the cleaning of such oil tanks, indicating the specific type of oil carried or utilized by the vessel as the case may be, both prior to ballasting and after discharging ballast;

(c) The separating of oil from water, or from other substances, in any mixture containing oil;

(d) The discharging of oil or oily mixtures from the vessel for the purpose of securing the safety of the vessel, or of preventing damage to any vessel or cargo, or of saving lives, indicating the specific type of oil involved; and

(e) The discharging of oil or oily mixtures from the vessel as a result of a collision or accident, indicating the specific type of oil involved.

Article 4.2. Every vessel not registered in the Sultanate but which receives or delivers oil from or to a port facility or oil transmission apparatus within the territorial waters of the Sultanate, shall maintain an oil record book within which the owner, master or other person in charge of the vessel shall record the name, number and capacity of the cargo and fuel tanks in the vessel. In addition, such person shall record in the oil record book the date, hour and specific geographical position of the vessel at the time of each of the events set forth in subparagraphs *(a)* through *(e)* in Article 4.1 of this Law, to the extent that any of such events occur while the vessel is within the pollution-free zone.

Article 4.3. The owner, master or other person in charge of a vessel required to maintain an oil record book under Article 4.1 or 4.2 of this Law shall, upon the request of the Minister, or a pollution control officer, make such book available for inspection either while the vessel is in port in the Sultanate or while the vessel is within the territorial waters of Oman.

Article 4.4. The owner, master or other person in charge of any vessel travelling through the waters of the pollution-free zone shall report to the Minister forthwith, the occurrence of any of the events set forth in Article 4.1 of this Law to the extent any of such events occur while the vessel is travelling within the pollution-free zone. Such reports shall be made as soon as practicable after the occurrence of the event or in such manner as the Minister shall prescribe by regulation.

Article 4.5. The owner or occupier of a place on land or an oil transmission apparatus located within Omani territorial waters from which a discharge of a pollutant into the pollution-free zone originates, shall report to the Minister forthwith the occurrence of any such discharge. Such reports shall include the type of pollutant, the time, the date and the specific geographical location where the event occurred and shall be made as promptly as possible after the occurrence of the event.

Article 4.6. Subject to such regulations as may be promulgated by the Minister, the owner of any Omani-registered vessel which carries a pollutant in bulk or any non-Omani vessel which carries a pollutant in bulk to or from any Omani port, shall submit to the Minister on or before the vessel's entry into the pollution-free zone or, in the case of a vessel which regularly receives or delivers oil from or to a port facility or oil transmission apparatus within the territorial waters of the Sultanate, on or before the vessel's first entry into the pollution-free zone and thereafter on or before January 1st of each year such vessel is subject to the terms of this Article, evidence of financial responsibility in the form of insurance or an indemnity bond or any other evidence of financial responsibility satisfactory to the Minister in an amount equal to the lesser of (i) the aggregate amount of ten Rials Omani for each ton of the vessel's tonnage or (ii) 4,000,000 Rials Omani. Such insurance, indemnity bond or other undertaking of financial responsibility shall remain in effect in accordance with its terms as submitted to the Minister and any changes or amendments thereto shall promptly be filed with the Minister.

Chapter V

Administration and enforcement

Article 5.1. A pollution control officer or any other person designated by the Minister for this purpose shall investigate and review the facts relating to any alleged violation of this Law and such person or persons shall, upon the completion thereof, determine: (i) whether a violation of this Law occurred and the sanctions, if any, to be imposed therefor; and (ii) whether civil liability accrued under Chapter VI hereof as a result of the discharge from a vessel, a place on land or an oil transmission apparatus as the case may be.

Article 5.2. The Minister may, independently or in conjunction with other interested ministries, departments and agencies of the Government of the Sultanate, do one or both of the following:

(a) Construct and maintain pollutant reception facilities on land or within the territorial waters of the Sultanate; and

(b) Promulgate regulations requiring vessels using ports within the Sultanate or travelling through the pollution-free zone to discharge or deposit in such pollutant reception facilities any ballast or any pollutant.

Article 5.3. The Minister may, independently or in conjunction with other interested ministries, departments and agencies of the Government of the Sultanate, promulgate regulations prescribing the type of equipment with which Omani-registered vessels and all or certain classes of non-Omani vessels which use Omani ports or pass through the pollution-free zone must be fitted in order to minimize the risk of pollution.

Article 5.4. Subject to the limitations set forth in this Article and such regulations as may be promulgated hereunder, the Minister shall authorize one or more pollution control officers to enforce a prohibition on the transfer of oil or other pollutants to or from vessels in the Omani territorial waters between the hours of 6:00 p.m. and 6:00 a.m. where such transfers have not been authorized by the Director General of Petroleum and Mineral Resources. The Minister may, however, upon reasonable notice to the Minister or a pollution control officer from persons wishing to effect night transfers of oil, suspend the prohibition in this Article.

Article 5.5. For purposes of taking emergency actions to eliminate pollution or ascertaining whether a provision of this Law or any regulation promulgated hereunder has been or is being complied with, any pollution control officer is empowered to go on board a vessel or an oil transmission apparatus in the pollution-free zone or enter a place on land in the Sultanate, to examine equipment or records, to require a person to answer questions relating to compliance with this Law, or to effect emergency measures under Article 5.7 of this Law regarding the elimination of any pollutant from the pollution-free zone.

Article 5.6. Any pollution control officer is empowered to arrest without warrant any person who has committed an offence under this Law or any regulations made hereunder for which a sentence of imprisonment may be imposed, and to take such person into custody to be dealt with according to the law.

Article 5.7. In the event of an accident to or in a vessel, a place on land or an oil transmission apparatus which results in or could result in large-scale pollution of the pollution-free zone, the Minister may authorize one or more pollution control officers for purposes of preventing, stopping or reducing pollution or the risk of pollution, to direct the owner, master, occupier or person in charge of such vessel, place on land or apparatus, as the case may be, to take or refrain from taking specific actions, or, if such actions prove to be inadequate, to take any and all necessary independent action, including but not limited to the sinking or the destruction of the vessel or the destruction of the place on land or oil transmission apparatus as the case may be.

Article 5.8. The Minister or any pollution control officer authorized by the Minister shall be empowered to detain or seize a vessel within the pollution-free zone in the name of the Government of the Sultanate:

(a) When a vessel violates Article 2.2 *(a)* or 2.4 *(a)* of this Law and the payment of the fine imposed under subparagraph *(b)* of each of those Articles or security for the payment of such fine is not delivered to the Minister in accordance with the conditions of Article 2.8 of this Law;

(b) When an accident to or in a vessel occurs which could result in large-scale pollution of the pollution-free zone and the Minister or a pollution control officer issue directives to the vessel under Article 5.7 of this Law which are not immediately carried out;

(c) When an owner, master or person in charge of the vessel to be seized violates Article 2.1 *(a)*, 2.3 *(a)* or 2.5 of this Law and payment of the fine imposed under Article 2.1 *(b)*, 2.3 *(b)* or 2.5 of this Law or security for the payment of such fine is not delivered to the Minister in accordance with the conditions of Article 2.11 of this Law; or

(d) When an owner, master, or person in charge of the vessel to be seized is civilly liable under Article 6.1 of this Law and payment of the amount due or security for payment of said amount is not delivered to the Minister in accordance with the conditions of Article 6.3 of this Law; or

(e) When the Minister shall have reason to believe that the fines which may be or have been imposed under Chapter II of the Law would not be paid if so imposed or will not be paid in accordance with the provisions of this Law.

Article 5.9. Where a vessel is seized or detained pursuant to Article 5.8 of this Law, the Minister or a pollution control officer so authorized by the Minister may order re-delivery of the vessel to the person(s) from whom it was seized if any amounts payable by such person(s) or security for the payment of said amounts are delivered to the Minister.

Article 5.10. Where a vessel is seized or detained pursuant to Article 5.8 of this Law and any fines imposed or any liability accrued under this Law are not paid within thirty days of the seizure, the Minister may recover such amounts, with costs, out of the proceeds of a public sale of the vessel and its cargo to be held pursuant to this Article not earlier than ten days after notice thereof has been published in the Official Gazette, or out of any security given pursuant to this Law, and any seized property not so sold and any surplus funds arising from any sale shall thereupon be re-delivered or paid as the case may be, to the person(s) from whom the property was seized.

Article 5.11. The Minister may demand any monies due as a result of: (i) a fine imposed under Article 2.1 *(b)*, 2.2 *(b)*, 2.3 *(b)*, 2.4 *(b)* or 2.5 of this Law or (ii) civil liability imposed under Article 6.1 of this Law. If such demand is not satisfied in accordance with the procedures set forth in this Law, the Minister may initiate a money action in the appropriate forum either within the Sultanate or in any other jurisdiction, to recover all monies due. Such an action may be brought by the Minister on behalf of either the Sultanate or any person injured by the pollution discharge, or both. In the event the Minister sues on behalf of an injured individual or class of persons, he shall maintain any proceeds recovered as a fund for the benefit of and distribute such funds to the person or persons who suffered damages.

Article 5.12. The Minister shall promptly remit to the Department of Finance of the Government of the Sultanate all monies collected pursuant to Article 5.11 of this Law except such amounts as are held for the benefit of person or persons who suffered damages.

Article 5.13. The Minister may appoint that number of pollution control officers and other persons which may be necessary to carry out the provisions of this Law and any regulations promulgated hereunder.

Article 5.14. The Minister may promulgate regulations exempting any vessels or classes of vessels or any person or classes of persons from any provision of this Law or of any regulation promulgated hereunder, either absolutely or subject to such conditions as the Minister shall determine, specifying the basis or other reason for such exemption and why such exemption is in the interest of the Sultanate.

Article 5.15. The Minister may, if so authorized by His Majesty the Sultan, represent the Government of the Sultanate in negotiations with any other government or international organization concerning any agreement or treaty which would assist the Minister in accomplishing the general pollution control objectives of this Law; provided, however, that accession to and ratification of any such agreement or treaty will require the express written approval of His Majesty the Sultan.

Article 5.16. The Minister shall promulgate such additional rules and regulations as may be required to carry out the policies, purposes and terms of this Law.

Article 5.17. Regulations promulgated by the Minister, amendments thereto and cancellations thereof shall become effective on the 30th day after publication thereof in the Official Gazette unless:

(a) His Majesty the Sultan decrees that such proposed regulations, amendments or cancellations shall become effective on some other date and such other date is published in the Official Gazette;

(b) His Majesty the Sultan amends such proposed regulations, amendments or cancellations in which case the regulations, amendments or cancellations, as so amended, shall be published in the Official Gazette and shall become effective on such 30th day or on such other day as may be set by His Majesty the Sultan; or

(c) His Majesty the Sultan revokes such proposed regulations, amendments or cancellations and such revocation is published in the Official Gazette.

Chapter VI

Civil liability for costs and damages

Article 6.1. If a determination is made pursuant to Article 5.1 of this Law that a discharge of a pollutant into the pollution-free zone originated from a vessel, a place on land, or oil transmission apparatus, then the owner of such vessel or the owner or occupier of such place on land or oil transmission apparatus, as the case may be, shall, subject to the limitations set forth in Articles 6.2 and 6.4 of this Law and without regard to whether there is a finding of culpability or negligence, be liable:

(a) For the costs incurred by the Government of the Sultanate or any other person in preventing, stopping, reducing or eliminating the pollution from the waters of the pollution-free zone and in restoring the ecology of the area to the condition existing prior to the discharge; and

(b) For the damages suffered by the Government of the Sultanate or any other person as a result of the discharge, in addition to the costs referred to in subparagraph *(a)* of this Article.

Article 6.2. Notwithstanding any other provision of this Law, the aggregate amount recoverable under Article 6.1 *(b)* of this Law in respect of any discharge of a pollutant into the pollution-free zone, whether it is a single discharge or a continuous discharge from a single source, from a vessel, place on land or oil transmission apparatus, or the imposition of liability on any person or persons in connexion with such discharge shall not exceed an aggregate of 4,000,000 Rials Omani, and in the case of liability arising from a discharge by a vessel, the lesser of an aggregate of 4,000,000 Rials Omani or the aggregate amount of ten Rials Omani for each ton of the vessel's tonnage.

Article 6.3. A written notice that a person is liable for specified costs incurred or damages suffered under Article 6.1 of this Law shall be delivered to the person by hand, or if that is impracticable, by mail or some other method of service reasonably designed to apprise the person of the liability, and unless payment of the amount or amounts specified in the notice or security for the payment of such amount or amounts is delivered to the Minister within 45 days of the service of such notice, the Minister may take such additional actions as are authorized and appropriate under this Law; unless, prior to such date, such person has appealed such determination in accordance with Article 6.6 of this Law.

Article 6.4. The occupier of a place on land shall be exempted from the liability to pay the costs or damages set forth in Article 6.1 of this Law, if it is proven that the discharge of a pollutant was caused by the act of a person who was in that place without the permission (express or implied) of the occupier.

Article 6.5. Nothing in this Law shall prohibit any private person from seeking compensation against any other person for damages suffered as a result of a discharge of a pollutant.

Article 6.6. If a determination is made pursuant to Article 6.1 of this Law, that a person is civilly liable, the person or persons adversely affected by such determination shall have the right to appeal that determination to the Committee for the Settlement of Maritime Disputes. If the determination is affirmed by the Committee, the person shall have a final right of recourse to the Council of Ministers. The decision of the Council shall be final.

Chapter VII

Effectiveness

Article 7.1. The provisions of any decree, law or regulation inconsistent with any provision hereof are hereby revoked.

. . .

12. SINGAPORE

CIVIL LIABILITY (OIL POLLUTION) ACT 1973[1]

. . .

2. (1) In this Act, unless the context otherwise requires—

"Authority" means the Port of Singapore Authority established under the Port of Singapore Authority Act;

"damage" includes loss;

"Director" means the Director of Marine appointed under section 6 of the Merchant Shipping Act and includes the Deputy Director of Marine appointed under that section;

"master" includes every person, except a pilot, having command or charge of a ship;

"offshore facility" means any facility of any kind located in, on or under any of the territorial waters of Singapore other than a ship;

"oil" means oil of any description and includes spirit produced from oil of any description, coal tar, oil refuse and oil mixed with waste;

"onshore facility" means any facility (but not limited to motor vehicles and rolling stock) of any kind located in, on or under any land within Singapore other than submerged land;

"owner", in relation to a ship, means the person registered as the owner of the ship, or in the absence of registration the person owning the ship except that, in relation to a ship owned by a State which is operated by a person registered as the ship's operator, it means the person registered as the operator;

"owner or operator", in relation to an offshore facility and an onshore facility, means any person owning or operating such offshore facility or onshore facility and in the case of an abandoned offshore facility, the person who owned or operated such facility immediately prior to such abandonment;

"port" has the same meaning as is assigned to it in the Port of Singapore Authority Act;

---

[1] Act No. 43 of 1973. All the provisions of this Act, except sections 6 and 11, have been brought into force in accordance with the information provided by the Chargé d'Affaires, a.i. of the Permanent Mission of Singapore to the United Nations in a note verbale of 9 July 1974.

"Port Master" means the Port Master appointed under section 35 of the Port of Singapore Authority Act and includes any Deputy Port Master appointed under that section;

"ship" includes every description of vessel used in navigation and includes a dump-barge and also includes an air cushioned vehicle;

"Surveyor-General" means the Surveyor-General of Ships appointed under section 8 of the Merchant Shipping Act.

(2) In relation to any damage or loss resulting from the discharge or escape of any oil from a ship references in this Act to the owner of the ship are references to the owner at the time of the occurrence or first of the occurrences resulting in the discharge or the escape.

(3) References in this Act to the area of Singapore include the territorial waters of Singapore.

(4) Any reference in this Act to the measures reasonably taken after the discharge or escape of oil for the purpose of preventing or reducing any damage caused by contamination resulting from such discharge or escape shall include actions taken to remove the oil from the water and foreshores or the taking of such other actions as may be necessary to minimize or mitigate damage to the public health or welfare, including but not limited to fish, shellfish, wildlife, and public and private property, foreshores and beaches.

(5) Any reference in this Act to the discharge or escape of any oil from a ship, offshore facility or onshore facility shall be construed as a reference to the discharge or escape of the oil from the ship, offshore facility or onshore facility at any place in or outside the area of Singapore.

3. (1) Where any oil is discharged or escapes from any ship (whether carried as part of a cargo of a ship or otherwise), offshore facility, or onshore facility—

(a) The owner of the ship; or

(b) The owner or operator of the offshore facility or onshore facility, shall be liable, except as otherwise provided by this Act;

(c) For any damage caused in the area of Singapore by contamination resulting from the discharge or escape;

(d) For the cost of any measures reasonably taken after the discharge or escape for the purpose of preventing or reducing any such damage in the area of Singapore; and

(e) For any damage caused in the area of Singapore by any measures so taken.

(2) Where any oil is discharged or escapes from two or more ships and—

(a) A liability is incurred under this section by the owner of each of them; but

(b) The damage or cost of which each of the owners would be liable cannot reasonably be separated from that for which the other or others would be liable,

the owners shall be liable, jointly and severally with the other or others, for the whole of the damage or cost for which the owners together would be liable under this section.

(3) For the purposes of this Act, where more than one discharge or escape results from the same occurrence or from a series of occurrences having the same origin, they shall be treated as one; but any measures taken after the first of them shall be deemed to have been taken after the discharge or escape.

(4) The Contributory Negligence and Personal Injuries Act shall apply in relation to any damage or cost for which a person is liable under this section, but which is not due to his fault, as if it were due to his fault.

4. The owner or operator of a ship, offshore facility, or onshore facility, from which oil has been discharged or has escaped, shall not incur any liability under section 3 if he proves that the discharge or escape—

(a) Resulted from an act of war, hostilities, civil war, insurrection or an exceptional, inevitable and irresistible natural phenomenon;

(b) Was due wholly to anything done or left undone by another person, not being a servant or agent of the owner or operator with intent to do damage; or

(c) Was, in the case of the discharge or escape of oil from a ship, due wholly to the negligence or wrongful act of the Government or the Authority in exercising its function of maintaining lights or other navigational aids for the maintenance of which it was responsible.

5. Where, as a result of any oil being discharged or escaping from a ship, offshore facility or onshore facility then, whether or not the owner or operator thereof incurs a liability under section 3,

(a) He shall not be liable otherwise than under that section for any such damage or cost as is mentioned therein; and

(b) No servant or agent of the owner or the operator nor any person performing salvage or cleaning operations with the agreement of the owner or operator shall be liable for any such damage or cost.

6. (1) Where the owner of a ship incurs a liability under section 3 by reason of a discharge or escape which occurred without his actual fault or privity—

(a) Section 295 of the Merchant Shipping Act shall not apply in relation to that liability; but

(b) His liability (that is to say, the aggregate of his liabilities under section 3 resulting from the discharge or escape) shall not exceed three hundred and seventy-five dollars for each ton of the ship's tonnage nor (where that tonnage would result in a greater amount) fifty million dollars.

(2) For the purposes of this section the tonnage of a ship shall be ascertained as follows:

(a) If the ship is a Singapore ship or British registered ship (whether registered in the United Kingdom or elsewhere) or a ship to which an Order under section 84 of the Merchant Shipping Act 1894 applies, its tonnage shall be taken to be its registered tonnage increased, where a deduction has been made for engine room space in arriving at that tonnage, by the amount of that deduction;

(b) If the ship is not such a ship as is mentioned in paragraph *(a)* and it is possible to ascertain what would be its registered tonnage if it were registered in Singapore, that paragraph shall apply (with the necessary modifications) as if the ship were so registered;

(c) If the ship is not such a ship as is mentioned in paragraph *(a)* and it is not possible to ascertain its tonnage in accordance with paragraph *(b)*, its tonnage shall be taken to be forty per cent of the weight (expressed in tons of two thousand two hundred and forty pounds) of oil which the ship is capable of carrying;

(d) If the tonnage of the ship cannot be ascertained in accordance with paragraph *(a), (b)* or *(c)* the Surveyor-General shall, if so directed by the court, certify what, on the evidence specified in the direction, would in his opinion be the tonnage of the ship if ascertained in accordance with those paragraphs, and the tonnage stated in his certificate shall be taken to be the tonnage of the ship.

7. No action to enforce a claim in respect of a liability incurred under section 3 shall be entertained by any court in Singapore unless the action is commenced not later than three years after the claim arose nor later than six years after the occurrence or first of the occurrences resulting in the discharge or escape by reason of which the liability was incurred.

8. Paragraph *(d)* of subsection (1) of section 3 of the High Court (Admiralty Jurisdiction) Act shall be construed as extending to any claim in respect of a liability incurred by the owner of a ship under this Act.

9. The provisions of this Act shall not apply in relation to any warship or any ship for the time being used by the government of any foreign country for other than commercial purposes.

10. (1) Where—

(a) After an escape or discharge of oil from a ship, offshore facility, or onshore facility, measures are reasonably taken for the purpose of preventing or reducing damage in the area of Singapore which may be caused by contamination resulting from the discharge or escape; and

(b) Any person incurs, or might but for the measures have incurred, a liability, otherwise than under section 3, for any such damage,

then, notwithstanding that paragraph *(d)* of subsection (1) of that section does not apply, he shall be liable for the cost of the measures, whether or not the person taking them does so for the protection of his interests or in the performance of a duty.

(2) For the purposes of section 295 of the Merchant Shipping Act, any liability incurred under this section shall be deemed to be a liability to damages in respect of such loss, damage or infringement mentioned in paragraph *(d)* of subsection (1) of that section.

11. (1) Where any liability is alleged to have been incurred by the owner of a Singapore or foreign ship in respect of any occurrence in respect of which his liability is limited under section 6, and several claims are made or apprehended in respect of that liability, then the owner may apply to the High Court, and the Court may determine the amount of the owner's liability

and may distribute that amount rateably among the several claimants, and may stay any proceedings pending in any other court in relation to the same matter, and may proceed in such manner and subject to such regulations as to making persons interested parties to the proceedings, and as to the exclusion of any claimants who do not come in within a certain time, and as to requiring security from the owner, and as to payment of any costs as the Court thinks just.

(2) No lien or other right in respect of any ship or property shall affect the proportions in which any amount is distributed among several claimants under this section.

12. Where the Director or the Port Master has reasonable cause to believe that any oil has been discharged or has escaped from any ship and the owner of the ship has incurred a liability under section 3, the Director or the Port Master may detain the ship and the ship may be so detained until the owner of the ship deposits with the Government or the Authority a sum of money or furnishes such security which would in the opinion of the Director or the Port Master be adequate to meet the owner's liability under that section.

13. (1) If any ship is detained under section 12 and the ship proceeds to sea before it is released by the Director or the Port Master, the master of the ship, and also the owner thereof and any person who sends the ship to sea, if that owner or person is party or privy to the act of sending the ship to sea, shall be guilty of an offence and shall be liable on conviction to a fine not exceeding fifty thousand dollars or to imprisonment for a term not exceeding two years or to both such fine and imprisonment.

(2) Any person authorized under this Act to detain a ship may, if he thinks it necessary, place a police guard on board.

14. (1) The Director, the Port Master or a police officer may arrest without warrant any person who has committed or whom he reasonably believes to have committed an offence under this Act and take him before a Magistrate's Court or a District Court, as the case may be, to be dealt with according to law.

(2) Any article concerning, by or for which an offence has been committed may be seized and taken to a police station, unless given up sooner by order of a Magistrate's Court or a District Court, until the charge is decided in due course of law.

15. No matter or thing done by the Director, the Port Master or an officer employed in the administration of this Act or other person acting under the direction of the Director or the Port Master shall, if the matter or thing was done *bona fide* for the purpose of executing this Act, subject them or any of them personally to any action, liability, claim or demand whatsoever.

16. (1) Proceedings for an offence under this Act may be brought only by or with the sanction of the Public Prosecutor.

(2) Any employee of the Authority or any police officer may conduct such a prosecution on behalf of the Authority.

(3) Any offence under this Act may be tried by a District Court or by a Magistrate's Court and such court shall, notwithstanding the provisions of the Criminal Procedure Code and any other written law, have jurisdiction to impose the maximum penalty provided for by this Act.

(4) Where a body corporate is guilty of an offence under this Act and the offence is proved to have been committed with the consent or connivance of, or to be attributable to any neglect on the part of, any director, manager, secretary or other similar officer of the body corporate or any person who was purporting to act in any such capacity he, as well as the body corporate, shall be guilty of the offence and shall be liable to be proceeded against and punished accordingly.

17. The Prevention of Pollution of the Sea Act, 1971 is hereby amended in the manner set out in the Schedule to this Act.[1]

13. SWEDEN

(a) [ACT NO. 1154 OF 17 DECEMBER 1971 TO PROHIBIT THE DISCHARGE (DUMPING) OF WASTE MATTER INTO WATER, AS AMENDED IN 1972, Articles 1-6 and 8][2]

(b) [ACT NO. 275 OF 2 JUNE 1972 CONCERNING MEASURES TO PREVENT THE POLLUTION OF WATER BY VESSELS, AS AMENDED ON 17 DECEMBER 1973][3]

(c) [ACT NO. 1198 OF 17 DECEMBER 1973 CONCERNING LIABILITY FOR OIL DAMAGE AT SEA][4]

(d) [ACT NO. 1199 OF 17 DECEMBER 1973 CONCERNING COMPENSATION FROM THE INTERNATIONAL OIL POLLUTION COMPENSATION FUND][5]

(e) [ROYAL ORDER NO. 278 OF 2 JUNE 1972 CONCERNING MEASURES TO PREVENT THE POLLUTION OF WATER BY VESSELS][6]

(f) [ORDER OF 6 JUNE 1972 BY THE NATIONAL ADMINISTRATION OF SHIPPING AND NAVIGATION CONCERNING MEASURES TO PREVENT THE POLLUTION OF WATER BY VESSELS, Paragraphs 1-3, 5 and 7-8][7]

14. TOGO

[LOI No 64-14 DU 11 JUILLET 1964 PORTANT REGLEMENTATION DE LA PECHE, articles 3 et 13][8]

---

[1] *Infra* Division III, 11.
[2] *Infra* Division III, 12 *(a)*.
[3] *Ibid.*, 12 *(b)*.
[4] *Ibid.*, 12 *(c)*.
[5] *Ibid.*, 12 *(d)*.
[6] *Ibid.*, 12 *(e)*.
[7] *Ibid.*, 12 *(f)*.
[8] *Infra* Division IV, 13.

15. UNION OF SOVIET SOCIALIST REPUBLICS

(a) DECREE NO. 5590-VIII of 26 FEBRUARY 1974, OF THE PRESIDIUM OF THE SUPREME SOVIET OF THE USSR RELATING TO GREATER RESPONSIBILITY FOR POLLUTION OF THE SEA BY SUBSTANCES HARMFUL TO HUMAN HEALTH OR TO THE LIVING RESOURCES OF THE SEA[1]

In order to intensify action to counter pollution of the internal maritime and territorial waters of the USSR and of the high seas by substances harmful to human health or to the living resources of the sea, the Presidium of the Supreme Soviet of the USSR hereby decrees that:

1. Pollution of the internal maritime and territorial waters of the USSR as a result of the unlawful discharge into such waters from ships or other floating structures, or as a result of failure to take the requisite steps to prevent the escape therefrom, of substances harmful to human health or to the living resources of the sea, or of mixtures containing more than the permitted concentration of such substances, or pollution of the high seas as a result of the discharge from Soviet ships or other floating structures, or as a result of failure to take the requisite steps to prevent the escape therefrom, of the aforementioned substances or mixtures in violation of international agreements to which the USSR is a party, shall be punishable by imprisonment for a term of not more than two years, or by correctional labour for a term of not more than one year, or by a fine of not more than 10,000 roubles.

Where such acts cause substantial harm to human health or to the living resources of the sea, they shall be punishable by imprisonment for a term of not more than five years, or by a fine of not more than 20,000 roubles.

2. Failure by the master of a ship or other floating structure to notify the administration of the nearest Soviet port of the imminent or actual emergency discharge from such ship or structure, or of the unavoidable escape therefrom, within the limits of the internal maritime or territorial waters of the USSR, of substances harmful to human health or to the living resources of the sea, or of mixtures containing more than the permitted concentration of such substances, shall be punishable by correctional labour for a term of not more than one year or by a fine of not more than 500 roubles.

3. The master or any other officer of a ship or other floating structure who is found guilty of failure to comply with the obligations prescribed by the laws in force with regard to entering in the ship's documents any operations relating to substances that are harmful to human health or to the living resources of the sea, or relating to mixtures containing more than the permitted concentration of such substances, of making false entries in the ship's documents concerning such operations, or of unlawfully refusing to

---

[1] Gazette of the Supreme Soviet of the Union of Soviet Socialist Republics, 1974, No. 10, p. 161. In force on 1 March 1974 in conformity with Article 4. Russian text provided by the Permanent Mission of the Union of Soviet Socialist Republics to the United Nations in a note verbale of 14 January 1975. Translation by the Secretariat of the United Nations.

produce such documents to the proper authorities shall be liable to an administrative fine of not more than 100 roubles.

The fines provided for in this article shall be levied in the manner prescribed by the Decree of the Presidium of the Supreme Soviet of the USSR, dated 21 June 1961, on the further limitation of the use of administrative fines.

. . .

(b) DECISION NO. 118 OF 14 FEBRUARY 1974 OF THE COUNCIL OF MINISTERS OF THE USSR RELATING TO GREATER EFFORTS TO COUNTER POL-LUTION OF THE SEA BY SUBSTANCES HARMFUL TO HUMAN HEALTH OR TO THE LIVING RESOURCES OF THE SEA[1]

In order to encourage greater efforts to counter marine pollution, to safeguard human health and to protect the living resources of the sea, the Council of Ministers of the USSR has decided that:

1. It shall be an obligation of Ministries and government departments to take steps to prevent pollution of the internal maritime and territorial waters of the USSR and of the high seas by oil, petroleum products and other substances harmful to human health or to the living resources of the sea as a result of the discharge or escape from ships and other floating structures of such substances or of mixtures containing such substances.

A list of the substances whose discharge is prohibited and of the limits of the permitted concentration of such substances in mixtures discharged shall be drawn up by the USSR Ministry of Land Improvement and Water Management in consultation with the USSR Ministry of Health and the USSR Ministry of Fisheries.

2. Operations relating to the substances and mixtures mentioned in paragraph 1 of this Decision which are carried out on board ships and other floating structures within the limits of the internal maritime or territorial waters of the USSR must be entered in the ship's documents in the cases and in the manner prescribed by the USSR Ministry of Land Improvement and Water Management in consultation with the USSR Ministry of Merchant Marine and the USSR Ministry of Fisheries, and operations as aforesaid carried out on board Soviet ships or other floating structures on the high seas shall be so entered in accordance with the rules laid down in international agreements to which the USSR is a party.

3. The masters of ships and other floating structures shall notify the administration of the nearest Soviet port of the imminent or actual emergency discharge from such ships or structures, or of the unavoidable escape therefrom, within the limits of the internal maritime or territorial waters of the USSR, of substances harmful to human health or to the living resources of the sea, or of mixtures containing more than the permitted concentration of such substances.

---

[1] Legislative Series of the Government of the Union of Soviet Socialist Republics, 1974, No. 6, p. 26. Russian text provided by the Permanent Mission of the Union of Soviet Socialist Republics to the United Nations in a note verbale of 14 January 1975. Translation by the Secretariat of the United Nations.

4. The masters of Soviet sea-going vessels and other floating structures and the captains of Soviet civil aircraft shall inform the competent Soviet authorities of all cases observed by them, either in the internal maritime or territorial waters of the USSR or on the high seas, which constitute violations of regulations for the prevention of water pollution laid down by the legislation of the USSR and the Union Republics and by international agreements to which the USSR is a party, and shall take action to substantiate evidence of such violations. The procedure for the transmittal of information as aforesaid shall be determined by the USSR Ministry of Land Improvement and Water Management in consultation with the USSR Ministry of Merchant Marine, the USSR Ministry of Fisheries and the USSR Ministry of Civil Aviation.

5. The competent officials of the authorities responsible for regulating the use of and safeguarding the waters subject to the jurisdiction of the USSR Ministry of Land Improvement and Water Management within the limits of the internal maritime and territorial waters of the USSR shall be empowered to:

(a) Stop, board and inspect ships and other floating structures in order to ascertain the reasons for and circumstances of the discharge or escape of substances harmful to human health or to the living resources of the sea or of mixtures containing more than the permitted concentration of such substances, and to verify the accuracy of entries in the ship's documents concerning operations relating to such substances and mixtures;

(b) Give binding instructions for the cessation of violations of established rules governing operations relating to substances harmful to human health or to the living resources of the sea or relating to mixtures containing more than the permitted concentration of such substances;

(c) Detain ships and other floating structures in the event of the unlawful discharge therefrom, or of failure to take the requisite steps to prevent the escape therefrom, within the limits of the internal maritime and territorial waters of the USSR, of substances harmful to human health or to the living resources of the sea or of mixtures containing more than the permitted concentration of such substances; draw up reports in the prescribed manner on violations of rules for the prevention of water pollution; institute administrative proceedings against offenders and bring charges for the criminal prosecution of offenders in accordance with the laws of the USSR and of the Union Republics.

Where necessary, the frontier guard in the areas where they are serving, shall assist the authorities responsible for regulating the use of and safeguarding waters in their activities to protect the internal maritime and territorial waters of the USSR from pollution.

6. The present Decision shall not apply to military vessels or military auxiliary vessels, to which special rules apply.

7. A draft decree on greater responsibility for pollution of the sea by substances harmful to human health or to the living resources of the sea shall be submitted by the Council of Ministers of the USSR to the Presidium of the · Supreme Soviet of the USSR.

94

16. UNITED KINGDOM OF GREAT BRITAIN AND NORTHERN IRELAND

(a) [PROTECTION OF WRECKS ACT 1973, Sections 2 and 3] [1]

(b) [DUMPING AT SEA ACT 1974] [2]

1. (1) Subject to the provisons of this section, no person, except in pursuance of a licence granted under section 2 below and in accordance with the terms of that licence—

(a) Shall dump substances or articles in United Kingdom waters; or

(b) Shall dump substances or articles in the sea outside United Kingdom waters from a British ship, aircraft, hovercraft or marine structure; or

(c) Shall load substances or articles on to a ship, aircraft, hovercraft or marine structure in the United Kingdom or United Kingdom waters for dumping in the sea, whether in United Kingdom waters or not; or

(d) Shall cause or permit substances or articles to be dumped or loaded as mentioned in paragraphs *(a)* to *(c)* above.

(2) Subject to subsections (3) to (5) below, substances and articles are dumped in the sea for the purposes of this Act if they are permanently deposited in the sea from a vehicle, ship, aircraft, hovercraft or marine structure, or from a structure on land constructed or adapted wholly or mainly for the purpose of depositing solids in the sea.

(3) A discharge incidental to or derived from the normal operation of a ship, aircraft, vehicle, hovercraft or marine structure or of its equipment does not constitute dumping for the purposes of this Act unless the ship, aircraft, vehicle, hovercraft or marine structure in question is constructed or adapted wholly or mainly for the purpose of the disposal of waste or spoil and the discharge takes place as part of its operation for that purpose.

(4) A deposit made by, or with the written consent of, a harbour authority or lighthouse authority, for the purpose of providing moorings or securing aids to navigation, does not constitute dumping for the purposes of this Act.

(5) A deposit made by or on behalf of a harbour authority in the execution of works of maintenance in their harbour does not constitute dumping for the purposes of this Act if it is made on the site of the works.

(6) Subject to subsections (7) to (9) below, any person who contravenes subsection (1) above shall be guilty of an offence and liable—

(a) On summary conviction to a fine of not more than £400 or to imprisonment for a term of not more than six months or to both; or

(b) On conviction on indictment, to imprisonment for not more than five years, or a fine, or to both.

---

[1] *Supra* Chapter II, 7 *(a)*.

[2] 1974 Chapter 20, 27 June 1974. Text provided by the Permanent Representative of the United Kingdom of Great Britain and Northern Ireland to the United Nations in a note verbale of 12 December 1974.

(7) It shall be a defence for a person charged with an offence under subsection (6) above to prove—

(a) That the substances or articles in question were dumped for the purpose of securing the safety of a ship, aircraft, hovercraft or marine structure or of saving life; and

(b) That he took steps within a reasonable time to inform the Minister that the dumping had taken place and of the locality and circumstances in which it took place and the nature and quantity of the substances or articles dumped,

unless the court is satisfied that the dumping was not necessary for any of the purposes mentioned above and was not a reasonable step to take in the circumstances.

(8) It shall be a defence for a person charged with an offence under subsection (6) above to prove—

(a) That he acted under instructions given to him by his employer; or

(b) That he acted in reliance on information given to him by others without any reason to suppose that the information was false or misleading,

and in either case that he took all such steps as were reasonably open to him to ensure that no offence would be committed.

(9) It shall be a defence for a person charged with an offence under subsection (6) above in relation to substances or articles dumped outside United Kingdom waters from a British ship, aircraft or hovercraft to prove that they were loaded on to it in a Convention State and that the dumping was authorized by a licence issued by the responsible authority in that State.

2. (1) In determining whether to grant a licence a licensing authority shall have regard to the need to protect the marine environment and the living resources which it supports from any adverse consequences of dumping the substances or articles to which the licence, if granted, will relate; and the authority shall include such conditions in a licence as appear to the authority to be necessary or expedient for the protection of that environment and those resources from any such consequences.

(2) The licensing authority may revoke a licence if it appears to the authority that the holder is in breach of a condition included in it.

(3) The licensing authority may vary or revoke a licence if it appears to the authority that the licence ought to be varied or revoked because of a change of circumstances relating to the marine environment or the living resources which it supports, including a change in scientific knowledge.

(4) The licensing authority may require an applicant for a licence to pay such fee on applying for it as may be determined by the authority with the consent of the Treasury.

(5) The licensing authority may require an applicant to supply such information and permit such examination and sampling of the substances or articles which he desires to dump, or of similar substances or articles, and to supply such information about the method of dumping which he desires to use, as in the opinion of the authority is necessary to enable the authority to

96

decide whether a licence should be granted and the conditions which any licence that is granted ought to contain.

(6) The licensing authority may require an applicant for a licence to pay such amount, in addition to any fee under subsection (4) above, as the licensing authority may, with the consent of the Treasury, determine, towards the expense of any tests which in the opinion of the authority are necessary to enable the authority to decide whether a licence should be granted and the conditions which any licence that is granted ought to contain, and in particular expense incurred in connexion with any monitoring to determine the effect that dumping may have or has had on the marine environment and the living resources which it supports.

(7) A licence—

(a) Shall specify the person to whom it is granted;

(b) Shall state whether it is to remain in force until revoked or is to expire at a time specified in the licence;

(c) Shall specify the quantity and description of substances or articles to which it relates; and

(d) May make different provision as to different descriptions of substances or articles.

(8) The licensing authority may transfer a licence from the holder to any other person on the application of that person or of the holder, but shall have power to include additional conditions in a licence on transferring it.

(9) Any person who for the purpose of procuring the grant or transfer of a licence, or in purporting to carry out any duty imposed on him as a condition of a licence, knowingly or recklessly makes a false statement or knowingly or recklessly produces, furnishes, signs or otherwise makes use of a document containing a false statement shall be guilty of an offence and liable on summary conviction to a fine not exceeding £400.

(10) A person who at the passing of this Act is authorized in writing by a licensing authority to dump substances or articles in the sea may continue to do so, so long as he complies with any conditions subject to which the authorization is given, until the authorization expires or is revoked, as if the authorization were a licence under this Act.

3. (1) Where a licensing authority proposes—

(a) To refuse a licence; or

(b) To include a condition in a licence, whether on granting or transferring it; or

(c) To require a payment under section 2 (6) above; or

(d) To vary or revoke a licence,

it shall be the authority's duty, when notifying the applicant for or holder of the licence of the proposal, also to notify him—

    (i) Of the reason for it; and

    (ii) Of his right under this section to make written representations relating to it.

(2) A notification of a proposal to vary or revoke a licence shall also include a notice that any written representations must be received by the licensing authority within 28 days of the receipt of the notification.

(3) A person who receives a notification of a proposal such as is mentioned in subsection (1) above may make written representations about it to the licensing authority.

(4) If a licensing authority receives such representations, and in the case of a proposal to vary or revoke a licence receives them within 28 days of the receipt of the notification of the proposal, the authority shall constitute a committee to consider the representations and shall appoint one of the members of the committee to be its chairman.

(5) Each licensing authority shall draw up and from time to time revise a panel of persons who are specially qualified in the authority's opinion to be members of such committees, and any such committee constituted by a licensing authority shall be drawn from members of the authority's panel.

(6) It shall be the duty of the chairman of a committee—

(a) To serve upon the person who made the representations under subsection (3) above a notice in writing requiring him to state within 14 days of the receipt of the notice whether he wishes to make oral representations to the committee; and

(b) To give him, not earlier than the date of the notice under paragraph *(a)* above, notice in writing of the place, date and time of the meeting of the committee.

(7) A notice under subsection (6) *(b)* above shall not specify a date for the meeting of the committee earlier than 21 days from the date of the notice, unless the person who made the representations has agreed to an earlier meeting.

(8) If the person who made the representations expresses a wish to make oral representations to the committee, they shall afford him an opportunity of so doing, either in person or by any person authorized by him in that behalf.

(9) The committee shall consider any representations made under subsection (3) or (8) above and shall make a report to the licensing authority after the close of their consideration, giving their findings of fact and their recommendations.

(10) Where representations relating to a proposal have been made under this section, the licensing authority may make a final decision relating to the proposal only after receiving and considering the committee's report on it.

(11) The licensing authority shall notify the person who made the representations of the authority's decision and the reasons for it and shall send him a copy of the committee's report.

(12) Subject to subsection (13) below, a licensing authority may pay to a person who makes representations under this section such sum as the authority considers appropriate in respect of costs or expenses incurred by him in connexion with the making of the representations and their consideration under this section.

(13) No payment shall be made under subsection (12) above where the final decision confirms the authority's original proposal without modifications.

(14) Each licensing authority, with the consent of the Minister for the Civil Service as to numbers, may appoint such staff for committees under this section as the authority thinks fit, and may make arrangements for securing that such of the authority's officers as the authority considers are required are available to assist any such committee.

4. (1) A licensing authority shall compile and keep available for public inspection free of charge at reasonable hours the notifiable particulars of any dumping licensed by them under this Act, and shall furnish a copy of any such notifiable particulars to any person on payment of such reasonable sum as the authority may with the consent of the Treasury determine.

(2) In subsection (1) above "notifiable particulars" means particulars which Her Majesty's Government in the United Kingdom are required to notify to the international organizations.

5. (1) Each licensing authority, with the consent of the Minister for the Civil Service as to numbers, may appoint enforcement officers for the purposes of this Act.

(2) An enforcement officer appointed under subsection (1) above is referred to in this Act as a "British enforcement officer".

(3) A British enforcement officer may be either an inspector appointed for the purposes of this Act or an officer of the licensing authority appointed to exercise and perform the powers and duties and such an inspector subject to such limitations as may be specified in the instrument appointing him; and the following provisions of this Act shall be construed, in reference to such an officer, as subject to any such limitations.

(4) A British enforcement officer may, for the purpose of enforcing this Act exercise, in relation to places and things liable to inspection under this Act, the powers conferred by subsections (7) to (10) below.

(5) Subject to subsection (6) below, the places and things liable to inspection under this Act are—

(a) Land (including land submerged at mean high water springs and buildings on land), vehicles, aircraft and hovercraft in the United Kingdom;

(b) Ships in ports in the United Kingdom; and

(c) British ships, aircraft, hovercraft and marine structures, wherever they may be,

in which a British enforcement officer has reasonable cause to believe that any substances or articles intended to be dumped in the sea are or have been present.

(6) The places liable to inspection under this Act do not include any private dwelling not used by or by permission of the occupier for the purpose of a trade or business.

(7) A British enforcement officer may at any reasonable time enter any place liable to inspection under this Act, and board any vehicle, ship, aircraft,

hovercraft or marine structure which is so liable, with or without persons and equipment to assist him in his duties.

(8) A British enforcement officer—

(a) May open any container and examine and take samples of any substances or articles;

(b) May examine equipment and require any person in charge of it to do anything which appears to the officer to be necessary for facilitating examination;

(c) May require any person to produce any licenses, records or other documents which relate to the dumping of substances or articles in the sea and which are in his custody or possession;

(d) May require any person on board a ship, aircraft, hovercraft or marine structure to produce any records or other documents which relate to it and which are in his custody or possession; and

(e) May take copies of any document produced under paragraph *(c)* or *(d)* above.

(9) For the purpose of boarding a vehicle, ship, aircraft, hovercraft or marine structure, a British enforcement officer may require the person in charge to do anything which will facilitate boarding, and the power conferred by this subsection includes power, in the case of a vehicle, ship or hovercraft, to require the person in charge to stop it.

(10) A British enforcement officer may require the attendance of a master of a ship, the commander of an aircraft, the captain of a hovercraft or the person in charge of a marine structure on board that ship, aircraft, hovercraft or structure, and may make any examination and inquiry which appears to him to be necessary.

(11) A British enforcement officer shall be furnished with a certificate of his appointment and on entering or boarding for the purposes of this Act any place or thing liable to inspection under this Act, shall, if so requested, produce the said certificate.

6. (1) The Minister and the Secretary of State may jointly by order declare—

(a) That any procedure which has been developed for the effective application of the London Convention, the Oslo Convention or any designated Convention and is specified in the order is an accepted procedure as between Her Majesty's Government in the United Kingdom and the Government of any Convention State so specified; and

(b) That the powers conferred by subsections (7) to (10) of section 5 above may be exercised, for the purpose of the enforcement of that procedure outside United Kingdom waters—

   (i) In relation to a British ship or hovercraft, by a person of any specified class appointed to enforce it by the Government of that state; and

   (ii) In relation to a ship or hovercraft of that State, by a British enforcement officer.

(2) A person belonging to a class specified in an order under this section is referred to in this Act as a "foreign enforcement officer", but any reference to a foreign enforcement officer in the following provisions of this Act shall be construed, in relation to any person of a class so specified, as applying to him only for the purposes of the procedure specified in the order as the procedure for whose enforcement his Government appointed him.

7. (1) A British or foreign enforcement officer shall not be liable in any civil or criminal proceedings for anything done in purported exercise of the powers conferred on him by this Act if the court is satisfied that the act was done in good faith and that there were reasonable grounds for doing it.

(2) Any person who—

(a) Without reasonable excuse fails to comply with any requirement imposed, or to answer any question asked, by a British or foreign enforcement officer under this Act;

(b) Without reasonable excuse prevents, or attempts to prevent, any other person from complying with any such requirement or answering any such question; or

(c) Assaults any such officer while exercising any of the powers conferred on him by or by virtue of this Act or obstructs any such officer in the exercise of any of those powers,

shall be guilty of an offence.

(3) A person guilty of an offence under this section shall be liable on summary conviction in the case of a first offence thereunder to a fine not exceeding £200 and in the case of a second or subsequent offence thereunder to a fine not exceeding £400.

8. (1) In any civil or criminal proceedings a written statement purporting to be a report made by a British or foreign enforcement officer on matters ascertained in the course of exercising his powers under this Act shall be admissible as evidence to the like extent as oral evidence to the like effect by that officer.

(2) Subsection (1) above shall be taken to be in addition to and not to derogate from the provisions of any other enactment relating to the reception or admissibility of documentary evidence.

9. (1) Where an offence under this Act which has been committed by a body corporate is proved to have been committed with the consent or connivance of, or to be attributable to any neglect on the part of, a director, manager, secretary or other similar officer of the body corporate, or any person who was purporting to act in any such capacity, he, as well as the body corporate, shall be guilty of that offence and be liable to be proceeded against and punished accordingly.

(2) Where the affairs of a body corporate are managed by its members, subsection (1) above shall apply in relation to the acts and defaults of a member in connexion with his functions of management as if he were a director of the body corporate.

(3) Proceedings for any offence under this Act may be taken, and the offence may for all incidental purposes be treated as having been committed, in any place in the United Kingdom.

10. (1) The powers conferred by subsection (7) to (10) of section 5 above shall be exercisable, with the consent of the appropriate authority, in relation to land in which there is a Crown interest or a Duchy interest but in which there is also an interest held otherwise than by or on behalf of the Crown.

(2) In subsection (1) above "Crown interest" means any interest belonging to Her Majesty in right of the Crown, or belonging to a government department, or held in trust for Her Majesty for the purposes of a government department; "Duchy interest" means an interest belonging to Her Majesty in the right of the Duchy of Lancaster, or belonging to the Duchy of Cornwall; and for the purposes of that subsection "the appropriate authority", in relation to any land—

(a) In the case of land belonging to Her Majesty in right of the Crown and forming part of the Crown Estate, means the Crown Estate Commissioners, and, in relation to any other land belonging to Her Majesty in right of the Crown, means the government department having the management of that land;

(b) In relation to land belonging to Her Majesty in right of the Duchy of Lancaster, means the Chancellor of the Duchy;

(c) In relation to land belonging to the Duchy of Cornwall, means such person as the Duke of Cornwall, or the possessor for the time being of the Duchy of Cornwall, appoints;

(d) In the case of land belonging to a government department or held in trust for Her Majesty for the purposes of a government department, means that department;

and, if any question arises as to what authority is the appropriate authority in relation to any land, that question shall be referred to the Treasury, whose decision shall be final.

11. (1) There shall be paid out of money provided by Parliament all sums required for the purpose of making payments on behalf of Her Majesty's Government in the United Kingdom to the international organizations.

(2) There shall also be paid out of money provided by Parliament—

(a) Such fees and allowances for members of committees under section 3 above;

(b) Such salaries and allowances for the staff of such committees;

(c) Such other expenses of such committees; and

(d) Such salaries or other remuneration for British enforcement officers,

as the licensing authority constituting any such committee or appointing such staff or officers may, with the consent of the Minister for the Civil Service, determine.

(3) There shall also be paid out of money provided by Parliament any expenses incurred under this Act by a licensing authority and not mentioned in subsection (1) or (2) above.

(4) Any receipts of a licensing authority under this Act shall be paid into the Consolidated Fund.

12. (1) In this Act, unless the context otherwise requires—

"British aircraft" means an aircraft registered in the United Kingdom;

"British enforcement officer" has the meaning assigned to it by section 5 (2) above;

"British hovercraft" means a hovercraft registered in the United Kingdom;

"British marine structure" means a marine structure owned by or leased to an individual resident in or a body corporate under the law of any part of the United Kingdom;

"British ship" means a vessel registered in the United Kingdom, or a vessel exempted from such registration under the Merchant Shipping Act 1894;[1]

"captain", in relation to a hovercraft, means the person who is designated by the operator to be in charge of it during any journey, or, failing such designation, the person who is for the time being lawfully in charge of it;

"commander", in relation to an aircraft, means the member of the flight crew designated as commander of that aircraft by the operator thereof, or, failing such a person, the person who is for the time being the pilot in command of the aircraft;

"Convention" includes an agreement or other arrangement;

"Convention State", in relation to the London Convention, the Oslo Convention or a designated Convention, means a State declared to be a party to that Convention by an order for the time being in force under subsection (3) below;

"designated Convention" means a Convention declared to be a designated Convention by an order for the time being in force under that subsection;

"dumping" has the meaning assigned to it by section 1 above;

"foreign enforcement officer" has the meaning assigned to it by section 6 (2) above;

"government department" includes a department of the Government of Northern Ireland;

"harbour authority" has the meaning assigned to it by section 57 of the Harbours Act 1964 or in Northern Ireland, section 38 of the Harbours Act (Northern Ireland) 1970;

"hovercraft" means a hovercraft within the meaning of the Hovercraft Act 1968;

"international organizations" means any organization established in pursuance of Article XIV of the London Convention or Article 16 of the Oslo Convention and any similar organization established in pursuance of a designated Convention;

"licensing authority" means—

(a) In relation to substances or articles which have been or are to be loaded in England or Wales, or in United Kingdom waters adjacent to England or Wales, the Minister;

---

[1] Reproduced in part in ST/LEG/SER.B/5 and Add.1, pp. 180-186.

(b) In relation to substances or articles which have been or are to be loaded in Scotland, or in United Kingdom waters adjacent to Scotland, the Secretary of State;

(c) In relation to substances or articles which have been or are to be loaded in Northern Ireland, or in United Kingdom waters adjacent to Northern Ireland, the Department of the Environment for Northern Ireland; and

(d) In relation to substances or articles which have been or are to be loaded outside the United Kingdom and outside United Kingdom waters, the Minister;

"lighthouse authority" means a local lighthouse authority or a general lighthouse authority within the meaning of section 634 of the Merchant Shipping Act 1894;

"Load" means load for dumping;

"the London Convention" means the Convention on the Prevention of Marine Pollution by Dumping of Wastes and Other Matter concluded at London in December 1972;[1]

"marine structure" means a platform or other man-made structure at sea;

"master", in relation to any ship, includes the person for the time being in charge of the ship;

"the Minister" means the Minister of Agriculture, Fisheries and Food;

"the Oslo Convention" means the Convention for the Prevention of Marine Pollution by Dumping from Ships and Aircraft concluded at Oslo in February 1972;[2]

"sea" includes any area submerged at mean high water springs, and also includes, so far as the tide flows at mean high water springs, an estuary or an arm of the sea and the waters of any channel, creek, bay or river; and

"United Kingdom waters" means any part of the sea within the seaward limits of United Kingdom territorial waters.

(2) Any reference in this Act to any other enactment is a reference thereto as amended, and includes a reference thereto as extended or applied by or under any other enactment, including this Act.

(3) The Minister and the Secretary of State may jointly by order declare—

(a) That any Convention relating to dumping in the sea to which Her Majesty's Government in the United Kingdom is a party is a designated Convention for the purposes of this Act; and

(b) That any State specified in the order is a party to the London Convention, the Oslo Convention or a designated Convention.

. . .

---

[1] Reproduced in ST/LEG/SER.B/16, p. 464.
[2] *Ibid.*, p. 457.

(c) [MERCHANT SHIPPING ACT 1974] [1]

(d) [OIL IN NAVIGABLE WATERS (EXCEPTIONS) REGULATIONS 1972, Regulations 3-5] [2]

(e) [OIL IN NAVIGABLE WATERS (RECORDS) REGULATIONS 1972, Regulations 2-5] [3]

(f) [PREVENTION OF OIL POLLUTION ACT 1971 (COMMENCEMENT) ORDER 1973] [4]

(g) [OFFSHORE INSTALLATIONS (CONSTRUCTION AND SURVEY) REGULATIONS 1974] [5]

[1] *Infra* Division III, 13 *(b)*.
[2] *Infra* Division III, 13 *(c)*.
[3] *Ibid., (d)*.
[4] See foot-note under the same title, *ibid., (e)*.
[5] *Infra,* Chapter IX, 6 *(c)*.

Chapter VIII

BROADCASTS FROM SHIPS IN THE TERRITORIAL SEA[1]

---

[1] No text concerning broadcasts from ships in the territorial sea was received during the period covered by this volume.

Chapter IX

EXPLOITATION OF MINERAL RESOURCES AND THE LAYING OF CABLES AND PIPELINES UNDER THE TERRITORIAL SEA[1]

1. BURMA

PETROLEUM RESOURCES (DEVELOPMENT AND REGULATION) ACT, 1957[2]

. . .

2. In this Act, unless there is anything repugnant in the subject or context—

(a) "Concession" includes an exploring licence, a prospecting licence or a mining lease granted under the provisions of this Act;

(b) "Concessionaire" means a person to whom a concession has been granted under the provisions of this Act and any other person deriving title under him;

(c) "Continental Shelf" means the sea-bed and subsoil of the submarine areas adjacent to the coast but outside the area of the territorial sea, to a depth of 200 metres (approximately 100 fathoms), or, beyond that limit, to where the depth of the superjacent waters admits of the exploitation of the natural resources of the said areas;

(d) "Exploring Licence" means a licence granted under the provisions of this Act conferring the right to search by geological or geophysical methods for rock strata that appear likely to contain petroleum and whose geological structure is favourable for its accumulation in commercial quantities and includes trenching, pitting and drilling for geological information but not test drilling for petroleum;

(e) "Mining Lease" means a lease granted under the provisions of this Act conferring the right to mine, bore, dig, drill, search for, win, work and extract petroleum and to carry away the same or refined products thereof;

(f) "Petroleum" includes any mineral oil or natural gas or relative hydro-carbon existing in its natural condition in rock strata. It does not include coal, oil-shale or other stratified deposits from which oil can be extracted;

(g) "President" means the President of the Union of Burma;

(h) "Prospecting Licence" means a licence granted under the provisions of this Act conferring the right to conduct the operations necessary for determining whether any geological structures favourable for accumulation of

---

[1] See also *infra* Divisions II and III. Some of the texts reproduced there may also be of relevance in relation to mineral resources exploitation and to the laying of cables and pipelines under the territorial sea.

[2] Act No. 55 of 1957. Text provided by the Permanent Representative of Burma to the United Nations in a note verbale of 30 April 1973.

petroleum are present and capable of yielding petroleum in commercial quantities. It includes detailed geological and geophysical investigation and the drilling of test wells to discover the configuration of the structure and the drilling of such number of wells as may be necessary to prove the extent of any apparently productive strata that may be discovered;

(i) "Union" means the Union of Burma.

3. All natural resources of petroleum in the Union, whether such natural resources are found—

(a) On, in, or under the surface of any land; or

(b) Under any water; or

(c) In any submerged land within the territorial waters of the Union; or

(d) Under the continental shelf; or

(e) The analogue in any island within the Union

shall be deemed to belong to the Union.

Provided that this section shall not affect the rights conferred by any existing grant in respect of petroleum.

4. (1) No person shall explore or prospect for or exploit any petroleum except under and in accordance with the conditions contained in a concession issued under this Act.

Explanation: For the purpose of this section any concession previously issued under any law for the time being in force and which is still valid shall be deemed to be a concession issued under this Act.

(2) Whoever contravenes the provisions of subsection (1) shall, on conviction before a Magistrate, be punishable with imprisonment for a term not exceeding six months or with fine not exceeding Kyat 1,000 or with both, and in addition the plant, machinery, tool, equipment, material and structure used in exploring or prospecting for petroleum or exploiting petroleum shall be liable to confiscation.

5. The operations of a concessionaire under the provisions of this Act shall always be subject to subsisting rights, if any, of any other person in respect of petroleum or other minerals.

6. Subject to the rights expressly granted in the concession, the President shall be at liberty to use or permit the use of the land in respect of which the concession has been granted for any purpose other than that for which such concession is granted.

7. (1) The President may by notification make rules consonant with this Act, and such rules shall have the force of law.

. . .

9. (1) For the purpose of ascertaining the position of the working, actual or prospective, of any area covered by a concession or an abandoned concession or for any other purpose mentioned in this Act or the rules made thereunder any officer authorized by the President in this behalf shall have the right to—

(a) Enter and inspect any area covered by a concession;

(b) Order the production of any document, book, register or record in the possession or power of any person having the control of or connected with petroleum operation in any such area; or

(c) Orally examine any person having the control or connected with petroleum operation in any such area.

. . .

10. No suit, criminal prosecution or other legal proceedings whatever shall lie against any public servant for having done or in good faith intended to be done under this Act or under any rule made thereunder.

11. The President shall not be responsible for any loss or damage which may occur owing to any action taken in good faith by any public servant under this Act or under any rule made thereunder.

12. The provisions of this Act and of any rule made thereunder shall have effect notwithstanding anything inconsistent therewith contained in any other law for the time being in force; but save as aforesaid the provisions of this Act shall be in addition to and not in derogation of any other law for the time being applicable to petroleum.

2. CAMBODIA

DECRET No 261/72-PRK EN DATE DU 20 MAI 1972 RELATIF A L'APPLICATION DE LA LOI MINIERE[1]

Titre I

Dispositions préliminaires

Article premier. Les modalités d'application du Kram No 380/68-CE[2] portant réglementation minière de la République khmère[3] sont fixées comme suit :

Article 2. Les gîtes de substances minérales ou fossiles renfermés dans le sein du territoire de la République khmère et de son plateau continental, ainsi que les gîtes existant à la surface du territoire et de son plateau continental, qui sont classés en mines, sont soumis au droit minier prévu à l'article 7 du Kram.

Article 3. L'octroi des permis de recherches ainsi que l'octroi des concessions des mines, permis ou concessions accordés à toute personne physique ou morale possédant les capacités techniques et financières pour la recherche ou l'exploitation des substances minérales ou fossiles classées en mines d'après l'article 3 de la loi, est soumis aux dispositions dans le présent Kret.

Article 4. Les zones désignées ou délimitées par Kret comme étant "zone interdite" ou "zone réservée" peuvent inclure des permis de recherches et des

---

[1] Texte communiqué par lettre en date du 11 septembre 1974 du représentant permanent de la République khmère auprès de l'Organisation des Nations Unies.

[2] Reproduit dans le document ST/LEG/SER.B/16, p. 88-90.

[3] Titre utilisé pour la période allant du 9 octobre 1970 au 30 avril 1975.

concessions antérieurement accordées; dans ce cas, l'Etat annule ces permis ou concessions pour la partie qui empiète sur la zone interdite ou réservée et verse une juste indemnisation aux permissionnaires ou concessionnaires; l'indemnité est établie par un accord amiable entre les intéressés et le Service des mines, ou à défaut d'accord amiable, par décision du Ministre chargé des mines sur rapport et proposition du chef du Service des mines.

Article 5. En application de l'article 5 du Kram No 380/68-CE, l'Etat a droit d'option pour la participation dans l'exploitation des substances minérales découvertes à la poursuite de l'exploration dans le cadre d'une association à créer avec le titulaire.

La quote-part de participation de l'Etat cambodgien avec le titulaire, à la date à laquelle il demande au Gouvernement la transformation du permis de recherches en concession, ne doit pas être inférieure à 20 p. 100 du capital investi.

Article 6. Les droits coutumiers visés par l'article 10 de loi, et qui sont relatifs à la recherche ou l'exploitation de substances classées en mines, se limitent à des travaux superficiels exécutés avec des moyens rudimentaires, à l'exclusion de tout travail de fouille en profondeur tel que tranchée, puits ou galerie.

Article 7. Dans le cas où des titulaires de concessions ou de permis se heurteraient à certaines personnes ou collectivités jouissant de droits coutumiers concernant l'exploitation de mines dans le périmètre couvert par ces concessions ou permis, les titulaires des titres miniers devront affranchir de ces droits coutumiers en payant aux intéressés une indemnité fixée, après examen sur place, par le Service des mines et ne pourront commencer les travaux qu'après paiement de cette indemnité.

Article 8. Les personnes physiques ou morales étrangères accréditées, au titre de l'article 12 de la loi, à rechercher ou à exploiter en République khmère des substances minérales ou fossiles classées en mines, ne peuvent exercer leurs activités qu'après acceptation, si le Ministre chargé des mines le juge nécessaire, de la nomination de techniciens khmers du Service des mines en poste permanent sur les lieux de recherche ou d'exploitation.

Ces techniciens désignés par le Ministre chargé des mines sur proposition du chef du Service des mines, devront remettre au Service des mines des rapports techniques de contrôle mensuels sur les travaux de recherche ou d'exploitation effectués.

Article 9. Les personnes physiques ou morales étrangères visées à l'article 12 de la loi ne pourront exercer leurs activités qu'après avoir prouvé qu'elles sont capables techniquement et financièrement de conduire elles-mêmes les travaux prévus, toute utilisation d'un prête-nom sur ce point est rigoureusement interdite.

...

Titre II

Les permis de recherches

Article 12. Le droit exécutif de recherche conféré par le permis de recherches est limité dans l'espace :

    a) En surface, à l'étendue matérialisée par le périmètre accordé;

b) En profondeur, par les faces d'une pyramide ayant pour base le carré du permis et pour sommet le centre du globe terrestre.

. . .

Titre III

La concession des mines

Article 32. Le droit exclusif d'exploitation conféré par la concession des mines est limité géographiquement :

a) En superficie, à l'étendue matérialisée par le périmètre accordé;

b) En profondeur, par les faces d'une pyramide ayant pour base la surface du carré du permis et pour sommet le centre du globe terrestre.

Article 33. Le droit à une concession ne peut être invoqué par le titulaire d'un permis de recherches de validité non expirée que pour les gisements qui ont été découverts au cours de cette validité à l'intérieur du périmètre de ce permis et pour la ou les substances pour lesquelles ce permis avait été délivré.

Aucune découverte ne pourra être prise en considération si le Service des mines n'a pas été mis en mesure d'en constater la réalité avant l'expiration dudit permis ou, le cas échéant, de son renouvellement ou de sa prorogation.

Après remise au Service des mines d'un rapport technique dont le bien-fondé est vérifié sur le terrain par les ingénieurs du Service des mines, le titulaire d'un permis de recherches pourra néanmoins étendre sa demande de concession à un seul bloc constituant le prolongement naturel du gisement découvert en dehors du périmètre du permis de recherches.

. . .

Article 39. La durée de validité d'une concession, conformément à l'article 40 de la loi, est de 4 ans au minimum et de 50 ans au maximum, pour les concessions d'une durée comprise entre 10 et 50 ans, le concessionnaire devra, avant l'expiration de la dixième année au plus tard, réduire de moitié la superficie de sa concession, et avant l'expiration de la vingtième année au plus tard, réduire de moitié cette nouvelle superficie de concession.

. . .

Article 45. Lorsque l'intérêt général l'exige, le Gouvernement peut se porter acquéreur exclusif des substances déjà extraites par un concessionnaire légal; dans ce cas, les tarifs de base réglant l'acquisition seront au moins égaux à ceux des cours moyens en vigueur au moment de l'opération. Les Services gouvernementaux chargés de l'acquisition devront aviser le concessionnaire de la décision au moins trois mois avant la date fixée pour l'opération. Cette décision devra dans tous les cas être prise en Conseil des ministres sur proposition du Ministre chargé des mines.

. . .

Titre IV

Relations entre titulaires de titres miniers et propriétaires du sol

Article 53. Le permissionnaire ou concessionnaire doit respecter et entretenir les voies de communication d'intérêt public qui existaient dans son permis ou sa concession antérieurement à l'obtention du titre minier; il doit laisser au public la libre utilisation de ces voies de communication sans prétendre indemnité.

. . .

Titre VI

Sécurité et hygiène des mines

Article 73. D'une manière générale, les exploitants de mines sont tenus de se conformer aux instructions réglementaires dans le cadre de la prévention des accidents du travail et de sauvegarde de la santé des travailleurs, telles qu'elles sont édictées dans le code du travail et prescrites par le Ministère de l'action sociale, du travail et de l'emploi, et conformément à la loi sur les explosifs.

De même, les responsables de recherches et d'exploitation minière sont tenus de se conformer à toutes dispositions adoptées sur le plan international en matière de prévention des risques de pollution pouvant résulter des travaux qu'ils entreprennent.

. . .

Titre VII

Pierres et métaux précieux et semi-précieux

Article 86. Les modalités relatives à la recherche, l'exploitation et la commercialisation des pierres et métaux précieux ou semi-précieux ainsi que des substances utiles à l'énergie atomique, font l'objet de Prakas pris par le Ministre chargé des mines.

Article 87. Les dispositions prévues par l'article 5 de la loi sont applicables à la recherche, l'exploitation et la commercialisation des pierres et métaux précieux et semi-précieux, ainsi que des substances utiles à l'énergie atomique; dans ce cas, les zones intitulées "zone à déterminer" à l'article 85 de la loi correspondent aux "zones réservées" de l'article 5; dans tous les cas, la recherche, l'exploitation ou la commercialisation des substances définies au titre VII et au titre VIII de la loi dans les zones réservées, sont monopoles d'Etat; en dehors des zones réservées, la recherche, l'exploitation et la commercialisation de ces substances sont libres dans la limite des permis ou concessions accordés et tombent sous le régime de la loi générale.

. . .

Titre VIII

Les hydrocarbures

Article 98. En plus des dispositions au titre VI de la loi minière du 16 décembre 1968, sont également applicables aux hydrocarbures (liquides ou gazeux), les dispositions générales du présent Kret en ce qui n'est pas contraire aux dispositions des articles suivants :

Article 99. Le permis "H" de recherches d'hydrocarbures et la concession "H" d'hydrocarbures sont accordés par Krets séparés pris en Conseil des ministres. Ces Krets seront pris après enquête et examen d'une convention d'établissement entre le Gouvernement et l'entreprise désireuse de rechercher ou d'exploiter des hydrocarbures sur le territoire khmer ou son plateau continental.

Article 100. Cette convention d'établissement sera établie comme un marché entre le Gouvernement cambodgien représenté par le Ministre chargé des mines, d'une part, l'entreprise pétitionnaire représentée par sa plus haute autorité hiérarchique responsable, d'autre part. Elle fixera les conditions dans lesquelles le titulaire procédera à la recherche d'hydrocarbures à l'intérieur du permis de recherches demandé ou de tout autre permis demandé ultérieurement : elle fixera également les conditions dans lesquelles, en cas de découverte, seront effectués l'exploitation des gisements, le stockage, le transport, l'évacuation et l'utilisation des produits extraits.

Article 101. Le titulaire signataire de cette convention d'établissement s'engagera à respecter les conventions et résolutions internationales en matière de pollution et notamment :

- La Convention de 1954 pour la prévention de la pollution des eaux de mer par les hydrocarbures,
- La Convention de 1958 sur le plateau continental, en ce qui concerne les dispositions relatives à la protection du milieu marin,
- La résolution 2467 B (XXIII) du 21 décembre 1968 de l'Assemblée générale des Nations Unies, relative à la prévention des risques de pollution pouvant résulter de l'exploitation des ressources minérales au large des côtes.

. . .

Article 107. La durée de validité d'une concession "H" conformément à l'article 82 de la loi est de quarante ans; cependant le concessionnaire devra, avant l'expiration de la dixième année de validité au maximum, réduire de moitié la superficie de sa concession, et avant l'expiration de la vingtième année de validité au maximum, réduire de moitié cette nouvelle superficie de concession.

. . .

Article 108. L'autorisation spéciale prévue à l'article 84 de la loi modifiant la superficie maximale qui peut être obtenue pour un permis "H" ou une concession "H", devra figurer expressément sur le Kret accordant le permis ou la concession demandé; la superficie accordée et les coordonnées du permis ou de la concession devront également figurer sur le Kret.

Titre IX

Fouilles et levés géophysiques

Article 109. On entend par fouille, dans le présent Kret, tout travail de creusement à partir de la surface du sol ou d'un escarpement vertical ou oblique, quel que soit le but poursuivi par le travail.

Article 110. La déclaration de tout travail de fouille d'une amplitude verticale, horizontale ou oblique supérieure à dix mètres est obligatoire, quel qu'en soit le maître d'oeuvre ou l'entrepreneur : simple particulier, entreprise privée, services publics.

Article 111. La déclaration de tout levé de mesures géophysiques est obligatoire sur toute l'étendue du territoire khmer et de son plateau continental, quel qu'en soit le maître d'oeuvre ou l'entrepreneur.

. . .

Titre X

Infractions et pénalités

Article 116. Les contraventions aux dispositions du présent Kret et toutes autres infractions à la loi minière seront poursuivies et jugées conformément aux dispositions du titre X de la loi et aux dispositions du Code de procédure en matière pénale en vigueur en République khmère.

Article 117. La procédure du jugement de tels délits se fera en collaboration étroite du Ministère chargé des mines et du Ministère de la justice; au cours des procédures, le chef du Service des mines, les ingénieurs et les techniciens dudit Service pourront être appelés à représenter l'autorité du Ministre chargé des mines en tant que plaignants, témoins, partie civile ou pour toute expertise pour laquelle ils seront requis par les autorités judiciaires.

Article 118. Sont abrogées toutes dispositions antérieures contraires à celles du présent Kret.

Article 119. Le Ministre d'Etat chargé de l'intérieur, le Ministre d'Etat chargé de la justice, le Ministre des finances, le Ministre de l'agriculture, le Ministre des travaux publics, le Ministre du travail et de l'action sociale et le Ministre de l'industrie, des ressources minières et des pêches maritimes, sont chargés, chacun en ce qui le concerne, de l'exécution du présent Kret.

3. DENMARK

ACT No. 285 of 7 JUNE 1972 CONCERNING THE EXPLOITATION OF STONE, GRAVEL AND OTHER NATURAL DEPOSITS IN THE GROUND IN THE TERRITORIAL SEA[1]

Chapter 1

Scope of the Act

Article 1. 1. The Act applies to stone, gravel, sand, clay, limestone, chalk, peat and similar specific deposits in the ground and to non-living natural deposits on the sea-bed and in the subsoil thereof. The Act is valid only with regard to raw materials which were subject to private economic exploitation in Denmark before 23 February 1932.

---

[1] Danish text provided by the Ministry of Foreign Affairs of Denmark in a note verbale of 4 January 1974. Translation by the Secretariat of the United Nations.

2. The purpose of the Act is to ensure:

(1) That the exploitation of these deposits is preceded by a comprehensive appraisal of the relevant social considerations, including in particular the extent of the resources, business and employment interests, the risk of damage or prejudice to health or to the water supply, the preservation of scenic beauty, scientific interests, the promotion of suitable urban development, attention to agricultural considerations, and the risk of coastal degradation, marine pollution, alteration of the pattern of currents and interference with navigation and fishing;

(2) Co-ordination of the treatment by the authorities of questions concerning the extraction of raw materials covered by the Act.

3. The Minister of Public Works may lay down regulations concerning the extraction of raw materials from the ground and the taking thereof from the territorial sea with due regard for the considerations set forth in paragraph 2.

. . .

Chapter 2

Deposits in the ground

. . .

Chapter 3

Deposits in the territorial sea

Article 9. Deposits in the territorial sea (marine materials) may be explored and exploited only under a permit from the Minister of Public Works.

Article 10. An exploration permit under article 9 may, *inter alia,* be made subject to the condition that the results of the exploration shall be reported to the Minister of Public Works and that they shall, in accordance with his detailed directions, be made available to the public.

Article 11. 1. An exploitation permit under article 9 shall be issued for a period of up to five years at a time and may, *inter alia,* specify the following conditions:

(1) That the Minister of Public Works may at any time impose restrictions as to the nature and quantity of the materials which may be taken, restrict or completely halt operations in particular areas or set general or local limits on the depth to which or short of which material may be taken;

(2) That the materials taken shall be discharged in a Danish port or at another landing place approved by the Minister;

(3) That the holder of the permit shall report, along lines laid down by the Minister, on the extraction operations and in particular on the sites and depths of excavation and the nature and quantity of the materials taken;

(4) That the holder of the permit shall submit to supervision of compliance with the instructions given in accordance with the Minister's detailed directions and shall bear the cost of such supervision; and

(5) That the holder of the permit shall pay a royalty to the State in connexion with the extraction operations.

Chapter 4

Penal provisions and provisions concerning entry into force

Article 12. 1. Any person who:

. . .

(4) Prospects for or takes marine materials without a permit under article 9; or

(5) Violates the conditions laid down under articles 10 and 11

shall be liable to a fine unless a severer penalty is incurred under other legislation.

2. Regulations issued under the Act may provide a penalty in the form of a fine for any breach of provisions in the regulations.

3. If the offence is committed by a joint-stock company or the like, the company as such may be held liable to a fine.

Article 13. 1. The date of entry into force of the Act shall be fixed by the Minister of Public Works.

2. Article 9 of Act No. 149 of 18 May 1906 on preservation of the coast, article 4, paragraph 1, sub-paragraph (3), of Act No. 195 of 26 May 1965 on salt water fishing and article 44, paragraphs 2 and 3, and article 45, paragraph 2, of Act No. 314 of 18 June 1969 on the preservation of nature are hereby repealed.

Article 14. The Act does not apply to the Faroe Islands or Greenland.

4. GHANA

(a) MINERALS ACT, 1962,[1] AS AMENDED UP TO 1968[2]

1. *Minerals, etc., to be vested in President.* Subject as hereinafter expressly provided, the entire property in and control of all minerals in, under or upon, any lands in Ghana, all rivers, streams and watercourses throughout Ghana and land covered by territorial waters, and of the continental shelf, are hereby declared to be vested in the President on behalf of the Republic of Ghana in trust for the People of Ghana:

Provided that nothing in this Act shall be deemed to affect—

(a) The validity of any prospecting, mining, dredging, water or ferry right, lawfully held by any person immediately before the commencement of

---

[1] Act 126 of 1962, 14 June 1962 (amended in 1963 and 1968). This Act as amended by the Territorial Waters and Continental Shelf Act, 1963 is reproduced in part in ST/LEG/SER.B/15, p. 359.

[2] The 1968 amendment was made by the Minerals Act and Regulations (Amendment) Decree, 1968 (N.L.C.D. 308 of 1968). Text provided by the Permanent Representative of Ghana to the United Nations in a note verbale of 5 July 1973.

this Act under any law (customary or otherwise), such person being hereinafter in this Act referred to as an "existing holder"; or

(b) Any lawful rights or interests in the land in, under or upon which the minerals are situated.

The rights or interests referred to in paragraph *(a)* or paragraph *(b)* immediately preceding, shall continue, subject to the provisions of any other enactment and to such conditions as may be prescribed.

2. *President to grant mining licences, etc.* (1) The President, subject to this Act and any other enactment, may after holding such inquiry as may be prescribed—

(a) Grant, upon payment of the appropriate rents and royalties and compliance with such conditions as may be prescribed, licences for—

   (i) prospecting minerals;

   . . .

   (iii) winning or obtaining minerals from any land;

   . . .; and

(b) Declare that any land is required for the purposes of such licence, subject to such conditions as may be prescribed, if the holder of such licence is unable to secure the use of such land by private agreement.

   . . .

(3) Where a declaration has been made in respect of land other than stool land under section 2 (1) *(b),* the first-mentioned land shall be deemed to be vested in the President on behalf of the Republic of Ghana in trust for the People of Ghana. The President may prescribe, by executive instrument in the form of an order, the terms for the use of land referred to in the preceding provisions of this subsection by the holder of a licence. . . .

   . . .

5. *Government's right of pre-emption of minerals, etc.* (1) Subject to subsection (3) of this section, the Government shall, on behalf of the Republic of Ghana in trust for the People of Ghana, have the right of pre-emption of all minerals raised, won, or gotten in Ghana or from lands covered by territorial waters and the continental shelf by any existing holder or by any holder of a licence granted under this Act and of products derived from the refining or treatment of such minerals.

(2) The Government may, by executive instrument in the form of an order, appoint any statutory corporation to act as the Government's agent for the exercise of the right of pre-emption conferred on the Government by subsection (1) of this section.

(3) The said right of pre-emption shall not be exercised with respect to petroleum or petroleum products except in the event of war or an emergency declared by the Government.

   . . .

12. *Interpretation.* In this Act, unless the context otherwise requires—

"minerals" includes minerals and ores of all kinds including precious stones, coal and petroleum;

. . .

"petroleum" means any petroleum fluid with or without sulphur content whether liquid or gaseous, and includes oil, natural gas, natural gasoline, condensates and related fluid hydro-carbons, and also asphalt and other solid petroleum hydro-carbons when dissolved in and producible with fluid petroleum;

. . .

"territorial waters" means the territorial waters of Ghana below low water mark;

. . .

(b) MINERALS (OFFSHORE) REGULATIONS, 1963,[1] AS AMENDED IN 1968[2]

1. *Application of regulations.* (1) These Regulations shall apply to the application for and grant of licences under the Act[3] to win or obtain minerals under the territorial waters of Ghana and from the continental shelf (such licences being hereinafter referred to collectively as "offshore licences" and individually as an "offshore prospecting licence" and an "offshore winning licence" respectively).

(2) Save as may be hereinafter expressly provided the Minerals Regulations, 1962 (L.I. 231) (hereinafter referred to as "the principal regulations") shall not apply to licences to which these Regulations apply.

2. *Applications for offshore licences.* (1) Every application for an offshore licence shall be made to the Minister in writing and shall—

(a) In the case of an application for an offshore prospecting licence be in Form 1 of the First Schedule to the principal regulations; or

(b) In the case of an application for an offshore winning licence, be in Form 3 of that Schedule,

and in each case shall contain the further particulars specified in the First Schedule to these Regulations.

(2) The provisions of paragraph *(b)* of regulation 1 of the principal regulations (which paragraph relates to applications by bodies corporate and persons not resident in Ghana) shall apply to applications for offshore licences.

---

[1] L.I. 257 of 1963; 12 March 1963.

[2] Amended by the Minerals Act and Regulations (Amendment) Decree, 1968 (N.L.C.D. 308 of 1968) and the Minerals Act and Regulations (Amendment) (No. 2) Decree, 1968 (N.L.C.D. 315 of 1968). Texts of these Decrees, together with that of the original Regulations, provided by the Permanent Representative of Ghana to the United Nations in a note verbale of 5 July 1973.

[3] "The Act" in these regulations means the Minerals Act, 1962 (Act 126 of 1962). The Act, as amended up to 1968 is reproduced in part *supra (a)*.

(3) Every application for an offshore licence shall be accompanied by the appropriate fee specified in the Second Schedule[1] hereto and shall be made by reference to any official plan issued for the purpose of the grant of offshore licences. Where no such official plan has been issued, the application shall be accompanied by a sketch plan identifying the area of the sea-bed in respect of which a licence is sought.

(4) Five copies of all applications, documents and sketch plans shall be submitted.

3. *Restrictions on grant of offshore licences.* (1) An offshore licence shall not be granted to any person unless that person is—

(a) Over the age of 21 or, where the licence is granted to a partnership, all the partners are over 21; and

(b) A citizen of Ghana, or in the case of partnership each partner is a citizen of Ghana, or where the licence is granted to a body corporate, that body has been established in accordance with the laws of Ghana and has its registered office in Ghana.

. . .

5. *Helium and radio-active minerals.* (1) No offshore licence shall include the right to extract helium from any gas produced in the course of operations under the licence, and, subject to any directions by the Minister, the right to such helium shall be reserved to the Republic.

(2) Such directions by the Minister may include a direction to the licensee to extract and deliver helium upon the payment to the licensee of the costs of separation and transport, to such organs of the Republic as the Minister may specify.

(3) The foregoing provisions of this regulation shall apply to any mineral containing uranium or thorium or other fissionable material, being a mineral won in the course of operations under a licence, as they apply to helium.

(4) Where any such mineral or helium is discovered in the course of operations under an offshore licence the licensee shall, without prejudice to the requirements of any other enactment,—

(a) Forthwith notify the Minister of such discovery; and

(b) Ensure that such mineral or helium is not removed from the site of such operations without the prior approval of the Minister.

6. *Agreements and arrangements between licensees.* (1) Any unit plan, pooling or drilling agreement or any other agreement or arrangement between two or more licensees to share or make common use of any of the facilities of any of those licensees for the purpose of, or in connexion with, the discovery, winning, development or transport of any mineral under an offshore licence shall be submitted to the Minister for his approval before that unit plan, agreement or arrangement is put into effect.

(2) The foregoing subregulation shall apply to any agreement or arrangement which relates solely to matters of a financial character if such

---

[1] Not reproduced here.

matters arise out of, or are connected with, any unit plan, arrangement or agreement referred to in that subregulation, and to any agreement for securing the conservation of any minerals or facilities.

7. *Limitations on term of offshore licences.* An offshore licence shall be granted for a term of not more than five years in the case of a prospecting licence or 10 years in the case of a winning licence, and may be renewed if the Minister is of the opinion, in the case of the last-mentioned licence, that operations under the renewed licence will produce economic quantities of the relevant mineral, or if drilling or well reworking operations are to be conducted thereunder, and if, in every case, the Minister grants his approval of the renewal.

7A. *Term of petroleum winning licences.* (1) An offshore licence for the winning of petroleum may be granted for a term of not more than 30 years and may be renewed for a further term of not more than 10 years, notwithstanding regulation 7 of these Regulations.

(2) The grant of the Commissioner's approval under the said regulation 7 shall not be required in the case of any licensee who complies fully with all the provisions of any such offshore licence concerning the renewal of the licence.

8. *Ancillary works.* (1) No licensee shall construct, place or maintain within the licensed area any building, structure or works of any description, whether fixed or floating, or dredge any channel or part of the sea-bed, or lay any pipeline, telephone line, electric line or cable, unless he has first submitted to the Minister five copies of a plan of the proposed building, structure or works, and that plan has been approved by the Minister.

(2) In approving a plan under this regulation the Minister may, following consultation with the Ministers responsible for Defence, Shipping, Ports, Public Construction, Telecommunications and Mining (or any of them), attach such conditions to the approval as he thinks fit.

(3) Where it is provided in any offshore licence that the licensee shall be entitled to exercise any rights and powers reasonably incidental to the rights granted him under that offshore licence the Commissioner shall not refuse to approve any plan of any proposed building, structure or works submitted to him under this regulation being a building, structure or works the construction, maintenance or placing of which within the licensed area is reasonably incidental to the exercise by the licensee of his rights under the said offshore licence.

9. *Directional drilling.* No licensee shall carry out any directional drilling unless the place from which the drilling commences and the parts of the sea-bed through which the drill penetrates are within or under an area covered by an offshore licence.

10. *Prohibition of pollution.* (1) Every licensee shall so conduct his operations as to ensure that—

(a) The sea is not polluted thereby;

(b) No organic life is damaged thereby; and

(c) That no mineral or water-bearing formations of the sea-bed are damaged thereby by the introduction therein of any extraneous matter.

(2) In order to comply with, but without prejudice to, the generality of the foregoing subregulation all waste products of wells shall be suitably disposed of.

11. *Interference with navigation and research.* No building, structure or works shall be erected or constructed by a licensee within the area of an offshore licence so as to interfere with, endanger or prejudice fishing, navigation or any oceanographic or scientific research.

12. *Subsurface storage of oil and gas.* (1) The subsurface storage of oil or gas within the area of the territorial waters of Ghana is hereby prohibited unless such oil or gas is stored under and in accordance with the terms and conditions of an authorization granted expressly in that behalf by the Minister.

. . .

14. *Information obtained by licensee.* Every licensee shall ensure that any geographical, geological, geophysical, seismographic or oceanographic information obtained by him in the course of operations under or in connexion with an offshore licence is furnished forthwith, in the case of information relating to the conformation of the sea-bed, to the Ministers responsible for Defence and Shipping, and in any other case to the Commissioners respectively responsible for Lands and Mineral Resources and for national research, or to any person designated by any of the aforesaid Ministers.

. . .

16. *Cesser of operations.* (1) Except where a shorter period of notice is specified in his offshore licence, every licensee shall give to the Commissioner not less than six months notice in writing of the licensee's intention to cease operations under his licence.

(2) Unless the Minister in any particular case otherwise directs, all wells, shafts boreholes, pipes and other openings shall, upon cesser of operations, be plugged by the licensee, and all buildings, structures and works removed so as not to interfere with, endanger, or prejudice fishing, navigation or any oceanographic or scientific research.

17. *Restriction on plugging and abandonment.* (1) Subject to the last foregoing regulation a licensee shall not abandon or plug any well, shaft or pipe unless he has satisfied the Minister on technical and economic grounds, that good reasons exist for doing so, and the Minister has granted his approval to the plugging or abandonment (as the case may be).

(2) In the event of a contravention of the foregoing subregulation by a licensee the Minister may direct the immediate termination of the licence.

(3) An approval under subregulation (1) of this regulation shall not be necessary in the case of a licensee who complies fully with all the terms of his offshore licence with respect to the abandonment or plugging of any wells, shafts boreholes, pipes and other openings.

18. *Restriction of operations in an emergency.* (1) Notwithstanding the terms of any offshore licence operations under that licence may be restricted or suspended if, either—

(a) The Minister responsible for Defence, for the purpose of the defence of the Republic; or

(b) The Minister of the Interior, for securing the internal security of the Republic,

so directs.

(2) Where any direction is given under the foregoing subregulation, the licensee concerned shall comply with that direction and with any conditions attached thereto.

19. *Platforms and other structures.* (1) No platform or other structure (whether fixed or floating) used by a licensee in an area covered by an offshore licence shall be manned by persons who are not citizens of Ghana except under and in accordance with the terms of an approval granted by the Minister responsible for the Interior after consultation with the Minister responsible for Defence.

(2) The licensee shall ensure that any such platform or other structure is lit at night in such manner as the Commissioner responsible for the Interior may direct.

(3) The licensee shall ensure that access to any such platform or other structure is given at all times to any public officer acting in the course of his duty and to any other person duly authorized as a servant or agent of the Republic to have access thereto.

. . .

20. *Ancillary rights.* (1) Where an applicant for an offshore licence is desirous of being granted an easement or other ancillary right or an authorization for the subsurface storage of oil or gas under regulation 12 a request in that behalf shall be included in the application.

. . .

21. *Application of the principal regulations.* (1) Regulation 2 of the principal regulations (which relates to publication of notices of applications) shall apply to applications for offshore licences subject to the modification that the District Commissioner referred to in paragraph *(b)* of that regulation shall be such District Commissioner as the Minister may think fit.

(2) Regulations 3 and 4 of the principal regulations (which relate respectively to the establishment of a Board to consider applications and the publication of decisions to grant or refuse applications) shall apply to applications and grants under these Regulations.

(3) Regulation 5 of the principal regulations (which relates to the renewal of prospecting licences) shall apply to the renewal of offshore prospecting licences and offshore winning licences.

(4) Regulation 10 of the principal regulations (which restricts the export of samples of minerals) shall apply to samples obtained in the exercise of rights under an offshore licence.

(5) Regulation 15 of the principal regulations (which relates to the execution of licences) shall apply to offshore licences.

21A. *Certain regulations not to apply to petroleum licences.* Unless the Commissioner otherwise decides regulations 3 (1) *(b)*, 4, 6 and 21 (1) (2) and (4) of these Regulations shall not apply in the case of offshore licences for the prospecting or winning of petroleum.

22. *Reports to Minister.* The holder of an offshore licence, subject to the terms of the licence, shall—

(a) Forthwith report in writing to the Minister the finding of any deposit of minerals; and

(b) Without prejudice to the foregoing paragraph, and subject to any directions by the Minister, furnish the Minister with a written report, by not later than the twentieth day of each month, of the results of the operations carried on by the licensee during the immediately preceding month.

. . .

FIRST SCHEDULE *Regulation 2*

Application for an Offshore Licence

Additional Information

1. Particulars of operations which applicant proposes to undertake.

2. Particulars of structure which applicant proposes to construct or erect.

3. Particulars of the means of communication which applicant proposes to establish—

(a) Between any structure in the licensed area and the shore;

(b) Between any one such structure and any other such structure; and

(c) Between any such structure and any vessel.

4. Whether applicant proposes to maintain a rescue service and, if so, particulars of that service.

5. Whether applicant proposes to tow into the licensed area any floating structure and, if so, from where and under what flag.

6. Particulars of all vessels applicant proposes to operate in connexion with the licence, including port of registration, flag, and net registered tonnage of the vessel.

7. Particulars of means proposed for conveying minerals to the shore (e.g. pipeline, overhead ropeway, barge, etc.)

8. Whether applicant requests an authorization under regulation 12 for subsurface storage.

5. TONGA

PETROLEUM MINING ACT 1969[1]

. . .

2. In this Act, unless the context otherwise requires—

---

[1] Act No. 3 of 7 August 1969. Given Royal assent on 28 January 1970. Text transmitted to the Secretary-General of the United Nations by the Acting Prime Minister and Minister for Foreign Affairs of Tonga, in a letter dated 25 June 1974.

"Minister" means the Minister of Lands;

"land" means any area of on-shore land within the Kingdom of Tonga and includes off-shore land adjacent to and contiguous with such on-shore land;

"on-shore land" means the surface area of the islands of Tongatapu, 'Eua, Ha'apai, Vava'u and other islands within the Kingdom of Tonga, including the foreshores of these islands;

"off-shore land" means all submerged lands lying within the extent and boundaries of the Kingdom of Tonga as defined by the Royal Proclamation of 11 June 1887,[1] namely, between the fifteenth and twenty-third and half degrees of south latitude and between the one hundred and seventy-third and one hundred and seventy-seventh degrees of west longitude;

"foreshore" means the land adjacent to the sea alternately covered and left dry by the ordinary flow and ebb of the tides and all land adjoining thereunto lying within fifty feet of the high water mark of the ordinary tides;

"licensee" means a person to whom an exploration licence under Section 7 is issued and includes his successors in title and the persons deriving title under him;

"exploration licence" means a licence issued under Section 7 authorising the licensee thereof to explore for petroleum;

"exploration work" means any work carried out in connection with exploration for petroleum;

"person" includes a company;

"petroleum" means—

(a) Any naturally occurring hydrocarbons, whether in gaseous, liquid or solid state, but excluding coal or bituminous shales or other stratified deposits from which oil can be extracted by destructive distillation;

(b) Any naturally occurring mixture of hydrocarbons, whether in gaseous, liquid or solid state;

(c) Any naturally occurring mixture of one or more hydrocarbons, whether in gaseous, liquid or solid state, and one or more of the following that is to say, hydrogen sulphide, nitrogen, helium and carbon dioxide and includes any petroleum as defined by paragraphs *(a)*, *(b)* or *(c)* of this definition that has been returned to its natural reservoir;

"petroleum agreement" means an agreement entered into by His Majesty in Council with any person who desires to explore, prospect and mine for petroleum in the Kingdom of Tonga in accordance with Sections 8 and 9.

3. (1) No persons shall explore, prospect or mine for petroleum or do any act with a view to such exploring, prospecting or mining upon any land except by virtue of an exploration licence or a petroleum agreement issued or entered into under the provisions of this Act.

(2) Any person who acts in contravention of this section shall be guilty of an offence and shall on conviction be liable to a term of imprisonment not

---

[1] *Supra* chapter I, 17 *(a)*.

exceeding two years, or to a fine not exceeding five thousand pa'anga or to both such imprisonment and fine; and all machinery, tools, plant, buildings and other property together with any minerals or other products which may be found upon or proved to have been obtained from the land so unlawfully explored, prospected or mined shall be liable to forfeiture.

4. (1) Any person desirous of exploring, prospecting or mining for petroleum may apply in accordance with the provisions of this Act for an exploration licence or a petroleum agreement in respect of any area of land.

(2) Every application for an exploration licence or for a petroleum agreement under this Act shall be considered and approved or refused, as the case may be, by His Majesty in Council.

5. (1) Every application shall be made in writing in the form set out in the Schedule1 to this Act and shall be addressed to the Minister for consideration by His Majesty in Council.

(2) Every application made under this section shall be accompanied by such fees as may be prescribed.

(3) There shall be attached to the application two copies of a recognised official map of the lands or any part thereof upon which shall be delineated the boundaries of the area in respect of which an exploration licence or petroleum agreement, as the case may be, is applied for; and in the case of an application for an exploration licence, such application shall be supported by evidence that the applicant intends to carry out exploration work on a serious basis over the area of land applied for.

(4) The applicant shall, upon request by the Minister, furnish such evidence as His Majesty in Council may consider necessary as to his financial and technical qualifications and as to his ability to comply with any terms and conditions in the exploration licence or, as the case may be, in the clauses of the petroleum agreement; and if such evidence shall not have been so furnished within three months of the request thereof, the application shall, unless His Majesty in Council otherwise determines, be deemed to have lapsed and become void.

(5) All information comprised in or furnished to His Majesty in Council in pursuance of an application made under this Act shall be treated as confidential.

(6) Where any person requires an exploration licence or a petroleum agreement in respect of two or more separate areas, a separate application shall be made in respect of each such area.

6. If a petroleum agreement has not been signed by the applicant company or its successor and such applicant company or its successor has not paid the fee in accordance with regulations within six months following the approval date of the application, the right of the applicant to such petroleum agreement shall lapse, unless His Majesty in Council considers that the delay is not attributable to the fault of such company.

---

1 Not reproduced here.

7. (1) His Majesty in Council may issue an exploration licence in respect of the whole or any part of the area of land applied for, and every exploration licence issued under this Act may, subject to the following provisos, authorise the licensee thereof to explore for petroleum over the whole or any part of the area of land specified in that licence:

Provided that an exploration licence shall not be issued in respect of an area of land which has already been covered by a petroleum agreement entered into under Section 8:

And provided further that nothing in this section shall prevent His Majesty in Council from issuing in respect of the same area of land more than one exploration licence or another exploration licence or licences to other person or persons.

(2) Every licensee of an exploration licence shall enjoy rights and liberty granted under his licence during the continuance thereof in common with other licensees to whom exploration licences in respect of the same area may have been issued or may hereafter be issued.

(3) Every exploration licence shall be for an initial period of two years and thereafter may be extended from time to time upon an application for the extension thereof made and supported by evidence that the licensee had in fact carried out during the currency of the licence exploration work upon a reasonable scale.

(4) The licensee of an exploration licence may at any time apply to His Majesty in Council for a petroleum agreement in respect of the whole or any part of the area held under his exploration licence; and upon the issue of a petroleum agreement covering such area or any part thereof all exploration licences covering such area or any part thereof shall determine without the Government of Tonga being liable to pay any compensation to licensees.

(5) An exploration licence shall be in the form and shall contain the terms and conditions of the model exploration licence to be made by His Majesty in Council under Section 12 (1) *(i):*

Provided that, in respect of any exploration licence, His Majesty in Council may make such modifications and exclusions and may add such additional clauses covering ancillary matters as His Majesty in Council may deem fit.

8. (1) Upon an application made in that behalf by any person desirous of exploring, prospecting and/or mining for petroleum His Majesty in Council may, subject to the provisions of Section 9 and the following subsection, enter with such person into a petroleum agreement in respect of any area or areas of land for which such application therefor has been made as herein provided.

(2) Save as provided in Section 9, every petroleum agreement shall cover an area of land not exceeding 4,000 square miles, or areas of land which in the aggregate do not exceed 4,000 square miles, and shall be in the form and shall contain terms and conditions of the model petroleum agreement to be made by His Majesty in Council under Section 12 (1) *(i):*

Provided that in respect of any petroleum agreement His Majesty in Council may make such modifications and exclusions and may add such additional clauses covering ancillary matters as to His Majesty in Council may seem fit.

9. (1) Subject to the provisions of subsection (2), His Majesty in Council may enter into a single petroleum agreement in respect of an area or areas of land notwithstanding that the total areas to be covered by such petroleum agreement may exceed 4,000 square miles as required by subsection (2) of section 8.

(2) Where the total area or areas covered by a single petroleum agreement which has been entered into exceeds 4,000 square miles, the obligations which the other party to such single petroleum agreement shall perform as expenditure commitments and fixed yearly payments under the agreement shall be increased proportionately in the same proportion as the area in excess thereof bears to the area of 4,000 square miles.

10. Nothing in this Act shall prevent more than one exploration licence or petroleum agreement being issued to or entered into with the same person.

11. His Majesty in Council shall, as soon as may be after the execution, surrender, determination or assignment of any petroleum agreement or the rights thereunder, issue a public notification of the fact stating the name of the person with whom such petroleum agreement was made, the name of any assignee and the situation of the area concerned.

12. (1) His Majesty in Council may make and when made vary, alter, amend, revoke or cancel regulations generally for the purposes of carrying into effect the provisions of this Act, and in particular such regulations may provide for—

    (i) The model exploration licence and the model petroleum agreement;

    (ii) The appointment, duties, privileges and powers of officers to enforce the provisions of this Act including an exploration licence and any petroleum agreement issued or entered into thereunder;

    (iii) The prescribing of fees to be paid in respect of the issue of an exploration licence and the entering into of any petroleum agreement;

    (iv) The prevention of fires in areas where oil mining is being carried on;

    (v) The establishment of safety areas around any petroleum reserve installations erected on the sea bed provided that no safety area around petroleum mining installations erected on the off-shore land shall exceed five hundred metres in radius;

    (vi) The general safety, health, working conditions and welfare of persons engaged in oil mining whether on-shore or off-shore; and

    (vii) The amendment of the Schedule.

(2) Any rules made in pursuance of paragraph (vi) of subsection (1) may provide that such rules shall be in addition to or in substitution for the provisions of the written law of the Kingdom relating to labour and any rules made thereunder relating to the matters specified in that paragraph.

(3) Any person who contravenes a provision of any regulations made under subsection 1 (iv), (v) and (vi) of this section shall be guilty of an offence and shall on conviction be liable to a term of imprisonment not

exceeding 2 years or to a fine not exceeding five thousand pa'anga or to both such imprisonment and fine.

13. (1) Where a licensee or a person who is a party to a petroleum agreement has been refused entry upon an alienated land by the holder thereof, such licensee or such person may make an application to the Minister for permission to enter upon such alienated land; and the Minister may subject to subsection (2) grant the permission applied for on condition that the applicant undertakes to pay compensation for all the damage which may have been caused to the land or crops or property therein or on such other conditions as the Minister may deem fit to impose.

(2) Before granting the permission referred to under subsection (1), the Minister shall grant to the holder of such alienated land the right of being heard, and the permission so granted shall be final and shall not be questioned in any court of law.

(3) Upon the production to the holder of such alienated land of the permission granted under subsection (1), such holder shall allow the person in whose favour the permission is granted or a person authorised by him to enter upon such land.

(4) If, after having been produced to him the permission referred to under subsection (1) the the holder of such alienated land refuses or fails to allow entry upon his land by the person in whose favour the permission is granted or a person authorised by him, such holder shall be guilty of an offence and upon conviction shall be liable to a fine not exceeding one thousand pa'anga and a further fine not exceeding twenty pa'anga for every day during which the refusal or the failure continues.

(5) For the purpose of this section the expression "holder" includes chargee, lessee, occupier or any person having interest in the land; and the expression "entry" includes the exercising of any rights contained in the licence or the petroleum agreement.

14. The basic financial, fiscal and other considerations stipulated in any petroleum agreement executed under this Act shall not be changed during its term by unilateral legislative or executive measures.

15. All references to petroleum exploration and prospecting licences and to petroleum mining leases occurring in the Minerals (Temporary Provisions) Act 1919-1968 shall on the coming into force of this Act be deemed to have been repealed.

6. UNITED KINGDOM OF GREAT BRITAIN AND NORTHERN IRELAND

(a) OFFSHORE INSTALLATIONS (LOGBOOKS AND REGISTRATION OF DEATH) REGULATIONS 1972[1]

Citation, commencement and interpretation

1. (1) . . .

---

[1] Dated 16 October 1972. *Statutory Instruments,* 1972 No. 1542. Came into operation on 30 November 1972.

(2) In these Regulations—

"installation logbook" means a logbook obtained from the Department of Trade and Industry; and

"manager" includes, where no manager is appointed pursuant to section 4 of the Act,[1] any person made responsible by the owner for safety, health and welfare on board an offshore installation.

(3) These Regulations shall not apply to installations registered as vessels (whether so registered in the United Kingdom or elsewhere) which are dredging installations or which are in transit to or from a station, or in relation to installations which are unmanned.

(4) The Interpretation Act 1889[2] shall apply to the interpretation of these Regulations as it applies to the interpretation of an Act of Parliament.

Logbooks

2. (1) An installation logbook shall be maintained on every offshore installation at all times when the installation is in waters to which the Act applies:

Provided that in the case of a fixed installation under construction or in course of assembly or dismantlement it shall be sufficient compliance with this Regulation to maintain the installation logbook on an attendant vessel.

(2) An installation logbook shall be maintained on an offshore installation notwithstanding that another logbook may be required to be maintained on it as a registered vessel.

3. (1) There shall be entered in every installation logbook before any other entry is made in the book—

(a) The registered name or other designation of the relevant installation;

(b) The name of the owner and the address to which communications for him are to be sent;

(c) The name of the person or persons appointed as manager;

and if at any time while the logbook is in use these entries are no longer correct they shall be amended appropriately.

(2) Entries shall be made in the installation logbook regarding every occurrence affecting or likely to affect the safety of the installation or the safety, health and welfare of persons on or working from the installation or involving the installation and endangering persons in its neighbourhood and in particular, but without prejudice to the generality of the foregoing, of—

(a) The assumption and relinquishment of responsibility by managers, manning changes, visits by vessels, aircraft and hovercraft and, in the case of a mobile offshore installation, of its movements and locations;

---

[1] "The Act" in these Regulations means the Mineral Workings (Offshore Installations) Act 1971, reproduced in part in ST/LEG/SER.B/16, pp. 107-112.

[2] 1889 c. 63.

(b) Adverse weather conditions, collisions, structural changes and major repairs, surveys and any other occurrence relevant to the safety, seaworthiness or stability of the installation;

(c) Safety drills, accidents and injuries to persons, and the occurrence of disease and death;

(d) Emergencies and apprehended emergencies and measures taken to meet or avoid them, whether relating to the installation or to personnel;

(e) The placing under restraint of any person pursuant to section 5 (6) of the Act;

(f) Any visit of an inspector appointed under section 6 (4) of the Act or other person acting at the direction of the Secretary of State and any action taken as a result of investigations made or notices served by such inspector or other person.

. . .

5. Where an entry is made in an installation logbook recording that a person has been placed under restraint on an installation the owner of the installation shall as soon as practicable notify the Secretary of State for Trade and Industry of the relevant occurrence.

. . .

Records of persons at an installation

7. (1) At all times when there is an obligation to maintain an installation logbook on any installation there shall also be maintained on the installation a separate continuous record of the persons on or working from the installation which shall include:

(a) The full names of every such person;

(b) The date and time of his arrival and, if he is no longer on or working from the installation, of his departure;

(c) The reason for his presence there;

(d) The name and address of his employer;

Provided that in the case of a fixed installation under construction or in course of assembly or dismantlement it shall be sufficient compliance with this Regulation to maintain such record on an attendant vessel.

. . .

(3) The owner of the installation shall maintain at a place ashore in the United Kingdom a record of the persons on or working from the installation and such record shall include the information specified in paragraph (1) together with the nationality, the date of birth and the usual residence of those persons and the name, address and relationship of their next-of-kin (if any).

(4) The owner of the installation shall, on demand, produce to the Secretary of State a copy of the record of persons required to be maintained by the manager of the installation pursuant to paragraph (1) or, if this is not practicable, a copy of the record of persons required to be maintained by the owner pursuant to paragraph (3), being in either case a copy certified by the owner or a person authorized by him as a true copy.

. . .

Registration of deaths and persons lost

8. Where any person

(a) Dies on an offshore installation or is lost from an installation in circumstances such that it is reasonable to believe that he has died; or

(b) Dies in or on a lifeboat, liferaft or other emergency survival craft belonging to an offshore installation or is lost therefrom in such circumstances as aforesaid; or

(c) Otherwise dies or is lost in such circumstances as aforesaid in the neighbourhood of an offshore installation while engaged in any operation connected with the installation;

and the death or loss is not required to be registered under the Merchant Shipping Act 1894[1] or under any regulations made under section 72 of the Merchant Shipping Act 1970[2] (which relates to returns of births and deaths in ships), a return of death in the form set out in the Schedule hereto shall be made in accordance with Regulation 9.

. . .

Offences and penalties

12. (1) A contravention of any requirement of Regulation 2 (1), 3, 6 (1), 7 (1) or 9 (1) shall be an offence for which the manager of the relevant installation at the time of the contravention shall be liable on summary conviction to a fine not exceeding £100.

(2) A contravention of any requirement of Regulation 2 (1), 5, 6, 7, 9 (2) or 10 shall be an offence for which the owner of the relevant installation shall be liable on summary conviction to a fine not exceeding £100.

. . .

(4) If any person wilfully refuses to give any information necessary for the maintenance of the records required to be maintained by Regulation 7, he shall be liable on summary conviction to a fine not exceeding £50.

(5) If any person wilfully enters any false information in a logbook or record required to be maintained by Regulation 7 or makes any false certificate in any return of death or, knowing such certificate to be false, sends the same as true to any person, he shall be liable on summary conviction to a fine not exceeding £400.

(6) It shall be a defence in any proceedings for an offence under paragraphs (1) and (2) of this Regulation for the person charged to prove:

(a) That he exercised all due diligence to prevent the commission of the offence; and

(b) That the relevant contravention was committed without his consent, connivance or wilful default.

---

[1] 1894 c. 60.

[2] 1970 c. 36.

(b) OFFSHORE INSTALLATIONS (INSPECTIONS AND CASUALTIES) REGULATIONS 1973[1]

Citation, commencement and interpretation

1. (1) These Regulations may be cited as the Offshore Installations (Inspectors and Casualties) Regulations 1973 and shall come into operation on 1 December 1973.

(2) In these Regulations unless the context otherwise requires—

"casualty" means a casualty or other accident involving loss of life or danger to life suffered by a person—

(a) Employed on, on or working from an offshore installation; or

(b) On or working from an attendant vessel, in the course of any operation undertaken on or in connexion with an offshore installation;

"disease" includes any ailment or adverse condition, whether of body or mind;

"equipment" means any plant, machinery, apparatus or system used, formerly used or intended to be used (whether on or from an offshore installation or on or from an attendant vessel) in the assembly, reconstruction, repair, dismantlement, operation, movement or inspection of an offshore installation of the inspection of the sea bed under or near an offshore installation;

"inspector" means a person appointed as an inspector under section 6 (4) of the Act;[2]

"manager" includes, where no manager is appointed pursuant to section 4 of the Act, any person made responsible by the owner for safety, health and welfare on board an offshore installation;

"offshore installation" includes any part of an offshore installation whether or not capable of being manned by one or more persons; and

"vessel" includes an aircraft, a hovercraft and any floating structure other than an offshore installation.

(3) The Interpretation Act 1889 shall apply to the interpretation of these Regulations as it applies to the interpretation of an Act of Parliament.

PART 1

Inspection of offshore installations

Functions and powers of inspectors

2. (1) For the purpose of ensuring that the provisions of the Act and of regulations thereunder are complied with, of investigating a casualty and

---

[1] Dated 2 November 1973. Statutory Instruments, 1973 No. 1842. Came into operation on 1 December 1973.

[2] Mineral Workings (Offshore Installations) Act 1971, partially reproduced in document ST/LEG/SER.B/16, pages 107-112.

generally assisting the Secretary of State in the execution of the Act, an inspector, at any time—

(a) May board an offshore installation and obtain access to all parts of it;

(b) May inspect an offshore installation and any equipment;

(c) May inspect the sea bed and subsoil under or near an offshore installation;

(d) May inspect and take copies from any certificate of insurance issued under regulations made under paragraph 4 (2) *(b)* or (3) of the Schedule to the Act or any copy thereof so required to be maintained on an offshore installation, from any installation logbook or other record required to be maintained under regulations made under paragraph 11 of that Schedule or from any other document relating to the operation or safety of an offshore installation or of any equipment;

(e) May test any equipment;

(f) Where a casualty has occurred or is apprehended, may dismantle any equipment or test to destruction or take possession of any equipment;

(g) May require the owner or manager or any person on board or near to an offshore installation to do or to refrain from doing any act as appears to the inspector to be necessary or expedient for the purpose of averting a casualty (whether the danger is immediate or not), or minimizing the consequences of a casualty.

(2) An inspector shall permit the owner or manager or any person nominated by the owner or manager to be present when any inspection, test or dismantlement is carried out under this Regulation.

(3) A requirement under paragraph (1) *(g)* above shall cease to have effect at the expiration of 3 days after the date on which it is given, unless the Secretary of State by notice given to the owner of the offshore installation extends its operation (with or without variation) for a further period or periods:

Provided that, before giving notice extending the operation of the requirement, the Secretary of State shall consult with the owner of the installation and shall consider any representations made by him.

3. (1) In connexion with any of his functions under Regulation 2 an inspector—

(a) May make such requirements of any person (including the owner and manager of the installation) as appear to the inspector to be required for the performance of those functions whether by himself or any other person acting at the direction of the Secretary of State:

Provided that before making a requirement in connexion with any of paragraphs (1) *(e)*, *(f)* or *(g)* of that Regulation, the inspector shall consult with the owner or manager with a view to maintaining safety and to minimizing interference with the operation of the installation;

(b) May require any person to produce to the inspector any article to which this Regulation applies and which is in his possession or custody;

(c) May make notes, take measurements, make drawings and take photographs of an offshore installation and of any article to which this Regulation applies;

(d) May require the owner or manager of the installation to furnish to him any article to which this Regulation applies (other than a document), or, in the case of any article on any vessel, may so require the master, captain or person in charge of the vessel;

(e) May require the owner or manager of an offshore installation or any person employed on or in connexion with the installation or equipment to carry out or to assist in carrying out any inspection, text or dismantlement of the offshore installation or of any equipment;

(f) May require the owner or manager of an offshore installation or the concession owner concerned to assist him in carrying out an inspection of the sea bed or subsoil under or near the installation; and

(g) May require the owner or manager to provide at any reasonable time conveyance to or from the installation of the inspector, any other person acting at the direction of the Secretary of State, any equipment required by the inspector for testing and any article of which he has taken possession pursuant to these Regulations.

(2) This Regulation applies to articles of the following descriptions, that is to say, any equipment or part thereof, a specimen of any material or substance (including a natural substance) on or near an offshore installation and any document of a description referred to in Regulation 2 (1) *(d)*.

4. (1) An inspector may require an owner or a manager of an offshore installation or any other person to furnish to him or to a person acting at the direction of the Secretary of State such information as he may reasonably demand in exercise of the inspector's functions under Regulation 2.

(2) Information required to be furnished under paragraph (1) may, and if so required by the inspector shall, be furnished in writing, and if furnished orally may be so furnished in the presence of any person whom the person furnishing the information reasonably desires to be present and, if practicable and that person so wishes, in the presence of the manager of the installation.

Duties of owners of offshore installations and others

5. (1) The owner or manager of an offshore installation shall provide an inspector and any other person acting at the direction of the Secretary of State with reasonable accommodation and means of subsistence while on board an offshore installation for the purposes of these Regulations.

(2) The owner or manager of an offshore installation and any other person, in relation to any offshore installation in any area in respect of which he is the concession owner, shall afford generally or so cause to be afforded to an inspector and any other person acting at the direction of the Secretary of State all such facilities and assistance (including the carrying out of any procedures by way of demonstration) as an inspector of such other person may reasonably require in performing the functions of an inspector under these Regulations; and an inspector or such other person may require accordingly.

134

Disclosure of information

6. A person acting at the direction of the Secretary of State (not being a person holding office under Her Majesty) shall not disclose to any other person any information obtained or received by him while acting at such direction—

(a) By virtue of these Regulations other than Regulation 4 (1), without the consent of the owner; or

(b) By virtue of Regulation 4 (1), without the consent of the person who furnished the information; or

(c) Under any provision of these Regulations, without the consent of the Secretary of State.

Offences under Part I

7. (1) Any person—

(a) Who fails to comply with any requirements made of him under this Part of these Regulations; or

(b) Who obstructs any other person in the performance of his functions, powers or duties under, or in complying with any requirement made of that person under, this Part of these Regulations, or

(c) Who, without permission granted by an inspector or other person acting at the direction of the Secretary of State, removes, conceals or tampers with any article of which possession has been taken by an inspector or such a person;

shall be guilty of an offence.

(2) An owner or manager who fails to provide accommodation and means of subsistence pursuant to Regulation 5 (1) shall be guilty of an offence.

(3) An owner, manager or concession owner who fails to afford or cause to be afforded facilities and assistance pursuant to Regulation 5 (2) shall be guilty of an offence.

(4) A person acting at the direction of the Secretary of State who discloses any information in contravention of Regulation 6 shall be guilty of an offence.

8. (1) It shall be a defence to a charge—

(a) Under Regulation 7 (1) *(a)* relating to failure to comply with a requirement made under Regulation 5 (2); or

(b) Under Regulation 7 (3) relating to failure to afford facilities or assistance under Regulation 5 (2);

to show that the person charged, being the manager of the offshore installation to which the charge relates, was acting, in respect of the facts alleged, under and in accordance with the provisions of subsections (4) or (6) of section 5 of the Act (which confers powers on the manager of an offshore installation).

(2) The fine which may be imposed under Regulation 7 (2) shall not exceed £100 and proceedings on indictment thereunder shall be excluded.

(3) The variations or revocation of any requirement given or made under any provision of these Regulations shall not affect liability for any offence committed before the variation or revocation takes effect.

. . .

(c) OFFSHORE INSTALLATIONS (CONSTRUCTION AND SURVEY) REGULATIONS 1974[1]

. . .

2. (1) In these Regulations and the Schedules hereto, unless the context otherwise requires—

"Certificate of Fitness" means a certificate issued by a Certifying Authority under Regulation 9;

"Certifying Authority" means the Secretary of State or any person, committee, society or other body of persons appointed by the Secretary of State pursuant to Regulation 4;

"environmental factors" mean the matters referred to in Part II of Schedule 2;

"equipment" means any plant, machinery, apparatus or system attached to or forming part of an offshore installation;

"fixed installation" means an offshore installation which is not a mobile installation;

"mobile installation" means an offshore installation which can be moved from place to place without major dismantling or modification, whether or not it has its own motive power;

"operations manual" means written particulars provided by the owner of an offshore installation for the information, guidance and instruction of the manager thereof in securing, in the case of a fixed installation, the safety of the installation when established at a station and, in the case of a mobile installation, the safety, seaworthiness and stability of the installation when moving to or from, or being located on, or removed from, or maintained at, a station;

"primary structure" means all structural components of an offshore installation, the failure of which would seriously endanger the safety of the installation;

"relevant waters" mean waters to which the Act[2] applies;

"seaworthiness" means the capacity of a mobile installation to withstand, while floating, all relevant environmental factors;

"survey" means an examination conducted by a surveyor of an offshore installation or any part thereof or of any equipment, including the scrutiny of

---

[1] Dated 17 February 1974. *Statutory Instruments* 1974. No. 289. Came into operation on 1 May 1974.

[2] Mineral Workings (Offshore Installations) Act 1971, partially reproduced in document ST/LEG/SER.B/16, pages 107-112.

any document, relevant thereto, and the conducting of any tests which a surveyor considers necessary in order to assess the integrity or safety of any item and whether any requirement of these Regulations has been complied with; and

"surveyor" means a surveyor appointed by a Certifying Authority.

(2) Nothing in these Regulations shall apply to an offshore installation which is a dredging installation and which is registered as a vessel (whether so registered in the United Kingdom or elsewhere) or to an offshore installation which can be navigated or operated when wholly submerged in water.

(3) The Interpretation Act 1889 shall apply to the interpretation of these Regulations as it applies to the interpretation of an Act of Parliament.

Certification of offshore installations

3. (1) On or after 31 August 1975:—

(a) No fixed installation shall be established in the relevant waters;

(b) No mobile installation shall be brought into those waters with a view to its being stationed there; and

(c) No fixed or mobile installation shall be maintained in those waters; unless there is in force in respect thereof a valid Certificate of Fitness.

(2) On or after the date specified in paragraph (1), no mobile installation shall be moved to a station in the relevant waters unless prior to moving the owner of the installation has obtained from a competent person a report on the environmental factors at that station and the owner has reasonable grounds for believing that the installation is capable of withstanding those factors.

4. The Secretary of State may appoint any person, committee, society or other body of persons to cause surveys and assessments to be made pursuant to these Regulations and to certify offshore installations as fit for any of the purposes specified in these Regulations.

5. (1) An application for a Certificate of Fitness in respect of an offshore installation, or for a renewal thereof, shall:—

(a) Be made by or on behalf of the owner of that installation;

(b) Be made to a Certifying Authority in the form specified in Part I of Schedule 1 duly completed and signed;

(c) Be accompanied by such information as may be necessary to enable the fees to be calculated in accordance with Regulation 13;

(d) Be accompanied by sufficient plans, drawings, specifications, reports and other documents and information to enable the Certifying Authority to ascertain whether the requirements specified in Schedule 2, or such of the same as are applicable to the installation and its equipment, have been complied with; and

(e) Be accompanied by the operations manual relating to the installation:

Provided that it shall be permissible to submit any document referred to in paragraphs *(d)* and *(e)* at any date prior to the grant of the Certificate of Fitness.

(2) If upon receipt of an application for a Certificate of Fitness in respect of an offshore installation, or for a renewal thereof, the Certifying Authority shall be of opinion that the application and the supporting documents and information comply with the requirements of paragraph (1), the Authority shall:—

(a) Cause to be carried out, or ensure that there has already been carried out, by a competent person, an independent assessment of the design and method of construction of the installation to ascertain whether the requirements specified in Schedule 2 hereto, or such of the same as are applicable to the installation and its equipment, have been complied with, and an independent assessment of the provisions of the operations manual to ascertain whether the information, guidance and instructions contained therein are adequate and appropriate in relation to the installation; and

(b) Cause to be carried out a major survey of the installation and its equipment in accordance with Regulation 8 (1) in order to ascertain whether the installation conforms to the design and method of construction referred to in sub-paragraph *(a)* and whether the requirements specified in Schedule 2, or such of the same as are applicable to the installation and its equipment, have been complied with.

Surveys of offshore installations

6. (1) A certifying Authority shall appoint, from among persons appearing to the Authority to be suitably qualified, surveyors whose duty it shall be to conduct the surveys required by these Regulations.

(2) In carrying out any such survey, a surveyor shall be accorded all necessary facilities therefor by the owner and manager of the installation concerned, and the installation and any of its equipment shall be submitted to such tests as may in the opinion of the surveyor be necessary to ascertain whether the requirements specified in Schedule 2, or such of the same as are applicable, have been complied with.

(3) On completing a survey, a surveyor shall make a declaration to the Certifying Authority giving the date of completion of his survey, the results thereof and his findings as to whether the installation complies with the requirements of Schedule 2, or such of the same as may be applicable, on a form specified by the Authority for that purpose, which form shall remain in the Authority's custody.

7. (1) If at any time while an application for a Certificate of Fitness is being considered by a Certifying Authority or while a Certificate of Fitness is in force any alteration should be made to any plan, drawing, specification or other document (apart from an operations manual), a copy of which was previously submitted pursuant to these Regulations, the owner of the installation concerned shall forthwith upon such alterations send particulars thereof to the Certifying Authority which is considering the application or which issued the certificate in force or both those Authorities (as the case may be).

(2) No alterations shall be made to the provisions of any operations manual, which has previously been submitted to a Certifying Authority, without the consent of that Authority.

138

(3) If at any time while an application for a Certificate of Fitness is being considered by a Certifying Authority or while a Certificate of Fitness is in force there occurs in respect of the offshore installation to which the application of certificate (as the case may be) relates any of the following events: —

(a) It is damaged, or is suspected of having been damaged, in a manner likely to impair the safety, strength, stability and, in the case of a mobile installation, seaworthiness of the installation; or

(b) It demonstrates signs of deterioration in its structure to an extent likely to impair the safety, strength, stability and, in the case of a mobile installation, seaworthiness of the installation; or

(c) Its equipment is subjected to any alteration, repair or replacement; the owner of the installation shall forthwith notify in writing the Certifying Authority which is considering the application or which issued the certificate in force or both those Authorities (as the case may be) of the occurrence of that event, giving whatever particulars may be required to enable the Authority concerned to determine whether or not an additional survey should be carried out.

(4) No repair, replacement, alteration or dismantlement shall be carried out in respect of any offshore installation at any time while a Certificate of Fitness is in force in respect of that installation unless the procedures specified in sub-paragraphs *(a)*, *(b)* and *(c)* of paragraph 1 of Part VII of Schedule 2 are observed in respect thereof, the references in those sub-paragraphs to "the Certifying Authority" being taken to refer to the Certifying Authority which issued the before-mentioned Certificate of Fitness and the reference therein to "such work" being taken to refer to such repair, replacement, alteration or dismantlement (as the case may be).

8. (1) In respect of every offshore installation in relation to which there is no Certificate of Fitness in force or in respect of which a Certificate of Fitness is in force and a renewal thereof is sought, there shall be carried out a survey (herein referred to as a "major survey") which shall include a thorough examination of the installation and its equipment in order to ascertain the matters specified in Regulation 5 (2) *(b)*:

Provided that a Certifying Authority may accept as part of a major survey the results of a survey carried out otherwise than under these Regulations if satisfied that the results so obtained are equivalent to those which would have been obtained in the course of a major survey:

Provided further that at any time after the installation has been subjected to a major survey a Certifying Authority may accept, instead of a subsequent major survey, a series of continuous surveys conducted in rotation in conjunction with the annual surveys required under paragraph (2) if satisfied that the results so obtained are equivalent to those which would have been obtained in the course of a major survey.

(2) *(a)* In respect of every installation in relation to which a Certificate of Fitness is in force, there shall be carried out on behalf of the Certifying Authority which issued that certificate surveys (hereinafter referred to as "annual surveys") of a selection of the members, joints and areas of the

primary structure of the installation, the parts of the installation referred to in Part V of Schedule 2 and its equipment, the selection being sufficient in number, disposition or extent (as the case may be) to provide reasonable evidence as to whether the installation and its equipment continue to comply with the requirements of Schedule 2, or such of the same as may be applicable.

(b) The first annual survey shall be carried out within not less than 9 nor more than 18 months after the date of issue of the Certificate of Fitness and thereafter similar surveys shall be carried out within not less than 9 nor more than 15 months of each anniversary of the date of issue of the certificate during the period in which it is in force.

(3) Upon receipt of a notification pursuant to Regulation 7 (3) of the occurrence in respect of an installation of any of the events specified therein, or if the Certifying Authority otherwise has reason to believe that any such event has occurred, the Certifying Authority may cause such additional survey of the installation and its equipment to be carried out as the Authority thinks fit to ascertain, in the case of an installation in respect of which an application for a certificate is being considered, whether any changes have been made or taken place sufficient to render no longer accurate the data which accompanied the application and, in the case of an installation in respect of which a Certificate of Fitness is in force, whether the installation and its equipment continue to comply with the requirements of Schedule 2, or such of the same as may be applicable.

Certificates of Fitness

9. (1) After considering all documents and other information submitted in pursuance of Regulation (5) (1) and all declarations of survey and the results of all assessments carried out in pursuance of Regulation (5) (2) the Certifying Authority may, if the Authority is satisfied that it is proper to do so, issue a Certificate of Fitness in accordance with these Regulations certifying that the offshore installation concerned is fit to be established or stationed (according to whether it is respectively a fixed or a mobile installation) and maintained in the relevant waters.

(2) A certificate of Fitness shall be in the form set out in Part II of Schedule 1 and may contain whatever limitations the Certifying Authority considers it appropriate to specify as respects the movement, location and operation of the installation to which it relates having regard to the design of the installation, the method of its construction, the materials employed in its construction and the environmental factors. The Certifying Authority shall issue two copies of the Certificate of Fitness to the owner of the installation.

(3) One copy of the current Certificate of Fitness shall be kept posted on board the installation to which it relates in such a position that it can be conveniently read, save for occasions when in pursuance of these Regulations any amendment or endorsement required to be made thereto is being effected.

(4) The Certifying Authority may amend any Certificate of Fitness by recording on the copy of the certificate referred to in paragraph (3) any changes which have occurred since it was issued, and a record of any survey

made in pursuance of Regulation 8 (2) or (3) in connexion with the installation to which the certificate relates shall be endorsed thereon on behalf of the Certifying Authority by the surveyor who carried it out. The surveyor shall also furnish the owner of the installation with a copy of the endorsement made by him.

10. (1) If, after considering the matters referred to in Regulation 9 (1), the Certifying Authority is not satisfied that a Certificate of Fitness may properly be issued, the Authority shall send a notification in writing to that effect to the owner of the offshore installation concerned giving the reasons for the conclusion, and shall at the same time send a copy of that notification to the Secretary of State.

(2) If, after considering any declaration of survey carried out in pursuance of Regulation 8 (2) or (3), or particulars of any alteration to a document submitted in pursuance of Regulation 7 (1), the Certifying Authority is of opinion that the installation is not, or is no longer, fit to be maintained in the relevant waters or in any part thereof to which it may be limited by the terms of the Certificate of Fitness issued in respect of it, the Authority shall send a notification in writing to that effect to the owner of the offshore installation concerned giving the reasons for forming that opinion, and shall at the same time send a copy of that notification to the Secretary of State.

11. (1) Subject to paragraph (2), the Secretary of State may terminate a Certificate of Fitness if he is satisfied that: —

(a) Information supplied in connexion with the application therefor was incorrect in a material particular; or

(b) The installation to which it relates is not, or is no longer, fit to be maintained in the relevant waters or in any part of such waters to which it may be limited by the terms thereof; or

(c) There has been a failure to observe any limitation contained therein respecting the movement, location or operation of the installation; or

(d) The installation to which it relates has been moved to a station contrary to the provisions of Regulation 3 (2); or

(e) There has been a failure to comply with any Regulation; or

(f) It has been superseded by a new Certificate of Fitness, or by an exemption made by the Secretary of State, issued in respect of the same installation; or

(g) The installation has in the opinion of the Secretary of State changed in character to such an extent that the issue of a new Certificate of Fitness is desirable.

(2) Before a Certificate of Fitness is terminated in accordance with paragraph (1), both the owner of the installation to which it relates, and the Certifying Authority which issued the certificate, shall be given notification in writing of the reasons for such termination, and the date on which it is to take effect, which shall not be less than 30 days after the date of issue of the said notification.

(3) A Certificate of Fitness shall be valid for such period as the Certifying Authority may specify, not exceeding 5 years from the date of completion of

the last major survey carried out pursuant to Regulation 8 (1) or of the last equivalent survey carried out in accordance with the second proviso to that Regulation, unless it is previously terminated by the Secretary of State in accordance with paragraph (1). The date of expiration shall be recorded on the certificate by the Certifying Authority.

Exemptions

12. (1) The Secretary of State may exempt any offshore installation or part of an offshore installation from all or any of the provisions of these Regulations and any such exemption may be made subject to any conditions which the Secretary of State sees fit to impose.

(2) Where an installation or part of an installation has been exempted in accordance with paragraph (1) but subject to a condition and the condition is not observed, the exemption shall not have effect and proceedings may be brought in respect of any breach of duty as if the exemption had not been made.

(3) When an installation or part of an installation has been exempted in accordance with paragraph (1), the Certifying Authority shall endorse a note of such exemption and of any conditions to which it is made subject on the Certificate of Fitness (if any) relating to that installation issued in accordance with Regulation 9.

. . .

SCHEDULE 2

. . .

Part II

Environmental considerations

1. Every offshore installation shall be capable of withstanding any combination of —

(a) Meteorological and oceanological conditions; and

(b) Properties and configuration of the sea bed and subsoil;

to which the installation may foreseeably be subjected at the place at which it is, or is intended to be, located, as assessed in accordance with paragraphs 2 and 3.

2. An assessment of the matters referred to in paragraph 1 shall be made by an competent person and (to such extent as may be relevant to the installation concerned) shall take into consideration —

(a) The water depth, the tidal range and the height of wind-induced and pressure-induced wave surges;

(b) The frequency and direction of winds and their respective speeds, averaging periods and heights above the surface of the sea;

(c) The heights, directions and periods of waves, the probability of their occurrence and the effect of currents, sea bed topography and other factors likely to modify their characteristics;

(d) The direction, speed and duration of tidal and other currents;

(e) Characteristics of the sea bed which may affect the foundations of the installation;

(f) Air and sea temperature extremes;

(g) The extent to which marine growth may form on the submerged sections of the installation; and

(h) The extent to which snow and ice may accumulate on or against the installation.

3. In assessing the matters referred to in paragraph 2—

(a) The minimum values to be ascribed by the competent person shall not be less than those likely to be exceeded on average once only in any period of 50 years; and

(b) Full account shall be taken of the records, predictions and other information available from the Institute of Oceanographic Science, the Meteorological Office of the Ministry of Defence or from any other body of comparable status fulfilling substantially the same functions or any of them.

. . .

(d) [OFFSHORE INSTALLATIONS (DIVING OPERATIONS) REGULATIONS 1974] [1]

---

[1] Dated 22 July 1974. *Statutory Instruments* 1974 No. 1229. Came into operation on 1 January 1975. Text not reproduced herein.

Subdivision B. The Contiguous Zone

1. DENMARK

[CUSTOMS ACT OF 1972, Article 110] [1]

. . .

2. TOGO

[RENSEIGNEMENTS CONCERNANT LA LEGISLATION
SUR LE DROIT DE LA MER] [2]

---

[1] *Supra* Subdivision A, Chapter IV, 1 *(a)*.
[2] *Supra* Subdivision A, Chapter I, 17 *(a)*.

Division II

THE CONTINENTAL SHELF[1]

1. ARGENTINA

(a) ACT NO. 20,489 OF 23 MAY 1973 REGULATING SCIENTIFIC AND TECH-NICAL RESEARCH ACTIVITIES CONDUCTED BY FOREIGNERS AND INTERNATIONAL ORGANIZATIONS[2]

In exercise of the powers conferred on him by article 5 of the Statute of the Argentine Revolution,

The President of the Argentine Nation approves and promulgates with the force of law:

Article 1. Scientific and technical research activities contemplated by foreign physical or legal persons or international organizations in waters subject to national sovereignty and in the sea-bed and subsoil of the submarine zones adjacent to Argentine territory to a depth of 200 metres or, beyond that limit, to where the depth of the superjacent waters permits the exploitation of the natural resources of such zones may be carried out only with the prior authorization of the National Executive Power.

Article 2. The authorization shall be granted through the Commander-in-Chief of the Navy. Whenever the research activities are, because of their nature, within the competence of other State, national or provincial agencies, the authorization shall be granted through them, and the Commander-in-Chief of the Navy shall be notified in the interest of the safety of navigation and defence and shall be empowered, to that end, to supervise any activities carried out.

Article 3. The agency through which an authorization is granted in pursuance of the foregoing articles shall receive a copy of the data or samples produced and shall have access to all the information derived from the scientific and technical research carried out in the maritime zones referred to in article 1, and to its interim and final results and it may appoint representatives to observe the operations and make certain that they comply with the conditions and limitations laid down by such agency.

Article 4. The agency through which the Executive Power grants the authorization may require that Argentine experts with instructions to attend or take part in the work shall be carried on board the components used in the research activities.

---

[1] See also *supra* Division I, Subdivision A, Chapter IX. Most of the texts reproduced there are of relevance also in relation to the continental shelf.

[2] Spanish text provided by the Permanent Mission of Argentina to the United Nations, in a note verbale of 28 June 1973. Translation by the Secretariat of the United Nations.

Article 5. The scientific and technical research activities shall be carried out in such a way as not to damage the marine natural resources or unnecessarily to endanger or hamper the exploitation or such marine resources, navigation or existing services or works of any kind.

Article 6. Infringements of the provisions of this Act and the regulations made under it and of the conditions, limitations and time-limits laid down in the relevant authorization may result in the revocation of the authorization, without prejudice to the imposition of the penalties provided for in this Act.

Article 7. Those responsible for the scientific and technical research activities who commit the offences referred to in article 6 shall be liable to a fine, and until such time as the fine is paid the components and equipment used for the work shall be impounded. Fines shall be imposed after summary proceedings arranged by the Executive Power through the Commander-in-Chief of the Navy have taken place at the Argentine Naval Prefecture; the amounts of the fines shall range from a minimum of $US 500 (five hundred) to a maximum of $US 100,000 (one hundred thousand) or their equivalent in another currency. The persons concerned may appeal against the fines imposed in conformity with the provisions of Act No. 19,549.

. . .

Article 9. A decree[1] embodying regulations shall establish the requirements, procedures, time-limits and conditions for the granting of authorizations and shall lay down the period during which the authority granting the authorization may not divulge information supplied to it by the researchers with a view to safeguarding their right to priority in publishing such information.

(b) DECREE NO. 4,915 OF 23 MAY 1973 REGULATING SCIENTIFIC AND TECHNICAL RESEARCH ACTIVITIES CONDUCTED BY FOREIGNERS AND INTERNATIONAL ORGANIZATIONS[2]

Considering Act No. 20,489[3] and

Considering that it is necessary to establish regulations under the Act on scientific and technical research carried out in waters subject to national sovereignty, in the sea-bed and subsoil of those waters and on the Argentine continental shelf,

The President of the Argentine Nation decrees:

Article 1. The persons concerned shall apply for the prior authorization to which articles 1 and 2 of the said Act refer to the Ministry of External Relations and Worship through their diplomatic representatives in Argentina or at the Argentine Embassy in their own countries. The Ministry of External Relations and Worship shall transmit the application to the competent State agency, depending on the nature of the research, and shall receive from it for

---

[1] See Decree No. 4,915 of 23 May 1973, reproduced *infra (b)*.

[2] Spanish text provided by the Permanent Mission of Argentina to the United Nations in a note verbale of 28 June 1973. Translation by the Secretariat of the United Nations.

[3] Reproduced *supra (a)*.

transmission to the applicant the decision of the Executive Power on the matter.

Article 2. The application for prior authorization shall be submitted to the Ministry of External Relations and Worship of the Argentine Embassy at least 180 days before the date on which activities are to begin. The Executive Power shall rule on it within 60 days of receiving the application through the Ministry of External Affairs and Worship. An applicant who has received no reply to his request within the period indicated above must regard it as rejected.

Article 3. Foreign nationals undertaking scientific and technical research activities under a contract concluded with or instructions issued by a State, national or provincial agency for the conduct of those tasks shall be exempt from the procedure laid down in the foregoing articles. In such cases the application shall be submitted directly by the public agency responsible for the contract or instructions to the agency competent to grant the authorization 90 days in advance.

Article 4. The application for prior authorization shall specify in the greatest possible detail:

(a) The physical and/or moral person or international organization under whose responsibility the research will be carried out;

(b) The physical and/or moral person or the international and/or private organization financing the research for which authorization is being sought;

(c) The physical person under whose direction the research in the maritime zones referred to in article 1 of the Act is to be carried out, and the scientific and technical staff who will participate, with a statement of their qualifications;

(d) The scientific and technical research operations to be carried out in the maritime zones referred to in article 1 of the Act and the land-based operations, with a time-table for their execution;

(e) The equipment and techniques which are to be used;

(f) The area of the maritime zones referred to in article 1 of the Act in which it is desired to carry out the research, which shall be defined by geographical co-ordinates, the places at which it is desired to carry out land-based activities, the Argentine ports which are to be called at and the itinerary in waters under Argentine jurisdiction;

(g) The dates between which it is desired to conduct the activities in the areas for which authorization is sought and the dates of stay on land and in Argentine ports;

(h) Description of the vessels from which the research is to be conducted, their sources of energy for propulsion and equipment, communication equipment, radio frequencies on which they will operate and international call-signs. In the case of semi-fixed platforms, a statement of the stabilizing systems and, for the towing vessel, the data mentioned above, photographs of all the components to be used;

(i) Accommodation available, in the components to be used, for Argentine observers and experts.

148

Article 6. The person who is to be responsible for the components from which the research is to be conducted shall be obliged to provide adequate accommodation and food, for such time as they remain on board, for the personnel assigned to them as observers or experts by instruction of the authority granting the authorization.

Article 7. Foreign vessels which are authorized to conduct research activities in waters within Argentine jurisdiction shall comply with the instructions of the Navigational Safety Communications Service and report their midday position in the official Argentine time-zone through the stations of that Service. They shall also, if they are covered by the provisions of the Convention for the Safety of Life at Sea, meet at all times the standards specified by that Convention. If they are not covered by it, they shall hold a certificate of satisfying requirements for the Safety of Life at Sea issued by the maritime authority of their respective countries. Compliance with this requirement may be verified by the Argentine maritime authorities when they deem it necessary. Failure to comply with this provision may result in the revocation of the authorization.

2. BURMA

[PETROLEUM RESOURCES (DEVELOPMENT AND REGULATION) ACT, 1957, Sections 2-7, 9 (1) and 10-12] [1]

3. CAMBODIA

(a) [DECRET N° 261/72-PRK EN DATE DU 20 MAI 1972 RELATIF A L'APPLICATION DE LA LOI MINIERE] [2]

(b) DECRET N° 439-72/PRK EN DATE DU 1er JUILLET 1972 PORTANT DELIMITATION DU PLATEAU CONTINENTAL KHMER [3]

Article premier. En application des clauses de la Convention de Genève du 29 avril 1958 sur le Plateau continental [4] à laquelle la République khmère [5] a adhéré et du Traité franco-siamois du 23 mars 1907 [6] et le Procès-Verbal de délimitation de la frontière du 8 février 1908, la limite extérieure du Plateau continental de la République khmère est fixée comme l'indique la carte No 1972 de la Marine française à l'échelle 1/1 096 000 annexée au présent Kret avec les coordonnées de ses points repères suivantes :

La délimitation latérale nord entre les zones du Plateau continental relevant de la souveraineté respective de la République khmère et de la

---

[1] *Supra* Division I, Subdivision A, Chapter IX, 1.

[2] *Supra* Division I, Subdivision A, Chapter IX, 2.

[3] Texte transmis par le représentant permanent de la République khmère auprès de l'Organisation des Nations Unies par note en date du 11 septembre 1974.

[4] *Recueil des Traités* de l'Organisation des Nations Unies, vol. 499, p. 311, et document ST/LEG/SER.B/15, p. 767.

[5] Title used for the period beginning 9 October 1970 and prior to 30 April 1975.

[6] De Martens, *Nouveau Recueil général des traités,* troisième série, tome II, No 15, p. 38.

Thaïlande est constituée par une ligne droite joignant le point frontière "A" sur la côte au plus haut sommet de l'île de Koh Kut "S" et se prolongeant jusqu'au point P; ces points A et P sont définis ci-après :

	Longitudes est Greenwich	Latitudes nord
POINT A		
Ce point étant le point frontière sur la côte (Traité de Bangkok du 23 mars 1907)	102° 54′ 81	11° 38′ 88
POINT P		
Point équidistant de la base cambodgienne A— Ilot Kusrovie et de la ligne de base thaïlandaise opposée	101° 20′ 00	11° 32′ 00

Article 2. La délimitation de la ligne médiane (direction Nord-Sud) est constituée par une ligne brisée partant du point P et passant successivement sur les points

$$P_{ck1} - P_{ck2} - P_{ck3} - P_{ck4} - P_{ck5} - P_{ck6} - P_{ck7} -$$
$$P_{ck8} - P_{ck9} - P_{ck10} - P_{ck11} - P_{ck12} - P_{ck13}$$

et B point frontière avec le Sud-Vietnam ci-après définis et reportés sur la carte jointe en annexe :

	Longitudes est Greenwich	Latitudes nord
P_{ck1}	101° 13′ 00	10° 16′ 00
Point équidistant d'une part de l'îlot cambodgien de Kusrovie et d'autre part des points thaïlandais suivants : îlot Koh Charn et point 8 Area 2 (Hin Bai).		
P_{ck2}	101° 29′ 00	10° 16′ 50
P_{ck3}	101° 36′ 00	9° 05′ 00
P_{ck4}	101° 57′ 50	8° 31′ 00
P_{ck5}	102° 59′ 50	7° 42′ 00
P_{ck6}	103° 21′ 00	7° 34′ 00
P_{ck7}	104° 08′ 00	9° 01′ 00
P_{ck8}	104° 01′ 00	9° 18′ 00
P_{ck9}	104° 08′ 50	9° 38′ 50

150

	Longitudes est Greenwich	Latitudes nord
P_{ck}10	104° 16' 50	9° 56' 00
P_{ck}11	104° 15' 00	10° 01' 00
P_{ck}12	104° 10' 50	10° 05' 00
P_{ck}13	104° 09' 00	10° 12' 00
B point frontière avec Sud-Vietnam	104° 26' 63	10° 25' 23

Article 3. La carte marine No 1972 de la Marine française – Edition 1949 à l'échelle 1/1 096 000 est jointe au présent Kret.

Toute référence au Kret implique en même temps une référence à la carte No 1972.

Article 4. Toutes dispositions contraires au présent Kret sont purement et simplement abrogées.

Article 5. Le Ministre des affaires étrangères et le Ministre de l'industrie, des ressources minières et des pêches maritimes sont chargés, chacun en ce qui le concerne, de l'exécution du présent Kret.

4. DENMARK

EXECUTIVE ORDER No. 141 OF 13 MARCH 1974 BY THE MINISTRY OF PUBLIC WORKS CONCERNING PIPELINE INSTALLATIONS IN THE AREA OF THE DANISH CONTINENTAL SHELF FOR THE TRANSPORT OF HYDRO-CARBONS[1]

In pursuance of Article 4 and article 5, paragraph 3, of Act No. 259 of 9 June 1971 concerning the continental shelf,[2] as amended by Act No. 278 of 7 June 1972,[3] it is hereby provided as follows:

Article 1. (1) The establishment and operation of pipeline installations in the area of the Danish continental shelf for the transport of hydrocarbons may only take place on the basis of a permit issued by the Minister for Public Works.

(2) This Executive Order shall not apply to local pipelines which form an integral part of an installation used for the extraction of hydrocarbons from the Danish continental shelf, or to other pipelines leading from such installations where they are situated inside a safety zone surrounding the installation.

---

[1] Came into force immediately in accordance with Article 7. Danish text transmitted by the Ministry of Foreign Affairs in a note verbale of 20 December 1974. Translation by the Secretariat of the United Nations.

[2] Reproduced in document ST/LEG/SER.B/16, pp. 138-140.

[3] *Idem.*

Article 2. A permit in pursuance of article 1 may be subject to such conditions as the following:

(1) That the pipeline installation is used only for the transport os specific categories of hydrocarbon,

(2) That further provisions to ensure the implementation of reasonable measures for the exploration of the continental shelf and utilization of its natural resources are complied with,

(3) That the pipeline is buried in the sea-bed so that its presence does not cause unwarranted interference with navigation and fisheries,

(4) That, where the pipeline is to cross existing pipelines or cables, the permit-holder reaches an appropriate agreement with the owner of such lines or cables to ensure indemnification of the owner in connexion with such crossing,

(5) That the pipeline installation is marked in accordance with directives to be laid down by the Directorate of Maritime Affairs, at no charge to the Danish State,

(6) That safety requirements to be prescribed in the permit or at a subsequent stage after the granting of the permit concerning the construction, establishment and operation of the pipeline installation are complied with,

(7) That the pipeline installation, both at the installation stage and during operation, is subject to inspection by Danish authorities, to be specified subsequently, whose orders and instructions shall be carried out,

(8) That the expenses connected with such inspection are refunded by the permit-holder,

(9) That the permit-holder establishes an emergency service to deal with the consequences of leakage of hydrocarbons and

(10) That the pipeline is maintained and inspected in accordance with the directives laid down on the subject by the inspecting authorities.

Article 3. An applicant for a permit in pursuance of article 1 may be required by the Minister for Public Works to communicate all information considered to be of importance for the processing of the application.

Article 4. (1) The permit-holder shall compensate for damage occasioned by the activities carried out on the basis of the permit, even if the damage is accidental.

(2) Where the injured party wilfully or through gross negligence contributes to the damage, the compensation may be reduced or may lapse.

(3) The permit-holder may be required, in the permit, to take out insurance for the full or partial coverage of liability for damages as provided in paragraph 1.

Article 5. Offences against article 1, paragraph 1, shall be punishable by a fine.

Article 6. Any disputes that may arise between the Danish State and the permit-holder on any question concerning the permit, shall be settled by the Danish courts. The venue, unless otherwise specified by the Minister for Public Works shall be Copenhagen.

. . .

5. FRANCE

DECRET No 71-361 DU 6 MAI 1971 PORTANT DISPOSITIONS PENALES POUR L'APPLICATION DE LA LOI No 68-1181 DU 30 DECEMBRE 1968 RELATIVE A L'EXPLORATION DU PLATEAU CONTINENTAL ET A L'EXPLOITATION DE SES RESSOURCES NATURELLES ET DU DECRET No 71-360 DU 6 MAI 1971 PRIS POUR SON APPLICATION[1]

Le Premier Ministre,

. . .

Vu la loi No 68-1181 du 30 décembre 1968[2] relative à l'exploration du plateau continental et à l'exploitation de ses ressources naturelles, ensemble le décret No 71-360 du 6 mai 1971[3] portant application de ladite loi;

Vu l'article R. 25 du code pénal;

. . .

Décrète :

Art. 1er. Les personnes énumérées au premier alinéa de l'article 11 de la loi susvisée du 30 décembre 1968 ne peuvent mettre en oeuvre aucun équipement susceptible d'être confondu avec une marque de signalisation maritime ou de nuire à l'observation d'une telle marque par les navigateurs.

Toute contravention au présent article sera punie d'un emprisonnement de six jours à un mois et d'une amende de 400 à 2 000 F ou de l'une de ces deux peines seulement.

Art. 2. La personne assumant la conduite des travaux d'exploration et d'exploitation à bord des installations et dispositifs visés à l'article 3-1° de la loi susvisée du 30 décembre 1968 est tenue, sous peine d'une amende de 180 à 1 080 F, de faire mentionner, par l'autorité maritime, sur le permis de circulation prévu à l'article 10 de la loi précitée, le nom et les qualifications de chacune des personnes dont la présence à bord est obligatoire en application des textes sur la sauvegarde de la vie humaine en mer.

Art. 3. Lorsque le registre des hydrocarbures prévu à l'article 27 du décret susvisé du 6 mai 1971 n'est pas tenu conformément aux prescriptions réglementaires ou comporte des mentions fausses, la personne assumant la conduite des travaux d'exploration ou d'exploitation à bord des installations ou dispositifs visés à l'article 3-1° de la loi susvisée du 30 décembre 1968 sera punie d'une amende de 1 000 à 2 000 F. En cas de récidive, un emprisonnement de 10 jours à un mois pourra, en outre, être prononcé.

Les mêmes peines seront applicables si le responsable refuse de communiquer le registre ou s'oppose au contrôle de celui-ci par les autorités compétentes.

Art. 4. Le présent décret est applicable dans les territoires d'outre-mer.

. . .

---

[1] *Journal officiel,* 15 mai 1971.

[2] Reproduite partiellement dans ST/LEG/SER.B/15, p. 356-359.

[3] Reproduit partiellement dans ST/LEG/SER.B/16, p. 146-150.

6. GHANA

(a) [MINERALS ACT, 1962, AS AMENDED UP TO 1968, Sections 1, 2 (1) and (3), 5 and 12][1]

(b) [MINERALS (OFFSHORE) REGULATIONS, 1963, AS AMENDED IN 1968, Regulations 1-3, 5-7, 7A, 8-12, 14, 16-19 (1)-(3), 20 (1), 21, 21A, 22 and the First Schedule][2]

(c) [TERRITORIAL WATERS AND CONTINENTAL SHELF DECREE, 1973, Sections 3 and 5][3]

7. GERMAN DEMOCRATIC REPUBLIC

(a) [EXCERPT FROM THE CONSTITUTION OF THE GERMAN DEMOCRATIC REPUBLIC OF 6 APRIL 1968 AS MODIFIED BY THE LAW OF 7 OCTOBER 1974][4]

(b) PROCLAMATION OF 26 MAY 1964 BY THE GOVERNMENT OF THE GERMAN DEMOCRATIC REPUBLIC ON THE CONTINENTAL SHELF ALONG THE BALTIC SEA COAST OF THE GERMAN DEMOCRATIC REPUBLIC[5]

The exploration and utilization of the natural resources of the sea-bed and the subsoil of the submarine areas adjacent to the Baltic Sea Coast of the German Democratic Republic outside the territorial sea are an unlimited sovereign right of the German Democratic Republic which derives from the generally recognized principle of international law of the rights of States over the natural resources of the continental shelf extending from their coasts.

This principle of international law is in conformity with the practice of States and has been confirmed specifically in the Geneva Convention on the Continental Shelf of 29 April 1958.

The Government of the German Democratic Republic declares that explicit approval by the competent authorities of the German Democratic Republic is required for any measures for the exploration and utilization of the continental shelf of the German Democratic Republic. The Government of the German Democratic Republic reserves the right to take appropriate measures against activities undertaken without the approval of the competent authorities of the German Democratic Republic.

The Government of the German Democratic Republic declares its readiness to enter into inter-State agreements on the delimitation of the continental shelf of the German Democratic Republic with respect to the continental shelf of neighbouring States on the Baltic Sea, in accordance with

---

[1] *Supra* Division I, Subdivision A, Chapter IX 4 *(a)*.

[2] *Ibid., (b)*.

[3] *Supra* Division I, Subdivision A, Chapter I, 5.

[4] *Supra* Division I, Subdivision A, Chapter I, 4 *(a)*.

[5] Legal Gazette of the German Democratic Republic, Part I, No. 6, p. 99; 26 May 1964. German text provided by the Permanent Mission of the German Democratic Republic in a note verbale of 19 December 1974. Translation by the Secretariat of the United Nations.

the principle of delimitation laid down in the Geneva Convention on the Continental Shelf of 29 April 1958. It expresses its conviction that the delimitation of the continental shelf in the Baltic Sea will open new possibilities for the exploration and utilization of the resources of the sea and will also further promote friendly co-operation between the States having Baltic Sea coasts.

(c) LAW OF 20 FEBRUARY 1967 ON THE EXPLORATION, EXPLOITATION AND DELIMITATION OF THE CONTINENTAL SHELF[1] AS MODIFIED BY THE LAW OF 11 JUNE 1968[2]

In accordance with the Geneva Convention on the Continental Shelf of 29 April 1958[3] (hereinafter called the Convention) and for the safeguarding and protection of the rights established by the Proclamation by the Government of the German Democratic Republic on the Continental Shelf of the Baltic Coast of the German Democratic Republic of 26 May 1974,[4] the following law is enacted:

Article 1. (1) The natural resources of the continental shelf of the German Democratic Republic are the property of the people;

(2) The exploration and utilization of the natural resources referred to in paragraph 1 are subject exclusively to the internal regulations of the German Democratic Republic and require special approval by the competent central authorities.

Article 2. In accordance with article 1 of the Convention, the term "continental shelf" shall mean:

> The sea-bed and the subsoil of the submarine areas adjacent to the coast but outside the area of the territorial sea, to a depth of 200 metres or, beyond that limit, to where the depth of the superjacent waters admits of the exploitation of the natural resources of the said areas.

Article 3. (1) The delimitation of the continental shelf in relation to other States whose coasts are opposite the coasts of the German Democratic Republic or which are adjacent to the German Democratic Republic shall be carried out in accordance with article 6 of the Convention in such a way that the boundary is formed by the median line every point of which is equidistant from the nearest points on the baselines from which the breadth of the territorial sea of each State is measured.

(2) The basis for the delimitation of the continental shelf of the German Democratic Republic shall be the baseline and its co-ordinates as they were laid down in the legal provisions concerning the safeguarding of the sea-frontier of the German Democratic Republic.

---

[1] GB1.I, p. 5. In force on 20 February 1967, in accordance with article 7. German text provided by the Permanent Mission of the German Democratic Republic to the United Nations in a note verbale of 19 December 1974. Translation by the Secretariat of the United Nations.

[2] GB1.I, p. 242: Ber. GB1.II, p. 827.

[3] United Nations, *Treaty Series,* Vol. 499, p. 311. Also ST/LEG/SER.B/15, p. 767.

[4] *Supra (b).*

Note: At the present time the regulation of 30 December 1961 concerning the safeguarding of the sea-frontier of the German Democratic Republic as modified on 19 March 1964 (published annually in the first issue of *Nautische Mitteilungen für Seefahrer* is in effect.

(3) The Council of Ministers may, if necessary, have the line of delimitation of the continental shelf incorporated in the charts of the German Democratic Republic.

Article 4. The protection of the sovereign rights of the German Democratic Republic over the natural resources of its continental shelf and the protection of the installations erected outside the territorial waters for the purpose of exploration and exploitation of the continental shelf shall be the responsibility of the competent State organ of the German Democratic Republic.

Article 5. (1) Any person who intentionally or negligently exploits, explores or utilizes the nationally owned natural resources of the continental shelf of the German Democratic Republic contrary to the legal provisions of the German Democratic Republic, or removes any extracted nationally owned natural resources, or commits any other act which may prejudice the protection of the rights of the German Democratic Republic over the exploration and exploitation of the continental shelf, shall be punishable by deprivation of liberty for up to five years, by being placed on probation, or by a fine of up to 100,000 marks;

(2) It shall be a punishable offence to attempt to commit such acts;

(3) Article 56 of the Criminal Code shall apply with respect to the confiscation of property;

(4) The criminal law of the German Democratic Republic shall apply with respect to offences within the meaning of this regulation.

Article 6. The Council of Ministers of the German Democratic Republic shall issue, on the basis of this law, the regulations needed for the exploration, utilization and protection of the natural resources of the continental shelf of the German Democratic Republic.

Article 7. This law shall enter into force on its publication.

8. GERMANY, FEDERAL REPUBLIC OF

ACT OF 24 JULY 1964 ON PROVISIONAL DETERMINATION OF RIGHTS RELATING TO THE CONTINENTAL SHELF[1], AS AMENDED ON 2 SEPTEMBER 1974.[2]

Article 1. Authorization shall be required for the exploration of the mineral resources of the German continental shelf as defined in the

---

[1] Reproduced in ST/LEG/SER.B/15, pp. 351-353.

[2] By the Act Amending the Act on the provisional determination of rights relating to the continental shelf, *BGBl* 1974, part I, p. 2149. In force as of 3 September 1974. Only the amended articles are reproduced here. Translation by the Secretariat of the United Nations.

Declaration by the Federal Government of 20 January 1964,[1] the extraction of such mineral resources, and all research activities relating to the continental shelf undertaken *in situ,* and the installation and operation of a transit pipeline in or on the German continental shelf. The rules of international law relating to the high seas and the continental shelf shall not be affected.

Article 2. (1) Authorization for the operation referred to in article 1, first sentence, shall be granted provisionally in accordance with the provisions of paragraphs (2)-(6).

(2) Pending definitive regulation of the question of competence, permits shall be issued:

1. As concerns technical and commercial mining operations, by the Central Bureau of Mines at Clausthal-Zellerfeld;

2. With regard to the regulation of the utilization of the superjacent waters of the continental shelf and the air space above those waters by the German Hydrographical Institute. Research activities which, by their nature, are manifestly not directed towards prospecting for mineral resources shall require only a permit in accordance with clause 2 of the first sentence; in other cases, such a permit may be issued only if the permit under clause 1 of the first sentence is produced.

(3) The permit may be issued subject to restrictions and conditions and may be subject to cancellation; conditions may also be imposed retrospectively. The permit shall be issued for a maximum period of three years and may, if the Act referred to in article 16, paragraph (2), has not yet come into force when the period expires, be renewed, provided that its total duration shall not exceed five years. A legal right to the granting or extension of authorization for the exploration and exploitation of mineral resources or for any research activities relating to the continental shelf undertaken *in situ* does not exist.

(4) The granting or extension of authorization for the installation and operation of a transit pipeline may be denied only where there is reason to fear a danger to human life or health or to material property, or a threat to overriding public interests, which cannot be prevented or removed by means of conditions or restrictions. A threat to overriding public interests shall exist, in particular, if the installation or operation of a transit pipeline would:

1. Hinder or impair the orderly exploration of the German continental shelf, the exploitation of its natural resources, navigation, fishing, the conservation of the living resources of the sea or the protection and use of underwater cables or pipelines;

2. Give reason to fear pollution of the sea; or

3. Create a threat to the security of the Federal Republic of Germany.

(5) Any restrictions and conditions attached to a permit issued in accordance with clause 1 of the first sentence of paragraph (2) must in

---

[1] Reproduced in ST/LEG/SER.B/15, p. 351.

substance conform at least to such provisions of Part Three, Section Two, and Part Nine, Section Two, of the General Mines Act for the Prussian States of 24 June 1865 (*Gesetzesammlung,* p. 705) and of orders made pursuant to article 197 thereof as are in force in *Land* Lower Saxony.

(6) The issue of a permit for the extraction of mineral resources in accordance with clause 1 of the first sentence of paragraph (2) may be subject to payment of a consideration. The amount of the consideration shall be assessed on the basis of the mining dues which would customarily be payable at the point in German territorial waters nearest to the place of extraction. The option provided for in the first sentence shall be exercised where the competitive position of enterprises engaged in mining in German territorial waters would otherwise be substantially affected. The consideration shall be paid to the Central Bureau of Mines at Clausthal-Zellerfeld; the party to whom the Central Bureau of Mines shall transfer moneys thus received shall be specified in the Act envisaged in article 16, paragraph (2).

9. IRAQ

[INFORMATION CONCERNING THE SOVEREIGNTY OVER IRAQ'S TERRITORIAL WATERS AND ITS CONTINENTAL SHELF][1]

10. IRELAND

(a) CONTINENTAL SHELF ACT, 1968[2]

1. In this Act—

"designated area" means an area standing designated for the time being by order under section 2 of this Act;

"the Minister" means the Minister for Industry and Commerce.

2. (1) Any rights of the State outside territorial waters over the sea bed and subsoil for the purpose of exploring such sea bed and subsoil and exploiting their natural resources are, subject to subsection (2) of this section, hereby vested in the Minister and shall be exercisable by the Minister.

(2) Whenever the Government so think fit and so direct, any rights referred to in subsection (1) of this section and specified in the direction shall be vested in and exercisable by a Minister of State specified in the direction other than the Minister.

(3) The Government may by order[3] designate any area as an area within which the rights referred to in subsection (1) of this section are exercisable.

(4) The Government may by order revoke or amend an order under this section, including an order under this subsection.

---

[1] *Supra* Division I, Subdivision A, Chapter I, 7.

[2] Act No. 14 of 11 June 1968. Text provided by the Permanent Representative of Ireland to the United Nations in a note verbale of 17 April 1974.

[3] Reproduced *Infra, (b).*

3. (1) *(a)* Any act or omission which—

(i) Takes place on an installation in a designated area or any waters within five hundred metres of such an installation; and

(ii) Would, if taking place in the State, constitute an offence under the law of the State,

shall be deemed, for all purposes relating to the offence, to take place in the State.

(b) Any act or omission which—

(i) Takes place on any waters in a designated area (not being waters within five hundred metres of an installation), or under or above any waters or installation in a designated area, in connexion with the exploration of the sea bed or subsoil or the exploitation of their natural resources; and

(ii) Would, if taking place in the State, constitute an offence under the law of the State,

shall be deemed, for all purposes relating to the offence, to take place in the State.

(2) *(a)* Any act or omission which—

(i) Takes place on an installation or any waters within five hundred metres of such installation, in a designated area; and

(ii) Would, if taking place in the State, constitute a wrong,

shall be deemed for all purposes relating to the wrong, to take place in the State.

(b) Any act or omission which—

(i) Takes place on any waters in a designated area (not being waters within five hundred metres of an installation), or under or above any waters or installation in a designated area, in connexion with the exploration of the sea bed or subsoil or the exploitation of their natural resources, and

(ii) Would, if taking place in the State, constitute a wrong,

shall be deemed, for all purposes relating to the wrong, to take place in the State.

(c) In this subsection "wrong" has the meaning assigned to it by the Civil Liability Act, 1961. (1961, No. 41)

(3) Any jurisdiction conferred on any court under this section shall be without prejudice to any jurisdiction exercisable apart from this section by that or any other court.

4. (1) The Minerals Development Acts, 1940 and 1960, shall apply in relation to minerals (within the meaning of those Acts) with respect to which the rights referred to in section 2 of this Act are exercisable as they apply in relation to those minerals in the State.

(2) The Petroleum and Other Minerals Development Act, 1960, shall apply in relation to petroleum (within the meaning of that Act) with respect

to which the rights referred to in the said section 2 are exercisable as it applies in relation to petroleum in the State.

5. (1) A person shall not construct, alter or improve any structure or works in or remove any object or material from a designated area without the consent of the Minister for Transport and Power.

(2) The Minister for Transport and Power may, as a condition of considering an application for consent under this section, require to be furnished with such plans and particulars as he may consider necessary and, on receipt of any such application, he may cause notice of the application, and of the time within which and the manner in which objections thereto may be made, to be published in such manner as he may consider appropriate for informing persons affected thereby, and, before granting his consent, may, if he thinks fit, appoint a person to hold an inquiry, and notice of the holding of the inquiry shall be given in accordance with the provisions of this Act.

(3) If the Minister for Transport and Power is of opinion that the action in respect of which his consent was sought would cause an obstruction or danger to navigation, he shall either refuse his consent thereto or grant his consent subject to such conditions as he may think proper.

(4) All expenses incurred by the Minister for Transport and Power in holding an inquiry under this section shall, unless that Minister with the sanction of the Minister for Finance otherwise directs (in which case they shall, to the extent of the direction, be defrayed out of moneys provided by the Oireachtas), be paid by the person who applied for the consent to which the inquiry related, and the amount to the expenses shall be fixed by the Minister for Finance and shall be recoverable by the Minister for Transport and Power from the person as a simple contract debt in any court of competent jurisdiction.

(5) The person holding an inquiry under this section may, if he so thinks proper, order the costs and expenses incurred by any person in relation to the inquiry to be paid by any other person who appeared or was represented at the inquiry and, if the person who incurred, or the person who is liable to pay, the costs so requires, the costs and expenses shall be taxed and ascertained by a taxing-master of the High Court and the amount of such costs and expenses when so taxed and ascertained shall be recoverable as a simple contract debt in any court of competent jurisdiction.

(6) Where a person erects a structure, or removes an object or materials, without the consent of the Minister for Transport and Power or fails to comply with a condition subject to which the consent of that Minister was given under this section and the erection, removal or failure constitutes, in the opinion of that Minister, an obstruction or danger to navigation, that Minister may serve a notice on the person requiring him, within such period (not being less than thirty days) as may be specified in the notice, to remove the structure or to carry out such other directions of that Minister as that Minister may think necessary, or, if it appears to that Minister urgently necessary so to do, may himself remove the structure or carry out the directions.

(7) If within the period specified in a notice under subsection (6) of this section, the person upon whom the notice is served fails to comply with the terms thereof, the Minister for Transport and Power may himself remove the structure to which the notice refers or carry out the directions contained in the notice, as the case may be.

(8) Where under subsection (6) or (7) of this section the Minister for Transport and Power removes any structure referred to in a notice under the said subsection (6) or carries out any direction contained in such a notice, that Minister may recover the expense thereof from the person upon whom the notice was served as a simple contract debt in any court of competent jurisdiction.

(9) A person who contravenes subsection (1) of this section or fails to comply with a condition subject to which a consent of the Minister for Transport and Power has been given under this section shall be guilty of an offence and shall be liable—

(a) On summary conviction to a fine not exceeding one hundred pounds; and

(b) On conviction on indictment to a fine of such amount as the court may consider appropriate.

6. (1) The Minister may, for the purpose of protecting any installation in a designated area, after consultation with the Minister for Transport and Power and the Minister for Agriculture and Fisheries, by order, subject to any exceptions provided by the order, prohibit ships from entering without his consent such part of that area as may be specified in the order.

(2) If a ship enters part of a designated area in contravention of an order under this section, its owner and master shall be guilty of an offence unless it is proved that the prohibition imposed by the order was not and would not on reasonable inquiry have become known to the master.

(3) A person guilty of an offence under this section shall be liable—

(a) On summary conviction to a fine not exceeding one hundred pounds or to imprisonment for a term not exceeding three months, or to both the fine and the imprisonment; and

(b) On conviction on indictment, to a fine of such amount as the court may consider appropriate or to imprisonment for a term not exceeding twelve months or to both the fine and the imprisonment.

(4) The Minister may by order revoke or amend an order under this section including an order under this subsection.

7. (1) If any soil to which section 10 of the Oil Pollution of the Sea Act, 1956,[1] applies or any mixture containing not less than one hundred parts of such oil in a million parts of the mixture is discharged or escapes into any part of the sea—

(a) From a pipe-line; or

(b) Otherwise than from a ship, as the result of any operation for the exploration of the sea bed and subsoil or the exploitation of their natural resources in a designated area,

[1] *Infra* Division III, 6 *(a)*.

the owner of the pipe-line or, as the case may be, the person carrying on the operations shall be guilty of an offence unless he proves, in the case of a discharge from a place in his occupation, that it was due to the act of a person who was there without his permission (express or implied) or, in the case of an escape, that he took all reasonable care to prevent it and that' as soon as practicable after it was discovered all reasonable steps were taken for stopping or reducing it.

(2) A person guilty of an offence under this section shall be liable—

(a) On summary conviction to a fine not exceeding one hundred pounds; and

(b) On conviction on indictment to a fine of such amount as the court may consider appropriate.

8. (1) Section 3 of the Submarine Telegraph Act, 1885, and Article IV and the first paragraph of Article VII of the Convention set out in the Schedule to that Act shall apply in relation to all submarine cables and pipe-lines under the high seas and the said section 3 shall be construed—

(a) as referring to telephonic as well as telegraphic communication, and

(b) in relation to pipe-lines and electricity cables, as if from "to which the Convention" to the end of subsection (1) were deleted.

(2) Sections 4 and 13 of the said Submarine Telegraph Act, 1885, are hereby repealed.

9. Any installation in a designated area and any waters within five hundred metres of such an installation shall be deemed, for the purposes of the Wireless Telegraphy Acts, 1926 and 1956, and any regulations made thereunder (subject, in the case of regulations made after the passing of this Act, to any contrary intention in the regulations), to be situated in the State.

10. The Minister for Social Welfare may by regulations make provision for—

(a) Treating as insurable employment for the purposes of the Social Welfare Acts, 1952 to 1967, any employment prescribed by the regulations which is employment in connexion with the exploitation of the resources mentioned in section 2 (1) of this Act or with the exploration of the sea bed and subsoil in any designated area notwithstanding that such employment is not employment in the State;

(b) Treating as insurable (occupational injuries) employment for the purposes of those Acts any such employment; and

(c) Modifying the provisions of those Acts in their application in the case of persons in such employment.

11. The Minister for Social Welfare may by regulations make provision—

(a) For treating as insurable employment for the purposes of the Insurance (Intermittent Unemployment) Acts, 1942 and 1963, any employment prescribed by the regulations which is employment in connexion with the exploration or exploitation of the kind mentioned in section 10 of this Act notwithstanding that such employment is not employment in the State; and

(b) For modifying the provisions of those Acts in their application in the case of persons in such employment.

12. (1) Whenever an inquiry is proposed to be held under this Act (Inquiries), notice of the holding thereof shall be given in such manner as the Minister for Transport and Power may direct.

(2) A person appointed to hold an inquiry under this Act may do all or any of the following things—

(a) Summon witnesses to attend before him at the inquiry;

(b) Examine on oath (which such person is hereby authorized to administer) witnesses attending before him at the inquiry;

(c) Require any such witnesses to produce any documents in their power or control the production of which such person considers necessary for the purposes of the inquiry.

(3) A witness at an inquiry under this Act shall be entitled to the same immunities and privileges as if he were a witness before the High Court.

(4) If a person—

(a) On being duly summoned to attend as a witness at an inquiry under this Act makes default in attending; or

(b) So being in attendance as a witness, refuses to take an oath lawfully required by the person holding the inquiry to be taken, or to produce any document in his power or control lawfully required by the person holding the inquiry to be produced by him, or to answer any question to which such authorized person may require an answer, he shall be guilty of an offence and shall be liable, on summary conviction, to a fine not exceeding fifty pounds or to imprisonment for a term not exceeding six months, or to both the fine and imprisonment.

13. (1) Proceedings for an offence under this Act (including an offence under another Act as applied by or under this Act and anything that is an offence by virtue of section 3 (1) of this Act) may be taken, and the offence may for all incidental purposes be treated as having been committed, in any place in the State.

(2) Where a body corporate or an unincorporated body of persons is guilty of such an offence and the offence is proved to have been committed with the consent or connivance of, or to be attributable to any neglect on the part of, any director, manager, secretary or other similar officer of the body or any person who was purporting to act in any such capacity he, as well as the body, shall be guilty of the offence and shall be liable to be proceeded against and punished accordingly.

(3) A member of the Garda Síochána shall in a designated area have all the powers, protection and privileges which he has in the State.

14. Every order and regulation made under this Act shall be laid before each House of the Oireachtas as soon as may be after it is made, and if a resolution annulling the order or regulation is passed by either House within the next subsequent twenty-one days on which that House has sat after the order or regulation is laid before it, the order or regulation shall be annulled

accordingly, but without prejudice to the validity of anything previously done thereunder.

15. The expenses incurred by the Minister or any other Minister of State in the administration of this Act shall, to such extent as may be sanctioned by the Minister for Finance, be paid out of moneys provided by the Oireachtas.

16. This Act may be cited as the Continental Shelf Act, 1968.

(b) CONTINENTAL SHELF (DESIGNATED AREAS) ORDER, 1974[1]

The Government, in exercise of the powers conferred on them by section 2 (3) of the Continental Shelf Act, 1968,[2] hereby order as follows:

. . .

2. The areas set out in the Schedule to this Order are hereby designated as areas within which the rights of the State outside the territorial seas over the sea bed and subsoil for the purpose of exploring such sea bed and subsoil and exploiting their natural resources may be exercised.

SCHEDULE

1. The area bounded by a line joining the following co-ordinates:

(1)	56° 00' N.	9° 24' W.
(2)	56° 00' N.	9° 48' W.
(3)	55° 40' N.	9° 48' W.
(4)	55° 40' N.	10° 24' W.
(5)	55° 20' N.	10° 24' W.
(6)	55° 20' N.	10° 48' W.
(7)	54° 50' N.	10° 48' W.
(8)	54° 50' N.	11° 12' W.
(9)	54° 50' N.	11° 12' W.
(10)	54° 40' N.	11° 24' W.
(11)	54° 30' N.	11° 24' W.
(12)	54° 30' N.	12° 00' W.
(13)	54° 20' N.	12° 00' W.
(14)	54° 20' N.	12° 12' W.
(15)	54° 10' N.	12° 12' W.
(16)	54° 10' N.	13° 36' W.
(17)	54° 00' N.	13° 36' W.
(18)	54° 00' N.	11° 00' W.
(19)	54° 40' N.	11° 00' W.
(20)	54° 40' N.	10° 24' W.
(21)	55° 00' N.	10° 24' W.
(22)	55° 00' N.	10° 12' W.
(23)	55° 20' N.	10° 12' W.
(24)	55° 20' N.	9° 36' W.
(25)	55° 50' N.	9° 36' W.
(26)	55° 50' N.	9° 24' W.
(27)	56° 00' N.	9° 24' W.

[1] S.I. No. 36 of 15 February 1974. Text provided by the Permanent Representative of Ireland to the United Nations in a note verbale of 17 April 1974.

[2] Reproduced *Supra, (a)*.

2. The area bounded by a line joining the following co-ordinates:

(1)	54° 00′ N.	13° 36′ W.
(2)	54° 00′ N.	14° 24′ W.
(3)	53° 50′ N.	14° 24′ W.
(4)	53° 50′ N.	14° 36′ W.
(5)	53° 40′ N.	14° 36′ W.
(6)	53° 40′ N.	14° 48′ W.
(7)	53° 30′ N.	14° 48′ W.
(8)	53° 30′ N.	15° 00′ W.
(9)	53° 20′ N.	15° 00′ W.
(10)	53° 20′ N.	15° 12′ W.
(11)	53° 10′ N.	15° 12′ W.
(12)	53° 10′ N.	15° 24′ W.
(13)	51° 00′ N.	15° 24′ W.
(14)	51° 00′ N.	15° 00′ W.
(15)	50° 50′ N.	15° 00′ W.
(16)	50° 50′ N.	14° 36′ W.
(17)	50° 30′ N.	14° 36′ W.
(18)	50° 30′ N.	14° 24′ W.
(19)	50° 20′ N.	14° 24′ W.
(20)	50° 20′ N.	14° 12′ W.
(21)	50° 10′ N.	14° 12′ W.
(22)	50° 10′ N.	14° 00′ W.
(23)	50° 00′ N.	14° 00′ W.
(24)	50° 00′ N.	13° 48′ W.
(25)	49° 50′ N.	13° 48′ W.
(26)	49° 50′ N.	13° 36′ W.
(27)	49° 20′ N.	13° 36′ W.
(28)	49° 20′ N.	13° 24′ W.
(29)	49° 10′ N.	13° 24′ W.
(30)	49° 10′ N.	13° 12′ W.
(31)	49° 00′ N.	13° 12′ W.
(32)	49° 00′ N.	13° 00′ W.
(33)	48° 50′ N.	13° 00′ W.
(34)	48° 50′ N.	12° 36′ W.
(35)	48° 40′ N.	12° 36′ W.
(36)	48° 40′ N.	11° 48′ W.
(37)	48° 50′ N.	11° 48′ W.
(38)	48° 50′ N.	11° 36′ W.
(39)	49° 00′ N.	11° 36′ W.
(40)	49° 00′ N.	11° 00′ W.
(41)	50° 00′ N.	11° 00′ W.
(42)	50° 00′ N.	12° 00′ W.
(43)	53° 00′ N.	12° 00′ W.
(44)	53° 00′ N	13° 36′ W.
(45)	54° 00′ N.	13° 36′ W.

11. MADAGASCAR

[ORDONNANCE No 73-060 DU 28 SEPTEMBRE 1973 FIXANT LES LIMITES DE LA MER TERRITORIALE ET DU PLATEAU CONTINENTAL DE LA REPUBLIQUE MALGACHE, article 2] [1]

---

[1] *Supra* Division I, Subdivision A, Chapter I, 10.

12. PHILIPPINES

[CONSTITUTION OF THE REPUBLIC, Article 1] [1]

13. TOGO

[RENSEIGNEMENTS CONCERNANT LA LEGISLATION
SUR LE DROIT DE LA MER] [2]

14. TONGA

CONTINENTAL SHELF ACT 1970 [3]

. . .

2. (1) Any rights exercisable by the Kingdom either inside or outside the limits of the Kingdom with respect to the seabed and subsoil and their natural resources are hereby vested in His Majesty.

(2) In relation to any petroleum outside the limits of the Kingdom and with respect to which those rights are exercisable, the Petroleum Mining Act 1969 [4] shall apply, subject to this Act, as it applies in relation to petroleum inside the limits of the Kingdom.

(3) In relation to minerals outside the limits of the Kingdom and with respect to which those rights are exercisable, the Minerals (Temporary Provisions) Act 1949-1968 shall apply, subject to this Act, as it applies in relation to minerals inside the limits of the Kingdom.

(4) His Majesty may from time to time by Order-in-Council designate any area as an area within which the rights mentioned in subsection (1) of this section are exercisable, and any area so designated is in this Act referred to as a designated area.

(5) In this section "petroleum" has the same meaning as in the Petroleum Mining Act 1969 and "minerals" has the same meaning as in the Minerals (Temporary Provisions) Act 1949-1968.

3. (1) The Premier may for the purpose of protecting any installation in a designated area by order published in the Gazette prohibit ships, subject to any exceptions provided by the order, from entering without his consent such part of that area as may be specified in the order.

(2) If any ship enters any part of a designated area in contravention of any order made under this section its owner or master shall be liable on conviction to a fine not exceeding one hundred pa'anga or to imprisonment for a term not exceeding one year, or to both, unless he proves that the

[1] *Ibid.*, 15.

[2] *Ibid.*, 17 *(a)*.

[3] Act No. 6 of 24 August 1970. Given Royal assent on 1 December 1970. Text transmitted to the Secretary-General of the United Nations by the Acting Prime Minister and Minister for Foreign Affairs of Tonga, in a letter dated 25 June 1974.

[4] *Supra* Division I, Subdivision A, Chapter IX, 5.

prohibition imposed by the order was not, and would not on reasonable inquiry have become, known to the master.

(3) Any order made under this section may be varied or revoked by a subsequent order, and any order may be annulled by the Legislative Assembly.

4. (1) Any act or omission which—

(a) Takes place on, under or above an installation in a designated area outside the limits of the Kingdom or any waters within five hundred metres of such an installation; and

(b) Would, if taking place inside the limits of the Kingdom, constitute an offence under the law in force inside those limits,

shall be treated for the purposes of that law as taking place inside those limits.

(2) His Majesty may by Order-in-Council make provision for the determination of questions arising out of acts or omissions taking place in a designated area, or in any part of such an area, in connexion with the exploration of the seabed or subsoil or the exploitation of their natural resources, and for conferring jurisdiction with respect to such questions on courts in the Kingdom.

(3) Any jurisdiction conferred on any court under this section shall be without prejudice to any jurisdiction exercisable apart from this section by that or any other court.

(4) Any Order-in-Council under this section may be varied or revoked by a subsequent Order-in-Council and such an Order may be annulled by the Legislative Assembly.

5. (1) No person shall without the consent in writing of the Premier in any designated area—

(a) Construct, alter or improve any works on, under or over any part of the seabed; or

(b) Remove any object or any material from any part of the seabed, so that any obstruction or danger to navigation is caused or is likely to result.

(2) Any application made to the Premier for such consent shall be supported by such plans and particulars as the Premier may consider necessary.

(3) If the Premier is of opinion that any operation in respect of which an application is made to him under this section will cause or is likely to result in any obstruction or danger to navigation he shall either refuse his consent or give his consent subject to such conditions as he may think fit having regard to the nature and extent of the obstruction or danger which it appears to him would otherwise be caused or be likely to result.

(4) A consent of the Premier under this section may be given so as to continue in force, unless renewed, only if the operation for which the consent is given is begun or completed within such period as may be specified in the consent; and any renewal of the consent may be limited in the like manner.

6. (1) Any person who—

(a) Carries out any operation in contravention of the provisions of subsection (1) of section 5 of this Act; or

(b) Fails to comply with any condition subject to which a consent of the Premier has been given under the section,

commits an offence and is liable on conviction to a fine not exceeding two thousand pa'anga.

(2) Without prejudice to any proceedings under subsection (1) of this section, where any person has constructed, altered or improved any works in contravention of the provisions of section 5 of this Act or has failed to comply with any condition subject to which a consent of the Premier was given under that section, the Premier may serve a notice on that person requiring him within such period, not being less than thirty days, as may be specified in the notice, to remove the works or make such alterations therein as may be specified in the notice, or, if it appears to the Premier urgently necessary so to do, the Premier may himself arrange for the works to be removed or altered, as the case may be.

(3) If within the period specified in any notice under subsection (2) of this section the person upon whom the notice is served fails to comply therewith, the Premier may himself arrange for the works to be removed or altered, as the case may be.

(4) In any case in which the Premier, exercising the powers conferred by either subsection (2) or subsection (3) of this section, arranges for works to be removed or altered, he shall be entitled to recover as a civil debt the expenses thereof, as certified by him, from the person by whom the works were constructed, altered or improved.

7. (1) If any oil or any mixture containing not less than one hundred parts of such oil in a million parts of the mixture is discharged or escapes into any part of the sea—

(a) From a pipeline; or

(b) (Otherwise than from a ship) as a result of any operations for the exploration of the seabed and subsoil or the exploitation of their natural resources in a designated area,

the owner of the pipeline or, as the case may be, the person carrying on the operations shall be guilty of an offence unless he proves, in the case of a discharge from a place in his occupation, that it was due to the act of a person who was there without his permission (express or implied) or, in the case of an escape, that he took all reasonable care to prevent it and that as soon as practicable after it was discovered all reasonable steps were taken for stopping or reducing it.

(2) This section applies to crude oil, fuel oil, lubricating oil and heavy diesel oil, as the same may be defined by the Premier by order made under this section, and to any other description of oil which may be so defined by the Premier having regard to the persistent character of that oil and the likelihood that it would cause pollution if discharged or allowed to escape into the sea.

Penalty: Two thousand pa'anga or imprisonment for two years or both.

8. (1) No person shall unlawfully and wilfully, or by culpable negligence, break or injure any submarine cable or pipeline to which this section applies:

Provided that in the application of this subsection to any submarine cable which is not a high voltage power cable this subsection shall have effect as if there were added thereto immediately after the word "applies" the words "in such manner as might interrupt or obstruct in whole or in part telegraphic or telephonic communication.".

(2) Any person who acts or attempts to act in contravention of subsection (1) of this section commits an offence and is liable on conviction—

(a) If he acted wilfully, to imprisonment for a term not exceeding five years or to a fine not exceeding five thousand pa'anga or to both such imprisonment and fine;

(b) If he acted by culpable negligence, to imprisonment for a term not exceeding three months or to a fine not exceeding one hundred pa'anga or to both such imprisonment and fine.

(3) Where a person does any act with the object of preserving the life or limb of himself or of any other person, or of preserving the vessel to which he belongs or any vessel, and takes all reasonable precautions to avoid injury to a submarine cable or pipeline, that person shall not be deemed to have acted unlawfully and wilfully within the meaning of subsection (1) of this section.

(4) A person shall not for the purposes of subsection (1) of this section be deemed to have unlawfully and wilfully broken or injured any submarine cable or pipeline, where in the bona fide attempt to repair another submarine cable or pipeline injury has been done to such first-mentioned cable or pipeline, or the same has been broken; but this subsection shall not apply so as to exempt such person from any liability arising whether by virtue of subsection (5) of this section or otherwise, to pay the cost of repairing such breakage or injury.

(5) In relation to any submarine cable or pipeline to which this section applies the provisions of Article IV and paragraph 1 of Article VII of the Submarine Telegraphs Convention set out in the Schedule to the Submarine Telegraph Act, 1885 (United Kingdom) as in force in Tonga shall have effect as those provisions have effect in relation to submarine cables to which that Act (as so in force) applies.

(6) In this section "vessel" means every description of vessel used in navigation, in whatever way it is propelled; and any reference to a vessel shall include a reference to a boat belonging to such vessel.

(7) This section applies to any submarine cable or pipeline laid in a designated area.

9. The Premier with the prior approval of His Majesty in Council may enter into agreements with or grant licenses to any person for the exploration by that person of the seabed or subsoil or the exploration of the resources thereof in any designated area upon such terms and conditions not

inconsistent with the provisions of this Act as may appear to the Premier to be proper.

10. (1) Proceedings for any offence under this Act (including an offence under any other law applied by or under this Act and anything which is an offence by virtue of subsection (1) of section 4 of this Act) may be taken, and such offence may for all incidental purposes be treated as having been committed, inside the limits of the Kingdom.

(2) Where a body corporate is guilty of such an offence and the offence is proved to have been committed with the consent or connivance of, or to be attributable to any neglect on the part of, any director, manager, secretary or other similar officer of the body corporate or any person who was purporting to act in any such capacity he, as well as the body corporate, shall be guilty of the offence and shall be liable to be proceeded against and punished accordingly.

(3) In the last preceding subsection, "director" in relation to any statutory corporation, the affairs of which are managed by its members, means a member of that corporation.

(4) A police officer shall on any installation in a designated area outside the limits of the Kingdom have all the powers, protection and privileges which he has inside the limits of the Kingdom.

15. UNION OF SOVIET SOCIALIST REPUBLICS

(a) REGULATIONS OF 11 JANUARY 1974 FOR SAFEGUARDING
THE CONTINENTAL SHELF OF THE USSR[1]

1. The purposes of safeguarding the continental shelf of the USSR shall be to defend the sovereign rights of the USSR over the continental shelf of the USSR with a view to exploring and exploiting its natural resources, which are the State property of the USSR, and to ensure that the conduct of research, the exploration and exploitation (harvesting and extraction) of natural resources and the conduct of other operations on the continental shelf of the USSR (hereinafter designated as "operations") shall be carried out in accordance with the laws of the USSR and of the Union Republics and with the agreements of the USSR and the Union Republics with other countries.

2. The conduct of operations on the continental shelf of the USSR shall be permitted after the same have been registered in the manner prescribed by the laws of the USSR.

The registration of operations conducted on the continental shelf of the USSR shall be effected by:

(a) The authorities of the Ministry of Geological Surveys of the USSR, in the case of research and exploration relating to the mineral and other non-living resources of the shelf;

---

[1] Decision No. 24 of 11 January 1974 of The Council of Ministers of the USSR. *Legislative Series of the Government of the Union of Soviet Socialist Republics,* 1974, No. 3, p. 18. Russian text provided by the Permanent Mission of the Union of Soviet Socialist Republics to the United Nations in a note verbale of 14 January 1975. Translation by the Secretariat of the United Nations.

(b) The authorities of the State Office of the USSR for the Supervision of Mining Technology (insofar as the issue of mining claims is concerned), in the case of the exploitation of the mineral and other non-living resources of the shelf;

(c) The fishery conservation authorities of the Ministry of Fisheries of the USSR, in the case of research concerning, and the exploration and harvesting of, living organisms on the shelf belonging to the sedentary species.

Compliance with the prescribed procedure for the registration of operations conducted on the continental shelf of the USSR shall not exempt foreign individuals and bodies corporate or Soviet organizations from the obligation to obtain the appropriate permit for the conduct of the operations in cases where such permit is required under the laws in force.

3. Protection of the natural resources of the continental shelf of the USSR shall be the responsibility of the fishery conservation authorities.

Where necessary, the frontier guard shall assist the fishery conservation authorities in their activities for the protection of the natural resources of the continental shelf of the USSR.

Those authorities of the Ministry of Geological Surveys of the USSR, the State Office for the Supervision of Mining Technology, the State Office for Sanitary Supervision and the Central Office of the Hydrometeorological Service of the Council of Ministers of the USSR that are responsible for state supervision of operations conducted on the continental shelf of the USSR shall provide the fishery conservation authorities, at their request, with the information required to ensure protection of the natural resources of the shelf, and shall take part in protecting the natural resources of the shelf in accordance with the State supervisory duties assigned to them.

4. For the purposes of protecting the natural resources of the continental shelf of the USSR, fishery conservation officials shall:

(a) Verify documents authorizing the conduct of operations on the shelf, and take action to terminate such operations in cases where they have not been registered in the prescribed manner;

(b) Take action to suspend operations on the shelf if the organizations and persons conducting the operations fail to comply with binding instructions to suspend the same given by authorities responsible for State supervision of the conduct of operations on the continental shelf of the USSR;

(c) Take offenders into custody and seize vessels, fishing gear and other technical equipment used by the offenders, and everything illegally harvested or extracted, and convey all of the aforesaid to an open port of the USSR;

(d) Draw up inspection and seizure reports and, where necessary, bring charges for the prosecution of offenders in accordance with the laws in force.

Instructions given by fishery conservation officials within the scope of their authority to protect the natural resources of the continental shelf of the USSR shall be binding on all organizations and nationals of the USSR and on foreign individuals and bodies corporate conducting operations on the continental shelf of the USSR.

5. The fishery conservation authorities shall be empowered to bring actions against State enterprises, organizations and establishments, collective farms and other co-operative and public organizations, against USSR nationals, and against foreign individuals and bodies corporate for the recovery of damages by the State for the harm, resulting from violations of the laws relating to the continental shelf of the USSR, done to living organisms belonging to the sedentary species.

The amount of the fines for damage done by the USSR nationals or by foreign individuals and bodies corporate as a consequence of the illegal harvesting of living organisms belonging to sedentary species shall be determined according to the prescribed schedule of fines.

In other cases, the amount of the fines for such damage shall be determined in the manner prescribed by the USSR Ministry of Fisheries in consultation with the USSR Ministry of Finance and the other organizations concerned.

6. State supervision of operations conducted on the continental shelf of the USSR shall be exercised by:

The authorities of the Ministry of Geological Surveys of the USSR, as regards compliance with the regulations for the conduct of research and the exploration of the mineral and other non-living resources of the shelf;

The authorities of the State Office for the Supervision of Mining Technology, as regards compliance with the regulations and requirements relating to the exploitation and protection of mineral and other non-living resources and to safety in the conduct of research and in the exploration and exploitation of the said resources of the shelf;

The fishery conservation authorities, as regards compliance with the regulations for the conduct of research and for the exploration, harvesting and protection on the shelf of living organisms belonging to the sedentary species;

The authorities of the State Office for Sanitary Supervision, as regards compliance with the requirements relating to the microbiological and hydrobiological composition of the waters above the shelf and of ground deposits (in areas where the water is used for human consumption);

The Central Office of the Hydrometeorological Service of the Council of Ministers of the USSR, as regards compliance with the requirements relating to the composition of the waters above the shelf and of ground deposits, including the degree of chemical and radioactive pollution thereof (the authorities responsible for the registration of operations relating to the conduct of research and the exploration and exploitation of the mineral and other non-living resources of the shelf shall inform the Central Office of the Hydrometeorological Service of the Council of Ministers of the USSR of the nature and location of such operations).

7. Officials of the authorities responsible for State supervision of operations conducted on the continental shelf of the USSR shall be empowered to:

(a) Visit and inspect without hindrance structures, installations, vessels and other means of transport (hereinafter designated as "vessels") which are

used in the conduct of operations on the shelf. Visits to areas and facilities subject to special arrangements shall be carried out in the prescribed manner;

(b) Obtain from organizations (persons) conducting operations on the shelf any information required and scrutinize documents relating to matters falling within the competence of the authority responsible for State supervision;

(c) Verify compliance with the appropriate regulations and requirements relating to the conduct of operations on the shelf and obtain explanations concerning any violations thereof;

(d) Give binding instructions for the elimination of such violations of the regulations and requirements relating to the conduct of operations on the shelf as are discovered, and, if such violations endanger human life, are apt to lead to accidents or are apt to cause substantial damage to the natural resources of the shelf or to the living resources of the sea, give binding instructions for the suspension of such operations, and, where necessary, submit to the appropriate authorities recommendations for the suspension thereof;

(e) Draw up inspection reports and institute administrative proceedings in the prescribed manner against offenders or bring charges against them before other authorities in accordance with the laws in force.

Officials of the authorities responsible for State supervision shall also have such other powers as are provided in the regulations concerning the various types of State supervision, the regulations (statutes) concerning the relevant authorities and other laws and regulations in force.

8. The authorities responsible for the protection of the natural resources of the continental shelf of the USSR and for State supervision of the conduct of operations on the shelf shall be guided in the performance of their duties by the provisions of the present Regulations, the regulations concerning the various types of State supervision and the regulations (statutes) concerning the relevant authorities, and by the provisions of other laws and regulations of the USSR and of the Union Republics and the provisions of the agreement of the USSR and the Union Republics with other States.

9. Organizations (persons) conducting operations on the continental shelf of the USSR shall be required, at the request of the fishery conservation authorities and the authorities responsible for State supervision of the conduct of operations on the continental shelf of the USSR, to provide for the transport of officials of those authorities to and from the place where the operations are being conducted.

10. Fishery conservation officials and officials of the authorities responsible for State supervision of the conduct of operations on the continental shelf of the USSR shall, in the performance of their official duties, carry the requisite official credentials.

Vessels of the fishery conservation authorities being used to protect the natural resources of the continental shelf of the USSR shall wear the pennant of the fishery conservation authorities of the USSR.

11. In order to stop a vessel in the cases provided for in these Regulations, vessels of the fishery conservation authorities shall give the signals prescribed by the International Code of Signals.

A vessel that has been signalled to stop shall do so. It may proceed after obtaining the necessary permission from the fishery conservation authorities.

12. The taking of offenders into custody and the seizure of vessels, fishing gear and other technical equipment and of everything illegally harvested or extracted shall be effected by the fishery conservation officials on their own initiative and at the request of the authorities responsible for State supervision of the conduct of operations on the continental shelf of the USSR.

13. In order to assist the fishery conservation authorities, the frontier guard, in the areas where they are serving, shall keep under observation the waters of the high seas which constitute the superjacent waters of the continental shelf of the USSR.

The frontier guard shall notify the fishery conservation authorities of all vessels found to be conducting operations on the shelf. The fishery conservation authorities shall notify the frontier guard of the time, place and type of operations permitted to be conducted on the shelf.

14. Where necessary, ships and other vessels of the frontier guard, in the areas where they are serving, shall assist the fishery conservation authorities, at their request, in seizing Soviet vessels that fail to comply with demands relating to the application of these Regulations which are made by officials of the said authorities.

15. Foreign non-military vessels that violate the regulations for the use of the continental shelf of the USSR and fail to obey the instructions of, or offer resistance to, officials of the fishery conservation authorities may, at the request of those authorities, be stopped by a ship or other vessel of the frontier guard.

The commanding officer of a ship or other vessel of the frontier guard shall, in such cases, be empowered to demand, at the request of the fishery conservation authorities, that the master of the foreign non-military vessel allow officials of the fishery conservation authorities on board to carry out an inspection, to stop illegal operations on the shelf and to proceed to an open port of the USSR. The commanding officer of the ship or other vessel of the frontier guard shall report to his command base any failure by a foreign non-military vessel to comply with such a demand and shall act in accordance with the instructions he receives.

16. Offenders whose identity cannot be immediately established, and vessels, fishing gear and other technical equipment which are used to conduct operations on the continental shelf of the USSR and whose ownership cannot be determined on inspection shall be taken into custody or seized, as the case may be, and be taken to an open port of the USSR for identification of the offenders and determination of the ownership of the vessels, fishing gear and other technical equipment seized.

17. On the occasion of the inspection, as provided in these Regulations, of vessels, structures and installations, examination may be made of: the ship's papers, navigational documents and documents relating to crew, passengers and cargo; working areas and cargo areas; technical and other

equipment used to conduct the operations; and everything harvested on or extracted from the shelf.

The inspection shall be carried out in the presence of the master of the vessel or of other crew members designated by him, or in the presence of a representative of the administration in charge of the operations on the shelf.

18. Inspection or seizure reports drawn up in accordance with these Regulations shall be signed by officials of the fishery conservation authorities or of the authorities responsible for State supervision of operations conducted on the continental shelf of the USSR and by the master of the vessel or a representative of the administration in charge of the operations on the shelf. Such reports shall be drawn up in the Russian language.

If the master of the vessel or the representative of the administration considers that the actions of the officials of the fishery conservation authorities or of the authorities responsible for State supervision of operations conducted on the continental shelf of the USSR are improper or not in accord with the contents of the report, he may make the corresponding reservation, in any language, in the report itself or in a separate document annexed thereto. If the master of the vessel or the representative of the administration refuses to sign the report, that fact shall be noted in the report.

19. Where a foreign non-military vessel is seized, the fishery conservation authorities shall take it, together with the members of its crew, any other persons on board the vessel, the fishing gear and other technical equipment used, and everything illegally harvested or extracted, to the nearest open port of the USSR.

20. The master of a seized foreign non-military vessel shall be compelled to surrender such ship's papers, navigational documents and documents relating to crew, passengers and cargo as are needed to explain the circumstances and nature of the offence. The documents so surrendered shall be recorded in a list, shall be fastened together in some secure manner, shall be sealed with the seal of the State inspector or of the master of the vessel of the fishery conservation authorities and the seal of the master of the seized vessel, and shall be attached to the report on the seizure of the vessel.

21. The fishery conservation authorities shall notify the frontier guard of the seizure of a foreign non-military vessel before the vessel crosses the State maritime frontier of the USSR, after which they shall act in concert with the frontier guard.

The fishery conservation authorities shall forthwith inform the Ministry of Foreign Affairs of the USSR of all cases which concern the taking into custody of individuals of foreign nationality, the examination of questions of the responsibility of foreign individuals and bodies corporate, and the seizure of vessels, fishing gear and other technical equipment used to conduct operations on the continental shelf of the USSR by foreign individuals and bodies corporate and of everything illegally harvested or extracted by them.

22. A seized foreign non-military vessel taken to an open port of the USSR shall remain there until the question of responsibility for violating the

laws relating to the continental shelf of the USSR has been settled according to the prescribed procedure.

Whenever a vessel seized by the fishery conservation authorities is taken into port, the said authorities shall so inform the harbour-master concerned.

If a seized foreign non-military vessel attempts to leave port without the necessary permission, the harbour-master shall forthwith notify the fishery conservation authorities and the frontier guard so that action can be taken to seize the vessel.

23. The responsibility for making arrangements for a seized foreign non-military vessel to be moored in a port of the USSR shall rest with the port administration.

The harbour-master shall take steps to ensure that the regulations governing the conduct of vessels in ports of the USSR are complied with by the seized vessel.

While a seized foreign non-military vessel is in a port of the USSR, the provision of necessary supplies and equipment for the vessel, and the provision of commercial and other services for persons on board, shall, at the request of the master of the vessel, be effected in the prescribed manner by the Inflot agency.

24. Crew members and other persons on board a seized foreign non-military vessel must remain on board the vessel while it is lying in a Soviet port, with the exception of persons to whom restrictive measures, taken in the prescribed manner, have been applied which preclude their being on board. In exceptional circumstances, crew members and other persons on board the vessel, in the manner provided by the laws in force, may be permitted by the frontier guard authorities to go ashore.

Persons against whom no charges have been brought may, with the consent of the fishery conservation authorities, leave the territory of the USSR in the manner prescribed by law.

25. Where, in the cases provided for by the laws in force, the confiscation of a foreign non-military vessel is ordered by a court, the fishery conservation authorities shall direct the persons on board the vessel, with the exception of those sentenced to imprisonment, to leave the territory of the USSR in the manner prescribed by law and shall notify the Ministry of Foreign Affairs of the USSR accordingly.

Cargo on board a confiscated vessel, if not liable to confiscation, seizure or attachment, shall be returned to the owner of the cargo at his expense.

26. Foreign non-military vessels which have been seized, other than those confiscated in the manner provided by law, shall, after payment of any sums due or after receipt of a written guarantee that they will be paid, be escorted by the frontier guard, at the request of the fishery conservation authorities—and after any documents confiscated in accordance with the present Regulations have been returned to the master of the vessel—to the boundary of the territorial sea of the USSR, and the fishery conservation authorities shall notify the Ministry of Foreign Affairs of the USSR accordingly.

Vessels owned by a foreign State shall not be subject to seizure under property claims except in the cases provided in article 61 of the Fundamentals of Civil Procedure of the USSR and the Union Republics.

27. Soviet vessels seized by the fishery conservation authorities in connexion with a violation of the laws relating to the continental shelf of the USSR shall be detained in an open port of the USSR in accordance with the general regulations governing the stay of ships in ports of the USSR.

Ships belonging to Soviet State, co-operative or public organizations may be detained in port by the fishery conservation authorities only for as long as is necessary to confiscate prohibited fishing gear and anything illegally harvested on or extracted from the shelf.

28. When found in the possession of offenders, prohibited fishing gear used on the continental shelf of the USSR, organisms belonging to the sedentary species illegally harvested on the shelf and products derived therefrom shall be confiscated by the fishery conservation officials.

Mineral and other non-living resources obtained illegally from the continental shelf of the USSR, and permitted fishing gear and other technical equipment used by offenders on the shelf—other than gear and equipment belonging to Soviet State, co-operative or public organizations—shall be placed under seal by the fishery conservation officials.

Cargo and other items which have been confiscated or placed under seal shall be kept by the fishery conservation authorities, or shall be handed over to other organizations to be kept by them, until the question of the responsibility of the offender is settled in the prescribed manner. Where illegally harvested organisms belonging to the sedentary species and products derived therefrom are highly perishable, the same shall be sold by the fishery conservation authorities at the established prices to Soviet enterprises or trading organizations. Receipts for the items sold shall be included with the other material relating to the offence.

Where the question of the responsibility of the offender is settled administratively, prohibited fishing gear shall be disposed of so that it can be used for the manufacture of permitted fishing gear or, where it cannot be used for other purposes, shall be destroyed; illegally harvested organisms belonging to the sedentary species and products derived therefrom shall be sold at the established prices to the appropriate Soviet enterprises and organizations.

29. The present Regulations shall not apply to foreign warships or military auxiliary vessels, to which special rules apply.

If a foreign warship or military auxiliary vessel is found to be engaged in operations of any kind on the continental shelf of the USSR, the fishery conservation authorities shall keep it under observation and shall report its activities to the appropriate higher authority and to the frontier guard.

(b) SCHEDULE FOR THE CALCULATION OF FINES IMPOSED FOR DAMAGE CAUSED TO LIVING ORGANISMS BELONGING TO THE SEDENTARY SPECIES, AND FORMING PART OF THE NATURAL RESOURCES OF THE CONTINENTAL SHELF OF THE USSR, AS A RESULT OF THE ILLEGAL HARVESTING OF SUCH SPECIES BY NATIONALS OF THE USSR OR BY FOREIGN INDIVIDUALS OR BODIES CORPORATE[1]

Organisms belonging to the sedentary species	*Amount of fine for illegal harvesting of organisms belonging to the sedentary species—per individual regardless of size, or per kg. raw weight (roubles)*
	Per individual
Crustaceans	
Kamchatka crab, blue crab, equispinous crab, arctic crab	5
Cutter crab, hairy crab, prickly crab	2
Other sedentary species of crustaceans	1
Molluscs	
Scallops	1
Oysters, mussels	0.5
Other bivalves and sedentary species of gastropod molluscs	0.4
Echinoderms	
Trepang, cucumaria	1
Sea urchins, starfish, brittle stars	0.2
Other sedentary species of echinoderms	0.1
Sedentary species of coelenterates	0.05
	Per kg.
Sedentary species of sponges	0.1
Sedentary species of seaweed	1
Marine grasses	0.2

16. UNITED KINGDOM OF GREAT BRITAIN AND NORTHERN IRELAND

(a) [OFFSHORE INSTALLATIONS (LOGBOOKS AND REGISTRATION OF DEATH) REGULATIONS 1972, Regulations 1 (2)-(4), 2, 5, 8 and 12 (1), (2) and (4)-(6)][2]

(b) [PETROLEUM (PRODUCTION) (AMENDMENT) REGULATIONS 1972][3]

---

[1] Decision No. 831 of 25 October 1974 of the Council of Ministers of the USSR. *Legislative Series of the Government of the Union of Soviet Socialist Republics,* 1974, No. 22, p. 132. Russian text provided by the Permanent Mission of the Union of Soviet Socialist Republics to the United Nations in a note verbale of 14 January 1975. Translation by the Secretariat of the United Nations.

[2] *Supra* Division I, Subdivision A, Chapter IX, 6 (a).

[3] Dated 10 October 1972. *Statutory Instruments* 1972 No. 1522. These regulations amend the Petroleum (Production) Regulations, as amended, which are reproduced in part in document ST/LEG/SER.B/15, pages 450-455 and B/16, p. 168. None of the provisions reproduced in those documents are affected by the new amendments.

(c) [OFFSHORE INSTALLATIONS (INSPECTIONS AND CASUALTIES) REGULA-TIONS 1973] [1]

(d) [OFFSHORE INSTALLATIONS (CONSTRUCTION AND SURVEY) REGULA-TIONS 1974] [2]

(e) [OFFSHORE INSTALLATIONS (DIVING OPERATIONS) REGULATIONS 1974] [3]

(f) CONTINENTAL SHELF (PROTECTION OF INSTALLATIONS) (NO. 6) ORDER 1973. [4]

. . .

2. (1) Subject to paragraph (2) of this Article, ships are prohibited from entering, without the consent of the Secretary of State, those areas (hereinafter referred to as "safety zones") specified in Schedule 2 hereto (being parts of areas designated by Orders in Council made under section 1 (7) of the Act). [5]

(2) Nothing in paragraph (1) of this Article shall apply to prohibit a ship from entering a safety zone:

(a) In connection with the repair of any submarine cable or pipeline in or near that safety zone;

(b) To provide services for, to transport persons or goods to or from, or under the authority of a government department to inspect, an installation in that safety zone;

(c) If it is a ship belonging to a general lighthouse authority and it enters to perform duties relating to the safety of navigation;

(d) When carrying out movements with a view to saving or attempting to save life or property;

(e) Owing to stress of weather; or

(f) When in distress.

. . .

SCHEDULE 2

Safety zones

The areas within a radius of 500 metres of each of the points having the following co-ordinates:

. . .

---

[1] *Supra* Division I, Subdivision A, Chapter IX, 6 *(b)*.

[2] *Supra* Division I, Subdivision A, Chapter IX, 6 *(c)*.

[3] *Supra* Division I, Subdivision A, Chapter IX, 6 *(d)*.

[4] Dated 22 February 1973. *Statutory Instruments,* 1973, No. 284. Came into operation on 2 April 1973. This order revoked all the Continental Shelf (Protection of Installations) Orders made during 1967-1972. For the texts of these Orders, see ST/LEG/SER.B/15, pp. 455-457 and ST/LEG/SER.B/16, pp. 168-169 and 171-172.

[5] "The Act" means the Continental Shelf Act 1964 (1964 c. 29), reproduced in part in ST/LEG/SER.B/15, pp. 445-447.

(g) CONTINENTAL SHELF (DESIGNATION OF ADDITIONAL AREAS) ORDER 1974[1]

. . .

2. The area defined in the Schedule to this Order is hereby designated as an area within which the rights of the United Kingdom outside territorial waters with respect to the sea-bed and subsoil and their natural resources are exercisable.

SCHEDULE

Article 2 of this Order applies to the area bounded by a line commencing at the co-ordinates numbered (42) in the Schedule to the Continental Shelf (Designation of Additional Areas) Order 1971 and joining the following co-ordinates on European Datum:

(1) 59° 50′ 00″ N.; 14° 30′ 00″ W.;
(2) 57° 00′ 00″ N.; 19° 30′ 00″ W.;

and thence by a line to the co-ordinates numbered (35), (36), (37), (38), (39), (40), (41) and (42) in the Schedule to the Continental Shelf (Designation of Additional Areas) Order 1971.[2]

(h) [CONTINENTAL SHELF (JURISDICTION) (AMENDMENT) ORDER 1974][3]

---

[1] Dated 6 September 1974. *Statutory Instruments* 1974 No. 1489. Text provided by the Permanent Representative of the United Kingdom of Great Britain and Northern Ireland to the United Nations in a note verbale of 12 December 1974.

[2] Reproduced in ST/LEG/SER.B/16, p. 170.

[3] Dated 6 September 1974. *Statutory Instruments* 1974 No. 1490. Came into operation on 3 October 1974. This order includes in the areas of the United Kingdom continental shelf those areas treated as Scottish areas for the purposes of the civil law of Scotland and the new areas designated as part of the shelf by the Continental Shelf (Designation of Additional Areas) Order 1974, reproduced in part *supra (g)*.

Division III

THE HIGH SEAS[1]

---

1. CANADA

(a) OIL POLLUTION PREVENTION REGULATIONS OF 21 SEPTEMBER 1971[2] AS AMENDED IN 1973[3]

. . .

Interpretation

2. In these Regulations,

"Canadian waters" means the territorial sea of Canada and all internal waters of Canada;

"discharge" includes, but not so as to limit its meaning, any spilling, leaking, pumping, pouring, emitting, emptying, throwing or dumping;

"heavy diesel oil" means diesel oil, other than those distillates of which more than 50 per cent by volume distills at a temperature not exceeding 340 degrees centigrade when tested by the *American Society for Testing and Materials, Standard Method D.86/59;*

"instantaneous rate of discharge of persistent oil content" means the rate of discharge of persistent oil in litres per hour at any instant divided by the speed of the ship in knots at that instant;

"loading facility" means any shore or sea installation that is used for the loading of oil or an oily mixture on to a ship; "mile" means a nautical mile of 6,080 feet (1,852 metres);

"nearest land" means the base line from which the territorial sea of the territory in question is established in accordance with the *Geneva Convention on the Territorial Sea and the Contiguous Zone,* 1958,[4] except that the base line off the eastern coast of Australia, shall be a line commencing at latitude 11° 00′ South, longitude 142° 08′ East; thence to latitude 10° 35′ South, longitude 142° 55′ East; thence to latitude 10° 00′ South, longitude 142° 00′ East; thence to latitude 9° 10′ South, longitude 143° 52′ East; thence to latitude 9° 00′ South, longitude 144° 30′ East; thence to latitude 13° 00′

---

[1] Some of the texts reproduced under Division II and Division IV also contain provisions relating to the high seas.

[2] P.C. 1971-2005. SOR/71-495, *Canada Gazette,* Part II, vol. 105, No. 19, 13 October 1971. These Regulations revoked the Oil Pollution Prevention Regulations of 17 September 1968 (P.C. 1968-1788) as amended in 1971.

[3] Amended by P.C. 1973-2566, 31 August 1973. SOR/73-500 (*ibid.,* vol. 107, No. 18, 26 September 1973).

[4] United Nations, *Treaty Series,* vol. 516, p. 205. Reproduced in ST/LEG/SER.B/15, pp. 721-728.

South, longitude 144° 00′ East; thence to latitude 15° 00′ South, longitude 146° 00′ East; thence to latitude 18° 00′ South, longitude 147° 00′ East; thence to latitude 21° 00′ South, longitude 153° 00′ East; thence to latitude 24° 42′ South, longitude 153° 15′ East.

"oil" means oil of any kind or in any form and, without limiting the generality of the foregoing, includes petroleum, fuel oil, sludge, oil refuse and oil mixed with wastes, but does not include dredged spoil;

"oily mixture" means a mixture with any oil content;

"persistent oil" means crude oil, fuel oil, heavy diesel oil and lubricating oil;

"persistent oily mixture" means a mixture with any content of persistent oil;

"pollution prevention officer" means a person designated as a pollution prevention officer pursuant to section 740 of the *Canada Shipping Act* as enacted by section 2 of *An Act to amend the Canada Shipping Act,*[1] Chapter 27 of the Statutes of Canada 1970-1971;

"steamship inspector" means a person appointed as a steamship inspector pursuant to section 366 of the *Canada Shipping Act;*

"tanker" means a ship in which the greater part of the cargo space is constructed or adapted for the carriage of liquid cargoes in bulk that is not, for the time being, carrying a cargo other than oil in that part of its cargo space;

"transfer operation" means

(a) The loading of oil or an oily mixture on to a ship from a loading facility or from another ship;

(b) The unloading of oil or an oily mixture from a ship to an unloading facility or on to another ship; or

(c) The transfer of oil or an oily mixture on board a ship; and

"unloading facility" means any shore or sea installation that is used for the unloading of oil or an oily mixture from a ship.

Prescription of Pollutants

3. For the purposes of Part XIX of the *Canada Shipping Act,* as enacted by section 2 of *An Act to amend the Canada Shipping Act,*[2] Chapter 27 of the Statutes of Canada 1970-1971, an oily mixture and a persistent oily mixture are prescribed to be pollutants.

Part I

Canadian Waters and Fishing Zones

4. This Part applies

(a) To all Canadian waters south of the sixtieth parallel of north latitude;

---

[1] Reproduced in part in ST/LEG/SER.B/16, pp. 196-207.
[2] *Idem.*

(b) To all Canadian waters north of the sixtieth parallel of north latitude that are not within a shipping safety control zone prescribed pursuant to the *Arctic Waters Pollution Prevention Act;*[1]

(c) To any fishing zones of Canada prescribed pursuant to the *Territorial Sea and Fishing Zones Act;*[2] and

(d) To all ships in waters described in paragraphs *(a)* to *(c)* other than ships of war held by or on behalf of Her Majesty in any right.

5. Subject to section 6,

(a) No person shall discharge from any ship; and

(b) No ship shall discharge

oil or an oily mixture into any of the waters described in paragraphs 4 *(a)* to *(c)*.

6. (1) Section 5 does not apply where oil or oily mixture is discharged from a ship

(a) For the purpose of saving life or preventing the immediate loss of a ship;

(b) Due to damage to or leakage from the ship as a result of stranding, collision or foundering if all reasonable precautions were taken

(i) To avoid the stranding, collision or foundering; and

(ii) To prevent or minimize the discharge; or

(c) Through the exhaust of an engine or by leakage from an underwater machinery component where such discharge is minimal, unavoidable and essential to the operation of the engine or component.

(2) Notwithstanding paragraph (1) *(c)*, section 5 applies where oil or an oily mixture is discharged directly into the water from the crankcase drain of a ship's engine that is manufactured on or after 1 January 1973.

7. Where a ship

(a) Discharges oil or an oily mixture into the water; or

(b) Is in danger of discharging or causing a discharge of oil or an oily mixture into the water,

other than in a manner described in paragraph 6 (1) *(c)*, the master of the ship shall forthwith report the discharge or the danger and the circumstances thereof by radio, or where a radio is not available, by the fastest means available to a pollution prevention officer or steamship inspector at the location listed in Schedule A[3] that is the closest to the ship.

---

[1] *Statutes of Canada,* 1969-1970, chap. 47. Reproduced in part in ST/LEG/SER.B/16, pp. 183-195.

[2] *Statutes of Canada,* 1964, chap. 22. The Act and its amendments are reproduced in part in ST/LEG/SER.B/15, pp. 52-54 and ST/LEG/SER.B/16, pp. 4-6.

[3] Schedule A is not reproduced here.

Part II

Waters other than Canadian Waters and Fishing Zones

8. This Part applies to all Canadian ships except

(a) Tankers of less than 150 tons, gross tonnage;

(b) Ships other than tankers, of less than 500 tons, gross tonnage;

(c) Ships engaged in the whaling industry, when actually employed in whaling operations; and

(d) Naval ships and ships for the time being used as naval auxiliaries, when they are in waters other than

(e) The waters described in paragraphs 4 *(a)* to *(c);* and

(f) Waters north of the sixtieth parallel of north latitude that are within a shipping safety control zone prescribed pursuant to the *Arctic Waters Pollution Prevention Act.*

9. Subject to sections 10 to 12, no ships shall discharge persistent oil or a persistent oily mixture into the water.

10. Persistent oil or a persistent oily mixture may be discharged into the water from a ship other than a tanker where

(a) The ship is proceeding en route;

(b) The instantaneous rate of discharge of persistent oil content does not exceed 60 litres per mile;

(c) The persistent oil content of the discharge is less than 100 parts per 1,000,000 parts of the mixture; and

(d) The discharge is made as far as practicable from land.

11. (1) Subject to subsections (2) and (3), persistent oil or persistent oily mixture may be discharged into the water from a tanker where

(a) The tanker is proceeding en route;

(b) The instantaneous rate of discharge of persistent oil content does not exceed 60 litres per mile;

(c) The total quantity of persistent oil discharged on the voyage does not exceed one fifteen thousandth of the total liquid cargo carrying capacity of the tanker; and

(d) The tanker is more than 50 miles from the nearest land.

(2) Water ballast from a cargo tank of a tanker may be discharged into the water where the tank has, since cargo was last carried therein, been cleaned so that any effluent therefrom, if it were discharged from a stationary tanker into clean calm water on a clear day, would produce no visible traces of persistent oil on the surface of the water.

(3) Persistent oil or a persistent oily mixture may be discharged into the water from machinery space bilges of a tanker where

(a) The tanker is proceeding en route;

(b) The instantaneous rate of discharge of persistent oil content does not exceed 60 litres per mile;

(c) The persistent oil content of the discharge is less than 100 parts per 1,000,000 parts of the mixture; and

(d) The discharge is made as far as practicable from land.

12. Section 9 does not apply where persistent oil or a persistent oily mixture is discharged into the water from a ship

(a) For the purpose of

(i) Securing the safety of a ship;

(ii) Preventing damage to a ship or its cargo; or

(iii) Saving life; or

(b) Due to damage or to unavoidable leakage from a ship, if all reasonable precautions have been taken after the occurrence of the damage or discovery of the leakage to prevent or minimize the discharge.

13. Where persistent oil or a persistent oily mixture is discharged into the water for a purpose specified in paragraph 12 *(a)* or in accordance with paragraph 12 *(b)*, the master of the ship shall forthwith report the discharge and the circumstances thereof to the Minister of Transport at Ottawa by radio or, where a radio is not available, by the fastest means available.

Part III

Cargo, Fuel and Ballast Handling

14. (1) Subject to subsection (2), this Part applies

(a) To the waters described in paragraphs 4 *(a)* to *(c)*;

(b) To all ships in the waters described in paragraphs 4 *(a)* to *(c)* except ships of war held by or on behalf of Her Majesty in any right; and

(c) To all loading facilities and unloading facilities in Canada.

(2) Sections 17 to 22 do not apply to

(a) Tankers of less than 150 tons, gross tonnage; or

(b) Ships other than tankers, of less than 500 tons, gross tonnage.

15. The owner of a ship described in subsection 14 (2) shall

(a) Appoint a person to be in charge of a transfer operation affecting that ship; and

(b) Ensure that all necessary precautions are taken to avoid the discharge of oil or an oily mixture into the water during the transfer operation.

16. (1) The owner of any ship, loading facility or unloading facility shall ensure that any flexible hose or pipe that may be used in a transfer operation is hydraulically tested manually to a pressure equal to one and one half times its maximum working pressure.

. . .

25. The owner of a loading facility or an unloading facility shall

(a) Appoint a person to be in charge of the facility; and

(b) Provide a sufficient number of persons at the facility to ensure compliance with the provisions of this Part.

. . .

27. In the event of any emergency related to a transfer operation, nothing in this Part shall prevent

(a) The master of a ship;

(b) The officer in charge of the transfer operation for a ship; or

(c) The person in charge of a transfer operation at

(i) A loading facility; or

(ii) An unloading facility,

from taking the most effective action that, in his opinion, is necessary to rectify or minimize the conditions that caused the emergency.

Part IV

General

28. (1) Sections 29, 31 and 32 apply to Canadian ships while in waters other than waters north of the sixtieth parallel of north latitude that are within a shipping safety control zone prescribed pursuant to the *Arctic Waters Pollution Prevention Act*.

(2) Sections 30 and 31 apply to ships other than Canadian ships while in waters described in paragraphs 4 *(a)* to *(c)*.

29. Every ship of 150 tons, gross tonnage, or over that carries oil as fuel or cargo shall carry an oil record book in the form specified in Schedule B[1] for that type of ship.

30. Every ship of 150 tons, gross tonnage, or over that carries oil as fuel or cargo shall carry

(a) An oil record book

(i) In the form specified in Schedule B, for that type of ship; or

(ii) In a form approved by the country of the ship's nationality for that type of ship; or

(b) An official log book, part of which shall be used as an oil record book, with provision for the entries as set out in Schedule B for that type of ship.

31. (1) The master of every ship to which sections 29 or 30 apply shall ensure that appropriate entries are recorded without delay in the oil record book or official log book of his ship, and that each page thereof is signed by himself and by the officer or officers in charge of the operations for which the entry is made.

. . .

(iv) Discharge overboard of bilge water containing oil that has accumulated in the machinery spaces while the ship was in port, and routine discharge at sea of bilge water containing oil; or

(v) Accidental or other exceptional discharge of oil or an oily mixture.

---

[1] Schedule B is not reproduced here.

32. Every ship that carries oil as fuel or cargo shall be fitted

(a) So as to prevent any oil from leaking or draining into the bilges; or

(b) With effective means to ensure that the oil in the bilges is not discharged in contravention of these Regulations.

Part V

Limitation on Cargo Tank Size

. . .

34. (1) This Part applies to every tanker that is

(a) A Canadian ship; and

(b) Not a Canadian ship and that is to be navigated in the waters described in paragraphs 4 *(a)* to *(c)*, in respect of which, on or after 1 January 1974

(c) A building contract has been entered into for its construction; or

(d) Where no building contract has been entered into for its construction, the keel is laid, or if no keel is laid, the tanker is in a similar stage of construction.

(2) This Part does not apply to naval ships or ships for the time being used as naval auxiliaries.

35. (1) The cargo carrying portion of a ship shall be divided into tanks so that the length of each tank shall not exceed the greater of 10 metres, and

(a) Where no longitudinal bulkhead is provided, 0.1L;

(b) Where a longitudinal bulkhead is provided at the centreline only, 0.15L; and

(c) Where two or more longitudinal bulkheads are provided;

(i) In the case of wing tanks, 0.2L; and

(ii) In the case of centre tanks

    (A) If bi/B is equal to or greater than 1/5, 0.2L; or

    (B) If bi/B is less than 1/5;

        (I) Where no longitudinal bulkhead is provided at the centre line, $(0.5\ bi/B + 0.1)L$; or

        (II) Where a longitudinal bulkhead is provided at the centre line, $(0.25\ bi/B + 0.15)L$.

(2) For the purposes of this section,

(a) "L" means length in metres;

(b) "B" means breadth in metres; and

(c) "bi" means width of adjacent wing tank in metres.

36. (1) The centre tanks and wing tanks of every ship shall be arranged in that ship so that if it sustains the maximum assumed damage by collision or stranding, as calculated in accordance with Schedule C, the maximum

hypothetical oil outflow from the ship, calculated in accordance with that Schedule, would not exceed the greater of

(a) 30,000 cubic metres; and

(b) $400 \sqrt[3]{\dfrac{\text{deadweight of ship}}{\text{in metric tons}}}$ $\left.\begin{array}{c} \\ \\ \end{array}\right\}$ the result of which shall be read as cubic metres and shall not exceed 40,000 cubic metres.

(2) The volume of a wing tank shall not exceed 75 per cent of the hypothetical oil outflow from the ship calculated in accordance with Schedule C.

(3) The volume of centre tank shall not exceed 50,000 cubic metres.

. . .

(b) NON-CANADIAN SHIPS COMPLIANCE CERTIFICATE REGULATIONS OF 6 MARCH 1973[1]

. . .

Interpretation

2. In these Regulations,

"Act" means the *Canada Shipping Act;*[2]

"Administration" means the Government of the State in which a ship is registered;

"Canadian waters" means the territorial sea of Canada and all internal waters of Canada;

"certificate" means a certificate issued pursuant to these Regulations;

"inspector" means a steamship inspector who has been designated as a pollution prevention officer pursuant to section 731 of the Act;

. . .

"master" includes every person having command or charge of any ship but does not include a pilot;

"oil" means oil of any kind or in any form and, without limiting the generality of the foregoing, includes petroleum, fuel oil, sludge, oil refuse and oil mixed with wastes, but does not include dredged spoil;

"owner", in relation to a ship, means the person having for the time being, either by law or by contract, the rights of the owner of the ship as regards the possession and use thereof;

---

[1] P.C. 1973-547. SOR/73-134, *Canada Gazette,* Part II, vol. 107, No. 6, 28 March 1973. Came into effect on 1 September 1973.

[2] *Revised Statutes of Canada,* 1970, chap. S-9. The Act as amended in 1971 is reproduced in part in ST/LEG/SER.B/16, pp. 196-207.

"Safety Convention" means the International Convention for the Safety of Life at Sea, 1960 signed at London on the 12th day of June, 1960;[1]

"steamship inspector" means a person appointed as a steamship inspector pursuant to section 366 of the Act;

"tanker" means a ship in which the greater part of the cargo space is constructed or adapted for the carriage of liquid cargoes in bulk that is not, for the time being, carrying a cargo other than oil in that part of its cargo space.

Application

3. (1) Subject to subsection (2), these Regulations apply to all ships in

(a) Canadian waters south of the sixtieth parallel of north latitude;

(b) Canadian waters north of the sixtieth parallel of north latitude that are not within a shipping safety control zone prescribed pursuant to the *Arctic Waters Pollution Prevention Act;*[2] and

(c) Any fishing zone of Canada prescribed pursuant to the *Territorial Sea and Fishing Zones Act.*[3]

(2) These Regulations do not apply to

(a) Ships registered in Canada;

(b) Ships other than tankers;

(c) Tankers of less than 500 tons, gross tonnage; and

(d) Naval ships and ships for the time being used as naval auxiliaries.

Certification

4. (1) Subject to section 5, an inspector, an officer of the Administration or a person authorized to survey ships by

(a) Lloyd's Register of Shipping;

(b) American Bureau of Shipping;

(c) Bureau Veritas;

(d) Det norske Veritas;

(e) Germanischer Lloyd; or

(f) Registro Italiano Navale

may issue a certificate to the owner or master of a ship that is in waters other than the waters described in paragraphs 3 (1) *(a)* to *(c).*

(2) Subject to section 5, an inspector may issue a certificate to the owner or master of a ship that is in the waters described in paragraphs 3 (1) *(a)* to *(c).*

---

[1] United Nations, *Treaty Series,* vol. 536, p. 27.

[2] *Statutes of Canada,* 1969-1970, chap. 47. Reproduced in part in ST/LEG/SER.B/16, pp. 183-195.

[3] *Statutes of Canada,* 1964, chap. 22. The Act and its amendments are reproduced in part in ST/LEG/SER.B/15, pp. 52-54 and ST/LEG/SER.B/16, pp. 4-6.

5. No certificate shall be issued to the owner or master of a ship unless

(a) In the case of a Safety Convention ship, the ship complies with section 1 of Schedule A;

(b) In the case of a ship other than a Safety Convention ship, the ship complies with section 2 or 3 of Schedule A, whichever is applicable;

(c) The ship has on board a valid load line certificate; and

(d) The ship complies with the provisions, relating to reconstruction, fitting and equipping of ships, in regulations made under the Act respecting navigating appliances, pollution prevention and limitations on the quantity of pollutants to be carried.

6. A certificate shall be in the form set out in Schedule B.[1]

7. Subject to sections 8 and 9, a certificate issued to the owner or master of a ship pursuant to sections 4 to 6 is a certificate that, pursuant to subsection 730 (2) of the Act, in the absence of any evidence to the contrary, is proof of the compliance of such ship with the requirements of the Act and regulations made thereunder relating to construction, fitting and equipping that are applicable to it or would be applicable to it if it were within the waters described in paragraphs 3 (1) *(a)* to *(c)*.

8. (1) Subject to subsection (2), a certificate shall be valid for a period of not more than two years from its date of issue.

(2) When an inspector conducts an inspection of a ship and is of the opinion

(a) That the ship does not comply with the essential conditions subject to which a certificate was issued for the ship; and

(b) That the ship is in danger of discharging or causing the discharge of a pollutant into the water,

he may endorse the certificate as invalid.

. . .

SCHEDULE A

1. A Safety Convention ship shall have on board

(a) A valid

(i) Cargo Ship Safety Construction Certificate, or

(ii) Passenger Ship Safety Certificate; and

(b) A valid Exemption Certificate, where the ship has been exempted from any of the provisions of the Safety Convention.

2. Subject to section 3, a ship, other than a Safety Convention ship, shall comply with the requirements of the Safety Convention with respect to the hull and machinery.

3. A ship, other than a Safety Convention ship, that operates solely in the Great Lakes and the St. Lawrence River as far seaward as a straight line drawn

(a) From Cap-des-Rosiers to West Point Anticosti Island; and

---

[1] Schedule B is not reproduced here.

(b) From Anticosti Island to the north shore of the St. Lawrence River along the meridian of longitude 63 degrees west

shall comply with the inspection requirements for the hull and machinery as required by

(c) The Act; or

(d) In the case of a ship registered in the United States, regulations made by that country.

. . .

2. FINLAND

(a) ACT No. 668 of 22 SEPTEMBER 1972 FOR THE PREVENTION OF OIL DAMAGE CAUSED BY SHIPS[1]

Chapter 1

Regulations concerning ships

Article 1. The discharge of oil or of an oily mixture into the water from a ship shall be prohibited in Finnish waters.

The discharge of oil or of an oily mixture into the water from Finnish tankers of 150 tons gross tonnage or more and from other Finnish ships of 500 tons gross tonnage or more shall also be prohibited outside Finnish waters to the extent prescribed by order.

Exceptions to the prohibition prescribed by the first paragraph which are insignificant from the point of view of the prevention of water pollution may be made by order.

Article 2. The provisions of article 1 shall not apply to the escape of oil, or of an oily mixture, resulting from damage to the ship or unavoidable leakage, if all reasonable precautions have been taken after the occurrence of the damage or discovery of the leakage for the purpose of preventing or minimizing the escape, nor to the discharge of oil or of an oily mixture into the water from a ship for the purpose of securing the safety of the ship, preventing damage to the ship or cargo, or saving life at sea.

Article 3. The meaning, for the purposes of this Act, of the expressions "oil" and "oily mixture" shall be defined by order.[2]

Article 4. Such regulations for the prevention of oil damage as relate to the structure, equipment, crews and use of ships may be made by order in so far as concerns:

(1) A Finnish or foreign tanker which transports oil along the coast of Finland in the coasting trade or in Finnish internal waters; or

---

[1] As provided in article 29, the Act came into effect on 1 November 1972 and superseded Act No. 289/57 of 26 August 1957, as amended, concerning measures for the prevention of oil damage caused by ships. Text provided by the Permanent Representative of Finland to the United Nations in a note verbale of 30 November 1973. Translation by the Secretariat of the United Nations.

[2] See *infra (b)*.

(2) any other Finnish ship if the regulations are based on an international agreement or on practice.

Article 5. The Inspector of Navigation may prohibit the departure of a ship or interrupt its voyage where there has been on board the ship a serious contravention of the provisions of this Act or of regulations made thereunder, or where there is a question of a restriction of navigation being imposed by virtue of article 6 of this Act, or where for any specific reason a direct risk of oil damage exists in relation to the voyage.

The Inspector of Navigation and the Maritime Patrol and Police Authority shall be entitled to take oil samples for the purpose of determining the origin of oil observed in the water and to interrupt the voyage of a ship for such time as is necessary to take an oil sample.

Article 6. The Shipping and Navigation Board shall restrict the navigation of tankers in Finnish waters when, owing to weather or ice conditions or the defective state of a ship or the large size of a ship in relation to the fairway, the Board considers such action necessary in order to avoid a clear risk of oil damage. In so far as possible, advance notice of the restrictions shall be given to navigators.

. . .

Chapter 2

Prevention of oil damage

Article 8. The organization and development of measures for the prevention of oil damage caused by ships shall be the responsibility of the Shipping and Navigation Board, which shall also be responsible for ensuring that the provisions of this Act and of the regulations made thereunder are complied with.

The local authorities (the commune) shall be responsible within their area of jurisdiction for the prevention of the damage referred to in the first paragraph, in accordance with the provisions of this Act.

For the purposes of this Act, the *authorities responsible for the prevention of oil damage* shall be the Shipping and Navigation Board, a director of preventive action appointed by the Board and, at the local level, the authority given responsibility by the commune for the direction of activities for the prevention of oil damage.

. . .

Article 10. In the case of ports which are regularly visited by tankers, or with especial frequency by other ships, the owner of the port shall provide the necessary equipment and facilities for preventing and limiting oil damage and shall arrange for trained staff to be available for servicing such equipment. The same shall apply, *mutatis mutandis,* to the owner of an industrial or storage establishment that deals with large quantities of oil in the course of its operations and to the owner of a shipyard that carries out ship repairs.

Further regulations concerning the equipment and facilities which must be provided and the extent thereof shall be made by the Ministry of Trade and Industry as required, due account being taken of: the traffic in the port, and especially the number of tankers putting in there; other circumstances having a bearing on the risk of oil damage; and the economic resources of the port, establishment or shipyard in question.

. . .

Article 13. The Ministry of Trade and Industry may make regulations concerning the obligations of the owner of a port or the owner of an establishment or shipyard as referred to in article 10 to take, in respect of tankers, reasonable advance measures for the prevention of oil damage, such as the provision of a containment boom or the posting of guards.

Article 14. Where oil has escaped from a ship into the water or there is a threat of oil leakage by reason of a ship running aground, being disabled by machine failure or suffering any other accident at sea, the master of ship, or, where the area of a port, establishment or shipyard as referred to in article 10 is affected, the owner thereof, shall forthwith report the oil damage or threat thereof to an authority responsible for the prevention of oil damage or to the police and shall take such immediate preventive measures as can reasonably be expected of him. The authorities responsible for the prevention of oil damage shall promptly take the necessary measures to prevent or minimize the damage in so far as the costs incurred by or the damage resulting from such measures are not manifestly disproportionate to the threatened economic or other loss.

In the event of oil escaping or threatening to escape from a ship into the water, the owner of a port, establishment or shipyard as referred to in article 10 shall make his equipment and facilities for the prevention of oil damage and the staff required for the operation thereof available to the authorities responsible for the prevention of oil damage if the said authorities so request.

Article 15. Where a ship, in Finnish waters, sinks, runs aground, springs a leak, is disabled by machine failure or otherwise becomes involved in a situation where there is a risk of oil damage, the Shipping and Navigation Board may direct that such rescue or other measures be taken in regard to the ship and its cargo as the Board considers reasonable for the purpose of preventing or minimizing oil damage. Before any such measures are taken, the Shipping and Navigation Board shall consult with representatives of the owner and of the insurers of the ship if this can be done without giving rise to harmful delay.

The provisions of the first paragraph shall apply to a ship owned by a foreign State only if such ship is being used for the purposes of merchant shipping at the time of the incident.

Article 16. A person who is liable for damage caused by oil that has escaped into the water, or who has brought about a situation as referred to in article 15, and a shipowner who, under article 11 of Act No. 167/39 (the Maritime Act), is liable for the actions of a person who has brought about such a situation, shall in addition be obliged to pay compensation to the authorities and to the owner or proprietor of the property that was exposed to danger for the costs incurred by the preventive measures and for damage caused to the ship, its cargo or other property on board the ship by the preventive measures, if the measures were not manifestly unnecessary or inappropriate in the light of the prevailing situation. Even where the shipowner is not liable for the actual or threatened oil damage, he shall be obliged to pay reasonable compensation corresponding to the benefits which he has obtained from the measures referred to in article 15.

If, in a case as referred to in article 15, the damage caused to the ship, its cargo or other property on board the ship exceeds what might ordinarily be expected in the conduct of rescue operations, and if no one can be regarded as liable for the damage in accordance with the provisions of the first paragraph, compensation for the excess portion of the damage shall be paid by the State.

Article 17. Where oil damage occurs, or there is a threat of it occurring, on the open sea or in the area of two or more communes, or where the oil damage or the threat thereof is so great that a commune cannot reasonably be required to carry out the preventive action alone, the Shipping and Navigation Board shall take over the action for the prevention of oil damage by appointing a director of preventive action and making the necessary staff, equipment and facilities available to him. In such a case, a commune shall be obliged, in accordance with the instructions of the Shipping and Navigation Board, to make its equipment and facilities for the prevention of oil damage and the staff required for the operation thereof available to the director of preventive action even outside the area of the commune. The corresponding obligation on the part of the owner of a port, establishment or shipyard as referred to in article 10 shall be governed by the provisions of article 14, second paragraph.

To the extent that preventive measures are carried out on the open sea, or to protect the area of another commune, or, in so far as a port, establishment or shipyard as referred to in article 10 is concerned, elsewhere than within or in the immediate vicinity of the area thereof, full compensation for the assistance in the prevention of oil damage which is rendered in pursuance of the foregoing provisions shall be paid by the State.

Article 18. The master of a ship which is the cause of oil damage or the threat thereof shall be obliged to give the authorities every assistance which in the circumstances can be demanded for the prevention of oil damage.

Chapter 3

Fund for Compensation for Oil Damage

Article 19. An extrabudgetary *Fund for Compensation for Oil Damage* shall be established for the payment of compensation for oil damage caused by ships and for the reimbursement of costs which are incurred for the prevention of such damage or which, in pursuance of article 17, second paragraph, are payable by the State. The Fund shall be administered by the Ministry of Trade and Industry, and decisions on the payment of compensation from the Fund shall be made by the Council of State.

. . .

Article 20. For the purposes of the Fund for Compensation for Oil Damage an *oil protection levy* shall be imposed on imported oil at the rate of 100 marks per 1,000 tons.

The oil protection levy shall be paid by the person who initially reports the oil to the customs authorities for customs clearance.

The oil protection levy shall be collected by the Customs Department in conformity with the relevant provisions of the customs regulations.

. . .

Chapter 4

Supplementary provisions

Article 25. Any person who wilfully or through gross negligence causes oil or an oily mixture to escape into the water in contravention of this Act shall, save where a more severe penalty is otherwise prescribed for such action, be liable, upon conviction, to a fine or to imprisonment for a term not exceeding two years.

Any person who otherwise commits an offence against the provisions of this Act or of the regulations made thereunder shall be liable, upon conviction, to a fine or to imprisonment for a term not exceeding six months.

If the offence was committed with the knowledge and consent of the shipowner, the shipowner shall be subject to the same penalties as the actual offender.

. . .

(b) ORDER No. 710 of 26 OCTOBER 1972 FOR THE PREVENTION OF OIL DAMAGE CAUSED BY SHIPS[1]

On the proposal of the Minister of Trade and Industry and by virtue of Act No. 668/72 of 22 September 1972 for the prevention of oil damage caused by ships,[2] it is hereby provided as follows:

Article 1. For the purposes of Act No. 668/72 for the prevention of oil damage caused by ships, of the present Order and of regulations made under the said Act and Order, and save as otherwise specifically provided:

"Oil" means crude oil, all oil products derived therefrom such as fuel oil, lubricating oil and motor spirits, and oil residues;

"Persistent oil" means crude oil, heavy fuel and diesel oil, lubricating oil and other oil products of a similar consistency, and oil residues;

"Light oil" means petrol, kerosene, light diesel oil and other oil products of a similar consistency;

"Heavy diesel oil" means diesel oil, other than those diesel oils of which more than 50 per cent by volume distils at a temperature not exceeding 340°C. when tested by A.S.T.M. Standard Method D. 86/59;

---

[1] Text provided by the Permanent Representative of Finland to the United Nations in a note verbale of 30 November 1973. Translation by the Secretariat of the United Nations. For the entry into force and the status of previous legislation, see article 12.

[2] *Supra (a).*

"Oily mixture" means a mixture which contains persistent oil, or a mixture with a light-oil content of more than 100 parts in 100,000 parts of the mixture;

"Ship" means any sea-going vessel of any type whatsoever, including floating craft, whether self-propelled or towed by another vessel;

"Tanker" means a ship in which the greater part of the cargo space is constructed or adapted for the carriage of liquid cargoes in bulk and which is not, for the time being, carrying a cargo other than oil in that part of its cargo space;

"Oil damage" means damage caused by the outflow of oil into the water from a ship.

The Act referred to in the first paragraph shall be designated in this Order as the "Oil Damage Act".

Article 2. In addition to what is provided in article 1, first paragraph, of the Oil Damage Act, the discharge of persistent oil or an oily mixture containing persistent oil into the water from a Finnish tanker of 150 tons gross tonnage or more and from any other Finnish ship of 500 tons gross tonnage or more shall also be prohibited outside Finnish waters.

Article 3. Notwithstanding the provisions of article 2, it shall be permissible on the open sea:

(1) for an oily mixture of less than 100 parts of oil in 1,000,000 parts of the mixture to be discharged from a ship under way, other than a tanker, if the amount of oil released into the water does not at any time exceed 60 litres per nautical mile covered by the ship and the discharge of the mixture into the water is made as far as practicable from the nearest land;

(2) for oily bilge-water to be discharged from the machinery spaces of a tanker, subject to the restrictions specified in subparagraph (1);

(3) for oil or an oily mixture to be discharged from a tanker in ballast when it is more than 50 nautical miles from the nearest land, if the amount of oil released into the water does not at any time exceed 60 litres per nautical mile covered by the ship and the total amount of oil released into the water while the ship is under way does not exceed 1/15,000th part of the cargo capacity of the tanker.

It shall also be permissible for ballast from the cargo tanks of tankers to be discharged into the water if the degree of cleanliness of the ballast is such that no trace thereof, even when the vessel is at rest, would be visible on a clean and calm water surface on a clear day.

The Ministry of Trade and Industry may completely prohibit the discharge of oil and oily mixtures into the waters of the Gulf of Finland, the Gulf of Bothnia and the Baltic Sea.

For the purposes of this article, the term "land", subject to the limits specified by the Shipping and Navigation Board, shall be considered to include the Great Barrier Reef off the north-east coast of Australia.

Article 4. Finnish tankers of 150 tons gross tonnage or more and other Finnish ships of 500 tons gross tonnage or more may not be used for navigation unless such tanker or ship, so far as is reasonable and practicable, is so fitted as to prevent oil from draining into the bilges of the ship or the ship is equipped with effective means to prevent oil in the bilges from being discharged into the sea in contravention of the provisions of the Oil Damage Act or of this Order.

The transport of water ballast in fuel tanks shall be permitted only if the stability of the ship cannot be ensured in any other manner.

. . .

Article 7. An *oil record book* in a form specified by the Shipping and Navigation Board shall be carried in a Finnish tanker of 150 tons gross tonnage or more and in any other Finnish ship of 500 tons gross tonnage or more in which oil is used as a fuel, and the entries in such record book shall be made by the master or, under his supervision, by another officer.

The competent authorities and, while the ship is in a foreign port, the competent foreign authorities may inspect the oil record book and may, on request, obtain from the master a certified true copy of any entry therein. Any action by the authorities in pursuance of the provisions of this paragraph shall be taken as expeditiously as possible, and the ship shall not be delayed.

The oil record book shall be kept in such a place as to be readily available for inspection, and it shall be preserved for a period of two years after the last entry has been made.

The provisions of the second paragraph shall also apply, *mutatis mutandis,* to the oil record book or corresponding entries of a foreign ship when the ship is in a Finnish port.

. . .

Article 12. This Order shall come into effect on 1 November 1972, provided that the provisions of article 5 shall apply only to:

— A ship for which the building contract is placed after 1 June 1973;

— A ship the delivery of which is after 1 January 1977; and

— As from 1 January 1975 or such later day as is specified by the Ministry of Trade and Industry, any other ship for which the building contract was placed after 1 January 1972.

Until such time as the Ministry of Trade and Industry provides otherwise, but not later than the end of the year 1973, oil or an oily mixture may be discharged into the water from a Finnish ship outside Finnish waters even if the limits prescribed by the first paragraph of article 3 are exceeded, on condition that it is not possible in practice to comply with the limits and that the oil or mixture cannot be retained on board until such port of destination is reached at which it would be possible for the oil or mixture to be removed from the ship. It shall be compulsory, however, in this connexion to comply with the limitations deriving from the International Convention of 1954 for the Prevention of Pollution of the Sea by Oil, as amended in 1962.[1]

---

[1] United Nations, *Treaty Series,* vol. 327, p. 3. The Convention of 1954 as amended in 1962 is reproduced in ST/LEG/SER.B/15, pp. 787-799.

This Order shall supersede Order No. 290/57 of 26 August 1957, as subsequently amended, on measures for the prevention of oil damage caused by ships.

3. FRANCE

LOI No 64-1331 DU DECEMBRE 1964 REPRIMANT LA POLLUTION DES EAUX DE LA MER PAR LES HYDROCARBURES[1], MODIFIEE PAR LA LOI No 73-477 DU 16 MAI 1973[2]

Article 1er. Sera puni d'une amende de 10 000 F à 100 000 F et d'un emprisonnement de trois mois à deux ans, ou de l'une de ces deux peines seulement, et, en cas de récidive, du double de ces peines, tout capitaine d'un bâtiment français soumis aux dispositions de la convention internationale pour la prévention de la pollution des eaux de la mer par les hydrocarbures, signée à Londres le 12 mai 1954, et de ses modificatifs[3], qui se sera rendu coupable d'infraction aux dispositions de l'article 3 de ladite convention relatif aux interdictions de rejet à la mer d'hydrocarbures ou de mélanges d'hydrocarbures.

Article 2. Sera puni d'une amende de 3 000 F à 30 000 F et, en cas de récidive, d'un emprisonnement de dix jours à six mois et d'une amende de 6 000 F à 60 000 F, ou de l'une de ces deux peines seulement, tout capitaine d'un bâtiment français non soumis aux dispositions de la convention internationale mentionnnée à l'article premier et appartenant aux catégories suivantes, à l'exception des bâtiments de la marine nationale, qui aura commis les actes interdits par les dispositions précitées :

a) Navires-citernes;

b) Autres navires, lorsque la puissance installée de leur machine propulsive dépasse un chiffre fixé par décret en Conseil d'Etat;

c) Engins portuaires, chalands et bateaux-citernes fluviaux, qu'ils soient automoteurs, remorqués ou poussés.

Article 3. Les peines visées aux articles 1er et 2 seront prononcées suivant la distinction faite auxdits articles lorsque les actes interdits à l'article 3 de la convention mentionnée à l'article 1er auront été commis, dans les eaux intérieures françaises fréquentées normalement par les bâtiments de mer, par le capitaine d'un bâtiment français auquel s'applique soit l'article 2 de ladite convention, soit l'article 2 de la présente loi.

Article 3 bis. Sans préjudice des peines prévues aux articles 1er, 2 et 3 à l'égard du capitaine, si l'infraction a été commise sur ordre du propriétaire ou de l'exploitant du navire, ce propriétaire ou cet exploitant sera puni des peines prévues auxdits articles, le maximum de ces peines étant toutefois porté au double.

---

[1] Reproduite dans ST/LEG/SER.B/15, p. 487-489.

[2] *Journal officiel,* 17 mai 1973. Aux termes de son article 3, la loi est applicable dans les territoires d'outre-mer.

[3] Nations Unies, *Recueil des Traités,* vol. 327, p. 3, et vol. 600, p. 332. Le texte anglais de la Convention modifié par les amendements de 1962 est reproduit dans ST/LEG/SER.B/15, p. 787-799.

Tout propriétaire ou exploitant d'un bâtiment qui n'aura pas donné au capitaine l'ordre écrit de se conformer aux dispositions de l'article 3 de la convention de Londres et aux obligations prévues aux articles 2 et 3 ci-dessus pourra être retenu comme complice de l'infraction prévue aux articles 1er, 2 et 3 ci-dessus.

Article 4. Dans les eaux territoriales françaises et dans les eaux intérieures françaises fréquentées normalement par les bâtiments de mer, les dispositions de la présente loi s'appliquent aux bâtiments étrangers même immatriculés dans un territoire relevant d'un gouvernement non contractant, et y compris les catégories de bâtiments énumérées à l'article 2 ci-dessus.

Article 5. Sont habilités a constater les infractions aux dispositions des articles 3 et 9 de la convention mentionnée à l'article 1er, aux dispositions réglementaires qui étendront l'application dudit article 9, et à celles de la présente loi :

Les administrateurs des affaires maritimes;

Les inspecteurs de la navigation et du travail maritimes;

Les inspecteurs-mécaniciens;

Les ingénieurs des ponts et chaussées et les ingénieurs des travaux publics de l'Etat chargés de services maritimes;

Les ingénieurs des mines et les ingénieurs des travaux publics de l'Etat affectés au service des mines des circonscriptions minéralogiques intéressées;

Les officiers de port et officiers de port adjoints;

Les agents des douanes;

Et, à l'étranger, les consuls de France, à l'exclusion des agents consulaires.

En outre, les infractions aux dispositions de l'article 3 de la convention pourront être constatées par les commandants des bâtiments de la marine nationale.

Sont chargés de rechercher les infractions constituant le délit de pollution des eaux de la mer, de recueillir à cet effet tous renseignements en vue de découvrir les auteurs de ces infractions et d'en rendre compte soit à un administrateur des affaires maritimes, soit à un officier de police judiciaire :

Les agents de la police de la navigation et de la surveillance des pêches maritimes;

Les commandants des navires océanographiques de l'Etat;

Les chefs de bord des aéronefs militaires, des aéronefs de la protection civile et des aéronefs de l'Etat affectés à la surveillance des eaux maritimes;

Les agents des services des phares et balises;

Les agents de l'institut scientifique et technique des pêches maritimes;

Et les agents de la police de la pêche fluviale.

Article 6. Les procès-verbaux dressés conformément à l'article 5 de la présente loi font foi jusqu'à preuve du contraire et ne sont pas soumis à l'affirmation. Ils sont transmis immédiatement au procureur de la République par l'agent verbalisateur qui en adresse en même temps copie à l'administrateur des affaires maritimes lorsqu'il s'agit de navires et à l'ingénieur en chef des ponts et chaussées ou au directeur départemental de l'équipement chargé du service maritime s'il s'agit d'engins portuaires ou de bâtiments fluviaux.

Les infractions aux dispositions de la convention mentionnée à l'article 1er et à celles de la présente loi sont jugées soit par le tribunal compétent du lieu de l'infraction, soit par celui dans le ressort duquel le bâtiment est attaché en douanes s'il est français, soit par celui dans le ressort duquel peut être trouvé le bâtiments s'il est étranger.

Article 7. L'administration conserve la faculté de poursuivre, selon la procédure des contraventions de grande voirie, la réparation des dommages causés au domaine public, sans qu'aucune peine puisse être prononcée par la juridiction administrative lorsque les faits incriminés sont constitutifs d'un des délits prévus aux articles 1er à 4 de la présente loi.

4. GERMANY, FEDERAL REPUBLIC OF

ORDINANCE OF 17 JULY 1973 BY THE MINISTER OF TRANSPORT CONCERNING THE CONDUCT OF VESSELS WITHIN DIVIDED-TRAFFIC AREAS ON THE HIGH SEAS[1]

Article 1

Area of application

This Ordinance shall be applicable on the high seas outside the area of application of the Regulations governing Maritime Shipping Routes, dated 3 May 1971,[2] amended by the First Ordinance Amending the Regulations governing Maritime Shipping Routes, dated 7 July 1972,[2] with respect to all vessels that are entitled to fly the federal flag.

Article 2

Divided-traffic areas

Divided-traffic areas within the meaning of this Ordinance are the shipping routes designated by the Federal Minister of Transport, in the *Bundesanzeiger* which are separated into one-way lanes by dividing lines or dividing zones or in some other way in which travel is permitted only on the side of the dividing line or dividing zone which is the right side in the direction of travel.

Article 3

Responsibility

(1) The master of the vessel and, in the case of pushing or towing units, the master of the unit shall be responsible for ensuring that the provisions of this Ordinance are observed.

---

[1] BGBl 1973, part I, p. 975. For the entry into force see Article 8. Translation by the Secretariat of the United Nations.

[2] *Supra*, Division I, Subdivision A, chapter II 4 *(b)*.

(2) The pilot shall also bear responsibility; he must so advise the persons mentioned in paragraph (1) as to enable them to observe the provisions of this Ordinance.

Article 4

Conduct within divided-traffic areas

(1) Within divided-traffic areas, vessels must use the one-way lane which lies to the right of the dividing line or dividing zone in the direction of travel. The vessel's course must be consistent with the general direction of traffic in the lane. All vessels must keep clear of the dividing line or dividing zone as far as possible.

(2) Vessels entering or leaving a one-way lane must, in general, use the ends of the lane. If a vessel finds it necessary to enter or leave a one-way lane in a lateral direction, its deviation from the direction of the lane must be at the smallest possible angle.

(3) Vessels must avoid crossing divided-traffic areas in so far as possible. If they are nevertheless obliged to do so, the crossing must, if possible, be at right angles to the general direction of traffic in the lane.

(4) Vessels may not travel in dividing zones or cross dividing lines except for the purpose of

1. Crossing a divided-traffic area (paragraph (3), second sentence);
2. Fishing within a dividing zone;
3. Emergency action to avoid imminent danger.

(5) Vessels travelling in the entrance and exit areas (approach zones) of a divided-traffic area must manoeuvre with particular caution.

(6) Areas between the coastline and the lateral boundary of a divided-traffic area (coastal navigation zones) may not in general be used by through traffic if the appropriate one-way lane of the adjacent divided-traffic area can be used without danger.

(7) Anchoring within divided-traffic areas or their approach zones must be avoided in so far as possible.

(8) Vessels not using divided-traffic areas must keep as far away from them as possible.

(9) Vessels engaged in fishing must not impede the passage of other vessels using one-way lanes in the prescribed direction.

(10) Vessels less than 20 metres in length and sailing vessels must not impede the safe passage of power-driven vessels using one-way lanes in the prescribed direction.

Article 5

Application of the rules of navigation

The Regulations for Preventing Collisions at Sea (annex B of the International Convention for the Safety of Life at Sea—Rules of Navigation—*Bundesgesetzblatt* 1965, II, p. 742) shall not be affected.

202

Article 6

Disciplinary offences

(1) A disciplinary offence within the meaning of article 15., paragraph (1), item 2, of the Act on the Functions of the Federal Government in matters of Maritime Shipping shall be deemed to have been committed by anyone who intentionally or negligently

1. As master of a vessel or master of a unit (article 3, paragraph (1))

    (a) Contrary to article 4, paragraph (1), first sentence, fails to use a one-way lane or, contrary to article 4, paragraph (1), second or third sentence, or paragraph (2), fails to use it in the prescribed manner;

    (b) Contrary to article 4, paragraph (3), crosses a divided-traffic area;

    (c) Contrary to article 4, paragraph (4), travels in a dividing zone or crosses a dividing line;

    (d) Contrary to article 4, paragraph (6), uses a coastal traffic zone;

    (e) Contrary to article 4, paragraph (7), anchors in a divided-traffic area or its approach zones;

    (f) Contrary to article 4, paragraph (8), fails to keep a clear distance from a divided-traffic area; or

    (g) Contrary to article 4, paragraph (9) or (10), impedes passage in a one-way lane; or

2. As a pilot, contrary to article 3, paragraph (2), fails to advise or incorrectly advises a person specified in article 3, paragraph (1).

(2) Competence for the prosecution and punishment of disciplinary offences under paragraph (1) shall be vested in the waterways and shipping administrations.

Article 7

In accordance with article 14 of the Third Transference Act, dated 4 January 1952 (*Bundesgesetzblatt* I, p. 1), in conjunction with article 21 of the Act on the Functions of the Federal Government in matters of Maritime Shipping and article 111 of the Act on Disciplinary Offences, this Ordinance shall also be valid in *Land* Berlin.

Article 8

This Ordinance shall enter into force on the first day of the second month following the date of its promulgation.

5. GHANA

[MINERALS (OFFSHORE) REGULATIONS 1963, AS AMENDED IN 1968
Regulations 10, 11, 16 (2) and 19 (2)] [1]

---

[1] *Supra* Division I, Subdivision A, chap. IX, 4 *(b)*.

6. IRELAND

(a) OIL POLLUTION OF THE SEA ACT, 1956[1]

Part I

Preliminary and general

. . .

3. In this Act:

"barge" includes a lighter or like vessel;

"Convention of 1954" means the International Convention for the Prevention of Pollution of the Sea by Oil, 1954;[2]

"discharge" in relation to oil or any oily mixture means any discharge or escape howsoever caused;

"harbour authority" means:

(a) in the case of a harbour to which the Harbours Act, 1946 (No. 9 of 1946), applies, the harbour authority under that Act,

(b) in the case of a harbour under the control and management of the Commissioners of Public Works in Ireland, the Commissioners, and

(c) in any other case, the person entitled to charge rates in respect of vessels entering or using the harbour;

"harbour master" includes a person appointed by a harbour authority for the purpose of enforcing the provisions of this Act;

"inspector" means a surveyor of ships or a person appointed under section 20;

"master", in relation to a vessel, means the person having the command or charge of the vessel for the time being;

"mile" means a nautical mile of six thousand and eighty feet;

"the Minister" means the Minister for Industry and Commerce;

"oil" means oil of any description, and includes spirit produced from oil, and coal tar;

"occupier", in relation to anything which has no occupier, means the owner, and, in relation to a railway wagon or road vehicle, means the person in charge of it;

"petroleum spirit" means petroleum to which the Petroleum Acts, 1871 and 1879, apply;

---

[1] Act No. 25 of 17 July 1956. In accordance with Commencement Order, 1957 (S.I. No. 203 of 14 October 1957), the Act came into force on 1 November 1957 with the exception of the provisions in Section 9, subsections (1) and (2) in what they concern Parts III and IV of the Schedule of the Act. These latter provisions came into effect on 1 August 1958 in accordance with Commencement (No. 2) Order, 1958 (S.I. No. 165 of 28 July 1958).

[2] United Nations, *Treaty Series*, Vol. 327, p. 3, and ST/LEG/SER.B/15, pp. 787-799.

"place of land" includes anything resting on the bed or shore of the sea or inland waters and also includes anything afloat, other than a vessel, if anchored or attached to the bed or shore;

"prescribed" means prescribed by regulations made by the Minister;

"transfer" in relation to oil means transfer in bulk;

other terms have the same meanings as in the Merchant Shipping Act, 1894.

4. (1) This Act does not apply to a vessel of the Irish Naval Exemptions Service, wholly manned by personnel of the Service.

(2) The Minister may exempt any vessels or classes of vessels from any of the provisions of this Act or of regulations thereunder, either absolutely or subject to such conditions as he thinks fit.

5. Every order and regulation made under this Act shall be laid before each House of the Oireachtas as soon as may be after it is made and, if a resolution annulling it is passed by either House within the next twenty-one days on which that House has sat after the instrument has been laid before it, the instrument shall be annulled accordingly but without prejudice to the validity of anything previously done under it.

6. (1) Fees under this Act shall be taken and collected in such manner as the Minister for Finance may from time to time direct and shall be paid into or disposed of for the benefit of the Exchequer in accordance with the directions of the Minister for Finance.

(2) The Public Offices Fees Act, 1879, shall not apply in respect of such fees.

7. The expenses incurred by the Ministry in the administration of this Act shall, to such extent as may be sanctioned by the Minister for Finance, be paid out of moneys provided by the Oireachtas.

8. The Oil in Navigable Waters Act, 1926 (No. 5 of 1926), is hereby repealed.

Part II

Prevention of oil pollution of the sea

9. (1) Subject to subsection (3), the sea areas specified in Parts I and III of the Schedule shall be prohibited zones for tankers.

(2) Subject to subsection (3), the sea areas specified in Parts II and IV of the Schedule shall be prohibited zones for ships other than tankers.

(3) The Minister may by order extend or reduce any prohibited zone or declare any specified sea area to be a prohibited zone for tankers or for other ships for the purpose of giving effect to any variation of sea areas in accordance with the Convention of 1954 or of implementing any subsequent Convention or of protecting the coasts of the State, and amend any order under this subsection.

10. (1) This section applies to crude oil, fuel oil and lubricating oil.

(2) This section shall also apply to any heavy diesel oil or other description of oil which may be prescribed.

(3) The owner and also the master of any ship registered in the State which discharges into a prohibited zone for that ship any oil to which this section applies or any mixture containing such oil, the oil in which fouls the surface of the sea, shall be guilty of an offence.[1]

(4) For this purpose, the oil in any oily mixture of less than one hundred parts of oil in one million parts of the mixture shall be deemed not to foul the surface of the sea.[2]

(5) The Minister may prescribe exceptions to subsection 3 either generally or for specified classes of ships or in relation to particular descriptions of oil or oily mixtures, or to their discharge in specified circumstances, or in relation to particular sea areas.

11. (1) If any oil or oily mixture is discharged (directly or indirectly) into the territorial seas of the State or into its inland waters navigable by sea-going vessels, then, if the discharge is:

(a) From a vessel, the owner and also the master of the vessel;

(b) From a place on land, the occupier of that place;

(c) From apparatus for transferring oil to or from a vessel, the person in charge of the apparatus,

shall be guilty of an offence.

(2) A harbour master may specify a place where the ballast water of a vessel in which a cargo of petroleum spirit has been carried may be discharged into the waters of the harbour at such times and on such conditions as he may direct. The discharge of ballast water containing no oil other than petroleum spirit in accordance with such directions shall not be an offence.

12. (1) Sections 10 and 11 shall not apply to:

(a) The discharge of oil or of an oily mixture from a vessel for the purpose of securing the safety of the vessel, preventing damage to the vessel or her cargo, or saving life, if such discharge was necessary and reasonable in the circumstances; or

(b) The escape of oil or of an oily mixture from a vessel, resulting from damage to the vessel or from any leakage, not due to any want of reasonable care, if all reasonable precautions have been taken after the occurrence of the damage or discovery of the leakage for the purpose of preventing or minimizing the escape.

(2) Section 11 shall not apply to the escape of oil or of an oily mixture from any place or apparatus, if the escape was not due to any want of reasonable care and if all reasonable steps have been taken after the discovery of the escape for the purpose of stopping or minimizing it.

---

[1] Subsections (3) and (4) of section 10 have been replaced by a new subsection (3), as provided in Section 6 of the Oil Pollution of the Sea (Amendment) Act, 1965. *Infra (b).*

[2] *Ibid.*

(3) Section 11 shall not apply to the discharge from any place of an effluent produced by operations for the refining of oil, if:

(a) It was not reasonably practicable to dispose of the effluent otherwise than by so discharging it; and

(b) All reasonably practicable steps had been taken for eliminating oil from the effluent; and

(c) In the event of the surface of the waters into which the mixture was discharged, or land adjacent to those waters, being fouled by oil at the time of the discharge, it is shown that the fouling was not caused or contributed to by oil contained in any effluent discharged at or before that time from that place.

13. (1) A harbour authority may provide, or cause to be provided, facilities for the discharge of oily residue from vessels using the harbour and arrange for its disposal.

(2) Whenever the Minister, after consultation with the harbour authority and with any organization appearing to him to be representative of owners of ships registered in the State, is of opinion that such facilities or arrangements are necessary at a particular harbour, or that the existing facilities are inadequate, he may require the harbour authority to make such provision, and within such time, as he may consider necessary and may extend the time for complying with any such requirement.

(3) A harbour authority shall not be obliged to make any facilities provided under this section available for tankers or for the discharge of oily residues for the purpose of enabling a vessel to undergo repairs or to allow the disposal of residue from which the water has not been effectively separated but, subject thereto, the facilities shall be available for all vessels using the harbour.

(4) A harbour authority, or any person by arrangement with a harbour authority, providing facilities for vessels in accordance with this section may make reasonable charges, and impose reasonable conditions, for the use of the facilities.

14. (1) If any oil or oily mixture:

(a) Is discharged from a vessel into the waters of a harbour for the purpose of securing the safety of the vessel, preventing damage to the vessel or her cargo, or saving life; or

(b) Is found to be escaping or to have escaped into such waters from a vessel as a result of damage to the vessel or leakage, or from any place on land,

the owner and the master of the vessel, or the occupier of the place, as the case may be, shall forthwith report the fact and cause of the occurrence to the harbour master.

(2) A person who fails to comply with subsection (1) shall be guilty of an offence and shall, on summary conviction, be liable to a fine not exceeding one hundred pounds.

15. (1) No oil shall be transferred between sunset and sunrise to or from a vessel in a harbour unless notice has previously been given in accordance with this section to the harbour master.

(2) Notice shall be given not less than three and not more than ninety-six hours before the transfer of oil begins but, where transfers are frequently carried out at a particular place, a general notice to that effect, covering a period of not more than twelve months from the date of the notice shall suffice.

(3) If any oil is transferred to or from a vessel in contravention of this section the master of the vessel, and, if the transfer is from or to a place on land, also, the occupier, shall be guilty of an offence and shall, on summary conviction, be liable to a fine not exceeding fifty pounds.

(4) This section shall not apply to the transfer of oil by or on the direction of the harbour master or the officer in charge of a fire brigade in the event of a fire.

16. (1) The Minister may make regulations requiring ships registered in the State to be so fitted, and to comply with such requirements, as to prevent or reduce the discharge of oil or oily mixtures into the sea.

(2) A surveyor of ships and such other persons as the Minister may appoint may carry out such tests as may be prescribed for the purpose of this section and, for such tests, may charge such fees as the Minister, with the consent of the Minister for Finance, may direct.

(3) The owner and also the master of a ship, in respect of which there is a contravention of regulations under this section, shall be guilty of an offence. The offence shall be a continuing offence and fresh proceedings in respect of it may be taken from time to time.

17. (1) The master of a ship registered in the State shall keep the prescribed records of:

(a) The discharge of any oil or oily mixture from the ship for the purpose of securing the safety of the ship, preventing damage to the ship or her cargo, or saving life;

(b) The escape of any oil or oily mixture from the ship, resulting from damage to the ship or leakage;

(c) The carrying out of prescribed operations, being:

(i) The ballasting of and discharge of ballast from cargo tanks or bunker fuel tanks, and the cleaning of such tanks; or

(ii) The separation of oil in any oily mixture; or

(iii) The disposal from the ship of any oil, water or other substance arising from such operations; or

(iv) The disposal of any oily residue.

(2) The Minister may make regulations requiring the keeping of prescribed records of the transfer of oil to or from any vessel, whether registered in the State or not, while within the territorial seas or inland waters of the State. Records of transfer of oil to or from a barge shall be kept, respectively, by the person by whom the oil is supplied or to whom it is

delivered. In every other case the records shall be kept by the master of the vessel.

(3) Regulations for the purposes of this section may provide for the custody, preservation, disposal and inspection of records and for such other ancillary matters as may be prescribed.

(4) Every person who contravenes this section or regulations under it shall be guilty of an offence and shall be liable, on summary conviction, to a fine not exceeding two hundred and fifty pounds.

(5) Every person who makes in a record any entry or alteration which is to his knowledge false or misleading in any material respect shall be guilty of an offence and shall, on summary conviction, be liable to a fine not exceeding two hundred and fifty pounds or to imprisonment for a term not exceeding six months or to both such fine and imprisonment.

18. (1) The Government may by order apply section 16 or subsection (1) of section 17 to ships registered in other countries while they are in a harbour in the State or within the territorial seas while on their way to or from such a harbour, unless their presence there is due to stress of weather or some other unforeseen and unavoidable circumstance.

(2) The Government may by order exempt from such application a ship of any country, if satisfied that the requirements of the law of that country are equally effective and that the ship complies with them.

(3) The Government may by order revoke an order under this section.

Part III

Enforcement and penalties

19. (1) The Minister, if satisfied:

(a) That the government of any country has accepted or denounced the Convention of 1954 or any subsequent Convention; or

(b) That any such Convention extends, or has ceased to extend, to any territory,

may by order so declare.

(2) In this section "ship to which the Convention applies" means a ship registered in:

(a) A country the government of which has been declared to have accepted the Convention of 1954 or any subsequent Convention and has not been subsequently declared to have denounced it; or

(b) A territory to which any such Convention has been declared to extend and to which it has not been subsequently declared to have ceased to extend.

(3) A surveyor of ships or any person empowered by warrant of the Minister may go on board any ship to which the Convention applies, while she is within a harbour in the State, may inspect the oil record book required by the Convention to be carried in the ship and may make a true copy of any

entry in the book and require the master of the ship to certify that it is a true copy.

(4) Any person who impedes a surveyor of ships or other person in the exercise of his functions under this section, or who, on being so required, fails to produce the oil record book for inspection or to certify a copy of an entry shall be guilty of an offence and shall, on summary conviction, be liable to a fine not exceeding fifty pounds.

(5) A person exercising functions under this section shall not unnecessarily detain or delay the vessel from proceeding on her voyage.

20. (1) A surveyor of ships shall be an inspector with the function of reporting to the Minister generally:

(a) Whether the requirements of this Act are being complied with;

(b) What measures have been taken for the prevention of the escape of any oil or oily mixtures;

(c) Whether the facilities in any harbour for reception of disposal of oily residue are adequate.

(2) The Minister may appoint any person to be an inspector with the function of reporting, either generally or in a particular case, under subsection (1).

21. (1) For the purpose of his functions, an inspector may:

(a) Go on board any vessel and inspect the vessel and her machinery, boats, equipment and articles on board the vessel and test any equipment with which under this Act she is required to be fitted, not unnecessarily detaining or delaying her from proceeding on her voyage;

(b) Enter and inspect any premises and any apparatus for the transfer of oil;

(c) By summons under his hand require any person to attend before him and examine him on oath (which the inspector is hereby authorized to administer);

(d) Require a witness to make and subscribe a declaration of the truth of the statements made by him at his examination;

(e) Require any person to produce to him any document in his power or control or make return to any inquiry;

(f) Copy any entry in any prescribed record and require the person by whom the record is.to be kept to certify the copy as a true copy of the entry.

(2) A witness before an inspector shall be entitled to the same immunities and privileges as if he were a witness before the High Court and shall be allowed such expenses as would be allowed to a witness attending that Court on subpoena; and any dispute as to the amount of those expenses shall be referred to a Taxing Master who shall, on request made to him under the hand of the inspector, ascertain and certify the amount of the expenses.

(3) If any person:

(a) On being summoned as a witness before an inspector and tendered the expenses to which he is entitled under this section, makes default in attending, or refuses to take an oath legally required by the inspector to be taken; or

(b) Refuses or neglects to make any answer, or to give any return or to produce any document, or to make or subscribe any declaration, or to certify a copy of any entry, which the inspector is entitled to require; or

(c) Wilfully impedes a person in the exercise of his functions under this section,

he shall be guilty of an offence and shall, on summary conviction, be liable to a fine not exceeding fifty pounds.

22. (1) Without prejudice to the powers conferred by section 21, a harbour master may, in the case of any vessel in the harbour:

(a) Go on board the vessel and inspect the vessel and her machinery, boats, equipment and articles on board the vessel for the purpose of ascertaining the circumstances relating to an alleged discharge of oil or oily mixture from the vessel into the waters of the harbour;

(b) Require the production of any prescribed record;

(c) Copy any entry in any prescribed record and require the person by whom the record is to be kept to certify the copy as a true copy of the entry,

but not unnecessarily detaining or delaying the vessel from proceeding on her voyage.

(2) If any person:

(a) Fails to comply with any such requirement; or

(b) Wilfully impedes a harbour master in the exercise of his functions under this section,

he shall be guilty of an offence and shall, on summary conviction, be liable to a fine not exceeding fifty pounds.

23. Every person who commits an offence under this Act for which no special penalty is provided shall:

(a) On summary conviction, be liable to a fine not exceeding five hundred pounds (together with, in the case of a continuing offence, a fine not exceeding fifty pounds for every day on which the offence is continued); or

(b) On conviction on indictment, be liable to a fine not exceeding five thousand pounds (together with, in the case of a continuing offence, a further fine not exceeding five hundred pounds for every day on which the offence is continued).

24. (1) Summary proceedings in respect of any offence under this Act may be brought and prosecuted by the Minister.

(2) Summary proceedings in respect of an offence in relation to a particular harbour or harbour master may be brought and prosecuted by the harbour authority.

(3) Notwithstanding subsection (4) of section 10 of the Petty Sessions (Ireland) Act, 1851, summary proceedings for the offence may be instituted:

(a) In every case, within twelve months from the date of the offence; and

(b) If at the expiry of that period the person to be charged is outside the State, within two months of the date on which he next enters the State.

(4) Without prejudice to any other jurisdiction, proceedings for an offence may be taken against a person at any place where he may be for the time being.

25. (1) A body corporate may be sent forward for trial on indictment for an offence under this Act with or without recognizances.

(2) On arraignment before the Central Criminal Court or the Circuit Court, the body corporate may enter in writing by its representative a plea of guilty or not guilty and if it does not appear by a representative appointed by it for the purpose, or, though it does so appear, fails to enter any plea, the court shall order a plea of not guilty to be entered and the trial shall proceed as though the body corporate had duly entered that plea.

(3) A statement in writing purporting to be signed by the secretary of the body corporate to the effect that the person named in the statement has been appointed as the representative of the body for the purpose of this section shall be admissible without further proof as evidence that that person has been so appointed.

(4) Any summons or other document required to be served for the purpose or in the course of proceedings under this section on a body corporate may be served by leaving it at or sending it by registered post to the registered office of that body or, if there be no such office in the State, by leaving it at, or sending it by registered post to, the body at any place in the State at which it conducts its business.

26. (1) Where a fine imposed on the owner or master of a vessel is not duly paid, the court may, without prejudice to any other powers for enforcing payment, direct the amount remaining unpaid to be levied by distress and sale of the vessel, her tackle, furniture and apparel.

(2) Where it appears to the court imposing a fine that any person has incurred or will incur expense in removing any pollution or making good any damage attributable to the offence, the court may order the whole or part of the fine to be paid to that person for or towards defraying the expense.

27. Every document purporting to be a record kept in pursuance of this Act or of the Convention of 1954 or any subsequent Convention or to be a true copy, certified as such by the person required to keep the record, of an entry therein shall, unless the country is shown, be presumed to be such and be admissible as evidence of the facts stated therein without further proof.

SCHEDULE. PROHIBITED ZONES

Part I

Initial Zones for Tankers

1. The whole of the sea which lies:

(a) Outside the territorial seas of the State; and

(b) Within 100 miles from the coast of Ireland, Great Britain, Belgium, the Netherlands, the Federal Republic of Germany or Denmark.

2. The whole of the sea which lies:

(a) South of latitude 62° north; and

(b) Within 50 miles from the coast of Norway.

3. So much of the Atlantic Ocean and of the English Channel, outside the territorial seas of the State, and outside the area specified in paragraph 1, as lies within a line drawn from a point on the Greenwich meridian 100 miles in a north-north-easterly direction from the Shetland Islands; thence northwards along the Greenwich meridian to latitude 64° north; thence westwards along the 64th parallel to longitude 10° west; thence to latitude 60° north, longitude 14° west; thence to latitude 54° 30′ north, longitude 30° west; thence to latitude 44° 20′ north, longitude 30° west; thence to latitude 48° north, longitude 14° west; thence eastwards along the 48th parallel to the coast of France.

Part II

Initial Zone for Vessels other than Tankers

1. The whole of the sea which lies:

(a) Outside the territorial seas of the State; and

(b) Within 100 miles from the coast of Ireland, Great Britain, Belgium, the Netherlands, the Federal Republic of Germany or Denmark, or within 100 miles from the coast of any of the Channel Islands.

2. The whole of the sea which lies:

(a) South of latitude 62° north; and

(b) Within 50 miles from the coast of Norway.

Part III

Additional Zones for Tankers

1. The whole of the sea which lies within 50 miles from land, exclusive of:

(a) The areas specified in Part I;

(b) The territorial seas of the State; and

(c) The Adriatic Sea and the areas specified in paragraph 3.

2. So much of the Adriatic Sea as lies within 50 miles from the coast of Albania, and so much of the remainder of the Adriatic Sea as lies within 30 miles from any other coast (the island of Vis being disregarded).

3. The whole of the sea which lies within 150 miles from the coasts of Australia, except off the north and west coasts of the Australian mainland between the point opposite Thursday Island and the point on the west coast at 20° south latitude.

Part IV

Additional Zones for Vessels other than Tankers

1. The whole of the sea which lies within 50 miles from land, exclusive of:

(a) The areas specified in Part II;

(b) The territorial seas of the State; and

(c) The Adriatic Sea.

2. So much of the Adriatic Sea as lies within 50 miles from the coast of Albania, and so much of the remainder of the Adriatic Sea as lies within 20 miles from any other coast (the island of Vis being disregarded).

(b) OIL POLLUTION OF THE SEA (AMENDMENT) ACT, 1965[1]

. . .

2. In this Act "the Principal Act" means the Oil Pollution of the Sea Act, 1956.[2]

3. (1) The owner and also the master of any ship registered in the State (being a ship of twenty thousand tons gross tonnage or more for which the building contract was entered into after the commencement of this section) which discharges oil or oily mixture anywhere at sea shall be guilty of an offence under the Principal Act.

(2) Subsection (1) of this section shall not apply in relation to—

(a) The discharge of oil or oily mixture from a ship outside the prohibited zones where special circumstances exist that, in the opinion of the master of the ship, make it neither reasonable nor practicable to retain the oil or oily mixture in the ship;

(b) The discharge of oil or oily mixture from a ship for the purpose of securing the safety of any ship, preventing damage to any ship or cargo, or saving life, if such discharge was necessary and reasonable in the circumstances; or

(c) The escape of oil or oily mixture from a ship, resulting from damage to the vessel or from any leakage, not due to any want of reasonable care, if all reasonable precautions have been taken after the occurrence of the damage or discovery of the leakage for the purpose of preventing or minimizing the escape.

(3) For the purpose of giving effect to any variation of the Convention of 1954 or to any subsequent convention, the Minister may by order apply the foregoing provisions of this section to ships of such classes as may be specified in the order.

(4) Subsection (5) of section 10 of the Principal Act shall apply in relation to subsection (1) of this section.

(5) In this section—

"oil" means oil to which section 10 of the Principal Act applies;

"oily mixture" means any mixture containing not less than one hundred parts of oil to which the said section 10 applies in a million parts of the mixture.

4. The sea areas which at the commencement of this section are prohibited zones for tankers shall be prohibited zones for all ships registered in the State.

5. (1) Whenever the Minister is of opinion that facilities for the discharge and reception of oil and oily residue from ships and arrangements for their

[1] Act No. 1 of 2 March 1965. In accordance with Oil Pollution of the Sea (Amendment) Act, 1965 (Commencement) Order, 1967 (S.I. No. 122 of 16 May 1967) this Act came into force on 18 May 1967.

[2] *Supra (a)*.

disposal are necessary at any premises occupied by an oil refinery, shipbuilding or ship repairing yard or that the existing facilities at such premises are inadequate, he may, after consultation with the owner of the refinery or yard, require the owner to make such provision and within such time as he may consider necessary and may extend the time for complying with any such requirement.

(2) If the owner of an oil refinery or shipbuilding or ship repairing yard fails to comply with the terms of a requirement under this section in relation to the refinery or yard, he shall be guilty of an offence under the Principal Act.

6. Section 10 of the Principal Act is hereby amended by the deletion of subsections (3) and (4) and the insertion of the following subsection:

"(3) The owner and also the master of any ship registered in the State which discharges into a prohibited zone for that ship any oil to which this section applies or any mixture containing not less than one hundred parts of oil to which this section applies in a million parts of the mixture shall be guilty of an offence."

7. Sections 10 and 11 of the Principal Act shall not apply to the discharge of oil or oily mixture from a ship for the purpose of securing the safety of any other ship or preventing damage to any other ship or cargo.

8. The provisions of section 17 of the Principal Act relating to the keeping of records of the discharge of oil and oily mixture shall apply to—

(a) The discharge of oil or oily mixture from a ship outside the prohibited zones where special circumstances exist which, in the opinion of the master of the ship, make it neither reasonable nor practicable to retain the oil or oily mixture in the ship; and

(b) The discharge of oil or oily mixture from a ship for the purpose of securing the safety of any other ship or preventing damage to any other ship or cargo.

9. (1) This Act may be cited as the Oil Pollution of the Sea (Amendment) Act, 1965.

(2) The Principal Act and this Act shall be construed together as one Act.

(3) The Principal Act and this Act may be cited together as the Oil Pollution of the Sea Acts, 1956 and 1965.

(c) OIL POLLUTION OF THE SEA ACT, 1956 (APPLICATION OF SECTION 10) REGULATIONS, 1957[1]

. . .

2. Section 10 of the Oil Pollution of the Sea Act, 1956 (No. 25 of 1956), shall apply to marine diesel oil other than distillates of which more than half the volume distils at a temperature not exceeding three hundred and

---

[1] S.I. No. 204 of 14 October 1957. In force as of 1 November 1957, as provided in article 1 (2) of the S.I.

forty degrees centigrade when tested by the American Society for Testing
Materials Standard Method D 153-54.

(d) OIL POLLUTION OF THE SEA ACT, 1956 (EXCEPTION FROM SECTION 10 (3)) REGULATIONS, 1958[1]

. . .

2. Every ship of under eighty tons gross tonnage registered in the State
(not being a tanker) which uses bunker fuel tanks for the carriage of ballast
water is hereby excepted from the operation of subsection (3) of section 10
of the Oil Pollution of the Sea Act, 1956[2], in respect of a discharge of a
mixture containing oil where the mixture consists only of oil from bunker
fuel tanks and ballast water, subject to the condition that the discharge is
made as far from land as is practicable and not to landward of the seaward
limits of the territorial seas of the State.

(e) OIL POLLUTION OF THE SEA ACT, 1956 (EXCEPTIONS AND EXEMPTIONS) REGULATIONS, 1957[3]

. . .

3. Every ship registered in the State is hereby excepted from the
operation of subsection (3) of section 10 of the Act[4] in respect of the
discharge from its bilges into a prohibited zone for such ship of a mixture
containing lubricating oil which has drained or leaked from machinery spaces
but no other oil to which that section applies.

4. Every ship registered in the State (not being a tanker) which uses
bunker fuel tanks for the carriage of ballast water and is proceeding to a port
in the State or to a port within a prohibited zone for such ship, being in
either case a port which has not adequate facilities to receive oil residues is
hereby excepted from the operation of subsection (3) of section 10 of the
Act[4] in respect of a discharge of a mixture containing oil where the mixture
consists only of oil from bunker fuel tanks and ballast water, subject to the
condition that the discharge is made as far from land as is practicable and not
to landward of the seaward limits of the territorial seas of the State.

5. Every vessel of less than eighty tons gross tonnage whether registered
or not and of whatever nationality is hereby exempted from the provisions of
subsection (1) of section 11 of the Act in respect of the discharge from its
bilges of a mixture containing lubricating oil which has drained or leaked
from machinery spaces but no other oil.

---

[1] S.I. No. 244 of 1 December 1958. In force as of 15 December 1958, as provided in
article 1 (2) of the S.I.

[2] *Supra (a)*.

[3] S.I. No. 205 of 14 October 1957. In force as of 1 November 1957, as provided in
article 1 (2) of the S.I.

[4] *Supra (a)*.

(f) OIL POLLUTION OF THE SEA ACT, 1956 (EXCEPTIONS AND EXEMPTIONS) (AMENDMENT) REGULATIONS, 1967[1]

. . .

2. Regulation 4 of the Oil Pollution of the Sea Act, 1956 (Exceptions and Exemptions) Regulations, 1957[2] shall not apply to a ship registered in the State of twenty thousand tons gross tonnage or more for which the building contract was entered into after the commencement of section 3 of the Oil Pollution of the Sea Act, 1965.[3]

(g) OIL POLLUTION OF THE SEA (RECORDS) REGULATIONS, 1957[4]

. . .

2. In these Regulations "the Act" means the Oil Pollution of the Sea Act, 1956 (No. 25 of 1956).

3. (1) The records to be kept in pursuance of subsection (1) of section 17 of the Act by the master of a ship registered in the State (not being a tanker) of eighty tons gross tonnage or over shall—

(i) As respects the matters specified in paragraph (a) and paragraph (b) of that subsection, be in the form set out in the First Schedule to these Regulations; and

(ii) As respects the matters specified in paragraph (c) of that subsection, be in the form set out in the Third Schedule to these Regulations.

(2) The records to be kept in pursuance of subsection (1) of section 17 of the Act by the master of a ship registered in the State, being a tanker, shall—

(i) As respects the matters specified in paragraph (a) and paragraph (b) of that subsection, be in the form set out in the First Schedule to these Regulations; and

(ii) As respects the matters specified in paragraph (c) of that subsection be in the form set out in the Second Schedule to these Regulations.

4. The records prescribed by these Regulations shall be retained in the ship for the duration of the voyage and shall be surrendered to the Superintendent of the Mercantile Marine Office with the ship's log.

---

[1] S.I. No. 126 of 16 May 1967. In force as of 18 May 1967, as provided in article 1 (2) of the S.I.

[2] Supra (e).

[3] Supra (b).

[4] S.I. No. 206 of 14 October 1957. In force as of 1 November 1957, as provided in article 1 (2) of the S.I.

FIRST SCHEDULE[1]

Accidental and other exceptional discharges or escapes of oil

1. Date and time of occurrence				
2. Place or position of ship at time of occurrence . .				
3. Approximate quantity and type of oil				
4. Circumstances of discharge or escape and general remarks				
Signature of Officer or Officers in charge of the operations concerned				
Date of entry				
Signature of Master				
Date				

SECOND SCHEDULE

Date of entry				
(a) Ballasting of and discharge of ballast from cargo tanks				
1. Identity number(s) of tank(s) concerned . .				
2. Type of oil previously contained in tank(s) .				
3. Date and place of ballasting				
4. Date and time of discharge of ballast water .				
5. Place or position of ship at time of discharge				
6. Approximate amount of oil-contaminated water transferred to slop tank(s)				
7. Identity number(s) of slop tank(s)				

[1] The three schedules reproduced here incorporate the changes made by S.I. No. 124 of 16 May 1967, Oil Pollution of the Sea (Records) (Amendment) Regulations, 1967, in force on 18 May 1967.

SECOND SCHEDULE *(continued)*

Date of entry					
(b) Cleaning of cargo tanks					
8. Identity number(s) of tank(s) concerned cleaned					
9. Type of oil previously contained in tank(s) .					
10. Identity number(s) of slop tank(s) to which washings transferred					
11. Dates and times of cleaning					
(c) Settling in slop tank(s) and discharge of water					
12. Identity number(s) of slop tank(s)					
13. Period of settling (in hours)					
14. Date and time of discharge of water					
15. Place or position of ship					
16. Approximate quantities of residue					
17. Approximate quantities of water discharged					
(d) Disposal of oily residues from slop tank(s) and other sources					
18. Date and method of disposal					
19. Place or position of ship at time of disposal .					
20. Sources and approximate quantities					

. . . .   Signature of Officer or Officers in charge of the operations concerned.

. . . .   Signature of Master.

THIRD SCHEDULE

(a) Ballasting, or cleaning during voyage, of bunker fuel tanks					
1. Identity number(s) of tank(s) concerned . .					
2. Type of oil previously contained in tank(s) .					
3. Date and place of ballasting					
Signature of Officer in charge of operations and date of entry					
Signature of Master and date					
4. Date and time of discharge of ballast or washing water					
5. Place or position of ship at time of disposal .					
6. Whether separator used; if so, give period of use					

THIRD SCHEDULE *(continued)*

7. Disposal of oily residue retained on board ..				
Signature of Officer in charge of operations and date of entry				
Signature of Master and date				
(b) Disposal of oily residues from bunker fuel tanks and other sources				
8. Date and method of disposal				
9. Place or position of ship at time of disposal .				
10. Sources and approximate quantities				
Signature of Officer in charge of operations and date of entry				
Signature of Master and date				

(h) OIL POLLUTION OF THE SEA (TRANSFER RECORDS)
REGULATIONS, 1957[1]

. . .

2. These Regulations shall apply to every vessel, whether registered in the State or not, which is capable of carrying in bulk, whether for cargo or bunker purposes, more than twenty-five tons of oil or which is capable of carrying in bulk as aforesaid more than five tons of oil in any one space or container.

3. (1) Subject to paragraph (2) of this Regulation, the master of every vessel to which these Regulations apply shall keep a record of the particulars specified in Regulation 4 of these Regulations relating to the transfer of oil to or from the vessel while within the territorial seas or inland waters of the State.

(2) In the case of the transfer of oil to or from a barge, the records shall be kept, respectively, by the person by whom the oil is supplied, or to whom it is delivered.

4. (1) The records required to be kept by Regulation 3 of these Regulations shall show clearly the following particulars:

(a) The name and port of registry (if any) of the vessel or barge;

(b) The date and time of transfer;

(c) The place of transfer;

(d) The amount and description of oil transferred;

(e) From what vessel, barge or place on land, and to what vessel, barge or place, the oil was transferred.

(2) The record of each operation shall be separately signed and dated by the person required by Regulation 3 of these Regulations to keep such record.

---

[1] S.I. No. 207 of 14 October 1957. In force as of 1 November 1957, as provided in article 1 (2) of the S.I.

(i) OIL POLLUTION OF THE SEA (SHIPS' EQUIPMENT) REGULATIONS, 1957[1]

. . .

2. These Regulations shall apply to every ship registered in the State which uses oil as fuel for either engines or boilers.

3. Every ship to which these Regulations apply shall be fitted so as effectively to prevent oil fuel from leaking or draining from machinery spaces into bilges unless the contents of the bilges are subjected to an effective means of separating the oil therefrom before they are pumped into the sea.

(j) OIL POLLUTION OF THE SEA ACT, 1956 (EXTENSION OF PROHIBITED ZONES) ORDER, 1961[2]

. . .

3. The prohibited zones for tankers and ships other than tankers for the purposes of the Oil Pollution of the Sea Act, 1956[3] are hereby extended so as to include so much of the Atlantic Ocean as lies within 100 miles from the coast of Canada.

(k) [CONTINENTAL SHELF ACT, 1968][4]

7. MONACO

LOI No 937 DU 16 JUILLET 1973 CONCERNANT LA REPRESSION DES ACTES DE POLLUTION DES EAUX DE LA MER PAR DES HYDROCARBURES PROVENANT DE NAVIRES[5]

Article premier. Sera passible d'un emprisonnement de six mois à trois ans et de l'amende prévue au chiffre 4 de l'article 26 du Code pénal, le capitaine d'un navire battant pavillon monégasque et relevant du champ d'application de la Convention internationale de Londres du 12 mai 1954, amendée[6], sur la prévention de la pollution des eaux de mer par les hydrocarbures, qui en violation des interdictions visées à l'article 3 de la Convention et sous réserve des exceptions prévues aux articles 4 et 5 de cette dernière aura procédé, fait ou laissé procéder au rejet à la mer d'hydrocarbures ou de mélanges d'hydrocarbures dans les zones déterminées par la Convention.

Le capitaine pourra, en outre, être frappé de l'interdiction de commander un navire pendant une durée qui n'excédera pas cinq années.

---

[1] S.I. No. 208 of 14 October 1957. In force as of 1 March 1958, as provided in article 1 (2) of the S.I.

[2] S.I. No. 104 of 25 May 1961. In force as of 15 June 1961 as provided in article 2 of the S.I. Order made pursuant to annex A of the International Convention for the Prevention of Pollution of the Sea by Oil, 1954 (United Nations, Treaty Series, vol. 327, p. 3 and ST/LEG/SER.B/15, p. 787).

[3] *Supra (a)*, Schedule.

[4] *Supra* Division II, 10 *(a)*.

[5] *Journal de Monaco,* No 6043 du 20 juillet 1973, p. 490 et 491.

[6] Nations Unies, *Recueil des Traités,* vol. 327, p. 3, et ST/LEG/SER.B/15, p. 787.

S'il s'agit d'un navire de plaisance et à défaut de capitaine mentionné en titre sur le rôle d'équipage ou sur le congé, les peines prévues au premier alinéa seront applicables à la personne qui avait, en fait, la responsabilité du navire au moment de l'infraction.

Indépendamment des peines encourues en application des trois alinéas ci-dessus, le propriétaire ou l'exploitant du navire qui aura donné l'ordre de procéder au rejet sera puni d'un emprisonnement de un an à cinq ans et du maximum de l'amende prévue au chiffre 4 de l'article 26 du Code pénal.

Dans tous les cas, lorsqu'il y aura récidive, outre l'application de l'article 40 du Code pénal, le maximum de l'amende prévue au chiffre 4 de l'article 26, lequel pourra être porté au triple, sera prononcé et l'interdiction de commander un navire pourra être ordonnée à titre définitif.

Article 2. Lorsque les infractions visées à l'article premier auront été commises à partir d'un navire battant pavillon monégasque et ne relevant pas, en raison de son tonnage réduit, du champ d'application de la Convention internationale de Londres, les dispositions de cet article sont néanmoins applicables si le navire transporte ou utilise pour sa propulsion des hydrocarbures ou mélanges d'hydrocarbures.

Toutefois, lorsque la puissance de l'appareil propulsif d'un navire autre qu'un navire-citerne est inférieure à un chiffre fixé par ordonnance souveraine, les peines portées à l'article premier sont réduites comme suit :

— Le capitaine est passible d'un emprisonnement de six jours à un mois et de l'amende prévue au chiffre 2 de l'article 26 du Code pénal, ou de l'une de ces deux peines seulement,

— Le propriétaire ou l'exploitant est passible d'un emprisonnement de six mois à trois ans et de l'amende prévue au chiffre 3 de l'article 26 du Code pénal.

En cas de récidive, outre l'application de l'article 40 dudit Code, le maximum de l'amende prévue au chiffre 3 de l'article 26 sera prononcé.

Article 3. Lorsqu'il y aura eu rejet d'hydrocarbures, ou de mélanges d'hydrocarbures dans les eaux intérieures ou dans la mer territoriale de Monaco, les peines prévues aux deux articles précédents seront prononcées, quel que soit le pavillon du navire, même si ce dernier est immatriculé dans un Etat non partie à la Convention internationale de Londres.

Article 4. Le capitaine d'un navire auquel s'applique l'article premier doit tenir le registre des hydrocarbures institué par l'article 9 de la Convention internationale de Londres; à défaut ou si le registre comporte des mentions sciemment inexactes, le capitaine est passible d'un emprisonnement de six jours à un mois et de l'amende prévue au chiffre 2 de l'article 26 du Code pénal ou de l'une de ces deux peines seulement.

Il encourt les mêmes peines s'il refuse de présenter le registre à toute requête des autorités compétentes ou s'il tente de s'opposer à ce qu'elles en prennent connaissance.

Article 5. Le capitaine d'un navire auquel s'applique l'article 2 doit tenir un registre des hydrocarbures dans les conditions fixées par une ordonnance souveraine; à défaut ou si le registre comporte des mentions sciemment inexactes, le capitaine est passible des peines portées à l'article précédent.

Il encourt les mêmes peines s'il refuse de présenter le registre à toute requête des autorités compétentes ou s'il tente de s'opposer à ce qu'elles en prennent connaissance.

Toutefois, les dispositions ci-dessus ne sont pas applicables aux navires autres que les navires-citernes dont la jauge brute est inférieure à 150 tonneaux.

Article 6. Il peut être interdit à tout navire dont le capitaine aura commis l'une des infractions prévues par la présente loi :

— Soit de naviguer pendant une durée de quinze jours à six mois, lorsque le navire bat pavillon monégasque;

— Soit d'user des ports de la Principauté pendant une durée de un mois à deux ans, lorsque le navire bat un pavillon autre que monégasque. S'il y a nouvelle infraction, même commise sous le commandement d'un autre capitaine, l'interdiction définitive peut être prononcée.

Article 7. Les infractions aux dispositions des articles 3 et 9 de la Convention internationale de Londres, à celles de la présente loi et aux mesures qui seront prises pour leur application seront constatées par les fonctionnaires des services de la marine, de la police maritime et des travaux publics concurremment avec les officiers de police judiciaire.

8. MOROCCO

[DAHIR PORTANT LOI No 1.73.211 DU 2 MARS 1973 FIXANT LA LIMITE DES EAUX TERRITORIALES ET DE LA ZONE DE PECHE EXCLUSIVE MAROCAINES, article 6][1]

9. NORWAY

ACT NO. 46 OF 16 JUNE 1972 CONCERNING MEASURES TO BE ADOPTED IN PURSUANCE OF THE INTERNATIONAL CONVENTION OF 29 NOVEMBER 1969 RELATING TO INTERVENTION ON THE HIGH SEAS IN CASES OF OIL POLLUTION CASUALTIES[2]

Section 1

The King may decide on the implementation of measures to be taken in pursuance of the International Convention adopted in Brussels on 29 November 1969 relating to Intervention on the High Seas in cases of Oil Pollution Casualties,[3] and may issue further administrative regulations in respect of such measures.

---

[1] *Supra* Division L, Subdivision A, chap. I, 14.

[2] English text provided by the Permanent Representative of Norway to the United Nations in a note verbale of 21 January 1974.

[3] Reproduced in ST/LEG/SER.B/16, pp. 439-447.

Section 2

This Act does not in any way restrict the right, pursuant to the law otherwise in force, to implement measures in Norwegian territorial waters to prevent or limit damage arising from oil pollution.

Section 3

This Act enters into force at such time as the King may decide.

10. OMAN

[MARINE POLLUTION CONTROL LAW] [1]

11. SINGAPORE

PREVENTION OF POLLUTION OF THE SEA ACT, 1971,[2] AS AMENDED
BY SECTION 17 OF THE CIVIL LIABILITY (OIL POLLUTION) ACT, 1973[3]

. . .

PART II. CRIMINAL LIABILITY FOR POLLUTING THE SEA

3. Discharge of oil into the sea

(1) If any oil or mixture containing oil is discharged from a Singapore ship into any part of the sea outside the territorial limits of Singapore, the owner, the agent or the master of such ship shall, subject to the provisions of this Act, be guilty of an offence under this Act and shall be liable on conviction to a fine of not less than five hundred dollars and not exceeding five hundred thousand dollars or to imprisonment for a term not exceeding two years or to both such fine and imprisonment.

. . .

4. Discharge of oil into Singapore waters

If any oil or mixture containing oil is discharged into Singapore waters from any vessel, or from any place on land, or from any apparatus used for transferring oil from or to any vessel (whether to or from a place on land or to or from another vessel):

(a) If the discharge is from a vessel, the owner, the master or the agent of the vessel; or

(b) If the discharge is from a place on land, the occupier of that place or if the discharge is caused by the act of another person who is in that place without the permission (express or implied) of the occupier, that person; or

---

[1] *Supra* Division I, Subdivision A, Chapter VII, 11.

[2] Reproduced in ST/LEG/SER.B/16, p. 224. Only the amended provisions are reproduced here.

[3] *Supra* Division I, Subdivision A, Chapter VII, 12.

(c) If the discharge is from appartus used for transferring oil from or to a vessel, the person in charge of the apparatus shall be guilty of an offence under this Act and shall be liable on conviction to a fine of not less than five hundred dollars and not more than five hundred thousand dollars or to imprisonment for a term not exceeding two years or to both such fine and imprisonment.

. . .

PART IV. MISCELLANEOUS PROVISIONS

13. Recovery of costs for removing refuse

(1) If any refuse, garbage, waste matter, substance of a dangerous or obnoxious nature or trade effluent is discharged or escapes from a vessel, the owner of the vessel shall be liable for the costs of any measure reasonably taken after the discharge or escape for the purpose of removing the same and for preventing or reducing any damage caused in Singapore by contamination resulting from the discharge or escape.

(2) Where the refuse, garbage, waste matter, substance of a dangerous or other obnoxious nature or trade effluent is discharged or escapes from two or more ships—

(a) The liability is incurred under this section by the owner of each of them; but

(b) The damage or cost for which each of the owners would be liable cannot reasonably be separated from that for which the other or others would be liable;

each of the owners shall be liable, jointly and severally with the other or others, for the whole of the damage or cost for which the owners together would be liable under this section.

14. Recovery of costs from operator or apparatus [Repealed]

15. Recovery of costs from occupier of land [Repealed]

. . .

17. Power to detain vessels

Notwithstanding any proceedings which may be instituted under section 4 or 6 of this Act, the Director or the Port Master may detain any vessel if the Director or the Port Master has reasonable cause to believe that any refuse, garbage, waste matter, substance of a dangerous or obnoxious nature or trade effluent has been discharged or has escaped from the vessel and that the owner of the vessel has incurred a liability under section 13 of this Act, and the vessel may be so detained until the owner of the vessel deposits with the Government or the Authority a sum of money or furnishes such security which would, in the opinion of the Director or the Port Master, be adequate to meet the owner's liability incurred under section 13 of this Act.

12. SWEDEN

(a) ACT NO. 1154 OF 17 DECEMBER 1971 TO PROHIBIT THE DISCHARGE (DUMPING) OF WASTE MATTER INTO WATER,[1] AS AMENDED IN 1972[2]

Article 1. Waste matter, whether solid, liquid or gaseous, may not be discharged (dumped) in the territorial sea of Sweden from a vessel, aircraft or other means of transport. Nor may such discharge be effected by a Swedish vessel or aircraft in the open sea. Waste matter intended to be discharged in the open sea may not be taken out of the country.

Article 2. This Act shall not apply to the discharge (dumping) of oil or oily mixtures as referred to in the Act (1972:275) concerning Measures to Prevent the Pollution of Water by Vessels[3] nor to waste matter produced through the operation of a vessel.

Article 3. The King, or such authority as the King may appoint, may permit derogations from article 1 if discharge (dumping) can be effected without adverse effects with respect to the protection of the environment. Conditions may be attached to such permission.

Should discharge (dumping) cause adverse effects which were not foreseen when the permission was granted, the authority which granted the permission may make regulations to remedy the adverse effects.

If conditions or regulations are disregarded, or if the adverse effects referred to in the second subparagraph cannot be remedied, the permission granted may be revoked.

Article 4. Supervision of the observance of this Act and of conditions laid down and regulations made under it shall be performed by such authority as the King may appoint.

The supervisory authority shall be entitled to receive, on demand, such information and such documents as may be required for the purpose of supervision.

For the purposes of supervision the authority shall have access to means of transport, premises or areas which are used in connexion with discharge (dumping) as aforesaid and shall be entitled to make investigations there.

Article 5. A fine or a sentence of not more than one year's imprisonment shall be imposed on any person who wilfully or through negligence

1. Acts in breach of article 1; or

2. Disregards conditions laid down or regulations made under article 3.

A person attempting to commit an act which is an offence under article 1 shall be answerable therefor under chapter 23 of the Criminal Code.

---

[1] *Swedish Code of Statutes,* 28 December 1971. Came into force on 1 January 1972.

[2] Amendment by the Act of 2 June 1972 to Amend the Act (1971:1154) to Prohibit the Discharge (Dumping) of Waste Matter into Water. The amending Act came into force on 15 June 1972. Swedish texts of the original Act and the amending Act provided by the Permanent Representative of Sweden to the United Nations in a note verbale of 13 March 1973. Translation by the Secretariat of the United Nations.

[3] *Infra (b).*

Article 6. A fine shall be imposed on any person who wilfully or through negligence

1. Fails to perform a duty incumbent upon him under article 4, second paragraph; or
2. Furnishes false information in cases as referred to in article 4, second paragraph, unless the act is punishable under the Criminal Code.

. . .

Article 8. The yield of an offence as referred to in article 5 shall be declared forfeit unless such declaration would be manifestly inequitable.

Property which has been used as a means of committing an offence as referred to in article 5 may be declared forfeit if so required for the purpose of preventing an offence or if special grounds therefor otherwise exist. The value of the property may be declared forfeit in place of the property itself.

. . .

(b) ACT NO. 275 OF 2 JUNE 1972 CONCERNING MEASURES TO PREVENT THE POLLUTION OF WATER BY VESSELS[1] AS AMENDED ON 17 DECEMBER 1973[2]

Prohibition of pollution by vessels

Article 1. Oil may not be discharged from a vessel in the territorial sea of Sweden. The outflow of oil from a vessel in the area of the territorial sea shall be prevented so far as is possible.

In the open sea what is stated in the first paragraph shall apply to tank vessels of a gross tonnage of not less than 150 register tons and to other vessels of a gross tonnage of not less than 500 register tons.

The King may ordain that the second paragraph shall likewise apply to vessels of a lesser gross tonnage than is specified in that paragraph.[3]

Article 2. Nothwithstanding article 1, second paragraph, the following may be discharged in the open sea:

1. An oily mixture from a vessel other than a tank vessel, on condition that

   The vessel is under way; that

   The mixture is never discharged at a rate greater than that corresponding to 60 litres of oil per nautical mile travelled by the vessel; that

[1] SFS 1972: 275, *Swedish Code of Statutes*, 15 June 1972. Came into force on 1 July 1972 and superseded Act No. 86 of 6 April 1956, reproduced in part in ST/LEG/SER.B/15, pp. 287-288. Swedish text provided by the Permanent Representative of Sweden to the United Nations in a note verbale of 13 March 1973. Translation by the Secretariat of the United Nations.

[2] Amendment by SFS 1973: 1201, *Swedish Code of Statutes*, 11 January 1974. Swedish text provided by the Permanent Representative of Sweden to the United Nations in a note verbale of 4 February 1974. Translation by the Secretariat of the United Nations.

[3] Royal Order No. 278 of 2 June 1972, *infra (e)*, paragraph 2.

The oil constitutes less than one ten-thousandth part of the mixture; and that

Discharge is effected as far from the nearest land as the circumstances allow.

2. Bilge water containing oil which has run out or leaked from a space occupied by the propelling machinery of a tank vessel, if the water is discharged in conformity with the requirements specified under paragraph 1;

3. Oil from a tank vessel other than oil as referred to under paragraph 2, on condition that

The vessel is under way; that

The oil is never discharged at a rate greater than that corresponding to 60 litres of oil per nautical mile travelled by the vessel; that

The aggregate quantity of oil that is discharged during a voyage in ballast does not exceed one fifteen-thousandth part of the vessel's load capacity; and that

The vessel is not less than 50 nautical miles from the nearest land.

The distance from the nearest land shall be computed from the baseline from which the territorial sea is measured, save as the King may prescribe otherwise.

Article 3. The term "oil" as used in this Act means crude oil, lubricating oil, diesel oil and other fuel oil in accordance with provisions to be enacted by the King.

The term "oily mixture" means any mixture that contains oil.

Article 4. In the matter of waste matter, other than oil, produced through the operation of a vessel, the King or such authority as the King may appoint may make regulations for the purpose of preventing pollution of the water.

Equipment of vessels, etc.

Article 5. The King or such authority as the King may appoint may make regulations concerning the construction and equipment of vessels for the purpose of preventing or limiting the pollution of water and concerning certificate showing that such regulations are complied with.

Article 6. The King may prescribe that a Swedish vessel may not be used for marine navigation if it is not constructed or not equipped in conformity with regulations as referred to in article 5 or if it lacks a certificate as referred to in that article.

The King or such authority as the King may appoint may prescribe that a vessel lacking a certificate as prescribed in article 5 or an equivalent document made out by a competent foreign authority may not enter or be in a part of Sweden's territorial sea or a loading or unloading point at sea which is under Swedish control.

Article 7. The King or such authority as the King may appoint may either prescribe that a Swedish vessel may not carry water in a fuel tank or may prescribe conditions governing such carriage.

Oil log

Article 8. On a Swedish tank vessel and on any other Swedish vessel of a gross tonnage of not less than 500 register tons using oil as its propellant fuel the master shall keep or supervise the keeping of an oil log complying with regulations to be made by the King or by such authority as the King may appoint. The King may ordain that an oil log shall likewise be kept on other Swedish vessels.

The oil log shall be kept readily accessible for inspection and shall be preserved for not less than three years after the date of the last entry.

Dumping stations

Article 9. In such public harbour as the King may designate there shall be an installation or arrangement for receiving oil residue and oily mixtures from vessels.

The King or such authority as the King may appoint shall make regulations concerning an installation or arrangement as referred to in the first paragraph.

Article 10. If the owner of a harbour fails to install or operate an installation or arrangement as referred to in article 9, the King or such authority as the King may appoint may install or operate the installation or arrangement at the owner's expense.

Special measures against pollution

Article 11. If oil or some other harmful substance comes out of a vessel or if there are reasonable grounds for fearing that this will happen, the National Administration of Shipping and Navigation *(Sjöfartsverket)* and such other authority as the King may appoint may notify the prohibitions and orders required for preventing or limiting the discharge. Such a decision may relate to:

1. A prohibition on the vessel's departure or continued voyage;
2. A prohibition on the use of particular equipment;
3. A requirement that the vessel shall follow a prescribed route;
4. A requirement that the vessel shall put in at or depart from a particular harbour or other place;
5. A requirement concerning the vessel's movement or operation;
6. A requirement that oil or some other harmful substance shall be lightered;
7. A requirement that loading, unloading, lightering or bunkering shall be discontinued; or
8. A requirement concerning some other measure to prevent or limit the discharge of oil or other harmful substances.

If a person fails to take within the time prescribed action incumbent upon him under a decision as referred to in the first paragraph, or if he cannot be notified of the decision without such delay as would jeopardize achievement of the purpose of the decision, the authority may cause the action to be taken at the cost of the vessel's owner or operator. The same shall likewise apply where, a decision having been notified in conformity with the first paragraph hereof, immediate action is required but cannot be expected to be taken by the party referred to in the decision.

The King or such authority as the King may appoint shall make regulations concerning what is to be regarded as harmful within the meaning of the first paragraph.

Article 12. A decision as referred to in article 11, first paragraph, shall contain particulars of the action required to be taken and of the time within which the action is required to have been taken. The decision shall be communicated to the master and the operator forthwith and if the decision relates to a foreign vessel, to the embassy or consulate of the foreign vessel's home country.

Article 12 a. Where those provisions of the Act (1973: 1198) concerning liability for oil damage at sea[1] which relate to an insurance obligation or an obligation to give security are not complied with in respect of a particular vessel, such authority as may be appointed by the King may prohibit the vessel from putting in at or departing from a particular harbour or off-shore terminal or, in the case of a Swedish vessel, may prohibit the vessel from continuing its voyage. The provisions of article 12, second sentence, shall apply to such prohibition.

Article 13. An authority which pursuant to article 11, first paragraph, or article 12 *a* has notified a prohibition on a vessel's departure or continued voyage shall, if the vessel is in the territorial sea of Sweden, report the decision forthwith to the police, customs and pilotage authorities. It shall be the duty of the said authorities to take such action as may be required to prevent the vessel's departure or continued voyage.

Where the prohibition applies to a Swedish vessel which is in the territorial sea of a foreign country, it shall be duty of the master to deliver the vessel's document of nationality to the Swedish consul at that consul's request.

Article 14. If a decision as referred to in article 11, first paragraph, has been notified in the National Administration of Shipping and Navigation by a person other than the head of the section responsible for matters relating to safety on vessels (the Director, Safety at Sea Section) or has been notified by another authority, it shall be submitted to the Director, Safety at Sea Section, forthwith.

Supervision

Article 15. In order to determine the origin of polluting oil, the police authority or the authority that is empowered to notify a decision under article 11, first paragraph, may take samples of oil on a vessel and for that purpose interrupt the vessel's voyage, unless material inconvenience would be caused by so doing.

---

[1] *Infra (c).*

Article 16. Supervision of the observance of the provisions of articles 5 and 7 concerning the construction and equipment of the vessel shall be performed in conformity with the Safety on Vessel Act (1965: 719)[1] in the matter of a vessel which is subject to regular supervision under that Act.

Article 17. The policy authority, the supervisory authority under the Safety on Vessels Act (1965: 719), the Customs authority and such authority as the King may appoint may inspect the oil log of a Swedish vessel. In the case of a foreign vessel that is in the territorial sea of Sweden the same shall apply in the matter of the oil log or of equivalent records thereto.

In the territorial sea of a foreign country the master of a Swedish vessel shall be under a duty to allow the proper foreign authority to inspect the oil log.

Article 18. In other respects supervision of the observance of this Act and of regulations made pursuant to the Act shall be the duty of such authority as the King may appoint.

Article 19. No proceedings may be instituted against a decision which, as provided in article 14, must be submitted to the Director, Safety at Sea Section. Proceedings against a decision notified by the Shipping and Navigation Administration through the Director, Safety at Sea Section, in a matter as referred to in article 11, first paragraph, or against a decision in a matter as referred to in article 12 *a,* shall be instituted in the Revenue Court *(kammarrätt)* by way of an appeal.

Proceedings against any other decision under this Act which was made by an authority other than a central administrative authority shall be instituted before the Shipping and Navigation Administration by way of an appeal.

Proceedings against a decision under this Act made by the Shipping and Navigation Administration or by some other authority, being a central administrative authority, in a matter other than as referred to in article 11, first paragraph, or in article 12 *a* shall be instituted before the King by way of an appeal.

Article 20. A decision under this Act shall be complied with forthwith unless otherwise provided in the decision. In the case of a decision which must be submitted to the Director, Safety at Sea Section, the Director may order that the decision shall remain in abeyance until further notice.

Provisions concerning liability etc.

Article 21. A fine or a sentence of not more than one year's imprisonment shall be imposed on any person who wilfully or through negligence acts in breach of

1. Article 1, unless the act is punishable under the Criminal Code;
2. A regulation as referred to in article 4; or
3. A prohibition or requirement as referred to in article 11, first paragraph, or a prohibition as referred to in article 12 *a.*

---

[1] Reproduced in part in ST/LEG/SER.B/15, pp. 182-185.

Article 22. Where the master or the officer to whom the master has assigned responsibility for supervision over the manipulation of oil or waste matter on board has failed in the supervision required to prevent the oil or waste matter from coming out of the vessel, in breach of this Act or of a regulation made under the Act, he shall be fined or be sentenced to not more than one year's imprisonment.

Article 23. A master who fails to keep an oil log in conformity with article 8 or who makes an incorrect entry in such a log shall be fined or be sentenced to not more than six months' imprisonment.

A master who acts in breach of a regulation made pursuant to article 6 or article 7 shall be fined.

Article 24. If oil or waste matter is discharged in breach of this Act or of a regulation made pursuant to the Act; or

If a prohibition as referred to in article 6 or article 7 is infringed; or

If a prohibition under article 11, first paragraph, is infringed or a requirement under that paragraph is disregarded, or a prohibition under article 12 *a* is infringed;

Then the operator or the owner of the vessel shall be judged as though he himself had performed the act if he had or should have had knowledge of the act.

Article 25. Cases concerning liability for offences as referred to in this Act may be heard by a district court *(tingsrätt)* that is the court having jurisdiction in accordance with chapter 19 of the Code of Judicial Procedure or articles 336 and 338 of the Maritime Act (1891: 35).[1]

Other provisions

Article 26. This Act shall apply to State-owned vessels not used in commercial service only to the extent prescribed by the King.

(c) ACT NO. 1198 OF 17 DECEMBER 1973 CONCERNING LIABILITY FOR OIL DAMAGE AT SEA[2]

Introductory provisions

Article 1. For the purposes of this Act:

"Oil damage" means, on the one hand, damage caused outside the ship by contamination resulting from oil from the ship and, on the other hand, the costs of preventive measures and damage caused by such measures;

"Incident" means any occurrence, or series of occurrences having the same origin, which causes oil damage;

---

[1] Partially reproduced in ST/LEG/SER.B/5 and Add.1, pp. 162-163. For the texts of articles 336 and 338 of the Maritime Act (1891: 35), see René Rodière, *Lois Maritimes Nordiques,* Institut de Droit comparé de Paris, 1972, at pages 314 and 318.

[2] SFS 1973: 1198, *Swedish Code of Statutes,* 11 January 1974. Swedish text provided by the Permanent Representative of Sweden to the United Nations in a note verbale of 4 February 1974. Translation by the Secretariat of the United Nations.

"Preventive measures" means any reasonable measures taken after an incident has occurred to prevent or minimize oil pollution damage;

"Ship's owner" means the person registered as the owner of the ship or, in the absence of registration, the person owning the ship; however, in the case of a ship owned by a State and operated by a company which in that State is registered as the ship's operator, "owner" shall mean such company;

"Franc" means a unit of value consisting of 65½ milligrams of gold of millesimal fineness nine hundred;

"Ship's tonnage" means the net tonnage of the ship with the addition of the amount deducted from the gross tonnage on account of engine room space for the purpose of ascertaining the net tonnage, or, in the case of a ship which cannot be ·measured in accordance with the normal rules of tonnage measurement, 40 per cent of the weight in tons of oil which the ship is capable of carrying;

"Liability Convention" means the Convention on Civil Liability for Oil Pollution Damage, adopted at Brussels on 29 November 1969;[1]

"Convention State" means a State which has acceded to the Liability Convention.

For the purposes of this Act, "ship" includes any seaborne craft of any type whatsoever.

Article 2. This Act shall apply to oil damage caused in Sweden or in another Convention State by a ship carrying oil in bulk as cargo (bulk cargo) and to the costs of preventive measures taken to prevent or minimize such damage in Sweden or another Convention State.

The applicability of the Act to warships and certain other ships owned by a State and to ships not carrying oil in bulk as cargo shall be governed by the provisions of article 22.

Compensation for measures in respect of oil damage shall be made in accordance with this Act even where an obligation to take the measures existed by virtue of a law or other legislative instrument.

This Act shall apply irrespective of any other provisions in force regarding the applicable law.

The provisions of this Act shall not apply in so far as their application would be incompatible with Sweden's obligations under international agreements.

Damages

Article 3. Compensation for oil damage shall be made by the ship's owner even though neither the owner nor any person for whom he is responsible was the author of the damage. Where an incident consists of a series of occurrences, liability shall attach to the person who was the ship's owner on the date of the first such occurrence.

---

[1] ST/LEG/SER.B/16, pp. 447-454.

No liability shall, however, attach to the owner if he proves that the damage:

1. Resulted from an act of war, hostilities, civil war, insurrection or a natural phenomenon of an exceptional, inevitable and irresistible character; or

2. Was wholly caused by an act done with intent to cause damage by a third party; or

3. Was wholly caused by the negligence or other wrongful act of any Swedish or foreign authority responsible for the maintenance of lights or other navigational aids in the exercise of that function.

In the event of the person who suffered the damage being also at fault or in the event of two or more ship's owners being jointly and severally liable, the provisions of chapter 5, articles 5 and 6, of the Damages Act (1972: 207) shall apply.

Article 4. No claim for compensation for oil damage under the compensation provisions of this Act shall be made against a ship's owner otherwise than in accordance with the Act.

A claim as referred to in the first paragraph may not be made against the operator of a ship who is not the owner thereof, nor against a charterer or any other person operating the ship in the place of the operator, nor against a shipper, consignee, cargo owner, pilot or any other person who, without being a member of the crew, performs work in the service of the ship. Where damage has occurred in connexion with the salvage of a ship or the cargo or in connexion with preventive measures, the foregoing provision shall apply also to the salvager or to the person carrying out the said measures unless the salvage operations or the preventive measures were undertaken contrary to the prohibition of a government authority or—if undertaken otherwise than by a government authority—despite the express and justified prohibition of the ship's owner or the cargo owner.

A claim as referred to in the first paragraph may likewise not be made against a person who is an employee of the ship's owner or of a person referred to in the second paragraph.

No claim for the recovery of amounts paid in compensation for oil damage under this Act may be brought against a pilot, a salvager or a person who has undertaken preventive measures, or against an employee as referred to in the third paragraph, except where the person against whom the claim is made caused the damage either wilfully or through gross negligence or where the claim is made against a salvager or a person who took preventive measures and such salvager or person violated a prohibition as referred to in the second paragraph, second sentence.

Article 5. A ship's owner shall be entitled to limit his liability under this Act in respect of any one incident to an amount of 2,000 francs for each ton of the ship's tonnage. However, such liability shall not in any event exceed 210 million francs. Such limitation shall not be allowed in the case of interest or compensation for court costs.

Where a demand is made for compliance with Sweden's obligations in relation to a State which has acceded to the Convention relating to the

234

Limitation of the Liability of Owners of Seagoing Ships, adopted at Brussels on 10 October 1957, the right of the owner to limit his liability shall be governed by the provisions of chapter 10 of the Maritime Act (1891:35, p. 1). The amount of liability shall be determined in accordance with article 235 of the Maritime Act.

If the incident occurred as a result of the actual fault or negligence of the ship's owner, he shall not be entitled to avail himself of the limitation of liability unless he committed such fault or was guilty of such negligence while acting as master or crew member of the ship.

Article 6. For the purpose of availing himself of the benefit of limitation provided for in article 5, first paragraph, the owner, his insurer or some other person acting on the owner's behalf shall, in accordance with this Act or with the applicable law of another Convention State, constitute a fund for the total sum representing the limit of his liability. The sum shall be converted into kronor at the official rate of exchange in effect on the date on which the fund is constituted.

The fund, in the case of Sweden, shall be constituted with the court in which action is brought under article 18. The fund can be constituted either by depositing the sum or by giving security that is acceptable to the court.

Where any person wishes to constitute a fund, the court, at the request of such person, shall render a decision as soon as possible on the size of the sum representing the limit of liability. The decision shall remain in effect until countermanded. Upon the expiry of the time-limit specified in article 7, first paragraph, the court shall make a final determination regarding the size of the sum.

An action against a decision on the sum representing the limit of liability or concerning the question of the acceptability of the security shall be brought separately.

Regulations concerning the constitution of a fund and the administration and distribution of the fund shall be made by the King.

Article 7. If a fund is constituted in Sweden, the court with which the fund is constituted shall, by notification, urge the claimants to present their claims in writing within a specified period which shall not be less than six months and to request that a specified amount be set aside for their account. The notification shall be inserted in the Official Gazette and in one or more newspapers in the part of the country where oil damage resulting from the incident in question occurred. If oil damage occurred in another Convention State, the notification shall also be inserted in the official gazette of such State. All known claimants shall be separately notified by letter.

A claimant who fails to present his claim within the period specified in the notification may not make a claim against the fund unless he either did not have, or could not be expected to have had, knowledge of the notification. Notwithstanding the foregoing provision, a claim as aforesaid may be made if the damage on the basis of which the claim is made occurred after the expiry of the time-limit or within such a short time before the expiry thereof that the claimant's failure to present his claim within the prescribed period cannot be construed as negligence on his part. The court may decide that a specified amount shall be set aside to cover such claims which have not been presented before the expiry of the time-limit but which can nevertheless be made against the fund. This amount shall be distributed when all such claims have been decided or when, as provided in article 10, no further actions for compensation may be brought.

Where the amount of established claims exceeds the aggregate amount of compensation payable under article 5, first paragraph, the amount of all such claims shall be reduced in the same proportion.

If a fund is constituted in Sweden and there is reason to believe that the amount of established claims will exceed the aggregate amount of compensation pertaining to the ship, the court may order that, provisionally, only a specified proportion of the amount of compensation shall be paid.

The fund shall be distributed even if the owner, as provided in article 5, third paragraph, is not entitled to limit his liability.

Article 8. If before the fund is distributed any person has paid compensation for oil damage, that person shall, up to the amount he has paid, acquire by subrogation the rights which the person so compensated would have enjoyed under this Act or the applicable law of another Convention State.

Where the owner or any other person establishes that he may be compelled to pay at a later date any such amount of compensation with regard to which he would have enjoyed a right of subrogation under the first paragraph had the compensation been paid before the fund was distributed, the court may order that a sum be provisionally set aside to enable him at such later date to enforce his claim against the fund.

Claims in respect of expenses incurred or sacrifices made by the owner voluntarily in connexion with preventive measures shall rank equally with other claims against the fund.

Article 9. Where a fund is constituted in accordance with article 6 and the owner is entitled to limit his liability, no claim for compensation may be brought against any other assets of the owner if such claim can be brought against the fund.

Where in a case as referred to in the first paragraph other property belonging to the owner has been arrested or attached in respect of a claim for compensation which can be brought against the fund, the said property shall be released. Any security furnished by the owner to avoid such arrest or attachment shall be returned to him.

Where a fund is constituted in another Convention State, the provisions of the first and second paragraphs shall apply only if the claimant has access to the court or authority administering the fund and the fund is actually available in respect of his claim.

Article 10. Rights of compensation under this Act shall be extinguished unless an action is brought within three years from the date when the damage occurred. However, in no case shall an action be brought after six years from the date of the incident which caused the damage or, where the incident consisted of a series of occurrences, from the date of the first such occurrence.

Article 11. The right to compensation from the International Oil Pollution Compensation Fund shall be governed by separate provisions.

Insurance

Article 12. The owner of a Swedish ship carrying more than 2,000 tons of oil in bulk as cargo shall be required to obtain and maintain insurance or give other adequate security to cover his liability under this Act or the applicable law of another Convention State within the limits prescribed by article 5, first paragraph. Such requirement shall not, however, be incumbent on the State.

The insurance or security referred to in the first paragraph must be approved by the King or an authority designated by the King.

If the requirements of the first paragraph have been complied with by the owner, the authority designated by the King shall issue a certificate attesting that this has been done. In the case of a ship owned by a State, the authority designated by the King shall issue a certificate stating that the ship is owned by the Swedish State and that its liability is covered within the limits prescribed by article 5, first paragraph.

The form of the certificate referred to in the third paragraph shall be determined by the King. The certificate shall be carried by the ship.

Article 13. Insurance or other adequate security covering the owner's liability under this Act or the applicable law of another Convention State within the limits prescribed by article 5, first or second paragraph, shall be in force in respect of a foreign ship entering or leaving a Swedish port, or arriving at or leaving an off-shore terminal in the Swedish territorial sea, if the ship actually carried more than 2,000 tons of oil in bulk as cargo. This provision shall not apply to a ship owned by a foreign State.

The ship shall carry a certificate showing that the insurance or security referred to in the first paragraph is in force. A ship owned by a foreign State shall carry a certificate stating that the ship is owned by that State and that the ship's liability is covered within the limits prescribed by article 5, first or second paragraph.

Regulations concerning the certificate referred to in the second paragraph shall be made by the King or an authority designated by the King.

Article 14. In so far as a person entitled to compensation is concerned, insurance as referred to in article 12 or 13 shall confer the right to bring a claim for compensation directly against the insurer.

The insurer may, however, avail himself of the defences which the owner himself would have been entitled to invoke or of the defence that the damage resulted from the wilful misconduct of the owner. The liability of the insurer shall in no case exceed the limits of liability prescribed in article 5, first or second paragraph.

An insurer shall not avail himself of any defence exceeding what is provided in the second paragraph by invoking against a person other than the owner a defence which he might have been entitled to invoke against the owner.

Article 15. Save as otherwise stipulated by the insurer, the insurance shall cover the liability incurred by the ship's owner under this Act or the applicable law or another Convention State.

Article 16. The provisions of articles 14 and 15 in respect of insurance shall apply, *mutatis mutandis*, to any other kind of security referred to in article 12 or 13.

Jurisdiction of courts and related matters

Article 17. Actions for compensation under this Act may be brought in Sweden only if oil pollution damage has occurred in Sweden or preventive measures have been taken to prevent or minimize such damage in Sweden.

Where a Swedish court has jurisdiction under the first paragraph, actions for compensation in respect of other oil damage resulting from the same incident may also be brought in Sweden.

Article 18. An action for compensation for oil damage which, according to article 17, may be brought in Sweden shall be brought in the maritime court situated nearest to the place where the damage occurred.

Where actions for compensation for damage that was caused by the same incident have been brought in two or more courts, one of such courts shall be designated to deal with all the actions.

Where a fund is constituted in Sweden under article 6 and the owner or insurer against whom actions for compensation have been brought in Sweden or in another Convention State is entitled to limit his liability, the court in which the fund is constituted shall determine all matters relating to the distribution of the sum representing the limit of liability.

Article 19. Where a judgement in an action for compensation for oil damage has been given in another Convention State and the courts of that State are competent under the Liability Convention in respect of actions to which the judgement relates, the judgement, when it has become final and enforceable in the State in which it was given, shall, upon application and save as otherwise provided in article 9 or article 18, third paragraph, be enforced in Sweden without any further determination of the case that was decided by the judgement. There shall be no obligation under this provision for the enforcement of a foreign judgement if the sum representing the limit of liability of the ship's owner would thereby be exceeded.

Applications for enforcement shall be made to the Svea court of appeal. An application shall be accompanied by:

1. The original or a certified true copy of the judgement;
2. A statement by the competent authority of the State in which the judgement was given that the judgement relates to compensation under the Liability Convention and that the judgement has become final and enforceable in the said State.

The aforementioned documents shall be certified as having been issued by a competent authority. The certification shall be issued by the Swedish Embassy or a Swedish consul or by the chief of the Department of Justice of the State in which the judgement was given. A relevant document which is drafted in a foreign language other than Danish or Norwegian shall be accompanied by a Swedish translation. The translation shall be notarized by a diplomatic or consular officer or by a Swedish notary public.

An application for enforcement shall not be approved without the other party to the proceedings having had an opportunity to express an opinion on the application.

If the application is approved, the judgement shall be enforced in the same manner as a Swedish judgement which has become final unless the Supreme Court, acting on an appeal from the judgement of the court of appeals, determines otherwise.

Article 20. Where, in accordance with the provisions of the Liability Convention, a fund is constituted in another Convention State under law of that State and the owner or insurer against whom an action or compensation has, under this Act, been brought in a Swedish court is entitled to limit his liability, the court, in its judgement in the action for compensation, shall order that judgement may not be enforced until after matters relating to the distribution of the fund have been determined in the foreign State according to the law of that State.

Penal provisions

Article 21. A ship's owner who wilfully or through negligence disregards the provisions of this Act concerning the obligation to obtain and maintain insurance or to give security shall be liable to a fine or to imprisonment for a term of not more than six months.

The same penalty shall apply to a ship operator who allows a ship to be used for navigation even though he was, or ought to have been, aware that the obligation in respect of insurance or the giving of security prescribed by this Act had not been complied with. For the purposes of this provision, an operator shall be deemed to include a person managing the ship's operation on the operator's behalf and the ship's master.

Failure to carry on board a ship, while it is being used for navigation, the certificate prescribed by article 12 or 13 shall be punishable by a fine, which shall be levied against the master of the ship.

Other provisions

Article 22. The provisions of this Act shall not apply to oil damage caused by warships or by other ships which, at the time of the incident, are owned or operated by a State and are being used only on government non-commercial service. Where, however, such a ship has caused oil pollution damage in Sweden, or where preventive measures have been taken to prevent or minimize such damage in Sweden, the provisions of article 1, article 2, third paragraph, and articles 3 to 5, 10 and 18 shall apply.

Where oil pollution damage has been caused in Sweden by a ship which, at the time of the incident, was not carrying oil in bulk as cargo, or where preventive measures have been taken to prevent or minimize such damage in Sweden, the provisions of article 1, article 2, third and fifth paragraphs, and articles 3, 10 and 18 shall apply. In such cases, the provisions of chapter 10 of the Maritime Act (1891: 35, p. 1) shall apply to the owner's right to limit his liability. The amount of liability shall be determined in accordance with the provisions of article 235 of the Maritime Act.

(d) ACT NO. 1199 of 17 DECEMBER CONCERNING COMPENSATION FROM THE INTERNATIONAL OIL POLLUTION COMPENSATION FUND[1]

Article 1. The provisions of articles 1-13 of the Convention on the Establishment of an International Fund for Compensation for Oil Pollution Damage, adopted at Brussels on 18 December 1971,[2] shall, in so far as they do not exclusively regulate the mutual obligations of the contracting States and subject to what is hereinafter provided, be given effect as Swedish law.

Article 2. Amounts paid by the Fund as compensation under article 4 or as indemnification under article 5 may be recovered by the Fund from the persons referred to in article 4, fourth paragraph, of the Act (1973: 1198) concerning liability for oil damage at sea[3] only under the conditions specified in the said article 4, fourth paragraph. Furthermore, such amounts may be recovered by the Fund from persons other than the owner or his guarantor only to the extent compatible with article 25, first paragraph, of the Act (1927: 77) concerning insurance contracts.

Article 3. An action for compensation for pollution damage which, under article 7, first or third paragraph, may be brought before a court in Sweden shall be brought before a court which, under article 18 of the Act (1973: 1198) concerning liability for oil damage at sea,[3] has jurisdictional competence over an action against the ship's owner in respect of the same incident.

Article 4. The notification referred to in article 7, sixth paragraph, shall be governed, *mutatis mutandis,* by those provisions of chapter 14, articles 12 and 13, of the Code of Judicial Procedure which relate to notice of legal proceedings.

Article 5. Enforcement under article 8 of a judgement given in an action for compensation for pollution damage shall be governed, *mutatis mutandis,* by the provisions of article 19 of the Act (1973: 1198) concerning liability for oil damage at sea.[4]

---

[1] SFS 1973: 1199, *Swedish Code of Statutes,* 11 January 1974. Swedish text provided by the Permanent Representative of Sweden to the United Nations in a note verbale of 4 February 1974. Translation by the Secretariat of the United Nations.

[2] *Infra* Part II, Division I, Subdivision A, 2.

[3] *Supra (c).*

[4] *Supra (c).*

(e) ROYAL ORDER NO. 278 OF 2 JUNE 1972 CONCERNING MEASURES
TO PREVENT THE POLLUTION OF WATER BY VESSELS[1]

Introductory provisions

Paragraph 1. The term "diesel oil" as used in the Act of 2 June 1972
(1972: 275)[2] concerning measures to prevent the pollution of water by
vessels, article 3, means diesel oil of which at least 50 per cent by volume
remains after distillation at a temperature not exceeding 340°C. when tested
by A.S.T.M. Standard Method D.86/59.

Prohibition of pollution by vessels

Paragraph 2. The provisions of the Act (1972: 275)[2] concerning
measures to prevent the pollution of water by vessels, article 1, second
paragraph, shall also apply in the case of a Swedish tank vessel having a gross
tonnage of less than 150 register tons and in the case of other Swedish vessels
having a gross tonnage of less than 500 register tons and an engine power of
not less than 400 horse-power effective. The National Administration of
Shipping and Navigation *(Sjöfartsverket)* may allow derogations from this
provision.

Paragraph 3. Off the north-east coast of Australia the distance from the
nearest land, as referred to in the Act (1972: 275) concerning measures to
prevent the pollution of water by vessels, article 2,[3] is computed from a line
drawn between the following points; that is to say:

South latitude	East longitude
11° 00'	142° 08'
10° 35'	141° 55'
10° 00'	142° 00'
9° 10'	143° 52'
9° 00'	144° 30'
13° 00'	144° 00'
15° 00'	146° 00'
18° 00'	147° 00'
21° 00'	153° 00'
24° 42'	153° 15'

---

[1] SFS 1972: 278, *Swedish Code of Statutes*, 15 June 1972. As provided in the
Statute, this Order came into force on 1 July 1972. It superseded Order No. 191 of
2 May 1958, reproduced in ST/LEG/SER.B/15, pp. 513-515. Swedish text provided by
the Permanent Representative of Sweden to the United Nations in a note verbale of 13
March 1973. Translation by the Secretariat of the United Nations.

[2] *Supra (b)*.

[3] *Ibid.* Until such time as the amendments of 1969 to the International Convention
of 1954 for the Prevention of Pollution of the Sea by Oil have entered into force, Act
No. 275 of 2 June 1972, article 2, shall apply in respect of a foreign vessel only if the
vessel's home country is a country which already applies the amended rules of the
Convention. Otherwise, discharge of oil from foreign vessels is subject, as appropriate, to
article 2 of Act No. 86 of 6 April 1956 (reproduced in ST/LEG/SER.B/15, pp. 287-288)
and of paragraph 1 of the annex to Order No. 191 of 2 May 1958 (*ibid.*, pp. 513-515).

Paragraph 4. Regulations under the Act (1972: 275) concerning measures to prevent the pollution of water by vessels, article 4, in respect of prohibiting the release of waste matter, other than oil, produced through the operation of a vessel shall be made by the Commander-in-Chief of the Navy in the case of warships and by the State Environment Protection Agency in the case of other vessels. Both authorities shall consult with each other in this matter and with the State Social Welfare Board and the Shipping and Navigation Administration.[1]

Equipment of vessels, etc.

Paragraph 5. Regulations under the Act (1972: 275) concerning measures to prevent the pollution of water by vessels, article 5, in respect of the construction and equipment of vessels and in respect of the certificate referred to in article VI a[2] of the 1954 International Convention for the Prevention of Pollution of the Sea by Oil shall be made by the Shipping and Navigation Administration in consultation with the State Environment Protection Agency.

The Shipping and Navigation Administration shall furnish to the Inter-Governmental Maritime Consultative Organization (IMCO) the information which, under item 2.3.4 of annex C to the Convention for the Prevention of Pollution of the Sea by Oil, is to be supplied by the government administration.

Paragraph 6. A Swedish vessel may be used for marine navigation only if it is constructed and equipped in conformity with the regulations made pursuant to the Act (1972: 275) concerning measures to prevent the pollution of water by vessels, article 5. A Swedish tank vessel having a gross tonnage of not less than 150 register tons may not be used for marine navigation if it lacks a certificate as prescribed in that article.

Paragraph 7. A tank vessel having a gross tonnage of not less than 150 register tons may not enter or be in such part of Sweden's territorial sea or such loading or unloading point at sea under Swedish control as the National Administration of Shipping and Navigation may designate if the vessel lacks a certificate as prescribed in the Act (1972: 275) concerning measures to prevent the pollution of water by vessels, article 5, or an equivalent document made out by a competent foreign authority. The National Administration of Shipping and Navigation may allow derogations from the prohibition if it is shown in some other way that the vessel fulfils the requirements of the

---

[1] Until such time as regulations by the commander-in-chief of the Swedish Navy and by the State Environment Protection Agency, both as referred to in this paragraph, have entered into force, the status of regulations pursuant to article 4 of Act No. 275 of 2 June 1972 shall attach to decisions by tne county administration *(länsstyrelsen)* which have been made pursuant to paragraph 3 of Order No. 191 of 2 May 1958 (ST/LEG/SER.B/15, pp. 513-515).

[2] Adopted by the Seventh Assembly of IMCO in Resolution A.246 (VII) of 15 October 1971.

242

International Convention of 1954 for the Prevention of Pollution of the Sea by Oil,[1] article VI a,[2] or if any special grounds exist.

Paragraph 8. A Swedish vessel may not carry water in a fuel tank. The National Administration of Shipping and Navigation may allow derogations from the prohibition.

Oil record book

Paragraph 9. Regulations under the Act (1972: 275) concerning measures to prevent the pollution of water by vessels, article 8, first paragraph, first sentence, in respect of the oil record book shall be made by the Shipping and Navigation Administration in consultation with the Customs Administration.

During the period that the oil log book must be preserved after the date of the last entry, it shall be kept on board the vessel or by whoever was the vessel's operator or owner at the time of the last entry.

Dumping stations

Paragraph 10. Installations for the reception of oil residues and oily mixtures shall be provided in the public harbour of the ports of Luleå, Stockholm, Norrköping, Malmö, Helsingborg and Göteborg.

Arrangements of a simpler type for the reception of limited amounts of oil residues shall be provided in the public harbour of the ports of Piteå, Skellefteå, Umeå, Härnösand, Sundsvall, Hudiksvall, Söderhamn, Gävle, Södertälje, Oskarshamn, Kalmar, Visby, Slite, Karlskrona, Trelleborg, Landskrona, Falkenberg, Lidköping, Karlstad, Kristinehamn, Västerås and Köping.

Regulations concerning the installations and arrangements referred to in the first and second paragraphs shall be made by the Shipping and Navigation Administration.

Special measures for the prevention of pollution

Paragraph 11. A decision under the Act (1972: 275) concerning measures to prevent the pollution of water by vessels, article 11, first paragraph, may be made by the Customs Administration if, in view of the need for prompt action to prevent, minimize or combat pollution, it is not possible to wait for a decision from the Shipping and Navigation Administration.

Paragraph 12. The regulations referred to in article 11, third paragraph, of the Act (1972: 275) concerning measures to prevent the pollution of water by vessels shall be made by the State Environment Protection Agency.

Supervision

Paragraph 13. To the extent that nothing is prescribed to the contrary, supervision of the observance of the Act (1972: 275) concerning measures to

[1] United Nations, *Treaty Series,* vol. 327, p. 3. The Convention as amended in 1962 is reproduced in ST/LEG/SER.B/15, pp. 787-799.

[2] Adopted by the Seventh Assembly of IMCO in Resolution A.246 (VII) of 15 October 1971.

prevent the pollution of water by vessels and of regulations made pursuant to the Act shall be performed by the commander-in-chief of the Swedish Navy in respect of naval vessels and by the National Administration of Shipping and Navigation in respect of other vessels.

Paragraph 14. Instructions for the exercise of supervision over the oil record books shall be issued by the Shipping and Navigation Administration in consultation with the National Police Administration and the Customs Administration.

Other provisions

Paragraph 15. The Act (1972: 275) concerning measures to prevent the pollution of water by vessels shall, except as regards its articles 5-8, 11-14, 16 and 17, likewise apply to a Swedish State-owned vessel not commercially operated.

Paragraph 16. Any regulation made pursuant to the Act (1972: 275) concerning measures to prevent the pollution of water by vessels or to this Order other than a regulation made by the commander-in-chief of the Swedish Navy shall be included in the publication *Underrättelser för Sjöfarande* ("Swedish Shipping Gazette").

(f) ORDER OF 6 JUNE 1972 BY THE NATIONAL ADMINISTRATION OF SHIPPING AND NAVIGATION CONCERNING MEASURES TO PREVENT THE POLLUTION OF WATER BY VESSELS[1]

Pursuant to the Royal Order (1972:278)[2] concerning measures to prevent the pollution of water by vessels, the National Administration of Shipping and Navigation has deemed it proper to direct as follows.

Paragraph 1. Where nothing is indicated to the contrary, this Order applies to Swedish vessels and foreign vessels in the territorial sea of Sweden and to Swedish vessels outside the territorial sea of Sweden.

Paragraph 2. A Swedish tank vessel having a gross tonnage of not less than 150 register tons shall conform to the regulations governing the arrangement of tanks and the limitation of their size contained in the International Convention in force for the Prevention of Pollution of the Sea by Oil, the text of which is annexed to this Order as *annex 1*.[3]

Paragraph 3. Except where it is manifestly unnecessary, a vessel shall be equipped with a bilge-water separator and with arrangements for the collection of oil, e.g. troughs or cofferdams under day's-supply tanks, separators, filters, cocks, shore connexions and other arrangements from which oil may leak. Such an arrangement in an engine space or pump room

---

[1] *Gazette of the National Administration of Shipping and Navigation,* Series A, No. 8, 30 June 1972. Came into force on 1 July 1972. Swedish text provided by the Permanent Representative of Sweden to the United Nations in a note verbale of 13 March 1973. Translation by the Secretariat of the United Nations.

[2] *Supra (e).*

[3] Annex I is not reproduced. For the text of the Convention as amended in 1962, see ST/LEG/SER.B/15, pp. 787-799.

shall be drained to a collecting tank for waste oil and oily water. The collecting tank shall be equipped with devices preventing oil-gas from escaping from the tank and thereby creating an explosion risk or other danger.

The oil drain outlet from the bilge-water separator shall be connected to the waste-oil collecting tank.

Arrangements shall be made to ensure that waste oil and oily water collected in gutters in the engine compartment and pump room are drained through a bilge-water separator to a collecting tank.

Collecting tanks for waste oil and oily water shall be equipped with internationally standardized connexions for discharging the tanks into reception (dumping) installations in harbours. The connexions shall meet the requirements laid down in IMCO resolution A 234 (VII), the text of which is annexed to this Order as *annex 2*.[1]

. . .

Paragraph 5. The Royal Order (1972:278) concerning measures to prevent the pollution of water by vessels states in its paragraph 6 that a Swedish vessel not fulfilling the requirements of paragraphs 3 and 4 may not be used for marine navigation.

Where a foreign vessel fails to meet the requirements of paragraphs 2, 3 and 4, the National Administration of Shipping and Navigation may require special safety measures to be taken on the vessel.

. . .

Paragraph 7. The duty to keep an oil log on a vessel is prescribed in the Act (1972:275) concerning Measures to Prevent the Pollution of Water by Vessels,[2] article 8.

The oil log on a tank vessel shall be kept in accordance with form A and on other vessels in accordance with form B, which are annexed to this Order as *annex 4* and *annex 5*[3] respectively.

Paragraph 8. An entry in the oil log shall be made tank by tank whenever one of the following measures is taken on the vessel:

(a) On a tank vessel:

1. Loading a cargo of oil;
2. Shifting of oil cargo *en route;*
3. Discharging of oil cargo;
4. Ballasting of cargo tanks;
5. Cleaning of cargo tanks;
6. Discharge of polluted ballast;
7. Discharge of water from slop tanks;
8. Disposal of oil residues;

---

[1] Annex 2 is not reproduced.

[2] *Supra (b).*

[3] Annexes 4 and 5 are not reproduced.

9. Discharge overboard of bilge-water containing oil that has collected in the engine space (pump room included) during a stay in port, and routine discharge at sea of bilge-water containing oil if it has not been recorded in some other appropriate log.

(b) On a vessel other than a tank vessel:

1. Ballasting or cleaning of fuel tanks;
2. Discharge of polluted ballast or spill water from tanks as referred to under 1;
3. Disposal of oil residues;
4. Discharge overboard of bilge-water containing oil that has collected in the engine space during a stay in port, and routine discharge at sea of bilge-water containing oil if it has not been recorded in some other appropriate log.

In the discharge or outflow of oil or oily mixtures for the purpose of preventing damage to the vessel or cargo or of saving human lives or because of damage to the vessel or unavoidable leakage, the circumstances surrounding and grounds for the discharge or outflow shall be recorded in the oil log.

. . .

13. UNITED KINGDOM OF GREAT BRITAIN AND NORTHERN IRELAND

(a) [DUMPING AT SEA ACT 1974][1]

(b) MERCHANT SHIPPING ACT 1974[2]

PART I

The International Oil Pollution Compensation Fund

1. (1) In this Part of this Act—

(a) The "Liability Convention" means the International Convention on Civil Liability for Oil Pollution Damage opened for signature in Brussels on 29 November 1969;[3]

(b) The "Fund Convention" means the International Convention on the Establishment of an International Fund for Compensation for Oil Pollution Damage opened for signature in Brussels on 18 December 1971;[4]

(c) "the Fund" means the International Fund established by the Fund Convention; and

(d) "Fund Convention country" means a country in respect of which the Fund Convention is in force.

---

[1] *Supra,* Division I, Subdivision A, Chapter VII, 16 *(b).*

[2] Chapter 43, 31 July 1974. As provided in section 24 (2), the Act shall come into force on such day as the Secretary of State may appoint by order made by statutory instrument.

[3] Reproduced in ST/LEG/SER.B/16, pp. 447-454.

[4] *Infra,* Part II, Division I, Subdivision A.3.

(2) If Her Majesty by Order in Council declares that any State specified in the Order is a party to the Fund Convention in respect of any country so specified the Order shall, while in force, be conclusive evidence that that State is a party to the Convention in respect of that country.

(3) In this Part of this Act, unless the context otherwise requires—

the "Act of 1971" means the Merchant Shipping (Oil Pollution) Act 1971;[1]

"damage" includes loss;

"discharge or escape", in relation to pollution damage, means the discharge or escape of oil carried by the ship;

"guarantor" means any person providing insurance or other financial security to cover the owner's liability of the kind described in section 10 of the Act of 1971;

"oil", except in sections 2 and 3, means persistent hydrocarbon mineral oil;

"owner" means the person or persons registered as the owner of the ship or, in the absence of registration, the person or persons owning the ship, except that in relation to a ship owned by a State which is operated by a person registered as the ship's operator, it means the person registered as its operator;

"pollution damage" means damage caused outside the ship carrying oil by contamination resulting from the escape or discharge of oil from the ship, wherever the escape or discharge may occur, and includes the cost of preventive measures and further damage caused by preventive measures;

"preventive measures" means any reasonable measures taken by any person after the occurrence to prevent or minimize pollution damage;

"ship" means any sea-going vessel and any seaborne craft of any type whatsoever carrying oil in bulk as cargo.

(4) For the purposes of this Part of this Act a ship's tonnage shall be the net tonnage of the ship with the addition of the amount deducted from the gross tonnage on account of engine room space for the purpose of ascertaining the net tonnage.

If the ship cannot be measured in accordance with the normal rules, its tonnage shall be deemed to be 40 per cent of the weight in tons (of 2240 lbs.) of oil which the ship is capable of carrying.

(5) For the purposes of this Part of this Act, where more than one discharge or escape results from the same occurrence or from a series of occurrences having the same origin, they shall be treated as one.

(6) In this Part of this Act a franc shall be taken to be a unit of 65½ milligrammes of gold of millesimal fineness 900.

(7) The Secretary of State may from time to time by order made by statutory instrument specify the amounts which for the purposes of this Part of this Act are to be taken as equivalent to any specified number of francs.

---

[1] Partially reproduced in ST/LEG/SER.B/16, pp. 260-263.

Contributions to Fund

2. (1) Contributions shall be payable to the Fund in respect of oil carried by sea to ports or terminal installations in the United Kingdom.

(2) Subsection (1) above applies whether or not the oil is being imported, and applies even if contributions are payable in respect of carriage of the same oil on a previous voyage.

(3) Contributions shall also be payable to the Fund in respect of oil when first received in any installation in the United Kingdom after having been carried by sea and discharged in a port or terminal installation in a country which is not a Fund Convention country.

(4) The person liable to pay contributions is—

(a) In the case of oil which is being imported into the United Kingdom, the importer; and

(b) Otherwise, the person by whom the oil is received.

(5) A person shall not be liable to make contributions in respect of the oil importer or received by him in any year if the oil so imported or received in the year does not exceed 150,000 tonnes.

(6) For the purpose of subsection (5) above—

(a) All the members of a group of companies shall be treated as a single person; and

(b) Any two or more companies which have been amalgamated into a single company shall be treated as the same person as that single company.

(7) The contributions payable by a person for any year shall—

(a) Be of such amount as may be determined by the Assembly of the Fund under Articles 11 and 12 of the Fund Convention and notified to him by the Fund;

(b) Be payable in such instalments, becoming due at such times, as may be so notified to him;

and if any amount due from him remains unpaid after the date on which it became due, it shall from then on bear interest, at a rate determined from time to time by the said Assembly, until it is paid.

(8) The Secretary of State may by regulations contained in a statutory instrument impose on persons who are or may be liable to pay contributions under this section obligations to give security for payment to the Secretary of State, or to the Fund.

Regulations under this subsection—

(a) May contain such supplemental or incidental provisions as appear to the Secretary of State expedient;

(b) May impose penalties for contravention of the regulations punishable on summary conviction by a fine not exceeding £400, or such lower limit as may be specified in the regulations; and

(c) Shall be subject to annulment in pursuance of a resolution of either House of Parliament.

(9) In this and the next following section, unless the context otherwise requires—

"company" means a body incorporated under the law of the United Kingdom, or of any other country;

"group" in relation to companies, means a holding company and its subsidiaries as defined by section 154 of the Companies Act 1948 (or for companies in Northern Ireland section 148 of the Companies Act (Northern Ireland) 1960), subject, in the case of a company incorporated outside the United Kingdom, to any necessary modifications of those definitions;

"importer" means the person by whom or on whose behalf the oil in question is entered for customs purposes on importation, and "import" shall be construed accordingly;

"oil" means crude oil and fuel oil, and

(a) "crude oil" means any liquid hydrocarbon mixture occurring naturally in the earth whether or not treated to render it suitable for transportation; and includes—

   (i) Crude oils from which distillate fractions have been removed; and
   (ii) Crude oils to which distillate fractions have been added;

(b) "fuel oil" means heavy distillates or residues from crude oil or blends of such materials intended for use as a fuel for the production of heat or power of a quality equivalent to the "American Society for Testing and Materials' Specification for Number Four Fuel Oil (Designation D 396-69)", or heavier.

"terminal installation" means any site for the storage of oil in bulk which is capable of receiving oil from waterborne transporation, including any facility situated offshore and linked to any such site.

(10) In this section "sea" does not include any waters on the landward side of the baselines from which the territorial sea of the United Kingdom is measured.

3. (1) For the purpose of transmitting to the Fund the names and addresses of the persons who under the last preceding section are liable to make contributions to the Fund for any year, and the quantity of oil in respect of which they are so liable, the Secretary of State may by notice require any person engaged in producing, treating, distributing or transporting oil to furnish such information as may be specified in the notice.

(2) A notice under this section may require a company to give such information as may be required to ascertain whether its liability is affected by subsection (6) of the last preceding section.

(3) A notice under this section may specify the way in which, and the time within which, it is to be complied with.

(4) In proceedings by the Fund against any person to recover any amount due under the last preceding section, particulars contained in any list transmitted by the Secretary of State to the Fund shall, so far as those particulars are based on information obtained under this section, be admissible as evidence of the facts stated in the list; and so far as particulars which are so admissible are based on information given by the person against

whom the proceedings are brought, those particulars shall be presumed to be accurate until the contrary is proved.

(5) If a person discloses any information which has been furnished to or obtained by him under this section, or in connexion with the execution of this section, he shall, unless the disclosure is made—

(a) With the consent of the person from whom the information was obtained; or

(b) In connexion with the execution of this section; or

(c) For the purposes of any legal proceedings arising out of this section or of any report of such proceedings,

be liable on summary conviction to a fine not exceeding £400.

(6) A person who—

(a) Refuses or wilfully neglects to comply with a notice under this section; or

(b) In furnishing any information in compliance with a notice under this section makes any statement which he knows to be false in a material particular, or recklessly makes any statement which is false in a material particular,

shall be liable—

(i) On summary conviction to a fine not exceeding £400; and

(ii) On conviction on indictment to a fine, or to imprisonment for a term not exceeding twelve months, or to both.

Compensation for persons suffering pollution damage

4. (1) The Fund shall be liable for pollution damage in the United Kingdom if the person suffering the damage has been unable to obtain full compensation under section 1 of the Act of 1971 (which gives effect to the Liability Convention)—

(a) Because the discharge or escape causing the damage—

(i) Resulted from an exceptional, inevitable and irresistible phenomenon; or

(ii) Was due wholly to anything done or left undone by another person (not being a servant or agent or the owner) with intent to do damage; or

(iii) Was due wholly to the negligence or wrongful act of a government or other authority in exercising its function of maintaining lights or other navigational aids for the maintenance of which it was responsible,

(and because liability is accordingly wholly displaced by section 2 of the Act of 1971), or

(b) Because the owner or guarantor liable for the damage cannot meet his obligations in full; or

(c) Because the damage exceeds the liability under section 1 of the Act of 1971 as limited—

(i) By section 4 of the Act of 1971; or

(ii) (where the said section 4 is displaced by section 9 of this Act) by section 503 of the Merchant Shipping Act 1894.[1]

(2) Subsection (1) above shall apply with the substitution for the words "the United Kingdom" of the words "A Fund Convention country" where—

(a) The headquarters of the Fund is for the time being in the United Kingdom, and proceedings under the Liability Convention for compensation for the pollution damage have been brought in a country which is not a Fund Convention country; or

(b) The incident has caused pollution damage both in the United Kingdom and in another Fund Convention country, and proceedings under the Liability Convention for compensation for the pollution damage have been brought in a country which is not a Fund Convention country or in the United Kingdom.

(3) Where the incident has caused pollution damage both in the United Kingdom and in another country in respect of which the Liability Convention is in force, references in this section to the provisions of the Act of 1971 shall include references to the corresponding provisions of the law of any country giving effect to the Liability Convention.

(4) Where proceedings under the Liability Convention for compensation for pollution damage have been brought in a country which is not a Fund Convention country and the Fund is liable for that pollution damage by virtue of subsection (2) *(a)* above, references in this section to the provisions of the Act of 1971 shall be treated as references to the corresponding provisions of the law of the country in which those proceedings were brought.

(5) For the purposes of this section an owner or guarantor is to be treated as incapable of meeting his obligations if the obligations have not been met after all reasonable steps to pursue the legal remedies available have been taken.

(6) Expenses reasonably incurred, and sacrifices reasonably made, by the owner voluntarily to prevent or minimize pollution damage shall be treated as pollution damage for the purposes of this section, and accordingly he shall be in the same position with respect to claims against the Fund under this section as if he had a claim in respect of liability under section 1 of the Act of 1971.

(7) The Fund shall incur no obligation under this section if—

(a) It proves that the pollution damage—

(i) Resulted from an act of war, hostilities, civil war or insurrection; or

(ii) Was caused by oil which has escaped or been discharged from a warship or other ship owned or operated by a State and used, at the

---

[1] Reproduced in part in ST/LEG/SER.B/5 and Add.1, pp. 180-186.

time of the occurrence, only on Government non-commercial service; or

(b) The claimant cannot prove that the damage resulted from an occurrence involving a ship identified by him, or involving two or more ships one of which is identified by him.

(8) If the Fund proves that the pollution damage resulted wholly or partly—

(a) From an act or omission done with intent to cause damage by the person who suffered the damage; or

(b) From the negligence of that person,

the Fund may be exonerated wholly or partly from its obligation to pay compensation to that person:

Provided that this subsection shall not apply to a claim in respect of expenses or sacrifices made voluntarily to prevent or minimize pollution damage.

(9) Where the liability under section 1 of the Act of 1971 is limited to any extent by subsection (5) of that section (contributory negligence), the Fund shall be exonerated to the same extent.

(10) The Fund's liability under this section shall be subject to the limits imposed by paragraphs 4, 5 and 6 of Article 4 of the Fund Convention which impose an overall liability on the liabilities of the owner and of the Fund, and the text of which is set out in Schedule 1 to this Act.

(11) Evidence of any instrument issued by any organ of the Fund or of any document in the custody of the Fund, or any entry in or extract from such a document, may be given in any legal proceedings by the production of a copy certified as a true copy by an official of the Fund; and any document purporting to be such a copy shall be received in evidence without proof of the official position or handwriting of the person signing the certificate.

(12) For the purpose of giving effect to the said provisions of Article 4 of the Fund Convention a Court giving judgement against the Fund in proceedings under this section shall notify the Fund, and—

(a) No steps shall be taken to enforce the judgement unless and until the court gives leave to enforce it;

(b) That leave shall not be given unless and until the Fund notifies the court either that the amount of the claim is not to be reduced under the said provisions of Article 4 of the Fund Convention, or that it is to be reduced to a specified amount; and

(c) In the latter case the judgement shall be enforceable only for the reduced amount.

Indemnification of shipowners

5. (1) Where a liability is incurred under section 1 of the Act of 1971 in respect of a ship registered in a Fund Convention country the Fund shall indemnify the owner and his guarantor for that portion of the aggregate amount of the liability which—

252

(a) Is in excess of an amount equivalent to 1500 francs for each ton of the ship's tonnage or of an amount of 125 million francs, whichever is the less; and

(b) Is not in excess of an amount equivalent to 2000 francs for each ton of the said tonnage or an amount of 210 million francs, whichever is the less.

(2) Where proceedings under the Liability Convention for compensation for pollution damage have been brought in a country which is not a Fund Convention country (but is a country in respect of which the Liability Convention is in force), and either—

(a) The incident has caused pollution damage in the United Kingdom (as well as in that other country); or

(b) The headquarters of the Fund is for the time being in the United Kingdom,

subsection (1) above shall apply with the omission of the words "under section 1 of the Act of 1971".

(3) The Fund shall not incur an obligation under this section where the pollution damage resulted from the wilful misconduct of the owner.

(4) In proceedings to enforce the Fund's obligation under this section the court may exonerate the Fund wholly or partly if it is proved that, as a result of the actual fault or privity of the owner—

(a) The ship did not comply with such requirements as the Secretary of State may by order prescribe for the purposes of this section; and

(b) The occurrence or damage was caused wholly or partly by that non-compliance.

(5) The requirements referred to in subsection (4) above are such requirements as appear to the Secretary of State appropriate to implement the provisions of—

(a) Article 5 (3) of the Fund Convention (marine safety conventions); and

(b) Article 5 (4) of the Fund Convention (which enables the Assembly of the Fund to substitute new conventions).

(6) An order made under subsection (4) above—

(a) May be varied or revoked by a subsequent order so made; or

(b) May contain such transitional or other supplemental provisions as appear to the Secretary of State to be expedient; and

(c) Shall be contained in a statutory instrument subject to annulment in pursuance of a resolution of either House of Parliament.

(7) Expenses reasonably incurred, and sacrifices reasonably made, by the owner voluntarily to prevent or minimize the pollution damage shall be treated as included in the owner's liability for the purposes of this section.

PART II

Oil tankers

10. (1) In this Part of this Act "the Conventions" means—

(a) Article VI *bis* and Annex C of the International Convention, signed in London on 12 May 1954, for the Prevention of Pollution of the Sea by Oil, which Article and Annex were added on 15 October 1971 by resolution of the Assembly of the Inter-governmental Maritime Consultative Organization;[1] and

(b) Any other international convention, or amendment of an international convention, which relates in whole or in part to prevention of pollution of the sea by oil, and which has been signed for the United Kingdom before the passing of this Act, or later.

(2) In this Part of this Act "Convention country" means a country in respect of which a State is a party to any of the Conventions.

(3) If Her Majesty by Order in Council declares that any State specified in the Order is a party to any of the Conventions in respect of any country so specified, the Order shall, while in force, be conclusive evidence that that State is a party to the Convention in respect of that country.

(4) In this Part of this Act—

"oil tanker" means a ship which is contructed or adapted primarily to carry oil in bulk in its cargo spaces (whether or not it is also so constructed or adapted as to be capable of carrying other cargoes in those spaces),

"United Kingdom oil tanker" means an oil tanker registered in the United Kingdom,

"oil" means crude oil, fuel oil (including diesel oil) and lubricating oil,

"port" includes an off-shore terminal, and references to entering or leaving a port shall include references to using or ceasing to use an off-shore terminal.

11. (1) For the purpose of preventing pollution of the sea by oil, the Secretary of State may make rules (called "oil tanker construction rules") prescribing requirements to be complied with by United Kingdom oil tankers in respect of their design and construction.

(2) The said rules may include such requirements as appear to the Secretary of State to implement any of the provisions of the Conventions, so far as they relate to prevention of pollution of the sea by oil.

This subsection applies whether or not the said provisions are for the time being binding on Her Majesty's Government in the United Kingdom.

(3) Oil tanker construction rules may provide—

(a) For oil tankers to be surveyed and inspected with a view to determining whether they comply with the rules;

(b) For a tanker which on a survey is found to comply to be issued with a certificate called a "tanker construction certificate"; and

---

[1] Adopted by the Seventh Assembly of IMCO in Resolution A.246 (VII) of 15 October 1971.

(c) For a tanker which is not required to comply with the rules to be issued with a certificate called a "tanker exemption certificate".

(4) Schedule 2 to this Act shall have effect for supplementing this Part of this Act.

(5) It is hereby declared that the oil tankers to which rules under this section may be applied include those designed or constructed before the rules come into force, and that the following provisions of this Part of this Act apply whether the oil tanker in question was designed or constructed before or after the relevant requirements as to design or construction came into force.

(6) Oil tanker construction rules shall be contained in a statutory instrument subject to annulment in pursuance of a resolution of either House of Parliament.

12. (1) No oil tanker shall proceed, or attempt to proceed, to sea unless—

(a) It is a certificated oil tanker (within the meaning of Schedule 3 to this Act); or

(b) It is not registered in the United Kingdom; and—

(i) If it were a United Kingdom oil tanker, it would qualify for the issue of a tanker exemption certificate; or

(ii) Its gross tonnage is less than 150 tons; or

(c) The Secretary of State has issued it with leave to sail.

(2) Where an application is made for leave to sail to be issued to an oil tanker, then—

(a) If the tanker is registered in the United Kingdom, the Secretary of State may issue it with leave to sail where he considers it appropriate to do so;

(b) If the tanker is not registered in the United Kingdom, the Secretary of State—

(i) Shall issue it with leave to sail if he is satisfied that it would qualify for the issue of a tanker construction certfificate if it were a United Kingdom oil tanker; and

(ii) May, if he is not so satisfied, issue it with leave to sail where he considers it appropriate to do so.

(3) Leave to sail issued under paragraph *(a)* or *(b)* (ii) of subsection (2) above may be issued subject to conditions imposed with a view to preventing or limiting the danger of oil pollution, including—

(a) Conditions as to the cargo with which the tanker may sail;

(b) A condition that the tanker sails only to a specified port in the United Kingdom or elsewhere.

(4) Subject to subsection (5) below, if—

(a) An oil tanker proceeds, or attempts to proceed, to sea in contravention of subsection (1) above; or

(b) Leave to sail having been issued to an oil tanker under this section subject to conditions, it proceeds to sea but the conditions are not complied with,

the owner and master of the tanker shall each be liable on summary conviction to a fine of not more than £10,000, or on conviction on indictment to a fine.

(5) In proceedings under subsection (4) above, it shall be a defence to prove that in order—

(a) To ensure the safety of the oil tanker; or

(b) To reduce the risk of damage to any other vessel or property,

it was necessary for the tanker to proceed to sea in contravention of subsection (1) above or, as the case may be, without complying with the conditions mentioned in paragraph *(b)* of section (4).

In this section "damage" does not include damage caused by contamination resulting from the escape or discharge of oil from a tanker.

13. (1) If it appears to the Secretary of State that an oil tanker is not certificated (within the meaning of Schedule 3 to this Act) he may direct the oil tanker—

(a) Not to enter any port in the United Kingdom (or not to enter one or more specified ports in the United Kingdom); or

(b) Not to enter all or any ports in the United Kingdom except subject to specified conditions.

(2) A direction may be given under this section in respect of an oil tanker which is for the time being in a port in the United Kingdom, so as to apply after it leaves that port.

(3) Directions under this section shall be addressed to the master or owner of the tanker, or to both, and may be communicated by any means which appear to the Secretary of State suitable for the purpose.

(4) Subject to subsection (5) below, if an oil tanker enters a port in the United Kingdom in contravention of a direction under this section, or without complying with any conditions imposed under this section, the owner and the master of the tanker shall each be liable on summary conviction to a fine not exceeding £15,000, or on conviction on indictment to a fine.

(5) In proceedings under subsection (4) above, it shall be a defence to prove that the tanker entered the port out of necessity due—

(a) To an emergency involving a threat to any person's life or the safety of the tanker; or

(b) To circumstances outside the control of the tanker's master.

PART III

Protection of shipping and trading interests

14. (1) The Secretary of State may exercise the powers conferred by this section if he is satisfied that a foreign government, or any agency or

authority of a foreign government, have adopted, or propose to adopt, measures or practices concerning or affecting the carriage of goods by sea which—

(a) Are damaging or threaten to damage the shipping or trading interests of the United Kingdom; or

(b) Are damaging or threaten to damage the shipping or trading interests of another country, and the Secretary of State is satisfied that action under this section would be in fulfilment of the international obligations of Her Majesty's Government to that other country.

(2) The Secretary of State may by order make provision for requiring persons in the United Kingdom carrying on any trade or business to provide the Secretary of State with all such information as he may require for the purpose of enabling him—

(a) To determine what further action to take under this section; and

(b) To ensure compliance with any orders or directions made or given under this section.

(3) The Secretary of State may by order provide for—

(a) Regulating the carriage of goods in ships and the rates which may or must be charged for carrying them;

(b) Regulating the admission and departure of ships to and from United Kingdom ports, the cargoes they may carry, and the loading or unloading of cargoes;

(c) Regulating the making and implementation of agreements (including charter-parties) whose subject matter relates directly or indirectly to the carriage of goods by sea, and requiring such agreements to be subject to the Secretary of State's approval in such cases as he may specify;

(d) Imposing charges in respect of ships which enter United Kingdom ports to load or unload cargo.

(4) In a case falling within subsection (1) *(a)* above, an order under subsection (3) above shall specify the measures or practices which in the opinion of the Secretary of State are damaging or threaten to damage shipping or trading interests of the United Kingdom.

(5) An order under this section may authorize the Secretary of State to give directions to any person for the purposes of the order.

Provided that this subsection shall not apply for the purpose of recovering charges imposed under subsection (3) *(d)* above.

(6) Any order or direction made or given under this section—

(a) May be either general or special, and may be subject to such conditions or exceptions as the Secretary of State specifies (including conditions and exceptions operating by reference to the giving or withholding of his approval for any course of action);

(b) May be in terms that require compliance either generally or only in specified cases;

(c) May be varied or revoked by a subsequent order, or as the case may be, a subsequent direction, so made or given,

and an order made pursuant to this section shall be contained in a statutory instrument.

(7) Before the Secretary of State makes an order under this section he shall consult such representatives of the shipping or trading interests of the United Kingdom, and such other persons, as appear to him appropriate.

(8) If a person discloses any information which has been furnished to or obtained by him under this section, or in connexion with the execution of this section, he shall, unless the disclosure is made—

(a) With the consent of the person from whom the information was obtained; or

(b) In connexion with the execution of this section; or

(c) For the purposes of any legal proceedings arising out of this section or of any report of such proceedings,

be liable on summary conviction to a fine not exceeding £400.

(9) A person who—

(a) Refuses or wilfully neglects to furnish any information which he is required to furnish under this section; or

(b) In furnishing any such information makes any statement which he knows to be false in a material particular, or recklessly makes any statement which is false in a material particular,

shall be liable on summary conviction to a fine not exceeding £400.

(10) A person who wilfully contravenes or fails to comply with any provision of an order or direction made or given pursuant to this section, other than a provision requiring him to give any information, shall be liable—

(a) On summary conviction to a fine of not more then £5,000;

(b) On conviction on indictment to a fine;

and where the order or direction requires anything to be done, or not to be done, by, to or on a ship, and the requirement is not complied with, the owner and master of the ship are each to be regarded as wilfully failing to comply, without prejudice to the liability of anyone else.

(11) In this section "foreign government" means the government of any country outside the United Kingdom; and references to ships are to ships of any registration.

(12) Schedule 4 to this Act shall have effect for supplementing this section, which in that Schedule is called "the principal section".

15. (1) No order shall be made in exercise of the powers conferred by subsection (3) of the last preceding section unless—

(a) A draft has been approved by resolution of each House of Parliament; or

(b) It is declared in the order that it appears to the Secretary of State that by reason of urgency it is necessary to make the order without a draft having been so approved.

(2) An order made in exercise of the powers conferred by the said subsection (3) without a draft having been approved by resolution of each House of Parliament shall cease to have effect at the expiration of a period of 28 days beginning with the date on which it was made unless before the expiration of that period it has been approved by resolution of each House of Parliament, but without prejudice to anything previously done, or to the making of a new order.

In reckoning for the purposes of this subsection any period of 28 days, no account shall be taken of any period during which Parliament is dissolved or prorogued or duing which both Houses are adjourned for more than four days.

(3) An order under the last preceding section which is not made in exercise of the powers conferred by subsection (3) of that section shall be subject to annulment in pursuance of a resolution of either House of Parliament.

(4) If an order under that section recites that it is not made in exercise of the powers conferred by the said subsection (3), the recital shall be conclusive.

PART IV

Submersible apparatus

16. (1) This Part of this Act applies to any submersible or supporting apparatus—

(a) Operated within waters which are in the United Kingdom or which are adjacent thereto and within the seaward limits of territorial waters; or

(b) Launched or operated from, or comprising, a ship registered in the United Kingdom or a British ship of a specified description (being a British ship which is not registered in the United Kingdom).

(2) In this section—

"apparatus" includes any vessel, vehicle or hovercraft, any structure, any diving plant or equipment and any other form of equipment;

"specified" means specified in regulations made by the Secretary of State for the purposes of this section,

"submersible apparatus" means any apparatus used, or designed for use, in supporting human life on or under the bed of any waters or elsewhere under the surface of any waters, and

"supporting apparatus" means any apparatus used or designed for use, in connexion with the operation of any submersible apparatus.

17. (1) The Secretary of State may make regulations—

(a) For the safety of submersible and supporting apparatus;

(b) For the prevention of accidents in or near submersible or supporting apparatus;

(c) For the safety, health and welfare of persons on or in submersible and supporting apparatus;

(d) For prohibiting or otherwise restricting the operation of any submersible apparatus except in accordance with the conditions of a licence granted under the regulations; and

(e) For the registration of submersible apparatus.

(2) Regulations made under this section shall be contained in a statutory instrument subject to annulment in pursuance of a resolution of either House of Parliament.

(3) Schedule 5 to this Act shall have effect for supplementing the provisions of this section.

SCHEDULES

SCHEDULE 1. OVERALL LIMIT ON LIABILITY OF FUND

Article 4—paragraphs 4, 5 and 6

4. *(a)* Except as otherwise provided in sub-paragraph *(b)* of this paragraph, the aggregate amount of compensation payable by the Fund under this Article shall in respect of any one incident be limited, so that the total sum of that amount and the amount of compensation actually paid under the Liability Convention for pollution damage caused in the territory of the Contracting States, including any sums in respect of which the Fund is under an obligation to indemnify the owner pursuant to Article 5, paragraph 1, of this Convention, shall not exceed 450 million francs.

(b) The aggregate amount of compensation payable by the Fund under this Article for pollution damage resulting from a natural phenomenon of an exceptional, inevitable and irresistible character shall not exceed 450 million francs.

5. Where the amount of established claims against the Fund exceeds the aggregate amount of compensation payable under paragraph 4, the amount available shall be distributed in such a manner that the proportion between any established claim and the amount of compensation actually recovered by the claimant under the Liability Convention and this Convention shall be the same for all claimants.

6. The Assembly of the Fund (hereinafter referred to as "the Assembly") may, having regard to the experience of incidents which have occurred and in particular the amount of damage resulting therefrom and to changes in the monetary values, decide that the amount of 450 million francs referred to in paragraph 4, sub-paragraph *(a)* and *(b)*, shall be changed; provided, however, that this amount shall in no case exceed 900 million francs or be lower than 450 million francs. The changed amount shall apply to incidents which occur after the date of the decision effecting the change.

SCHEDULE 2. OIL TANKERS

Surveys, inspections and certificates

1. (1) Oil tanker construction rules may provide for any surveys or inspections under the rules to be undertaken, and certificates to be issued, in such circumstances as may be specified in the rules, by persons appointed by such organizations as may be authorized for the purpose by the Secretary of State.

(2) Sub-paragraph (1) above shall have effect notwithstanding section 86 of the Merchant Shipping Act 1894 (which requires certain surveys and measurements to be carried out by officers of the Secretary of State).

(3) The rules may apply any of the following provisions of the Merchant Shipping Act 1894 with such exceptions or modifications as may be prescribed by the rules, that is—

(a) Section 272(2) (surveyor to deliver declaration of survey to owner);

(b) Section 273 (owner to deliver declaration to Secretary of State);

(c) Section 275 (appeal to court of survey);

(d) Section 276 and sections 278 to 281 (provisions about certificates);

(e) Section 282 (forgery of certificate or declaration of survey).

Duty to notify alterations

2. (1) The rules may require the owner of a United Kingdom oil tanker to notify the Secretary of State of any alteration to the tanker which may affect the question of its qualification or continued qualification for a tanker construction certificate or a tanker exemption certificate.

(2) If any person contravenes the rules by failing to notify such an alteration, he shall be guilty of an offence and liable on summary conviction to a fine not exceeding £1,000.

Clearance of outgoing tanker

3. (1) Before a certificated oil tanker proceeds to sea, the master of the tanker shall produce the certificate to the officer of customs from whom a clearance for the ship is demanded.

(2) Before any oil tanker which is not certificated proceeds to sea, the master of the tanker shall produce to the officer of customs from whom a clearance for the ship is demanded evidence to the satisfaction of the officer that the departure will not be in contravention of section 12 of this Act.

(3) A clearance shall not be granted, and the tanker may be detained, until the certificate or other evidence is so produced.

Inspection of foreign tanker

4. (1) For the purpose of determining whether an oil tanker not registered in the United Kingdom is certificated, or whether, if it were a United Kingdom oil tanker, it would qualify for the issue of a tanker construction certificate or a tanker exemption certificate, a competent officer may at all reasonable times go on board the tanker and inspect any part of it, and call for the production of any document carried in the tanker.

(2) An officer exercising powers under this paragraph shall not unnecessarily detail or delay a tanker but may, if he considers it necessary in order to determine—

(a) Whether the tanker should be issued with leave to sail under section 12 of this Act, or whether leave to sail should be issued subject to any conditions under subsection (3) of that section; or

(b) Whether an order should be issued in respect of the tanker under section 13 of this Act,

require the tanker to be taken into dock for a survey of its hull, cargo-spaces or fuel-tanks.

(3) If any person obstructs an officer acting under this paragraph, or fails to comply with a requirement made under sub-paragraph (2) above, or fails to produce a document carried in the tanker when called on by the officer to produce it, he shall be guilty of an offence and liable on summary conviction to a fine of not more than £100.

(4) In this paragraph "competent officer" means an officer of the Secretary of State authorized by him to act thereunder.

(5) Nothing in this paragraph prejudices section 76 of the Merchant Shipping Act 1970 (general powers of inspection).

Offences

5. (1) Oil tanker construction rules may provide for the punishment of any contravention of or failure to comply with the rules by making a person liable on summary conviction to a fine not exceeding £100, or such lower limit as may be specified in the rules.

(2) This paragraph is without prejudice to liability for any offence against the rules for which a punishment is provided by some other provision of this Act.

Fees

6. Oil tanker construction rules—

(a) May, with the approval of the Treasury, prescribe the fees payable in respect of surveys and inspections carried out, and certificates issued, under the rules;

(b) Shall, subject to sub-paragraph *(c)* below, provide for all fees payable under the rules to be paid to the Secretary of State; and

(c) May, in the case of surveys and inspections carried out, and certificates issued, by persons appointed by organizations authorized under paragraph 1 above, provide for fees to be payable to those persons or organizations.

SCHEDULE 3. CERTIFICATED OIL TANKERS

1. In Part II of this Act a "certificated oil tanker" means one falling within paragraphs 2, 3 or 4 below.

2. An oil tanker is certificated if it is a United Kingdom oil tanker in respect of which a tanker construction certificate or a tanker exemption certificate is in force.

3. (1) An oil tanker registered in a Convention country (other than the United Kingdom) is certificated if a certificate corresponding to a tanker construction certificate or tanker exemption certificate duly issued under the law of that country is in force in respect of the tanker.

(2) The Secretary of State may by order in a statutory instrument declare that for the purposes of this paragraph a certificate of a kind specified in the order is one which corresponds to a tanker construction certificate or tanker exemption certificate, and is of a kind which is issued under the law of a Convention country so specified.

(3) An order under this paragraph shall, while the order is in force, be conclusive evidence of the facts stated in the order.

4. (1) An oil tanker is certificated if a certificate of a prescribed kind issued under the law of a country which is not a Convention country is in force as respects the oil tanker.

(2) In this paragraph "prescribed" means prescribed by order of the Secretary of State contained in a statutory instrument.

5. An order made under this Schedule may be varied or revoked by a subsequent order so made.

SCHEDULE 4. PROTECTION OF SHIPPING AND TRADING INTERESTS

Customs powers

1. (1) An order made under the principal section with the consent of the Commissioners of Customs and Excise may provide for the enforcement and execution of any order or direction under the principal section by officers of customs and excise.

(2) Officers of customs and excise acting under any provision made under sub-paragraph (1) above shall have power to enter any premises or vessel.

(3) Section 53 of the Customs and Excise Act 1952 (power to refuse or cancel clearance of ship or aircraft) shall apply as if the principal section and this Schedule were contained in that Act.

Orders imposing charges

2. (1) An order under subsection (3) *(d)* of the principal section—

(a) May apply to ships of any description specified in the order, and may apply in particular to ships registered in a specified country, or ships carrying specified goods or cargoes; and

(b) May contain such provisions as appear to the Secretary of State expedient to enable the Commissioners of Customs and Excise to collect any charge imposed by the order; and

(c) May apply any of the provisions of the customs Acts which relate to duties of customs, subject to any modifications or exceptions specified in the order.

(2) The charge so imposed may be a fixed amount, or may be an amount depending on the tonnage of the ship.

(3) Any such charge shall be payable to the Secretary of State.

Criminal proceedings

3. A person shall not be guilty of an offence against any provision contained in or having effect under the principal section or this Schedule by reason only of something done by that person wholly outside the area of the United Kingdom unless that person is a British subject or a company incorporated under the law of any part of the United Kingdom.

Interpretation

4. In the principal section "port" includes an off-shore terminal, and references to entering or leaving a port shall include references to using or ceasing to use an off-shore terminal.

SCHEDULE 5. REGULATIONS RELATING TO SUBMERSIBLE AND SUPPORTING APPARATUS

1. (1) In this Schedule "regulations" means regulations made under section 17 of this Act, and "prescribed" means prescribed by regulations.

(2) Nothing in this Schedule shall be taken to prejudice the generality of section 17 of this Act.

Registration of submersible apparatus

2. Regulations made by virtue of section 17 (1) *(e)* of this Act may make provision—

(a) For all matters relevant to the maintenance of a register of submersible apparatus;

(b) Without prejudice to sub-paragraph *(a)* above, for the period for which any registration or exemption is to remain effective without renewal, the alteration or cancellation in any prescribed circumstances of registration or exemption or of any conditions attached thereto, the person by whom and manner in which applications in connexion with any registration or exemption are to be made, and information and evidence to be furnished in connexion with any such application;

(c) For the marking or other means of identification of any submersible apparatus;

(d) For the issue of certificates of registration or exemption, and the custody, surrender, production or display of the certificates or copies of them;

(e) For matters arising out of the termination of any registration or exemption, or any conditions attached thereto.

Offences

3. (1) Subject to sub-paragraph (2) below, regulations—

(a) May provide for the creation of offences and for their punishment on summary conviction or on conviction on indictment; and

(b) May afford, in respect of any description of offence created by the regulations, such defence (if any) as may be prescribed.

(2) The punishment for an offence created by regulations shall be—

(a) On summary conviction a fine not exceeding £400;

(b) On conviction on indictment imprisonment for a term not exceeding 2 years, or a fine, or both,

but without prejudice to any further restriction contained in the regulations on the punishments which can be awarded and without prejudice to the exclusion by the regulations of proceedings on indictment.

Exemptions from regulations

4. (1) The operation of any regulations may be excluded in whole or in part in relation to any class or description of submersible or supporting apparatus by regulations, or in relation to any particular apparatus by the direction of the Secretary of State given in such manner as he thinks appropriate.

(2) Any exemption or exclusion by regulations or by directions of the Secretary of State under this paragraph may be made subject to the imposition of conditions specified by the regulations or directions.

(3) Where, in pursuance of this paragraph, a person is exempted or excluded from the requirements of the provisions of regulations but, subject to a condition, and the condition is not observed, the exemption or exclusion shall not have effect, and accordingly proceedings may be brought in respect of any offence created by the regulations.

General

5. Regulations–

(a) May provide for their operation anywhere outside the United Kingdom and for their application to persons, whether or not British subjects, and to companies, whether or not incorporated under the law of any part of the United Kingdom;

(b) May provide that in any proceedings for an offence under the regulations an averment in any process of the fact that anything was done or situated within waters to which this Act applies shall, until the contrary is proved, be sufficient evidence of that fact as stated in the averment;

(c) May provide that proceedings for any offence under the regulations may be taken, and the offence be treated for all incidental purposes as having been committed, in any place in the United Kingdom;

(d) May provide for any provisions of the Merchant Shipping Acts 1894 to 1970 relating to inquiries and investigations into shipping casualties to apply (with such modifications as may be specified) in relation to casualties involving any submersible apparatus which is not a ship as they apply to ships;

(e) May provide that specified provisions of any enactment (other than this Act) shall, in such circumstances as may be prescribed, not have effect in relation to such class or description of, or to such particular, submersible or supporting apparatus as may be prescribed;

(f) May make different provision for different classes or descriptions of submersible or supporting apparatus and for different circumstances;

(g) May contain such supplemental, and incidental provisions as appear to the Secretary of State to be expedient, including provision for requiring the payment of fees in connexion with the making of applications and the granting of licences or issue of certificates, or other matters.

(c) OIL IN NAVIGABLE WATERS (EXCEPTIONS) REGULATIONS 1972[1]

. . .

3. *Interpretation.* (1) In these Regulations,

In relation to all land other than the part of the coast of Australia specified below, "from the nearest land" means from the nearest baseline from which the territorial sea of any territory is established in accordance with the Geneva Convention on the Territorial Sea and the Contiguous Zone, 1958.

In relation to the part of the North-eastern coast of Australia which lies between points 11° 00' S., 142° 08' E. and 24° 42'S., 153° 15'E., "from the nearest land" means from the nearest of the straight lines joining consecutively the following points: 11° 00' S., 142° 08' E.; 10° 35' S.; 141° 55' E.; 10° 00' S., 142° 00' E.; 9° 10' S., 143° 52' E.; 9° 00' S., 144° 30' E.; 13° 00' S.; 144° 00' E.; 15° 00' S., 146° 00' E.; 18° 00' S., 147° 00' E.; 21° 00' S., 153° 00' E.; 24° 42' S.; 153° 15' E.;

---

[1] Dated 8 December 1972. *Statutory Instruments,* 1972 No. 1928. Came into operation on 5 January 1973. By these Regulations, the Oil in Navigable Waters (Exceptions) Regulations 1967, reproduced in **ST/LEG/SER.B/15**, pp. 537-539, were revoked.

"Instantaneous rate of discharge of oil content" when expressed in litres per mile means the rate of discharge of oil in litres per hour at any instant divided by the speed of the ship in knots at the same instant;

"Mile" means an international nautical mile that is to say a distance of 1,852 metres;

"Proceeding" means in relation to any voyage making way through the water in the normal course of that voyage;

"Tanker" means a vessel the greater part of the cargo space of which is constructed or adapted for the carriage of liquid cargoes in bulk and which is either carrying a cargo of oil in bulk in that part of its cargo space or has on board oil residues from a cargo of oil in bulk previously carried;

"ballast voyage" means any voyage of a tanker on which that tanker is not carrying oil in bulk as cargo but has on board oil residues from a cargo of oil in bulk carried on the voyage immediately preceding that voyage.

(2) The Interpretation Act, 1889[1] shall apply to the interpretation of these Regulations as if these Regulations and the Regulations hereby revoked were Acts of Parliament.

4. *Exceptions for ships other than tankers and for tankers in relation to their machinery space bilges.* (1) This Regulation applies to ships other than tankers, and to tankers in relation only to discharge of oil or mixtures containing oil from their machinery space bilges.

(2) Every ship to which this Regulation applies is hereby excepted from the operation of section 1 (1) of the principal Act[2] as amended by the Oil in Navigable Waters Act, 1971[3] (hereinafter called "the 1971 Act") if all the following conditions are satisfied:

(i) The ship is proceeding on a voyage;

(ii) The instantaneous rate of discharge of oil content does not exceed 60 litres per mile;

(iii) The oil content of the discharge is less than 100 parts per 1,000,000 parts of the mixture; and

(iv) The discharge is made as far as practicable from the nearest land.

5. *Exception for tankers.* (1) Every tanker is hereby excepted from the operation of section 1 (1) of the Principal Act as amended by the 1971 Act provided that either

(a) All the following conditions are satisfied;

(i) The tanker is proceeding on a ballast voyage;

---

[1] 1889 c. 63.

[2] "The principal Act" in these Regulations means the Oil in Navigable Waters Act 1955 (1955 c. 25). The Act, as amended in 1963, is reproduced in part in ST/LEG/SER.B/15, pp. 520-530.

[3] 1971 c. 21. The Oil in Navigable Waters Acts 1955 (principal Act), 1963 and 1971 were repealed through their consolidation into the Prevention of Oil Pollution Act 1971 (reproduced in part in ST/LEG/SER.B/16, pp. 242-259) which entered into force on 1 March 1973.

    (ii) The instantaneous rate of discharge of oil content does not exceed 60 litres per mile;

    (iii) The total quantity of oil discharged during the voyage does not exceed 1/15,000 of the total oil cargo carrying capacity of the tanker; and

    (iv) The tanker is more than 50 miles from the nearest land; or

(b) All the following conditions are satisfied:

    (i) The tanker is proceeding on a voyage immediately following a ballast voyage and still has on board oil residues from a cargo of oil in bulk previously carried; and

    (ii) The only oil discharged is oil from those oil residues; and

    (iii) Conditions (ii) and (iv) of subparagraph (1) *(a)* of this Regulation are satisfied; and

    (iv) The total quantity of oil discharged during that voyage and the immediately preceding ballast voyage does not exceed 1/15,000 of the total oil cargo carrying capacity of the tanker; or

(c) The discharge consists only of ballast from a cargo tank which since the cargo was last carried therein, has been so cleaned that any effluent therefrom, if it were discharged from a stationary tanker into clean calm water on a clear day, would produce no visible traces of oil on the surface of the water.

(2) This Regulation does not apply to discharge of oil or mixtures containing oil from the machinery space bilges of tankers.

(d) OIL IN NAVIGABLE WATERS (RECORDS) REGULATIONS 1972[1]

. . .

2. *Interpretation and revocation.* (1) In these Regulations—

"tanker" means a vessel the greater part of the cargo space of which is constructed or adapted for the carriage of liquid cargoes in bulk and which is either carrying a cargo of oil in bulk in that part of its cargo space or has on board oil residues from a cargo of oil in bulk previously carried.

"tons" means tons gross tonnage.

(2) The Interpretation Act 1889[2] shall apply to the interpretation of these Regulations as if these Regulations and the Regulations hereby revoked were acts of Parliament.

. . .

---

[1] Dated 8 December 1972. *Statutory Instruments,* 1972 No. 1929. Came into operation on 5 January 1973. By these Regulations, the Oil in Navigable Waters (Records and Reports) Regulations 1967, reproduced in part in ST/LEG/SER.B/15, pp. 539-540, were revoked.

[2] 1889 c. 63.

3. *Records: tankers.* (1) The master of every ship to which section 7 (1) of the principal Act[1] applies, being a tanker, shall carry on board ship an oil record book, and shall record in such book the following matters, namely—

(a) Any of the following operations carried out on board or in connexion with the ship, namely—

(i) Loading of oil cargo;

(ii) Transfer of oil cargo during a voyage;

(iii) Discharge of oil cargo;

(iv) Ballasting of cargo tanks;

(v) Cleaning of cargo tanks;

(vi) Discharge of dirty ballast;

(vii) Discharge of water from slop tanks;

(viii) Disposal of oil residues;

(ix) Discharge overboard of oily bilge water which has accumulated in machinery spaces including pump rooms whilst in port;

(x) Subject to subparagraph (3), the routine discharge at sea of oily bilge water;

(b) Any occasion on which oil or a mixture containing oil is discharged from a ship for the purpose of securing the safety of any vessel or of preventing damage to any vessel or cargo, or of saving life;

(c) Any occasion on which oil or a mixture containing oil is found to be escaping, or to have escaped, from the ship in consequence of damage to the ship, or by reason of leakage.

(2) Entries shall be made in the said book in respect of the operations specified in subparagraph *(a)* of paragraph (1) above, and in respect of every occasion specified in subparagraphs *(b)* and *(c)* of that paragraph in the form and containing the particulars set out in Schedule 1 to these Regulations.

(3) (i) The requirement to keep a record in the form required by paragraphs (1) and (2) of this Regulation shall not apply to any discharge referred to in paragraph (1) *(a)* (x) of this Regulation, in so far as it relates to the discharge of oily bilge water from machinery spaces, including pump rooms, if such discharge has been entered in the engine room log book or deck log book.

(ii) Any entry relating to the discharge of oily bilge water from machinery spaces, including pump rooms, whether made in the oil record book or in the engine room log book or deck log book, shall state whether the discharge was made through a separator. Where the pump discharging such bilge water starts automatically and discharges through a separator at all times it will be sufficient to enter each day "Automatic discharge from bilges through a separator".

---

[1] For the meaning and the status of the "principal Act", see foot-notes to Regulation 4 of the Regulations reproduced under *(a) supra.*

4. *Records: ships other than tankers.* (1) The master of every ship to which section 7 (1) of the principal Act applies of 80 tons or more which uses oil fuel, not being a tanker, shall carry on board ship an oil record book and shall record in such book the following matters, namely—

(a) Any of the following operations carried out on board or in connexion with the ship, namely—

(i) Ballasting or cleaning of bunker fuel tanks;

(ii) Discharge of dirty ballast or cleaning water from bunker fuel tanks;

(iii) Disposal of oil residues;

(iv) Discharge overboard of oily bilge water which has accumulated in machinery spaces including pump rooms whilst in port;

(v) Subject to subparagraph (3), the routine discharge at sea of oily bilge water;

(b) Any occasion on which oil or a mixture containing oil is discharged from the ship for the purpose of securing the safety of any vessel or of preventing damage to any vessel or cargo, or of saving life;

(c) Any occasion on which oil or a mixture containing oil is found to be escaping or to have escaped, from the ship in consequence of damage to the ship, or by reason of leakage.

(2) Entries shall be made in the said book in respect of the operations specified in subparagraph *(a)* of paragraph (1) above, and in respect of every occasion specified in subparagraphs *(b)* and *(c)* of that paragraph in the form and containing the particulars set out in Schedule 2 to these Regulations.

(3) (i) The requirements to keep a record in the form required by paragraphs (1) and (2) of this Regulation shall not apply to any discharge referred to in paragraph (1) *(a)* (v) of this Regulation, in so far as it relates to the discharge of oily bilge water from machinery spaces, including pump rooms, if such discharge has been entered in the engine room log book or deck log book.

(ii) Any entry relating to the discharge of oily bilge water from machinery spaces, including pump rooms, whether made in the oil record book or in the engine room log book or deck log book, shall state whether the discharge was made through a separator.

Where the pump discharging oily bilge water starts automatically and discharges through a separator at all times it will be sufficient to enter each day "Automatic discharge from bilges through a separator".

5. *Retention, custody and disposal of records.* (1) Every master of a ship in respect of which records are required to be kept pursuant to the preceding Regulations shall retain the records in his custody in the ship until the expiration of the period of two years next following the date of the last entry therein:

Provided that if the principal place of business of the owners of the ship is in the United Kingdom the master may at any time within that period transmit the records of the owners at that place of business.

(2) Records transmitted to the owners of a ship pursuant to the proviso to paragraph (1) of this Regulation shall be retained by them in their custody

at their principal place of business in the United Kingdom until the expiration of the period of two years next following the date of the last entry therein.

. . .

(e) [PREVENTION OF OIL POLLUTION ACT 1971
(COMMENCEMENT) ORDER 1973][1]

---

[1] Dated 12 February 1973. *Statutory Instruments*, 1973 No. 203 (C.6). This Order brought into operation the Prevention of Oil Pollution Act 1971 (1971 c. 60) on 1 March 1973. The Act of 1971 is reproduced in part in ST/LEG/SER.B/16, pp. 242-259.

Division IV

FISHING AND CONSERVATION OF THE
LIVING RESOURCES OF THE SEA[1]

1. ARGENTINA

ACT NO. 17,500 OF 25 OCTOBER 1967 CONCERNING THE PROMOTION
OF FISHERIES,[2] AS AMENDED BY ACT NO. 20,136 OF 5 FEBRUARY 1973[3]

Article 1. The living resources of the maritime zones under Argentine
sovereignty are the property of the national State, which shall authorize their
exploitation in accordance with this Act and its implementing regulations.

Article 2. The resources referred to in the preceding article shall be
exploited only by vessels flying the Argentine flag and with the prior
authorization of the competent authority.

. . .

Article 12. Any contravention of this Act and the regulations issued in
pursuance of it shall be punished by the following penalties:

(a) In the case of national enterprises or vessels:

1. A fine of from five hundred (500) to two hundred thousand
   (200,000) pesos;
2. Confiscation of fishing nets and equipment;
3. Confiscation of the fish catch;
4. Revocation of fishing licence.

These penalties shall be cumulative.

(b) In the case of vessels flying a foreign flag:

1. A fine of $US 5,000 (five thousand) to $US 100,000 (one hundred
   thousand) or the equivalent in Argentine currency at the exchange
   rate ruling at the time of the payment, which shall be made by the
   agent responsible for commissioning the vessel or its owner *in
   solidum;*
2. Confiscation of the fish catch;
3. Confiscation of fishing nets and equipment.

The first two of these penalties shall be cumulative, the competent
authority having discretion to add the third penalty also.

---

[1] Texts under this Division cover both the territorial sea and the high seas. For texts
relating to sedentary fisheries on the continental shelf, see also *supra* Division II.

[2] Reproduced in part in ST/LEG/SER.B/15, p. 569.

[3] Spanish text provided by the Permanent Mission of Argentina to the United
Nations in a note verbale of 3 April 1973. Translation by the Secretariat of the United
Nations.

The penalties shall be imposed after summary proceedings to enable the right to a defence to be exercised by the Ministry of Agriculture and Livestock Breeding, in the case of those referred to in subparagraph *(a)*, and by the competent maritime authority, in the case of those referred to in subparagraph *(b)*, and shall be subject to appeal before the competent national judge having jurisdiction over the place at which the contravention was committed within five (5) days of notification of the penalty. In the case of contraventions committed by vessels flying a foreign flag, the maritime authority may order that they be impounded in an Argentine port until the fine is paid.

. . .

2. CANADA

(a) TUNA FISHERY REGULATIONS OF 22 SEPTEMBER 1966,[1] AS AMENDED UP TO 1973[2]

. . .

2. In these Regulations, "tuna" means any fish known by the name of tuna and includes fish of the species yellowfin *(Thunnus albacares)*, bluefin *(Thunnus thynnus)*, blackfin *(Thunnus atlanticus)*, albacore *(Thunnus alalunga)*, bigeye *(Thunnus obesus)*, skipjack *(Euthynnus pelamis)*, common bonito *(Sarda sarda)*, Pacific bonito *(Sarda chiliensis)* or false albacore *(Euthynnus alletteratus)*.

3. (1) No person on board a fishing vessel that is subject to the laws of Canada shall fish for, transport, process or have in his possession any tuna except under a licence for such vessel issued by the Minister.

(2) The Minister may, in any licence, impose such terms and conditions, not inconsistent with these Regulations, as he deems proper and the holder of the licence shall comply with those terms and conditions.

(3) Every licence issued under these Regulations expires on the 31st day of December next following the day on which it is issued.

(4) The fees for a licence are

(a) For a vessel under one hundred feet in over-all length, $15; and

(b) For a vessel one hundred feet or more in over-all length, $25.

(5) The provisions in this section shall not apply to vessels from British Columbia ports fishing for the species albacore *(Thunnus alalunga)* in the waters of the eastern Pacific Ocean north of 32° 30′ north latitude.

---

[1] P.C. 1966-1979. SOR/66-449, *Canada Gazette*, Part II, vol. 100, No. 19, 12 October 1966.

[2] Amendments were made by P.C. 1968-1775. SOR/68-431 (*ibid.*, vol. 102, No. 19, 9 October 1968), P.C. 1969-698. SOR/69-180 (*ibid.*, vol. 103, No. 9, 14 May 1969), P.C. 1972-2600. SOR/72-467 (*ibid.*, vol. 106, No. 22, 22 November 1972) and P.C. 1973-202. SOR/73-62 (*ibid.*, vol. 107, No. 3, 14 February 1973).

4. (1) No person shall fish for, transport, process or have in his possession any yellowfin from 30 September to 31 December in any year in the area described in the Schedule.[1]

(2) Notwithstanding subsection (1), a person, in the course of fishing for tuna other than yellowfin, may take a quantity of yellowfin not exceeding 15 per cent by pound weight of all tuna on the vessel.

5. No person shall fish for tuna in the Gulf of St. Lawrence, being the area of the sea defined as Zone 1 in the *Fishing Zones of Canada (Zones 1, 2 and 3) Order*,[2] except by rod, line and hooks.

6. Any closed time or fishing quota that is fixed by these Regulations may be varied by order of the Minister.

. . .

(b) SEAL PROTECTION REGULATIONS OF 19 MAY 1966,[3] AS AMENDED UP TO 1973 [4]

. . .

3. [Repealed].

. . .

9. . . .

(3) No vessel sealing licence shall be issued in respect of any vessel that has an over-all length of more than 65 feet unless such a licence in respect of that vessel was issued in 1970 or 1971.

. . .

11. (1) The combined annual quota for harp seals in the Front Area is 60,000 for persons hunting from or by means of a vessel that is more than 65 feet in over-all length.

(2) No person hunting from or by means of a vessel that is more than 65 feet in over-all length shall take or kill harp seals in the Gulf Area.

(3) The combined annual quota for harp seals in the Front and Gulf Areas is 30,000 for persons operating from the shore or hunting from or by means of a vessel that is 65 feet or less in over-all length.

(4) When the annual quotas prescribed in subsections (1) and (3) for the Areas referred to therein have been reached or when the Minister is of the opinion that such quotas are about to be reached, the Minister shall by order direct that the taking or killing of harp seals in such Areas shall cease.

. . .

[1] The Schedule is not reproduced here.

[2] P.C. 1971-366, 25 February 1971. SOR/71-81, *ibid.*, vol. 105, No. 5, 10 March 1971. Reproduced in part in ST/LEG/SER.B/16, pp. 286-288.

[3] P.C. 1966-904. SOR/66-235, *Canada Gazette*, Part II, vol. 100, No. 11, 8 June 1966.

[4] The latest amendments were made by P.C. 1973-578, 13 March 1973. SOR/73-159 (*ibid.*, vol. 107, No. 6, 28 March 1973). The Regulations as amended up to 1968 are reproduced in part in ST/LEG/SER.B/15, pp. 609-611 and ST/LEG/SER.B/16, pp. 284-285. Only the relevant sections amended thereafter are reproduced here.

13. (1) Subject to subsection (2) no person shall take or kill by any means

(a) Harp seals in the Gulf Area or the Front Area from the 25th day of April, in any year, to the 11th day of March next following, both days inclusive; or

(b) Hood seals in the Front Area from the 25th day of April, in any year, to the 19th day of March next following, both days inclusive.

(2) Subject to subsection (3), a resident of a province adjacent to the Gulf Area or the Front Area operating from the shore or from a vessel having an over-all length of 65 feet or less may take or kill seals at any time.

(3) No person hunting seals pursuant to subsection (2) shall take or kill seals except in waters along the shore of that part of the province in which he resides.

(4) The Minister may, by order, vary the closed season prescribed in subsection (1).

(5) When the Minister considers it necessary for conservation purposes he may, by order, prohibit the taking or killing of seals in any part of the Gulf Area or the Front Area.

. . .

(c) WHALING REGULATIONS OF 19 MARCH 1964,[1]
AS AMENDED UP TO 1973[2]

. . .

Conservation

7. (1) Subject to these Regulations, no person shall

(a) Engage in whaling for

 (i) Any grey whale or right whale; or

 (ii) Any whale on the Atlantic coast of Canada; or

(b) Leave any place or port on the Atlantic coast of Canada with the intention of engaging in whaling, unless that person is an Indian or Eskimo and the meat and other products of the whale are to be used exclusively for local consumption by Indians or Eskimos.

(2) The Minister or any person acting on his behalf may issue a permit to take whales for scientific purposes.

(3) Subparagraph (1) *(a)* (ii) and paragraph (1) *(b)* do not apply to whaling by coastal residents for pilot (pothead), minke or other non-commercial species of whales where the meat and other products of the whales are to be used exclusively for local consumption.

---

[1] P.C. 1964-400. SOR/64-117, *Canada Gazette*, Part II, vol. 98, No. 7, 8 April 1964.

[2] The latest amendments were made by P.C. 1972-474. SOR/72-74, (*ibid.*, vol. 106, No. 7, 12 April 1972) and P.C. 1973-833. SOR/73-193 (*ibid.*, vol. 107, No. 8, 25 April 1973). The regulations as amended up to 1967 are reproduced in part in ST/LEG/ SER.B/15, p. 608. Only the relevant sections amended thereafter are reproduced here.

8. (1) No person shall kill or attempt to kill any blue whale

(a) In the North Atlantic Ocean;

(b) In the waters south of the Equator; or

(c) In the North Pacific Ocean or its dependent waters north of the Equator for a period of four years from the beginning of the 1972 season.

(2) No person shall kill or attempt to kill any humpback whales,

(a) In the North Atlantic Ocean;

(b) In the waters south of the Equator; or

(c) In the North Pacific Ocean or its dependent waters north of the Equator for a period of three years from the beginning of the 1971 season.

. . .

(4) The number of baleen whales taken during the 1972-73 open season in waters south of 40° South Latitude by factory ships or whale catchers attached to factory ships shall not exceed

(a) One thousand nine hundred and fifty fin whales;

(b) Five thousand sei and Bryde's whales in the aggregate; and

(c) Five thousand minke whales.

(5) No person shall use a factory ship or a whale catcher attached to a factory ship for the purpose of killing or attempting to kill baleen whales in any waters south of 40° South Latitude after the date determined by the Bureau of International Whaling Statistics as the date on which the maximum catch of whales permitted by subsection (4) is reached.

(6) The number of whales taken in the 1973 open season in the North Pacific Ocean and its dependent waters shall not exceed

(a) Six hundred and fifty fin whales (exclusive of catch in the East China Sea);

(b) Three thousand sei and Bryde's whales in the aggregate; and

(c) Six thousand male and four thousand female sperm whales.

(7) The number of sperm whales taken in the Southern Hemisphere in the 1972-73 pelagic season and the 1973 coastal season shall not exceed eight thousand male and five thousand female sperm whales.

(8) For the purpose of subsection (7), "pelagic season" means the season during which whales that are caught are processed on a factory ship and "coastal season" means the season during which such whales are processed at a land station.

9. No person shall take or kill calves or suckling whales or female whales that are accompanied by calves or suckling whales.

10. (1) No person shall use a whale catcher, helicopter or other aircraft attached to a factory ship for the purpose of killing or attempting to kill sperm or minke whales in the North Atlantic and North Pacific Oceans except during the open seasons prescribed in subsection (2) with respect to such whales.

(2) The open season in any year is, for

(a) Sperm whales in the North Atlantic Ocean, from 1 May to 31 December, both dates inclusive;

(b) Sperm whales in the North Pacific Ocean, from 1 April to 30 November, both dates inclusive; and

(c) Minke whales in the North Pacific Ocean, from 1 April to 30 September, both dates inclusive.

(3) No person shall use a whale catcher, helicopter or other aircraft attached to a land station for the purpose of killing or attempting to kill sperm or baleen whales in the North Atlantic or North Pacific Ocean except during the open seasons hereinafter prescribed in subsection (4) with respect to such whales.

(4) The open season in any year is, for

(a) Baleen (except minke) whales in the North Atlantic Ocean, from 15 May to 14 November, both dates inclusive;

(b) Baleen (except minke) whales in the North Pacific Ocean, from 1 April to 30 September, both dates inclusive;

(c) Sperm whales in the North Atlantic Ocean from 1 April to 30 November, both dates inclusive;

(d) Sperm whales in the North Pacific Ocean, from 1 April to 30 November, both dates inclusive; and

(e) Minke whales in the North Atlantic Ocean, from 1 May to 31 October, both dates inclusive.

(5) No person shall use a factory ship or a whale catcher attached to a factory ship for the purpose of killing, attempting to kill or treating baleen whales, other than minke whales, in any waters south of 40° South Latitude except during the period commencing on the twelfth day of December in any year and terminating on the seventh day of April next following, both days inclusive.

(6) No person shall use a factory ship or a whale catcher attached to a factory ship for the purpose of killing, attempting to kill or treating baleen whales, other than minke whales, in

(a) Waters north of 66° North Latitude except those waters from 150° East Longitude eastwards to 140° West Longitude between 66° North Latitude and 72° North Latitude;

(b) The Atlantic Ocean and its dependent waters north of 40° South Latitude;

(c) The Pacific Ocean and its dependent waters east of 150° West Longitude between 40° South Latitude and 35° North Latitude;

(d) The Pacific Ocean and its dependent waters west of 150° West Longitude between 40° South Latitude and 20° North Latitude; and

(e) The Indian Ocean and its dependent waters north of 40° South Latitude.

(7) [Repealed].

(8) No person shall use a factory ship or a whale catcher attached to a factory ship for the purpose of killing, attempting to kill or treating sperm whales in the waters between 40° South Latitude and 40° North Latitude.

(8a) [Repealed].

. . .

(d) NORTH PACIFIC FISHERIES CONVENTION REGULATIONS OF 12 JUNE 1973[1]

Short title

1. These Regulations may be cited as the North Pacific Fisheries Convention Regulations.

Interpretation

2. In these Regulations,

"Convention" means the International Convention for the High Seas Fisheries of the North Pacific Ocean[2] and the Protocol thereto;

"Minister" means the Minister of the Environment.

Prohibition

3. No person aboard a Canadian fishing vessel shall fish for, load, process, transport or have in his possession salmon in that area of the Bering Sea that lies east of the line starting from Cape Prince of Wales on the west coast of Alaska, thence running westward to 168° 58′ 22.59″ west longitude, thence due south to a point 65° 15′ 00″ north latitude, thence along the Great Circle Course which passes through 51° north latitude and 167° east longitude, to its intersection with meridian 175° west longitude, thence south along a provisional line which follows this meridian to the territorial waters limit of Atka Island.

4. Every person who violates section 3 is liable upon summary conviction to a fine not exceeding five thousand dollars or to imprisonment for a term not exceeding three months or to both.

Powers of protection officers

5. (1) A protection officer may, except within the territorial waters of another country, seize any Canadian fishing vessel and any goods found thereon including equipment, fishing gear or fish by means of or in relation to which section 3 has been violated.

(2) A protection officer shall take delivery of any Canadian fishing vessel seized and delivered by a duly authorized official of the United States or of Japan pursuant to Article X of the Convention.

---

[1] P.C. 1973-1479; 12 June 1973. SOR/73-318, *Canada Gazette* Part II, Vol. 107, No. 12, 27 June 1973. Adopted pursuant the North Pacific Fisheries Convention Act of 14 May 1953, reproduced in part in ST/LEG/SER.B/15, pp. 599-600. They supersede the North Pacific Fisheries Convention Regulations of 3 June 1954 reproduced in ST/LEG/SER.B/15, pp. 601-602.

[2] United Nations, *Treaty Series,* Vol. 205, page 65, and also in ST/LEG/SER.B/8, pp.57-63 and ST/LEG/SER.B/15, p. 840.

6. Subject to these Regulations, a protection officer who has the custody of any fishing vessel or goods that were seized in respect of an alleged violation of section 3 shall retain them in his custody or shall deliver them into the custody of such person as the Minister may direct.

7. Where fish or other perishable goods are seized in respect of an alleged violation of section 3, the protection officer or other person having the custody thereof may, with the consent of the person from whom they were seized, sell them, and the proceeds of the sale thereof shall be paid to the Receiver General or deposited in a chartered bank to the credit of the Receiver General.

Powers of court

8. Where a person is convicted of a violation of section 3, the convicting court or judge may, in addition to any other penalty imposed, order that

(a) The fishing vessel and any goods found thereon by means of or in relation to which the violation was committed; and

(b) If any of the person's goods have been sold under section 7, the proceeds of the sale thereof

be forfeited, and upon the making of such order the fishing vessel, goods and proceeds are forfeited to Her Majesty in right of Canada.

9. Where proceedings in respect of an alleged violation of section 3 have been instituted against a person, the court or judge may, with the consent of the protection officer who has the custody of any fishing vessel or goods that were seized in respect of the alleged violation, order that the vessel or goods be delivered into the custody of the person upon security by bond with two sureties, in an amount and form satisfactory to the court or judge, until the disposition of the prosecution.

Disposal of fishing vessel and goods after conviction

10. Any fishing vessel, goods or proceeds of sale ordered to be forfeited under section 8 shall be disposed of at such time and in such manner as the Minister directs.

Return of fishing vessel and goods

11. Where

(a) The Minister decides not to prosecute a person in respect of an alleged violation of section 3; or

(b) No proceedings against a person in respect of an alleged violation of section 3 have been instituted within three months after the date of the alleged violation,

any fishing vessel or goods seized from the person in respect of the alleged violation and any proceeds of the sale of his goods under section 7 shall be returned or paid to that person.

12. Subject to section 13, where a person is convicted of a violation of section 3, any fishing vessel or goods seized from that person in respect of the violation and any proceeds of the sale of his goods under section 7 shall be returned or paid to the person after the conclusion of the proceedings against

him unless the court or judge has ordered that the vessel, goods or proceeds of sale be forfeited under section 8.

13. (1) Where a person is convicted of a violation of section 3 and a fine is imposed in respect of the conviction, any fishing vessel or goods seized from the person may

(a) Be detained until the fine has been paid;

(b) If the fine remains unpaid for a period of thirty days, be sold under execution in satisfaction of the fine; or

(c) After the expiration of the time allowed by the court or judge for payment of the fine, be sold under execution in satisfaction of the fine.

(2) When a person is convicted of a violation of section 3 and a fine is imposed in respect of the conviction, the proceeds of the sale of the person's goods under section 7 may be applied in satisfaction of the fine.

(e) INTERNATIONAL FISHING VESSEL INSPECTION REGULATIONS OF 4 SEPTEMBER 1973[1] AS AMENDED UP TO 1974[2]

. . .

Interpretation

2. In these Regulations,

"Act" means the *Northwest Atlantic Fisheries Convention Act;*[3]

"fishing vessel" means a Canadian fishing vessel or a fishing vessel of a foreign government;

"foreign government" means a government designated by section 3;

"foreign inspector" means a person authorized by a foreign government to carry out inspections pursuant to subsection 3.1 (2) of the Act;

"inspection flag" means a flag or pennant in the shape, size and colours set out in Schedule II;[4]

"inspection officer" means a foreign inspector or a protection officer;

"Minister" means the Minister of Fisheries for Canada.

Designation of Foreign Governments Authorized to Carry Out Inspections

3. The government of a country set out in column I of an item of Schedule I may authorize a person to carry out inspections pursuant to subsection 3.1 (2) of the Act on board Canadian fishing vessels while the vessels are within the Convention area but outside Canadian territorial waters.

---

[1] P.C. 1973-2587. SOR/73-510, *Canada Gazette,* Part II, vol. 107, No. 18, 26 September 1973.

[2] Amended by P.C. 1974-1550, 16 July 1974. SOR/74-428, *Canada Gazette,* Part II, Vol. 108, No. 15, 14 August 1974.

[3] 2-3 Eliz., Chap. 18, 4 March 1954.

[4] Schedule II is not reproduced here.

280

Powers of Inspection Officers

4. An inspection officer may carry out inspections pursuant to sub-sections 3.1 (2) and (3) of the Act on board a fishing vessel of a country set out in column I of an item of Schedule I subject to the inspection limitations specified in column II of that item.

Identification of Ships Carrying Inspection Officers

5. Whenever a ship in the Convention[1] area carries an inspection officer, that ship shall fly an inspection flag.

. . .

Identification of Inspection Officers

6. (1) While carrying out his duties under subsections 3.1 (2) or (3) of the Act,

(a) Every foreign inspector shall carry an identification card issued to him for that purpose by the foreign government that authorized him to carry out those duties; and

(b) Every protection officer shall carry an identification card in the form set out in Schedule III.[2]

(2) Every inspection officer shall produce his identification card upon the request of the master of a fishing vessel that he boards for the purpose of carrying out an inspection.

7. (1) Every fishing vessel in the Convention area shall stop or heave to when signalled to do so by a ship flying an inspection flag.

(2) For the purpose of subsection (1), the signal requiring a fishing vessel to stop or heave to is the hoisting of the International Code flag S.Q.3.

8. The master of any fishing vessel that is within the Convention area shall give to an inspection officer all reasonable assistance requested by him for the purpose of carrying out inspections pursuant to subsection 3.1 (3) of the Act.

9. A protection officer shall, within seven days, report to the Minister any failure by the master of a fishing vessel to comply with section 7.

10. The master of any Canadian fishing vessel that has any net or portion thereof sealed by an inspection officer shall keep the same on board his fishing vessel until it has been checked by a protection officer.

Reporting

. . .

Penalties

12. Every person who violates these Regulations is liable on summary conviction to a fine not exceeding one thousand dollars or to imprisonment for a term not exceeding one month or to both.

---

[1] Northwest Atlantic Fisheries Convention of 8 February 1949. United Nations, *Treaty Series,* Vol. 157, page 157, and ST/LEG/SER.B/15, pp. 832-838.

[2] Schedule III is not reproduced here.

SCHEDULE I

Column I Country	Column II Inspection Limitations
1. Bulgaria	No inspection permitted
2. Denmark	None
3. France	None
4. Federal Republic of Germany	None
5. Iceland	No inspection permitted
6. Italy	None
7. Japan	None
8. Norway	None
9. Poland	None
10. Portugal	None
11. Romania	None
12. Spain	None
13. Union of Soviet Socialist Republics	None
14. United Kingdom	None
15. United States	None

(f) NORTHWEST ATLANTIC FISHERIES REGULATIONS
OF 15 JANUARY 1974[1] AS AMENDED[2]

Short title

1. These Regulations may be cited as the Northwest Atlantic Fisheries Regulations.

Interpretation

2. In these Regulations,

"American plaice" means a fish of the species Hippoglossoides platessoides (Fab.); (plie du Canada)

"billfish" means a fish of the species Scomberesox saurus; (balaou)

"capelin" means a fish of the species Mallotus villosus; (Capelan)

"cod" means a fish of the species Gadus morhua (L); (morue)

"cod-end" means a bag-like extension attached to the after end of the belly of a trawl net and used to retain the catch; (cul)

---

[1] P.C. 1974-75, 15 January 1974. SOR/74-59, *Canada Gazette,* Part II, Vol. 108, No. 3, 13 February 1974. Adopted pursuant the Northwest Atlantic Fisheries Convention Act of 4 March 1954 (reproduced in part in ST/LEG/SER.B/15, pp. 600-601). To give effect to the Northwest Atlantic Fisheries Convention, done in Washington on 8 February 1949 (reproduced in United Nations, *Treaty Series,* Vol. 157, page 157 and in ST/LEG/SER.B/15, pp. 832-838).

[2] P.C. 1974-470, 5 March 1974. SOR/74-143, *Canada Gazette,* Part II, Vol. 108, No. 6, 27 March 1974; P.C. 1974-1201, 30 May 1974. SOR/74-337, *Canada Gazette,* Part II, Vol. 108, No. 12, 26 June 1974 and P.C. 1974-2122, 24 September 1974. SOR/74-547, *Canada Gazette,* Part II, Vol. 108, No. 19, 9 October 1974.

"division" means a division of a subarea described in Schedule I; (division)

"dogfish" means a fish of the species the family name of which is (Squalidae); (aiguillat)

"finfish" means any of several species of fish having fins; (poisson à nageoires)

"goods" means fish, fishing gear, rigging and other equipment; (effets)

"government vessel" has the same meaning as in the Coastal Fisheries Protection Act; (bâtiment du gouvernement)

"Greenland halibut" means a fish of the species Reinhardtius hyppoglossus (Walb.); (flétan du Groenland)

"haddock" means a fish of the species Melanogrammus aeglefinus (L); (aiglefin)

"halibut" means a fish of the species Hippoglossus hyppoglossus (L.); (flétan)

"herring" means a fish of the species Clupea harengus (L.); (hareng)

"mackerel" means a fish of the species Scomber scombrus; (maquereau bleu)

"menhaden" means a fish of the species Brevoortia tyrannus; (alose tyran)

"Minister" means the Minister of Fisheries for Canada; (Ministre)

"pollock" means a fish of the species saithe or Pollachius virens (L.) (goberge)

"redfish" means a fish of the species Sebastes marinus; (sébaste)

"red hake" means a fish of the species Urophycis chuss; (merluche écureuil)

"Regional Director" means the Regional Director of Fisheries for the Maritimes Region or the Newfoundland Region; (directeur régional)

"regulated species" means a species of fish set out in column II of Schedule II or column I of Schedule IV; (espèce réglementée)

"shark" means any of several species of fish belonging to the order Pleurotremata (Squaliformes); (requin)

"silver hake" means a fish of the species Merluccius bilinearis; (merluche argentée)

"squid" means cephalopods of the species Illex illecebrasus and Loligo pealei; (calmar)

"trawl net" means any large bag net dragged in the sea by a vessel or vessels for the purpose of taking fish; (chalut)

"tuna" has the same meaning as in section 2 of the Tuna Fishery Regulations; (thon)

"vessel" means a Canadian fishing vessel as defined in the Coastal Fisheries Protection Act; (bateau)

"white hake" means a fish of the species Urophycis tenuis (Mitch.); (merluche blanche) "winter flounder" means a fish of the species Pseudopleuronectes americanus (Walb.); (plie rouge)

"witch flounder" means a fish of the species Ghyptocephalus cynoglossus (L.); (plie grise)

"yellowtail flounder" means a fish of the species Limanda ferruginea (Storer). (limande à queue jaune)

Application

3 These Regulations apply to commercial fishing in the Convention area by citizens or residents of Canada by means of vessels.

Mesh size restrictions

4. (1) Subject to subsection (2), no person on board a vessel shall fish for or take from a subarea set out in column I of an item of Schedule II any species of fish set out in column II of that item except by means of a net described in column III of that item having a mesh size that is

(a) In the cod-end, not less than the size set out in column IV of that item opposite that net; and

(b) In any part of the net other than the cod-end, not less than the size set out in column V of that item opposite that net.

(2) A person fishing in a subarea set out in column I of item 3, 4 or 5 of Schedule II for a species of fish other than a species set out in column II of that item and using a net that does not meet the requirements of subsection (1) may catch and retain any species of fish set out in column II of that item if the quantity of any species so retained does not exceed the greater of five thousand pounds and ten per cent of the total weight of fish on board his vessel.

(3) For the purposes of this section, mesh size means

(a) In respect of the cod-end of a net, the average of the measurements of any twenty consecutive meshes running parallel to the long axis of the cod-end, beginning at the after end of the cod-end, and at least ten meshes from the lacings; and

(b) In respect of any part of a net other than the cod-end, the average of the measurements of any twenty consecutive meshes that are at least ten meshes from the lacings.

(4) The measurements referred to in subsection (3) shall be made by inserting into the meshes a flat wedge-shaped gauge having a taper of two inches in eight inches and a thickness of three thirty-seconds of an inch with a weight of eleven pounds attached.

5. (1) Subject to subsection (2), no person on board a vessel that is operating in subarea 3, 4 or 5 shall use any device by means of which the openings in the mesh in any part of a trawl net are obstructed or the size of the mesh is diminished.

(2) For the purpose of preventing wear and tear to a trawl net, a person may attach

(a) To the underside of the cod-end, hides, canvas, netting or any similar material; and

(b) To the topside of the cod-end;

(i) A piece of netting the width of which is at least one and one-half times the width of the area of the cod-end that is covered, the width being measured at right angles to the long axis of the cod-end, and the mesh size of which, being the average of the measurements of twenty consecutive meshes across the netting, is not less than the mesh size required by section 4 if the piece of netting is fastened to the cod-end only along the forward and lateral edges of the netting in a manner that will permit it to extend;

(A) Where a splitting strap is used, over not more than that part of the cod-end between the fourth mesh forward of the splitting strap and the fourth mesh from the cod line mesh; and

(B) Where a splitting strap is not used, over not more than one-third of the cod-end measured from not closer than four meshes in front of the cod line mesh; or

(ii) At the rear portion thereof, a rectangular piece of netting made of twine of the same material and size as that of the cod-end, the width of which is the same as the width of the cod-end and the mesh size of which is twice as large as the mesh size of the cod-end, if the piece of netting is fastened to the cod-end along the forward, lateral and rear edges of the netting in a manner that will permit the meshes of that piece of netting to exactly overlie the meshes of the cod-end over which it extends.

Closed seasons

6. (1) No person in command of, and no crew member on, a fishing vessel shall, during March, April or May in any year, fish with any

(a) Otter trawl or similar device;

(b) Gill net;

(c) Hook and line; or

(d) Any other gear that is capable of taking any demersal species of fish

in any portion of subarea 5 or division 4X of subarea 4 bounded by the straight lines connecting the geographical coordinates of points listed in Schedule III in the order in which they are listed.

(2) Subsection (1) does not apply to any person fishing with a hook having a gape of not less than one and three-sixteenths of an inch (three centimetres) in those portions of subarea 5 bounded by the geographical coordinates of points listed in items 1 and 2 of Schedule III.

7. (1) No person shall, during the month of April in any year, fish for red hake or white hake in that portion of subarea 5 bounded by the meridian of 69° 00' west longitude, the parallel of 39° 50' north latitude, the meridian of 71° 40' west longitude and the parallel of 42° 20' north latitude.

(2) A person fishing during the period and in the waters described in subsection (1) for any species of fish other than the species referred to in that subsection may catch and retain fish of the species referred to in that subsection if the quantity so retained in the aggregate does not exceed the greater of five thousand pounds and ten per cent of the total weight of fish on board his vessel.

7.1. No person shall, by means of a vessel that is more than one hundred and forty-five feet in overall length, fish for any demersal species of fish from 1 July to 31 December, both dates inclusive, in any year, in that portion of subarea 5 that is north of 40° 20' north latitude, south of 43° 17' north latitude and west of a straight line drawn from a point at 68° 15' west longitude and 40° 20' north latitude to a point at 70° 00' west longitude and 43° 17' north latitude.

Fishing quotas

8. (1) No person shall, in any year, fish for a species of fish set out in column I of an item of Schedule IV in an area or portion thereof set out in column II of that item after notice is given in respect of that species stating that the annual quota set out in column III of that item, opposite that area or portion thereof, has been, or is about to be, reached.

(2) The notice referred to in subsection (1) may be given by the Regional Director and shall be published in a daily newspaper in each of the Provinces of New Brunswick, Nova Scotia, Prince Edward Island and Newfoundland within seven days of the day it is given.

Incidental catches

9. Where a notice has been given pursuant to section 8 in respect of a species of fish set out in column I of an item of Schedule IV and an area or portion thereof set out in column II of that item, a person fishing in that area or portion thereof for a species of fish other than the species mentioned in the notice may catch and retain fish of that other species if the quantity so retained does not exceed the greater of five thousand pounds and ten per cent of the total weight of fish on board his vessel.

Recording and reporting catches

10. (1) The master of every vessel in excess of twenty-five tons gross tonnage that is fishing in the Convention Area for any species of fish specified in these Regulations shall maintain a record in which he shall record daily the estimated weight of the catch of each species of fish and the area in which the catch was taken.

(2) A copy of the record of catch referred to in subsection (1) shall be given to the purchaser of the catch at the time of sale and the purchaser shall forward that copy and a copy of the sales slip to the Minister.

Haddock

11. (1) Subject to subsection (2), no person shall fish for haddock in division 4V, 4W or 4X of subarea 4 or in subarea 5.

(2) A person fishing for species other than haddock in a division or subarea referred to in subsection (1) may catch and retain haddock if the quantity so retained does not exceed the greater of five thousand pounds and ten per cent of the total weight of fish on board his vessel.

Scallops

12. (1) Subject to subsection (2), no person fishing in any Northwest Atlantic Fisheries Convention subarea with a vessel over sixty-five feet in length shall fish for, catch or retain any sea scallops (Placopecten magellanicus Gmelin)

(a) The shell sizes of which are less than 81.5 mm. (3 1/4 inches) measured from the hinge to the opposite edge of the shell; or

(b) The meats of which weigh on the average less than 7.5 grams based on an average count of not more than sixty scallop meats per pound.

(2) A person fishing for sea scallops in an area or portion thereof referred to in subsection (1) and with a vessel described in that subsection may catch and retain scallops the average weight of the meats of which is less than that specified in paragraph (1) (b) if the number of such scallops does not exceed five per cent of the total number of scallops retained by that person while so fishing, the percentage being determined on the basis of not less than eight representative samples, each sample weighing not less than one pound.

(3) Any person who catches a sea scallop the shell size of which is less than that specified in paragraph (1) (a) shall return it to the water immediately.

Herring

13. (1) Subject to subsection (2), no person shall, in those portions of division 4W of subarea 4 south of 44° 52′ north latitude, in those portions of division 4X of subarea 4 south of 43° 50′ north latitude and in subarea 5, catch and retain any herring that is less than nine inches in length measured from the tip of the nose to the end of the caudal fin.

(2) A person fishing for herring in the areas specified in subsection (1) may catch and retain herring the length of which is less than that specified in subsection (1) if the number of such herring does not exceed twenty-five per cent of the total number of herring caught and retained by that person while so fishing, the percentage being determined on the basis of not less than four representative samples, each sample weighing not less than twenty-five pounds.

Enforcement

14. (1) A protection officer may

(a) Require a vessel to bring to;

(b) Board the vessel; and

(c) Examine under oath the master or any member of the crew of the vessel concerning its cargo and voyage.

(2) Where a protection officer boards a vessel pursuant to paragraph (1) (b), the master of the vessel shall provide any assistance required by the protection officer.

(3) For the purpose of subsection (1), the signal requiring a vessel to bring to is

(a) The hoisting of a rectangular flag known as the International Code Flag "L", which flag is divided vertically and horizontally into quarters and coloured so that

    (i) Both the upper quarter next to the staff and the lower quarter next to the fly are yellow; and

    (ii) Both the lower quarter next to the staff and the upper quarter next to the fly are black;

(b) The flashing of a light to indicate the International Morse Code Letter "L", which consists of one short flash followed by one long flash followed by two short flashes; or

(c) The sounding of a horn or whistle to indicate the International Morse Code Letter "L", which consists of one short blast followed by one long blast followed by two short blasts.

Offences

15. Every person who,

(a) Being the master or person in command of a vessel, fails without legal excuse to bring to when required to do so by a protection officer or by a signal of a government vessel;

(b) Being on board a vessel, refuses to answer under oath any question asked him by a protection officer;

(c) Being on board a vessel that has been required by a protection officer or by a signal of a government vessel to bring to, throws overboard or destroys any part of the vessel's cargo, outfit or equipment;

(d) Resists or wilfully obstructs any protection officer in the execution of his duty; or

(e) Violates any other provision of these Regulations,

is guilty of an offence and is liable on summary conviction to a fine not exceeding one thousand dollars or to imprisonment for a term not exceeding one month or to both.

Seizure of goods

16. (1) Whenever a protection officer suspects on reasonable grounds that an offence under these Regulations has been committed, he may seize any vessel or any goods found on board the vessel by means of or in relation to which he reasonably believes the offence was committed.

(2) Subject to this section, any vessel or goods seized under subsection (1) shall be retained in the custody of the protection officer making the seizure or shall be delivered into the custody of such person as the Minister directs.

(3) Where fish or other perishable articles are seized under subsection (1), the protection officer or other person having the custody thereof may sell them, and the proceeds of the sale shall be paid to the Receiver General or deposited in a chartered bank to the credit of the Receiver General.

(4) Where any vessel or goods have been seized under subsection (1) and proceedings in respect of the offence have been instituted, the court or judge may, with the consent of the protection officer who made the seizure, order the vessel or goods to be returned to the person from whom they were seized upon the giving to Her Majesty of security by bond, with two sureties, in an amount and form satisfactory to the Minister.

. (5) Any vessel or goods seized under subsection (1) and the proceedings of any sale made under subsection (3) shall be returned or paid to the person from whom the vessel or goods were seized if the Minister decides not to institute proceedings in respect of the offence, and in any event shall be so returned or paid upon the expiration of three months from the day of seizure unless before that time proceedings in respect of the offence are instituted.

17. (1) Where a person is convicted of an offence under these Regulations, the convicting court or judge may, in addition to any other penalty imposed, order that

(a) Any vessel or any goods on board the vessel by means of or in relation to which the offence was committed; or

(b) The whole or any part of the proceeds of any sale made under subsection 16 (3)

be forfeited, and upon the making of the order the goods or proceeds so ordered to be forfeited are forfeited to Her Majesty.

(2) Where, at the conclusion of any proceedings in respect of an offence under these Regulations, any vessel or goods seized under subsection 16 (1) or proceeds of a sale made under subsection 16 (3) are not ordered to be forfeited, the vessel or goods shall be returned or the proceeds paid to the person from whom the vessel or goods were seized, unless there has been a conviction and a fine imposed, in which case

(a) The vessel or goods may be detained until the fine is paid;

(b) The vessel or goods may be sold under execution in satisfaction of the fine; or

(c) The proceeds may be applied in payment of the fine.

(3) Any vessel, goods or proceeds forfeited pursuant to subsection (1) may be disposed of as the Minister directs.

Protection of persons claiming interest in goods seized

18. Section 59 of the Fisheries Act applies, with such modifications as the circumstances may require, in respect of any vessel or goods forfeited under section 17 as though the vessel or goods were articles forfeited under subsection 58 (5) of that Act.

SCHEDULE I

Divisions of Subareas

1. *Division 2J of subarea 2.* That portion of the Convention area bounded on the north by the parallel of 55° 20′ north latitude; on the east by a rhumb line drawn in a northwesterly direction from a point at 52° 15′ north latitude and 42° 00′ west longitude to a point at 61° 00′ north latitude and 59° 00′ west longitude; on the south by the parallel of 52° 15′ north latitude; and on the west by the Canadian territorial waters off the coast of the Province of Newfoundland.

2. *Division 3K of subarea 3.* That portion of the Convention area bounded on the north by the parallel of 52° 15′ north latitude; on the east by the meridian of 42° 00′ west longitude; on the south by the parallel of 49° 15′ north latitude; and on the west by the Canadian territorial waters off the coast of the Province of Newfoundland.

3. *Division 3L of subarea 3.* That portion of the Convention area bounded on the north by the parallel of 49° 15′ north latitude; on the east by the meridian of 46° 30′ west longitude; on the south by the parallel of 46° 00′ north latitude; and on the west by a straight line drawn from a point at 46°00′ north latitude and 54° 30′ west longitude to Cape St. Mary's in the Province of Newfoundland and by the Canadian territorial waters off the coast of the Province of Newfoundland.

3.1. *Division 3M of subarea 3.* That portion of the Convention area bounded on the north by the parallel of 49° 15′ north latitude; on the east by the meridian of 42° 00′ west longitude; on the south by the parallel of 39° 00′ north latitude; and on the west by the meridian of 46° 30′ west longitude.

4. *Division 3N of subarea 3.* That portion of the Convention area bounded on the north by the parallel of 46° 00′ north latitude; on the east by the meridian of 46° 30′ west longitude; on the south by the parallel of 39° 00′ north latitude; on the southwest by a rhumb line drawn from a point at 39° 00′ north latitude and 50° 00′ west longitude to a point at 47° 50′ north latitude and 60° 00′ west longitude; and on the west by the meridian of 51° 00′ west longitude.

5. *Division 3O of subarea 3.* That portion of the Convention area bounded on the north by the parallel of 46° 00′ north latitude; on the east by the meridian of 51° 00′ west longitude; on the southwest by a rhumb line drawn from a point at 39° 00′ north latitude and 50° 00′ west longitude to a point at 47° 50′ north latitude and 60° 00′ west longitude; and on the west by the meridian of 54° 30′ west longitude.

6. *Division 3Ps of subarea 3.* That portion of the Convention area bounded on the north by the Canadian territorial waters off the coast of the Province of Newfoundland; on the east by a line drawn from Cape St. Mary's in the Province of Newfoundland to a point 46° 00′ north latitude and 54° 30′ west longitude and by the meridian of 54° 30′ west longitude; on the southwest by a rhumb line drawn from a point at 39° 00′ north latitude and 50° 00′ west longitude to a point at 47° 50′ north latitude and 60° 00′ west longitude; on the northwest by a straight line drawn from a point at 46° 50′ north latitude and 58° 50′ west longitude to Burgeo Island in the Province of Newfoundland.

7. *Division 3Pn of subarea 3.* That portion of the Convention area bounded on the north by the Canadian territorial waters off the coast of the Province of Newfoundland; on the southeast by a straight line drawn from Burgeo Island in the Province of Newfoundland to a point at 46° 50′ north latitude and 58° 50′ west longitude; on the southwest by a rhumb line drawn from a point at 39° 00′ north latitude and 50° 00′ west longitude to a point at 47° 50′ north latitude and 60° 00′ west longitude; and on the northwest by a straight line drawn from Cape Ray in the Province of Newfoundland to Cape North in the Province of Nova Scotia.

7.1. *Division 4T of subarea 4.* That portion of the Convention area bounded on the south and west by the territorial waters of Canada along the coasts of the Provinces of Nova Scotia, Prince Edward Island, New Brunswick and Quebec, on the north and northwest by a line beginning at Pointe des Monts and running due east to a point at 49° 25′ north latitude and 64° 40′ west longitude, thence along a rhumb line in a eastsoutheasterly direction to a point at 47° 50′ north latitude and 60° 00′ west longitude, and on the east by a line from the last mentioned point to Cape North in the Province of Nova Scotia.

7.2. *Division 4Vn of subarea 4.* That portion of the Convention area bounded on the west by the territorial waters of Canada off the Province of Nova Scotia and a line drawn from Cape North to a point 47° 50′ north latitude and 60° 00′ west longitude, on the northeast by a rhumb line drawn from the last mentioned point to a point 39° 00′ north latitude and 50° 00′ west longitude, and on the south by the parallel of 45° 40′ north latitude.

8. *Division 4Vs of subarea 4.* That portion of the Convention area bounded on the north by the parallel of 45° 40′ north latitude; on the northeast by a rhumb line drawn from a point at 39° 00′ north latitude and 50° 00′ west longitude to a point at 47° 50′ north latitude and 60° 00′ west longitude; on the south by the parallel of 39° 00′ north latitude; and on the west by the meridian of 59° 00′ west longitude, the parallel of 44° 10′ north latitude and the meridian of 60° 00′ west longitude.

9. *Division 4W of subarea 4.* That portion of the Convention area bounded on the north by the parallel of 45° 40′ north latitude; on the east by the meridian of 60° 00′ west longitude, the parallel of 44° 10′ north latitude and the meridian of 59° 00′ west longitude; on the south by the parallel of 39° 00′ north latitude; on the west by the meridian of 63° 20′ west longitude and a straight line drawn from a point at 63° 20′ west longitude and 44° 20′ north latitude to Cape Sambro in the Province of Nova Scotia; and on the northwest by the Canadian territorial waters off the coast of the Province of Nova Scotia.

10. *Division 4X of subarea 4.* That portion of the Convention area bounded on the north by the Canadian territorial waters off the coast of the Provinces of Nova Scotia and New Brunswick; on the east by a straight line drawn from Cape Sambro in the Province of Nova Scotia to a point at 44° 20′ north latitude and 63° 20′ west longitude and the meridian of 63° 20′ west longitude; on the south by the parallel of 39° 00′ north latitude; on the west by the meridian of 65° 40′ west longitude, by a rhumb line drawn from a point at 42° 00′ north latitude and 65° 40′ west longitude to a point at 42° 20′ north latitude and 66° 00′ west longitude, by the parallel of 42° 20′ north latitude, by the meridian of 67° 40′ west longitude, by the parallel of 43° 50′ north latitude and by the meridian of 66° 54′ 11.23″ west longitude to its intersection with the parallel of 44° 46′ 35.43″ north latitude.

11. *Division 5Y of subarea 5.* That portion of the Convention area bounded on the north and west by the outer limits of the territorial waters off the east coast of the United States; on the east by the meridian of 66° 55′ 11.23″ west longitude, by the parallel of 43° 50′ north latitude, by the meridian of 67° 40′ west longitude and by the meridian of 70° 00′ west longitude from 42° 20′ north latitude to Cape Cod; and on the south by the parallel of 42° 20′ north latitude.

12. *Division 5Ze of subarea 5.* That portion of the Convention area bounded on the north by the parallel of 42° 20′ north latitude; on the northeast by a rhumb line drawn from a point at 42° 20′ north latitude and 66° 00′ west longitude to a point 42° 00′ north latitude and 65° 40′ west longitude; on the east by the meridian of 65° 40 west longitude; on the south by the parallel of 39° 00′ north latitude; and on the west by the meridian of 70° 00′ west longitude and the outer limits of the territorial waters off the east coast of the United States.

13. *Division 5Zw of subarea 5.* That portion of the Convention area bounded on the north by the outer limits of the territorial waters off the east coast of the United States; on the east by the meridian of 70° 00′ west longitude; on the south by the parallel of 39° 00′ north latitude; and on the west by the meridian of 71° 40′ west longitude.

SCHEDULE II

Mesh sizes of nets

Column I Part of Convention Area	Column II Regulated Species	Column III Type of Net	Column IV Mesh Size (Cod-end of Net)	Column V Mesh Size (Generally)
1. Subarea 1	Cod Haddock Redfish Halibut Witch flounder	Seine net . . . . Such part of any trawl net as is made of cotton, hemp, polyamide fibres or polyester fibres . . .	4 3/8 in. 4 3/4 in.	4 3/8 in. 4 3/4 in.
	American plaice Greenland halibut	Such part of any trawl net as is made of any other material not mentioned above	5 1/8 in.	5 1/8 in.
2. Subarea 2	Cod Haddock Redfish Halibut	Seine net . . . . Such part of any trawl net as is made of cotton, hemp, polyamide fibres or polyester fibres . . .	4 3/8 in. 4 3/4 in.	4 3/8 in. 4 3/4 in.
	Witch flounder American plaice Greenland halibut	Such part of any trawl net as is made of any other material not mentioned above	5 1/8 in.	5 1/8 in.

3. Subarea 3	Cod
	Haddock
	Redfish, except in
	  Divisions 3N, 30,
	  3Ps and 3Pn
		Seine net
		
		Such part of any trawl net as is made of cotton, hemp, polyamide fibres or polyester fibres . . .
			4 3/8 in.
			
			4 3/4 in.
				4 3/8 in.
				
				4 3/4 in.

	Halibut Witch flounder Yellowtail flounder American plaice Greenland halibut Pollock White hake	Such part of any trawl net as is made of any other material not mentioned above	5 1/8 in.	5 1/8 in.

SCHEDULE II *(continued)*

Mesh sizes of nets

Column I Part of Convention Area	Column II Regulated Species	Column III Type of Net	Column IV Mesh Size (Cod-end of Net)	Column V Mesh Size (Generally)
4. Subarea 4	Cod Haddock Witch flounder Winter flounder American plaice	Seine net		4 3/8 in.
		Such part of any trawl net as is made of cotton, hemp, polyamide fibres or polyester fibres ...	4 3/4 in.	4 1/8 in.
	Yellowtail flounder	Such part of any trawl net as is made of any other material not mentioned above	5 1/8 in.	4 1/2 in.
5. Subarea 5	Cod Haddock Yellowtail flounder	Seine net		4 3/8 in.
		Such part of any trawl net as is made of cotton, hemp, polyamide fibres or polyester fibres ...	4 3/4 in.	4 1/8 in.
		Such part of any trawl net as is made of any other material not mentioned above	5 1/8 in.	4 1/2 in.

SCHEDULE III

Geographical coordinates of points

Column I Longitude	Column II Latitude
1. (1) 69° 55′ West	42° 10′ North
(2) 69° 10′ West	41° 10′ North
(3) 68° 30′ West	41° 35′ North
(4) 68° 45′ West	41° 50′ North
(5) 69° 00′ West	41° 50′ North
2. (1) 67° 00′ West	42° 20′ North
(2) 67° 00′ West	41° 15′ North
(3) 65° 40′ West	41° 15′ North
(4) 65° 40′ West	42° 00′ North
(5) 66° 00′ West	42° 20′ North
3. (1) 65° 44′ West	42° 04′ North
(2) 64° 30′ West	42° 40′ North
(3) 64° 30′ West	43° 00′ North
(4) 66° 32′ West	43° 00′ North
(5) 66° 32′ West	42° 20′ North
(6) 66° 00′ West	42° 20′ North

293

SCHEDULE IV

Fishing quotas

Column I Species	Column II Area or Portion Thereof		Column III Annual quota in metric tons
1. American Plaice	(a)	Subarea 2 and Division 3K of Subarea 3	(a) 2,500
	(b)	Divisions 3L, 3N and 3O of Subarea 3	(b) 48,000
	(c)	Division 3M of subarea 3	(c) 800
	(d)	Division 3Ps of subarea 3	(d) 8,800
2. Cod	(a)	Division 2J of subarea 2 and divisions 3K and 3L of subarea 3 ...	(a) 60,000
	(b)	Division 3M of subarea 3	(b) 3,000
	(c)	Divisions 3N and 3O of subarea 3 .	(c) 15,000
	(d)	Division 3Ps of subarea 3	(d) 40,000
	(e)	Division 4T of subarea 4 during the whole year and division 4Vn of subarea 4 during the period 1 January to 30 April	(e) 46,000
	(f)	Division 4Vn of Subarea 4 during the period 1 May to 30 December .	(f) 5,808
	(g)	Division 4Vs and 4W of subarea 4 .	(g) 24,250
	(h)	Divisions 5Ze and 5Zw of subarea 5	(h) 4,820
3. Finfish (not including menhaden, tuna, billfish or any species of shark except dogfish) and squid		Subarea 5	25,000
4. Herring	(a)	Division 5Y of subarea 5	(a) 6,000
	(b)	Division 5Ze of subarea 5	(b) 2,980
	(c)	Division 4X of Subarea 4 and that portion of division 4W of subarea 4 south of 44° 52' north latitude .	(c) 67,500
	(d)	Division 4V of subarea 4 and that portion of division 4W of subarea 4 north of 44° 52' north latitude .	(d) 39,800
5. Mackerel	(a)	Division 4V, 4W and 4X of subarea 4	(a) 20,000
	(b)	Subarea 5	(b) 8,000
6. Pollock		Divisions 4V, 4W and 4X of subarea 4 and subarea 5	34,000
7. Redfish	(a)	Division 3M of subarea 3	(a) 1,000
	(b)	Divisions 3L and 3N of subarea 3 .	(b) 3,000
	(c)	Division 3O of subarea 3	(c) 3,000
	(d)	Division 3P of subarea 3	(d) 9,500

SCHEDULE IV *(continued)*

Fishing quotas

Column I Species	Column II Area or Portion Thereof	Column III Annual quota in metric tons
	(e) Divisions 4V, 4W and 4X of sub-area 4	*(e)* 20,000
	(f) Subarea 5	*(f)* 414
	(g) Subarea 2 and Division 3K of subarea 3	*(g)* 3,500
8. Silver hake	Divisions 4V, 4W and 4X of subarea 4 .	2,000
9. Witch flounder	*(a)* Division 2J of subarea 2 and divisions 3K and 3L of subarea 3 ...	*(a)* 6,000
	(b) Divisions 3N and 3O of subarea 3 .	*(b)* 4,500
	(c) Division 3Ps of subarea 3	*(c)* 2,500
10. Yellowtail flounder	Divisions 4V, 4W and 4Y of subarea 3 .	32,400
11. Yellowtail floun-der, Witch flounder and American plaice	Divisions 4V, 4W and 4Y of subarea 4 .	20,000 in the aggregate
12. Greenland halibut	Subarea 2 and Divisions 3K and 3L of subarea 3	7,000
13. Capelin	*(a)* Subarea 2 and Division 3K of Subarea 3	*(a)* 10,000
	(b) Divisions 3L, 3N, 3O and 3Ps of subarea 3	*(b)* 20,000

(g) INTERNATIONAL PACIFIC HALIBUT CONVENTION REGULATIONS
OF 26 FEBRUARY 1974[1]

Section 1

Regulatory areas

(a) The "convention waters" include the territorial waters and the high seas off the western coasts of Canada and the United States of America and are divided into the following areas. All bearings are magnetic and all positions are determined by the most recent charts issued by the United States Coast and Geodetic Survey or National Ocean Survey.

[1] P.C. 1974-345, 26 February 1974. SOR/74-132, *Canada Gazette,* Part II, Vol. 108, No. 5, 13 March 1974. These Regulations implement the Regulations of the International Pacific Halibut Commission adopted pursuant to the Pacific Halibut Fishery Convention between Canada and the United States of America, signed on 2 March 1953 (United Nations, *Treaty Series,* Vol. 222, p. 77. Reproduced in part in ST/LEG/SER.B/8, pp. 51-53). In accordance with Section 13, the regulations reproduced in this volume are to be effective each succeeding year until superseded. They supersede all previous regulations of the Commission, including those of 1971 reproduced in part in ST/LEG/SER.B/16, pp. 288-291.

(b) Area 2 includes all convention waters east of a line running northwest one-quarter west (309°) from Cape Spencer Light (latitude 58° 11' 57" N., longitude 136° 38' 18" W.) and south and east of a line running south one-quarter east (174°) from said light.

(c) Area 3 includes all convention waters north and west of Area 2, excluding the Bering Sea.

(d) Area 4 includes all convention waters in the Bearing Sea. Areas 4A, 4B, 4C, 4D-East and 4E include all waters in the Bering Sea east of 175° W. Area 4D-West includes all waters in the Bering Sea west of 175° W.

(e) The boundary between Area 3 and Area 4 is from Cape Kabuch Light (latitude 54° 49' 00" N., longitude 163° 21' 36" W.) to Cape Sarichef Light (latitude 54° 36' 00" N., longitude 164° 55' 42" W.); then to a point in Pumicestone Bay on Unalaska Island (latitude 52° 59' 48" N., longitude 168° 55' 06" W.); then to Sequam Island Light (latitude 52° 23' 16" N., longitude 172° 26' 15" W.); then to Cape Amagalik (latitude 51° 40' 40" N., longitude 178° 07' 00" W.); then to Aleut Point (latitude 51° 38' 20" N., longitude 178° 37' 20" E.); then to Cape Wrangell, the westernmost extremity of Attu Island (latitude 52° 55' 20" N., longitude 172° 26' 50" E.); then west northwest.

(f) Area 4E includes all convention waters in the Bering Sea that are east of a line from Cape Sarichef Light (latitude 54° 36' 00" N., longitude 164° 55' 42" W.); to a point northeast of St. Paul Island (latitude 57° 15' 00" N., longitude 170° 00' 00" W.); and south of a line from the latter point to Cape Newenham (latitude 58° 39' 00" N., longitude 162° 10' 25" W.).

Section 2

Commercial fishing for halibut

The regulations and requirements in sections 3 to 11 pertain only to commercial fishing. The regulations for sport fishing are listed in section 12.

Section 3

Fishing seasons

(a) In Areas 2 and 3 the halibut fishing season shall commence at 1500 hours on 17 May and terminate at 0600 hours on a date to be determined and announced under paragraph *(b)* of section 5 of these Regulations, or at 0600 hours on 15 September, whichever is earlier.

(b) In Areas 4A, 4B, 4C and 4D-East the first halibut fishing season shall commence at 1800 hours on 1 April and terminate at 0600 hours on 19 April; the second season shall commence at 1800 hours on 15 September and terminate at 0600 hours on 30 September.

(c) In Area 4D-West the halibut fishing season shall commence at 1800 hours on 1 April and terminate at 0600 hours on 15 November.

(d) Area 4E in south-eastern Bering Sea is closed to halibut fishing, and no person shall fish for halibut therein or have halibut in his possession therein except in the course of a continuous transit across the area.

(e) All hours of opening and closing shall be Pacific Daylight Time in Areas 2 and 3 and Pacific Standard Time in Area 4.

Section 4
Closed seasons

(a) All convention waters shall be closed to commercial halibut fishing except as provided in section 3 of these Regulations, and the retention and landing of any halibut caught during any closed period shall be prohibited.

(b) These Regulations shall not prohibit the fishing for species of fish other than halibut during the closed halibut seasons, provided that it shall be unlawful for a vessel to have halibut aboard, or for any person to have halibut in his possession while so engaged. Nor shall these Regulations prohibit the International Pacific Halibut Commission, hereafter referred to as "the Commission", from conducting or authorizing fishing operations for research purposes.

Section 5
Catch limits

(a) The quantities of halibut to be taken during the halibut fishing season shall be limited to 13,000,000 pounds in Area 2 to 12,000,000 pounds in Area 3.

(b) The Commission will determine and announce the dates on which the catch limits will be attained in each area. Fishing for halibut in the area will be prohibited after that date.

Section 6
Size limits

(a) No person, firm or corporation may retain or have in possession any halibut that with head on is less than 32 inches as measured in a straight line, passing over the pectoral fin, from the tip of the lower jaw to the extreme end of the middle of the tail, or with head off is less than 24 inches as measured from the base of the pectoral fin, at its most anterior point, to the extreme end of the middle of the tail (see illustration).[1]

(b) Possession of halibut or portions from halibut below the minimum size is prohibited.

Section 7
Licensing of vessels

(a) All vessels of any tonnage which shall fish for halibut in any manner or hold halibut in possession in any area, or which shall transport halibut otherwise than as a common carrier documented by the Government of Canada or the United States for the carriage of freight, must be licensed by the Commission, provided that vessels of less than five net tons or vessels which use hook and line gear other than setlines need not be licensed.

(b) The halibut license must be carried on the vessel at all times and shall be subject to inspection by customs and fishery officers of the Government of Canada or the United States (hereinafter called the Governments) or by representatives of the Commission.

---

[1] Not reproduced in this volume.

(c) The halibut license shall be issued without fee by the customs officers of the Government of Canada or the United States or by representatives of the Commission or by fishery officers of the Government of Canada or the United States at places where there are neither customs officers nor representatives of the Commission.

(d) The halibut license of any vessel fishing for halibut in Area 4 must be validated at Sand Point, Alaska, both prior to such fishing and prior to unloading any halibut at any port other than Sand Point, Alaska. This validation shall be by United States customs or fishery officers or by a representative of the Commission.

(e) A halibut license shall not be valid for halibut fishing nor for possession of halibut in any area closed to halibut fishing except while in transit to an area open to halibut fishing, or to or within a port of sale. The license shall be invalid for the possession of halibut if the licensed vessel is fishing or attempting to fish for any species of fish in any area closed to halibut fishing.

(f) Any vessel which is not required to be licensed for halibut fishing under paragraph *(a)* of this section of these Regulations shall not possess any halibut of any origin in any area closed to halibut fishing except while in actual transit to or within a port of sale.

(g) No person on any vessel shall fish for halibut or have halibut in his possession, unless said vessel has a valid license issued in conformity with the provisions of this section.

(h) The captain or operator of any vessel holding a license under these Regulations shall keep an accurate log of all fishing operations including date, locality, amount of gear used and amount of halibut taken daily in each such locality. This log record shall be retained for a period of two years and shall be open to inspection by authorized representatives of the Commission.

(i) The captain, operator or any other person engaged on shares in the operation of any vessel licensed under these Regulations may be required by the Commission or by any officer of the Governments to certify to the correctness of such log record to the best of his information and belief and to support the certificate by a sworn statement.

Section 8

Statistical return by dealers

(a) All persons, firms or corporations that buy halibut or receive halibut from fishing or transporting vessels or other carrier shall keep records of each purchase or receipt of halibut, showing date, locality (statistical area), name of vessel, person, firm or corporation purchased or received from and the amount in pounds according to trade categories of the halibut.

(b) These records shall be retained for a period of two years and shall be open to inspection by any enforcement officer of the Governments or by any authorized representative of the Commission. Such persons, firms or corporations may be required to certify to the correctness of such records and to support the certificate by a sworn statement.

(c) The possession of halibut known to have been taken by a vessel without a valid halibut license is prohibited.

Section 9

Fishing gear

(a) Halibut are permitted to be taken only with hook and line gear. The retention or possession of halibut taken with any other gear, such as nets or pots, is prohibited.

(b) The retention or possession of halibut is prohibited when any commercial fishing gear other than hook and line gear or nets used solely for the capture of bait are on board.

Section 10

Retention of tagged halibut

Nothing contained in these Regulations shall prohibit any vessel at any time from retaining and landing a halibut which bears a Commission tag at the time of capture, provided that the halibut with the tag still attached is reported at the time of landing and made available for examination by representatives of the Commission or by enforcement officers of the State, Provincial or Federal Governments.

Section 11

Supervision of unloading and weighing

The unloading and weighing of halibut may be subject to the supervision of customs or other authorized officers to assure the fulfilment of the provisions of these Regulations.

Section 12

Sport fishing for halibut

(a) Sport fishing is permitted from 1 March to 31 October in all convention waters. The daily catch by any person is limited to one halibut of any size, caught with a hook attached to a handline or rod.

(b) It is illegal for any person to possess sport-caught halibut aboard a vessel when other fish or shellfish aboard said vessel are destined for commercial use (sale, trade or barter).

(c) Nothing in these Regulations shall restrict the right of the Government of Canada or of the state fisheries agencies of the United States of America to establish additional restrictive measures for the halibut sport fishery.

Section 13

Previous regulations superseded

These Regulations shall supersede all previous regulations of the Commission. These Regulations shall be effective each succeeding year, until superseded.

(h) COASTAL FISHERIES PROTECTION REGULATIONS
OF 19 MARCH 1974[1] AS AMENDED[2]

Short title

1. These Regulations may be cited as the Coastal Fisheries Protection Regulations.

Interpretation

2. In these Regulations,

"Act" means the Coastal Fisheries Protection Act;[3]

"Minister" means the Minister of Fisheries for Canada;

"license" means a license issued pursuant to these Regulations;

"permit" means a permit issued pursuant to these Regulations.

Licenses and permits

3. (1) The Minister may issue any license or permit referred to in these Regulations.

(2) A person designated by the Minister may issue a permit referred to in section 5.

Entering Canadian ports

4. (1) A United States fishing vessel may, under the authority of a license, enter any port on the Atlantic coast of Canada for the purpose of purchasing bait, supplies or outfits.

(2) A foreign fishing vessel, other than a United States fishing vessel, may, under the authority of a license, enter any port in the Province of Nova Scotia or Newfoundland during the period stated in the license for the purpose of purchasing bait, supplies or outfits.

(3) A license issued under this section is valid only during the calendar year in which it is issued.

(4) A fee of one dollar shall be paid upon application for a license issued under this section.

5. Subject to the customs laws of Canada, fish on board a disabled foreign fishing vessel entering any port on the Atlantic coast of Canada for repairs may, under the authority of a permit, be unloaded, landed or trans-shipped.

6. Subject to the customs and immigration laws of Canada, a foreign fishing vessel may, under the authority of a permit, enter any Canadian port

---

[1] P.C. 1974-605, 19 March 1974. SOR/74-173, *Canada Gazette,* Part II, Vol. 108, No. 7, 10 April 1974. These regulations supersede the regulations of 17 January 1957 as amended up to 1973, reproduced in ST/LEG/SER.B/15, pp. 602-603.

[2] P.C. 1974-1199, 30 May 1974, SOR/74-335, *Canada Gazette,* Part II, Vol. 108, No. 12, 26 June 1974.

[3] Partially reproduced in ST/LEG/SER.B/15, p. 599 and in ST/LEG/SER.B/16, pp. 282-283.

(a) To discharge or take on board a crew member or passenger of that vessel or of any other fishing vessel registered under the same national flag; or

(b) To unload, land, re-embark or trans-ship any equipment, other than fishing gear, of that vessel or of any other fishing vessel registered under the same national flag.

Entering Canadian fisheries waters

7. A United States fishing vessel may pass through the Canadian fisheries waters known as the "Inland Passage" in the Province of British Columbia under the following conditions:

(a) All fishing gear shall be removed from its normal position of operation on board the vessel and stowed in such a manner that it is not in readiness for fishing; and

(b) The vessel shall comply with any directions given to it by a protection officer.

8. A United States fishing vessel may, under the authority of a permit, enter Canadian fisheries waters off the coast of British Columbia to take on board or trans-ship pink salmon.

9. A United States sport fishing vessel may enter Canadian fisheries waters for sport fishing subject to the fisheries and customs laws of Canada.

10. A fishing vessel of any state that is a party to a fisheries conservation convention with Canada and the crew thereof may, under the authority of a permit, enter Canadian fisheries waters for the purpose of scientific research or engaging in experimental fisheries operations, and do all or any of the things described in paragraphs 3 (2) *(a)* to *(e)* of the Act, subject to the conditions set out in the permit

Signal to bring to

11. For the purpose of section 7 of the Act, the signal requiring a fishing vessel to bring to is

(a) The hoisting of a rectangular flag known as the International Code Flag "L", which flag is divided vertically and horizontally into quarters and coloured so that

   (i) Both the upper quarter next to the staff and the lower quarter next to the fly are yellow; and

   (ii) Both the lower quarter next to the staff and the upper quarter next to the fly are black;

(b) The flashing of a light to indicate the International Morse Code Letter "L", which consists of one short flash followed by one long flash followed by two short flashes; or

(c) The sounding of a horn or whistle to indicate the International Morse Code Letter "L", which consists of one short blast followed by one long blast followed by two short blasts.

Fishing zones

12. Fishing vessels of the United States may fish in the fishing zones established by section 4 of the Territorial Sea and Fishing Zones Act.

3. DENMARK

(a) ACT NO. 570 OF 21 DECEMBER 1972 ON THE PROHIBITION OF SALMON FISHING IN THE NORTH-WEST ATLANTIC[1]

Article 1. 1. In pursuance of the recommendations made by the International Commission for the Northwest Atlantic Fisheries, the Minister of Fisheries may establish regulations prohibiting, as from 1 January 1976, the fishing of salmon in those parts of the Atlantic waters to which article 1 of the Convention of 8 February 1949 for the Northwest Atlantic Fisheries[2] applies (Notice No. 3 of 8 February 1951, *Lovtidende C*) and which lie outside the national fishing limits.

2. In respect of Danish nationals or companies, etc., domiciled elsewhere in the realm than in Greenland, the Minister of Fisheries may also establish similar regulations for that part of the area covered by the Convention lying between 12 and 3 nautical miles from the coast or from the baselines established off Greenland.

3. As regards the Faroe Islands, the regulations referred to in paragraphs 1 and 2 shall be established after consultation with and with the approval of the local government of the Faroe Islands.

. . .

(b) ACT NO. 413 OF 13 JUNE 1973 ON COMMERCIAL FISHING, TRAPPING AND HUNTING IN GREENLAND[3]

Article 1. 1. Commercial fishing, trapping and hunting in the sea off Greenland within a distance of 12 nautical miles from the boundary line set by the Minister for Greenland may be engaged in only by:

(1) Persons who are resident in Greenland and have a regular connexion with the Greenland community;

(2) Institutions and associations the management of which consists exclusively of persons referred to in subparagraph (1);

(3) Jointly-owned shipping companies not less than two thirds of the shares in which and the majority of the capital of which are owned by persons referred to in subparagraph (1), and the managing owner of which is a person referred to in subparagraph (1);

(4) Joint-stock companies and other limited liability companies which have elected a board of directors, if at least two thirds of the board and the majority of the partners consist of persons referred to in subparagraph (1) and if the majority of the company's capital is owned by persons referred to in subparagraph (1).

---

[1] Danish text provided by the Ministry of Foreign Affairs in a note verbale of 4 January 1974. Translation by the Secretariat of the United Nations.

[2] United Nations, *Treaty Series,* vol. 157, p. 157. Reproduced in ST/LEG/SER.B/15, pp. 832-838.

[3] Danish text provided by the Ministry of Foreign Affairs of Denmark in a note verbale of 4 January 1974. Translation by the Secretariat of the United Nations. For the status of previous legislation, see article 12.

2. Where institutions, associations or companies are partners in a jointly-owned shipping company or in a company as referred to in paragraph 1, subparagraph (4), each partner must meet the requirements to be able to engage in commercial fishing, trapping and hunting independently.

. . .

5. Persons, etc., other than those referred to in paragraph 1 may not, without permission from the Minister or from the Governor of Greenland by authorization of the Minister, process or trans-ship fish or fish products in the area referred to in paragraph 1, or transport fish or fish products directly from the sea through that area to landing places in Greenland.

6. Only vessels registered as having their home port in Greenland may be used for the purposes referred to in paragraphs 1 and 5.

7. In very exceptional circumstances the Minister may depart from the provisions of paragraphs 1 and 6 when such departure is considered important for the development of the Greenland fishing industry.

8. The Minister may lay down regulations[1] under which persons and companies, etc., not covered by paragraph 1, but covered by article 1, paragraph 1, of Act No. 233 of 3 June 1967 on commercial trapping, fishing and hunting in Greenland,[2] may continue, until 31 December 1977, to engage in the activities referred to in paragraphs 1 and 5, and for that purpose may use vessels registered as having their home port in another part of the Kingdom.

. . .

Article 4. 1. The Minister for Greenland may, for the land territory and territorial waters of Greenland, lay down regulations concerning:

(1) The protection of animal and fish varieties, including regulations concerning:

(a) Closed seasons;

(b) Protected areas;

(c) Quantitative restrictions on the catch and restrictions on the input;

(d) Prohibitions on catching;

(e) Minimum sizes;

(f) The supply and use of implements and accessories;

(g) Prohibition of the use of certain appliances, types of appliances and catching methods;

(h) The apportionment, including apportionment at the national level, of the quantities that may be caught and of the input;

(2) Fishing rules;

(3) Measures to check observance of the regulations.

. . .

---

[1] See, e.g., *infra (c)*.

[2] Reproduced in part in ST/LEG/SER.B/15, pp. 627-629.

Article 5. Vessels equipped for fishing, trapping or hunting which enter the sea area mentioned in article 1, paragraph 1, without being entitled to fish, trap or hunt in that area shall have all their fishing, trapping or hunting gear stowed inboard and the boats aboard the vessel in their normal position.

Article 6. The Fishery Inspection Service of the Office of Naval Defence and the Greenland authorities may cause fishing vessels or vessels used to transport fish to be stopped and boarded so that official actions, including examination of ship's papers and inspection of fishing gear and catches, may be carried out, and they may require gear to be brought in for the purposes of official inspection. Furthermore, such vessels may be ordered to accompany the inspecting vessel to port for the purposes of search or the unloading of the catch.

Article 7. 1. Any breach of article 1, paragraphs 1-3, 5 and 6, article 3, paragraph 1, and article 5, or failure to comply with an order given in pursuance of article 6 may give rise to a warning or be punishable by a fine.

2. Regulations made under the Act may provide that violation of provisions of the regulations may also give rise to a warning or be punishable by a fine.

3. Confiscation shall be governed by the provisions of the Criminal Code. However, gear may be confiscated by reason both of a wilful offence and of an offence due to negligence. In addition, the catch or the value thereof may be confiscated even if it cannot be proved with certainty to have resulted entirely from the unlawful conduct.

Article 8. 1. If a reasonable presumption exists that a vessel has been used in connexion with an offence covered by article 7, the vessel may be seized by the authorities mentioned in article 6.

2. Outside the sea area referred to in article 1, paragraph 1, a foreign vessel may be stopped, searched or seized if a reasonable presumption exists that the offence was committed within the area or if pursuit was begun while the vessel was still within the area and was thereafter continued without interruption.

Article 9. 1. A vessel which is seized in pursuance of this Act may, if in the commission of the offence it was used by persons, companies, etc., other than those referred to in article 1, paragraph 1, be detained together with all gear until the amounts due in respect of fines, confiscation and costs have been paid or security for the payment thereof has been furnished. If payment is not made or security furnished within two months after the final disposition of the case, satisfaction may be sought against the vessel and gear.

. . .

Article 11. The Act shall be without prejudice to any rights granted to foreign nationals in Greenland under international agreements entered into before the Act came into force.

Article 12. Act No. 223 of 3 June 1967 on commercial trapping, fishing, and hunting in Greenland[1] is repealed. Notice No. 528 of 3 December 1969

---

[1] Reproduced in part in ST/LEG/SER.B/15, pp. 627-629.

on the regulation of fishing in Greenland waters, Notice No. 529 of 3 December 1969 on the admission of foreign vessels to Greenland waters for fishing, etc.,[1] and Notice No. 241 of 2 June 1972 on the prohibition of the use of certain means of transport for hunting in Greenland remain, however, in force.

(c) EXECUTIVE ORDER NO. 436 OF 23 JULY 1973 CONCERNING DANISH AND FAROESE FISHERIES IN GREENLAND WATERS[2]

Pursuant to article 1, paragraphs 5 and 8, of Act No. 413 of 13 June 1973 on Commercial Fishing, Trapping and Hunting in Greenland,[3] it is hereby ordered as follows:

Article 1. 1. This Notice shall apply to the following persons and establishments not resident in Greenland and having no regular connexion with the Greenland community:

(1) Danish nationals;

(2) Institutions and associations the management of which consists exclusively of Danish nationals who are resident in Denmark;

(3) Jointly-owned shipping companies at least two thirds of which are owned by Danish nationals and the managing owner of which is a Danish national and is resident in Denmark;

(4) Joint-stock companies and other with limited-liability companies which have elected a board of directors, if at least two thirds of the board consists of Danish nationals who are resident in Denmark;

(5) Other companies in which at least two thirds of the partners are Danish nationals who are resident in Denmark.

2. Where institutions, associations or companies are partners in a jointly-owned shipping company or in a company as referred to in paragraph 1 (5), each partner must meet the requirements of this Notice to be able to engage in fishing operations independently.

Article 2. The persons and establishments referred to in paragraph 1 shall be allowed to engage in the activities specified hereunder (see, however, the exceptions in articles 3 to 5); they may do so only until 31 December 1977 and only with vessels registered in Denmark:

(1) To engage in commercial fishing within 12 nautical miles from the baselines established in the Order on the delimitation of the territorial waters of Greenland;

---

[1] Reproduced in ST/LEG/SER.B/16, pp. 296-297.

[2] This Executive Order, in accordance with article 8 thereof, came into force on 24 July 1973, the day after its publication in the Official Gazette *(Lovtidende)*. It repealed Notice No. 530 of 3 December 1969 concerning commercial trapping, fishing and hunting in Greenland, reproduced in part in ST/LEG/SER.B/16, pp. 297-298. Danish text provided by the Ministry of Foreign Affairs of Denmark in a note verbale of 4 January 1974. Translation by the Secretariat of the United Nations.

[3] *Supra (b).*

(2) To process and trans-ship fish and fish products within the area mentioned in (1) above;

(3) To transport fish and fish products directly from the sea through the area mentioned in (1) above to landing places in Greenland.

Article 3. Commercial fishing may not be engaged in the areas mentioned in the annex [1] to this Notice ("closed areas").

Article 4. Commercial fishing involving the use of fixed fishing tackle attached to land may not be carried on within a distance of 3 nautical miles from the baselines established in the Order on the delimitation of the territorial waters of Greenland.

Article 5. Commercial salmon and sea-trout fishing may not be carried on inside the baselines established in the Order on the delimitation of the territorial waters of Greenland.

Article 6. The Governor of Greenland may, in special cases, grant to persons other than those mentioned in article 1 specific permission to engage in the activities mentioned in article 2 (2) and (3).

Article 7. Any violation of the provisions of this Notice or of the conditions of the authorizations granted pursuant to the Notice may lead to a warning or fine. Such cases shall be tried, moreover, in accordance with the rules laid down in the Act on commercial fishing, trapping and hunting in Greenland.

. . .

(d) EXECUTIVE ORDER NO. 25 OF 28 JANUARY 1974 FOR THE FAROE ISLANDS CONCERNING THE REGULATION OF FISHERIES IN THE NORTH-EAST ATLANTIC OCEAN[2]

Article 1. This Executive order shall apply, in accordance with the provisions of the North-East Atlantic Fisheries Convention,[3] to fisheries in waters situated within

1. Those parts of the Atlantic and Arctic Oceans and their dependent seas which lie north of 36° north latitude and between 42° west longitude and 51° east longitude, but excluding

(a) The Baltic Sea and Belts lying to the south and east of lines drawn from Hasenore Head to Gniben Point, from Korshage to Spodsbjerg and from Gilbierg Head to the Kullen; and

(b) The Mediterranean Sea and its dependent seas as far as the point of intersection of the parallel of 36° north latitude and the meridian of 5° 36' west longitude.

---

[1] The annex is not reproduced in this volume.

[2] Issued by the Ministry of Fisheries on 28 January 1974. In force immediately in accordance with article 20. It superseded a prior Executive Order of 7 February 1973 on the same subject. Danish text transmitted by the Ministry of Foreign Affairs of Denmark in a note verbale of 20 December 1974. Translation by the Secretariat of the United Nations.

[3] Reproduced in document ST/LEG/SER.B/15, pages 853-857.

2. That part of the Atlantic Ocean north of 59° north latitude and between 44° west longitude and 42° west longitude.

Article 2. The Convention area referred to in article 1 shall be divided into three regions, indicated on the attached map and defined as follows:

Region 1. The part of the Convention area bounded on the south by a line running from a point 59° north latitude 44° west longitude due east to the meridian of 42° west longitude; thence due east to the meridian of 4° west longitude; thence due north to the parallel of 64° north latitude; thence due east to the coast of Norway; thence north and east along the coast of Norway and along the coast of the Soviet Union as far as the meridian of 51° east longitude.

Region 2. The part of the Convention area situated north of 48° north latitude and not covered by region 1.

Region 3. The part of the Convention area between 36° and 48° north latitude.

Article 3. 1. No vessel may carry on board or use any kind of trawl, Danish seine or other net towed through the water where the size of the mesh in any part of the net is smaller than that specified in articles 4 to 7 (cf., however, articles 8 to 10).

2. The size of the mesh shall correspond to the maximum width of a flat gauge 2 mm thick which can pass easily through the mesh stretched diagonally lengthwise when the net is wet.

Article 4. In region 1 the minimum size shall be as follows:

1. In the case of those waters situated east of the meridian of Greenwich:

(a) In the case of Danish seines of any material: 110 mm.

(b) In the case of those parts of trawl nets made of cotton, hemp, polyamide fibre or polyester fibre: 120 mm.

(c) In the case of those parts of trawl nets made of any materials other than those mentioned in subparagraph *(b)*: 130 mm.

2. In the case of those waters situated west of the meridian of Greenwich:

(a) In the case of Danish seines of any material: 110 mm.

(b) In the case of those parts of trawl nets made of cotton, hemp, polyamide fibre or polyester fibre: 120 mm.

(c) In the case of those parts of trawl nets made of any materials other than those mentioned in subparagraph *(b)*: 130 mm.

Article 5. In region 2 the minimum mesh size shall be as follows:

(1) In the case of Danish seines of any material and in the case of trawl nets made of single twine without manila or sisal: 70 mm.

(2) In the case of trawl nets made of double twine without manila or sisal: 75 mm.

(3) In the case of trawl nets made of manila or sisal: 80 mm.

Article 6. In region 3 the minimum mesh size of Danish seines or trawl nets shall be 60 mm.

Article 7. Throughout the entire Convention area outside the national fishery limits the following regulations shall apply with respect to gear used for salmon fishing: drift nets, fixed nets and Danish seines shall have a mesh-gauge no smaller than 160 mm. Hooks shall have an opening no smaller than 1.9 cm and the snell (suspended) shall have a minimum strength equivalent to 0.6 monofilament nylon. The use of all kinds of trawl, monofilament netting and trolling line shall be prohibited.

Article 8. (1) Notwithstanding the foregoing regulations concerning mesh size, cordage or similar materials may be attached to the underside of the cod-end of a trawl net to prevent or reduce wear and tear.

(2) In those waters where the prescribed minimum mesh size is 100 mm or more, a rectangular protective bag of netting may, until 31 December 1975, also be affixed to the upper side of the cod-end of the trawl net to prevent or reduce wear and tear, subject to the following requirements:

(i) The netting may not have a mesh-gauge smaller than that prescribed for the net itself.

(ii) The netting may only be attached to the cod-end in front and along the sides and shall be attached in such a way that, in front, it only extends as far as four meshes before the splitting strap and, behind, ends at least four meshes before the cod-line. If a splitting strap is not used, the net may cover no more than a third of the cod-end, measured from the front edge to at least four meshes before the cod-line.

(iii) The number of meshes in the width of the netting shall be no less than one and a half times as large as in the width of the part of the cod-end which it covers. Both widths shall be measured at right angles to the longitudinal axis of the cod-end.

Article 9. (1) Vessels, fishing for mackerel, all clupeoid species, sand eel, Norway pout poutassou, capelin, smelt, eel, greater weever, horse-mackerel, shrimp, deep-water shrimp, deep-water lobster or molluscs, may, for the purpose of such fishing, carry on board and use seines with a smaller mesh-gauge than that indicated in articles 4 to 6.

(2) However, vessels engaging in the type of fishing referred to in paragraph 1 in waters west of the line between Hanstholm and Lindesnes, may not carry nets with a mesh-gauge ranging between 50 mm and the minimum size specified in articles 4 to 6.

Article 10. Notwithstanding the provisions of article 5, until 1 January 1980 vessels with a motor power not exceeding 150 hp, engaged in fishing for whiting in the waters east of a line running between Hanstholm and Lindesnes may use nets with a mesh-gauge smaller than that indicated in article 5 and land whiting under the minimum size indicated in article 13 without any restriction as to quantity. Such catches may not include fish other than the species mentioned in article 13.

Article 11. The National Executive may permit fishing gear not meeting the requirements laid down in articles 4 to 9, to be carried and used when this is done with a view to transplantation or for scientific purposes.

Article 12. The Act of the Legislative Assembly's concerning fishing in the fishery zone shall not be affected by the provisions of this Executive Order.

Article 13. (1) The following minimum dimensions for the species of fish enumerated below, measured from the tip of the snout to the extreme end of the tail fin, are prescribed for the Convention area (cf. arts. 1 and 2):

	Region 1 cm.	Region 2 cm.	Region 3 cm.
Salmon (Salmo salar)	60	60	60
Atlantic cod (Gadus morhua)	34	30	
Haddock (Melanogrammus aeglefinus)	31	27	
Whiting (Merlangus merlangus)	23	23	
European hake (Merluccius merluccius)	30	30	30
European plaice (Pleuronectus platessa)	25	25	
Common dab (Limanda limanda)	15	15	
Witch (Glyptocephalus cynoglossus)	28	28	
Lemon sole (Microstomus kitt)	25	25	
Sole (Solea solea)	24	24	24
Turbot (Psetta maxima)	30	30	
Brill (Scophthalmus rhombus)	30	30	
Fluke (Lepidorhombus whiffiagonis)	25	25	

(2) The provisions of paragraph 1 shall not apply to fish caught in the Faroese fishery zone with a handline or long line.

(3) The regulations laid down in other fishery legislation concerning the minimum size of certain species of fish shall not be affected by this Executive Order where they are stricter.

Article 14. (1) Salmon fishing shall not be permitted in the Convention area (cf. arts. 1 and 2) outside the national fishery limits

(i) Between the parallels of 63° and 68° north latitude east of the meridian of Greenwich and east of the meridian of 22° east longitude;

(ii) In region 2 south of the parallel of 62° north latitude between 2° east longitude and 11° west longitude;

(iii) Within an area defined by the following lines: from 27° west longitude along the parallel of 62° north latitude to 11° west longitude; thence due north to 68° north latitude, thence due west to 27° west longitude and thence due south to 62° north latitude.

(2) In regions 1 and 2 salmon fishing shall not be permitted outside the national fishery limits during the period from 1 July to 5 May inclusive.

Article 15. (1) Herring fishing in the North Sea and the Skagerrak shall not be permitted during the period from 1 February to 15 June 1974 inclusive. In this connexion the Skagerrak and the North Sea are bounded in the north by the parallel of 62° north latitude, in the west by the meridian of 4° west longitude from 62° north latitude to the Scottish coast, and in the English Channel by 1° west longitude and in the east by a line running from Skagen to Pater Noster Lighthouse.

(2) Notwithstanding the provisions of paragraph 1, any landing of fish may contain up to 10 per cent in weight of herring.

(3) The Faroese National Executive may, after consultation with the Minister for Fisheries allow a certain amount of herring to be caught during the close season for special consumption purposes in accordance with decisions by the North-East Atlantic Fisheries Commission.

Article 15A. Purse seines may not be used for herring fishing in the Celtic Sea. In this connexion the Celtic Sea is bounded in the north by 52° 30' north latitude, in the south by 49° north latitude, in the east by 5° west longitude, and in the west by 9° west longitude.

Article 15B. (1) Herring fishing shall not be permitted in that part of regions 1 and 2 which is bounded to the west and south by the following lines, along 11° west longitude due south to 63° north latitude; thence due west to 15° west longitude; thence due south to 60° north latitude; thence due east to 5° west longitude; thence due north to 60° 30' north latitude; thence due east to 4° west longitude; thence due north to 62° north latitude; thence due east to the Norwegian coast.

(2) The Faroese National Executive may, after consultation with the Minister for Fisheries, allow a certain amount of herring to be caught in the protected area for special consumption purposes in accordance with a decision by the North-East Atlantic Fisheries Commission.

(3) The provisions of paragraph 1 shall not apply to catches in the Faroese fishery zone of the local, early summer-spawning herring.

Article 16. (1) In the case of mackerel caught in the North Sea, the Skagerrak and the Kattegat, and which are not considered to be for human consumption, these shall be a minimum size of 30 cm, measured from the tip of the snout to the extreme end of the tail fin. In this connexion, the North Sea, the Skaggerak and the Kattegat are bounded in the north from 62° north latitude to the Scottish coast; in the English Channel by the parallel of 51° north latitude and in the east by the lines running between Hasenore and Gniben Point, Korshage and Spodsbjerg and Gilbierg Head and the Kullen.

(2) Nothwithstanding the provisions of paragraph 1, any landing of mackerel may contain up to 20 per cent in weight of mackerel under the prescribed minimum size.

Article 17. (1) Fish or parts of fish which do not conform to the minimum size prescribed in article 13, and protected fish caught in the close season (cf. articles 14 and 15) may not be killed, kept on board, landed, stored, sold, offered for sale or taken from one place to another, but shall immediately be returned to the sea as far as possible in a condition fit for survival.

(2) In the types of fishing referred to in article 9, however, catches not considered to be for human consumption may contain up to 10 per cent in weight of the species of fish mentioned in article 13, paragraph 1, except for salmon under the minimum size prescribed in article 13. Similarly, in the aforesaid types of fishing the minimum size for whiting shall be 20 cm.

(3) The National Executive may permit the catching, landing and transport of fish under the prescribed minimum size where the catch is made with a view to transplantation or for the purpose of scientific research.

Article 18. (1) Control over the implementation of the provisions of this Executive Order and the rules laid down in connexion therewith shall be exercised by the police or such organs or persons as are authorized to that effect by the National Executive.

(2) Pursuant to a decision by the North-East Atlantic Fisheries Commission, the supervisory functions referred to in paragraph 1 may be exercised outside the fishery limits also by inspectors especially authorized for the purpose by authorities of another member country.

(3) Vessels with the inspectors referred to in paragraph 2 on board shall fly a pennant with two yellow and two blue fields with the letters NE in the upper yellow field.

(4) Upon orders from one of the control authorities referred to in paragraphs 1 and 2 any vessel, fishing or dealing with fish in the Convention area shall stop unless it is engaged in putting out gear, fishing with gear or hauling in gear, in which case it shall stop as soon as the hauling-in process is completed. The master of the fishing vessel shall permit the inspector and, if necessary, a witness to go on board. The master shall also assist the inspector in such inspection of catch and gear both on and below deck and examination of ship's papers as the inspector may find necessary in order to verify that the provisions of this Executive Order have been complied with. The inspector shall be entitled to request such explanations as he may find necessary.

Article 19. (1) Offences against article 3, paragraph 1, article 7, article 8, paragraph 2, article 10, second sentence, article 14, article 15, paragraphs 1 and 2, article 15A, article 15B, article 16 and article 18, paragraph 4, shall be punishable by a fine.

(2) The regulations of the Civil Criminal Code shall apply with respect to confiscation. A catch may be confiscated even if it cannot be definitely established that it derives in its entirety from the unlawful circumstance.

(3) Undersized fish and protected fish shall be set free in the open sea by the supervisory authorities immediately after the impounding or seizure in accordance with Chapter 68 of the Code of Civil Procedure provided that the person charged with the offence admits the offence and provided that the fish are in a condition fit for survival.

(4) Half of the fines shall go to the Treasury and the other half to the Relief Fund for Disabled Fishermen.

(e) EXECUTIVE ORDER NO. 26 OF 28 JANUARY 1974 BY THE MINISTRY OF FISHERIES CONCERNING THE REGULATION OF FISHERIES IN THE NORTH-EAST ATLANTIC OCEAN[1] AS AMENDED[2]

Articles 1-11[3]

Article 12. The provisions contained in Chapter IV A of the Act on Salt-Water Fisheries[4] concerning the use of certain types of fishing gear shall not be affected by the provisions of this Executive Order.

Article 13. (1) The following minimum dimensions for the species of fish enumerated below, measured from the tip of the snout to the extreme end of the tail fin, are prescribed for the Convention area (cf. arts. 1 and 2):[5]

	Region		
	1 cm.	2 cm.	3 cm.
Salmon (Salmo salar)	60	60	60
Atlantic cod (Gadus morhua)	34	30	
Haddock (Melanogrammus aeglefinus)	31	27	
Whiting (Merlangus merlangus)	23	23	
European hake (Merluccius merluccius)	30	30	30
European plaice (Pleuronectus platessa)	25	25	
Common dab (Limanda limanda)	15	15	
Witch (Glyptocephalus cynoglossus)	28	28	
Lemon sole (Microstomus kitt)	25	25	
Sole (Solea solea)	24	24	24
Turbot (Psetta maxima)	30	30	
Brill (Scophthalmus rhombus)	30	30	
Fluke (Lepidorhombus whiffiagonis)	25	25	

(2) The regulations laid down in other fishery legislation concerning the minimum size of certain species of fish shall not be affected by this Executive Order where they are stricter.

Article 14. (1) Salmon fishing shall not be permitted in the Convention area (cf. arts. 1 and 2) outside the national fishery limits

(i) Between the parallels of 63° and 68° north latitude, east of the meridian of Greenwich and east of the meridian of 22° east longitude;

---

[1] This Executive Order does not apply to Greenland and the Faroe Islands as provided in article 21. In force as of the day after its publication in the Official Gazette *(Lovtidende)* in accordance with article 20. It superseded a prior Executive Order of 24 January 1973 on the same subject. Danish text transmitted by the Ministry of Foreign Affairs of Denmark in a note verbale of 20 December 1974. Translation by the Secretariat of the United Nations.

[2] By Executive Order No. 86 of 25 February 1974 by the Ministry of Fisheries.

[3] Identical to Articles 1-11 of Executive Order No. 25 of 28 January 1974, *supra (d)*.

[4] Reproduced in ST/LEG/SER.B/15, pages 623-627.

[5] *Supra (d)*.

(ii) In region 2 south of the parallel of 62° north latitude between 2° east longitude and 11° west longitude;

(iii) Within an area defined by the following lines: from 27° west longitude along the parallel of 62° north latitude to 11° west longitude; thence due north to 68° north latitude; thence due west to 27° west longitude and thence due south to 62° north latitude.

(2) In regions 1 and 2 salmon fishing shall not otherwise be permitted outside the national fishery limits during the period from 1 July to 5 May inclusive.

Article 15. (1) Herring fishing in the North Sea and the Skagerrak shall not be permitted during the period from 1 February to 15 June 1974 inclusive. In this connexion the Skagerrak and the North Sea are bounded in the north by the parallel of 62° north latitude, in the west by the meridian of 4° west longitude from 62° north latitude to the Scottish coast, and in the English Channel by 1° west longitude and in the east by a line running from Skagen to Pater Noster Lighthouse.

(2) Notwithstanding the provisions of paragraph 1, any landing of fish may contain up to 10 per cent in weight of herring.

(3) The Minister for Fisheries may allow a certain amount of herring to be caught during the close season for special consumption purposes in accordance with decisions by the North-East Atlantic Fisheries Commission.

Article 15A. (1) Herring fishing shall not be permitted in that part of regions 1 and 2 which is bounded to the west and south by the following lines, along 11° west longitude due south to 63° north latitude; thence due west to 15° west longitude; thence due south to 60° north latitude, thence due east to 5° west longitude; thence due north to 60° 30' north latitude; thence due east to 4° west longitude; thence due north to 62° north latitude; thence due east to the Norwegian coast.

(2) The Minister for Fisheries may allow a certain amount of herring to be caught in the protected area for special consumption purposes in accordance with a decision by the North-East Atlantic Fisheries Commission.

(3) The provisions of paragraph 1 shall not apply to catches in the Faroese fishery zone of the local, early summer-spawning herring.

Article 16. (1) In the case of mackerel caught in the North Sea, the Skagerrak and the Kattegat, and which are not considered to be for human consumption, there shall be a minimum size of 30 cm, measured from the tip of the snout to the extreme end of the tail fin. In this connexion the North Sea, the Skagerrak and the Kattegat are bounded in the north by the parallel of 62° north latitude, in the west by the parallel of 4° west latitude from 62° north latitude to the Scottish coast; in the English Channel by the parallel of 51° north latitude and in the east by lines running between Hasenore and Sniben Point, Korshage and Spodsbjerg and Gilbierg Head and the Kullen.

(2) Notwithstanding the provisions of paragraph 1, any landing of mackerel may contain up to 20 per cent in weight of mackerel under the prescribed minimum size.

Article 17. (1) Fish or parts of fish which do not conform to the minimum size prescribed in article 13, and protected fish caught within the close season (cf. articles 14 and 15) may not be killed, kept on board, landed, stored, sold, offered for sale or taken from one place to another, but shall immediately be returned to the sea as far as possible in a condition fit for survival.

(2) In the types of fishing referred to in article 9, however, catches not considered to be for human consumption may contain up to 10 per cent in weight of the species of fish mentioned in article 13, except for salmon under the minimum size prescribed in article 13. Similarly, in the aforesaid types of fishing the minimum size for whiting shall be 20 cm.

(3) As far as the Danish fishery zone is concerned, the exception mentioned in paragraph 2 shall apply only to haddock, common dab, whiting, witch and fluke.

(4) The Minister for Fisheries may permit the catching, landing and transport of fish under the prescribed minimum size where the catch is made with a view to transplantation or for the purpose of scientific research.

Article 18. (1) Supervision of the implementation of the provisions of this Executive Order and the rules laid down in connexion therewith shall be exercised by the police, the fishery control authorities and masters of the ships and vessels coming under the Ministry of Fisheries who are authorized to that effect by the Minister for Fisheries.

(2) Pursuant to a decision by the North-East Atlantic Fisheries Commission, the supervisory functions referred to in paragraph 1 may be exercised outside the fishery limits also by inspectors especially authorized for the purpose by authorities of another member country.

(3) Undersized fish and protected fish shall be set free in the open sea by the fishery control authorities immediately after the impounding or seizure (cf. chap. 68 of the Code of Civil Procedure) provided that the person charged with the offence admits the offence and provided that the fish are in a condition fit for survival.

(4) Upon orders from one of the control authorities referred to in paragraphs 1 and 2, any vessel, fishing or dealing with fish in the Convention area shall stop unless it is engaged in putting out gear, fishing with gear or hauling in gear, in which case it shall stop as soon as the hauling-in process is completed. The master of the fishing vessel shall permit the inspector and, if necessary, a witness to go on board. The master shall also assist the inspector in such inspection of catch and gear both on and below deck and examination of ship's papers as the inspector may find necessary in order to verify the provisions of this Executive Order have been complied with. The inspector shall be entitled to request such explanations as he may find necessary.

Article 19. 1. Offences against article 3, paragraph 1, article 8, paragraph 2, article 9, paragraph 2, article 10, second sentence, article 14, article 15, paragraphs 1 and 2, article 15A, paragraph 1, article 16, article 17, paragraphs 1, 2 and 3, and article 18, paragraph 4, shall be punishable by a fine.

2. The regulations of the Civil Criminal Code shall apply with respect to confiscation. A catch may be confiscated even if it cannot be definitely established that it derives in its entirety from the unlawful circumstance.

3. Undersized fish and protected fish shall be set free in the open sea by the fishery control authorities immediately after the impounding or seizure (cf. chap. 68 of the Code of Civil Procedure) provided that the person charged with the offence admits the offence and provided that the fish are in a condition fit for survival.

4. Half of the fines shall go to the Treasury and the other half shall be paid to the Ministry of Fisheries for apportionment between the relief fund of the Danish Fishery Association and the relief fund of the Deep-Sea Fishery Association of Denmark in the proportion of two thirds and one third respectively.

. . .

(f) EXECUTIVE ORDER NO. 118 OF 12 MARCH 1974 BY THE MINISTRY OF FISHERIES CONCERNING THE REGULATION OF FISHERIES IN THE NORTH-WEST ATLANTIC OCEAN[1] AS AMENDED[2]

Article 1. 1. This Executive Order shall apply to catches of fish in those parts of the Atlantic Ocean area outside the Greenland fishery zone which are covered by article 1 of the Convention of 8 February 1949 for the North-West Atlantic Fisheries (cf. annex 1 (I) of the Executive Order).

2. The Convention area referred to in paragraph 1 is divided, pursuant to article 1, paragraph 3, of the Convention, into five sub-areas (cf. annex 1, (II and III) of this Executive Order).

Article 2. 1. The following species of fish may be caught in the parts of the Convention area specified below only with the authorization of the Minister for Fisheries or of such person as he may authorize to that effect.

---

[1] In force as of 17 March 1974 in accordance with article 9. It superseded a prior Executive Order of 12 September 1973 on the same subject. Danish texts of this Order and of the amendments thereto by Executive Order No. 458 of 6 September 1974 were provided by the Ministry of Foreign Affairs of Denmark in a note verbale of 20 December 1974. Translation by the Secretariat of the United Nations.

[2] By Executive Order No. 458 of 6 September 1974 by the Ministry of Fisheries. In force as of the day after its publication in the Official Gazette *(Lovtidende).*

	Parts of the Convention area for which authorization is required (cf. annex 1, III)
(a) *Species of fish*	
Atlantic cod (Gadus morhua)	1; 2; 3K, L, M, N, O, Ps; 4T, V, W
Rat-tail (Cryophaenoides rupestris)	2; 3
Capelin (Mallotus villosus)	2; 3K, L, N, O, Ps
Greenland halibut (Reinhardtius hippoglossoides)	2; 3K, L
Witch (Glyptocephalus cynoglossus)	2J; 3K, L, N, O, Ps; 4V, W, X
Long rough dab (Hippoglossoides platessoides) .	2; 3K, L, N, O, Ps; 4V, W, X
Yellowtail flounder (Limanda ferruginea)	3L, N, O; 4V
Redfish (Sebastes marinus)	2; 3K, L, M, N, O, P; 4V, W, X
Haddock (Melanogrammus aeglefinus)	4V, W, X
Herring (Clupea harengus)	4V, W, X
Silver hake (Merluccius bilinearis)	4V, W, X
Saithe (Pollachius virens)	4V, W, X
Atlantic mackerel (Scomber scombrus)	4V, W, X
Great silver smelt (Argentina silus)	4V, W, X

(b) *In sub-area 5 all species of fish except for menhaden, tuna, sail-fish, spearfish, marlin, sharks, except for picked dogfish, and cuttle-fish.*

2. In connexion with the authorization referred to in paragraph 1 special conditions may be prescribed for the conduct of fishing activities, including

(a) Limits on the total catch quantity for one or more species of fish, applicable to the individual water areas and/or vessels;

(b) Duty to report on the catch;

(c) Minimum size of fish;

(d) Protected areas;

(e) Close seasons

in accordance with the decisions taken by the Commission for the North-West Atlantic Fisheries (ICNAF).

Article 3. 1. No vessel may carry on board or use any kind of trawl or Danish seine where the mesh size in any part of the net is smaller than that specified in articles 4 to 5 (cf., however, article 6).

2. The mesh shall be measured when stretched and when the net is wet, in the manner described in paragraph 3. The mesh size shall be estimated as an average of measurements of 20 connected meshes.

3. The mesh size shall be measured with a flat wedge-shaped gauge 2 mm thick, as shown in annex 2,[1] inserted in the meshes at a pressure of 5 kg.

Article 4. 1. In sub-area 1, outside the Greenland fishery zone, and in sub-areas 2 and 3, the minimum size of mesh used in fishing for cod,

---

[1] Not reproduced in this volume.

haddock, red fish, Atlantic halibut, Greenland halibut, witch and long rough dab, and in sub-area 3 for saithe, tusk and yellowtail flounder shall be as follows:

(1) In Danish seines of any material: 110 mm;

(2) In those parts of trawl nets which are made of hemp (but not manila), polyamide fibre or polyester fibre: 120 mm;

(3) In those parts of trawl nets which are made of manila or materials other than those mentioned in subparagraph (2): 130 mm.

2. Notwithstanding the foregoing provisions vessels engaged in fishing for red fish in sub-areas 3N, 3O and 3P may use nets with a mesh-gauge smaller than that indicated in paragraph 1. Such catches may contain up to 10 per cent in weight of the other species of fish mentioned.

Article 5. 1. In sub-areas 4 and 5 the minimum mesh size used in fishing for cod, haddock and yellowtail flounder, and in sub-area 4 for witch, winter flounder and long rough dab shall be as follows:

(1) In Danish seines of any material: 110 mm;

(2) In the whole trawl net except for the cod-end

(i) In those parts which are made of cotton, hemp (but not manila), polyamide or polyester fibre: 120 mm;

(ii) In those parts which are made of manila or materials other than those mentioned in subparagraph (2) b i: 130 mm.

2. Notwithstanding the foregoing provisions vessels engaged in fishing in sub-area 4 for species of fish other than those mentioned in this paragraph, for which nets with a mesh size smaller than that indicated in paragraph 1 are used, shall be permitted catches containing up to 10 per cent in weight of the species of fish mentioned.

3. Notwithstanding the foregoing provisions vessels engaged in fishing in sub-area 5 for species of fish other than cod and haddock, for which nets with a mesh size smaller than that indicated in paragraph 1 are used, shall be permitted catches containing up to 10 per cent in weight of cod and haddock.

Article 6. 1. Notwithstanding the foregoing regulations concerning mesh size, cordage or similar material may be attached to the underside of the cod-end to prevent or reduce wear and tear.

2. To prevent or reduce wear and tear a protective net meeting the requirements laid down in annex 3[1] may also be affixed to the upper side of the cod-end of the trawl net.

Article 7. 1. Supervision of the implementation of the provisions of this Executive Order or the rules laid down in connexion therewith shall be exercised by the police, the fishery control authorities, the fishery inspection authorities, or in the case of the Faroe Islands such persons as are authorized to that effect by the National Executive of the Faroe Islands.

2. Pursuant to a decision by the Commission for the North-West Atlantic Fisheries the supervisory functions referred to in paragraph 1 may be

---

[1] Not reproduced in this volume.

exercised outside the fishery limits also by inspectors especially authorized for the purpose by authorities of another member country.

3. Vessels with the inspectors referred to in paragraph 2 on board shall fly a pennant with two yellow and two blue fields with the letters NW in the upper yellow field.

4. Upon orders from one of the control authorities referred to in paragraphs 1 and 2, any vessel, fishing or dealing with fish in the Convention area shall stop unless it is engaged in putting out gear, fishing with gear or hauling in gear, in which case it shall stop as soon as the hauling-in process is completed. The master of the fishing vessel shall permit the inspector and, if necessary, a witness to go on board. The master shall also assist the inspector in such inspection of catch and gear both on and below deck and examination of ship's papers as the inspector may find necessary in order to verify that the rules laid down in this Executive Order have been complied with. The inspector shall be entitled to request such explanations as he may find necessary.

Article 8. 1. Offences against the provisions of this Executive Order or the rules laid down in connexion therewith shall be punishable by a fine.

2. The regulations of the Civil Criminal Code and the Criminal Law for Greenland shall apply with respect to confiscation. A catch may be confiscated even if it cannot be definitely established that it derives in its entirety from the unlawful circumstance.

3. Half of the fine shall go to the Treasury and the other half shall be paid to the Ministry of Fisheries for apportionment between the relief fund of the Danish Fishery Association and the relief fund of the Deep-sea Fishery Association of Denmark in the proportion of two thirds and one third respectively. However, in the case of persons or companies domiciled in Greenland or the Faroe Islands, the last-mentioned half shall be paid, in the case of Greenland, to the Governor of Greenland and shall be allotted to KNAPP's assistance fund (Carl Egede's Fund) for distribution and assistance to distressed fishermen and their survivors and, in the case of the Faroe Islands, to the Relief Fund for Disabled Fishermen.

. . .

ANNEX I

I.

The area covered by the Convention of 8 February 1949 concerning the North-West Atlantic Fisheries,[1] hereinafter referred to as "the Convention area", shall be all waters, except territorial waters, bounded by a line beginning at a point on the coast of Rhode Island in 71° 40' west longitude; thence due south to 39° 00' north latitude; thence due east to 42° 00' west longitude; thence due north to 59° 00' north latitude; thence due west to 44° 00' west longitude; thence due north to the coast of Greenland; thence along the west coast of Greenland to 78° 10' north latitude; thence southward to a point in 75° 00' north latitude and 73° 30' west longitude; thence along a rhumb line to a point in 69° 00' north latitude and 59° 00' west longitude; thence due south to 61° 00' north

---

[1] Reproduced in ST/LEG/SER.B/15, pp. 832-838. The Convention area is defined in article 1, *ibid.,* p. 832.

318

latitude; thence due west to 64° 30′ west longitude; thence due south to the coast of Labrador; thence in a southerly direction along the coast of Labrador to the southern terminus of its boundary with Quebec; thence in a westerly direction to the coast of Quebec, and in an easterly and southerly direction along the coasts of New Brunswick, Nova Scotia, and Cape Breton Island to Cabot Strait; Maine, New Hampshire, Massachusetts, and Rhode Island to the point of the beginning.

II.

The sub-areas referred to in article I, paragraph 3, of the Convention[1] shall be as follows:

sub-area 1

That portion of the Convention area which lies to the north and east of a line extending from a point (1) in 75° 00′ north latitude and 73° 30′ west longitude to a point (2) in 69° 00′ north latitude and 59° 00′ west longitude; east of 59° 00′ west longitude and to the north and east of a line running from 61° 00′ north latitude and 59° 00′ west longitude to 52° 15′ north latitude and 42° 00′ west longitude.

sub-area 2

That portion of the Convention area lying to the south and west of sub-area 1 defined above and to the north of the parallel of 52° 15′ north latitude.

sub-area 3

That portion of the Convention area lying south of the parallel of 52° 15′ north latitude; and to the east of a line extending due north from Cape Bauld on the north coast of Newfoundland to 52° 15′ north latitude to the north of the parallel of 39° 00′ north latitude; and to the east and north of a line extending in a northwesterly direction which passes through (1) 43° 30′ north latitude, 55° 00′ west longitude, in the direction of (2) 47° 50′ north latitude, 60° 00′ west longitude, until it intersects a straight line connecting Cape Ray, on the coast of Newfoundland, with Cape North on Cape Breton Island, thence in a northeasterly direction along said line to Cape Ray.

sub-area 4

That portion of the Convention area lying to the west of sub-area 3 defined above, and to the east of a line described as follows: beginning at the terminus of the international boundary between the United States of America and Canada in Grand Manan Channel, at a point in 44° 46′ 35.34″ north latitude, 66° 54′ 11.23″ west longitude; thence due south to the parallel of 43° 50′ north latitude; thence due west to the meridian of 67° 40′ west longitude; thence due south to the parallel of 42° 20′ north latitude; thence due east to a point in 66° 00′ west longitude; thence along a line in a southeasterly direction to 42° 00′ north latitude, 65° 40′ west longitude; thence due south to the parallel of 39° 00′ north latitude.

sub-area 5

That portion of the Convention area lying west of sub-area 4 defined above.

III. *Division of the sub-areas*

re sub-area 1

1 A − That part of the sub-area situated north of 68° 50′ north latitude (Christianshab).

1 B − That part of the sub-area situated between 66° 15′ north latitude (5 nautical miles north of Umanarsugssuak and 68° 50′ north latitude) (Christianshab).

---

[1] *Ibid.*, Annex, Section 1.

1 C – That part of the sub-area situated between 64° 15′ north latitude (4 nautical miles north of Godthab and 66° 15′ north latitude (5 nautical miles north of Umanarsugssuak).

1 D – That part of the sub-area situated between 62° 30′ north latitude (Frederikshab Isblink) and 64° 15′ north latitude (4 nautical miles north of Godthab).

1 E – That part of the sub-area situated between 60° 45′ north latitude (Cape Desolation) and 62° 30′ north latitude (Frederikshab Isblink).

1 F – That part of the sub-area situated south of 60° 45′ north latitude (Cape Desolation).

re sub-area 2

2 G – That part of the sub-area situated north 57° 40′ north latitude (Cape Mugford).

2 H – That part of the sub-area situated between 55° 50′ north latitude (Hopedale) and 57° 40′ north latitude (Cape Mugford).

2 J – That part of the sub-area situated south of 55° 20′ north latitude (Hopedale).

re sub-area 3

3 K – That part of the sub-area situated north of 49° 15′ north latitude (Cape Freels, Newfoundland).

3 L – That part of the sub-area situated between the coast of Newfoundland from Cape Freels to Cape St. Mary and a line described as follows: from Cape Freels due east to 46° 40′ west longitude; thence along a line to Cape St. Mary, Newfoundland.

3 M – That part of the sub-area situated south of 49° 30′ north latitude and east of 46° 30′ west longitude.

3 N – That part of the sub-area situated south of 46° 00′ north latitude and between 46° 30′ west longitude and 51° west longitude.

3 O – That part of the sub-area situated south of 46° 00′ north latitude and between 51° 00′ west longitude and 54° 30′ west longitude.

3 P – That part of the sub-area situated south of the coast of Newfoundland and west of a line extending from Cape St. Mary, Newfoundland, to 46° 00′ north latitude, 54° 30′ west longitude; thence due south to the boundary line between sub-areas 3 and 4. Sub-area 3 P shall be divided into two parts: a north-western and a south-eastern part, defined as follows:

3 Pn – The north-western part—that part of sub-area 3 P situated north-west of a line extending from Burgeo Island, Newfoundland, approximately south-west of 46° 50′ north latitude and 58° 50′ west longitude.

3 Ps – The south-eastern part of sub-area 3 P situated south-east of the line delimiting 3 Pn.

re sub-area 4

4 R – That part of the sub-area situated between the coast of Newfoundland from Cape Bauld to Cape Ray and a line described as follows: from Cape Bauld due north to 52° 15′ north latitude; thence due west to the coast of Labrador; thence along the coast of Labrador to the terminus of the Labrador-Quebec boundary line; thence along a line in a south-westerly direction to 49° 25′ north latitude, 60° 00′ west longitude; thence due south to 47° 50′ north latitude, 60° 00′ west longitude; thence along a line in a south-easterly direction to the point of intersection of a straight line between Cape North, Nova Scotia and Cape Ray, Newfoundland; thence to Cape Ray, Newfoundland.

4 S – That part of the sub-area situated between the south coast of the Province of Quebec from the terminus of the Labrador-Quebec boundary line to Pte. des Monts and a line described as follows: from Pte. des Monts due east to 49° 25′ north latitude,

64° 40′ west longitude; thence along a line in an east-southeasterly direction to 47° 50′ north latitude, 60° 00′ west longitude; thence due north to 49° 25′ north latitude; 60° 00′ west longitude; thence along a line in a north-easterly direction to the terminus of the Labrador-Quebec boundary line.

4 T – That part of the sub-area situated between the coasts of Nova Scotia, New Brunswick and Quebec from Cape North to Pte. des Monts and a line described as follows: from Pte. des Monts due east to 49° 25′ north latitude, 64° 40′ west longitude; thence along a line in an east-southeasterly direction to 47° 50′ north latitude, 60° 00′ west longitude; thence along a line in a southerly direction to Cape North, Nova Scotia.

4 V – That part of the sub-area situated between the coast of Nova Scotia between Cape North and Fourchu and a line described as follows: from Fourchu along a line in a southerly direction to 45° 40′ north latitude, 60° 00′ west longitude; thence due south along 60° 00′ west longitude to 44° 10′ north latitude; thence due east to 59° 00′ west longitude; thence due south to 39° 00′ north latitude; thence due east to a point where the boundary line between sub-areas 3 and 4 meets the parallel of 39° 00′ north latitude; thence along the boundary line between sub-areas 3 and 4 and a line continuing in a northwesterly direction to 47° 50′ north latitude, 60° 00′ west longitude; thence along a line in a southerly direction to Cape North, Nova Scotia.

Sub-area 4 V shall be divided into two parts: a northern and a southern part defined as follows:

4 Vn – The northern part—that part of sub-area 4 V situated north of 45° 40′ north latitude.

4 Vs – The southern part—that part of sub-area 4 V situated south of 45° 40′ north latitude.

4 W – That part of the sub-area situated between the coast of Nova Scotia between Halifax and Fourchu and a line described as follows: from Fourchu along a line in a southerly direction to 45° 40′ north latitude, 60° 00′ west longitude; thence due south along 60° 00′ west longitude to 44° 10′ north latitude; thence due east to 59° 00′ west longitude; thence due south to 39° 00′ north latitude; thence due west to 63° 20′ west longitude; thence due north to a point on that meridian at 44° 20′ north latitude; thence along a line in a north latitude; thence along a line in a northwesterly direction to Halifax, Nova Scotia.

4 X – That part of the sub-area situated between the boundary lines of sub-areas 4 and 5 and the coasts of New Brunswick and Nova Scotia from the terminus of the boundary line between New Brunswick and Maine to Halifax and a line described as follows: from Halifax along a line in a southeasterly direction to 44° 20′ north latitude, 63° 20′ west longitude; thence due south to 39° 00′ north latitude; thence due west to 65° 40′ west longitude.

re sub-area 5

5 Y – That part of the sub-area situated between the coasts of Maine, New Hampshire and Massachusetts from the boundary between Maine and New Brunswick to 70° west longitude at Cape Cod (at approx. 42° north latitude) and a line described as follows: from Cape Cod at 70° west longitude (at approx. 42° north latitude) due north to 42° 20′ north latitude; thence due east to 67° 40′ west longitude at the boundary line of sub-areas 4 and 5; thence along the boundary line to the boundary line of Maine and New Brunswick.

5 Z – That part of the sub-area situated south and east of sub-area 5 Y. Sub-area 5 Z shall be divided into two parts: an eastern and a western part defined as follows:

5 Ze – The eastern part—that part of sub-area 5 Z situated east of 70° 00′ west longitude.

5 Zw – The western part—that part of sub-area 5 Z situated west of 70° 00′ west longitude.

(g) EXECUTIVE ORDER No. 251 OF 20 MAY 1974 BY THE MINISTRY OF FISHERIES CONCERNING THE REGULATION OF FISHERIES IN WATERS OFF THE FAROE ISLANDS[1]

Article 1. This Executive Order shall apply, in accordance with the provisions of the Arrangement between Denmark, Belgium, France, Norway, Poland, the United Kingdom and the Federal Republic of Germany, signed on 18 December 1973, concerning fisheries in waters off the Faroe Islands,[2] to those waters situated within a line drawn due east from 15° west longitude along the parallel of 63° north latitude to 4° west longitude; thence due south to 60° 30' north latitude; thence due west to 5° west longitude; thence due south to 60° north latitude; thence due west to 15° west longitude; thence due north to 63° north latitude.

Article 2. 1. Fisheries in the area referred to in article 1 shall be regulated as follows:

2. In the case of persons or companies and the like domiciled in the Faroe Islands the annual catch of cod and haddock may not exceed 32,000 tons of whole, uncleaned fish.

3. Such further regulations as may be necessary for the implementation of the provisions contained in paragraph 2 shall be established by the National Executive of the Faroe Islands.

4. In the case of persons or companies and the like domiciled in the realm outside the Faroe Islands, fishing for demersal fish species, including flat-fish and gadids, may take place only with the authorization of the Minister for Fisheries.

5. Special provisions concerning the conduct of fishing activities may be established in connexion with the authorization mentioned in paragraph 4, covering such matters as:

(a) Limits on the total catch quantity applicable to the individual area and/or vessel.

(b) Duty to report on the catch.

Article 3. 1. Trawl fishing may not take place in the areas indicated below during the periods specified:

Area 1:

8 nautical miles from the fishery limit between a line 0° true from Eidiskoleor and a line 90° true from Bispur: 15 February to 15 May.

Area 2:

18 nautical miles from the fishery limit between a line 90° true from Bispur and a line 90° true from Akraberg: 1 June to 30 November.

---

[1] In force as of the day after its publication in the Official Gazette *(Lovtidende).* Danish text transmitted by the Ministry of Foreign Affairs in a note verbale of 20 December 1974. Translation by the Secretariat of the United Nations.

[2] *Infra* Part II, Division IV, Subdivision A, 6.

Area 3:

(a) 12 nautical miles from the fishery limit between a line 150° true from Akraberg and a line 190° true from Akraberg.

(b) 6 nautical miles from the fishery limit between a line 190° true from Akraberg and a line 240° true from Ørnanipan:

1 April to 30 June and 1 October to 31 December.

Area 4:

12 nautical miles from the fishery limit between a line 240° true from Trøllhøvdi and a line 320° true from Bardid: 1 December to 31 March and 1 May to 31 May.

Area 5:

The area within the 200 metre isobath in the waters situated within a line drawn due east from 10° west longitude along the parallel of 60° north latitude to 8° west longitude; thence due north to 60° 30' north latitude; thence due east to 7° 30' west longitude; thence due north to a point at 61° 15' north latitude, 7° 30' west longitude; thence in a northwesterly direction to a point at 61° 30' north latitude, 8° 00' west longitude; thence due west to 10° west longitude; thence due south to 60° north latitude: 1 March to 31 March.

2. The areas referred to in paragraph 1 are indicated on Danish map No. 80 (SUB-AREA 1-5).*

Article 4. 1. Notwithstanding the provisions of article 3, the National Executive of the Faroe Islands may permit small Faroese ships to engage in trawl fishing within areas 2, 3 and 4 during the periods in which trawl fishing is not otherwise permitted. The overall annual catch of cod and haddock on the basis of such permits may not exceed:

In area 2: 1,250 tons;
In area 3: 1,250 tons;
In area 4: 500 tons.

2. The catch quantities indicated in paragraph 1 shall be included in the permissible catch of cod and haddock for persons or companies and the like domiciled in the Faroe Islands (cf. article 2, paragraph 2).

3. Further regulations for the conduct of trawl fishing activities in pursuance of paragraph 1 shall be laid down by the National Executive of the Faroe Islands.

Article 5. Supervision of the implementation of the provisions contained in this Executive Order and the rules laid down in connexion therewith shall be exercised by the police, the fishery control authorities, the fishery inspection authorities or, in the case of the Faroe Islands, such persons as are authorized to that effect by the National Executive of the Faroe Islands.

Article 6. 1. Offences against article 3 and against the regulations established in pursuance of article 2, paragraphs 3 and 5, and article 4, paragraph 3, shall be punishable by a fine.

---

* Map No. 80 is not reproduced here.

2. Half of the fines shall go to the Treasury and the other half shall be paid to the Relief Fund for Disabled Fishermen. However, in the case of persons or companies domiciled in the realm outside the Faroe Islands the latter half shall be paid as follows: in the case of Greenland, to the Governor of Greenland and allotted to KNAPP's assistance fund (Carl Egede's Fund) for distribution and assistance to distressed fishermen and their survivors, and in other cases to the Ministry of Fisheries for further apportionment between the relief fund of the Danish Fishery Association and the relief fund of the Deep-Sea Fishery Association of Denmark in the proportion of two thirds and one third respectively.

. . .

(h) EXECUTIVE ORDER NO. 283 OF 7 JUNE 1974 BY THE MINISTRY FOR GREENLAND CONCERNING SALMON FISHING IN THE GREENLAND FISHERY ZONE[1]

Article 1. This Executive Order shall apply to commercial salmon fishing carried on in the Greenland fishery zone west of Kap Farval by Greenland, Danish and Faroese fishermen.

Article 2. (1) Salmon fishing may take place only with the authorization of the Minister for Greenland or such person as he may authorize to that effect. In connexion with such authorization an apportionment of the quantities may be made among the persons having such authorization.

(2) Authorizations for the persons specified in article 3, paragraph 1 (1) may not be granted where the main occupation of such persons lies outside the fields of fishing, trapping and sheep farming.

Article 3. (1) Salmon fishing shall be limited to the following annual catch quantities (whole fish):

(i)   In the case of persons residing in Greenland and having a permanent connexion with the Greenland community, or companies and the like domiciled in Greenland: 1,050 tons.
(ii) In the case of persons domiciled in the areas specified below and who only own boats measuring no more than 26 Danish feet, in addition:
Nanortalik commune − 20 tons.
Egedesminde and Kangasdtsiaq communes and Ikamiut − 20 tons.
Umanak commune − 5 tons.
Upernavik commune − 5 tons.
These catches shall be sold to coastal installations in the area concerned.
(iii) In the case of persons or companies and the like domiciled in the realm outside Greenland: 846 tons.

----
[1] Danish text transmitted by the Ministry of Foreign Affairs of Denmark in a note verbale of 20 December 1974. Translation by the Secretariat of the United Nations.

(2) The aforesaid catch quantities shall be reduced by the amount of salmon caught in the ICNAF area outside the Greenland fishery zone. The ICNAF area is described in the annex to this Executive Order.[1]

(3) Notice of the discontinuance of fishing in accordance with the aforesaid quotas shall be given by the Governor of Greenland over the radio and in the press.

Article 4. Supervision of the implementation of the provisions of this Executive Order shall be exercised by the police, the fishery control authorities, the fishery inspection authorities or, in the case of the Faroe Islands, such persons as are authorized to that effect by the National Executive of the Faroe Islands.

Article 5. (1) Offences against the provisions of this Executive Order may entail a warning or a fine.

(2) The regulations contained in the Civil Criminal Code and the Criminal Law for Greenland shall apply. With respect to confiscation a catch may be confiscated even if it cannot definitely be established that it derives in its entirety from the unlawful circumstance.

(3) Half of the fines shall go to the Treasury and the other half shall be paid to the Ministry of Fisheries for further apportionment between the relief fund of the Danish Fishery Association and the relief fund of the Deep-Sea Fishery Association of Denmark in the proportion of two thirds and one third respectively. However, in the case of persons or companies domiciled in Greenland or the Faroe Islands the latter half shall be paid as follows: in the case of Greenland, to the Governor of Greenland and allotted to KNAPP's assistance fund (Carl Egedes Fund) for distribution and assistance to distressed fishermen and their survivors, and in the case of the Faroe Islands to the Relief Fund for Disabled Fishermen.

(i) EXECUTIVE ORDER NO. 326 OF 24 JUNE 1974 BY THE MINISTRY OF FISHERIES CONCERNING THE REGULATION OF SALMON FISHING IN THE NORTH-WEST ATLANTIC OCEAN [2]

Article 1. (1) During the period up to 31 December 1974 salmon fishing in the ICNAF area[3] outside the Greenland fishery zone may only take place with the authorization of the Minister for Fisheries or such person as he may authorize to that effect, and shall be limited to the following catch quantities:

  (i) In the case of persons or companies and the like domiciled in Greenland: 1,100 tons (whole fish).

---

[1] The annex is not reproduced in this volume. For the area referred to in this provision see *supra (f)*, Annex 1 (I). See also Article 1 of the International Convention for the North-west Atlantic Fisheries of 8 February 1949, reproduced in ST/LEG/SER.B/15, p. 832.

[2] Danish text transmitted by the Ministry of Foreign Affairs of Denmark in a note verbale of 20 December 1974. Translation by the Secretariat of the United Nations.

[3] See *Supra (f)*, Annex I (I). See also Article 1 of the International Convention for the North-west Atlantic Fisheries of 8 February 1949, reproduced in part in ST/LEG/SER.B/15, p. 832.

(ii) In the case of persons or companies and the like domiciled in the realm outside Greenland: 846 tons (whole fish).

(2) In connexion with the authorization referred to in paragraph 1 an apportionment of the aforesaid catch quantities may be made among the persons having such authorization.

(3) The catch quantities referred to in paragraph 1 shall be reduced by the quality of salmon fished in the Greenland fishery zone.

Article 2. Supervision of the implementation of the provisions of this Executive Order shall be exercised by the police, the fishery control authorities, the fishery inspection authorities or, in the case of the Faroe Islands, such persons as are authorized to that effect by the National Executive of the Faroe Islands.

Article 3. (1) Offences against the provisions of this Executive Order shall be punishable by a fine.

(2) The regulations contained in the Civil Criminal Code and in the Criminal Law for Greenland shall apply with respect to confiscation. The catch may be confiscated even if it cannot be definitely established that it derives in its entirety from the unlawful circumstance.

(3) Half of the fines shall go to the Treasury and the other half shall be paid to the Ministry of Fisheries for further apportionment between the relief fund of the Danish Fishery Association and the relief fund of the Deep-Sea Fishery Association of Denmark in the proportion of two thirds and one third respectively. However, in the case of persons or companies domiciled in Greenland or the Faroe Islands, the latter half shall be paid as follows: in the case of Greenland, to the Governor of Greenland and allotted to KNAPP's assistance fund (Carl Egedes Fund) for distribution and assistance to distressed fishermen and their survivors and, in the case of the Faroe Islands, to the Relief Fund for Disabled Fishermen.

4. FRANCE

(a) [LOI No 71-1060 DU 24 DECEMBRE 1971 RELATIVE A LA DELIMITATION DES EAUX TERRITORIALES FRANCAISES, ARTICLE 4][1]

(b) LOI No 72-620 DU 5 JUILLET 1972 RELATIVE A LA CONSERVATION DES RESSOURCES BIOLOGIQUES DE LA MER AU LARGE DU DEPARTEMENT DE LA GUYANE[2]

Art. 1er. — En vue d'assurer la conservation des ressources biologiques de la mer au large du département de la Guyane et en attendant l'entrée en vigueur de conventions ou accords internationaux appropriés, l'application des dispositions du décret du 9 janvier 1852[3] modifié sur l'exercice de la pêche maritime est étendue à une zone de 80 milles marins mesurés à partir des lignes de base servant, pour ce département, à la délimitation des eaux territoriales.

---

[1] *Supra,* Division I, Subdivision A, Chapter I, 3 *(a).*

[2] *Journal officiel,* 9 juillet 1972.

[3] Reproduit partiellement dans ST/LEG/SER.B/6, p. 492 et 493.

Art. 2. – Dans la partie de la zone définie à l'article premier ci-dessus qui s'étend au-delà des eaux territoriales, des mesures sont prises, en tant que de besoin, dans des conditions fixées par décret, pour limiter la pêche des diverses espèces d'animaux marins. L'application de ces mesures aux navires des Etats étrangers est faite en tenant compte de la situation géographique de ces Etats et des habitudes de pêche de leurs ressortissants.

Dans la même partie de zone, la pêche peut être interdite par décret aux navires des Etats qui n'autorisent pas l'exercice de la pêche par les navires français dans des conditions comparables.

Art. 3. – Les dispositions du décret du 9 janvier 1852 modifié, à l'exception de celles qui concernent le montant des pénalités, sont applicables à la constatation et à la répression des infractions aux mesures prises pour l'application des dispositions du premier alinéa de l'article 2 ci-dessus.

Les dispositions de la loi du 1er mars 1888 modifiée[1], ayant pour objet d'interdire aux étrangers la pêche dans des eaux territoriales, sont applicables à la constatation et à la répression des infractions aux dispositions du deuxième alinéa de l'article 2 ci-dessus.

(c) ARRETE DU 28 DECEMBRE 1973 RELATIF A L'INTERDICTION DE PECHE A CERTAINES SAISONS DANS LA ZONE DE LA CONVENTION SUR LES PECHERIES DE L'ATLANTIQUE DU NORD-OUEST[2]

Article premier. Il est interdit de capturer de l'églefin dans les sous-secteurs 4 V, 4 W et 4 X, et dans le secteur 5 de la zone de la convention internationale des pêcheries du Nord-Ouest Atlantique[3].

Toutefois ne sera pas considéré comme contraire aux dispositions de l'alinéa précédent le fait d'avoir, à bord des navires recherchant essentiellement d'autres espèces, des églefins, capturés à titre accessoire, à condition que ces derniers ne dépassent pas soit 10 p. 100 en poids par rapport au poids total des captures se trouvant à bord, soit le chiffre forfaitaire de 2 268 kg, le chiffre le plus favorable pouvant être retenu.

Article 2. Il est interdit d'utiliser tous engins permettant de capturer des espèces de fonds pendant les mois de mars, avril et mai de chaque année dans les zones suivantes :

1. Partie du sous-secteur 4 X délimitée par les lignes joignant les points suivants.

65″ 44′ O., 42″ 04′ N.	65″ 32′ O., 43″ 20′ N.
64″ 30′ O., 42″ 40′ N.	66″ 32′ O., 42″ 20′ N.
64″ 30′ O., 43″ 00′ N.	66″ 00′ O., 42″ 20′ N.
66″ 32′ O., 43″ 00′ N.	

[1] Reproduite partiellement, *ibid.*, p. 497.

[2] *Journal officiel*, 27 février 1974, p. 2305. Arrêté pris compte tenu des recommandations adoptées par la Commission internationale des pêcheries de l'Atlantique du Nord-Ouest le 16 juin 1973.

[3] Reproduite dans le *Recueil des Traités* de l'Organisation des Nations Unies, vol. 157, p. 157, et dans ST/LEG/SER.B/15, p. 832-838.

2. Parties du secteur 5 délimitées par les lignes joignant les points suivants.

a) 69″ 55′ O., 42″ 10′ N.	*b)* 67″ 00′ O., 42″ 20′ N.
69″ 10′ O., 41″ 10′ N.	67″ 00′ O., 41″ 15′ N.
68″ 30′ O., 41″ 35′ N.	65″ 40′ O., 41″ 15′ N.
68″ 45′ O., 41″ 50′ N.	65″ 40′ O., 42″ 00′ N.
69″ 00′ O., 41″ 50′ N.	66″ 00′ O., 42″ 20′ N.

Article 3. Il est interdit de capturer du merlu rouge et du merlu argenté pendant le mois d'avril dans la zone délimitée par les coordonnées 69″ 00′ O., 39″ 50′ N. et 71″ 10′ O., 40″ 20′ N.

Toutefois, ne sera pas considéré comme contraire aux dispositions de l'alinéa précédent le fait d'avoir, à bord des navires recherchant d'autres espèces de fonds dans cette zone, des merlus rouges et des merlus argentés capturés à titre accessoire à condition que ces derniers ne dépassent pas 10 p. 100 en poids par rapport au poids total des captures réalisées au cours de chaque voyage dans ladite zone.

Article 4. Les infractions au présent arrêté seront passibles des peines prévues à l'article 8 (1″) du décret du 9 janvier 1852 modifié sur l'exercice de la pêche maritime.

. . .

(d) ARRETE DU 28 DECEMBRE 1973 RELATIF A LA TAILLE MARCHANDE DE CERTAINES ESPECES CAPTUREES DANS LA ZONE DE LA CONVENTION SUR LES PECHERIES DE L'ATLANTIQUE DU NORD-OUEST[1]

Article premier. Il est interdit de pêcher, de faire pêcher et de garder à bord dans la zone de la convention sur les pêcheries de l'Atlantique du Nord-Ouest les poissons et coquillages qui ne seraient pas parvenus aux dimensions fixées, suivant les espèces et les secteurs, au tableau ci-dessous.

Cette interdiction vise également l'achat, la vente, le transport et l'emploi à un usage quelconque de ces produits.

Espèces	*Secteurs*	*Dimension et méthode utilisée pour la mesurer*
Hareng	4 et 5	22,7 cm mesurés du haut du museau à l'extrémité de la nageoire caudale.
Coquilles Saint-Jacques . .	5 Z	95 mm mesurés d'un bord à l'autre de la coquille à partir de la charnière.

En outre, le poids moyen de la chair de coquilles Saint-Jacques devra être inférieur à 11,3 grammes.

---

[1] *Journal officiel*, 27 février 1974, p. 2306. Arrêté prix compte tenu des recommandations adoptées par la Commission internationale des pêcheries de l'Atlantique du Nord-Ouest lors de ses réunions de février et juin 1972.

Article 2. Toutefois, ne sera pas considéré comme contraire aux dispositions de l'article précédent le fait d'avoir à bord d'un navire, dans un des secteurs visés au tableau ci-dessus, des harengs d'une dimension inférieure à 22,7 cm à condition qu'ils ne dépassent pas 10 p. 100 en poids par rapport au total des captures de harengs réalisées par ce même navire au cours de l'année dans les secteurs 4 et 5.

Article 3. Les infractions au présent arrêté seront poursuivies et réprimées conformément aux articles 7 et 16 du décret susvisé du 9 janvier 1852.

. . .

(e) ARRETE DU 28 DECEMBRE 1973 RELATIF AUX CONDITIONS DE CAPTURE DE CERTAINES ESPECES DANS LA ZONE D'APPLICATION DE LA CONVENTION SUR LES PECHERIES DE L'ATLANTIQUE DU NORD-OUEST[1]

Article premier. Les captures effectuées dans la zone de la convention internationale des pêcheries du Nord-Ouest Atlantique, tant par les bateaux immatriculés dans un port métropolitain que par ceux immatriculés à Saint-Pierre et Miquelon, ne devront pas dépasser pour l'année 1974 les quantités fixées, suivant les espèces et les secteurs ou groupes de secteurs, au tableau figurant à l'annexe 1.

Article 2. Les captures effectuées dans la zone et par les bateaux visés à l'article premier du présent arrêté ne devront pas dépasser en 1974, en ce qui concerne les espèces, secteurs ou groupes de secteurs énumérés au tableau figurant à l'annexe 2, le montant maximum autorisé pour l'ensemble des pays membres de la Commission internationale des pêcheries du Nord-Ouest Atlantique auxquels un contingent particulier n'a pas été alloué.

Article 3. Les patrons pêcheurs devront consigner chaque jour sur le carnet de pêche tenu à bord de chaque navire opérant dans les secteurs visés aux articles premier et 2 du présent arrêté les renseignements portant sur la position du navire, les quantités des espèces capturées et leur destination, le type d'engin utilisé et son temps d'utilisation ainsi que les quantités de captures rejetées à la mer.

Les armateurs à la pêche rendront compte, tous les quinze jours au moins, au secrétariat général de la marine marchande (direction des pêches maritimes) des résultats des captures réalisées dans les conditions définies au tableau 1 annexé au présent arrêté.

Ils lui rendront également compte des résultats des captures réalisées dans les conditions définies au tableau 2 annexé au présent arrêté dès que les captures atteindront le chiffre de 100 tonnes, et au-delà, chaque fois qu'elles atteindront à nouveau ce chiffre de 100 tonnes.

Article 4. Lorsque le total des captures réalisées dans les conditions définies au tableau 1 visé à l'article premier du présent arrêté atteindra, pour chaque espèce, le chiffre maximum prévu dans chaque secteur ou groupe de secteurs, un arrêté interdira la pêche de cette espèce dans ce secteur ou groupe de secteurs.

---

[1] *Ibid.* Arrêté pris compte tenu des recommandations adoptées par la Commission internationale des pêcheries de l'Atlantique du Nord-Ouest les 14 et 16 juin 1973 et le 19 octobre 1973.

Article 5. Le montant des captures réalisées dans les conditions définies au tableau 2 visé à l'article 2 du présent arrêté sera régulièrement notifié au secrétaire exécutif de la Commission internationale des pêcheries du Nord-Ouest Atlantique. Lorsque ce dernier aura fait connaître que le total des captures ainsi notifié par l'ensemble des pays membres de la Commission visés à l'article 2 atteint, pour une espèce dans un secteur ou groupe de secteurs, le montant maximum autorisé en 1974, un arrêté interdira la pêche de cette espèce dans ce secteur ou groupe de secteurs.

Article 6. Les infractions aux dispositions de l'article 3 seront passibles des peines prévues à l'article R. 26 (15″) du code pénal.

. . .

TABLEAU I

Espèces	*Secteurs et sous-secteurs*	*Maximum de captures autorisées aux navires français* *Tonnes*
Morue	1	6 300
	2 G et H	500
	2 J, 3 K et L	51 100
	3 M	8 000
	3 N et O	1 000
	3 PS	5 300
	4 VS et 4 W	1 500
Carrelet américain ou balai	3 L, N et O	900
Sébaste	3 P	2 500
	4 V W X	1 000
Plie cynoglosse	3 PS	400
Carrelet américain ou balai, plie cyno- glosse, limande ferrugineuse	4 V W et X	300

TABLEAU II

Espèces	*Secteurs et sous-secteurs*	*Maximum de captures autorisées pour l'ensemble des pays visés à l'article 2* *Tonnes*
Limande ferrugineuse	3 L, N et O	600
Sébaste	3 M	9 000
	3 L et N	1 700
	3 O	1 200
	3 P	
Plie cynoglosse	2 J, 3 K et L	1 100
	3 N et O	600
Merlu argenté	4 V W et X	8 000
Lieu noir	4 V W et X et 5 . . .	4 100
Hareng	4 V et W	700

330

(f) ARRETE DU 2 AVRIL 1974 RELATIF AUX CONDITIONS DE CAPTURE DU HARENG DANS LA ZONE DE LA CONVENTION SUR LES PECHERIES DE L'ATLANTIQUE DU-NORD-EST (MER CELTIQUE)[1]

Article premier. La pêche du hareng est interdite du 1er avril 1974 au 31 mars 1975 dans la zone limitée :

Au nord, par le 52″ 30′ de latitude nord, entre les côtes irlandaises et anglaises;

A l'ouest, le long des côtes de l'Irlande jusqu'à la jonction des points 51″ 30′ de latitude nord et 9″ de longitude ouest, puis plein sud jusqu'à la jonction des points 50″ de latitude nord et 9″ de longitude ouest;

Au sud, de la jonction des points 50″ de latitude nord et 9″ de longitude ouest jusqu'à la jonction des points 50″ de latitude nord et 7″ de longitude ouest;

A l'est, de la jonction des points 50″ de latitude nord et 7″ de longitude ouest à la jonction des points 50″ 30′ de latitude nord et 7″ de longitude ouest, puis plein est de ce point à l'intersection des points 50″ 30′ de latitude nord et 6″ de longitude ouest, puis plein nord de ce point à la jonction des points 51″ de latitude nord et 6″ de longitude ouest, puis plein est de ce point à la jonction des points 51″ de latitude nord et 5″ de longitude ouest, puis plein nord de ce point à la côte anglaise.

Article 2. Toutefois, pendant la période et dans la zone visée à l'article premier, des captures de hareng n'excédant pas 5 000 tonnes pourront être effectuées par les pêcheurs détenant une autorisation de pêche sur le contingent ainsi fixé. La délivrance et le retrait de ces autorisations seront soumis aux conditions fixées aux articles 3 à 5 de l'arrêté du 19 janvier 1973 modifié susvisé.

Article 3. Les directeurs des affaires maritimes, au Havre, Nantes et Bordeaux sont chargés, chacun en ce qui le concerne, de l'exécution du présent arrêté. . . .

5. GHANA

[TERRITORIAL WATERS AND CONTINENTAL SHELF DECREE, 1973, SECTION 2][2]

---

[1] *Journal officiel,* 1er juin 1974, p. 5973. Arrêté pris compte tenu des recommandations adoptées par la Commission des pêcheries de l'Atlantique du Nord-Est à Londres en décembre 1973. La Convention sur les pêcheries de l'Atlantique du Nord-Est est reproduite dans le *Recueil des Traités* de l'Organisation des Nations Unies, vol. 496, p. 157, et dans le document ST/LEG/SER.B/15, p. 853-857.

[2] *Supra* Division I, Subdivision A, Chapter 1, 5.

6. ICELAND

(a) LAW No. 44 OF 5 APRIL 1948, CONCERNING THE SCIENTIFIC CONSER-
VATION OF THE CONTINENTAL SHELF FISHERIES, AS AMENDED UP TO
1974 [1]

Article 1. The Ministry of Fisheries shall issue regulations establishing
explicitly bounded conservation zones within the limits of the continental
shelf of Iceland; or in the ocean up to 200 nautical miles outside baselines;
wherein all fisheries shall be subject to Icelandic rules and control; provided
that the conservation measures now in effect shall in no way be reduced. The
Ministry shall further issue the necessary regulations for the protection of the
fishing grounds within the said zones. The Fiskifélag Islands (Fisheries
Society) and the Atvinnudeild Háskóla Islands (University of Iceland
Industrial Research Laboratories) shall be consulted prior to the promulgation of the said regulations.

The regulations shall be revised in the light of scientific research.

. . .

Article 3. Violations of the regulations promulgated under Article 1 of
the present law shall be punishable in accordance with the provisions of law
No. 62 of 18 May 1967, as amended, relative to prohibition of fishing with
trawl and mid-water trawl, law No. 40 of 9 June, 1960 concerning a limited
permission for fishing with Danish seine-netting within the fisheries jurisdiction of Iceland under scientific supervision, law No. 33 of 19 June 1922,
as amended, on the right to fish within the fisheries jurisdiction or in case of
violations not applicable to the aforementioned laws, shall be punishable by
fines of from kr. 10,000.00 to kr. 1,000,000.00.

(b) REGULATIONS OF 15 JULY 1975 BY THE MINISTRY OF FISHERIES
CONCERNING THE FISHERY LIMITS OFF ICELAND [2]

Article 1. The fishery limits off Iceland shall be drawn 200 nautical
miles outside base-lines drawn between the following points:

1.	Horn	66° 27' 4 N., 22° 24' 3 W.
2.	Ásbúdharrif	66° 08' 1 N., 20° 11' 0 W.
3.	Siglunes	66° 11' 9 N., 18° 49' 9 W.
4.	Flatey	66° 10' 3 N., 17° 50' 3 W.
5.	Lágey	66° 17' 8 N., 17° 06' 8 W.
6.	Raudhinúpur	66° 30' 7 N., 16° 32' 4 W.
7.	Rifstangi	66° 32' 3 N., 16° 11' 8 W.
8.	Hraunhafnartangi	66° 32' 2 N., 16° 01' 5 W.
9.	Langanes	66° 22' 7 N., 14° 31' 9 W.

[1] By law No. 45 of 13 May 1974. In effect immediately in accordance with
article 3 thereof. English text of law provided by the Permanent Representative of
Iceland to the United Nations in a note verbale of 12 July 1974. Only the amended
articles are reproduced here. See also ST/LEG/SER.B/1, pp. 12-13; ST/LEG/SER.B/6,
pp. 513-514 and ST/LEG/SER.B/8, pp. 10-11.

[2] In force as of 15 October 1975 in accordance with article 8. English text provided
by the Permanent Representative of Iceland to the United Nations in a letter dated 23
July 1975.

10.	Glettinganes	65° 30' 5 N., 13° 36' 3 W.
11.	Nordhfjardharhorn	65° 10' 0 N., 13° 30' 8 W.
12.	Gerpir	65° 04' 7 N., 13° 29' 6 W.
13.	Hólmur	64° 58' 9 N., 13° 30' 6 W.
14.	Setusker	64° 57' 7 N., 13° 31' 5 W.
15.	Thursasker	64° 54' 1 N., 13° 36' 8 W.
16.	Ystibodhi	64° 35' 2 N., 14° 01' 5 W.
17.	Selsker	64° 32' 8 N., 14° 07' 0 W.
18.	Hvitingar	64° 23' 9 N., 14° 28' 0 W.
19.	Stokksnes	64° 14' 1 N., 14° 58' 4 W.
20.	Hrollaugseyjar	64° 01' 7 N., 15° 58' 7 W.
21.	Hvítingar	63° 55' 7 N., 16° 11' 3 W.
22.	Ingólfshöfdhi	63° 47' 8 N., 16° 38' 5 W.
23.	Hvalsíki	63° 44' 1 N., 17° 33' 5 W.
24.	Medhallandssandur I	63° 32' 4 N., 17° 55' 6 W.
25.	Medhallandssandur II	63° 30' 6 N., 17° 59' 9 W.
26.	Mýrnatangi	63° 27' 4 N., 18° 11' 8 W.
27.	Kötlutangi	63° 23' 4 N., 18° 42' 8 W.
28.	Lundadrangur	63° 23' 5 N., 19° 07' 5 W.
29.	Surtsey	63° 17' 6 N., 20° 36' 3 W.
30.	Eldeyjardrangur	63° 43' 8 N., 22° 59' 4 W.
31.	Geirfugladrangur	63° 40' 7 N., 23° 17' 1 W.
32.	Skálasnagi	64° 51' 3 N., 24° 02' 5 W.
33.	Bjargtangar	65° 30' 2 N., 24° 32' 1 W.
34.	Kópanes	65° 48' 4 N., 24° 06' 0 W.
35.	Bardhi	66° 03' 7 N., 23° 47' 4 W.
36.	Straumnes	66° 25' 7 N., 23° 08' 4 W.
37.	Kögur	66° 28' 3 N., 22° 55' 5 W.
38.	Horn	66° 27' 9 N., 22° 28' 2 W.

Limits shall also be drawn around the following points 200 nautical miles seaward:

39.	Kolbeinsey	67° 08' 8 N., 18° 40' 6 W.
40.	Hvalbakur	64° 35' 8 N., 13° 16' 6 W.
41.	Grimsey, from its outermost points and rocks.	

Each nautical mile shall be equal to 1852 metres.

Where the distance between base-lines of the Faeroes and Greenland on the one hand and Iceland on the other is less than 400 nautical miles, the fishery limits of Iceland shall be demarcated by the equidistance line. These Regulations shall not be enforced for the time being or until further notice in the area outside the equidistance line between the base-lines of Jan Mayen and Iceland.

Article 2. Within the fishery limits all fishing activities by foreign vessels shall be prohibited in accordance with the provisions of Law No. 33 of 19 June 1922, concerning Fishing inside the Fishery Limits.[1]

Article 3. Icelandic vessels using bottom trawl, mid-water trawl or Danish seine-netting are prohibited from fishing inside the fishery limits in the following areas and periods:

1. Off the North East Coast during the period 1 April to 1 June in an area which in the west is demarcated by a line drawn true North from

---

[1] Reproduced in part in ST/LEG/SER.B/6, pp. 510-512.

Rifstangi (Base-point 7), in the east by a line which is drawn true North-East from Langanes (Base-point 9) and in the north by a line drawn 50 nautical miles outside base-lines.

2. All year within a line drawn 12 nautical miles from Kolbeinsey (67° 08' 8 N., 18° 40' 6 W.).

Icelandic vessels are prohibited from all fishing in the following areas and periods:

1. Off the South Coast during the period 20 March to 1 May in an area demarcated by lines drawn between the following points:

(a) 63° 32' 0 N., 21° 25' 0 W.
(b) 63° 00' 0 N., 21° 25' 0 W.
(c) 63° 00' 0 N., 22° 00' 0 W.
(d) 63° 32' 0 N., 22° 00' 0 W.

2. Fishing with any gear is prohibited within the fishery limits off the West-Fjords in an area which in the west is demarcated by a line true 340° from point 66° 57' N. and point 23° 36' W. and in the east by a line true 0° from point 67° 01' N. and 22° 24' W. In the south a line is drawn between the points mentioned and in the north the area is demarcated by a line drawn 50 nautical miles outside base-lines.

The Ministry of Fisheries will determine the necessary rules for the protection of the fishstocks within the fishery limits. Action will be taken upon receipt of proposals from the Marine Research Institute and the Fisheries Association of Iceland.

If in a given area there occurs the catch of small fish to the extent considered undesirable or dangerous the Ministry of Fisheries, upon receiving the advice of the Marine Research Institute, will take the measures required. The Ministry will then announce the closure of specified areas during longer or shorter periods for all trawling and other fishing to the extent required. The advice of the Marine Research Institute shall always be available before such restrictions are abolished.

With these exceptions Icelandic vessels using bottom trawl, mid-water trawl or Danish seine-netting shall be allowed to fish within the fishery limits in accordance with the provisions of Law No. 102 of 27 December 1973, concerning Fishing with Trawl and Mid-water Trawl, or special provisions made before these Regulations become effective.

Article 4. Trawlers shall have all their fishing gear properly stowed aboard while staying in areas where fishing is prohibited, i. e. that trawl panels are properly secured and trawlnets fastened.

Article 5. Fisheries statistics shall be forwarded to the Fiskifélag Islands (Fisheries Association of Iceland) in the manner prescribed by Law No. 55 of 27 June 1941, concerning Catch and Fisheries Reports.

If the Ministry of Fisheries envisages the possibility of overfishing, the Ministry may limit the number of fishing vessels and the maximum catch of each vessel.

Article 6. Violation of the provisions of these Regulations shall be subject to penalties provided for by Law No. 102 of 27 December 1973, concerning Fishing with Trawl, Mid-water Trawl and Danish Seine-netting, Law No. 33 of 19 June 1922, concerning Fishing inside the Fishery Limits, as amended, or if the provisions of said Laws do not apply, to fines from kr. 10,000.00 to kr. 1,000,000.00.

Article 7. These Regulations are promulgated in accordance with Law No. 44 of 5 April 1948, concerning the Scientific Conservation of the Continental Shelf Fisheries, cf. Law No. 45 of 13 May 1974.[1] When these Regulations become effective, Regulations No. 189 of 14 July 1972,[2] concerning the Fishery Limits off Iceland, as amended by Regulations No. 362 of 4 December 1973, shall cease to be effective.

. . .

7. IRAN

PROCLAMATION OF 30 OCTOBER 1973 CONCERNING THE OUTER LIMIT OF THE EXCLUSIVE FISHING ZONE OF IRAN IN THE PERSIAN GULF AND THE SEA OF OMAN[3]

Whereas the coastal communities of Iran have throughout history been engaged in fishing activities in the seas adjacent to the Iranian coast; and

Whereas under Article 7 of the law of 12 April 1959 on the territorial sea of Iran,[4] fishing and other rights of Iran beyond the limits of its territorial sea have been reaffirmed; and

Whereas the natural resources of the seas adjacent to the Iranian coast are of vital importance to the economic and social progress of Iran;

Now, therefore, in order to safeguard the fishing rights and interests of Iran in the seas adjacent to its coast and the coasts of its Islands, it is hereby proclaimed that:

(1) The outer limits of the exclusive fishing zone of Iran in the Persian Gulf shall be the outer limits of the superjacent waters of the continental shelf of Iran.

(a) In areas where the continental shelf of Iran has been delimited under bilateral agreements with other States, the outer limits of the exclusive fishing zone of Iran shall correspond to the outer limits of the continental shelf of Iran as specified in those agreements.

(b) Where the outer limits of the continental shelf of Iran has not yet been delimited under bilateral agreements, unless otherwise agreed, the outer limits of the superjacent waters of the continental shelf of Iran shall be, for the purpose of delimitating the exclusive fishing zone of Iran, the median line every point of which is equidistant from the nearest points of the baselines from which the breadth of the territorial seas of the parties concerned are measured.

---

[1] *Supra (a).*

[2] Reproduced in ST/LEG/SER.B/16, pp. 301-303.

[3] English text provided by the Permanent Representative of Iran to the United Nations in a note verbale of 23 November 1973.

[4] Reproduced in ST/LEG/SER.B/16, pp. 10-11.

(2) The outer limits of the exclusive fishing zone of Iran in the sea of Oman shall be 50 nautical miles from the baseline from which the breadth of the territorial sea of Iran is measured.

In areas where the exclusive fishing zone of Iran and that of another coastal State may overlap, unless otherwise agreed, the boundary shall be the median line every point of which is equidistant from the nearest points of the baselines from which the breadth of the territorial seas of the parties concerned are measured.

(3) Fishing and all related activities by non-Iranians in the exclusive fishing zone of Iran are prohibited unless prior authorization is obtained from the Government of Iran.

(4) The outer limits of the exclusive fishing zones of Iran in the Persian Gulf and the Sea of Oman shall be drawn on Maritimes Charts.

(5) The provisions of this proclamation shall be without prejudice to the right of international navigation exercised in accordance with the rules and principles of International Law.

8. MADAGASCAR

[ORDONNANCE No 73-060 DU 28 SEPTEMBRE 1973 FIXANT LES LIMITES DE LA MER TERRITORIALE ET DU PLATEAU CONTINENTAL DE LA REPUBLIQUE MALGACHE, article 2] [1]

9. MEXICO

(a) ACT OF 29 DECEMBER 1971 ON TAXES AND ON FEES FOR FISHERIES [2]

Chapter I

Subject and scope of the taxes

Article 1. The taxes established in this Act shall apply to the exploitation in national waters of flora and fauna in general, irrespective of the method used for that purpose.

Article 2. It shall be presumed that, in the absence of proof to the contrary, when vessels carrying products referred to in this Act put into national ports the exploitation was carried out in national waters.

Article 3. Individuals or bodies corporate and national or foreign economic entities in any of the situations envisaged in this Act shall be liable to the taxes.

Article 4. All persons who, in whatever capacity or for whatever purpose, have in their possession or transport exploited products, shall be severally liable for the payment of taxes, with the exception of those who acquire such products after processing or for domestic consumption.

---

[1] *Supra* Division I, Subdivision A, Chapter I, 10.

[2] *Diario Oficial,* 30 December 1971. Came into effect on 1 January 1972. This Act revoked the Act of 31 December 1951 on Taxes on Fisheries and all the provisions relating thereto. Translation by the Secretariat of the United Nations.

Chapter II

Rules and manner of payment of the taxes

Article 5. All persons who operate from vessels flying the Mexican flag or use fishing devices of any kind shall pay taxes in cash at the rate of 2 per cent of the official price of the taxable products.

. . .

Article 10. Persons operating from vessels flying a foreign flag under an authorization from the Secretariat for Industry and Commerce, in accordance with the provisions of the Federal Act on Fishèries Development, shall pay the tax in cash in respect of each journey at the rate of 225 pesos per net register ton or fraction of the vessel.

The maximum duration of each journey shall be as follows:

I.   Fifteen days for vessels up to 40 tons;

II. Thirty days for vessels between 40 and 80 tons;

III. Sixty days for vessels between 80 and 150 tons; and

IV. Ninety days for vessels over 150 tons.

. . .

Article 12. Fisheries offices shall not issue authorizations to ships flying a foreign flag without prior proof that they have met their tax obligations.

. . .

Chapter V

Fees for exploitation activities, sport fishing and commercial sport fishing

Article 17. For the purpose of conducting the activities of exploiting the flora and fauna of national waters using any types of vessels or devices, application shall be made for the appropriate permit for each activity at the appropriate fisheries office before the activities begin.

. . .

Chapter VI

Violations and penalties

Article 18. Failure to comply with the obligations established in this Act shall be punished in accordance with the provisions of the Fiscal Code of the Federation, with the following exceptions:

I. Non-payment of taxes shall be punishable by a fine amounting to three times the unpaid tax;

In the absence of proof to the contrary, non-payment of taxes on exploited products shall be presumed unless they are covered by documentation attesting the payment of taxes;

II. When a person operating under a fishing authorization issued for a vessel flying a foreign flag is found to be shipping products liable to the tax to another vessel or landing them at a national port, a fine of from 25,000 to 100,000 pesos shall be imposed on the offender;

III. When a person using a vessel flying the Mexican flag is found to be trans-shipping exploited products to a vessel flying a foreign flag, a fine of from 5,000 to 15,000 pesos shall be imposed on the offender;

IV. When any person transports in vessels flying a foreign flag any type of exploited products outside the holds, refrigerated compartments and other places authorized in the fishery registration certificate of the vessel, a fine of from 5,000 to 15,000 pesos shall be imposed on him.

. . .

(b) FEDERAL ACT OF 10 MAY 1972 ON FISHERIES DEVELOPMENT[1]

Chapter I

General provisions

Article 1. This Act implements article 27 of the Constitution relative to the regulation, development and use of aquatic flora and fauna as natural entities susceptible of appropriation, with a view to achieving an equitable distribution of the national wealth and securing its conservation. The natural resources in question may be exploited by persons or companies constituted in conformity with the laws of Mexico only by virtue of a concession, permit or authorization issued by the Federal Executive. This Act concerns:

I. Fisheries;

II. The protection of aquatic flora and fauna;

III. Resources research and the culture of aquatic species;

IV. The processing of fishery products;

V. The regulation of the home and export markets for fishery production.

. . .

Article 3. For the purposes of this Act, fishing shall mean the act of taking or catching by any authorized process species or biological entities whose environment is water, and any prior or subsequent acts related thereto.

Article 4. Prior acts shall be those whose direct purpose is fishing and subsequent acts shall be those performed directly on species taken or caught and shall include processing.

Article 5. This Act shall regulate and develop fisheries in:

I. Nationally-owned inland waters;

II. Waters of the territorial sea;

III. Extraterritorial waters in the case of vessels flying the Mexican flag;

IV. Exclusive or preferential zones so declared by the Federation;

V. Waters overlying the continental shelf;

VI. The continental shelf; and

VII. Waters of the high seas.

---

[1] *Diario Oficial,* 25 May 1972. Came into effect on 9 June 1972. This act revoked the Fisheries Act of 16 January 1950, as amended, and other legal provisions which were inconsistent therewith. Translation by the Secretariat of the United Nations.

These matters shall also be regulated by the respective Acts and international treaties and agreements which have been or may be concluded in accordance with article 133 of the Constitution.

Article 6.   Fisheries shall be classified as follows:

I.   Fishing for domestic consumption purposes;

II.   Commercial fishing;

III.   Fishing for scientific research purposes;

IV.   Sport fishing.

Article 7.   Fishing shall be deemed to be for domestic consumption purposes when it is conducted on a non-profit basis and for the purpose of obtaining food products for subsistence consumption by the person concerned and members of his household.

No concession or permit shall be required for fishing for domestic consumption purposes and such fishing may be carried on even in waters covered by a concession. It shall likewise be exempt from any fiscal dues.

Article 8.   Fishing shall be deemed to be commercial when it is conducted by individuals or bodies corporate for the purposes of gain, by fishery production and co-operative societies and *ejido* communities.

Article 9.   Fishing shall be deemed to be for scientific research purposes when it is conducted on a non-profit basis and its purpose is the study of, experimentation with, or cultivation or restocking of fishery species.

Article 10.   Fishing shall be deemed to be sport fishing when it is conducted on a non-profit basis for recreational purposes and with such gear as the Regulations may determine.

The following species shall be reserved exclusively for sport fishing: marlin, sailfish, shad, dory, dorado and any other species that may be prescribed on the advice of the National Fisheries Institute.

. . .

Chapter V

Concessions, permits and authorizations

Article 25.   A concession or permit shall be required for commercial and sport fishing and for the cultivation of species whose normal environment is water.

A concession shall be granted when the technical, economic and social study of the fishery submitted by the applicant and approved by the Secretariat for Industry and Commerce, the nature of the proposed activities and the level of investment demonstrate that a period of not less than two years is required to ensure stability and safety in the conduct of the undertaking. In other cases permits shall be granted. A concession shall be required, in all cases,

I.   For the cultivation and development of species whose normal environment is water. Species reserved to fisheries production co-operative societies shall be cultivated by such societies only; and

II. For sport fishing associations and clubs.

Decisions regarding the grant of concessions shall be issued within not more than 120 days.

. . .

Article 27. Concessions and permits may be granted to:

I. Mexicans by birth or by naturalization;

II. Fishery production and *ejido* fishery production co-operatives;

III. Decentralized agencies or enterprises in which the State is a shareholder;

IV. Commercial companies satisfying the following requirements:

(a) That they are constituted under Mexican law and have their registered office in Mexico;

(b) That their share certificates are registered;

(c) That not less than 51 per cent of the share capital with voting rights is subscribed by Mexicans or by Mexican companies whose articles of association provide that shares may not be held by aliens;

(d) That the articles of association provide that the majority of the directors shall be nominated by the Mexican shareholders and that only persons of Mexican nationality shall be nominated.

Article 28. The period of validity of concessions shall be not less than five years and not more than twenty years. Upon expiry the concession may be extended.

Article 29. The period of validity of permits shall be two calendar years. They may be renewed by the local fishery offices and may not be transferred.

Article 30. Permits may be granted for sport or scientific fishing to foreign nationals who comply with the conditions laid down in article 27 (1) of the Constitution, the Organic Art thereof and other pertinent legislation. Fishing permits for a period in excess of 48 hours shall be validated at the first Mexican port at which the vessel concerned calls.

Article 31. No foreign Government may be a shareholder in or establish in its favour any right in respect of concessions or permits. Any acts in contravention of this provision shall be *ipso facto* null and void, and such assets and rights as the said foreign Government may thereby have acquired shall revert to the Mexican nation.

This provision shall appear in all concessions and permits.

. . .

Article 37. Commercial fishing by foreign vessels in national waters shall be prohibited. However, the Secretariat for Industry and Commerce may, by way of exception, grant permits on a trip-by-trip basis, to foreign vessels, which satisfy the following requirements:

I. That they leave the territorial waters within the specified time;

II. That they do not land the products caught in the national territory;

III. That at least 50 per cent of the crew are of Mexican nationality;

IV. That the Mexican crew are engaged on Mexican territory, at wages and with benefits equal to those received by the non-Mexican crew whenever these are higher than or otherwise superior to those prevailing in Mexico;

V. That the person responsible produces evidence as to the net tonnage capacity of the hold in the form of a certificate from the National Fisheries Register;

VI. That no commercial fishing for sardine, anchoveta (Peruvian anchovy) and species reserved to co-operatives shall be undertaken;

VII. That live sardine is not caught for bait in areas prohibited by the Secretariat for Industry and Commerce;

VIII. That no commercial fishing is carried on in areas reserved pursuant to this Act; and

IX. That a cash bond is deposited by way of guaranteeing compliance with the foregoing requirements.

The general prohibition shall be waived in the case of sport fishing. Contravention of any of the foregoing provisions shall result in forfeiture of the relevant bond to an amount to be determined by the Secretariat for Industry and Commerce according to the seriousness of the offence, without prejudice to other penalties that may apply.

Article 38. The following obligations shall devolve upon all persons engaging in fisheries:

I. To take or catch only authorized species in the areas prescribed by the Secretariat for Industry and Commerce;

II. To observe the prescriptions of the Secretariat for Industry and Commerce with respect to minimum sizes and weights of species;

III. To observe the maximum volume of operations specified in the concession or permit;

IV. To co-operate with the Secretariat for Industry and Commerce and, as appropriate, the Secretariat for Water Resources in their operations in the reproduction, cultivation and restocking of species;

V. To admit on board vessels and processing plant research personnel and persons undergoing training in fishing;

VI. In the case of commercial fishing, to keep a register in which are to be entered in chronological order the volume caught, the species taken or caught, and the grounds worked;

VII. To submit returns, annually in the case of concession holders, and for each trip in the case of permit holders, on the full utilization of the fisheries;

VIII. To notify the appropriate Fisheries Office of the arrival and landing of catches;

IX. To furnish to the appropriate authorities any information required pursuant to the relevant legislation;

X. To allow and facilitate inspection by officers accredited by the appropriate authorities subject to the procedures provided for by the Constitution in order to establish that the persons concerned have complied with their obligations;

XI. In the case of ocean-going fishing vessels, to keep the documents and logs prescribed by the relevant legislation, and

XII. To comply with all other provisions of this Act and of other relevant legislation.

. . .

Article 41. The transport of fishery products within the national territory shall be carried out in Mexican vehicles covered by the "Fisheries Director" to be issued by the Secretariat for Industry and Commerce. Holders of permits for sport and scientific fishing and fishing for household consumption purposes shall be exempted from the foregoing. In the event of there being no Mexican vessels suitable for the transport of fishery products, the Secretariat for Industry and Commerce may authorize foreign vessels for that purpose provided that they satisfy the requirements laid down by other competent authorities. The said foreign vessels shall be subject to the inspection and control referred to in this Act and other relevant provisions.

. . .

Chapter VI

Forfeitures and revocation of concessions, and cancellation of permits and authorizations

Article 44. The following shall constitute grounds for the forfeiture of concessions:

I. Failure to initiate operations within the period laid down;

II. Failure to initiate investment, construction of works and installations or the purchase of equipment within the periods laid down;

III. Failure to complete the works and installations by the specified dates.

Article 45. The following shall constitute grounds for the revocation of concessions:

I. Failure to adhere to the established investment plan;

II. Suspension, without justified cause, of operations for more than 30 consecutive days;

III. The use of part or all of the production for purposes other than those specified in the concession, this Act and other pertinent provisions;

IV. Repeated falsification of fishery data;

. . .

VI. Failure, without justified cause, to observe the general technical requirements prescribed by the Secretariat for Industry and Commerce within the time laid down for so doing;

VII. Transfer of the concession, in contravention of the provisions of this Act; and

Chapter X

Offences

Article 78. The following shall constitute violations:

I. To conduct commercial fishing, scientific research or sport fishing without the relevant concession or permit;

II. To take or catch species during the declared closed season;

III. To use prohibited devices, gear or methods of fishing;

IV. To gather, keep or market nests or roe of fishery species without the authorization of the Secretariat for Industry and Commerce, or to destroy them;

V. To take or catch animals of a smaller size or weight than that prescribed by the Secretariat for Industry and Commerce;

VI. To catch, without authorization, species reserved for sport fishing;

VII. To take, catch or destroy fishery species in or at areas or sites designated as refuges or for cultivation or to interfere with the ecology of such areas or sites;

VIII. To have on board vessels intended for fishing any prohibited devices or fishing gear, explosives or contaminants;

IX. To install fixed fishing gear or to erect works in waters under Federal jurisdiction without the authorization of the Secretariat for Industry and Commerce or the Secretariat for Water Resources;

X. To employ for taking or catching methods that have not been authorized by the Secretariat for Industry and Commerce;

XI. To trade in the products of domestic, sport or scientific fishing;

. . .

XIV. To export or import fishery products without the permission of the Secretariat for Industry and Commerce;

XV. To set up floating plants for the processing of fishery products without the authorization of the Secretariat for Industry and Commerce;

XVI. To manufacture fertilizer, meal, oil or other industrial products from fishery species without the authorization of the Secretariat for Industry and Commerce;

XVII. To cause the death, degeneration or injuring of fishery species, save in the case of authorized taking or catching or for purposes of scientific research;

. . .

XIX. To trans-ship fishery products to any other vessel without the authorization of the Secretariat for Industry and Commerce, save in the event of an accident;

XX. To land commercial fishery products from foreign vessels without the authorization of the Secretariat for Industry and Commerce, save in the event of an accident;

. . .

XXII. Other cases of failure to comply with this Act, as specified in Chapter XII.

Article 79. The pollution of waters shall be governed by the provisions of the Federal Act on the Prevention and Control of Environmental Pollution.[1]

. . .

Chapter XII

Penalties

Article 88. Contraventions of the provisions of this Act shall be punished by the Secretariat for Industry and Commerce as set forth in the following articles:

Article 89. Fines shall be imposed as follows:

I. 50-1,000 pesos for contraventions of articles 21, 32 (III), 38 (V) and (VI), 81 and 83;

II. 1,000-5,000 pesos for contraventions of articles 36 (II) and (III), 38 (I), (II), (IV), (VII) and (VIII), 41, 66, 71 and 78 (I), (V), (VII) and (X);

III. 5,000-10,000 pesos for contraventions of articles 24, 38 (III), 68 (I), (II) and (III), and 78 (XX);

IV. 10,000-25,000 pesos for contraventions of articles 37, 40, 41 and 78 (IV), (VI), (XIV) and (XV); and

V. 100-20,000 pesos for contraventions of article 78 (VIII), (XI), (XII), (XIII), (XVIII), (XIX) and (XXI), and for any other violation of the provisions of this Act.

Article 90. For the second and subsequent offences, the amount of the fine shall be doubled.

By second and subsequent offences shall be understood the repetition of the same act if the said act involves the violation of the same provision.

Article 91. In addition to the fines provided for in article 89, one or more of the following penalties may be imposed at the same time:

I. Confiscation of the fishery products, means of transport, fishing devices and gear, for violations of articles 38 (I), 41 and 69 (VI), (VII), (VIII) and (XIX);

II. Temporary closure for up to 30 days for violations of articles 25 (I), 36 (II) and (III) and 78 (VI), (XIV), (XV) and (XVI).

For the second and subsequent first offences permanent closure may be imposed;

III. Revocation of concessions or cancellation of permits for violations of articles 38 (III) and 78 (VI), (VII) and (X).

. . .

Article 93. Fishing in territorial waters and exclusive fishing zones by foreign vessels not in possession of the relevant permit shall be punishable by a fine of from 75,000 to 300,000 pesos and confiscation of the fishing gear

---

[1] Dated 12 March 1971. Came into effect on 24 March 1971. *Diario Oficial,* 23 March 1971, pp. 8-11.

and the species on board. The vessels shall be impounded in the appropriate Mexican port until the fine has been paid.

. . .

10. MOROCCO

[DAHIR PORTANT LOI No. 1.73.211 DU 2 MARS 1973 FIXANT LA LIMITE DES EAUX TERRITORIALES ET DE LA ZONE DE PECHE EXCLUSIVE MARO-CAINES, articles 4-6] [1]

11. PAKISTAN

PRESIDENTIAL PROCLAMATION OF 20 MARCH 1973 EXTENDING THE EXCLUSIVE FISHERY ZONE[2]

Whereas the coastal communities of Pakistan have from time immemorial been engaged in fishing activities in the high seas adjacent to its territorial waters;

And whereas certain areas of these high seas provide fisheries which contribute ·to the food and means of livelihood of large sections of the population;

And whereas Pakistan has special interests and rights in the exploitation of fisheries adjacent to its coast;

Now, therefore, in partial modification of the earlier Proclamation of 19th February 1966[3] in respect of exclusive fishing rights, I, Zulfikar Ali Bhutto, President of the Islamic Republic of Pakistan do hereby proclaim and declare that—

Pakistan shall have an exclusive fishery zone in areas of the high seas adjacent to the territorial waters of Pakistan up to a distance of 50 nautical miles from the coast-line.

12. SWEDEN

(a) ACT NO. 596 of 1 DECEMBER 1950 CONCERNING FISHERY RIGHTS,[4] AS AMENDED UP TO 1973 [5]

Article 1. This Act relates to the right to fish in the territorial sea of Sweden and in the Swedish fishery zone.

---

[1] *Supra* Division I, Subdivision A, Chapter I, 14.

[2] Text provided by the Permanent Representative of Pakistan to the United Nations in a note verbale of 24 April 1973.

[3] Reproduced in ST/LEG/SER.B/15, p. 661.

[4] Reproduced in part in ST/LEG/SER.B/6, pp. 565-567. The Act as amended in 1960 and 1967 is reproduced in part in ST/LEG/SER.B/15, pp. 669-670.

[5] The 1973 amendment was made by the Act of 23 November 1973 to Amend the Act (1950: 596) respecting Fishery Rights, published in *Swedish Code of Statutes,* 4 December 1973. The amendment, which relates only to article 1, is to come into effect on the date as the King will determine. Swedish text provided by the Permanent Representative of Sweden to the United Nations in a note verbale of 17 December 1973. Translation by the Secretariat of the United Nations.

The fishery zone shall comprise such area of the sea up to eight nautical miles or 14,816 metres outside the territorial limits along the coast of Sweden as the King shall determine.

The provisions of this Act relating to fishing in public waters shall also apply to the fishery zone, subject however to the restrictions arising from the Continental Shelf Act.[1]

In respect of any area within which fishing is regulated by an agreement with a foreign State the provisions of this Act shall to the extent that they conflict with that agreement not apply.

. . .

(b) ORDER OF 8 JANUARY 1971 BY THE NATIONAL BOARD OF FISHERIES INCORPORATING CERTAIN REGULATIONS CONCERNING FISHING IN THE AREA COVERED BY THE NORTH-EAST ATLANTIC FISHERIES CONVENTION AND IN THE ÖRESUND CHANNEL[2]

Pursuant to a Convention (the North-East Atlantic Fisheries Convention)[3] concluded on 24 January 1959 between Sweden and a number of other European countries for the purpose of ensuring the conservation of the fish stocks and the rational exploitation of the fisheries in the Convention area, and pursuant to Royal Order No. 500 of 13 August 1965 concerning regulation of the size of mesh of fishing nets, minimum size of fish, etc., the Board of Fisheries hereby directs as follows.

Introductory provisions

Paragraph 1. This Order relates to fishing in the area covered by the North-East Atlantic Fisheries Convention and in the Öresund Channel.

The Convention sea comprises—subject to the exceptions indicated below—the parts of the Atlantic Ocean and the Arctic Ocean and their dependent seas which lie north of 36 degrees north latitude and between 42 degrees west longitude and 51 degrees east longitude, together with the part of the Atlantic Ocean which lies north of 59 degrees north latitude and between 42 degrees and 44 degrees west longitude.

The Convention area does not include the Baltic Sea, the Belts and the Öresund Channel to the south and east of lines drawn from Hasenöre Head to Gniben Point, from Korshage to Spodsbjerg and from Gilbjerg Head to the Kullen, nor the Mediterranean Sea and its dependent inland seas.

The Convention area is divided into the following regions:

. . .

---

[1] Reproduced in part in ST/LEG/SER.B/15, pp. 437-441.

[2] *Swedish Code of Statutes,* 8 February 1971. Came into force on 9 February 1971. Swedish text provided by the Permanent Representative of Sweden to the United Nations in a note verbale of 13 March 1973. Translation by the Secretariat of the United Nations.

[3] United Nations, *Treaty Series,* vol. 486, p. 157. Reproduced in part in ST/LEG/SER.B/15, pp. 853-857.

The Öresund Channel comprises the area between the boundary of the Convention area and the line from Falsterbo Light to Stevns Light.

Paragraph 2. The word "vessel" as used in this Order means any vessel or boat employed in fishing for sea fish or in the treatment of sea fish.

Size of mesh of fishing nets

Paragraph 3. When fishing in the parts specified below of the Convention area a Swedish vessel may not, except as stated in paragraph 4, carry on board or use any trawl, seine or other net towed or hauled at or near the bottom of the sea unless the inside length, between the end knots, of the meshes in the net is at least as stated below.

. . .

Paragraph 4. Notwithstanding the provisions of paragraph 3, nets having meshes of a size smaller than the size there specified may be used in fishing for mackerel, clupeoid fishes, sand eels *(Ammodytes),* Norway pout *(Gadus esmarkii),* smelts, eels, great weevers *(Trachinus draco),* capelin *(Mallotus villosus),* poutassou or blue whiting *(Gadus poutassou),* horse mackerel *(Trachurus trachurus),* prawns, Norway lobsters and molluscs on condition that the gear is not used for the purpose of catching fish and crustaceans of kinds other than those just named.

For the conservation of the stocks of deep-water prawns *(Pandalus borealis)* the specific regulation relating thereto shall apply.

What is stated in the first subparagraph hereof shall however not apply to fishing for horse mackerel and poutassou (blue whiting) in region III or in fishing for poutassou in that part of region II which lies south of 52 degrees 30 minutes north latitude and west of 7 degrees west longitude.

In the Convention area other than the area east of the line Hanstholm—Lindesnäs, no fishing gear having in the cod-end meshes of a size between 50 millimetres and the dimensions specified in paragraph 3 for region II may be carried on board or used on Swedish vessels.

. . .

Minimum sizes of certain kinds of fish

Paragraph 6. Fish of the kinds indicated below which have been caught in the Convention area and whose length, in the ungutted condition, from the tip of the snout to the extreme end of the tail fin is less than that indicated for each individual area in the following list may not be retained on board a Swedish vessel, or be killed, but shall be returned to the sea immediately.

. . .

Paragraph 7. No one may import into the Kingdom or in the Kingdom land, deal in, offer for sale, sell, or buy for purposes of resale fish which have been caught within the areas specified in paragraph 1 and whose length is of less than the minimum dimension prescribed in paragraph 6 for fish of the kind concerned.

If in fishing in conformity with paragraph 4 fishes specified in paragraph 6 have been caught which are of less than the prescribed minimum size, the undersized fish may until the end of the year 1973 and notwithstanding the regulations laid down in the foregoing be retained on board, killed, landed, dealt in, offered for sale, sold, or bought for purposes of resale if they do not constitute more than 10 per cent by weight of every landing or part thereof not intended to be used as fish for human consumption. Whitings of a length between 20 and 23 centimetres shall however not be regarded as undersized in this connexion.

Notwithstanding the provisions in paragraph 3, fishing nets having a mesh size smaller than the size there prescribed may until the end of the year 1979 be used in fishing for whitings in the Kattegatt and the Skagerrak east of a straight line from Hanstholm to Lindesnäs if the engine power of the vessel does not exceed 150 horse-power. During the same period, whitings which have been caught in fishing performed in the manner described which are of less than the prescribed minimum size may, notwithstanding the aforesaid provisions, be retained on board, killed, landed, dealt in, offered for sale, sold, or bought for purposes of resale on condition that the catch landed does not contain fish other than fish of the kinds enumerated in paragraph 6.

The regulations laid down in paragraph 6 and in the foregoing shall not apply to whitings caught with the hook in Swedish waters.

Provisions concerning salmon fishing

Paragraph 8. The following shall apply throughout the Convention area but outside the fishery limits of the States concerned.

Caught salmon whose length from the tip of the snout to the extreme end of the tail fin is less than 60 centimetres may not be retained on board, but shall be returned to the sea immediately.

Trawl nets, nets of fully-drawn nylon, spoon baits or whiffing-lines may not be used in salmon fishing.

Drift-nets, anchored nets and seines used in salmon fishing shall have a mesh size of not less than 160 mm measured as prescribed in paragraph 3.

The aperture of the salmon hook shall be of not less than 19 mm and the gut of the salmon hook shall be of a strength corresponding at least to that of a fully-drawn nylon line 0.6 mm thick.

Paragraph 9. In regions I and II but outside the fishery limits of the States concerned, salmon fishing is prohibited from 1 July to 5 May, both dates included; it is moreover prohibited altogether between 63 and 68 degrees north latitude east of the prime meridian and east of 22 degrees east longitude.

. . .

Paragraph 14. After authorization by the Board of Fisheries, undersized fish may be caught and be retained on board a Swedish vessel for the purpose of transplantation to other areas.

The provisions of this Order shall not apply to fishing performed for scientific purposes. Undersized fish caught during such fishing may be retained on board, killed and landed, but may not be sold.

. . .

(c) ROYAL ORDER OF 19 NOVEMBER 1971 CONCERNING REGULATION OF THE SIZE OF MESH OF FISHING NETS, MINIMUM SIZE OF FISH, ETC.[1]

His Majesty the King has deemed it proper to ordain in the matter of the Order (1965:500) concerning regulation of the size of mesh of fishing nets, minimum size of fish, etc., that

The present paragraphs 2-4 shall be numbered 6-8; that

The new paragraphs 6-8 shall be worded as shown hereunder; and that

Four new paragraphs, numbered 2-5, together with an annex, all worded as shown thereunder, shall be inserted in the Order.

In consequence hereof the Order will be worded as shown below as from the date on which the present Order enters into force.

Paragraph 1. The Board of Fisheries *(Fiskeristyrelsen)* shall enact the provisions, governing, *inter alia,* the size of mesh of fishing nets and the minimum size of fish, necessitated by Sweden's accession to the North-East Atlantic Fisheries Convention,[2] on 24 January 1959 and to an Agreement with Denmark and the Federal Republic of Germany, signed on behalf of Sweden on 20 December 1962, concerning measures to preserve stocks of salmon in the Baltic Sea.[3]

The Board of Fisheries shall likewise enact provisions on the same subjects for the Swedish sea fisheries.

Paragraph 2. Supervision of the observance of provisions enacted pursuant to paragraph 1 shall be performed within the North-East Atlantic Fisheries Convention area outside the territorial sea of Sweden and the Swedish fishing zone in conformity with the recommendation concerning international control activity which was adopted by the North-East Atlantic Fisheries Commission at its seventh session at Reykjavik from 7 to 13 May 1968. The wording of the recommendation is as shown in the annex hereto.[4] Paragraphs 3 to 6 shall apply in the implementation of the recommendation.

. . .

Paragraph 6. A fine or a sentence of not more than six months' imprisonment shall be imposed on any person who

---

[1] *Swedish Code of Statutes,* 10 December 1971. Entered into force on 1 January 1972. It amends a prior Order (1965: 500) on the same subject. Swedish text provided by the Permanent Representative of Sweden to the United Nations in a note verbale of 13 March 1973. Translation by the Secretariat of the United Nations.

[2] United Nations, *Treaty Series,* vol. 486, p. 157. Reproduced in part in ST/LEG/SER.B/15, pp. 853-857.

[3] Reproduced *ibid.,* pp. 859-861.

[4] Annex is not reproduced here.

1. Wilfully or through negligence acts in breach of a provision which has been enacted pursuant to paragraph 1; or

2. Resists or otherwise seeks by force to hinder an inspector as referred to in the recommendation in the performance of his duty or who fails to obey directions given by such inspector, unless the act is punishable under the Criminal Code.

Paragraph 7. Fish which have been caught or have otherwise been the object of an act conflicting with a provision enacted pursuant to paragraph 1 shall be declared forfeit unless such declaration would be manifestly inequitable.

If, in a batch of fish, fish are found which, under the first subparagraph of this paragraph, should be declared forfeit on the grounds that they are of less than the prescribed minimum size, and the owner of the batch does not immediately have the other fish sorted by a trustworthy person at his own expense, the other fish also shall be declared forfeit, unless such declaration would be manifestly inequitable.

Fishing gear which has been used to help in the commission of a breach of a provision which has been enacted pursuant to paragraph 1 may be declared forfeit if so required for the purpose of preventing a breach or if special grounds therefore otherwise exist.

The value of the fish or gear may be declared forfeit in place of the actual fish or gear.

Paragraph 8. The provisions of articles 34-37 and 40 of the Fisheries Act *(Fiskeristadgan)* (1954:607)[1] shall apply as appropriate in the matter of a breach as referred to in this Order.

(d) ROYAL ORDER OF 23 NOVEMBER 1973 CONCERNING THE EXTENT OF THE SWEDISH FISHERY ZONE[2]

His Majesty the King ordains, pursuant to the Act (1950:596) respecting the Fishery Rights, article 1,[3] as follows:

Paragraph 1. The Swedish fishery zone shall comprise the area of the sea outside the territorial limits up to eight nautical miles or 14,816 metres from those limits.

The fishery zone shall however

1. Not extend further than the territorial limits of a foreign State;

2. In the area nearest to the limits with Norway not extend beyond straight lines between the most westerly point on the outermost limits of

---

[1] Reproduced in part in ST/LEG/SER.B/15, pp. 671-673.

[2] *Swedish Code of Statutes,* 4 December 1973. Entered into force on 1 January 1974, on which date the Royal Notice of 5 September 1968 (1968: 486) concerning the extent of the Swedish fishery zone, reproduced in part in ST/LEG/SER.B/16, p. 330, ceased to have effect. Swedish text provided by the Permanent Representative of Sweden to the United Nations in a note verbale of 17 December 1973. Translation by the Secretariat of the United Nations.

[3] *Supra (a).*

Sweden's territorial sea towards Norway, the point 58° 53' 34.0" N., 10° 38' 25.0" E. and the point 58° 45' 41.3" N., 10° 35' 40.0" E.;

3. Extend in the Kattegatt not further than up to a line on which all points lie at the same distance from the nearest points on the low-water lines on the Swedish coast and the Danish coast;

4. In the Öresund Channel not extend beyond the line in the longitudinal direction of the Channel which is specified in the Joint Declaration with Denmark, made on 30 January 1932, concerning certain circumstances relating to the frontier in the Öresund Channel;[1]

5. Extend in the Baltic Sea, including the Åland Sea, the Sea of Bothnia and the Gulf of Bothnia not further than up to a line on which all points lie at the same distance from the nearest points on the baselines from which the width of the territorial sea of Sweden and a foreign State, respectively, are reckoned.[2]

Paragraph 2. The outermost limits of the fishery zone shall be marked by the National Administration of Shipping and Navigation *(sjöfartsverket)* on nautical charts available to the public.

. . .

. . .

13. TOGO

LOI No 64-14 DU 11 JUILLET 1964 PORTANT REGLEMENTATION DE LA PECHE[3]

Article premier. – Le Gouvernement exerce la surveillance et la police de la pêche dans l'intérêt général.

Chapitre 1 – De la pêche maritime

Article 2. – Les établissements de pêches industrielles, à l'exclusion des pêcheries traditionnelles, les parcs, les dépôts de coquillages formés sur le rivage de la mer, le long des côtes, sur les lagunes et sur les rives des lagunes sont soumis à autorisation dans les conditions qui seront fixées par décret en conseil des ministres. Les infractions audit décret seront passibles d'une amende de 12 000 francs à 120 000 francs.

Article 3. – L'utilisation des plages ou parties de plages et délimitation des zones réservées au bain, au tourisme, à l'industrie, au rejet des eaux résiduaires ou à tout autre usage seront réglementées par décret.

L'occupation de ces zones peut donner lieu à perception de redevances dans les conditions qui seront fixées par décret en conseil des ministres.

---

[1] Reproduced in ST/LEG/SER.B/6, pp. 792-794.

[2] Notwithstanding these new provisions, fishing from a fishing vessel whose home State is Denmark, Finland, Poland, the Soviet Union, the German Democratic Republic or the Federal Republic of Germany may be carried out in the Swedish fishery zone in the waters specified in paragraph 1, subparagraph 5, until the end of 1975, unless his Majesty the King ordains otherwise.

[3] Texte transmis par la Mission permanente du Togo auprès de l'Organisation des Nations Unies par note en date du 23 mai 1973.

Article 4. — La pêche est interdite aux navires étrangers dans les eaux territoriales togolaises en deçà d'une limite fixée à 12 milles marins au large de la laisse de basse mer.

Article 5. — Si le capitaine d'un navire étranger ou les hommes de son équipage sont surpris en action de pêche dans les eaux territoriales togolaises, le capitaine est puni d'une amende de 120 000 francs à 1 200 000 francs CFA.

Article 6. — En cas de récidive, la peine d'amende peut être portée au double; en outre, la confiscation des engins et des produits de la pêche est obligatoirement prononcée et le capitaine est passible d'un emprisonnement de quinze jours à trois mois.

Il y a récidive lorsque, dans les deux années précédant la constatation du délit, il a été rendu contre le contrevenant un jugement en application de l'article 4 de la présente loi.

Article 7. — En cas d'infraction à l'article 4 de la présente loi, le navire peut être saisi et retenu jusqu'à entier paiement des frais de garde et d'entretien, des frais de justice et des amendes.

Passé le délai de trois mois à compter du jour où le jugement est devenu définitif, le navire peut être vendu par autorisation de justice.

Article 8. — Les dispositions qui précèdent ne portent pas atteinte à la libre circulation des navires de pêche étrangers naviguant ou mouillant dans les eaux territoriales togolaises.

Chapitre II. — De la pêche fluviale

. . .

Chapitre III. — De la pêche par explosifs ou drogues

Article 10. — Il est interdit de faire usage pour la pêche maritime ou pour la pêche fluviale d'explosifs ou matières explosives de quelque nature que ce soit, de drogues pouvant détruire, enivrer ou modifier le comportement normal des poissons, crustacés, coquillages ou animaux aquatiques quelconques.

Sont prohibés la vente, le transport et le colportage du produit des pêches interdites au paragraphe précédent.

Lorsque les produits de la pêche ont toutes les apparences d'avoir été obtenus à l'aide d'explosifs ou de drogues, la preuve contraire incombe aux détenteurs de ces produits.

Article 11. — Toute infraction aux dispositions de l'article 10 sera punie d'une peine d'emprisonnement d'un an à cinq ans et d'une amende de 50 000 francs à 500 000 francs ou de l'une de ces deux peines seulement.

La confiscation des explosifs ou drogues et du produit de la pêche sera obligatoire. En outre, le tribunal pourra ordonner la confiscation des navires ou bateaux ayant servi au délit et des véhicules ayant servi au transport des explosifs ou drogues ou du produit de la pêche prohibée.

352

Article 12. − Le bénéfice de la transaction est exclu en matière de pêche par explosifs ou drogues.

Article 13. − La pêche maritime ou fluviale à l'aide de feux, d'engins éclairants ou d'engins électriques peut être interdite ou réglementée par décret en conseil des ministres.

Le rejet à la mer et la décharge dans la limite des eaux territoriales de tous produits toxiques et notamment des hydrocarbures sont passibles des peines prévues à l'article 28 ci-après.

Chapitre IV. − De la constatation et de la poursuite des infractions

Article 14. − Les agents assermentés des services des pêches, des eaux et forêts, de l'élevage et des douanes, les officiers de police judiciaire et les personnes commissionnées par arrêtés ministériels et dûment assermentées constatent les infractions en matière de pêche maritime ou de pêche fluviale.

. . .

Article 16. − Les délits en matière de pêche seront prouvés par procès-verbaux qui feront foi jusqu'à preuve contraire.

Article 17. − Les agents visés à l'article 14 sont autorisés à saisir les instruments de pêche prohibés ainsi que le produit des pêches frauduleuses. Ces engins prohibés ne peuvent être remis sous caution. Ils sont déposés au greffe et détruits après jugement définitif.

Article 18. − En cas de refus de la part des délinquants de remettre immédiatement les filets ou engins prohibés après sommation, le tribunal pourra prononcer une peine d'amende d'un montant double de la valeur des engins prohibés. Cette amende ne se confond pas avec les peines sanctionnant le délit de pêche.

. . .

Article 28. − Les infractions aux décrets pris pour l'application de la présente loi seront passibles d'une amende de 12 000 à 120 000 francs et d'un emprisonnement de quinze jours à six mois ou de l'une de ces deux peines seulement. La confiscation des engins de pêche et des poissons peut être prononcée s'il y a lieu.

Article 29. − Les peines prévues par la présente loi pourront être portées au double lorsque les délits auront été commis la nuit.

. . .

14. TONGA

FISHERIES PROTECTION ACT, 1973[1]

. . .

─────────
[1] Act No. 10 of 6 August 1973. Given Royal assent on 7 September 1973. Text transmitted to the Secretary-General of the United Nations by the Acting Prime Minister and Minister for Foreign Affairs of Tonga in a letter dated 25 June 1974.

2. In this Act—

"Court" means the Supreme Court;

"fish" means any aquatic animal, whether piscine or not, and includes shell-fish, crustaceans, sponge, holothurian (beche-de-mer) and turtle, and the young and eggs thereof;

"Fisheries Protection Officer" means any person as specified in section 4 of this Act;

"fishing" means taking, hunting, pursuing, catching, killing or possessing any fish, or attempting to do any of these things, and "to fish" has a corresponding meaning,

"foreign fishing vessel" means any vessel used commercially for fishing or for the processing or storage of fish which is either not registered in Tonga or is owned or controlled by a person or persons not ordinarily resident in Tonga, but does not include any canoe or any vessel used for the transport of fish or fish products as part of its general cargo;

"Minister" means such Minister as may be appointed to administer this Act;

"territorial waters of the Kingdom" means all waters within the area bounded by the fifteenth and twenty-third and half degrees of south latitudes and the one hundred and seventy-third and the one hundred and seventy-seventh degrees of west longitudes, and also within the area bounded by the Proclamation made on the 15th day of June, 1972 affirming and proclaiming Teleki Tonga and Teleki Tokelau part of the Kingdom of Tonga.

3. (1) A foreign fishing vessel shall not enter within the territorial waters of the Kingdom, except for a purpose recognized by international law, or by any convention, treaty or arrangement for the time being in force between Tonga and any Foreign State, or because of stress of weather or other unavoidable circumstances.

(2) If a foreign fishing vessel enters the territorial waters of the Kingdom, it—

(a) Shall return outside of the territorial waters of the Kingdom as soon as the purpose for which it entered them has been fulfilled;

(b) Shall not fish or attempt to fish while within the territorial waters of the Kingdom;

(c) Shall not load, unload or tranship any fish while within these limits;

(d) Shall stow its fishing gear in accordance with regulations issued by the Minister; and

(e) Shall obey such other regulations as may from time to time be issued by the Minister.

(3) In the event of contravention of this section in the case of a foreign fishing vessel—

(a) The master of the foreign fishing vessel shall be liable to a fine not exceeding T$100,000 or imprisonment for a term not exceeding five years or both;

(b) The Court may on conviction of the master of the foreign fishing vessel of an offence under this section also order the forfeiture to the Government of Tonga of the foreign fishing vessel and of any fish and tackle, engines, nets, gear, apparatus, cargo and stores.

(4) The foregoing provisions of this section shall not prohibit or restrict fishing by foreign fishing vessels in areas within the territorial waters of the Kingdom with respect to which special provision for fishing by such vessels is made by any arrangement between the Government of Tonga and the Government of the country in which such vessels are registered or the owners of such vessels.

4. The following persons shall be Fisheries Protection Officers for the purposes of this Ordinance, that is to say—

(a) Members of the Police Force;

(b) Commissioned officers of the Tonga Defence Services;

(c) Persons in command or charge of any vessel or aircraft operated by or on behalf of the Tonga Defence Services;

(d) Any other person appointed as a Fisheries Protection Officer by the Minister.

5. For the purposes of enforcing the provisions of this Act a Fisheries Protection Officer shall have the following powers, that is—

(a) He may with or without a warrant stop, board and search any foreign fishing vessel reasonably suspected of being used for the purposes of fishing and may examine any fish on the boat and the equipment of the boat including the fishing gear and require persons on the boat to do anything which appears to him to be necessary for facilitating such examination;

(b) Where it appears that any contravention of the provisions of this Act has taken place, he may, with or without a warrant, arrest any person whom he believes has committed any such contravention, and if the Fisheries Protection Officer arresting that person is not a police officer, he shall without unnecessary delay make over that person to a police officer;

(c) Where it appears that any contravention of the provisions of this Act has taken place, he may, with or without a warrant, seize the fishing vessel in relation to which the contravention took place together with its tackle, engines, nets, gear, apparatus, cargo and stores and may take the same and the crew of the fishing vessel to the port which appears to him to be the nearest convenient port and may detain the same and the crew until the completion of proceedings for the contravention;

(d) Where it appears that any fish have been taken or are possessed in contravention of this Act, he may seize same and if adequate facilities are not available to preserve such fish pending the completion of proceedings for the contravention, he may take all necessary steps for the sale of such fish at its reasonable market value, the net proceeds of such sale to be paid to the Registrar of the Supreme Court pending the making of a final order by the Court in respect of the forefeiture or otherwise of that fund;

(e) Where it appears that any contravention of the provisions of this Act has taken place, he may engage in hot pursuit of the vessel or fishing vessel in relation to which the contravention took place or of its mother ship; and such

hot pursuit shall be in accordance with the provisions of Article 23 of the Convention on the High Seas signed at Geneva on 29th day of April 1958,[1] which Article 23 is set out in the Schedule annexed hereto.[2]

6. Any person who—

(a) Wilfully obstructs any Fisheries Protection Officer in the exercise of any of his powers under this Act; or

(b) Fails to comply with any lawful requirement imposed or to answer any lawful enquiry made by any Fisheries Protection Officer under this Ordinance; or

(c) Being on board any vessel being pursued or about to be boarded by any Fisheries Protection Officer throws overboard or destroys any fish, fishing gear or any other thing whatsoever

shall be guilty of an offence against this Act and shall be liable to a fine of one thousand pa'anga or to imprisonment for two years or to both such fine and imprisonment, and if said offence takes place on board or alongside a fishing vessel, the master of the fishing vessel shall be guilty of a like offence and liable to a like penalty.

7. No Fisheries Protection Officer shall be personally liable in respect of any act done or omitted to be done by him in good faith in the execution or purported execution of his powers and duties under this Act.

8. Where a fine is imposed on the master or member of the crew of a foreign fishing vessel who is convicted of an offence under this Act or on any person or persons convicted under this Act of an offence which took place while he or she or they were on board or alongside a foreign fishing vessel, the Court may order—

(a) That the said vessel be detained for a period of three months from the date of the conviction or until the fine is paid, whichever occurs first; and

(b) In the event of non-payment of the fine within the said period of three months, that the said vessel and fish, tackle, engines, nets, gear, apparatus, cargo and stores be forfeited to the Government, and that notwithstanding the fact that the value of same exceeds the amount of the fine.

9. Notwithstanding any provision in any other Ordinance or Act the Supreme Court will have exclusive jurisdiction in all prosecutions brought under this Act and in all other matters relative thereto.

10. The Minister may with the consent of Cabinet make such regulations as seem to him expedient for carrying into effect any or all of the purposes or provisions of this Act and such regulations, when published in the Gazette shall have the force and effect of law.

---

[1] United Nations *Treaty Series*, vol. 450, p. 82, and also ST/LEG/SER.B/15, pp. 800-807.

[2] Not reproduced in this volume.

15. UNION OF SOVIET SOCIALIST REPUBLICS

(a) [REGULATIONS OF 11 JANUARY 1974 FOR SAFEGUARDING THE CON-
TINENTAL SHELF OF THE USSR.] [1]

(b) [SCHEDULE FOR THE CALCULATION OF FINES IMPOSED FOR DAMAGE
CAUSED TO LIVING ORGANISMS BELONGING TO THE SEDENTARY
SPECIES, AND FORMING PART OF THE NATURAL RESOURCES OF THE
CONTINENTAL SHELF OF THE USSR, AS A RESULT OF THE ILLEGAL
HARVESTING OF SUCH SPECIES BY NATIONALS OF THE USSR OR BY
FOREIGN INDIVIDUALS OR BODIES CORPORATE] [2]

16. UNITED KINGDOM OF GREAT BRITAIN
AND NORTHERN IRELAND

(i) FOREIGN SEA-FISHERY OFFICERS (NORTH-EAST ATLANTIC
FISHERIES COMMISSION SCHEME) ORDER 1969,[3] AS AMENDED[4]

. . .

SCHEDULE 1

Part I

. . .

Reservations

(a) As between the Union of Soviet Socialist Republics and other Contracting States
the provisions of the Scheme relating to inspection of gear or catch below deck do not
apply.

[*(b)* of the original Order has been repealed.]

[*(c)* of the original Order has been repealed.]

. . .

---

[1] *Supra* Division II, 15 *(a)*.

[2] *Supra* Division II, 15 *(b)*.

[3] *Statutory Instruments,* 1969 No. 1822. Reproduced in part in ST/LEG/SER.B/16,
pp. 353-356.

[4] Amended by the Foreign Sea-Fishery Officers (North-East Atlantic Fisheries
Commission Scheme) Variation Order 1972 (*Statutory Instruments,* 1972, No. 758), the
Foreign Sea-Fishery Officers (North-East Atlantic Fisheries Commission Scheme)
Variation (No. 2) Order 1973 (*ibid.,* 1973 No. 127); the Foreign Sea-Fishery Officers
(North-East Atlantic Fisheries Commission Scheme) Variation (No. 3) Order 1973 (*ibid.,*
1973 No. 789) and the Foreign Sea-Fishery Officers (North-East Atlantic Fisheries
Commission Scheme) Variation (No. 4) Order 1973 (*ibid.,* 1973 No. 1701). Except for
the texts reproduced here, the original Order remains unchanged.

SCHEDULE 2

Foreign Countries which are parties to the Scheme

1. Belgium	6. Poland	10. Union of Soviet Socialist Republics
2. Denmark	7. Portugal	
3. France	8. Spain	11. Federal Republic of Germany
4. Iceland		
5. Norway	9. Sweden	12. The Netherlands

(ii) [HADDOCK (RESTRICTIONS ON LANDING) ORDER 1972] [1]

(iii) [SEA FISHING (NORTHWEST ATLANTIC) LICENSING ORDER 1972] [2]

(iv) [SALMON AND MIGRATORY TROUT (RESTRICTIONS ON LANDING) ORDER 1972] [3]

(v) FISHING BOATS (EUROPEAN ECONOMIC COMMUNITY) DESIGNATION ORDER 1972 [4]

. . .

2. *Interpretation.* (1) In this Order

"the Act" means the Fishery Limits Act 1964; [5]

---

[1] Dated 24 November 1972. *Statutory Instruments,* 1972, No. 1793. Came into operation on 22 December 1972. This Order, which was made under section 6 and 15 of the Sea Fish (Conservation) Act 1967, implemented a recommendation of the Northwest Atlantic Fisheries Commission by prohibiting the landing in the United Kingdom of haddock caught in a specified area of the Northwest Atlantic during the period 22 December 1972 to 31 December 1972. For the text of the 1967 Act, see ST/LEG/SER.B/16, pp. 334-340.

[2] Dated 30 November 1972. *Ibid.,* 1972, No. 1857. Came into operation on 1 January 1973 and ceased to have effect on 1 January 1974. This Order, which implemented the recommendation of the International Commission for the Northwest Atlantic Fisheries, appointed 1 January 1973 as the date from which no British fishing boat should fish for specified types of fish in specified areas of the Northwest Atlantic.

[3] Dated 14 December 1972. *Ibid.,* 1972, No. 1966. Came into operation on 15 February 1973. This Order, made under the powers contained in section 6 of the Sea Fish (Conservation) Act 1967 (1967 c. 84), prohibits the landing in Great Britain of salmon and migratory trout caught in certain waters specified in the order for ten years. For the text of the 1967 Act, see ST/LEG/SER.B/16, pp. 334-340.

[4] Dated 21 December 1972. *Ibid.,* 1972, No. 2026. Came into operation on 1 January 1973. This Order revoked the Fishing Boats (Federal Republic of Germany) Designation Order 1964, the Fishing Boats (Belgium) Designation (Amendment) Order 1965 and the Fishing Boats (Netherlands) Designation (No. 2) Order 1966, all of which are reproduced in ST/LEG/SER.B/15, and the Fishing Boats (Belgium) Designation (Amendment) Order 1967 and the Fishing Boats (France) Designation (Amendment) Order 1967, which are reproduced in ST/LEG/SER.B/16. It also revoked in part the Fishing Boats (France) Designation Order 1965, the Fishing Boats (Republic of Ireland) Designation Order 1965 and the Fishing Boats (Belgium) Designation Order 1965, all of which are reproduced in ST/LEG/SER.B/15.

[5] 1964 c. 72. Reproduced in part in ST/LEG/SER.B/15, pp. 676-679.

"the baselines" means the baselines from which the territorial sea adjacent to the United Kingdom is measured as prescribed by the Territorial Waters Order in Council 1964;[1]

"the Community States" means the Kingdom of Belgium, the Kingdom of Denmark, the Federal Republic of Germany, the French Republic, the Republic of Ireland, the Italian Republic, the Grand Duchy of Luxembourg and the Kingdom of the Netherlands;

"demersal fish" means all sea fish other than salmon, migratory trout, mackerel, clupeoid fish, sand eels, Norway pout, smelts, eels, great weevers, crustaceans and molluscs (other than squids);

"the exclusive fishery limits" means the United Kingdom fishery limits to a distance of 6 miles from the baselines;

"fishing boat" means a vessel of whatever size and in whatever way propelled which is for the time being employed in sea fishing;

"the Ministers" means the Minister of Agriculture, Fisheries and Food and the Secretaries of State concerned with the sea fishing industry in Scotland and Northern Ireland respectively;

"the outer belt" means the United Kingdom fishery limits other than the exclusive fishery limits;

"the outer belt appurtenant to" in relation to a coast or island means that part of the outer belt which is within 12 miles of the baseline along such coast or round such island;

"the reserved waters" means the areas comprising the waters within those parts of the outer belt described in Schedule 1[2] to this Order;

"United Kingdom fishery limits" means those parts of the fishery limits of the British Islands which are adjacent to the United Kingdom.

. . .

4. *General and special fishing rights.* For the purpose of giving effect to the Treaty relating to the accession of the United Kingdom to the European Economic Community (in so far as sea fishing by fishing boats is provided for under that Treaty), and for the purposes of section 1 (3) of the Act (which empowers the Ministers by order to designate any country outside the United Kingdom, the Channel Islands and the Isle of Man, and the area in which and descriptions of sea fish for which fishing boats registered in that country may fish in the outer belt) the Ministers:

(a) As respects the area consisting of so much of the outer belt as does not include the reserved waters hereby designate (i) each of the Community States, (ii) that area and (iii) sea fish of all descriptions;

(b) As respects the reserved waters, hereby designate (i) each of the Community States specified in column 1 of Schedule 3[3] to this Order, (ii) such parts of reserved waters as are in relation to each such State specified in column 2 of that Schedule and (iii) such descriptions of sea fish as are in relation to such States and such parts, specified in column 3 of that Schedule.

. . .

---

[1] 1965 III, p. 6452A. Reproduced *ibid.*, pp. 129-131.

[2] Schedules are not reproduced here.

[3] Schedules are not reproduced here.

(vi) SALMON AND MIGRATORY TROUT (PROHIBITION OF FISHING) ORDER 1972[1]

. . .

2. *Interpretation.* (1) In this order—

"exclusive fishery limits" means the waters surrounding England and Wales to a distance of six miles from the baselines from which the breadth of the territorial sea is measured.

. . .

3. During the period 15 February 1973 to 14 February 1983 both days inclusive, fishing for salmon or migratory trout within the area of sea specified in the Schedule to this order is hereby prohibited.

4. In accordance with the provisions of section 5 (3) of the Sea Fish (Conservation) Act 1967)[2] it is hereby declared that this order is not made for the sole purpose of giving effect to such a convention or agreement as is mentioned in section 5 (1) of that Act.

SCHEDULE

The area of sea (excluding the exclusive fishery limits) contained within a line drawn from the coast of England along the southern boundary of the mouth of the River Tweed to the eastmost point of that boundary; thence due east to the intersection with the boundary of the fishery limits of the British Islands; thence along that boundary in a clockwise direction around the coast of England and Wales to the intersection with the parallel of latitude 54° 30' north in the Irish Sea; thence eastwards along that parallel until it meets the coast of England.

(vii) SALMON AND MIGRATORY TROUT (PROHIBITION OF FISHING) (NO. 2) ORDER 1972[3]

. . .

3. (1) During the period 15 February 1973 to 14 February 1983, both days inclusive, fishing for salmon or migratory trout by a specified method within the area of sea specified in the schedule to this order is hereby prohibited.

(2) In this Article—

"specified method" means a method of fishing with drift-net, trawl net, seine net, troll or long-line, but does not include beach seining or fishing from the shore by net and coble;

"drift-net" means any length of net allowed to float or drift being either attached to or released from a fishing boat and not being a length of net attached to or held on the shore.

---

[1] Dated 14 December 1972. *Statutory Instruments,* 1973 No. 188. Came into operation on 15 February 1973.

[2] 1967 c. 84. Reproduced in part in ST/LEG/SER.B/16, pp. 334-340.

[3] Dated 18 December 1972. *Statutory Instruments,* 1973 No. 207. Came into operation on 15 February 1973.

4. In accordance with the provisions of section 5 (3) of the Sea Fish (Conservation) Act 1967[1] it is hereby declared that this order is not made for the sole purpose of giving effect to such a convention or agreement as is mentioned in section 5 (1) of that Act.

SCHEDULE

1. The area of sea within the fishery limits of the British Islands lying west of the meridian of longitude 3° west and north of the parallel of latitude 54° 30' north, excluding—

(a) The waters within so much of the exclusive fishery limits as are adjacent to England but not nearer to any point on the coast of Scotland than to any point on the coast of England;

(b) The waters within that area, being waters within so much of those fishery limits as are mentioned in section 4 (2) of the Fishery Limits Act 1964.[2]

2. The area of sea within those fishery limits lying east of the meridian of longitude 3° west and north of the southern boundary of the mouth of the River Tweed and of a line drawn due east from the eastmost point of that boundary.

(viii) SALMON AND MIGRATORY TROUT (NORTH-EAST ATLANTIC) ORDER 1972[3]

. . .

3. *Prohibition.* During the period 15 February 1973 to 14 February 1983, both days inclusive, fishing for salmon or migratory trout within the area of sea specified in the Schedule to this order (being part of the area to which the North-East Atlantic Fisheries Convention[4] applies) is hereby prohibited.

4. In accordance with the provisions of section 5 (3) of the Sea Fish (Conservation) Act 1967[5] it is hereby declared that this order is not made for the sole purpose of giving effect to such a convention or agreement as is mentioned in section 5 (1) of that Act.

SCHEDULE

Those areas of the Atlantic and Arctic Oceans and seas adjacent to those oceans which lie outside the fishery limits of the British Islands, north of 36° north latitude, between 42° west longitude and 51° east longitude and north of 59° north latitude between 44° west longitude and 42° west longitude, but excluding the Mediterranean and Baltic Seas and Belts lying to the south and east of lines drawn from Hasenore Head, Denmark, to Gniben Point, Denmark, from Korshage, Denmark to Spodsbierg, Denmark and from Gilbierg Head, Denmark, to Kullen, Sweden.

---

[1] 1967 c. 84. Reproduced in part in ST/LEG/SER.B/16, pp. 334-340.

[2] 1964 c. 72. Reproduced in part in ST/LEG/SER.B/15, pp. 676-679.

[3] Dated 14 December 1972. *Statutory Instruments,* 1973 No. 189. Came into operation on 15 February 1973.

[4] United Nations, *Treaty Series,* vol. 486, p. 157. Reproduced in ST/LEG/SER.B/15, pp. 853-857.

[5] 1967 c. 84. Reproduced in part in ST/LEG/SER.B/16, pp. 334-340.

(ix) SALMON AND MIGRATORY TROUT (ENFORCEMENT) ORDER 1973[1]

. . .

4. *Powers of British Sea-fishery Officers.* For the purpose of the enforcement of (i) The Salmon (Northwest Atlantic) Order 1971 [2] (ii) The Salmon and Migratory Trout (North-East Atlantic) Order 1972,[3] (iii) The Salmon and Migratory Trout (Prohibition of Fishing) Order 1972,[4] (iv) The Salmon and Migratory Trout (Prohibition of Fishing) (No. 2) Order 1972,[5] and (v) The Salmon and Migratory Trout (Restrictions on Landing) Order 1972,[6] there are hereby conferred on every British sea-fishery officer the powers of a British sea-fishery officer under section 8 (2) to (4) of the Sea Fisheries Act 1968.[7]

(x) [SEA FISH (CONSERVATION) (ISLE OF MAN) ORDER 1973] [8]

(xi) [SEA FISH (CONSERVATION) (MANX BOATS) ORDER 1973] [9]

(xii) [HAKE (REGULATION OF LANDING) ORDER 1973] [10]

(xiii) CONSERVATION OF SEALS (SCOTLAND) ORDER 1973[11]

. . .

3. *Prohibition of killing, injuring or taking common seals.* On and after the date of the commencement of this order there is hereby prohibited the

---

[1] Dated 12 February 1973. *Statutory Instruments,* 1973 No. 210. Came into operation on 13 March 1973. This order revoked the Salmon and Migratory Trout (Enforcement) Order 1971 (*ibid.,* 1971 No. 627) and the Salmon and Migratory Trout (Enforcement) Order 1972 (*ibid.,* 1972 No. 112).

[2] *Ibid.,* 1971 No. 171.

[3] *Ibid.,* 1973 No. 189.

[4] *Ibid.,* 1973 No. 188.

[5] *Ibid.,* 1973 No. 207.

[6] *Ibid.,* 1972 No. 1966.

[7] 1968 c. 77. Reproduced in part in ST/LEG/SER.B/16, pp. 345-349.

[8] Dated 16 February 1973. *Statutory Instruments,* 1973 No. 237. Came into operation on 1 April 1973. This Order extended sections 1, 3 and 5 of the Sea Fish (Conservation) Act 1967 (1967 c. 84) and certain ancillary provisions to the Isle of Man with exceptions, adaptations and modifications. For the 1967 Act, see ST/LEG/SER.B/16, pp. 334-340.

[9] Dated 16 February 1973. *Statutory Instruments,* 1973 No. 238. Came into operation on 1 April 1973. This Order applied sections 4 and 5 of the Sea Fish (Conservation) Act 1967 to the British fishing boats registered in the Isle of Man.

[10] Dated 28 February 1973. *Ibid.,* 1973 No. 347. Came into operation on 1 April 1973. This Order prohibited the landing in the United Kingdom of red hake and silver hake caught in a specified area of the North-West Atlantic during the period 1 April 1973 to 30 April 1973, thus implementing a recommendation of the International Commission for the North-West Atlantic Fisheries.

[11] Dated 15 June 1973, *Ibid.,* 1973 No. 1079 (S.81). Came into operation on 1 September 1973.

killing, injuring or taking of common seals, that is to say seals of the species known as Phoca **Vitulina, in the County** of Zetland and the territorial waters adjacent thereto.

(xiv) SEA FISHERIES (SCOTLAND) BYELAW (NO. 86) 1973[1]

. . .

2. *Methods of fishing permitted in a defined area of the Moray Firth.* Notwithstanding the provisions of—

(a) Byelaw (No. 10) made by the Fishery Board for Scotland on 27 September 1892 and confirmed by the Secretary for Scotland on 22 November 1892[2] (prohibition of trawling in Moray Firth); and

(b) Sea Fisheries (Scotland) Byelaw (No. 81) 1963[3] (conditional permitting of trawling in part of Moray Firth)

it shall be lawful to use the methods of fishing known as beam trawling and otter trawling in that area of the Moray Firth comprising that part lying to the west of a line from Duncansby Head to Rattray Point except such parts thereof as are within the fishery limits of the British Islands appurtenant to the coast of Scotland between Duncansby Head and Rattray Point.

(xv) [HERRING (NORTH YORKSHIRE COAST) (PROHIBITION OF FISHING) ORDER 1973][4]

(xvi) [HERRING (ISLE OF MAN) (PROHIBITION OF FISHING) ORDER 1973][5]

(xvii) FOREIGN SEA-FISHERY OFFICERS ORDER 1973 [6]

. . .

Interpretation

2. (1) In this order—

"the Act" means the Sea Fisheries Act 1968;[7]

"the baselines" means the lines drawn round the coast of Iceland so as to join successively, in the order in which they are there set out, the points

---

[1] Dated 25 June 1973. *Statutory Instruments,* 1973 No. 1122 (S.85). Came into operation on 31 August 1973.

[2] *Statutory Rules and Orders,* 1892, p. 1010.

[3] *Statutory Instruments,* 1968, No. 1011.

[4] Dated 19 July 1973, *Ibid.,* 1973 No. 1259. Came into operation on 20 August 1973. This Order prohibited fishing for herring in an area of sea adjacent to the North Yorkshire coast within the fishery limits of the British Islands for the period 20 August 1973 to 30 September 1973.

[5] Dated 22 August 1973. *Ibid.,* 1973 No. 1496. Came into operation on 1 October 1973. This Order prohibited fishing for herring in waters adjacent to the Isle of Man within the fishery limits of the British Islands but excluding the territorial waters during the period 1 October 1973 to 17 November 1973.

[6] Dated 27 November 1973. *Statutory Instruments,* 1973 No. 1998. Came into operation 1 December 1973.

[7] Reproduced in part in ST/LEG/SER.B/16, pp. 345-349.

identified by the co-ordinates of latitude and longitude in Schedule 1 to this order;

"the Convention" means the Interim Agreement between Her Majesty's Government in the United Kingdom and the Government of Iceland constituted by the Exchange of Notes of 13 November 1973 (b); [1]

"the Convention area" means the area to which the Convention applies being the area described in Schedule 2 to this order;

"mile" means nautical mile;

"the 12 mile line" means a line drawn round the coast of Iceland 12 miles from the baselines and extended seawards by lines drawn 12 miles from and around the Island of Grimsey (from its outermost headlands and skerries) and around Hvalbakur (64° 35.8' north latitude 13° 16.7' west longitude).

"the 50 mile line" means a line drawn round the coast of Iceland 50 miles from the baselines and extended seawards by lines drawn 50 miles around Hvalbakur (64° 35.8' north latitude 13° 16.7' west longitude) and Kolbeinsey (67° 07.5' north latitude 18° 36' west longitude).

. . .

Foreign Sea-Fishery Officers

3. In relation to the Convention there are hereby specified as foreign sea-fishery officers, entitled to exercise in relation to British fishing boats anywhere within the Convention area the powers referred to in section 9 of the Act, coastguard officers duly appointed by the Government of Iceland to enforce the provisions of the Convention.

SCHEDULE 2

. . .

The area between the 12 mile line and the 50 mile line but excluding therefrom the area within a radius of 12 miles from Kolbeinsey (67° 07.5' north latitude 18° 36' west longitude).

(xviii) SEA-FISHING (SPECIFIED NORTHERN WATERS) PROHIBITION ORDER 1973 [2]

. . .

Interpretation

2. (1) In this order—

"the baselines" means the lines drawn round the coast of Iceland so as to join successively, in the order in which they are there set out, the points identified by the co-ordinates of latitude and longitude in Schedule 1 to this order;

---

[1] In force immediately upon conclusion. United Nations, *Treaty Series,* Vol. 903, No. 12886. Cmnd. 5484.

[2] Dated 27 November 1973. *Statutory Instruments,* 1973 No. 1999. Came into operation on 1 December 1973. This Order gives effect to an Interim Agreement made on 13 November 1973 and now in force between the Governments of the United Kingdom and Iceland.

364

"mile" means nautical mile;

"the 12 mile line" means a line drawn round the coast of Iceland 12 miles from the baselines and extended seawards by lines drawn 12 miles from and around the Island of Grimsey (from its outermost headlands and skerries) and around Hvalbakur (64° 35.8′ north latitude 13° 16.7′ west longitude);

"the 50 mile line" means a line drawn round the coast of Iceland 50 miles from the baselines and extended seawards by lines drawn 50 miles around Hvalbakur (64° 35.8′ north latitude 13° 16.7′ west longitude) and Kolbeinsey (67° 07.5′ north latitude 18° 36′ west longitude).

. . .

Prohibition

3. (1) There is hereby prohibited, in relation to any area defined in column 1 of Part I of Schedule 2 to this order, for the period specified in column 2 of that Part opposite the area so defined, all fishing for sea fish within that area.

(2) Without prejudice to paragraph (1) of this Article, there is hereby also prohibited in relation to any area defined in column 1 of Part II of Schedule 2 (being an area included in, or partly included in, an area as defined in column 1 of Part I of Schedule 2) for the period specified in column 2 of the said Part II opposite the area so defined, all fishing for sea fish within that area.

Enforcement

4. For the purpose of the enforcement of this order there are hereby conferred on every British sea-fishery officer the powers of a British sea-fishery officer under section 8 (2) and (3) of the Sea Fisheries Act 1968.[1]

. . .

[1] Reproduced in part in ST/LEG/SER.B/16, pp. 345-349.

SCHEDULE 2

Part I

Column 1 Area	Column 2 Period
An area off the north-west coast of Iceland between the 12 mile line and the 50 mile line, and between the meridian of 22° 24′ west longitude anti-clockwise to the parallel of 65° 30′ north latitude.	The months of September and October in the years 1974 and 1975.
An area off the south-west coast of Iceland between the 12 mile line and the 50 mile line, and between the parallel of 65° 30′ north latitude anti-clockwise to the meridian of 20° 30′ west longitude.	From the date of the coming into operation of this order until 31 December 1973 (both dates inclusive); the months of November and December in the year 1974; 1 November 1975 to 13 November 1975 (both dates inclusive).

Part I (continued)

Column 1	Column 2
Area	Period
An area off the south coast of Iceland between the 12 mile line and the 50 mile line, and between the meridian of 20° 30' west longitude anti-clockwise to the meridian of 14° 30' west longitude.	The months of May and June in the years of 1974 and 1975.
An area off the south-east coast of Iceland between the 12 mile line and the 50 mile line, and between the meridian of 14° 30' west longitude anti-clockwise to a line drawn 045 from Bjarnarey (65° 47.1' north latitude 14° 18.2' west longitude).	The months of January and February in the years 1974 and 1975.
An area off the north-east coast of Iceland between the 12 mile line and the 50 mile line, and between a line drawn 045° from Bjarnarey anti-clockwise to the meridian of 16° 11.8' west longitude.	The months of July and August in the years 1974 and 1975.
An area off the north coast of Iceland between the 12 mile line and the 50 mile line, and between the meridian of 16° 11.8' west longitude anti-clockwise to the meridian of 22° 24' west longitude, but excluding therefrom the area within a radius of 12 miles from Kolbeinsey (67° 07.5' north latitude 18° 36' west longitude).	The months of March and April in the years 1974 and 1975.

Part II

Column 1	Column 2
Area	Period
An area off the north-west coast of Iceland demarcated by— – a line drawn between the positions 66° 57' north latitude 23° 36' west longitude and 67° 01' north latitude 22° 24' west longitude; – a line drawn 340° from the position 66° 57' north latitude 23° 36' west longitude; – the meridian of 22° 24' west longitude; – the 50 mile line.	From the date of the coming into operation of this order until 13 November 1975 (both dates inclusive).

Part II (continued)

Column 1	Column 2
Area	Period
An area off the south coast of Iceland demarcated by— – the meridian of 22° 00′ west longitude; – the parallel of 63° 00′ north latitude; – the meridian of 21° 25′ west longitude; – the 12 mile line.	20 March to 20 April (both dates inclusive) in the years 1974 and 1975.
An area off the north-east coast of Iceland demarcated by— – the meridian of 16° 11.8′ west longitude; – the 12 mile line; – a line drawn 045° from Langanes (66° 22.7′ north latitude 14° 31.9′ west longitude); – the 50 mile line.	1 April to 1 June (both dates inclusive) in the years 1974 and 1975.
An area off the north-west coast of Iceland between the 12 mile line and a line drawn 20 miles from the baselines, and between the meridian of 22° 24′ west longitude anti-clockwise to the parallel of 65° 30′ north latitude.	From the date of the coming into operation of this order until 13 November 1975 (both dates inclusive).
An area off the east coast of Iceland between the 12 mile line and a line drawn 20 miles from the baselines, and demarcated in the south by the 12 mile line around Hvalbakur (64° 35.8′ north latitude 13° 16.7′ west longitude) and in the north by a line drawn 045° from Bjarnarey (65° 47.1′ north latitude 14° 18.2′ west longitude).	From the date of the coming into operation of this order until 13 November 1975 (both dates inclusive).
An area off the north coast of Iceland demarcated by— – a line drawn between the positions 66° 39.7′ north latitude 22° 24′ west longitude and 66° 23.8′ north latitude 18° 50′ west longitude; – the 12 mile line.	From the date of the coming into operation of this order until 13 November 1975 (both dates inclusive).

(xix) SEA FISHING (SPECIFIED NORTHERN WATERS)
LICENSING ORDER 1973[1]

. . .

Interpretation

2. (1) In this order—

"the Act" means the Sea Fish (Conservation) Act 1967;[2]

"the baselines" means the lines drawn round the coast of Iceland so as to join successively, in the order in which they are there set out, the points identified by the co-ordinates of latitude and longitude in Schedule 1 to this order;

"mile" means nautical mile;

"the 12 mile line" means a line drawn round the coast of Iceland 12 miles from the baselines and extended seawards by lines drawn 12 miles from and around the Island of Grimsey (from its outermost headlands and skerries) and around Hvalbakur (64° 35.8' north latitude 13° 16.7' west longitude);

"the 50 mile line" means a line drawn round the coast of Iceland 50 miles from the baselines and extended seawards by lines drawn 50 miles around Hvalbakur (64° 35.8' north latitude 13° 16.7' west longitude) and Kolbeinsey (67° 07.5' north latitude 18° 36' west longitude).

"the specified area" means the area described in Schedule 2 to this Order.

. . .

Appointed Day

4. The appointed day for the purpose of section 4 of the Act (which provides for the licensing of British fishing vessels in relation to fishing by way of trade or business in specified areas) in conjunction with this order is the day on which this order comes into operation.

Area and Period

5. This order applies to fishing for sea fish in the specified area for the period beginning with the day on which this order comes into operation and ending on 13 November 1975 (both dates inclusive).

Provided that nothing in this order shall authorize a licence under section 4 of the Act to be granted in respect of any part of the specified area in any period in which fishing for sea fish in such part is prohibited by the Sea Fishing (Specified Northern Waters) Prohibition Order 1973 *(c)*.

Enforcement

6. For the purposes of the enforcement of section 4 of the Act in conjunction with this order there are hereby conferred on every British sea-fishery officer the powers of a British sea-fishery officer under section 8 (2) and (3) of the Sea Fisheries Act 1968.

. . .

---

[1] Dated 29 November 1973. *Statutory Instruments,* 1973 No. 2000. Came into operation on 1 December 1973. It revoked the Sea Fishing (Specified Northern Waters) Licensing Order 1972, *ibid.,* 1972 No. 1477.

[2] Reproduced in part in ST/LEG/SER.B/16, pp. 334-340.

SCHEDULE 2

The area of sea between the 12 mile line and the 50 mile line but excluding therefrom the area within a radius of 12 miles from Kolbeinsey (67° 07.5′ north latitude 18° 36′ west longitude).

(xx) HADDOCK (RESTRICTIONS ON LANDING) ORDER 1973[1]

. . .

Interpretation

2. (1) In this Order—

"the specified waters" means the waters described in Schedule 1 to this Order.

. . .

Prohibition on Landing

3. Except as hereinafter provided, the landing in the United Kingdom of haddock (Melanogrammus aeglefinus) caught in the specified waters is hereby prohibited.

Exception from the Prohibition on Landing

4. (1) There shall be excepted from the prohibition contained in Article 3 of this Order the landing in the United Kingdom of haddock caught in the specified waters provided that:

(i) The haddock were caught in the course of fishing for sea fish of any description other than haddock; and

(ii) The haddock so caught are comprised in a catch the whole or part of which was taken in the specified waters and do not exceed in weight one-tenth of the total weight of the catch landed in the United Kingdom or, if only part of the catch was taken in the specified waters, one-tenth of the total weight of that part landed as aforesaid.

(2) Notwithstanding the exception contained in Article 4 (1) of this Order the prohibition contained in Article 3 of this Order shall apply to the landing in the United Kingdom of haddock caught during the period 1 March 1974 to 31 May 1974 (both dates inclusive):

(a) In those parts of the specified waters described in Part I of Schedule 2 to this Order; or

(b) In that part of the specified waters described in Part II of Schedule 2 to this Order with hooks having a gape of less than 3 centimetres.

Powers of British Sea-Fishery Officers

5. For the purpose of the enforcement of this Order there are hereby conferred on every British sea-fishery officer the powers of a British sea-fishery officer under section 8 (2) and (3) of the Sea Fisheries Act 1968.[2]

---

[1] Dated 29 November 1973. *Statutory Instruments,* 1973 No. 2004. Came into operation on 1 January 1974. It implements a recommendation of the International Commission for the North-West Atlantic Fisheries.

[2] Reproduced in part in ST/LEG/SER.B/16, pp. 345-349.

SCHEDULE 1

The area bounded by the coasts of Nova Scotia, west of Halifax; New Brunswick; Maine; New Hampshire; Massachusetts and Rhode Island, to a point 71° 40′ west longitude; and thence by straight lines connecting the following co-ordinates in the order listed:

39° 00′ north, 71° 40′ west;
39° 00′ north, 63° 20′ west;
44° 20′ north, 63° 20′ west;
Halifax, Nova Scotia.

SCHEDULE 2

Part I

Those two parts of the Northwest Atlantic Ocean which are respectively bounded by straight lines connecting the following co-ordinates in the order listed: ·

(a) 42° 20′ north, 67° 00′ west;
41° 15′ north, 67° 00′ west;
41° 15′ north, 65° 40′ west;
42° 00′ north, 65° 40′ west;
42° 20′ north, 66° 00′ west.

(b) 42° 04′ north, 65° 44′ west;
42° 40′ north, 64° 30′ west;
43° 00′ north, 64° 30′ west;
43° 00′ north, 66° 32′ west;
42° 20′ north, 66° 32′ west;
42° 20′ north, 66° 00′ west.

Part II

That part of the Northwest Atlantic Ocean bounded by straight lines connecting the following co-ordinates in the order listed:

42° 10′ north, 69° 55′ west;
41° 10′ north, 69° 10′ west;
41° 35′ north, 68° 30′ west;
41° 50′ north, 68° 45′ west;
41° 50′ north, 69° 00′ west.

(xxi) HERRING (ATLANTO-SCANDIAN) (PROHIBITION OF FISHING) ORDER 1973[1]

. . .

Prohibition

3. During the period from 1 January 1974 to 31 December 1974, both dates inclusive, fishing for herring (Clupea harengus) within the areas of sea specified in the Schedule to this order (being parts of an area to which the North-East Atlantic Fisheries Convention[2] applies) is hereby prohibited.

---

[1] 21 November 1973. *Statutory Instruments,* 1973 No. 2020. Came into operation on 1 January 1974. It implements a recommendation of the International Commission for the North-West Atlantic Fisheries.

[2] Reproduced in part in ST/LEG/SER.B/15, pp. 853-857.

370

Enforcement

4. For the purpose of the enforcement of this order, there are hereby conferred on every British sea-fishery officer the powers of a British sea-fishery officer under section 8 (2) and (3) of the Sea Fisheries Act 1968.[1]

. . .

SCHEDULE

Areas to which the Order relates

(1) The areas of sea lying between longitudes 11° W. and 68° 30′ E. to the north of a line running from a position longitude 11° W. and latitude 63° N. in an easterly direction along the parallel of latitude 63° N. to longitude 4° W. thence due south to latitude 62° N. thence due east to the coast of Norway; and

(2) The areas of sea bounded by a line drawn east from the meridian of 15° W. longitude along the parallel of 60° N. latitude to the meridian of 5° W. longitude thence due north to the parallel of 60° 30′ thence due east to the meridian of 4° W. longitude thence due north to the parallel of 63° N. latitude thence due west to the meridian of 15° W. longitude thence due south to the parallel of 60° N. latitude.

(xxii) SEA FISHING (NORTH-WEST ATLANTIC) LICENSING
ORDER 1973[2]

. . .

Interpretation

2. (1) In this Order "the Act" means the Sea Fish (Conservation) Act 1967.[3]

. . .

Appointed day

3. The appointed day for the purposes of section 4 of the Act (which prohibits the use of British fishing boats for fishing by way of trade or business in any area specified in an order made under that section as from a day appointed by the order except under the authority of a licence) in conjunction with this Order, is 10 January 1974.

Area

4. This Order applies to fishing for all sea fish in the areas of sea specified in the Schedule to this Order.

Enforcement

5. For the purpose of the enforcement of section 4 of the Act in conjunction with this Order, there are hereby conferred on every British

---

[1] *Supra* 8 *(b)*, footnote.

[2] Dated 7 December 1973. *Statutory Instruments* 1973 No. 2084. Came into operation on 10 January 1974. Implements recommendations of the International Commisson for the North-West Atlantic Fisheries.

[3] Reproduced in part in ST/LEG/SER.B/16, pp. 334-340.

sea-fishery officer the powers of a British sea-fishery officer under section 8 (2) and (3) of the Sea Fisheries Act 1968.[1]

SCHEDULE

Specified areas to which the Order applies:

(a) [waters to which the International Convention for the North-West Atlantic Fisheries applies] [2]

(b) All waters, except territorial waters, bounded by a line beginning at a point on the coast of Rhode Island in 71° 40′ west longitude; thence due south to 39° north latitude; thence due east to 65° 40′ west longitude; thence due south to 35° north latitude; thence due west to the coast of North Carolina; thence in a northerly direction along the coasts of North Carolina, Virginia, Maryland, Delaware, New Jersey, New York, Connecticut, and Rhode Island to the point of beginning.

(xxiii) SEA FISHING (FAROES REGION) LICENSING AND PROHIBITION OF FISHING METHOD ORDER, 1973[3]

. . .

Interpretation

2. (1) In this order:

"The Act" means the Sea Fish (Conservation) Act 1967;

"Faroes Region" means the area described in Schedule 1 to this order, comprising the statistical area Vb of the International Council for the Exploration of the Sea;

"Fishing Zone" means the area within the existing 12 mile Faroese fishing limits.

. . .

Prohibition

4. The fishing for sea fish by trawl in any of the specified sub-areas described in Column 1 of Schedule 2 to this order during the periods shown against these areas in Column 2 of that Schedule is hereby prohibited.

Enforcement

5. For the purposes of the enforcement of sections 4 and 5 of the Act in conjunction with this order there are hereby conferred on every British sea-fishery officer the powers of a British sea-fishery officer under section 8 (2) and (2) of the Sea Fisheries Act 1968.[4]

---

[1] *Ibid.*, pp. 345-349.

[2] United Nations, *Treaty Series,* vol. 157, p. 157; also ST/LEG/SER.B/15, p. 832.

[3] Dated 21 December 1973. *Statutory Instruments,* 1973 No. 2185. Came into operation on 1 January 1974.

[4] Reproduced in part in ST/LEG/SER.B/16, pp. 345-349.

SCHEDULE I

Faroes Region

International Council for the Exploration of the Sea Statistical Area Vb

The area of sea bounded by a line drawn east from the meridian of 15° west longitude along the parallel of 60° north latitude to the meridian of 5° west longitude thence due north to the parallel of 60° 30′ thence due east to the meridian of 4° west longitude thence due north to the parallel of 63° north latitude thence due west to the meridian of 15° west longitude thence due south to the parallel of 60° north latitude.

SCHEDULE II

Specified sub-areas to which the order applies

Column 1 *Description*	*Column 2* *Close Period* *(all dates inclusive)*
Sub-area 1: 8 nautical miles from the limit of the fishing zone between a line 0° true from Eidiskoll and a line 90° true from Bispur.	15th February to 15th May
Sub-area 2: 18 nautical miles from the limit of the fishing zone between a line 90° true from Bispur and a line 90° true from Akrabergi.	1st June to 30th November

Sub-area 3:
  (a) 12 nautical miles from the limit of the fishing zone between a line 150° true from Akrabergi and a line 190° true from Akrabergi, and
  (b) 6 nautical miles from the limit of the fishing zone between a line 190° true from Akrabergi and a line 240° true from Ørnanipuni.
	1st April to 30th June and 1st October to 31st December

Sub-area 4: 12 nautical miles from the limit of the fishing zone between a line 240° true from Trøllhøvda and a line 320° true from Bardi.	1st December to 31st March and 1st May to 31st May
Sub-area 5: Faroe Bank (ICES sub-Division Vb2) within the 200 m. isobath.	1st March to 31st March

(xxiv) MACKEREL (REGULATION OF LANDING) ORDER 1974[1]

. . .

[1] Dated 8 March 1974. *Statutory Instruments*, 1974 No. 397. Came into operation on 10 April 1974. It implements a recommendation of the North-East Atlantic Fisheries Commission.

Interpretation

2. (1) In this Order—

"specified waters" means those waters of the North-East Atlantic Ocean comprising the International Council for the Exploration of the Sea statistical areas IIIa and IV which areas are described in the Schedule to this Order; "undersized mackerel" means mackerel *(Scomber scombrus)* of a length less than 30 centimetres measured from tip of snout to extreme end of tail fin.

. . .

Prohibition on landing

3. Subject to Article 4 of this Order, the landing in the United Kingdom of any undersized mackerel caught in the specified waters is hereby prohibited.

Exception from prohibition on landing

4. Notwithstanding the prohibition contained in Article 3 of this Order undersized mackerel caught in the specified waters may be landed in the United Kingdom if:

(a) They are landed for the purpose of human consumption; or

(b) They are landed for any other purpose and do not exceed in weight, in respect of each landing, one fifth of the total weight of the mackerel caught in the specified waters.

Enforcement

5. For the purpose of the enforcement of this Order, there are hereby conferred on every British sea-fishery officer the powers of a British sea-fishery officer under section 8 (2) to (4) of the Sea Fisheries Act 1968.[1]

SCHEDULE

(a) *International Council for the Exploration of the Sea statistical area IIIa*

The area of sea bounded by a line drawn south from a point on the coast of Norway at 7° E. longitude to 57° 30″ N. latitude, thence due east to 8° E. longitude, thence due south to 57° N. latitude, thence due east to the coast of Denmark, thence in a northerly and easterly direction along the coast of Denmark to the Skaw, thence south to Hasenore Head, thence to Gniben Point, thence in an easterly direction along the coast to Gilbierg Head, thence to The Kullen in Sweden, thence in a northerly direction along the coasts of Sweden and Norway to 7° E. longitude.

(b) *International Council for the Exploration of the Sea statistical area IV*

The area of sea bounded by a line drawn from a point on the coast of Scotland at 4° W. longitude, thence due north to 62° N. latitude, thence due east to the coast of Norway, thence in a southerly direction along the west coast of Norway to 7° E. longitude, thence due south to 57° 30″ N. latitude, thence due east to 8° E. longitude, thence due south to 57° N. latitude, thence due east to the coast of Denmark, thence in a westerly direction along the coasts of Denmark, Germany, Holland, Belgium and France to 51° N. latitude, thence due west to the coast of England, thence in a northerly direction along the east coast of England and Scotland to the point of origin.

---

[1] Reproduced in part in ST/LEG/SER.B/16, pp. 345-349.

(xxv) [FOREIGN SEA-FISHERY OFFICERS (INTERNATIONAL COMMISSION FOR THE NORTHWEST ATLANTIC FISHERIES SCHEME) VARIATION ORDER 1974][1]

(xxvi) NORTH SEA HERRING (RESTRICTION ON LANDING) ORDER 1974[2]

. . .

Prohibiton of landings

2. As from 16 June 1974 the landing in the United Kingdom of any herring (clupea harengus) caught in the waters comprised in the North Sea being the area described in the Schedule to this order, is prohibited, but this prohibition shall not apply to the landing of herring so caught, which are landed within 24 hours of being so caught, and herring which, though not so landed, were, immediately on being so caught, packed in ice in boxes, stored in a refrigerated sea water tank or otherwise processed in such a way as to secure preservation for human consumption.

. . .

Powers of British Sea-Fishery Officers

3. For the purposes of the enforcement of this order there are hereby conferred on every British sea-fishery officer all the powers of a British sea-fishery officer under section 8 (2) to (4) of the Sea Fisheries Act 1968.[3]

SCHEDULE

The North Sea

The area of sea contained within a line drawn from a position having the co-ordinates of 62° north latitude and 4° west longitude, due south to the north coast of Scotland, thence generally south-eastwards along the north and east coasts of Scotland and the east coast of England, thence westwards along the south coast of England to the meridian of 1° west longitude, thence due south to the coast of France, thence generally in a north-easterly direction along the coasts of France, Belgium, the Netherlands, the Federal Republic of Germany and Denmark to Skagen Point, thence along a rhumb line to the Pater Noster Lighthouse on the coast of Sweden, thence generally in a north-westerly, south-westerly and northerly direction along the coasts of Sweden and Norway to the parallel of 62° north latitude, thence due west to the meridian of 4° west longitude.

(xxvii) NORTHWEST ATLANTIC (DEMERSAL FISH) ORDER 1974[4]

. . .

---

[1] Dated 9 April 1974. *Statutory Instruments,* 1974 No. 701. Came into operation on 14 May 1974. This Order rpovides for the elimination of reservation *(a)* in Part I of Schedule 1 of the Foreign Sea-Fishery Officers (International Commission for the Northwest Atlantic Fisheries Scheme) Order 1971, reproduced in part in document ST/LEG/SER.B/16, pp. 359-361.

[2] Dated 20 May 1974, *Statutory Instruments,* 1974 No. 881. Came into operation 16 June 1974.

[3] Reproduced in part in ST/LEG/SER.B/16, pp. 345-349.

[4] Dated 25 June 1974, *Statutory Instruments,* 1974 No. 1100. Came into operation on 29 July 1974.

Interpretation

2. (1) In this Order "demersal fish" means all sea fish other than salmon, migratory trout, mackerel, clupeoid fish, Norway pout, smelts, crustaceans and molluscs.

. . .

Prohibition

3. During the periods 29 July 1974 to 31 December 1974 and 1 July to 31 December in every subsequent year (all dates inclusive) the fishing for demersal fish in the area of sea specified in the Schedule to this Order (being part of the area to which the International Convention for the North-west Atlantic Fisheries[1] applies) is hereby prohibited

Enforcement

4. For the purpose of the enforcement of this Order, there are hereby conferred on every British sea-fishery officer the powers of a British sea-fishery officer under section 8 (2) and (3) of the Sea Fisheries Act 1968.[2]

SCHEDULE

The area to which the order applies

All waters, except territorial waters, bounded by a line beginning at a point on the coast of Rhode Island in 71° 40' west longitude; thence due south to 40° 20' north latitude; thence due east to 68° 15' west longitude; thence in a north-westerly direction to a point in 70° 00' west longitude, 43° 17' north latitude; thence due west to the coast of Maine, thence in a southerly direction along the coasts of Maine, New Hampshire, Massachusetts and Rhode Island to the point of beginning.

17. WESTERN SAMOA

FISHERIES PROTECTION ACT 1972[3]

. . .

2. *Interpretation.* In this Act, if not inconsistent with the context—

"Court" means any Court of competent jurisdiction in Western Samoa:

"Fish" means any marine animal and includes molluscs, crustaceans and all other forms of marine animal life:

"Fishing" means taking, hunting, pursuing, catching, illing or possessing any fish, and "to fish" has a corresponding meaning:

"Fisheries officer" means any fisheries officer employed in the Fisheries Division of the Department of Agriculture, Forests and Fisheries, and includes the Director, Deputy Director, and Chief Fisheries Officer:

---

[1] United Nations, *Treaty Series,* vol. 157, p. 157; also ST/LEG/SER.B/16, pp. 832-838.

[2] Reproduced in part in ST/LEG/SER.B/16, pp. 345-349.

[3] Act No. 2 of 21 March 1972. Text transmitted through the Charge d'Affaires a.i. of New Zealand to the United Nations in a note verbale of 9 July 1974.

"Foreign fishing vessel" means any fishing vessel owned or controlled by a person or persons not ordinarily resident in Western Samoa:

"Marine officer" means any officer employed in the Marine Department:

"Minister" means the Minister of Agriculture, Forests and Fisheries, or such other Minister as may from time to time be charged with the administration of this Act:

"Police officer" means a commissioned officer of Police, and includes any sergeant, corporal and constable acting with the authority of a commissioned officer of Police:

"Western Samoan waters" comprise the territorial sea of Western Samoa and any other waters in which Western Samoa for the time being has the right to control fishing.

3. *Administration.* The general administration of this Act shall be under the control and direction of the Minister, who may delegate, either generally or particularly, all or any of the powers conferred on him under this Act.

4. *Prohibition* against foreign fishing vessels. It shall be an offence for the master or any crew member of a foreign fishing vessel to engage in fishing or to possess any fish or to engage in activities in support of a foreign fishery fleet within Western Samoan waters except as expressly provided in an agreement or convention to which Western Samoa is a party provided that the Minister may grant exemptions from this prohibition in special cases if he considers such exemption is desirable for purposes of fishery research or is otherwise in the national interest.

5. *Penalty and forfeiture.* (1) Any person committing an offence against this Act shall be liable on conviction to a fine not exceeding one hundred thousand tālā, or imprisonment for a term not exceeding five years, or both.

(2) When any person is convicted of an offence under this Act every vessel employed in any manner in connexion with the offence, together with its tackle, engines, nets, gear, apparatus, cargo and stores, and all fish taken or possessed contrary to this Act or the monetary value thereof or the net proceeds of sale thereof may be ordered by the convicting Court to be forfeited to the Government Samoa and all things so forfeited shall be disposed of as the Minister thinks fit with the net proceeds of realization thereof to be paid into the Public Account.

6. *Apprehension of offenders.* (1) Any Fisheries officer, Police officer, or Marine officer shall have the power—

(a) With or without a warrant, to arrest any person committing in his sight or presence an offence against this Act;

(b) With or without a warrant to board and search any vessel and, if as a result of such search he has reasonable cause to believe that any person on board has committed an offence against this Act, then to arrest such person;

(c) To seize any vessel, together with its tackle, engines, nets, gear, apparatus, cargo and stores, used or employed in breach of the provisions of this Act or which it reasonably appears to have been so used or employed;

(d) To seize all fish taken or possessed in breach of this Act, and if adequate facilities are not available to preserve such fish pending the determination of the Court proceedings in respect of the taking or possessing of such fish, then to take all necessary steps for the sale of such fish at its reasonable market value, the net proceeds of such sale to be paid to the Registrar of the Court pending the making of a final order by the Court in respect of the forfeiture or otherwise of that fund.

(2) All persons, if called upon to assist any officer in the execution of any power vested in him by the preceding subsection, are hereby authorized and required to render such assistance.

7. *Discharge of seized fish on security.* Notwithstanding anything herein contained, the Minister may discharge any fish seized under this Act on receiving suitable and adequate security for the equivalent value of the fish, by way of bond, guarantee or other stipulation, conditioned for payment of such equivalent value in the event that such amount shall be adjudged by the Court to be forfeited to the Government of Western Samoa.

8. *Reward to informers and others.* The Minister may direct and the Financial Secretary is hereby empowered to pay—

(a) To any person, other than an Officer mentioned in section 6 of this Act, who submits to any such officer original information concerning the commission of any offence against this Act, leading to any penalty or forfeiture incurred in respect of such offence; and

(b) To any person or the dependents of any person who renders assistance to any officer pursuant to subsection 2 of section 6 hereof, and who in so doing suffers personal injury or death, a reward of not more than five thousand tālā, and in no case exceeding one half of the amount of such penalty or forfeiture.

9. *Regulations.* The Head of State acting on the advice of Cabinet may from time to time make regulations for any purpose for which regulations are required or contemplated by this Act and for giving full effect to the provisions of this Act.

Part II
TREATIES

Division I

THE TERRITORIAL SEA AND THE CONTIGUOUS ZONE[1]

Subdivision A. Multilateral Treaties

1. PROTOCOL OF ACCESSION TO THE SANTIAGO DECLARATION ON THE "MARITIME ZONE", DONE AT QUITO ON 6 OCTOBER 1955[2]

Considering that the Declaration on the "Maritime Zone",[3] signed at Santiago on 18 August 1952 by the Governments of Chile, Ecuador and Peru, contains principles and rules which affect other countries of the continent and that therefore, the adherence to those principles and rules by the American countries which are in agreement therewith should be facilitated,

The Governments of Ecuador, Chile and Peru,

Agree, by this Protocol, to open the Declaration on the Maritime Zone, signed at Santiago, Chile, on 18 August 1952, to American States for accession, as regards the basic principles contained in the paragraphs of the said Declaration reading as follows:

"Governments are bound to ensure for their peoples access to necessary food supplies and to furnish them with the means of developing their economy.

"It is therefore the duty of each Government to ensure the conservation and protection of its natural resources and to regulate the use thereof to the greatest possible advantage of its country.

"Hence it is likewise the duty of each Government to prevent the said resources from being used outside the area of its jurisdiction so as to endanger their existence, integrity and conservation to the prejudice of peoples so situated geographically that their seas are irreplaceable sources of essential food and economic materials."

And as regards the rules which flow from these principles as a result of the decision to preserve for and make available to their respective peoples the

---

[1] For the texts touching upon the territorial sea and the contiguous zone in connexion with exploration for and exploitation of the continental shelf, marine pollution, and fishing and conservation of living resources, see *infra* Divisions II, III and IV, respectively.

[2] Spanish text provided by the Permanent Mission of Ecuador to the United Nations in a note verbale of 16 October 1973. Translation by the Secretariat of the United Nations.

[3] Reproduced in ST/LEG/SER.B/6, pp. 723-724.

natural resources of the maritime zone adjacent to their coasts, such rules being embodied in the following declaration:

"Owing to the geological and biological factors affecting the existence, conservation and development of the marine fauna and flora of the waters adjacent to the coasts of the declarant countries, the former extent of the territorial sea and contiguous zone is insufficient to permit the conservation, development and use of those resources, to which the coastal countries are entitled.

"The Governments of Chile, Ecuador and Peru therefore proclaim as a principle of their international maritime policy that each of them possesses sole sovereignty and jurisdiction over the area of sea adjacent to the coast of its own country and extending not less than 200 nautical miles from the said coast. Their sole jurisdiction and sovereignty over the zone thus described includes sole sovereignty and jurisdiction over the sea-bed and subsoil thereof.

"This Declaration shall not be construed as disregarding the necessary restrictions on the exercise of sovereignty and jurisdiction imposed by international law to permit the innocent and inoffensive passage of vessels of all nations through the zone aforesaid."

The three Governments declared that adherence to the principle that coastal States have the right and the duty to protect, conserve and use the resources of the sea adjacent to their coasts shall not be affected by the exercise of the right which each State also has to fix the extent and limits of its Maritime Zone. Therefore, in effecting such adherence, each State may determine the extent and manner of delimitation of its respective zone, in relation to all or part of its coast, in accordance with the particular geographical configuration, the size of each sea, and the geological and biological factors affecting the existence, conservation and development of the marine fauna and flora of its waters.

Adherence as aforesaid shall not apply in respect of paragraph VI of the Santiago Declaration, since its terms are determined by the geographical and biological similarities prevailing in the coastal maritime zones of the signatory States, and consequently, are not characteristic of America as a whole.

2. AGREEMENT ON CO-OPERATION WITH REGARD TO MARITIME MERCHANT SHIPPING, DONE AT BUDAPEST ON 3 DECEMBER 1971[1]

The Governments of the People's Republic of Bulgaria, the Czechoslovak Socialist Republic, the German Democratic Republic, the Hungarian People's Republic, the Polish People's Republic, the Socialist Republic of Romania and the Union of Soviet Socialist Republics (hereinafter referred to as the "Contracting Parties"),

Desiring to promote the further development and strengthening of co-operation between their countries with regard to maritime merchant shipping, and

---

[1] Legislative Series of the Government of the USSR, 1974, No. 9, p. 49. Entered into force on 17 June 1973 in accordance with article 17. Translation by the Secretariat of the United Nations. Received for registration with the Secretariat on 20 May 1974.

Being convinced that such co-operation is conducive to the attainment of the purposes set out in the Charter of the United Nations,

Have agreed as follows:

Article 1

The Contracting Parties shall make every effort to develop and strengthen the existing co-operation between their countries in the field of maritime merchant shipping.

Article 2

In accordance with article 1 of this Agreement, the Contracting Parties shall encourage bilateral and multilateral co-operation between the government departments responsible in their countries for marine transport activities and between shipping organizations and enterprises in order to develop their countries' marine transport and, in particular, to:

Make fuller and more efficient use of the merchant marine and maritime ports to meet the demand for international marine transport;

Develop co-operation in the field of chartering;

Expand economic, scientific and technological relations and the exchange of experience;

Exchange views regarding the activities of international organizations dealing with shipping problems, and to enter into international agreements on marine transport.

Article 3

The Contracting Parties reaffirm their adherence to the principles of the freedom of merchant shipping, and their determination to oppose any discriminatory measures in that field that would hinder the normal development of shipping.

Article 4

The Contracting Parties shall promote the effective development of international merchant shipping and, in particular, the successful solution of the economic, scientific, technological and legal problems that arise in that field. They express their readiness to co-operate in the attainment of the aforementioned goals with other countries on the basis of the principles of equality, non-interference in domestic affairs and mutual benefit.

Article 5

1. The Contracting Parties agree:

To encourage participation by their vessels in marine transport between the ports of their countries;

To co-operate in removing obstacles that might hinder participation by vessels of the Contracting Parties in transport between the ports of their countries;

Not to prevent vessels of the Contracting Parties from participating in marine transport between the ports of one of the Contracting Parties and the ports of third countries.

2. The provisions of paragraph 1 shall not affect the right of vessels of third countries to participate in transport between the ports of one of the Contracting Parties and the ports of the other Contracting Parties.

Article 6

1. Vessels flying the flag of any of the Contracting Parties shall, in the ports of those Parties, be accorded, on a basis of reciprocity, the most favourable treatment that is accorded to national vessels engaged in international traffic, or, also on a basis of reciprocity, the most favourable treatment accorded to the vessels of other countries in all matters relating to entry into, stay in and departure from port; the use of ports for loading and unloading operations; embarkment and disembarkment of passengers; and the use of navigational services.

2. The provisions of paragraph 1 shall not apply: to ports that are not declared open for calls for foreign vessels; to pilotage operations; to such transport and other operations reserved by law to national organizations as cabotage, towing, rescue and salvage; or to compliance with customs, administrative, sanitary and phytosanitary regulations and formalities in effect in the ports.

3. In all navigational matters not specifically mentioned in this Agreement, the Contracting Parties shall extend to each other most favoured nation treatment.

Article 7

1. The Contracting Parties shall, on a basis of reciprocity, take steps to facilitate and expedite marine transport, to shorten the time spent by vessels in port, and to simplify as much as possible the customs, administrative, sanitary and phytosanitary formalities in effect in the ports.

2. The customs and fiscal authorities of the Contracting Parties shall, on a basis of reciprocity, refrain from imposing duties and fees on such items of equipment and machinery and on such spare parts and ship's stores on board vessels which are required for the operation and maintenance of the vessel and its machinery, and on stores intended for use and consumption on board by members of the crew and passengers.

3. Items of equipment and machinery, spare parts and ship's stores sent through the territory of any Contracting Party shall not be liable to the imposition of duties and fees provided they are intended exclusively for the normal operation of vessels flying the flag of one of the Contracting Parties and lying in ports of another Contracting Party.

Article 8

In the use of vessels flying the flag of a Contracting Party in whose territory there are no maritime ports for merchant shipping, the provisions of articles 6 and 7 of the Agreement shall apply irrespective of the conditions concerning reciprocity contained in those articles.

Article 9

1. The Contracting Parties shall accord reciprocal recognition to the tonnage certificates and other ship's documents issued or recognized by the competent authorities of the State whose flag the vessel is flying.

2. Marine fees and taxes shall be calculated and levied on the basis of the tonnage certificates or equivalent documents currently in force that are carried on board the vessels.

Article 10

Shipping establishments, organizations and enterprises of one of the Contracting Parties shall, on a basis of reciprocity, be exempt in the territory of the other Contracting Parties from taxes on profits and income derived by such establishments, organizations and enterprises from the operation of vessels belonging to them or chartered by them for the purposes of international marine transport.

Article 11

1. If a vessel flying the flag of one of the Contracting Parties is wrecked, runs aground, is driven ashore or suffers any other damage off the shore of any other Contracting Party, the necessary assistance and facilities shall be granted to the vessel, its crew, passengers and cargo by the competent authorities of the latter Party in the same measure as they would be granted to a vessel flying the flag of that Party.

2. If a vessel flying the flag of one of the Contracting Parties suffers damage or is in distress in the territorial or internal maritime waters of any other Contracting Party, the competent authorities of the latter Party may grant permission for the rescue vessels and equipment of the first Contracting Party to provide assistance to the vessel, its crew, passengers and cargo in accordance with its own domestic laws.

3. A vessel which has suffered damage or been in distress, and the cargo, stores and other property of that vessel, shall not be subject in the territory of another Contracting Party to port fees, taxes and customs duties provided the vessel has come there for purposes other than commercial operations, and its cargo, stores and other property have been brought there for purposes other than use or consumption in the territory of that Party.

4. The foregoing provisions shall not affect the levying of pilotage fees or payments made for actual services provided to a vessel that has suffered damage or been in distress.

Article 12

The Contracting Parties shall accord reciprocal recognition to the seamen's identity cards issued by the competent authorities of the State whose flag the vessel is flying.

Persons who are in possession of the aforementioned identity cards and whose names appear on the vessel's crew list shall be entitled to go ashore in a port of any of the Contracting Parties for a temporary stay in the territory of the port town while the vessel is lying in that port.

The stay of seamen in the territory of the port town shall be regulated by the relevant rules in effect in the port of call.

Article 13

1. All disputes between shipping establishments, organizations or enterprises of the Contracting Parties arising out of contractual and other civil law relationships that come into being between them in the course of co-operation for the purpose of this Agreement shall be subject to arbitration and shall not come within the jurisdiction of the State courts.

Disputes as aforesaid shall be submitted to arbitration in the country of the defendant or, by agreement between the shipping establishments, organizations or enterprises of the Contracting Parties, to arbitration in a third country that is a Party to the present Agreement.

2. The provisions of paragraph 1 of this article shall not extend to such disputes in respect of civil-law relationships as fall within the exclusive jurisdiction of the State courts or other authorities by virtue of international agreements concluded between the Parties, or to such disputes in respect of civil-law relationships as fall within the exclusive jurisdiction of the State courts or other national authorities by virtue of the domestic legislation of the Contracting Parties.

3. State-owned merchant vessels flying the flag of one of the Contracting Parties shall not be liable to seizure of attachment in the ports of the other Contracting Parties in connexion with the civil disputes referred to in paragraphs 1 and 2 of this article.

Article 14

The competent authorities of each of the Contracting Parties shall furnish necessary assistance to agencies in their territory representing shipping organizations and enterprises and establishments connected with shipping of other Contracting Parties in the discharge of the functions of those agencies.

The activities of such agencies shall be subject to the relevant laws and regulations in force in the territory of the country in which they are situated.

Article 15

After this Agreement has come into force, any State may become a party to it.

The accession of other States may take place on the basis of an understanding between them and the Contracting Parties.

Article 16

This Agreement has been concluded for an unlimited period.

A Contracting Party may denounce this Agreement by notifying the depositary accordingly in writing not less than six months before the end of the current calendar year. The denunciation shall take effect from 1 January of the following calendar year.

Article 17

This Agreement shall come into force 30 days after the Governments of the signatory States notify the depositary that the procedures required under their legislation for the Agreement to come into force have been completed.

Article 18

This Agreement may be amended subject to the consent of all the Contracting Parties in accordance with the procedure set out in article 17.

Article 19

This Agreement shall be deposited with the Government of the Union of Soviet Socialist Republics which shall act as depositary for the Agreement.

The depositary shall transmit certified copies of this Agreement to all the signatory States.

3. INTERNATIONAL CONVENTION ON THE ESTABLISHMENT OF AN INTERNATIONAL FUND FOR COMPENSATION FOR OIL POLLU-TION DAMAGE, DONE AT BRUSSELS ON 18 DECEMBER 1971[1]

The States Parties to the present Convention,

Being parties to the International Convention on Civil Liability for Oil Pollution Damage, adopted at Brussels on 29 November 1969[2]

Conscious of the dangers of pollution posed by the world-wide maritime carriage of oil in bulk,

Convinced of the need to ensure that adequate compensation is available to persons who suffer damage caused by pollution resulting from the escape or discharge of oil from ships,

Considering that the International Convention of 29 November 1969, on Civil Liability for Oil Pollution Damage, by providing a régime for compensation for pollution damage in Contracting States and for the costs of measures, wherever taken, to prevent or minimize such damage, represents a considerable progress towards the achievement of this aim,

Considering however that this régime does not afford full compensation for victims of oil pollution damage in all cases while it imposes an additional financial burden on shipowners,

Considering further that the economic consequences of oil pollution damage resulting from the escape or discharge of oil carried in bulk at sea by

---

[1] Text provided by the Permanent Representative of Sweden to the United Nations in a note verbale of 4 February 1975.

[2] Reproduced in ST/LEG/SER.B/16, pp. 447-454.

ships should not exclusively be borne by the shipping industry but should in part be borne by the oil cargo interests,

Convinced of the need to elaborate a compensation and indemnification system supplementary to the International Convention on Civil Liability for Oil Pollution Damage with a view to ensuring that full compensation will be available to victims of oil pollution incidents and that the shipowners are at the same time given relief in respect of the additional financial burdens imposed on them by the said Convention,

Taking note of the Resolution on the Establishment of an International Compensation Fund for Oil Pollution Damage which was adopted on 29 November 1969 by the International Legal Conference on Marine Pollution Damage,

Have agreed as follows:

General Provisions

Article 1

For the purposes of this Convention

1. "Liability Convention" means the International Convention on Civil Liability for Oil Pollution Damage, adopted at Brussels on 29 November 1969.

2. "Ship", "Person", "Owner", "Oil", "Pollution Damage", "Preventive Measures", "Incident" and "Organization", have the same meaning as in Article I of the Liability Convention, provided however that, for the purposes of these terms, "Oil" shall be confined to persistent hydrocarbon mineral oils.

3. "Contributing Oil" means crude oil and fuel oil as defined in subparagraphs *(a)* and *(b)* below:

(a) "Crude Oil means any liquid hydrocarbon mixture occurring naturally in the earth whether or not treated to render it suitable for transportation. It also includes crude oils from which certain distillate fractions have been removed (sometimes referred to as "topped crudes") or to which certain distillate fractions have been added (sometimes referred to as "spiked" or "reconstituted" crudes).

(b) "Fuel Oil" means heavy distillates or residues from crude oil or blends of such materials intended for use as a fuel for the production of heat or power of a quality equivalent to the "American Society for Testing and Materials' Specification for Number Four Fuel Oil (Designation D 396-69)", or heavier.

4. "Franc" means the unit referred to in Article V, paragraph 9 of the Liability Convention.

5. "Ship's tonnage" has the same meaning as in Article V, paragraph 10, of the Liability Convention.

6. "Ton", in relation to oil, means a metric ton.

7. "Guarantor" means any person providing insurance or other financial security to cover an owner's liability in pursuance of Article VII, paragraph 1, of the Liability Convention.

8. "Terminal installation" means any site for the storage of oil in bulk which is capable of receiving oil from waterborne transportation, including any facility situated off-shore and linked to such site.

9. Where an incident consists of a series of occurrences, it shall be treated as having occurred on the date of the first such occurrence.

Article 2

1. An International Fund for compensation for pollution damage, to be named "The International Oil Pollution Compensation Fund" and hereinafter referred to as "The Fund", is hereby established with the following aims:

(a) To provide compensation for pollution damage to the extent that the protection afforded by the Liability Convention is inadequate;

(b) To give relief to shipowners in respect of the additional financial burden imposed on them by the Liability Convention, such relief being subject to conditions designed to ensure compliance with safety at sea and other conventions;

(c) To give effect to the related purposes set out in this Covention.

2. The Fund shall in each Contracting State be recognized as a legal person capable under the laws of that State of assuming rights and obligations and of being a party in legal proceedings before the courts of that State. Each Contracting State shall recognize the Director of the Fund (hereinafter referred to as "The Director") as the legal representative of the Fund.

Article 3

The Convention shall apply:

1. With regard to compensation according to Article 4, exclusively to pollution damage caused on the territory including the territorial sea of a Contracting State, and to preventive measures taken to prevent or minimize such damage;

2. With regard to indemnification of shipowners and their guarantors according to Article 5, exclusively in respect of pollution damage caused on the territory, including the territorial sea, of a State Party to the Liability Convention by a ship registered in or flying the flag of a Contracting State and in respect of preventive measures taken to prevent or minimize such damage.

Compensation and indemnification

Article 4

1. For the purpose of fulfilling its function under Article 2, paragraph 1 *(a)*, the Fund shall pay compensation to any person suffering pollution damage if such person has been unable to obtain full and adequate compensation for the damage under the terms of the Liability Convention,

(a) Because no liability for the damage arises under the Liability Convention;

(b) Because the owner liable for the damage under the Liability Convention is financially incapable of meeting his obligations in full and any financial security that may be provided under Article VII of that Convention does not cover or is insufficient to satisfy the claims for compensation for the damage; an owner being treated as financially incapable of meeting his obligations and a financial security being treated as insufficient if the person suffering the damage has been unable to obtain full satisfaction of the amount of compensation due under the Liability Convention after having taken all reasonable steps to pursue the legal remedies available to him;

(c) Because the damage exceeds the owner's liability under the Liability Convention as limited pursuant to Article V, paragraph 1, of that Convention or under the terms of any other international Convention in force or open for signature, ratification or accession at the date of this Convention.

Expenses reasonably incurred or sacrifices reasonably made by the owner voluntarily to prevent or minimize pollution damage shall be treated as pollution damage for the purposes of this Article.

2. The Fund shall incur no obligation under the preceding paragraph if:

(a) It proves that the pollution damage resulted from an act of war, hostilities, civil war or insurrection or was caused by oil which has escaped or been discharged from a warship or other ship owned or operated by a State and used, at the time of the incident, only on Government non-commercial service; or

(b) The claimant cannot prove that the damage resulted from an incident involving one or more ships.

3. If the Fund proves that the pollution damage resulted wholly or partially either from an act or omission done with intent to cause damage by the person who suffered the damage or from the negligence of that person, the Fund may be exonerated wholly or partially from its obligation to pay compensation to such person provided, however, that there shall be no such exoneration with regard to such preventive measures which are compensated under paragraph 1. The Fund shall in any event be exonerated to the extent that the shipowner may have been exonerated under Article III, paragraph 3 of the Liability Convention.

4. *(a)* Except as otherwise provided in subparagraph *(b)* of this paragraph, the aggregate amount of compensation payable by the Fund under this Article shall in respect of any one incident be limited, so that the total sum of that amount and the amount of compensation actually paid under the Liability Convention for pollution damage caused in the territory of the Contracting States, including any sums in respect of which the Fund is under an obligation to indemnify the owner pursuant to Article 5, paragraph 1, of this Convention, shall not exceed 450 million francs.

(b) The aggregate amount of compensation payable by the Fund under this Article for pollution damage resulting from a natural phenomenon of an **exceptional, inevitable and irresistible character shall not exceed 450 million francs.**

5. Where the amount of established claims against the Fund exceeds the aggregate amount of compensation payable under paragraph 4, the amount available shall be distributed in such a manner that the proportion between any established claim and the amount of compensation actually recovered by the claimant under the Liability Convention and this Convention shall be the same for all claimants.

6. The Assembly of the Fund (hereinafter referred to as "the Assembly") may, having regard to the experience of incidents which have occurred and in particular the amount of damage resulting therefrom and to changes in the monetary values, decide that the amount of 450 million francs referred to in paragraph 4, sub-paragraphs *(a)* and *(b)*, shall be changed; provided, however, that this amount shall in no case exceed 900 million francs or be lower than 450 million francs. The changed amount shall apply to incidents which occur after the date of the decision effecting the change.

7. The Fund shall, at the request of a Contracting State, use its good offices as necessary to assist that State to secure promptly such personnel, material and services as are necessary to enable the State to take measures to prevent or mitigate pollution damage arising from an incident in respect of which the Fund may be called upon to pay compensation under this Convention.

8. The Fund may on conditions to be laid down in the Internal Regulations provide credit facilities with a view to the taking of preventive measures against pollution damage arising from a particular incident in respect of which the Fund may be called upon to pay compensation under this Convention.

Article 5

1. For the purpose of fulfilling its function under Article 2, paragraph 1 *(b)*, the Fund shall indemnify the owner and his guarantor for that portion of the aggregate amount of liability under the Liability Convention which:

(a) Is in excess of an amount equivalent to 1,500 francs for each ton of the ship's tonnage or of an amount of 125 million francs, whichever is the less; and

(b) Is not in excess of an amount equivalent to 2,000 francs for each ton of the said tonnage or an amount of 210 million francs, whichever is the less,

provided, however, that the Fund shall incur no obligation under this paragraph where the pollution damage resulted from the wilful misconduct of the owner himself.

2. The Assembly may decide that the Fund shall, on conditions to be laid down in the Internal Regulations, assume the obligations of a guarantor in respect of ships referred to in Article 3, paragraph 2, with regard to the portion of liability referred to in paragraph 1 of this Article. However, the Fund shall assume such obligations only if the owner so requests and if he maintains adequate insurance or other financial security covering the owner's liability under the Liability Convention up to an amount equivalent to 1,500 francs for each ton of the ship's tonnage or an amount of 125 million francs, whichever is the less. If the Fund assumes such obligations, the owner shall in

each Contracting State be considered to have complied with Article VII of the Liability Convention in respect of the portion of his liability mentioned above.

3. The Fund may be exonerated wholly or partially from its obligations under paragraph 1 towards the owner and his guarantor if the Fund proves that as a result of the actual fault or privity of the owner:

(a) The ship from which the oil causing the pollution damage escaped did not comply with the requirements laid down in:

(i) The International Convention for the Prevention of Pollution of the Sea by Oil, 1954, as amended in 1962; or

(ii) The International Convention for the Safety of Life at Sea, 1960; or

(iii) The International Convention on Load Lines, 1966; or

(iv) The International Regulations for Preventing Collisions at Sea, 1960; or

(v) Any amendments to the above-mentioned Conventions which have been determined as being of an important nature in accordance with Article XVI (5) of the Convention mentioned under (i), Article IX *(e)* of the Convention mentioned under (ii) or Article 29 (3) *(d)* or (4) *(d)* of the Convention mentioned under (iii), provided, however, that such amendments had been in force for at least twelve months at the time of the incident;

and

(b) The incident or damage was caused wholly or partially by such non-compliance.

The provisions of this paragraph shall apply irrespective of whether the Contracting State in which the ship was registered or whose flag it was flying is a Party to the relevant Instrument.

4. Upon the entry into force of a new Convention designed to replace, in whole or in part, any of the Instruments specified in paragraph 3, the Assembly may decide at least six months in advance a date on which the new Convention will replace such Instrument or part thereof for the purpose of paragraph 3. However, any State Party to this Convention may declare to the Director before that date that it does not accept such replacement; in which case the decision of the Assembly shall have no effect in respect of a ship registered in, or flying the flag of, that State at the time of the incident. Such a declaration may be withdrawn at any later date and shall in any event cease to have effect when the State in question becomes a party to such new Convention.

5. A ship complying with the requirements in an amendment to an Instrument specified in paragraph 3 or with requirements in a new Convention, where the amendment or Convention is designed to replace in whole or in part such Instrument, shall be considered as complying with the requirements in the said Instrument for the purposes of paragraph 3.

6. Where the Fund, acting as a guarantor by virtue of paragraph 2, has paid compensation for pollution damage in accordance with the Liability Convention, it shall have a right of recovery from the owner if and to the

extent that the Fund would have been exonerated pursuant to paragraph 3 from its obligations under paragraph 1 to indemnify the owner.

7. Expenses reasonably incurred and sacrifices reasonably made by the owner voluntarily to prevent or minimize pollution damage shall be treated as included in the owner's liability for the purposes of this Article.

Article 6

1. Rights to compensation under Article 4 or indemnification under Article 5 shall be extinguished unless an action is brought thereunder or a notification has been made pursuant to Article 7, paragraph 6, within three years from the date when the damage occurred. However, in no case shall an action be brought after six years from the date of the incident which caused the damage.

2. Nothwithstanding paragraph 1, the right of the owner or his guarantor to seek indemnification from the Fund pursuant to Article 5, paragraph 1, shall in no case be extinguished before the expiry of a period of six months as from the date on which the owner or his guarantor acquired knowledge of the bringing of an action against him under the Liability Convention.

Article 7

1. Subject to the subsequent provisions of this Article, any action against the Fund for compensation under Article 4 or indemnification under Article 5 of this Convention shall be brought only before a court competent under Article IX of the Liability Convention in respect of actions against the owner who is or who would, but for the provisions of Article III, paragraph 2, of that Convention, have been liable for pollution damage caused by the relevant incident.

2. Each Contracting State shall ensure that its courts possess the necessary jurisdiction to entertain such actions against the Fund as are referred to in paragraph 1.

3. Where an action for compensation for pollution damage has been brought before a court competent under Article IX of the Liability Convention against the owner of a ship or his guarantor, such court shall have exclusive jurisdictional competence over any action against the Fund for compensation or indemnification under the provisions of Article 4 or 5 of this Convention in respect of the same damage. However, where an action for compensation for pollution damage under the Liability Convention has been brought before a court in a State Party to the Liability Convention but not to this Convention, any action against the Fund under Article 4 or under Article 5, paragraph 1, of this Convention shall at the option of the claimant be brought either before a court of the State where the Fund has its headquarters or before any court of a State Party to this Convention competent under Article IX of the Liability Convention.

4. Each Contracting State shall ensure that the Fund shall have the right to intervene as a party to any legal proceedings instituted in accordance with Article IX of the Liability Convention before a competent court of that State against the owner of a ship or his guarantor.

5. Except as otherwise provided in paragraph 6, the Fund shall not be bound by any judgment or decision in proceedings to which it has not been a party or by any settlement to which it is not a party.

6. Without prejudice to the provisions of paragraph 4, where an action under the Liability Convention for compensation for pollution damage has been brought against an owner or his guarantor before a competent court in a Contracting State, each party to the proceedings shall be entitled under the national law of that State to notify the Fund of the proceedings. Where such notification has been made in accordance with the formalities required by the law of the court seized and in such time and in such a manner that the Fund has in fact been in a position effectively to intervene as a party to the proceedings, any judgment rendered by the court in such proceedings shall, after it has become final and enforceable in the State where the judgment was given, become binding upon the Fund in the sense that the facts and findings in that judgment may not be disputed by the Fund even if the Fund has not actually intervened in the proceedings.

Article 8

Subject to any decision concerning the distribution referred to in Article 4, paragraph 5, any judgment given against the Fund by a court having jurisdiction in accordance with Article 7, paragraphs 1 and 3, shall, when it has become enforceable in the State of origin and is in that State no longer subject to ordinary forms of review, be recognized and enforceable in each Contracting State on the same conditions as are prescribed in Article X of the Liability Convention.

Article 9

1. Subject to the provisions of Article 5, the Fund shall, in respect of any amount of compensation for pollution damage paid by the Fund in accordance with Article 4, paragraph 1, of this Convention, acquire by subrogation the rights that the person so compensated may enjoy under the Liability Convention against the owner or his guarantor.

2. Nothing in this Convention shall prejudice any right of recourse or subrogation of the Fund against persons other than those referred to in the preceding paragraph. In any event the right of the Fund to subrogation against such person shall not be less favourable than that of an insurer of the person to whom compensation or indemnification has been paid.

3. Without prejudice to any other rights of subrogation or recourse against the Fund which may exist, a Contracting State or agency thereof which has paid compensation for pollution damage in accordance with provisions of national law shall acquire by subrogation the rights which the person so compensated would have enjoyed under this Convention.

Contributions

Article 10

1. Contributions to the Fund shall be made in respect of each Contracting State by any person who, in the calendar year referred to in

Article 11, paragraph 1, as regards initial contributions and in Article 12, paragraphs 2 *(a)* or *(b)*, as regards annual contributions, has received in total quantities exceeding 150,000 tons:

(a) In the ports or terminal installations in the territory of that State contributing oil carried by sea to such ports or terminal installations; and

(b) In any installations situated in the territory of that Contracting State contributing oil which has been carried by sea and discharged in a port or terminal installation of a non-Contracting State, provided that contributing oil shall only be taken into account by virtue of this sub-paragraph on first receipt in a Contracting State after its discharge in that non-Contracting State.

2. *(a)* For the purposes of paragraph 1, where the quantity of contributing oil received in the territory of a Contracting State by any person in a calendar year when aggregated with the quantity of contributing oil received in the same Contracting State in that year by any associated person or persons exceeds 150,000 tons, such person shall pay contributions in respect of the actual quantity received by him notwithstanding that that quantity did not exceed 150,000 tons.

(b) "Associated person" means any subsidiary or commonly controlled entity. The question whether a person comes within this definition shall be determined by the national law of the State concerned.

Article 11

1. In respect of each Contracting State initial contributions shall be made of an amount which shall for each person referred to in Article 10 be calculated on the basis of a fixed sum for each ton of contributing oil received by him during the calendar year preceding that in which this Convention entered into force for that State.

2. The sum referred to in paragraph 1 shall be determined by the Assembly within two months after the entry into force of this Convention. In performing this function the Assembly shall, to the extent possible, fix the sum in such a way that the total amount of initial contributions would, if contributions were to be made in respect of 90 per cent of the quantities of contributing oil carried by sea in the world, equal 75 million francs.

3. The initial contributions shall in respect of each Contracting State be paid within three months following the date at which the Convention entered into force for that State.

Article 12

1. With a view to assessing for each person referred to in Article 10 the amount of annual contributions due, if any, and taking account of the necessity to maintain sufficient liquid funds, the Assembly shall for each calendar year make an estimate in the form of a budget of:

(i) *Expenditure*

(a) Costs and expenses of the administration of the Fund in the relevant year and any deficit from operations in preceding years;

(b) Payments to be made by the Fund in the relevant year for the satisfaction of claims against the Fund due under Article 4 or 5, including repayment on loans previously taken by the Fund for the satisfaction of such claims, to the extent that the aggregate amount of such claims in respect of any one incident does not exceed 15 million francs;

(c) Payments to be made by the Fund in the relevant year for the satisfaction of claims against the Fund due under Article 4 or 5, including repayments on loans previously taken by the Fund for the satisfaction of such claims, to the extent that the aggregate amount of such claims in respect of any one incident is in excess of 15 million francs;

(ii) *Income*

(a) Surplus funds from operations in preceding years, including any interest;

(b) Initial contributions to be paid in the course of the year;

(c) Annual contributions, if required to balance the budget;

(d) Any other income.

2. For each person referred to in Article 10 the amount of his annual contribution shall be determined by the Assembly and shall be calculated in respect of each Contracting State:

(a) In so far as the contribution is for the satisfaction of payments referred to in paragraph 1 (i) *(a)* and *(b)* on the basis of a fixed sum for each ton of contributing oil received in the relevant State by such persons during the preceding calendar year; and

(b) In so far as the contribution is for the satisfaction of payments referred to in paragraph 1 (i) *(c)* of this Article on the basis of a fixed sum for each ton of contributing oil received by such person during the calendar year preceding that in which the incident in question occurred, provided that State was a party to this Convention at the date of the incident.

3. The sums referred to in paragraph 2 above shall be arrived at by dividing the relevant total amount of contributions required by the total amount of contributing oil received in all Contracting States in the relevant year.

4. The Assembly shall decide the portion of the annual contribution which shall be immediately paid in cash and decide on the date of payment. The remaining part of each annual contribution shall be paid upon notification by the Director.

5. The Director may, in cases and in accordance with conditions to be laid down in the Internal Regulations of the Fund, require a contributor to provide financial security for the sums due from him.

6. Any demand for payments made under paragraph 4 shall be called rateably from all individual contributors.

Article 13

1. The amount of any contribution due under Article 12 and which is in arrear shall bear interest at a rate which shall be determined by the Assembly

for each calendar year provided that different rates may be fixed for different circumstances.

2. Each Contracting State shall ensure that any obligation to contribute to the Fund arising under this Convention in respect of oil received within the territory of that State is fulfilled and shall take any appropriate measures under its law, including the imposing of such sanctions as it may deem necessary, with a view to the effective execution of any such obligation; provided, however, that such measures shall only be directed against those persons who are under an obligation to contribute to the Fund.

3. Where a person who is liable in accordance with the provisions of Articles 10 and 11 to make contributions to the Fund does not fulfil his obligations in respect of any such contribution or any part thereof and is in arrear for a period exceeding three months, the Director shall take all appropriate action against such person on behalf of the Fund with a view to the recovery of the amount due. However, where the defaulting contributor is manifestly insolvent or the circumstances otherwise so warrant, the Assembly may, upon recommendation of the Director, decide that no action shall be taken or continued against the contributor.

4. CONVENTION ON THE PROTECTION OF THE ENVIRONMENT BETWEEN DENMARK, FINLAND, NORWAY AND SWEDEN (WITH PROTOCOL) DONE AT STOCKHOLM ON 19 FEBRUARY 1974[1]

Article 1

For the purpose of this Convention, environmentally harmful activities shall mean the discharge from the soil or from buildings or installations of solid or liquid waste, gas or any other substance into water-courses, lakes or the sea and the use of land, the seabed, buildings or installations in any other way which entails, or may entail environmental nuisance by water pollution or any other effect on water conditions, sand drift, air pollution, noise, vibration, changes in temperature, ionizing radiation, light etc.

The Convention shall not apply in so far as environmentally harmful activities are regulated by a special agreement between two or more of the Contracting States.

Article 2

In considering the permissibility of environmentally harmful activities, the nuisance which such activities entail or may entail in another Contracting State shall be equated with a nuisance in the State where the activities are carried out.

Article 3

Any person who is affected or may be affected by a nuisance caused by environmentally harmful activities in another Contracting State shall have the

---

[1] Finnish text provided by the Ministry of Foreign Affairs of Denmark in a note verbale of 20 December 1974. English text reproduced from text provided by the Embassy of Sweden at Washington, D.C. and published in *International Legal Materials*, Vol. XIII, No. 3, May 1974, pp. 591-597.

right to bring before the appropriate Court or **Administrative Authority** of that State the question of the permissibility of such activities, including the question of measures to prevent damage, and to appeal against the decision of the Court or the Administrative Authority to the same extent and on the same terms as a legal entity of the State in which the activities are being carried out.

The provisions of the first paragraph of this Article shall be equally applicable in the case of proceedings concerning compensation for damage caused by environmentally harmful activities. The question of compensation shall not be judged by rules which are less favourable to the injured party than the rules of compensation of the State in which the activities are being carried out.

Article 4

Each State shall appoint a special authority (supervisory authority) to be entrusted with the task of safeguarding general environmental interests in so far as regards nuisances arising out of environmentally harmful activities in another Contracting State.

For the purpose of safeguarding such interests, the supervisory authority shall have the right to institute proceedings before or be heard by the competent Court or Administrative Authority of another Contracting State regarding the permissibility of the environmentally harmful activities, if an authority or other representative of general environmental interests in that State can institute proceedings or be heard in matters of this kind, as well as the right to appeal against the decision of the Court or the Administrative Authority in accordance with the procedures and rules of appeal applicable to such cases in the State concerned.

Article 5

If the Court or the Administrative Authority examining the permissibility of environmentally harmful activities (examining authority) finds that the activities entail or may entail nuisance of significance in another Contracting State, the examining authority shall, if proclamation or publication is required in cases of that nature, send as soon as possible a copy of the documents of the case to the supervisory authority of the other State, and afford it the opportunity of giving its opinion. Notification of the date and place of a meeting or inspection shall, where appropriate, be given well in advance to the supervisory authority which, moreover, shall be kept informed of any developments that may be of interest to it.

Article 6

Upon the request of the supervisory authority, the examining authority shall, in so far as compatible with the procedural rules of the State in which the activities are being carried out, require the applicant for a permit to carry out environmentally harmful activities to submit such additional particulars, drawings and technical specifications as the examining authority deems necessary for evaluating the effects in the other State.

Article 7

The supervisory authority, if it finds it necessary on account of public or private interests, shall publish communications from the examining authority in the local newspaper or in some other suitable manner. The supervisory authority shall also institute such investigations of the effects in its own State as it deems necessary.

Article 8

Each State shall defray the cost of the activities of its supervisory authority.

Article 9

If, in a particular case, the supervisory authority has informed the appropriate Court or Administrative Authority of the State in which the activities are being carried out that in the case concerned the duties of the supervisory authority shall be discharged by another authority, the provisions of this Convention relating to supervisory activities shall, where appropriate, apply to that authority.

Article 10

If necessary for determining the damage caused in another State by environmentally harmful activities, the supervisory authority of that other State shall upon request of the examining authority of the State in which the activities are being carried out make arrangements for on-site inspection. The examining authority or an expert appointed by it may be present at such an inspection.

Where necessary, more detailed instructions concerning inspections such as referred to in the preceding paragraph shall be drawn up in consultation between the countries concerned.

Article 11

Where the permissibility of environmentally harmful activities which entail or may entail considerable nuisance in another Contracting State is being examined by the Government or by the appropriate Minister or Ministry of the State in which the activities are being carried out, consultations shall take place between the States concerned if the Government of the former State so requests.

Article 12

In cases such as those referred to in Article 11, the Government of each State concerned may demand that an opinion be given by a Commission which, unless otherwise agreed, shall consist of a chairman from another Contracting State to be appointed jointly by the parties and three members from each of the States concerned. Where such a Commission has been appointed, the case cannot be decided upon until the Commission has given its opinion.

Each State shall remunerate the members it has appointed. Fees or other remuneration of the Chairman as well as any other costs incidental to the activities of the Commission which are not manifestly the responsibility of one or the other State, shall be equally shared by the States concerned.

Article 13

This Convention shall also apply to the continental shelf areas of the Contracting States.

Article 14

This Convention shall enter into force six months from the date on which all the Contracting States have notified the Swedish Ministry for Foreign Affairs that the constitutional measures necessary for the entry into force of the Convention have been implemented. The Swedish Ministry for Foreign Affairs shall notify the other Contracting States of the receipt of such communications.

Article 15

Actions or cases relevant to this Convention, which are pending before a Court or an Administrative Authority on the date when this Convention enters into force, shall be dealt with and judged according to provisions previously in force.

Article 16

Any Contracting State wishing to denounce this Convention shall give notice of its intention in writing to the Swedish Government, which shall forthwith inform the other Contracting States of the denunciation and of the date on which notice was received.

The denunciation shall take effect twelve months from the date on which the Swedish Government received such notification or on such later date as may be indicated in the notice of denunciation.

This Convention shall be deposited with the Swedish Ministry for Foreign Affairs, which shall send certified copies thereof to the Government of each Contracting State.

PROTOCOL

In connection with the signing today of the Nordic Environmental Protection Convention the duly authorized signatory agreed that the following comments on its application shall be appended to the Convention.

In the application of *Article 1* discharge from the soil, or from buildings or installations of solid or liquid waste gases or other substances into water-courses, lakes or the sea shall be regarded as environmentally harmful activities only if the discharge entails or may entail a nuisance to the surroundings.

The right established in *Article 3* for anyone who suffers injury as a result of environmentally harmful activities in a neighbouring State to institute proceedings for compensation before a court or administrative authority of that State shall, in principle, be regarded as including the right to demand the purchase of his real property.

Article 5 shall be regarded as applying also to applications for permits where such applications are referred to certain authorities and organizations for their opinion but not in conjunction with proclamation or publication procedures.

The Contracting States shall require officials of the supervisory authority to observe *professional secrecy* as regards trade secrets, operational devices or business conditions of which they have become cognizant in dealing with cases concerning environmentally harmful activities in another State.

5. [CONVENTION ON THE PROTECTION OF THE MARINE ENVIRON-MENT OF THE BALTIC SEA AREA, DONE AT HELSINKI ON 22 MARCH 1974] [1]

6. [CONVENTION FOR THE PREVENTION OF MARINE POLLUTION FROM LAND BASED SOURCES, DONE AT PARIS ON 4 JUNE 1974] [2]

---

[1] *Infra* Division III, Subdivision A, 4.
[2] *Infra* Division III, Subdivision A, 5.

Subdivision B. Bilateral Treaties

1. (i) AGREEMENT CONCERNING THE SOVEREIGNTY OVER THE ISLANDS OF AL-'ARABIYAH AND FARSI AND THE DELIMITATION OF THE BOUNDARY LINE SEPARATING THE SUBMARINE AREAS BETWEEN THE KINGDOM OF SAUDI ARABIA AND IRAN, DONE AT TEHERAN ON 24 OCTOBER 1968[1]

The Royal Government of Saudi Arabia . . . and the Imperial Government of Iran . . .

Desirous of resolving the difference between them regarding sovereignty over the islands of Al-'Arabiyah and Farsi and

Desirous further of determining in a just and accurate manner the boundary line separating the respective submarine areas over which each Party is entitled by international law to exercise sovereign rights,

Now therefore and with due respect to the principles of the law and particular circumstances,

And after exchanging the credentials, have agreed as follows:

Article 1

The Parties mutually recognize the sovereignty of Saudi Arabia over the island of Al-'Arabiyah and of Iran over the island of Farsi. Each island shall possess a belt of territorial sea 12 nautical miles in width, measured from the line of lowest low water on each of the said islands. In the area where these belts overlap, a boundary line separating the territorial seas of the two islands shall be drawn so as to be equidistant throughout its length from the lowest low water lines on each island.

Article 2

The boundary line separating the submarine areas which appertain to Saudi Arabia from the submarine areas which appertain to Iran shall be a line established as hereinafter provided. Both Parties mutually recognize that each possesses over the sea-bed and subsoil of the submarine areas on its side of the line sovereign rights for the purpose of exploring and exploiting the natural resources therein.

---

[1] United Nations, *Treaty Series*, vol. 696, p. 212. Came into force on 29 January 1969 by the exchange of the instruments of ratification in accordance with article 5. Official translation signed by both Parties.

Article 3

The boundary line referred to in article 2 shall be:

(a) Except in the vicinity of Al-'Arabiyah and Farsi, the said line is determined by straight lines between the following points whose latitude and longitude are specified herein below:

Point	North Latitude	East Longitude
1	27° 10.0'	50° 54.0'
2	27° 18 5'	50° 45.5'
3	27° 26.5'	50° 37.0'
4	27° 56.5'	50° 17.5'
5	28° 08.5'	50° 06.5'
6	28° 17.6'	49° 56.2'
7	28° 21.0'	49° 50.9'
8	28° 24.7'	49° 47.8'
9	28° 24.4'	49° 47.4'
10	28° 27.9'	49° 42.0'
11	28° 34.8'	49° 39.7'
12	28° 37.2'	49° 36.2'
13	28° 40.9'	49° 33.5'
14	28° 41.3'	49° 34.3'

(b) In the vicinity of Al-Arabiyah and Farsi, a line laid down as follows:

At the point where the line described in paragraph *(a)* intersects the limit of the belt of territorial sea around Farsi, the boundary shall follow the limit of that belt on the side facing Saudi Arabia until it meets the boundary line set forth in article 1 which divides the territorial seas of Farsi and Al-'Arabiyah; thence it shall follow that line easterly until it meets the limit of the belt of territorial sea around Al-'Arabiyah; thence it shall follow the limit of that belt on the side facing Iran until it intersects again the line described in paragraph *(a)*.

The map prepared by the A. M. Service Corps of Engineers U.S. Army compiled in 1966 was used and shall be used as the basis for the measurement of the co-ordinates described above and the boundary line is illustrated in a copy of the said map signed and attached hereto.

Article 4

Each Party agrees that no oil drilling operations shall be conducted by or under its authority, within a zone extending five hundred (500) meters in width in the submarine areas on its side of the boundary line described in article 3, said zone to be measured from said boundary.

. . .

(ii) EXCHANGES OF LETTERS

Ia

Your Excellency:

With reference to the offshore boundary agreement signed by us today (hereinafter referred to as "the Agreement") on behalf of our respective

Governments, I have the honour to propose the following technical arrangement to facilitate the determination of geographical locations offshore in the Marjan-Fereydoun area:

As soon as possible after the entry into force of the Agreement a joint technical committee of four members shall be established composed of two experts appointed by each Government. This committee shall be charged with establishing agreed positions defined by co-ordinates of latitude and longitude with reference to the map attached to the Agreement, for the following offshore at which tangible markers of various kinds already exist:

On the Iranian Side:

1. The well site known as Fereydoun 3
2. The well site known as Fereydoun 2

On the Saudi Arabian Side:

3. The well site known as Fereydoun 7, or in case there shall be no tangible markers therein, the well site known as Marjan 1. It is understood that whenever a new well is drilled on the Saudi Arabian side with tangible markers on it and conveniently close to the boundary line, such a well shall also be included in the reference points, thus making the number of the reference points four all together.

The positions for these points fixed by the committee shall be regarded as accepted by both Governments if neither Government objects within one month after the committee has presented its reports, which reports shall be submitted to both Governments on the same date.

Thereafter, for all purposes arising under the Agreement positions for oil operations in the Marjan-Fereydoun area carried on under the authority of either Government shall be established by reference to these points in accordance with standard survey techniques.

If the foregoing proposal is acceptable to Your Excellency, this letter and your reply to that effect shall constitute an agreement between our respective Governments, effective on the date on which the Agreement comes into force.

With assurance of my high esteem.

Teheran on 2nd Sha'ban 1388 corresponding to 2nd Aban 1347 and 24th October 1968.

For the Royal Government of Saudi Arabia:

Ahmed ZAKI YAMANI
Minister of Petroleum
and Mineral Resources

His Excellency Dr. Manoochehr Eghbal
Chairman of the Board and General Managing
    Director of the National Iranian Oil Company
    and Representative of the Imperial Government of Iran

IIa

Your Excellency:

I have the honour to inform Your Excellency that I have received Your Excellency's letter of the following text:

[See letter Ia]

I have the pleasure to convey to Your Excellency my Government's approval of the contents of your letter, the text of which is hereabove stated, considering that the said letter and my reply thereto shall constitute an agreement between our respective Governments, effective on the date on which the Agreement comes into force.

With renewed assurance of my high esteem.

Teheran on 2nd Sha'ban 1388 corresponding to 2nd Aban 1347 and 24th October 1968.

For the Imperial Government of Iran:

Dr. Manoochehr EGHBAL
Chairman of the Board and General
Managing Director of the
National Iranian Oil Company

His Excellency Ahmed Zaki Yamani
Minister of Petroleum and Mineral Resources
Representative of the Royal Government
of Saudi Arabia

Ib

Your Excellency:

With reference to the offshore boundary agreement signed by us today on behalf of our respective Governments, I have the honour to propose, for the more effective implementation of this Agreement (hereinafter referred to as "the Agreement") the following understandings:

(a) The oil drilling operations which are prohibited by article 4 of the Agreement within the zone therein described (hereinafter referred to as "the Prohibited Area") shall include exploitation carried out directly from the Prohibited Area and shall also extend to all drilling operations which could be carried out within the Prohibited Area from installations which are themselves located outside it.

The term "oil drilling operations" as used in article 4 of the Agreement shall mean drilling operations for oil and/or gas.

Our two Governments shall ensure that the wells drilled in the immediate vicinity of the Prohibited Area shall be vertical wells, however, when a deviation is technically inevitable at a reasonable cost, such a deviation shall not be deemed as encroachment on the Agreement, provided that the deviation is within the minimum range of good drilling practice and further provided that the party concerned does not contemplate, by such deviation, the violation of the provisions set forth in the Agreement and this letter.

Should our two Governments mutually agree that gas injection and/or drilling an observation well is technically beneficial and advisable for the Marjan-Fereydoun reservoir, our two Governments shall agree on the location, the conducting of drilling the wells and their operations in the Prohibited Area for the sole purpose specified in this paragraph, provided that the wells to be drilled shall be conducted by each Government, directly or through its authorized agent, on its respective side of the Prohibited Area under the terms and conditions to be agreed upon by our two Governments.

(b) Our two Governments shall, directly or through authorized agents, exchange with each other all obtained directional survey information during the course of drilling operations carried out as from the effective date of the Agreement within two kilometers of the boundary line. This exchange shall be made on a reciprocal and continuous basis.

(c) Each Government shall ensure that the companies operating under its respective authority shall not carry out operations that may, for technical inconsistency with the conservation rules according to sound oil industry practice, be considered harmful to the oil and gas reservoir in the Marjan-Fereydoun area.

This letter and Your Excellency's reply thereto shall constitute an agreement between our respective Governments, to become effective on the date on which the Agreement enters into force.

With renewed assurance of my high esteem.

Teheran on 2nd Sha'ban 1388 corresponding to 2nd Aban 1347 and 24th October 1968.

For the Royal Government of Saudi Arabia:

Ahmed ZAKI YAMANI
Minister of Petroleum
and Mineral Resources

His Excellency Dr. Manoochehr Eghbal
Chairman of the Board and General Managing
    Director of the National Iranian Oil Company
    and Representative of the Imperial Government of Iran

IIb

Your Excellency:

I have the honour to inform Your Excellency that I have received Your Excellency's letter of the following text:

[See letter IIa]

I have the pleasure to convey to Your Excellency my Government's approval of the contents of your letter, the text of which is hereabove stated, considering that the said letter and my reply thereto shall constitute an agreement between our respective Governments, effective on the date on which the Agreement comes into force.

With renewed assurance of my high esteem.

Teheran on 2nd Sha'ban 1388 corresponding to 2nd Aban 1347 and 24th October 1968.

For the Imperial Government of Iran:

Manoochehr EGHBAL
Chairman of the Board and
General Managing Director of the
National Iranian Oil Company

His Excellency Shaikh Ahmed Zaki Yamani
Minister of Petroleum and Mineral Resources
and Representative of the Royal Government
of Saudi Arabia

2. TREATY BETWEEN THE FEDERAL REPUBLIC OF GERMANY AND THE REPUBLIC OF LIBERIA ON THE USE OF LIBERIAN WATERS AND PORTS BY THE NUCLEAR SHIP "OTTO HAHN", DONE AT BONN ON 27 MAY 1970[1]

The Republic of Liberia and the Federal Republic of Germany,

Desiring to promote and having a mutual interest in the peaceful uses of nuclear energy, including its application to the merchant marine,

Have agreed as follows:

Article 1

(1) Each entry of N.S. "Otto Hahn" (hereinafter designated as the "Ship") at present operated by the "Gesellschaft für Kernenergieverwertung in Schiffbau und Schiffahrt mbH, Hamburg", into waters extending to a distance of 24 nautical miles from the base line of the coast of the Republic of Liberia (hereinafter designated as "Liberian waters") and into Liberian ports, and the use thereof shall be subject to the prior approval in writing of the Government of the Republic of Liberia.

---

[1] BGBl 1971 II, p. 953, English text, which is authentic, provided by the Permanent Representative of the Federal Republic of Germany to the United Nations in a note verbale dated 4 March 1975.

The Federal Republic of Germany has concluded additional treaties concerning navigation by nuclear ships with the Netherlands, on 28 October 1968 (BGBl 1969 II, p. 1121); Portugal, on 29 January 1971 (BGBl 1972 II, p. 57); Argentina, on 21 March 1972 (BGBl 1972 II, p. 68); Brazil, on 7 June 1972 (BGBl 1974 II, p. 685).

(2) The Government of the Federal Republic of Germany shall notify the Government of the Republic of Liberia of any change of the operator of the Ship.

Article 2

Unless this Treaty expressly provides otherwise, the visits of the Ship to Liberian waters and ports shall be governed by the principles and procedures set forth in Chapter VIII of the Safety of Life at Sea International Convention of 1960 and in Annex C to the Final Act of the Safety of Life at Sea International Conference of 1960.

Article 3

The Government of the Republic of Liberia shall upon request of the operator determine the Liberian waters and the port or ports to be visited. It shall further designate the Authorities responsible for the acceptance arrangements, the stay and the special control under Regulation 11 of Chapter VIII of the Safety of Life at Sea Convention.

Article 4

(1) To enable the Government of the Republic of Liberia to consider the grant of approval for entry and use of Liberian waters and ports by the Ship, the operator of the Ship shall submit a Safety Assessment as required by Regulation 7 of Chapter VIII of the Safety of Life at Sea Convention and by the Recommendations contained in Annex C to the Final Act of the Safety of Life at Sea International Conference of 1960.

(2) As soon as practicable after receipt of the Safety Assessment and of the operator's request as mentioned in Article 3, the Government of the Republic of Liberia shall notify the Government of the Federal Republic of Germany of those Liberian waters and ports which the Ship may enter and use in accordance with this Treaty and on such further conditions as may be agreed.

Article 5

(1) The Government of the Republic of Liberia shall make arrangements with the appropriate local Authorities for the use of Liberian waters and ports by the Ship.

(2) Control of public access to the Ship shall be the responsibility of the Master of the Ship. Special regulations relating to such control shall be issued by the Master. They shall be subject to the approval of the appropriate Liberian Authorities.

(3) The Master of the Ship shall comply with local regulations as far as these regulations are not contrary to the Safety Assessment and the Operating Manual instructions for the reactor. The Master shall further comply with the instructions given by local Authorities in as far as these instructions, in his opinion, do not jeopardize the safety of the reactor. Should he be unable to comply, the Master shall immediately notify the designated governmental

Authorities of the Republic of Liberia. Such Authority may then prohibit the further use of Liberian waters and ports by the Ship.

(4) The Master of the Ship shall immediately notify the local Authorities of any event which may prolong the agreed stay of the Ship in the port.

Article 6

While the Ship is within Liberian waters and ports, the designated Liberian Authorities shall have normal access to the Ship. They shall further have access to its operating records and to the Operating Manual instructions for the reactor in order to determine whether the Ship has been operated and is being operated in accordance with the Operating Manual, as well as for the purpose of the special control required by Regulation 11 of Chapter VIII of the Safety of Life at Sea Convention.

Article 7

Unless the appropriate Liberian Authorities have expressly given their prior approval to a release of radioactive products or waste, there shall be no release of any radioactive products or waste from the Ship during its stay in Liberian waters or ports.

Article 8

(1) Unless the appropriate Liberian Authorities have expressly given their prior approval, there shall be no maintenance, repair and servicing of the Ship's nuclear installation in Liberian waters; however, normal crew maintenance is excepted.

(2) The use of contractors for maintenance, repair and servicing of the nuclear installation in Liberian waters or ports shall be restricted to those contractors having the specific approval of the appropriate Liberian Authorities for the rendering of such services.

(3) The appropriate Liberian Authorities must be notified of each such maintenance, repair and servicing of the nuclear installation to be carried out in Liberian waters or ports. Repairs which will prolong the agreed stay of the Ship in the port or which will affect the capability of the Ship to sail under its own steam shall only be carried out with the agreement of the appropriate Liberian Authorities.

(4) Such approval as mentioned in this article shall not create any liability on the part of the Liberian Government.

Article 9

An immediate report, such as is required by Chapter VIII, Regulation 12, of the Safety of Life at Sea Convention, shall be made to the designated Liberian Authorities by the Master of the Ship in the event of any accident or the existence of any condition likely to lead to an environmental hazard while the Ship is in or is approaching Liberian waters or ports.

Article 10

(1) If, in the opinion of the designated Liberian Authorities, there is an immediate environmental hazard while the Ship is in or is approaching Liberian waters or ports, the Master of the Ship shall comply with the instructions of these Authorities.

(2) If, for reasons of safety, he is unable to comply with the instructions of these Authorities, he shall immediately notify the designated governmental Authority of the Republic of Liberia. Such Authority may then prohibit the further use of Liberian waters and ports by the Ship.

Article 11

If the Ship strands, runs aground or sinks in Liberian waters and ports the competent Authorities of the Federal Republic of Germany shall, after consultation and with the assistance of the competent Liberian Authorities, take all necessary measures to prevent any possible risk of nuclear damage.

Article 12[1]

The terms "nuclear damage", "nuclear incident", "nuclear fuel" and "radioactive products or waste" as used in Articles 13-20 of this Treaty shall have the same meaning as in the Convention on the Liability of Operators of Nuclear Ships opened for signature in Brussels on May 25, 1962, hereinafter referred to as "the Convention".

Article 13

Liability for nuclear damage caused by a nuclear incident involving the nuclear fuel of, or radioactive products or waste produced in, the Ship shall be governed by Article II, para. 1 of Article III, Article IV, Article VIII and paras. 1 and 2 of Article X of the Convention as well as by the following Articles of this Treaty, provided, however, that the liability mentioned in para. 1 of Article III of the Convention shall be limited to DM 400 million (four hundred million).

Article 14

(1) Rights of compensation under Article 13 of this Treaty shall be extinguished if an action is not brought within ten years from the date of the nuclear incident.

(2) Where nuclear damage is caused by nuclear fuel, radioactive products or waste which were stolen, lost, jettisoned, or abandoned, the period established in para. 1 shall also be computed from the date of the nuclear incident causing the nuclear damage, but the period shall in no case exceed a period of twenty years from the date of the theft, loss, jettison or abandonment.

---

[1] The definitions referred to in this Article are reproduced after the text of this Convention.

(3) If the period established in para. (1) and the period established in para. (2) have not been exceeded the rights of compensation under Article 13 of this Treaty shall be subject to a prescription period of three years from the date on which the person who claims to have suffered a nuclear damage had knowledge or ought reasonably to have had knowledge of the damage and of the person liable for the damage.

Article 15

In each case of nuclear damage caused by the Ship the Liberian Government and the Government of the Federal Republic of Germany shall immediately initiate negotiations with a view to reaching a satisfactory settlement of the claim between the parties.

Article 16

(1) The Federal Republic of Germany shall ensure the payment of claims for compensation for nuclear damage established under this Treaty against the operator of the Ship by providing the necessary funds up to a maximum amount of DM 400 million (four hundred million). Funds shall be provided only to the extent that the yield of the insurance or other financial security is inadequate to satisfy such claims.

(2) The Government of the Federal Republic of Germany shall, upon request of the Liberian Government, make the amount available three months after the judgement against the operator has become final.

Article 17

The provisions of national legislation or international conventions on the limitation of shipowners' liability shall not apply to claims established under Article 13 of this Treaty.

Article 18

(1) Any definite judgement passed by Liberian courts on a nuclear incident caused by the Ship shall be recognized in the Federal Republic of Germany if, under para. 1 of Article X of the Convention, jurisdiction lies with the Liberian courts.

(2) Recognition of a judgement may be refused only if

(a) The judgement was obtained by fraud;

(b) A legal proceeding between the same parties and on account of the same subject matter is pending before a court in the Federal Republic of Germany and if application was first made to this court;

(c) The judgement is contrary to a definite decision passed by a court in the Federal Republic of Germany on the subject matter between the same parties;

(d) The operator of the Ship did not enter an appearance in the proceeding and if the document instituting the proceeding was served on him not effectively according to the laws of the Republic of Liberia, or not on him personally in the Republic of Liberia or not by granting him German legal assistance or not in due time for the operator of the Ship to defend himself, or if the operator can prove that he was unable to defend himself because, without any fault on his part, he did not receive the document for the institution of the legal proceeding or received it too late.

(3) In no event will the merits of any case be subject to review.

Article 19

Any judgement passed by Liberian courts, which are recognized according to Article 18 of this Treaty and which are enforceable under Liberian law, shall be enforceable in the Federal Republic of Germany as soon as the formalities required by the law of the Federal Republic of Germany have been complied with.

Article 20

Articles 13-19 of this Treaty shall apply to nuclear damage occurring within Liberian territory or Liberian waters, if the nuclear incident has occurred

(a) Within Liberian territory or Liberian waters; or

(b) Outside Liberian territory or Liberian waters during a passage to or from a Liberian port or to or from Liberian waters.

Article 21

If a multilateral international agreement or national legislation of one of the Contracting Parties becomes effective, concerning any matters governed by this Treaty, the Contracting Parties shall, in due course, initiate negotiations for a revision of this Treaty.

Article 22

(1) Disputes concerning the interpretation or application of this Treaty shall, if possible, be settled by the Governments of the two Contracting Parties.

(2) If a dispute cannot thus be settled it shall upon the request of either Contracting Party be submitted to an arbitral tribunal.

(3) Such arbitral tribunal shall be constituted in each individual case as follows: each Contracting Party shall appoint one member, and these two members shall agree upon a national of a third State as their chairman to be appointed by the Governments of the two Contracting Parties. Such members shall be appointed within two months, and such chairman within three months, from the date on which either Contracting Party has informed the other Contracting Party of its desire to submit the dispute to an arbitral tribunal.

(4) If the periods specified in paragraph 3 have not been observed, either Contracting Party may, in the absence of any other relevant arrangement, invite the President of the International Court of Justice to make the necessary appointments. If the President is a national of either Contracting

414

Party, if he is otherwise prevented from discharging the said function or if he is not accepted by one of the parties, the Vice-President should make the necessary appointments. If the Vice-President is a national of either Contracting Party, and if he, too, is prevented from discharging the said function or if he is not accepted by one of the parties, the Member of the International Court of Justice next in seniority who is not a national of either Contracting Party shall make the necessary appointments.

(5) The arbitral tribunal shall reach its decisions by a majority of votes. Such decisions shall be binding. Each Contracting Party shall bear the cost of its own member and of its representatives in the arbitral proceeding; the cost of the chairman and the remaining costs shall be borne in equal parts by both Contracting Parties. The arbitral tribunal may make a different regulation concerning costs. In all other respects, the arbitral tribunal shall determine its own procedure.

Article 23

The provisions of this Treaty shall not prejudice the rights, claims and legal views of the Contracting Parties with regard to the limits of the territorial sea and with regard to their jurisdiction on the high sea.

Article 24

This Treaty shall also apply to Land Berlin, provided that the Government of the Federal Republic of Germany does not make a contrary declaration to the Government of the Republic of Liberia within three months from the date of entry into force of this Treaty.

Article 25

(1) The present Treaty is subject to ratification; the instruments of ratification shall be exchanged as soon as possible in Monrovia.

(2) The present Treaty shall enter into force on the date of exchange of the instruments of ratification.

Article 26

This Treaty may be denounced subject to six months notice.

DONE at Bonn on 27 May 1970 in duplicate in the English and German languages, both texts being equally authentic.

DEFINITIONS[1]

Article I

For the purposes of this Convention,

1.–4. ...

5. "Nuclear fuel" means any material which is capable of producing energy by a self-sustaining process of nuclear fission and which is used or intended for use in a nuclear ship.

6. "Radioactive products or waste" means any material, including nuclear fuel, made radioactive by neutron irradiation incidental to the utilization of nuclear fuel in a nuclear ship.

7. "Nuclear damage" means loss of life or personal injury and loss or damage to property which arises out of or results from the radioactive properties or a combination of radioactive properties with toxic, explosive or other hazardous properties of nuclear fuel or of radioactive products or waste; any other loss, damage or expense so arising or resulting shall be included only if and to the extent that the applicable national law so provides.

8. "Nuclear incident" means any occurrence or series of occurrences having the same origin which causes nuclear damage.

9.–12. ...

Article II

(1) The operator of a nuclear ship shall be absolutely liable for any nuclear damage upon proof that such damage has been caused by a nuclear incident involving the nuclear fuel of, or radioactive products or waste produced in, such ship.

(2) Except as otherwise provided in this Convention no person other than the operator shall be liable for such nuclear damage.

(3) Nuclear damage suffered by the nuclear ship itself, its equipment, fuel or stores shall not be covered by the operator's liability as defined in this Convention.

(4) The operator shall not be liable with respect to nuclear incidents occurring before the nuclear fuel has been taken in charge by him or after the nuclear fuel or radioactive products or waste have been taken in charge by another person duly authorized by law and liable for any nuclear damage that may be caused by them.

---

[1] *Supra* Articles 12, 13-20. Convention on the Liability of Operators of Nuclear Ships opened for signature in Brussels on May 25, 1962 (Article I, paras. 5, 6, 7, 8; Article II; Article III, para. 1; Article IV; Article VIII, Article X, paras. 1 and 2). For text see: Conference Diplomatique de Droit Maritime, Onzième Session (2e phase), Bruxelles 1962 (Ad. Goemaere, Brussels, 1963), pp. 707-33. See also International Conventions on Civil Liability for Nuclear Damage, IAEA Legal Series No. 4 (Vienna, 1966) pp. 36-46).

(5) If the operator proves that the nuclear damage resulted wholly or partially from an act or omission done with intent to cause damage by the individual who suffered the damage, the competent courts may exonerate the operator wholly or partially from his liability to such individual.

(6) Notwithstanding the provisions of paragraph 1 of this Article, the operator shall have a right of recourse:

(a) If the nuclear incident results from a personal act or omission done with intent to cause damage in which event recourse shall lie against the individual who has acted, or omitted to act, with such intent;

(b) If the nuclear incident occurred as a consequence of any wreckraising operation, against the person or persons who carried out such operation without the authority of the operator or of the State having licensed the sunken ship or of the State in whose waters the wreck is situated;

(c) If recourse is expressly provided for by contract.

Article III, paragraph 1

(1) The liability of the operator as regards one nuclear ship shall be limited to 1,500 million francs in respect of any one nuclear incident, notwithstanding that the nuclear incident may have resulted from any fault or privity of that operator, such limit shall include neither any interest nor costs awarded by a court in actions for compensation under this Convention.

(2)–(4) ...

Article IV

Whenever both nuclear damage and damage other than nuclear damage have been caused by a nuclear incident and one or more other occurrences and the nuclear damage and such other damage are not reasonably separable, the entire damage shall, for the purposes of this Convention, be deemed to be the nuclear damage exclusively caused by the nuclear incident. However, where damage is caused jointly by a nuclear incident covered by this Convention and by an emission of ionizing radiation or by an emission of ionizing radiation in combination with the toxic, explosive or other hazardous properties of the source of radiation not covered by it, nothing in this Convention shall limit or otherwise affect the liability, either as regards the victims or by way of recourse or contribution, of any person who may be held liable in connection with the emission of ionizing radiation or by the toxic, explosive or other hazardous properties of the source of radiation not covered by this Convention.

Article VIII

No liability under this Convention shall attach to an operator in respect to nuclear damage caused by a nuclear incident directly due to an act of war, hostilities, civil war or insurrection.

Article X

(1) Any action for compensation shall be brought, at the option of the claimant, either before the courts of the licensing State or before the courts of the Contracting State or States in whose territory nuclear damage has been sustained.

(2) If the licensing State has been or might be called upon to ensure the payment of claims for compensation in accordance with paragraph 2 of Article III of this Convention, it may intervene as party in any proceedings brought against the operator.

(3) . . .

3. TREATY TO RESOLVE PENDING BOUNDARY DIFFERENCES AND MAINTAIN THE RIO GRANDE AND COLORADO RIVER AS THE INTERNATIONAL BOUNDARY BETWEEN THE UNITED MEXICAN STATES AND THE UNITED STATES OF AMERICA, DONE AT MEXICO CITY ON 23 NOVEMBER 1970[1]

The United Mexican States and the United States of America,

Animated by a spirit of close friendship and mutual respect and desiring to:

Resolve all pending boundary differences between the two countries,

. . .

And finally, considering that it is in the interest of both countries to delimit clearly their maritime boundaries in the Gulf of Mexico and in the Pacific Ocean,

Have resolved to conclude this Treaty concerning their fluvial and maritime boundaries and for such purpose have named their plenipotentiaries:

. . .

Who, . . . have agreed as follows:

. . .

Article V

The Contracting States agree to establish and recognize their maritime boundaries in the Gulf of Mexico and in the Pacific Ocean in accordance with the following provisions:

A. The international maritime boundary in the Gulf of Mexico shall begin at the centre of the mouth of the Rio Grande, wherever it may be located; from there it shall run in a straight line to a fixed point, at 25° 57' 22.18" North latitude, and 97° 8' 19.76" West longitude, situated approximately 2,000 feet seaward from the coast; from this fixed point the maritime boundary shall continue seaward in a straight line the delineation of

---

[1] United Nations, *Treaty Series*, vol. 830, No. 11873. Came into force on 18 April 1972 by the exchange of the instruments of ratification in accordance with article IX. ·

which represents a practical simplification of the line drawn in accordance with the principle of equidistance established in articles 12 and 24 of the Geneva Convention on the Territorial Sea and the Contiguous Zone.[1] This line shall extend into the Gulf of Mexico to a distance of 12 nautical miles from the baseline used for its delineation. The international maritime boundary in the Gulf of Mexico shall be recognized in accordance with the map entitled International Maritime Boundary in the Gulf of Mexico, which the Commission shall prepare in conformity with the foregoing description and which, once approved by the Governments, shall be annexed to and form a part of this Treaty.[2]

B. The international maritime boundary in the Pacific Ocean shall begin at the westernmost point of the mainland boundary; from there it shall run seaward on a line the delineation of which represents a practical simplification, through a series of straight lines, of the line drawn in accordance with the principle of equidistance established in articles 12 and 24 of the Geneva Convention on the Territorial Sea and the Contiguous Zone. This line shall extend seaward to a distance of 12 nautical miles from the baselines used for its delineation along the coast of the mainland and the islands of the Contracting States. The international maritime boundary in the Pacific Ocean shall be recognized in accordance with the map entitled International Maritime Boundary in the Pacific Ocean, which the Commission shall prepare in conformity with the foregoing description and which, once approved by the Governments, shall be annexed to and form a part of this Treaty.

C. These maritime boundaries, as they are shown in maps of the Commission entitled International Maritime Boundary in the Gulf of Mexico and International Maritime Boundary in the Pacific Ocean, shall be recognized as of the date on which this Treaty enters into force. They shall permanently represent the maritime boundaries between the two Contracting States; on the north side of these boundaries Mexico shall not, and on the south side of them the United States shall not, for any purpose claim or exercise sovereignty, sovereign rights or jurisdiction over the waters, air space, or sea-bed and subsoil. Once recognized, these new boundaries shall supersede the provisional maritime boundaries referred to in the Commission's Minute No. 229.

D. The establishment of these new maritime boundaries shall not affect or prejudice in any manner the positions of either of the Contracting States with respect to the extent of internal waters, of the territorial sea, or of sovereign rights or jurisdiction for any other purpose.

E. The Commission shall recommend the means of physically marking the maritime boundaries and of the division of work for construction and maintenance of the markers. When such recommendations have been approved by the two Governments the Commission shall construct and maintain the markers, the cost of which shall be equally divided between the Contracting States.

. . .

---

[1] United Nations, *Treaty Series*, vol. 516, p. 205. Also ST/LEG/SER.B/15, pp. 721-728.

[2] The map is not reproduced in this volume.

4. AGREEMENT BETWEEN FINLAND AND SWEDEN, CONCERNING FRONTIER RIVERS, SIGNED AT STOCKHOLM ON 16 SEPTEMBER 1971[1]

With a view to ensuring that frontier watercourses are used in the manner most in keeping with the interests of the two States and their frontier areas, the Government of Finland and the Government of Sweden have concluded the following Agreement regulating certain matters relating to water rights and fishing rights in connexion with the said watercourses.

Chapter 1. General provisions

Article 1

The Agreement shall be applicable to the following waters:

The Rivers Könkämä and Muonio and the portion of the River Torne and the lakes through which the State frontier between Finland and Sweden runs *(frontier rivers);*

The special effluents formed by the various branches at the mouth of the River Torne;

The part of the Gulf of Bothnia lying between the Finnish and Swedish parishes of Lower Torne.

The provisions of the Agreement relating to fishing shall be applicable within a special area, as indicated in chapter 5, article 1.

Article 2

The Agreement shall cover:

Measures that involve hydraulic construction works within the meaning of chapter 3 or water regulation within the meaning of chapter 4 or that may cause pollution within the meaning of chapter 6, where such measures are carried out in frontier rivers;

Measures of the same nature which are carried out within the area of application defined above in article 1, first paragraph, in either State and may produce effects in the other State;

Fishing in the special area defined in chapter 5, article 1.

. . .

Article 3

In the light of the considerations set out in detail in this Agreement, the waters covered by the Agreement shall be used in such a manner that both countries derive benefit from the frontier watercourses and that the interests of the frontier areas are promoted as effectively as possible. Particular importance shall be accorded to the interests of nature conservancy; the greatest possible attention shall be given to the preservation of fish stocks and the prevention of water pollution.

. . .

---

[1] Entered into force on 1 January 1972 in accordance with chapter 10, article 3. United Nations, *Treaty Series*, vol. 825, No. I-11827.

Chapter 2. Frontier River Commission

Article 1

For purposes of the application of the Agreement, a permanent commission *(the Finnish-Swedish Frontier River Commission)* shall be established jointly by the two States.

Article 2

The Frontier River Commission shall have six members, of whom the Government of each State shall appoint three. Members shall be appointed for a fixed term. One member from each State shall be a legal expert with experience as a judge, and one shall be a technical expert; the third member shall be a person with an intimate knowledge of conditions in the frontier areas, being appointed in the case of Finland on the basis of a recommendation from the county administration of Lappland county and in the case of Sweden on the basis of a recommendation from the county administration of Norrbotten county.

The Governments of the two States shall alternately designate one of their members to serve as Chairman or Vice-Chairman of the Commission for a term of one year.

One or more alternates who meet the qualifications established for members shall be appointed for each member in accordance with the procedure applicable in the case of members.

Secretarial and other personnel required by the Commission shall be made available to it.

. . .

Chapter 3. Hydraulic construction works

. . .

Article 2

Hydraulic construction works shall be carried out in such a way that their purpose is achieved without unreasonable cost and with the least possible damage and inconvenience to other interests in either State. Due regard shall be given to proposed future projects that may be affected by the installation.

Article 3

Where any person would suffer damage or inconvenience as a result of hydraulic construction works, the works shall be carried out only if they can be shown to bring public or private benefit that substantially outweighs the inconvenience.

Where the construction would result in a substantial deterioration in the living conditions of the population or cause a permanent change in natural conditions such as might entail substantially diminished comfort for people living in the vicinity or a significant nature conservancy loss or where significant public interests would be otherwise prejudiced, the construction shall be permitted only if it is of particular importance for the economy or for the locality or from some other public standpoint.

Compensation pursuant to chapter 7 shall be paid in respect of any damage or inconvenience.

Article 4

In deciding whether projected construction is to be carried out, conditions in both States shall be given equal weight.

. . .

Article 7

Where hydraulic construction works are such that they may have a harmful effect on fishing, the person carrying out the construction shall take or pay for such measures as are reasonably called for in order to protect the fish stock or maintain fishing of an equal standard.

. . .

Article 9

In carrying out hydraulic construction works, care shall be taken to ensure that, apart from occasional, temporary turbidity, no pollution occurs that causes any significant inconvenience.

. . .

Chapter 5. Fishing

Article 1

The following provisions shall be applicable to fishing within the area formed by the frontier rivers with their branches and effluents and the parts of the Gulf of Bothnia lying between the Finnish and Swedish parishes of Lower Torne north of latitude 65° 35′ N. *(fishery zone of the River Torne).*

The part of the fishery zone of the River Torne lying north of the mouth of the river defined as a straight line between the tip of Hellälä north point on the Finnish side and the tip of Virtakari point, the nearest site on the opposite Swedish side, shall be called the river zone; the part lying south of that line shall be called the sea zone. The effluents of the River Torne shall be part of the river zone.

. . .

Article 3

Within the sea zone there shall, in addition to fish channels, established in conformity with the law of each State, be reserve zones. These shall consist of the waters to a distance of 200 metres on each side of the following straight lines:

(a) From Kraaselikari in front of the river mouth bearing 196° to a point 65° 45.85′ N., 24° 06.45′ E., thence to 65° 44.0′ N., 25° 10.0′ E., thence to 65° 40.55′ N., 24° 11.95′ E., thence between Sarvenkataja and Linnanklupu bearing 193°;

(b) From the point of intersection of the line running from Kraaselikari as indicated in *(a)* and latitude line 65° 46.0' N. to 65° 46.05' N., 25° 02.75' E., thence bearing 213.5° to 65° 44.0' N., 23° 59.50' E., thence to 65° 42.0' N., 24° 01.70' E., thence to 65° 36.0' N., 23° 59.25' E., thence bearing 160°;

(c) From 65° 44.0' N., 23° 59.50' E. along the 213.5° bearing line referred to in *(b)* to 65° 39.0' N., 23° 51.50' E., thence to 65° 38.0' N., 23° 50.65' E., thence bearing 171°;

(d) From the point of intersection of the bearing line referred to in *(b)* and latitude line 65° 44.60' N. to 65° 44.50' N., 23° 50.30' E., thence to 65° 43.60' N., 23° 48.50' E., thence to 65° 42.80' N., 23° 48.70' E., thence to 65° 41.40' N., 23° 46.85' E., thence bearing 200°;

(e) From the 65° 44.0' N., 24° 10.0' E. deflection point referred to in *(a)* to 65° 43.95' N., 24° 14.15' E., thence to west of Vähä Huituri and Iso Huituri bearing 160°;

(f) From the 65° 43.95' N., 24° 14.15' E. deflection point referred to in *(e)* to 65° 43.80' N., 24° 19.40' E., thence to 65° 42.30' N., 24° 22.85' E., thence bearing 172°.

The co-ordinates refer to Swedish chart No. 417 (Haparanda), all editions 1960-1967.

The extent of the reserve zones is indicated on the chart annexed to the Declaration of 1 April 1967 amending the regulations accompanying the Declaration of 10 May 1927 by Sweden and Finland concerning the adoption of regulations for fishing in the fishery zone of the Torne (Tornio) River.

The county authorities in Norrbotten county and Lappland country shall be responsible for taking the necessary steps on their respective sides of the State frontier to mark out the position of the reserve zones in the water.

Fishing gear and other devices may not, save in the case of measures for which permission has been obtained in accordance with the provisions of this Agreement relating to hydraulic construction works, be set up or used in such a manner as might hinder fishing in the reserve zones or otherwise prevent fishing from proceeding there.

Article 4

All fishing with large bow-purse nets, bottom nets and *mocka* nets or other gear designed for catching salmon or sea trout shall be forbidden within the portion of the sea zone lying between the mouth of the river and a line drawn from the south shore of the mouth of the bay of Salmis through the southernmost points of the islands of Kraaseli and Tirro and the northwest point of Sell Islands up to the southwest point of Björk Island.

Fishing gear more than 200 metres in length may not be set up on either side of the strait between the islands of Stora Tervakari and Hamppuleiviskä.

Chapter 6. Protection against water pollution

Article 1

No solid or liquid wastes or other substances may be discharged into waters, to a greater extent than is permitted under this Agreement where such discharge results in harmful aggradation, a harmful change in the nature of the water, damage to fish stocks, diminished comfort for the population or endangerment of their health or other such damage or inconvenience to public or private interests.

Article 2

The applicable provisions shall be, in addition to those of this chapter, the provisions of the legislation concerning health, construction and nature conservancy of the State in which the discharge occurs or is to occur and the provisions of that State's special protective legislation against specific types of water pollution.

. . .

Chapter 7. Compensation

Article 1

Any person who is granted the right under this Agreement to use property belonging to a third party, to use water power belonging to a third party or to take measures which otherwise cause damage or inconvenience to property belonging to a third party shall be liable to pay compensation for the property used or for the loss, damage or inconvenience caused.

Save as otherwise provided, compensation shall be fixed at the same time that permission is granted for the measure in question.

Article 2

The Frontier River Commission may also take decisions otherwise than in connexion with applications' for permission on questions of compensation arising from measures falling within the scope of this Agreement.

Compensation for damage and inconvenience resulting from the measures referred to in chapter 3, article 21, shall, in the absence of agreement, be fixed by the Frontier River Commission

Article 3

Save as otherwise provided in this Agreement, the law of the State in which the property used is situated or in which loss, damage or inconvenience otherwise occurs shall apply in respect of the grounds for compensation, the right of the owner of property used or damaged to demand payment and the manner and time of payment of compensation.

. . .

Chapter 10. Final provisions

Article 1

Any dispute between the two States concerning the interpretation and application of this Agreement shall be settled in accordance with the Convention concluded between Finland and Sweden on 27 June 1924 concerning the establishment of a permanent Commission for investigation and conciliation.

Article 2

This Agreement, which has been drawn up in duplicate in the Swedish and Finnish languages, shall be ratified. The instruments of ratification shall be exchanged at Helsinki as soon as possible.

The Swedish and Finnish texts are equally authentic.

Article 3

The Agreement shall enter into force on 1 January 1972.

Article 4

Upon the entry into force of this Agreement, the following shall cease to have effect:

The Convention of 10 May 1927 between Finland and Sweden concerning the joint exploitation of the salmon fisheries in the Tornea and Muonio Rivers;

The Declaration of 8 September 1966 by Finland and Sweden concerning the application of the Convention of 10 May 1927 concerning the joint exploitation of the salmon fisheries in the Tornea and Muonio Rivers;

The Declaration of 10 May 1927 by Finland and Sweden concerning the adoption of regulation for fishing in the fishery zone of the Tornea River.

Article 5

If any installation or project referred to in this Agreement is built or carried out before the Agreement enters into force or is built or carried out subsequently pursuant to a decision of a court or other authority based on previously applicable provisions, the previously applicable provisions shall be applied in determining the legality of the installation or project and the associated rights and obligations. However, the provisions of this Agreement concerning review shall apply to the said installation or project.

Cases or other matters which, at the time of the entry into force of this Agreement, are pending in court or before any other authority and which affect questions covered by the Agreement shall be dealt with and decided in accordance with the previously applicable provisions.

The Kiviranta trap may be deployed and operated pursuant to the rules applicable heretofore for one year from the entry into force of the Agreement.

Article 6

The Agreement shall cease to have effect at the end of the year falling two years after denunciation of the Agreement by either State. Upon such denunciation, the States shall, in order to prevent injury to public interests and private rights, begin negotiations on the continued existence of installations extending across the State frontier which were built pursuant to the Agreement.

5. [AGREEMENT BETWEEN AUSTRALIA AND INDONESIA CONCERNING CERTAIN BOUNDARIES BETWEEN PAPUA NEW GUINEA AND INDONESIA, DONE AT CANBERRA ON 26 JANUARY 1973, Articles 7 and 8][1]

6. AGREEMENT BETWEEN DENMARK AND SWEDEN CONCERNING THE PROTECTION OF THE SOUND (ORESUND) FROM POLLUTION, SIGNED AT COPENHAGEN ON 5 APRIL 1974[2]

The Governments of Denmark and Sweden,

Believing that the Sound and the adjoining parts of the Baltic Sea and the Kattegat are of great importance *inter alia* to fisheries and recreational activities,

Having signed the Nordic Convention on the Protection of the Environment of 19 February 1974[3] and the Convention on the Protection of the Baltic Sea Environment of 22 March 1974,[4]

Believing that, in addition to the provisions of the aforesaid Conventions, there is a need for special measures effectively to protect the Sound from pollution and other influences that could endanger or impair its usefulness for the aforesaid purposes or otherwise damage its biological environment,

Have agreed as follows,

Article 1

For the purposes of this Agreement the term "the Sound" shall mean the area of water bounded in the north by a line drawn between Gilbierg Head and the Kullen, and in the south by a line drawn between Stevn lighthouse and Falsterbo Point.

Article 2

Effective measures shall be carried out in each country to reduce the pollution of the Sound caused by direct or indirect discharges. The scope of these measures shall be determined in the light of technological feasibility and

---

[1] *Infra* Division II, Subdivision B, 7.

[2] Danish text transmitted by the Ministry of Foreign Affairs of Denmark in a note verbale of 20 December 1974. Translation by the Secretariat of the United Nations. Received for registration with the Secretariat on 10 February 1975.

[3] *Supra* Subdivision A, 4.

[4] *Infra* Division III, Subdivision A, 4.

having regard both to public and private interests. To this end the following minimum requirements shall apply to purification treatment until further notice:

1. *Discharge of municipal waste water*

Direct or indirect discharge into the Sound of waste water from built-up areas may take place only where the waste water has undergone more thorough treatment than mechanical treatment (sludge separation).

Discharge into water areas with bad water-renewal properties may take place only after biological or chemical treatment reducing the content of organic matter, measured by biochemical oxygen consumption, by at least 90 per cent and the phosphate content either by an average of 90 per cent or to the equivalent of an effluent concentration averaging 0.5 mg of total phosphorus per litre. In the event of any dispute arising between the countries as to which areas are covered by this paragraph, such dispute shall be referred to the Commission mentioned in article 6.

2. *Discharge of industrial waste water*

Effective measures shall be undertaken to eliminate or substantially reduce any form of pollution from industries with direct waste water discharges which may be detrimental to the Sound. Such measures shall be designed to achieve the same aims as are sought with respect to the discharge of municipal waste.

Industries connected with municipal waste water systems shall institute effective internal measures for the elimination or substantial reduction of the discharge of all kinds of pollutant that may be damaging to the treatment process or to the receiver.

In determining what demands can be made for such measures, account shall be taken of such guidelines concerning the content of various substances in the waste water and similar matters as may be proposed by the Commission mentioned in article 6.

3. *Other guidelines*

In addition to the measures specifically indicated above, for the treatment of waste water or other restrictions on the discharge of pollutants into the Sound, the following guidelines shall be followed for the protection of the Sound.

(a) Improved treatment measures shall, in principle, be designed to keep pace with the growth of the population and the rise in industrial production. An effort shall be made to reduce both domestic and industrial pollution.

(b) The discharge of agricultural waste shall be supervised and kept under control.

Article 3

Measures to meet the minimum requirements indicated in article 2 for the treatment of municipal and industrial waste water shall be instituted as soon as possible and shall be implemented within five years after the signing of this

Agreement. The continual increase in the discharge of pollutants into the Sound necessitates prompt action to deal with the question of further treatment measures. This question shall be taken up by the Commission mentioned in article 6. The Commission shall, in particular, consider the need for reduction of nutritive salts also upon discharge into the water areas of the Sound other than those referred to in article 2, item 1, second section, and propose the necessary preventive measures in that respect by the end of 1977 at the latest.

Article 4

In order to control the direct discharge of waste water into the Sound from densely built-up areas and industries, each country shall adopt appropriate measures to gauge the amounts of water discharged and to ensure the regular sampling of major pollutants contained therein. For the purpose of control over the introduction into the Sound of waste water from the larger watercourses, hydrological monitoring stations should be established in the lower parts of the watercourses and regular monitoring of water quality should be undertaken.

The effects of discharges of waste water on the water, bottom sediment and organisms in the Sound should be regularly investigated within the discharge areas. Hydrological, chemical and biological studies should be made to determine the pollution situation in the Sound as a whole and in adjoining water areas and may serve as a basis for determining the need for further measures to counteract the pollution of the Sound.

Article 5

The question of special measures to prevent discharges in connexion with ferry traffic between the two countries shall be taken up by the Commission mentioned in article 6 as soon as possible.

Article 6

A Danish-Swedish Commission shall be established to deal with co-operation concerning the protection of the Sound from pollution. The Commission shall consist of six members and their alternates, of which each Government shall designate three. One of the members of the Commission designated by each Government shall represent the municipalities concerned. Each country may also designate experts to participate in the work and meetings of the Commission.

The chairmanship of the Commission shall alternate between the countries each year. The secretariat functions of the Commission shall be undertaken by the country which holds the chairmanship. Each country shall defray its own expenses in connexion with the work of the Commission.

The Commission shall establish its own rules of procedure.

The Commission shall establish such committees as it deems necessary.

Article 7

The Commission shall have the following tasks:

(a) It shall actively follow the fulfilment by each country of the requirements connected with this Agreement.

(b) It shall examine the need for additions to or changes in the set of goals established in this agreement.

(c) It shall promote co-ordination of ongoing research and study projects of importance to the protection of the Sound and, where necessary, initiate further projects.

(d) It shall propose such other measures as may be conducive to the reduction of pollution in the Sound.

(e) At the request of the Government of one of the two countries it shall give an opinion on questions falling within its purview.

(f) It shall report regularly to the Governments of the two countries on its activities and otherwise report in an appropriate manner on the pollution situation in the Sound.

Article 8

Proposals made by the Commission in accordance with article 7, *(a)* to *(d)*, shall be submitted to the Governments of the two countries or to competent authorities in the two countries. The proposals shall, if necessary, be accompanied by information concerning the manner in which expenses connected with their implementation should, in the Commission's opinion, be apportioned between the two countries.

Article 9

The Protocol signed by the Parties on 27 February and 1 March 1960 concerning a long-term programme for studies in the Sound shall cease to have effect forthwith. The Commission shall take a decision concerning the transfer of the work tasks which were previously the responsibility of the Sound Water Committee established under the aforesaid Protocol.

Article 10

This Agreement shall be subject to ratification. The Agreement shall enter into force when the two Governments have notified one another, by an exchange of notes in Stockholm, that they have ratified it. After the Agreement has been in force for ten years, it may be terminated by either party by written notice to that effect to the other party.

The Agreement shall expire one year after notice of termination.

Division II

THE CONTINENTAL SHELF

Subdivision A. Multilateral Treaties

1. [PROTOCOL OF ACCESSION TO THE SANTIAGO DECLARATION ON THE "MARITIME ZONE", DONE AT QUITO ON 6 OCTOBER 1955][1]

2. AGREEMENT BETWEEN THAILAND, INDONESIA AND MALAYSIA RELATiNG TO THE DELIMITATION OF THE CONTINENTAL SHELF BOUNDARIES IN THE NORTHERN PART OF THE STRAITS OF MALACCA, DONE AT KUALA LUMPUR ON 21 DECEMBER 1971[2]

Article I

1. The boundaries of the continental shelves of Thailand, Indonesia and Malaysia in the northern part of the Straits of Malacca shall start from a point whose co-ordinates are latitude 5° 57'.0 N. longitude 98° 01'.5 E. (hereinafter referred to as "the Common Point").

2. The boundary of the continental shelves of Thailand and Indonesia shall be formed by the straight lines drawn from the Common Point in a north-westerly direction to a point whose co-ordinates are latitude 6° 21'.8 N. longitude 97° 54'.0 E. and from there in a westerly direction to a point whose co-ordinates are latitude 7° 05'.8 N. longitude 96° 36'.5 E. as specified in the Agreement between the Government of the Kingdom of Thailand and the Government of the Republic of Indonesia relating to the delimitation of a continental shelf boundary between the two countries in the northern part of the Straits of Malacca and in the Andaman Sea, signed at Bangkok on the 17th day of December, 1971.

3. The boundary of the continental shelves of Indonesia and Malaysia shall be formed by the straight line drawn from the Common Point in a southward direction to Point 1 specified in the Agreement signed at Kuala Lumpur on the 27th day of October, 1969, between the Government of the Republic of Indonesia and the Government of Malaysia relating to the delimitation of the continental shelves between the two countries whose co-ordinates are latitude 5° 27'.0 N. longitude 98° 17'.5 E.

---

[1] *Supra* Division I, Subdivision A, 1.

[2] English text, which is authentic, provided by the Permanent Representative of Thailand to the United Nations in a note verbale of 15 November 1974.

4. The boundary of the continental shelves of Thailand and Malaysia shall be formed by the straight lines drawn from the Common Point in a north-easterly direction to a point whose co-ordinates are latitude 6° 18'.0 N. longitude 99° 06'.7 E. and from there in a south-easterly direction to a point whose co-ordinates are latitude 6° 16'.3 N. longitude 99° 19'.3 E. and from there in a north-easterly direction to a point whose co-ordinates are latitude 6° 18'.4 N. longitude 99° 27'.5 E.

5. The co-ordinates of the points specified above are geographical co-ordinates derived from the British Admiralty Charts No. 793 and No. 830 and the straight lines connecting them are indicated on the chart attached as Annexure "A" to this Agreement.

6. The actual location of the above-mentioned points at sea shall be determined by a method to be mutually agreed upon by the competent authorities of the respective Governments concerned.

7. For the purposes of paragraph (6), "competent authorities" in relation to the Kingdom of Thailand means the Director of the Hydrographic Department, Thailand, and includes any person authorized by him; in relation to the Republic of Indonesia the Chief of the Co-ordinating Body for National Survey and Mapping, Republic of Indonesia, and includes any person authorized by him; and in relation to Malaysia the Director of National Mapping, Malaysia, and includes any person authorized by him.

Article II

Each Government hereby undertakes to ensure that all the necessary steps shall be taken at the domestic level to comply with the terms of this Agreement.

Article III

If any single geological petroleum or natural gas structure extends across the boundary line or lines referred to in Article I and the part of such structure which is situated on one side of the said line or lines is exploitable, wholly or in part, from the other side or sides of the said line or lines, the Governments concerned shall seek to reach agreement as to the manner in which the structure shall be most effectively exploited.

Article IV

Any dispute between the three Governments arising out of the interpretation or implementation of this Agreement shall be settled peacefully by consultation or negotiation.

Article V

This Agreement shall be ratified in accordance with the legal requirements of the three countries.

Article VI

This Agreement shall enter into force on the date of the exchange of the Instruments of Ratification.

Done in triplicate at Kuala Lumpur the twenty first day of December, 1971, in the Thai, Indonesian, Malaysian and English languages. In the event of any conflict between the texts, the English text shall prevail.

3. [CONVENTION ON THE PROTECTION OF THE ENVIRONMENT BETWEEN DENMARK, FINLAND, NORWAY AND SWEDEN (WITH PROTOCOL), DONE AT STOCKHOLM ON 19 FEBRUARY 1974][1]

---

[1] *Supra* Division I, Subdivision A, 4.

Subdivision B. Bilateral Treaties

1. [AGREEMENT CONCERNING THE SOVEREIGNTY OVER THE ISLANDS OF AL-'ARABIYAH AND FARSI AND THE DELIMITATION OF THE BOUNDARY LINE SEPARATING THE SUBMARINE AREAS BETWEEN THE KINGDOM OF SAUDI ARABIA AND IRAN, DONE AT TEHERAN ON 24 OCTOBER 1968, Articles 2-4 and the Exchanges of Letters][1]

2. AGREEMENT BETWEEN THE GOVERNMENT OF THE COMMONWEALTH OF AUSTRALIA AND THE GOVERNMENT OF THE REPUBLIC OF INDONESIA ESTABLISHING CERTAIN SEA-BED BOUNDARIES, DONE AT CANBERRA ON 18 MAY 1971[2]

The Government of the Commonwealth of Australia and the Government of the Republic of Indonesia,

Desiring to strengthen the bonds of friendship between the two countries; and

Desiring particularly to co-operate in delimiting by agreement the boundaries of certain areas of sea-bed in which the two countries respectively exercise sovereign rights for the exploration and exploitation of the natural resources,

Have agreed as follows:

Article 1

In the Arafura Sea eastwards of Longitude 133° 23' East, the boundary between the area of sea-bed that is adjacent to and appertains to the Commonwealth of Australia and the area that is adjacent to and appertains to the Republic of Indonesia shall be the straight lines shown on chart[3] "A" annexed to this Agreement, commencing at the point of Latitude 9° 52' South, Longitude 140° 29' East (Point A1), and thence connecting the points specified hereunder in the sequence so specified:

A2. The point of Latitude 10° 24' South, Longitude 139° 46' East
A3. The point of Latitude 10° 50' South, Longitude 139° 12' East
A4. The point of Latitude 10° 24' South, Longitude 138° 38' East
A5. The point of Latitude 10° 22' South, Longitude 138° 35' East
A6. The point of Latitude 10° 09' South, Longitude 138° 13' East
A7. The point of Latitude 9° 57' South, Longitude 137° 45' East
A8. The point of Latitude 9° 08' South, Longitude 135° 29' East
A9. The point of Latitude 9° 17' South, Longitude 135° 13' East
A10. The point of Latitude 9° 22' South, Longitude 135° 03' East
A11. The point of Latitude 9° 25' South, Longitude 134° 50' East
A12. The point of Latitude 8° 53' South, Longitude 133° 23' East

[1] *Supra* Division I, Subdivision B, 1.

[2] Text provided by the Permanent Representative of Australia to the United Nations in a note verbale of 29 March 1973.

[3] The chart is not reproduced in this volume.

433

Article 2

The two Governments have not provided in this Agreement for the delimitation of the respective areas of adjacent sea-bed westward of Longitude 133° 23′ East, and have left this question for discussion at further talks to be held at a mutually convenient date.[1]

Article 3

1. Off the southern coast of the island of New Guinea (Irian) westwards of Longitude 140° 49′ 30″ East, the boundary between the area of sea-bed that is adjacent to and appertains to the Territory of Papua and the area that is adjacent to and appertains to the Republic of Indonesia shall be the straight line shown on chart "A" annexed to this Agreement, connecting the point of Latitude 9° 24′ 30″ South, Longitude 140° 49′ 30″ East (Point B1) with the point of Latitude 9° 52′ South, Longitude 140° 29′ East (Point A1).

2. The two Governments have not provided in this Agreement for the drawing of a boundary line between the point B1 referred to in paragraph 1 of this article and the point at which the land boundary between the Territory of Papua and West Irian meets the southern coast of the island of New Guinea (Irian), and have left this question for further discussion as and when agreed.[2]

Article 4

1. Off the northern coast of the island of New Guinea (Irian), the boundary between the area of sea-bed that is adjacent to and appertains to the Trust Territory of New Guinea and the area that is adjacent to and appertains to the Republic of Indonesia shall lie along the straight line shown on chart "B"[3] annexed to this Agreement, connecting the point at which the land boundary between the Trust Territory and West Irian meets the northern coast of the island of New Guinea (Irian) (Point C1) with the point of Latitude 2° 08′ 30″ South, Longitude 141° 01′ 30″ East (Point C2). If any lines are drawn extending this line northward, they shall be drawn on the same principle, that is to say the principle of equidistance.

2. The lines referred to in paragraph 1 of this article are to be taken as indicating the direction in which the lateral boundary of the respective areas of sea-bed is agreed to lie.

3. This article shall not in any way affect any agreement that may subsequently be made between the two Governments delimiting the lateral boundary of the territorial sea as between the Trust Territory of New Guinea and the Republic of Indonesia.

Article 5

For the purpose of this Agreement, "sea-bed" includes the subsoil thereof, except where the context otherwise requires.

---

[1] See the agreement of 9 October 1972, reproduced *infra* 6.

[2] See the agreement of 26 January 1973, reproduced *infra* 7.

[3] The chart is not reproduced in this volume.

Article 6

1. The co-ordinates of the points specified in articles 1, 3 and 4 of this Agreement are geographical co-ordinates, and the actual location of the points and of the lines joining them shall be determined by a method to be agreed upon by the competent authorities of the two Governments.

2. For the purpose of paragraph 1 of this article the competent authorities in relation to the Commonwealth of Australia shall be the Director of National Mapping and any person acting with his authority, and in relation to the Republic of Indonesia shall be the Chief of the Co-ordinating Body for National Survey and Mapping (Ketua Badan Koordinasi Survey dan Pemetaan Nasional) and any person acting with his authority.

Article 7

If any single accumulation of liquid hydrocarbons or natural gas, or if any other mineral deposit beneath the sea-bed, extends across any of the lines that are specified in articles 1, 3 and 4 of this Agreement, and the part of such accumulation or deposit that is situated on one side of the line is recoverable in fluid form wholly or in part from the other side of the line, the two Governments will seek to reach agreement on the manner in which the accumulation or deposit shall be most effectively exploited and on the equitable sharing of the benefits arising from such exploitation.

Article 8

Any dispute between the two Governments arising out the interpretation or implementation of this Agreement shall be settled peacefully by consultation or negotiation.

Article 9

This Agreement is subject to ratification in accordance with the constitutional requirements of each country, and shall enter into force on the day on which the Instruments of Ratification are exchanged.

3. AGREEMENT BETWEEN THE FEDERAL REPUBLIC OF GERMANY AND THE UNITED KINGDOM OF GREAT BRITAIN AND NORTHERN IRELAND RELATING TO THE DELIMITATION OF THE CONTINENTAL SHELF UNDER THE NORTH SEA BETWEEN THE TWO COUNTRIES, DONE AT LONDON ON 25 NOVEMBER 1971[1]

The Federal Republic of Germany and the United Kingdom of Great Britain and Northern Ireland;

Desiring to establish the common boundary between their respective parts of the Continental Shelf under the North Sea;

---

[1] United Nations, *Treaty Series,* vol. 880, No. I-12626. Also BGBl 1972 II, p. 897.

Have agreed as follows:

Article 1

(1) The dividing line between that part of the Continental Shelf which appertains to the Federal Republic of Germany and that part which appertains to the United Kingdom of Great Britain and Northern Ireland shall be arcs of Great Circles between the following points in the sequence given below:

1. 55° 45' 54.0" N.   03° 22' 13.0" E.
2. 55° 50' 06.0" N.   03° 24' 00.0" E.
3. 55° 55' 09.4" N.   03° 21' 00.0" E.

The positions of the points in this article are defined by latitude and longitude on European Datum (1st Adjustment 1950).

(2) In the south the termination point of the dividing line shall be point No. 1, which is the point of intersection of the dividing lines between the Continental Shelves of the Federal Republic of Germany, the United Kingdom of Great Britain and Northern Ireland, and the Kingdom of the Netherlands.

(3) In the north the termination point of the dividing line shall be point No. 3, which is the point of intersection of the dividing lines between the Continental Shelves of the Federal Republic of Germany, the United Kingdom of Great Britain and Northern Ireland, and the Kingdom of Denmark.

(4) The dividing line has been drawn on the chart[1] annexed to this Agreement.

Article 2

Should any dispute arise concerning the position of any installation or other device or a well's intake in relation to the dividing line, the Contracting Parties shall in consultation determine on which side of the dividing line the installation or other device or the well's intake is situated.

Article 3

(1) If any single geological mineral oil or natural gas structure or field, or any single geological structure or field of any other mineral deposit extends across the dividing line and the part of such structure or field which is situated on one side of the dividing line is exploitable, wholly or in part, from the other side of the dividing line, the Contracting Parties shall seek to reach agreement as to the exploitation of such structure or field.

(2) In this Article the term "mineral" is used in its most general, extensive and comprehensive sense and includes all non-living substances occurring on, in or under the ground, irrespective of chemical or physical state.

---

[1] Not reproduced in this volume.

Article 4

Where a structure or field referred to in Article 3 of this Agreement is such that failure to reach agreement between the Contracting Parties would prevent maximum ultimate recovery of the deposit or lead to unnecessary competitive drilling, then any question upon which the Contracting Parties are unable to agree concerning the manner in which the structure or field shall be exploited or concerning the manner in which the costs and proceeds relating thereto shall be apportioned, shall, at the request of either Contracting Party, be referred to a single Arbitrator to be jointly appointed by the Contracting Parties. The decision of the Arbitrator shall be binding upon the Contracting Parties.

Article 5

This Agreement shall also apply to Land Berlin, provided that the Government of the Federal Republic of Germany has not made a contrary declaration to the Government of the United Kingdom within three months from the date of entry into force of this Agreement.

Article 6

(1) This Agreement shall be ratified. Instruments of ratification shall be exchanged at London as soon as possible.

(2) This Agreement shall enter into force on the 30th day after the exchange of instruments of ratification.

In witness whereof the Plenipotentiaries, duly authorised thereto, have signed this Agreement.

Done in duplicate at London this 25th day of November, 1971, in the German and English languages, both texts being equally authoritative.

4. AGREEMENT BETWEEN THAILAND AND INDONESIA RELATING TO THE DELIMITATION OF A CONTINENTAL SHELF BOUNDARY BETWEEN THE TWO COUNTRIES IN THE NORTHERN PART OF THE STRAITS OF MALACCA AND IN THE ANDAMAN SEA, DONE AT BANGKOK ON 17 DECEMBER 1971[1]

Article I

(1) The boundary between the continental shelves of Thailand and Indonesia in the northern part of the Straits of Malacca and in the Andaman Sea is the straight line drawn from a point whose co-ordinates are latitude 6° 21'.8 N. longitude 97° 54'.0 E. (hereinafter referred to as point 1) in a westerly direction to a point whose co-ordinates are latitude 7° 05'.8 N. longitude 96° 36'.5 E. (hereinafter referred to as point 2).

(2) The boundary line between point 1 and the Common Point specified in the Memorandum of Understanding signed at Bangkok on 15 October

---

[1] English text, which is authentic, provided by the Permanent Representative of Thailand to the United Nations in a note verbale of 15 November 1974.

1970 by the representatives of Indonesia, Malaysia and Thailand shall be formally included in a tripartite agreement to be concluded shortly among the three Governments.

(3) The co-ordinates of the points specified in paragraph (1), which are geographical co-ordinates, and the straight line connecting them are indicated on the chart attached as an Annex to this Agreement.

(4) The actual location of the above-mentioned points at sea shall, at the request of either Government, be determined by a method to be mutually agreed upon by the competent authorities of the two Governments.

(5) For the purpose of paragraph (4), the term "competent authorities" in relation to the Kingdom of Thailand refers to Chao Krom Uthoksat (Director of the Hydrographic Department) and includes any person authorized by him; and in relation to the Republic of Indonesia refers to Ketua Badan Koordinasi Survey dan Pemetaan Nasional (Chief of the Co-ordinating Body for National Survey and Mapping) and includes any person authorized by him.

Article II

If any single geological petroleum or natural gas structure extends across the straight line referred to in Article I and the part of such structure which is situated on one side of the said line is exploitable, wholly or in part, from the other side of the said line, the two Governments shall seek to reach agreement as to the manner in which the structure shall be most effectively exploited.

Article III

Any dispute between the two Governments arising out of the interpretation or implementation of this Agreement shall be settled peacefully by consultation or negotiation.

Article IV

This Agreement shall be ratified in accordance with the legal requirements of the two countries.

Article V

This Agreement shall enter into force on the date of the exchange of the Instruments of Ratification.

Done in duplicate at Bangkok, this seventeenth day of December, one thousand nine hundred and seventy one, in the Thai, Indonesian and English languages. In the event of any conflict between the texts, the English text shall prevail.

5. (i) AGREEMENT BETWEEN FINLAND AND SWEDEN CONCERNING THE DELIMITATION OF THE CONTINENTAL SHELF IN THE GULF OF BOTHNIA, THE ÅLAND SEA AND THE NORTHERN-MOST PART OF THE BALTIC SEA, DONE AT STOCKHOLM ON 29 SEPTEMBER 1972[1]

The Government of the Republic of Finland and the Government of the Kingdom of Sweden,

Having decided to establish the boundary between the areas of the continental shelf in the Gulf of Bothnia, the Åland Sea and the northernmost part of the Baltic Sea over which Finland and Sweden respectively exercise sovereign rights for the purposes of the exploration and utilization of natural resources,

Having regard to the provisions of the Geneva Convention of 1958 on the Continental Shelf,[2]

Have agreed as follows:

Article 1

The boundary between the areas of the continental shelf over which Finland and Sweden respectively exercise sovereign rights for the purposes of the exploration and utilization of natural resources shall in principle be a median line between the baselines from which the breadth of the territorial sea of each country is measured. Departures from this principle have, however, been made in order to take into account, as special circumstances within the meaning of the Geneva Convention, the boundary lines which were established, on the one hand, in the year 1811 in the topographic description of the frontier drawn up after the Peace of Fredrikshamn and, on the other hand, in the Convention of 20 October 1921 relating to the non-fortification and neutralization of the Åland Islands. In order to arrive at a practical and expedient delineation of the boundary, the boundary shall be drawn in the form of straight lines between the points which are specified in articles 2 to 4.

Article 2

The northern starting point of the boundary shall be the point where the outer boundary of the Swedish territorial sea meets the sea frontier between Finland and Sweden. The co-ordinates of the point are:

65° 31.8′ N.   24° 08.4′ E. (point 1)

---

[1] Entered into force on 15 January 1973 in accordance with article 7. Finnish and Swedish texts of the Agreement and the Protocol provided by the Permanent Representative of Finland in a note verbale of 30 November 1973. Translation by the Secretariat of the United Nations. Received for registration with the Secretariat on 20 May 1975.

[2] United Nations, *Treaty Series*, vol. 499, p. 311. Reproduced in ST/LEG/SER.B/15, pp. 767-770.

From this point the boundary coincides with the Finnish sea frontier to the point where the outer boundary of the Finnish territorial sea meets the sea frontier. The co-ordinates of the point are:

65° 30.9' N.   24° 08.2' E. (point 2)

Article 3

From point 2 the boundary passes through the following points:

63° 40.0' N.	21° 30.0' E. (point 3)
63° 31.3' N.	20° 56.4' E. (point 4)
63° 29.1' N.	20° 41.8' E. (point 5)
63° 20.0' N.	20° 24.0' E. (point 6)
62° 42.0' N.	19° 31.5' E. (point 7)
60° 40.7' N.	19° 14.1' E. (point 8)
60° 22.5' N.	19° 09.5' E. (point 9)
60° 22.3' N.	19° 09.5' E. (point 10)

Point 9 is the·point of intersection between the outer boundary of the Swedish territorial sea and the straight line between point 8 and Märket (point 16 in the 1921 Åland Convention).

From point 9 to point 10, the boundary coincides with the Swedish sea frontier. Point 10 is the point of intersection between the outer boundary of the Finnish territorial sea and the straight line between point 8 and Märket.

Article 4

South of point 10 the boundary resumes at the point where the territorial sea of Finland and that of Sweden cease to be contiguous. The co-ordinates of the point are:

60° 14.2' N.   19° 06.5' E. (point 11)

From point 11 the boundary coincides with the Finnish sea frontier to a point the co-ordinates of which are:

60° 13.0' N.   19° 06.0' E. (point 12)

From point 12 the boundary passes through the following points:

60° 11.5' N.	19° 05.2' E. (point 13)
59° 47.7' N.	19° 39.4' E. (point 14)
59° 47.5' N.	19° 39.7' E. (point 15)
59° 45.2' N.	19° 43.0' E. (point 16)
59° 26.7' N.	20° 09.4' E. (point 17)

Between points 14, 15 and 16 the boundary coincides with the Finnish sea frontier.

Article 5

Points 8, 13, 15 and 17 as defined in articles 3 and 4 are identical with points 17, 15, 14 and 13, respectively, in the 1921 Åland Convention.

Article 6

The positions of points 1 to 17 as defined in articles 2 to 4 are indicated on the three annexed Finnish charts, namely:

No. 3, scale 1: 350,000, edition 1969 II;

No. 5, scale 1: 350,000, edition 1971 II;

No. 904, scale 1: 200,000, edition 1971 III.

All the co-ordinates given in this Agreement correspond to the co-ordinate system of these charts.

Article 7

This Agreement shall be ràtified. The Agreement shall come into force when the two Governments have notified each other through an exchange of notes, which shall take place at Helsinki, that they have ratified the Agreement.

(ii) PROTOCOL, DATED 29 SEPTEMBER 1972

In connexion with the signing this day of the Agreement between Finland and Sweden concerning the delimitation of the continental shelf in the Gulf of Bothnia, the Åland Sea and the northernmost part of the Baltic Sea, the undersigned plenipotentiaries have agreed that if natural resources on the sea-bed or in the subsoil thereof extend on both sides of the boundary line defined in articles 2 to 4 of the Agreement and the natural resources situated in the area of the continental shelf belonging to one State can be exploited wholly or in part from the area belonging to the other State, both States shall at the request of either State enter into discussions on the most effective means of utilizing such natural resources and on the manner in which the proceeds are to be apportioned.

The plenipotentiaries have in addition agreed that the further extension of the boundary into the Baltic Sea will be taken up for discussion at a later time.

. . .

6. AGREEMENT BETWEEN THE GOVERNMENT OF THE COMMON-WEALTH OF AUSTRALIA AND THE GOVERNMENT OF THE REPUBLIC OF INDONESIA ESTABLISHING CERTAIN SEA-BED BOUNDARIES IN THE AREA OF THE TIMOR AND ARAFURA SEAS, SUPPLEMENTARY TO THE AGREEMENT OF 18 MAY 1971, DONE AT JAKARTA ON 9 OCTOBER 1972[1]

The Government of the Commonwealth of Australia, and the Government of the Republic of Indonesia,

Recalling the Agreement between the two Governments, signed on the eighteenth day of May One thousand nine hundred and seventy-one,

---

[1] Text provided by the Permanent Representative of Australia to the United Nations in a note verbale of 29 March 1973.

establishing sea-bed boundaries in the Arafura Sea and in certain areas off the coasts of the island of New Guinea (Irian),[1]

Recalling further that in the aforesaid Agreement the two Governments left for later discussion the question of the delimitation of the respective areas of adjacent sea-bed in the Arafura and Timor Seas westward of longitude 133 degrees 23′ east,

Resolving, as good neighbours and in a spirit of co-operation and friendship, to settle permanently the limits of the areas referred to in the preceding paragraph within which the respective Government shall exercise sovereign rights with respect to the exploration of the sea-bed and the exploitation of its natural resources,

Have agreed as follows:

Article 1

In the area to the south of the Tanimbar Islands, the boundary between the area of sea-bed that is adjacent to and appertains to the Commonwealth of Australia and the area of sea-bed that is adjacent to and appertains to the Republic of Indonesia shall be the straight lines shown on the chart annexed to this Agreement commencing at the point of latitude 8 degrees 53′ south, longitude 133 degrees 23′ east (point A12, specified in the Agreement between the two countries dated the eighteenth day of May One thousand nine hundred and seventy-one), thence connecting in a westerly direction the points specified hereunder in the sequence so specified:

A13. The point of latitude 8 degrees 54′ south, longitude 133 degrees 14′ east
A14. The point of latitude 9 degrees 25′ south, longitude 130 degrees 10′ east
A15. The point of latitude 9 degrees 25′ south, longitude 128 degrees 00′ east
A16. The point of latitude 9 degrees 28′ south, longitude 127 degrees 56′ east

Article 2

In the area south of Roti and Timor Islands, the boundary between the area of sea-bed that is adjacent to and appertains to the Commonwealth of Australia and the area of sea-bed that is adjacent to and appertains to the Republic of Indonesia shall be the straight lines, shown on the chart annexed to this Agreement commencing at the point of latitude 10 degrees 28′ south, longitude 126 degrees 00′ east (point A17), and thence connecting in a westerly direction the points specified hereunder in the sequence so specified:

A18. The point of latitude 10 degrees 37′ south, longitude 125 degrees 41′ east
A19. The point of latitude 11 degrees 01′ south, longitude 125 degrees 19′ east
A20. The point of latitude 11 degrees 07′ south, longitude 124 degrees 34′ east
A21. The point of latitude 11 degrees 25′ south, longitude 124 degrees 10′ east
A22. The point of latitude 11 degrees 26′ south, longitude 124 degrees 00′ east
A23. The point of latitude 11 degrees 28′ south, longitude 123 degrees 40′ east
A24. The point of latitude 11 degrees 23′ south, longitude 123 degrees 26′ east
A25. The point of latitude 11 degrees 35′ south, longitude 123 degrees 14′ east

---

[1] Reproduced *supra* 2.

Article 3

The lines between points A15 and A16 and between points A17 and A18 referred to in article 1 and article 2, respectively, indicate the direction of those portions of the boundary. In the event of any further delimitation agreement or agreements being concluded between Governments exercising sovereign rights with respect to the exploration of the sea-bed and the exploitation of its natural resources in the area of the Timor Sea, the Government of the Commonwealth of Australia and the Government of the Republic of Indonesia shall consult each other with a view to agreeing on such adjustment or adjustments, if any, as may be necessary in those portions of the boundary lines between points A15 and A16 and between points A17 and A18.

Article 4

The Government of the Commonwealth of Australia and the Government of the Republic of Indonesia mutually acknowledge the sovereign rights of the respective Governments in and over the sea-bed areas within the limits established by this Agreement and that they will cease to claim or to exercise sovereign rights with respect to the exploration of the sea-bed and the exploitation of its natural resources beyond the boundaries so established.

Article 5

For the purpose of this Agreement, "sea-bed" includes the subsoil thereof, except where the context otherwise requires.

Article 6

1. The co-ordinates of the points specified in articles 1 and 2 of this Agreement are geographical co-ordinates, and the actual location of these points and of the lines joining them shall be determined by a method to be agreed upon by the competent authorities of the two Governments.

2. For the purpose of paragraph 1 of this article, the competent authorities in relation to the Commonwealth of Australia shall be the Director of National Mapping and any person acting with his authority, and in relation to the Republic of Indonesia shall be the Chief of the Co-ordinating Body for National Survey and Mapping (Ketua Badan Koordinasi Survey dan Pemetaan Nasional) and any person acting with his authority.

Article 7

If any single accumulation of liquid hydrocarbons or natural gas, or if any other mineral deposit beneath the sea-bed, extends across any of the lines that are specified or described in articles 1 and 2 of this Agreement, and the part of such accumulation or deposit that is situated on one side of the line is recoverable in fluid form wholly or in part from the other side of the line, the two Governments will seek to reach agreement on the manner in which the accumulation or deposit shall be most effectively exploited and on the equitable sharing of the benefits arising from such exploitation.

Article 8

1. Where the Government of the Commonwealth of Australia has granted an exploration permit for petroleum or a production licence for petroleum under the Petroleum (Submerged Lands) Acts of the Commonwealth of Australia[1] over a part of the sea-bed over which that Government ceases to exercise sovereign rights by virtue of this Agreement, and that permit or licence is in force immediately prior to the entry into force of this Agreement, the Government of the Republic of Indonesia or its authorized agent shall, upon application by the registered holder of the permit or licence, or where there is more than one registered holder, by the registered holders acting jointly, be willing to offer and to negotiate a production sharing contract under Indonesian law to explore for and to produce oil and natural gas in respect of the same part of the sea-bed on terms that are not less favourable than those provided under Indonesian law in existing production sharing contracts in other parts of the sea-bed under Indonesian jurisdiction.

2. An application for negotiation in accordance with paragraph 1 of this article must be made by the registered holder or holders within nine months after the entry into force of this Agreement. If no application is made within this period, or if an offer made in accordance with paragraph 1 of this article is, after negotiation, not accepted by the permittee or licensee, the Government of the Republic of Indonesia shall have no further obligation to the registered holder or holders of a permit or licence to which paragraph 1 of this article applies.

3. For the purpose of this article, "registered holder" means a company that was a registered holder of an exploration permit for petroleum or a production licence for petroleum, as the case may be under the Petroleum (Submerged Lands) Acts of the Commonwealth of Australia immediately prior to the entry into force of this Agreement.

Article 9

Any dispute between the two Governments arising out of the interpretation or implementation of this Agreement shall be settled peacefully by consultation or negotiation.

Article 10

This Agreement is subject to ratification in accordance with the constitutional requirements of each country, and shall enter into force on the day on which the Instruments of Ratification are exchanged.

7. AGREEMENT BETWEEN AUSTRALIA AND INDONESIA CONCERNING CERTAIN BOUNDARIES BETWEEN PAPUA NEW GUINEA AND INDONESIA, DONE AT CANBERRA ON 26 JANUARY 1973[2]

Australia and Indonesia,

Recognizing the desirability of having boundaries of political and physical permanence between Papua New Guinea and Indonesia,

[1] Reproduced in part in ST/LEG/SER.B/15, pp. 319-335.

[2] Text provided by the Permanent Representative of Australia to the United Nations in a note verbale of 29 March 1973.

Considering the desirability of demarcating more precisely in certain respects the land boundaries on the island of New Guinea (Irian) as described in articles I, II, III and IV of the Convention between Great Britain and the Netherlands dated the sixteenth day of May One thousand eight hundred and ninety-five,

. . .

Recalling that in the Agreement between the Australian and Indonesian Governments dated the eighteenth day of May One thousand nine hundred and seventy-one (in this Agreement called "the 1971 Sea-bed Agreement")[1] the two Governments left for further discussion the question of the sea-bed boundary line between the point of Latitude 9° 24′ 30″ South, Longitude 140° 49′ 30″ East (Point B1 shown on the chart[2] annexed to this Agreement and on chart "A" annexed to the 1971 Sea-bed Agreement) and the point at which the land boundary between the Territory of Papua and West Irian meets the southern coast of the island of New Guinea (Irian),

As good neighbours and in a spirit of friendship and co-operation,

Have agreed as follows:

. . .

Article 3

Immediately off the southern coast of the island of New Guinea (Irian), the boundary between the area of sea-bed that is adjacent to and appertains to Papua New Guinea and the area that is adjacent to and appertains to Indonesia shall be the straight lines shown on the chart annexed to this Agreement commencing at the point of Latitude 9° 24′ 30″ South, Longitude 140° 49′ 30″ East (Point B1) and thence connecting the points specified hereunder in the sequence so specified:

B2. The point of Latitude 9° 23′ South, Longitude 140° 52′ East
B3. The point of Latitude 9° 08′ 08″ South, Longitude 141° 01′ 10″ East referred to in article 1 *(c)* of this Agreement.

Article 4

The point B3 referred to in articles 1 *(c)* and 3 of this Agreement is the present location of the point of intersection of the meridian of Longitude 141° 01′ 10″ East with the mean low water line on the southern coast of the island of New Guinea (Irian). If the point B3 ceases to be the point of such intersection the land boundary referred to in article 1 *(c)* and the sea-bed boundary referred to in article 3 shall meet and terminate at the point at which the straight lines connecting the points MM14, B3 and B2 shown on the chart annexed to this Agreement intersect the mean low water line on the southern coast.

Article 5

For the purpose of this Agreement "sea-bed" includes the subsoil thereof, except where the context otherwise requires.

---

[1] Reproduced *supra* 2.
[2] The chart is not reproduced in this volume.

Article 6

If any single accumulation of liquid hydrocarbons or natural gas, or if any other mineral deposit beneath the sea-bed, extends across any of the sea-bed boundary lines that are referred to in this Agreement, and the part of such accumulation or deposit that is situated on one side of the line is recoverable in fluid form wholly or in part from the other side of the line, the Governments of Australia and Indonesia will seek to reach agreement on the manner in which the accumulation or deposit shall be most effectively exploited and on the equitable sharing of the benefits arising from such exploitation.

Article 7

Off the northern and southern coasts of the island of New Guinea (Irian) the lateral boundaries of the respective territorial seas and exclusive fishing zones shall so far as they extend coincide with the sea-bed boundary lines referred to in article 3 of this Agreement and in article 4 of the 1971 Sea-bed Agreement.

Article 8

1. Vessels or other craft permitted by the laws of Papua New Guinea to navigate on that part of the Bensbach River flowing within Papua New Guinea shall for the purpose of entering or leaving the river have a right of passage through the adjacent Indonesian waters.

2. For the purpose of access to the mouth of the Bensbach River, the authorities of Papua New Guinea and Indonesia shall keep open and mark any channel that may be necessary for safe navigation.

Article 9

1. The co-ordinates of the points specified in this Agreement are geographical co-ordinates. The actual location of any points or lines referred to in this Agreement which have not yet been determined shall be determined by a method to be agreed upon by the competent authorities of the Government of Australia and the Government of Indonesia.

2. For the purpose of paragraph 1 of this article the competent authorities shall be the Director of National Mapping of Australia and any person acting with his authority and the Chief of the Co-ordinating Body for National Survey and Mapping (Ketua Badan Koordinasi Survey dan Pemetaan Nasional) of Indonesia and any person acting with his authority.

Article 10

Any dispute between the Governments of Australia and Indonesia arising out of the interpretation or implementation of this Agreement shall be settled peacefully in accordance with the procedures mentioned in Article 33 of the Charter of the United Nations.

Article 11

1. This Agreement is subject to ratification in accordance with the constitutional requirements of each country, and shall enter into force on the day on which the Instruments of Ratification are exchanged.

2. It is understood that the approval of the House of Assembly of Papua New Guinea to this Agreement shall be obtained before Australian ratification of the Agreement.

8. AGREEMENT BETWEEN CANADA AND DENMARK RELATING TO THE DELIMITATION OF THE CONTINENTAL SHELF BETWEEN GREENLAND AND CANADA, DONE AT OTTAWA ON 17 DECEMBER 1973[1]

The Government of Canada and the Government of the Kingdom of Denmark,

Having decided to establish in the area between Greenland and the Canadian Arctic Islands a dividing line beyond which neither Party in exercising its rights under the Convention on the Continental Shelf of 29 April 1958[2] will extend its sovereign rights for the purpose of exploration and exploitation of the natural resources of the continental shelf,

Have agreed as follows:

Article I

The dividing line in the area between Greenland and the Canadian Arctic Islands, established for the purpose of each Party's exploration and exploitation of the natural resources of that part of the continental shelf which in accordance with international law appertains to Denmark and to Canada respectively, is a median line which has been determined and adjusted by mutual agreement.

Article II

1. In implementation of the principle set forth in Article I, the dividing line in the area between latitude 61° 00′ N. and latitude 75° 00′ N. (Davis Strait and Baffin Bay) shall be a series of geodesic lines joining the following points:

Point No.	Latitude	Longitude
1	61° 00′ 0	57° 13′ 1
2	62° 00′ 5	57° 21′ 1
3	62° 02′ 3	57° 21′ 8
4	62° 03′ 5	57° 22′ 2
5	62° 11′ 5	57° 25′ 4

---

[1] In force on 13 March 1973 in accordance with article VII. Received for registration with the Secretariat on 6 September 1974.

[2] United Nations, *Treaty Series,* vol. 499, page 311, and document ST/LEG/SER.B/15, pp. 767-770.

448

Point No.	Latitude	Longitude
6	62° 47' 2	57° 41' 0
7	63° 22' 8	57° 57' 4
8	63° 28' 6	57° 59' 7
9	63° 35' 0	58° 02' 0
10	63° 37' 2	58° 01' 2
11	63° 44' 1	57° 58' 8
12	63° 50' 1	57° 57' 2
13	63° 52' 6	57° 56' 6
14	63° 57' 4	57° 53' 5
15	64° 04' 3	57° 49' 1
16	64° 12' 2	57° 48' 2
17	65° 06' 0	57° 44' 1
18	65° 08' 9	57° 43' 9
19	65° 11' 6	57° 44' 4
20	65° 14' 5	57° 45' 1
21	65° 18' 1	57° 45' 8
22	65° 23' 3	57° 44' 9
23	65° 34' 8	57° 42' 3
24	65° 37' 7	57° 41' 9
25	65° 50' 9	57° 40' 7
26	65° 51' 7	57° 40' 6
27	65° 57' 6	57° 40' 1
28	66° 03' 5	57° 39' 6
29	66° 12' 9	57° 38' 2
30	66° 18' 8	57° 37' 8
31	66° 24' 6	57° 37' 8
32	66° 30' 3	57° 38' 3
33	66° 36' 1	57° 39' 2
34	66° 37' 9	57° 39' 6
35	66° 41' 8	57° 40' 6
36	66° 49' 5	57° 43' 0
37	67° 21' 6	57° 52' 7
38	67° 27' 3	57° 54' 9
39	67° 28' 3	57° 55' 3
40	67° 29' 1	57° 56' 1
41	67° 30' 7	57° 57' 8
42	67° 35' 3	58° 02' 2
43	67° 39' 7	58° 06' 2
44	67° 44' 2	58° 09' 9
45	67° 56' 9	58° 19' 8
46	68° 01' 8	58° 23' 3
47	68° 04' 3	58° 25' 0
48	68° 06' 8	58° 26' 7
49	68° 07' 5	58° 27' 2
50	68° 16' 1	58° 34' 1
51	68° 21' 7	58° 39' 0
52	68° 25' 3	58° 42' 4
53	68° 32' 9	59° 01' 8
54	68° 34' 0	59° 04' 6
55	68° 37' 9	59° 14' 3
56	68° 38' 0	59° 14' 6
57	68° 56' 8	60° 02' 4
58	69° 00' 8	60° 09' 0
59	69° 06' 8	60° 18' 5

Point No.	Latitude	Longitude
60	69° 10' 3	60° 23' 8
61	69° 12' 8	60° 27' 5
62	69° 29' 4	60° 51' 6
63	69° 49' 8	60° 58' 2
64	69° 55' 3	60° 59' 6
65	69° 55' 8	61° 00' 0
66	70° 01' 6	61° 04' 2
67	70° 07' 5	61° 08' 1
68	70° 08' 8	61° 08' 8
69	70° 13' 4	61° 10' 6
70	70° 33' 1	61° 17' 4
71	70° 35' 6	61° 20' 6
72	70° 48' 2	61° 37' 9
73	70° 51' 8	61° 42' 7
74	71° 12' 1	62° 09' 1
75	71° 18' 9	62° 17' 5
76	71° 25' 9	62° 25' 5
77	71° 29' 4	62° 29' 3
78	71° 31' 8	62° 32' 0
79	71° 32' 9	62° 33' 5
80	71° 44' 7	62° 49' 6
81	71° 47' 3	62° 53' 1
82	71° 52' 9	63° 03' 9
83	72° 01' 7	63° 21' 1
84	72° 06' 4	63° 30' 9
85	72° 11' 0	63° 41' 0
86	72° 24' 8	64° 13' 2
87	72° 30' 5	64° 26' 1
88	72° 36' 3	64° 38' 8
89	72° 43' 7	64° 54' 3
90	72° 45' 7	64° 58' 4
91	72° 47' 7	65° 00' 9
92	72° 50' 8	65° 07' 6
93	73° 18' 5	66° 08' 3
94	73° 25' 9	66° 25' 3
95	73° 31' 1	67° 15' 1
96	73° 36' 5	68° 05' 5
97	73° 37' 9	68° 12' 3
98	73° 41' 7	68° 29' 4
99	73° 46' 1	68° 48' 5
100	73° 46' 7	68° 51' 1
101	73° 52' 3	69° 11' 3
102	73° 57' 6	69° 31' 5
103	74° 02' 2	69° 50' 3
104	74° 02' 6	69° 52' 0
105	74° 06' 1	70° 06' 6
106	74° 07' 5	70° 12' 5
107	74° 10' 0	70° 23' 1
108	74° 12' 5	70° 33' 7
109	74° 24' 0	71° 25' 7
110	74° 28' 6	71° 45' 8
111	74° 44' 2	72° 53' 0
112	74° 50' 6	73° 02' 8
113	75° 00' 0	73° 16' 3

The positions of the above mentioned points have been computed from straight baselines along the coast of the Canadian Arctic Islands and of Greenland.

This part of the dividing line is illustrated on the chart attached to this Agreement as Annex I.[1]

2. In *Nares Strait* the dividing line shall be two series of geodesic lines joining the following points:

	Point No.	Latitude	Longitude
Series A:	114	76° 41' 4	75° 00' 0
	115	77° 30' 0	74° 46' 0
	116	78° 25' 0	73° 46' 0
	117	78° 48' 5	73° 00' 0
	118	79° 39' 0	69° 20' 0
	119	80° 00' 0	69° 00' 0
	120	80° 25' 0	68° 20' 0
	121	80° 45' 0	67° 07' 0
	122	80° 49' 2	66° 29' 0
Series B:	123	80° 49' 8	66° 26' 3
	124	80° 50' 5	66° 16' 0
	125	81° 18' 2	64° 11' 0
	126	81° 52' 0	62° 10' 0
	127	82° 13' 0	60° 00' 0

The positions of the above mentioned points are defined by latitude and longitude on Canadian Hydrographic Service Charts 7071 of 31 July 1964 and 7072 of 30 April 1971.

This part of the dividing line has been drawn on the charts attached to this Agreement as Annexes 2 and 3.[1]

3. That portion of the dividing line joining point 113 to point 114 is a geodesic line.

4. For the time being the Parties have not deemed it necessary to draw the dividing line further north than point No. 127 or further south than point No. 1. The dividing line is illustrated on the plan attached to this Agreement as Annex 4.[1]

Article III

In view of the inadequacies of existing hydrographic charts for certain areas and failing a precise determination of the low-water line in all sectors along the coast of Greenland and the eastern coasts of the Canadian Arctic Islands, neither Party shall issue licences for exploitation of mineral resources in areas bordering the dividing line without the prior agreement of the other Party as to the exact determination of the geographic co-ordinates of points of that part of the dividing line bordering upon the areas in question.

---

[1] Not reproduced in this volume.

Article IV

1. The Parties undertake to co-operate and to exchange all relevant data and measurements with a view to obtaining and improving the hydrographic and geodetic knowledge necessary for more precise charting and mapping of the region covered by this Agreement. When knowledge is obtained enabling the Parties to estimate the datum shift between the 1927 North American Datum and the Qornoq Datum, the geographic co-ordinates of points listed in Article II shall be adjusted and re-listed in relation to both the 1927 North American Datum and the Qornoq Datum.

2. If new surveys or resulting charts or maps should indicate that the dividing line requires adjustment, the Parties agree that an adjustment will be carried out on the basis of the same principles as those used in determining the dividing line, and such adjustment shall be provided for in a Protocol to this Agreement.

Article V

If any single geological petroleum structure or field, or any single geological structure or field of any other mineral deposit, including sand and gravel, extends across the dividing line and the part of such structure or field which is situated on one side of the dividing line, the Parties shall seek to reach an agreement as to the exploitation of such structure or field.

Article VI

Should international law concerning the delimitation of national jurisdiction over the continental shelf be altered in a manner acceptable to both Parties which could have an effect upon the dividing line in the area between 67° and 69° North latitude, each of the Parties shall waive jurisdiction over any part of the continental shelf which appertains to the other Party on the basis of the new agreed rules of international law concerning the delimitation of national jurisdiction over the continental shelf.

Article VII

1. This Agreement is subject to ratification. Instruments of ratification shall be exchanged at Copenhagen as soon as possible.

2. This Agreement shall enter into force on the date of the exchange of instruments of ratification.

In witness whereof the undersigned, duly authorized for this purpose by their respective Governments, have signed the present Agreement and affixed thereto their seals.

Done in two copies at Ottawa in the English, French and Danish languages, each version being equally authentic, this 17th day of December, 1973.

9. AGREEMENT BETWEEN SUDAN AND SAUDI ARABIA RELATING
TO THE JOINT EXPLOITATION OF THE NATURAL RESOURCES OF
THE SEA-BED AND SUB-SOIL OF THE RED SEA IN THE COMMON
ZONE, DONE AT KHARTOUM ON 16 MAY 1974[1]

Article I

For the purposes of the present Agreement the following expressions shall
have the meanings hereunder assigned to them:

(1) "Sea-bed" includes the sea-bed and sub-soil of the Red Sea.

(2) "Natural resources" comprise the non-living substances including the
hydrocarbon and the mineral resources.

(3) "Territorial Sea" means the Territorial Sea as defined in the laws of
the two Governments.

(4) "The Competent Minister" means the Minister appointed by the
Government of the Kingdom of Saudi Arabia and the Minister appointed by
the Government of the Democratic Republic of the Sudan to represent each
of them in the Joint Commission.

Article II

The two Governments covenant to co-operate through all ways and means
to explore and exploit the natural resources of the sea-bed of the Red Sea.

Article III

The Government of the Kingdom of Saudi Arabia recognizes that the
Government of the Democratic Republic of the Sudan has exclusive sovereign
rights in the area of the sea-bed adjacent to the Sudanese Coast and extending
eastwards to a line where the depth of the superjacent waters is uninterruptedly one thousand meters. The Government of the Kingdom of Saudi
Arabia claims no rights in this area.

Article IV

The Government of the Democratic Republic of the Sudan recognizes
that the Government of the Kingdom of Saudi Arabia has exclusive sovereign
rights in the area of the sea-bed adjacent to the Saudi Arabian Coast and
extending westwards to a line where the depth of the superjacent waters is
uninterruptedly one thousand meters. The Government of the Democratic
Republic of the Sudan claims no rights in this area.

Article V

The two Governments recognize that the area of the sea-bed lying
between the two areas defined in Articles III and IV above is common to
both Governments and shall hereafter be known as the Common Zone. The

---

[1] Entered into force on 26 August 1974 in accordance with article XVII. English
text provided by the Permanent Representative of Sudan to the United Nations in a
letter dated 29 October 1974. Received for registration with the Secretariat on 31
October 1974.

two Governments have equal sovereign rights in all the natural resources of the Common Zone which rights are exclusive to them. No part of the territorial sea of either Government shall be included in the Common Zone.

Article VI

The two Governments confirm that their equal sovereign rights in the Common Zone embrace all the natural resources therein and that they alone have the right to exploit such resources. The two Governments undertake to protect their sovereign rights and defend them against third parties.

Article VII

To ensure the prompt and efficient exploitation of the natural resources of the Common Zone there shall be established a Commission referred to hereafter as the Joint Commission. The Joint Commission shall be charged with the following functions:

(a) To survey, delimit and demarcate the boundaries of the Common Zone.

(b) To undertake the studies concerning the exploration and the exploitation of the natural resources of the Common Zone.

(c) To encourage the specialized bodies to undertake operations for the exploration of the natural resources of the Common Zone.

(d) To consider and decide, in accordance with the conditions it prescribes, on the applications for licences and concessions concerning exploration and exploitation.

(e) To take the steps necessary to expedite the exploitation of the natural resources of the sea-bed in the Common Zone.

(f) To organize the supervision of the exploitation at the production stage.

(g) To make such regulations as may be necessary for the discharge of the functions assigned to it.

(h) To prepare the estimates for all the expenses of the Joint Commission.

(i) To undertake any other functions or duties that may be entrusted to it by the two Governments.

Article VIII

The Joint Commission established under Article VII of this Agreement shall be a body corporate enjoying in the Kingdom of Saudi Arabia and the Democratic Republic of the Sudan such legal capacity as may be necessary for the exercise of all the functions assigned to it.

Article IX

The Joint Commission shall consist of an equal number of representatives from each of the two Countries and each side in the Joint Commission shall be headed by the competent Minister. The Regulations shall lay down the Joint Commission's rules of procedure.

454

Article X

The Joint Commission shall have a sufficient number of officials. The Joint Commission shall determine their number and terms of service.

Article XI

The seat of the Joint Commission shall be the city of Jeddah in the Kingdom of Saudi Arabia. The Joint Commission may, however, hold meetings at any other place it decides upon.

Article XII

The Government of the Kingdom of Saudi Arabia shall provide such funds as would enable the Joint Commission to discharge effectively the functions entrusted to it. The Government of the Kingdom of Saudi Arabia shall recover such funds from the returns of the production of the Common Zone and in a manner to be agreed upon between the two countries.

Article XIII

Whereas the Government of the Democratic Republic of the Sudan has concluded on 15 May 1973 an Agreement whereby it has given exploration licences to Sudanese Minerals Limited and the West German Company of Preussag which Agreement has created legal obligations on the Government of the Democratic Republic of the Sudan, the two Governments have agreed that the Joint Commission shall decide on this matter in such a manner as to preserve the rights of the Government of the Democratic Republic of the Sudan and in the context of the regime established by this Agreement for the Common Zone.

Article XIV

In the event that any accumulation or deposit of a natural resource extends across the boundary of the exclusive sovereign rights area of either Government and the Common Zone, the Joint Commission shall determine the manner in which it is to be exploited provided that any decision taken shall guarantee for the Government involved an equitable share in the proceeds of the exploitation of such accumulation or deposit.

Article XV

The application of this Agreement shall not affect the status of the high seas or obstruct navigation therein within the limits provided for by the established rules of public international law.

Article XVI

If a dispute arises respecting the interpretation or implementation of this Agreement or the rights and obligations it creates, the two Governments shall seek to settle such dispute by amicable means.

If the settlement of the dispute through amicable means fails, the dispute shall be submitted to the International Court of Justice. The parties accept the compulsory jurisdiction of the International Court of Justice in this respect.

If one of the two Governments takes a measure which is objected to by the other, the objecting Government may ask the International Court of Justice to indicate interim measures to be taken to stop the measure objected to or to allow its continuance pending the final decision.

Article XVII

This Agreement is subject to ratification in accordance with the constitutional requirements of each Government and shall enter into force on the day on which the instruments of ratification are exchanged.

Division III

THE HIGH SEAS[1]

Subdivision A. Multilateral Treaties

1. PROTOCOL RELATING TO INTERVENTION ON THE HIGH SEAS IN CASES OF MARINE POLLUTION BY SUBSTANCES OTHER THAN OIL, DONE AT LONDON ON 2 NOVEMBER 1973[2]

The Parties to the present Protocol,

Being Parties to the International Convention relating to Intervention on the High Seas in Cases of Oil Pollution Casualties done at Brussels on 29 November 1969,[3]

Taking into account the resolution on International Co-operation concerning Pollutants other than oil adopted by the International Legal Conference on Marine Pollution Damage, 1969,[4]

Further taking into account that pursuant to the resolution, the Inter-Governmental Maritime Consultative Organization has intensified its work, in collaboration with all interested international organizations, on all aspects of pollution by substances other than oil,

Have agreed as follows:

Article I

1. Parties to the present Protocol may take such measures on the high seas as may be necessary to prevent, mitigate or eliminate grave and imminent danger to their coastline or related interests from pollution or threat of pollution by substances other than oil following upon a maritime casualty or acts related to such a casualty, which may reasonably be expected to result in major harmful consequences.

---

[1] Some of the texts reproduced under Divisions II and IV may also cover questions concerning the high seas.

[2] Text provided by the Permanent Representative of the United Kingdom to the United Nations in a note verbale of 12 December 1974 as well as by the Ministry of Foreign Affairs of Denmark in a note verbale of 20 December 1974.

[3] Reproduced in ST/LEG/SER.B/16, pp. 439-447.

[4] Official Records of the International Legal Conference on Marine Pollution Damage, 1969. London, IMCO, Publication No. 1973.7 (E), page 184.

2. "Substances other than oil" as referred to in paragraph 1 shall be:

(a) Those substances enumerated in a list which shall be established by an appropriate body designated by the Organization and which shall be annexed to the present Protocol; and

(b) Those other substances which are liable to create hazards to human health, to harm living resources and marine life, to damage amenities or to interfere with other legitimate uses of the sea.

3. Whenever an intervening Party takes action with regard to a substance referred to in paragraph 2 *(b)* that Party shall have the burden of establishing that the substance under the circumstances present at the time of the intervention could reasonably pose a grave and imminent danger analogous to that posed by any of the substances enumerated in the list referred to in paragraph 2 *(a)*.

Article II

1. The provisions of paragraph 2 of Article I and Articles II to VIII of the Convention Relating to Intervention on the High Seas in Cases of Oil Pollution Casualties, 1969 and the Annex thereto as they relate to oil shall be applicable with regard to the substances referred to in Article I of the present Protocol.

2. For the purpose of the present Protocol the list of experts referred to in Articles III *(c)* and IV of the Convention shall be extended to include experts qualified to give advice in relation to substances other than oil. Nominations to the list may be made by Member States of the Organization and by Parties to the present Protocol.

Article III

1. The list referred to in paragraph 2 *(a)* of Article I shall be maintained by the appropriate body designated by the Organization.

2. Any amendment to the list proposed by a Party to the present Protocol shall be submitted to the Organization and circulated by it to all Members of the Organization and all Parties to the present Protocol at least three months prior to its consideration by the appropriate body.

3. Parties to the present Protocol whether or not Members of the Organization shall be entitled to participate in the proceedings of the appropriate body.

4. Amendments shall be adopted by a two-thirds majority of only the Parties to the present Protocol present and voting.

5. If adopted in accordance with paragraph 4 above, the amendment shall be communicated by the Organization to all Parties to the present Protocol for acceptance.

6. The amendment shall be deemed to have been accepted at the end of a period of six months after it has been communicated, unless within that period an objection to the amendment has been communicated to the Organization by not less than one-third of the Parties to the present Protocol.

7. An amendment deemed to have been accepted in accordance with paragraph 6 above shall enter into force three months after its acceptance for all Parties to the present Protocol, with the exception of those which before that date have made a declaration of non-acceptance of the said amendment.

Article IV

1. The present Protocol shall be open for signature by the States which have signed the Convention referred to in Article II or acceded thereto, and by any State invited to be represented at the International Conference on Marine Pollution 1973. The Protocol shall remain open for signature from 15 January 1974 until 31 December 1974 at the Headquarters of the Organization.

2. Subject to paragraph 4, the present Protocol shall be subject to ratification, acceptance or approval by the States which have signed it.

3. Subject to paragraph 4, this Protocol shall be open for accession by States which did not sign it.

4. The present Protocol may be ratified, accepted, approved or acceded to only by States which have ratified, accepted, approved or acceded to the Convention referred to in Article II.

Article V

1. Ratification, acceptance, approval or accession shall be effected by the deposit of a formal instrument to that effect with the Secretary-General of the Organization.

2. Any instrument of ratification, acceptance, approval or accession deposited after the entry into force of an amendment to the present Protocol with respect to all existing Parties or after the completion of all measures required for the entry into force of the amendment with respect to all existing Parties shall be deemed to apply to the Protocol as modified by the amendment.

Article VI

1. The present Protocol shall enter into force on the ninetieth day following the date on which fifteen States have deposited instruments of ratification, acceptance, approval or accession with the Secretary-General of the Organization, provided however that the present Protocol shall not enter into force before the Convention referred to in Article II has entered into force.

2. For each State which subsequently ratifies, accepts, approves or accedes to it, the present Protocol shall enter into force on the ninetieth day after the deposit by such State of the appropriate instrument.

Article VII

1. The present Protocol may be denounced by any Party at any time after the date on which the Protocol enters into force for that Party.

2.   Denunciation shall be effected by the deposit of an instrument to that effect with the Secretary-General of the Organization.

3.   Denunciation shall take effect one year, or such longer period as may be specified in the instrument of denunciation, after its deposit with the Secretary-General of the Organization.

4.   Denunciation of the Convention referred to in Article II by a Party shall be deemed to be a denunciation of the present Protocol by that Party. Such denunciation shall take effect on the same day as the denunciation of the Convention takes effect in accordance with paragraph 3 of Article XII of that Convention.

Article VIII

1.   A conference for the purpose of revising or amending the present Protocol may be convened by the Organization.

2.   The Organization shall convene a conference of Parties to the present Protocol for the purpose of revising or amending it at the request of not less than one-third of the Parties.

Article IX

1.   The present Protocol shall be deposited with the Secretary-General of the Organization.

2.   The Secretary-General of the Organization shall:

(a) Inform all States which have signed the present Protocol or acceded thereto of:

   (i) Each new signature or deposit of an instrument together with the date thereof;

   (ii) The date of entry into force of the present Protocol;

   (iii) The deposit of any instrument of denunciation of the present Protocol together with the date on which the denunciation takes effect;

   (iv) Any amendments to the present Protocol or its Annex and any objection or declaration of non-acceptance of the said amendment;

(b) Transmit certified true copies of the present Protocol to all States which have signed the present Protocol or acceded thereto.

Article X

As soon as the present Protocol enters into force, a certified true copy thereof shall be transmitted by the Secretary-General of the Organization to the Secretariat of the United Nations for registration and publication in accordance with Article 102 of the Charter of the United Nations.

Article XI

The present Protocol is established in a single original in the English, French, Russian and Spanish languages, all four texts being equally authentic.

2. INTERNATIONAL CONVENTION FOR THE PREVENTION OF POL-LUTION FROM SHIPS, 1973 (WITH PROTOCOLS I AND II), DONE AT LONDON ON 2 NOVEMBER 1973[1]

The Parties to the Convention,

Being conscious of the need to preserve the human environment in general and the marine environment in particular,

Recognizing that deliberate, negligent or accidental release of oil and other harmful substances from ships constitutes a serious source of pollution,

Recognizing also the importance of the International Convention for the Prevention of Pollution of the Sea by Oil, 1954,[2] as being the first multilateral instrument to be concluded with the prime objective of protecting the environment, and appreciating the significant contribution which that Convention has made in preserving the seas and coastal environment from pollution,

Desiring to achieve the complete elimination of international pollution of the marine environment by oil and other harmful substances and the minimization of accidental discharge of such substances,

Considering that this object may best be achieved by establishing rules not limited to oil pollution having a universal purport,

Have agreed as follows:

Article 1

General Obligations under the Convention

(1) The Parties to the Convention undertake to give effect to the provisions of the present Convention and those Annexes thereto by which they are bound, in order to prevent the pollution of the marine environment by the discharge of harmful substances or effluents containing such substances in contravention of the Convention.

(2) Unless expressly provided otherwise, a reference to the present Convention constitutes at the same time a reference to its Protocols and to the Annexes.

Article 2

Definitions

For the purposes of the present Convention, unless expressly provided otherwise:

(1) "Regulations" means the Regulations contained in the Annexes to the present Convention.

---

[1] Text provided by the Permanent Representative of the United Kingdom to the United Nations in a note verbale of 12 December 1974 as well as by the Ministry of Foreign Affairs of Denmark in a note verbale of 20 December 1974.

[2] United Nations, *Treaty Series*, vol. 327, page 3, and ST/LEG/SER.B/15, pp. 787-799.

462

(2) "Harmful substance" means any substance which, if introduced into the sea, is liable to create hazards to human health, to harm living resources and marine life, to damage amenities or to interfere with other legitimate uses of the sea, and includes any substance subject to control by the present Convention.

(3) *(a)* "Discharge", in relation to harmful substances or effluents containing such substances, means any release howsoever caused from a ship and includes any escape, disposal, spilling, leaking, pumping, emitting or emptying.

(b) "Discharge" does not include:

(i) Dumping within the meaning of the Convention on the Prevention of Marine Pollution by Dumping of Wastes and Other Matter done at London on 29 December 1972;[1] or

(ii) Release of harmful substances directly arising from the exploration, exploitation and associated off-shore processing of sea-bed mineral resources; or

(iii) Release of harmful subtances for purposes of legitimate scientific research into pollution abatement or control.

(4) "Ship" means a vessel of any type whatsoever operating in the marine environment and includes hydrofoil boats, air-cushion vehicles, submersibles, floating craft and fixed or floating platforms.

(5) "Administration" means the Government of the State under whose authority the ship is operating. With respect to a ship entitled to fly a flag of any State, the Administration is the Government of that State. With respect to fixed or floating platforms engaged in exploration and exploitation of the sea-bed and subsoil thereof adjacent to the coast over which the coastal State exercises sovereign rights for the purposes of exploration and exploitation of their natural resources, the Administration is the Government of the coastal State concerned.

(6) "Incident" means an event involving the actual or probable discharge into the sea of a harmful substance, or effluents containing such a substance.

(7) "Organization" means the Inter-Governmental Maritime Consultative Organization.

Article 3

Application

(1) The present Convention shall apply to:

(a) Ships entitled to fly the flag of a Party to the Convention; and

(b) Ships not entitled to fly the flag of a Party but which operate under the authority of a Party.

(2) Nothing in the present Article shall be construed as derogating from or extending the sovereign rights of the Parties under international law over the sea-bed and subsoil thereof adjacent to their coasts for the purposes of exploration and exploitation of their natural resources.

---

[1] Reproduced in ST/LEG/SER.B/16, pages 464-474.

(3) The present Convention shall not apply to any warship, naval auxiliary or other ship owned or operated by a State and used, for the time being, only on government non-commercial service. However, each Party shall ensure by the adoption of appropriate measures not impairing the operations or operational capabilities of such ships owned or operated by it, that such ships act in a manner consistent, so far as is reasonable and practicable, with the present Convention.

Article 4

Violation

(1) Any violation of the requirements of the present Convention shall be prohibited and sanctions shall be established therefor under the law of the Administration of the ship concerned wherever the violation occurs. If the Administration is informed of such a violation and is satisfied that sufficient evidence is available to enable proceedings to be brought in respect of the alleged violation, it shall cause such proceedings to be taken as soon as possible, in accordance with its law.

(2) Any violation of the requirements of the present Convention within the jurisdiction of any Party to the Convention shall be prohibited and sanctions shall be established therefor under the law of that Party. Whenever such a violation occurs, that Party shall either:

(a) Cause proceedings to be taken in accordance with its law; or

(b) Furnish to the Administration of the ship such information and evidence as may be in its possession that a violation has occurred.

(3) Where information or evidence with respect to any violation of the present Convention by a ship is furnished to the Administration of that ship, the Administration shall promptly inform the Party which has furnished the information or evidence, and the Organization, of the action taken.

(4) The penalties specified under the law of a Party pursuant to the present Article shall be adequate in severity to discourage violations of the present Convention and shall be equally severe irrespective of where the violations occur.

Article 5

Certificates and Special Rules on Inspection of Ships

(1) Subject to the provisions of paragraph (2) of the present Article a certificate issued under the authority of a Party to the Convention in accordance with the provisions of the Regulations shall be accepted by the other parties and regarded for all purposes covered by the present Convention as having the same validity as a certificate issued by them.

(2) A ship required to hold a certificate in accordance with the provisions of the Regulations is subject while in the ports or off-shore terminals under the jurisdiction of a Party to inspection by officers duly authorized by that Party. Any such inspection shall be limited to verifying that there is on board a valid certificate, unless there are clear grounds for believing that the condition of the ship or its equipment does not correspond substantially with

the particulars of that certificate. In that case, or if the ship does not carry a valid certificate, the Party carrying out the inspection shall take such steps as will ensure that the ship shall not sail until it can proceed to sea without presenting an unreasonable threat of harm to the marine environment. That Party may, however, grant such a ship permission to leave the port or off-shore terminal for the purpose of proceeding to the nearest appropriate repair yard available.

(3) If a Party denies a foreign ship entry to the ports or off-shore terminals under its jurisdiction or takes any action against such a ship for the reason that the ship does not comply with the provisions of the present Convention, the Party shall immediately inform the consul or diplomatic representative of the Party whose flag the ship is entitled to fly, or if this is not possible, the Administration of the ship concerned. Before denying entry or taking such action the Party may request consultation with the Administration of the ship concerned. Information shall also be given to the Administration when a ship does not carry a valid certificate in accordance with the provisions of the Regulations.

(4) With respect to the ships of non-Parties to the Convention, Parties shall apply the requirements of the present Convention as may be necessary to ensure that no more favourable treatment is given to such ships.

Article 6

Detection of Violations and Enforcement of the Convention

(1) Parties to the Convention shall co-operate in the detection of violations and the enforcement of the provisions of the present Convention, using all appropriate and practicable measures of detection and environmental monitoring, adequate procedures for reporting and accumulation of evidence.

(2) A ship to which the present Convention applies may in any port or off-shore terminal of a Party, be subject to inspection by officers appointed or authorized by that Party for the purpose of verifying whether the ship has discharged any harmful substances in violation of the provisions of the Regulations. If an inspection indicates a violation of the Convention, a report shall be forwarded to the Administration for any appropriate action.

(3) Any Party shall furnish to the Administration evidence, if any, that the ship has discharged harmful substances or effluents containing such substances in violation of the provisions of the Regulations. If it is practicable to do so, the competent authority of the former Party shall notify the master of the ship of the alleged violation.

(4) Upon receiving such evidence, the Administration so informed shall investigate the matter, and may request the other Party to furnish further or better evidence of the alleged contravention. If the Administration is satisfied that sufficient evidence is available to enable proceedings to be brought in respect of the alleged violation, it shall cause such proceedings to be taken in accordance with its law as soon as possible. The Administration shall promptly inform the Party which has reported the alleged violation, as well as the Organization, of the action taken.

(5) A Party may also inspect a ship to which the present Convention applies when it enters the ports or off-shore terminals under its jurisdiction, if a request for an investigation is received from any Party together with sufficient evidence that the ship has discharged harmful substances or effluents containing such substances in any place. The report of such investigation shall be sent to the Party requesting it and to the Administration so that the appropriate action may be taken under the present Convention.

Article 7

Undue Delay to Ships

(1) All possible efforts shall be made to avoid a ship being unduly detained or delayed under Articles 4, 5 and 6 of the present Convention.

(2) When a ship is unduly detained or delayed under Articles 4, 5 and 6 of the present Convention, it shall be entitled to compensation for any loss or damage suffered.

Article 8

Reports on Incidents Involving Harmful Substances

(1) A report of an incident shall be made without delay to the fullest extent possible in accordance with the provisions of Protocol I to the present Convention.

(2) Each Party to the Convention shall:

(a) Make all arrangements necessary for an appropriate officer or agency to receive and process all reports on incidents; and

(b) Notify the Organization with complete details of such arrangements for circulation to other Parties and Member States of the Organization.

(3) Whenever a Party receives a report under the provisions of the present Article, that Party shall relay the report without delay to:

(a) The Administration of the ship involved; and

(b) Any other State which may be affected.

(4) Each Party to the Convention undertakes to issue instructions to its maritime inspection vessels and aircraft and to other appropriate services, to report to its authorities any incident referred to in Protocol I to the present Convention. That Party shall, if it considers it appropriate, report accordingly to the Organization and to any other party concerned.

Article 9

Other Treaties and Interpretation

(1) Upon its entry into force, the present Convention supersedes the International Convention for the Prevention of Pollution of the Sea by Oil, 1954, as amended,[1] as between Parties to that Convention.

---

[1] United Nations, *Treaty Series*, vol. 327, p. 3; also ST/LEG/SER.B/15, pp. 787-799.

(2) Nothing in the present Convention shall prejudice the codification and development of the law of the sea by the United Nations Conference on the Law of the Sea convened pursuant to resolution 2750 C (XXV) of the General Assembly of the United Nations nor the present or future claims and legal views of any State concerning the law of the sea and the nature and extent of coastal and flag State jurisdiction.

(3) The term "jurisdiction" in the present Convention shall be construed in the light of international law in force at the time of application or interpretation of the present Convention.

Article 10

Settlement of Disputes

Any dispute between two or more Parties to the Convention concerning the interpretation or application of the present Convention shall, if settlement by negotiation between the Parties involved has not been possible, and if these Parties do not otherwise agree, be submitted upon request of any of them to arbitration as set out in Protocol II to the present Convention.

Article 11

Communication of Information

(1) The Parties to the Convention undertake to communicate to the Organization:

(a) The text of laws, orders, decrees and regulations and other instruments which have been promulgated on the various matters within the scope of the present Convention;

(b) A list of non-governmental agencies which are authorized to act on their behalf in matters relating to the design, construction and equipment of ships carrying harmful substances in accordance with the provisions of the Regulations;

(c) A sufficient number of specimens of their certificates issued under the provisions of the Regulations;

(d) A list of reception facilities including their location, capacity and available facilities and other characteristics;

(e) Official reports or summaries of official reports in so far as they show the results of the application of the present Convention; and

(f) An annual statistical report, in a form standardized by the Organization, of penalties actually imposed for infringement of the present Convention.

(2) The Organization shall notify Parties of the receipt of any communications under the present Article and circulate to all Parties any information communicated to it under subparagraphs (1) *(b)* to *(f)* of the present Article.

Article 12

Casualties to Ships

(1) Each Administration undertakes to conduct an investigation of any casualty occurring to any of its ships subject to the provisions of the Regulations if such casualty has produced a major deleterious effect upon the marine environment.

(2) Each Party to the Convention undertakes to supply the Organization with information concerning the findings of such investigation, when it judges that such information may assist in determining what changes in the present convention might be desirable.

Article 13

Signature, Ratification, Acceptance, Approval and Accession

(1) The present Convention shall remain open for signature at the Headquarters of the Organization from 15 January 1974 until 31 December 1974 and shall thereafter remain open for accession. States may become Parties to the present Convention by:

(a) Signature without reservation as to ratification, acceptance or approval; or

(b) Signature subject to ratification, acceptance or approval, followed by ratification, acceptance or approval; or

(c) Accession.

(2) Ratification, acceptance, approval or accession shall be effected by the deposit of an instrument to that effect with the Secretary-General of the Organization.

(3) The Secretary-General of the Organization shall inform all States which have signed the present Convention or acceded to it of any signature or of the deposit of any new instrument of ratification, acceptance, approval or accession and the date of its deposit.

Article 14

Optional Annexes

(1) A State may at the time of signing, ratifying, accepting, approving or acceding to the present Convention declare that it does not accept any one or all of Annexes III, IV and V (hereinafter referred to as "Optional Annexes") of the present Convention. Subject to the above, Parties to the Convention shall be bound by any Annex in its entirety.

(2) A State which has declared that it is not bound by an Optional Annex may at any time accept such Annex by depositing with the Organization an instrument of the kind referred to in Article 13 (2).

(3) A State which makes a declaration under paragraph (1) of the present Article in respect of an Optional Annex and which has not subsequently accepted that Annex in accordance with paragraph (2) of the present Article shall not be under any obligation nor entitled to claim any privileges under

the present Convention in respect of matters related to such Annex and all references to Parties in the present Convention shall not include that State in so far as matters related to such Annex are concerned.

(4) The Organization shall inform the States which have signed or acceded to the present Convention of any declaration under the present Article as well as the receipt of any instrument deposited in accordance with the provisions of paragraph (2) of the present Article.

Article 15

Entry into Force

(1) The present Convention shall enter into force twelve months after the date on which not less than 15 States, the combined merchant fleets of which constitute not less than fifty per cent of the gross tonnage of the world's merchant shipping, have become parties to it in accordance with Article 15.

(2) An Optional Annex shall enter into force twelve months after the date on which the conditions stipulated in paragraph (1) of the present Article have been satisfied in relation to that Annex.

(3) The Organization shall inform the States which have signed the present Convention or acceded to it of the date on which it enters into force and of the date on which an Optional Annex enters into force in accordance with paragraph (2) of the present Article.

(4) For States which have deposited an instrument of ratification, acceptance, approval or accession in respect of the present Convention or any Optional Annex after the requirements for entry into force thereof have been met but prior to the date of entry into force, the ratification, acceptance, approval or accession shall take effect on the date of entry into force of the Convention or such Annex or three months after the date of deposit of the instrument whichever is the later date.

(5) For States which have deposited an instrument of ratification, acceptance, approval or accession after the date on which the Convention or an Optional Annex entered into force, the Convention or the Optional Annex shall become effective three months after the date of deposit of the instrument.

(6) After the date on which all the conditions required under Article 16 to bring an amendment to the present Convention or an Optional Annex into force have been fulfilled, any instrument of ratification, acceptance, approval or accession deposited shall apply to the Convention or Annex as amended.

Article 16

Amendments

(1) The present Convention may be amended by any of the procedures specified in the following paragraphs.

(2) Amendments after consideration by the Organization:

(a) Any amendment proposed by a Party to the Convention shall be submitted to the Organization and circulated by its Secretary-General to all

Members of the Organization and all Parties at least six months prior to its consideration;

(b) Any amendment proposed and circulated as above shall be submitted to an appropriate body by the Organization for consideration;

(c) Parties to the Convention, whether or not Members of the Organization, shall be entitled to participate in the proceedings of the appropriate body;

(d) Amendments shall be adopted by a two-thirds majority of only the Parties to the Convention present and voting;

(e) If adopted in accordance with subparagraph *(d)* above, amendments shall be communicated by the Secretary-General of the Organization to all the Parties to the Convention for acceptance;

(f) An amendment shall be deemed to have been accepted in the following circumstances:

(i) An amendment to an Article of the Convention shall be deemed to have been accepted on the date on which it is accepted by two-thirds of the Parties, the combined merchant fleets of which constitute not less than fifty per cent of the gross tonnage of the world's merchant fleet;

(ii) An amendment to an Annex to the Convention shall be deemed to have been accepted in accordance with the procedure specified in subparagraph *(f)* (iii) unless the appropriate body, at the time of its adoption, determines that the amendment shall be deemed to have been accepted on the date on which it is accepted by two-thirds of the Parties, the combined merchant fleets of which constitute not less than fifty per cent of the gross tonnage of the world's merchant fleet. Nevertheless, at any time before the entry into force of an amendment to an Annex to the Convention, a Party may notify the Secretary-General of the Organization that its express approval will be necessary before the amendment enters into force for it. The latter shall bring such notification and the date of its receipt to the notice of Parties;

(iii) An amendment to an Appendix to an Annex to the Convention shall be deemed to have been accepted at the end of a period to be determined by the appropriate body at the time of its adoption, which period shall be not less than ten months, unless within that period an objection is communicated to the Organization by not less than one-third of the Parties or by the Parties the combined merchant fleets of which constitute not less than fifty per cent of the gross tonnage of the world's merchant fleet whichever condition is fulfilled;

(iv) An amendment to Protocol I to the Convention shall be subject to the same procedures as for the amendments to the Annexes to the Convention, as provided for in subparagraphs *(f)* (ii) or *(f)* (iii) above;

(v) An amendment to Protocol II to the Convention shall be subject to the same procedures as for the amendments to an Article of the Convention, as provided for in subparagraph *(f)* (i) above;

(g) The amendment shall enter into force under the following conditions:

(i) In the case of an amendment to an Article of the Convention, to Protocol II, or to Protocol I or to an Annex to the Convention not under the procedure specified in subparagraph *(f)* (iii), the amendment accepted in conformity with the foregoing provisions shall enter into force six months after the date of its acceptance with respect to the Parties which have declared that they have accepted it;

(ii) In the case of an amendment to Protocol I, to an Appendix to an Annex or to an Annex to the Convention under the procedure specified in subparagraph *(f)* (iii), the amendment deemed to have been accepted in accordance with the foregoing conditions shall enter into force six months after its acceptance for all the Parties with the exception of those which, before that date, have made a declaration that they do not accept it or a declaration under subparagraph *(f)* (ii), that their express approval is necessary.

(3) Amendment by a Conference:

(a) Upon the request of a Party, concurred in by at least one-third of the Parties, the Organization shall convene a Conference of Parties to the Convention to consider amendments to the present Convention.

(b) Every amendment adopted by such a Conference by a two-thirds majority of those present and voting of the Parties shall be communicated by the Secretary-General of the Organization to all Contracting Parties for their acceptance.

(c) Unless the Conference decides otherwise, the amendment shall be deemed to have been accepted and to have entered into force in accordance with the procedures specified for that purpose in paragraph (2) *(f)* and *(g)* above.

(4) *(a)* In the case of an amendment to an Optional Annex, a reference in the present Article to a "Party to the Convention" shall be deemed to mean a reference to a Party bound by that Annex.

(b) Any Party which has declined to accept an amendment to an Annex shall be treated as a non-Party only for the purpose of application of that amendment.

(5) The adoption and entry into force of a new Annex shall be subject to the same procedures as for the adoption and entry into force of an amendment to an Article of the Convention.

(6) Unless expressly provided otherwise, any amendment to the present Convention made under this Article which relates to the structure of a ship shall apply only to ships for which the building contract is placed, or in the absence of a building contract, the keel of which is laid, on or after the date on which the amendment comes into force.

(7) Any amendment to a Protocol or to an Annex shall relate to the substance of that Protocol or Annex and shall be consistent with the Articles of the present Convention.

(8) The Secretary-General of the Organization shall inform all Parties of any amendments which enter into force under the present Article, together with the date on which each such amendment enters into force.

(9) Any declaration of acceptance or of objection to an amendment under the present Article shall be notified in writing to the Secretary-General of the Organization. The latter shall bring such notification and the date of its receipt to the notice of the Parties to the Convention.

Article 17

Promotion of Technical Co-operation

The Parties to the Convention shall promote, in consultation with the Organization and other international bodies, with assistance and co-ordination by the Executive Director of the United Nations Environment Programme, support for those Parties which request technical assistance for:

(a) The training of scientific and technical personnel;

(b) The supply of necessary equipment and facilities for reception and monitoring;

(c) The facilitation of other measures and arrangements to prevent or mitigate pollution of the marine environment by ships; and

(d) The encouragement of research;

preferably within the countries concerned, so furthering the aims and purposes of the present Convention.

Article 18

Denunciation

(1) The present Convention or any Optional Annex may be denounced by any Parties to the Convention at any time after the expiry of five years from the date on which the Convention or such Annex enters into force for that Party.

(2) Denunciation shall be effected by notification in writing to the Secretary-General of the Organization who shall inform all the other Parties of any such notification received and of the date of its receipt as well as the date on which such denunciation takes effect.

(3) A denunciation shall take effect twelve months after receipt of the notification of denunciation by the Secretary-General of the Organization or after the expiry of any other longer period which may be indicated in the notification.

Article 19

Deposit and Registration

(1) The present Convention shall be deposited with the Secretary-General of the Organization who shall transmit certified true copies thereof to all States which have signed the present Convention or acceded to it.

(2) As soon as the present Convention enters into force, the text shall be transmitted by the Secretary-General of the Organization to the Secretary-General of the United Nations for registration and publication, in accordance with Article 102 of the Charter of the United Nations.

472

Article 20

Languages

The present Convention is established in a single copy in the English, French, Russian and Spanish languages, each text being equally authentic. Official translations in the Arabic, German, Italian and Japanese languages shall be prepared and deposited with the signed original.

ANNEXES TO THE INTERNATIONAL CONVENTION FOR THE PREVENTION OF POLLUTION FROM SHIPS, 1973

ANNEX I. REGULATIONS FOR THE PREVENTION OF POLLUTION BY OIL

Chapter I. General

Regulation 1. Definitions

For the purposes of this Annex:

(1) "Oil" means petroleum in any form including crude oil, fuel oil, sludge, oil refuse and refined products (other than petrochemicals which are subject to the provisions of Annex II of the present Convention) and, without limiting the generality of the foregoing, includes the substances listed in Appendix I to this Annex.

(2) "Oily mixture" means a mixture with any oil content.

(3) "Oil fuel" means any oil used as fuel in connexion with the propulsion and auxiliary machinery of the ship in which such oil is carried.

(4) "Oil tanker" means a ship constructed or adapted primarily to carry oil in bulk in its cargo spaces and includes combination carriers and any "chemical tanker" as defined in Annex II of the present Convention when it is carrying a cargo or part cargo of oil in bulk.

(5) "Combination carrier" means a ship designed to carry either oil or solid cargoes in bulk.

(6) "New ship" means a ship:

(a) For which the building contract is placed after 31 December 1975; or

(b) In the absence of a building contract, the keel of which is laid or which is at a similar stage of construction after 30 June 1976; or

(c) The delivery of which is after 31 December 1979; or

(d) Which has undergone a major conversion:

  (i) For which the contract is placed after 31 December 1975; or

  (ii) In the absence of a contract, the construction work of which is begun after 30 June 1976; or

  (iii) Which is completed after 31 December 1979.

(7) "Existing ship" means a ship which is not a new ship.

(8) "Major conversion" means a conversion of an existing ship:

(a) Which substantially alters the dimensions or carrying capacity of the ship; or

(b) Which changes the type of the ship; or

(c) The intent of which in the opinion of the Administration is substantially to prolong its life; or

(d) Which otherwise so alters the ship that if it were a new ship, it would become subject to relevant provisions of the present Convention not applicable to it as an existing ship.

(9) "Nearest land". The term "from the nearest land" means from the baseline from which the territorial sea of the territory in question is established in accordance with international law, except that, for the purposes of the present Convention "from the nearest land" off the north eastern coast of Australia shall mean from a line drawn from a point on the coast of Australia in

latitude 11° South, longitude 142° 08′ East to a point in latitude 10° 35′ South,
longitude 141° 55′ East, thence to a point latitude 10° 00′ South,
longitude 142° 00′ East, thence to a point latitude 9° 10′ South,
longitude 143° 52′ East, thence to a point latitude 9° 00′ South,
longitude 144° 30′ East, thence to a point latitude 13° 00′ South,
longitude 144° 00′ East, thence to a point latitude 15° 00′ South,
longitude 146° 00′ East, thence to a point latitude 18° 00′ South,
longitude 147° 00′ East, thence to a point latitude 21° 00′ South,
longitude 153° 00′ East, thence to a point on the coast of Australia in latitude 24° 42′ South, longitude 153° 15′ East.

(10) "Special area" means a sea area where for recognized technical reasons in relation to its oceanographical and ecological condition and to the particular character of its traffic the adoption of special mandatory methods for the prevention of sea pollution by oil is required. Special areas shall include those listed in Regulation 10 of this Annex.

(11) "Instantaneous rate of discharge of oil content" means the rate of discharge of oil in litres per hour at any instant divided by the speed of the ship in knots at the same instant.

(12) "Tank" means an enclosed space which is formed by the permanent structure of a ship and which is designed for the carriage of liquid in bulk.

(13) "Wing tank" means any tank adjacent to the side shell plating.

(14) "Centre tank" means any tank inboard of a longitudinal bulkhead.

(15) "Slop tank" means a tank specifically designated for the collection of tank drainings, tank washings and other oily mixtures.

(16) "Clean ballast" means the ballast in a tank which since oil was last carried therein, has been so cleaned that effluent therefrom if it were discharged from a ship which is stationary into clean calm water on a clear day would not produce visible traces of oil on the surface of the water or on adjoining shore lines or cause a sludge or emulsion to be deposited beneath the surface of the water or upon adjoining shore lines. If the ballast is discharged through an oil discharge monitoring and control system approved by the Administration, evidence based on such a system to the effect that the oil content of the effluent did not exceed 15 parts per million shall be determinative that the ballast was clean, notwithstanding the presence of visible traces.

(17) "Segregated ballast" means the ballast water introduced into a tank which is completely separated from the cargo oil and oil fuel system and which is permanently allocated to the carriage of ballast or to the carriage of ballast or cargoes other than oil or noxious substances as variously defined in the Annexes of the present Convention.

(18) "Length" (L) means 96 per cent of the total length on a waterline at 85 per cent of the least moulded depth measured from the top of the keel, or the length from the fore side of the stem to the axis of the rudder stock on that waterline, if that be greater. In ships designed with a rake of keel the waterline on which this length is measured shall be parallel to the designed waterline. The length (L) shall be measured in metres.

(19) "Forward and after perpendiculars" shall be taken at the forward and after ends of the length (L). The forward perpendicular shall coincide with the foreside of the stem on the waterline on which the length is measured.

(20) "Amidships" is at the middle of the length (L).

(21) "Breadth" (B) means the maximum breadth of the ship, measured amidships to the moulded line of the frame in a ship with a metal shell and to the outer surface of the hull in a ship with a shell of any other material. The breadth (B) shall be measured in metres.

(22) "Deadweight" (DW) means the difference in metric tons between the displacement of a ship in water of a specific gravity of 1.025 at the load water line corresponding to the assigned summer freeboard and the lightweight of the ship.

(23) "Lightweight" means the displacement of a ship in metric tons without cargo, oil fuel, lubricating oil, ballast water, fresh water and feedwater in tanks, consumable stores, passengers and their effects.

(24) "Permeability" of a space means the ratio of the volume within that space which is assumed to be occupied by water to the total volume of that space.

(25) "Volumes" and "areas" in a ship shall be calculated in all cases to moulded lines.

Regulation 2. Application

(1) Unless expressly provided otherwise, the provisions of this Annex shall apply to all ships.

(2) In ships other than oil tankers fitted with cargo spaces which are constructed and utilized to carry oil in bulk of an aggregate capacity of 200 cubic metres or more, the requirements of Regulations 9, 10, 14, 15 (1), (2) and (3), 18, 20 and 24 (4) of this Annex for oil tankers shall also apply to the construction and operation of those spaces, except that where such aggregate capacity is less than 1,000 cubic metres the requirements of Regulation 15 (4) of this Annex may apply in lieu of Regulation 15 (1), (2) and (3).

(3) Where a cargo subject to the provisions of Annex II of the present Convention is carried in a cargo space of an oil tanker, the appropriate requirements of Annex II of the present Convention shall also apply.

(4) *(a)* Any hydrofoil, air-cushion vehicle and other new type of vessel (near-surface craft, submarine craft, etc.) whose constructional features are such as to render the application of any of the provisions of Chapters II and III of this Annex relating to construction and equipment unreasonable or impracticable may be exempted by the Administration from such provisions, provided that the construction and equipment of that ship provides equivalent protection against pollution by oil, having regard to the service for which it is intended.

(b) Particulars of any such exemption granted by the Administration shall be indicated in the Certificate referred to in Regulation 5 of this Annex.

(c) The Administration which allows any such exemption shall, as soon as possible, but not more than ninety days thereafter, communicate to the Organization particulars of same and the reasons therefor, which the Organization shall circulate to the Parties to the Convention for their information and appropriate action, if any.

Regulation 3. Equivalents

(1) The Administration may allow any fitting, material, appliance or apparatus to be fitted in a ship as an alternative to that required by this Annex if such fitting, material, appliance or apparatus is at least as effective as that required by this Annex. This authority of the Administration shall not extend to substitution of operational methods

to effect the control of discharge of oil as equivalent to those design and construction features which are prescribed by Regulations in this Annex.

(2) The Administration which allows a fitting, material, appliance or apparatus, as an alternative to that required by this Annex shall communicate to the Organization for circulation to the Parties to the Convention particulars thereof, for their information and appropriate action, if any.

Regulation 4. Surveys

(1) Every oil tanker of 150 tons gross tonnage and above, and every other ship of 400 tons gross tonnage and above shall be subject to the surveys specified below:

(a) An initial survey before the ship is put in service or before the certificate required under Regulation 5 of this Annex is issued for the first time, which shall include a complete survey of its structure, equipment, fittings, arrangements and material insofar as the ship is covered by this Annex. This survey shall be such as to ensure that the structure, equipment, fittings, arrangements and material fully comply with the applicable requirements of this Annex.

(b) Periodical surveys at intervals specified by the Administration, but not exceeding five years, which shall be such as to ensure that the structure, equipment, fittings, arrangements and material fully comply with the applicable requirements of this Annex. However, where the duration of the International Oil Pollution Prevention Certificate (1973) is extended as specified in Regulation 8 (3) or (4) of this Annex, the interval of the periodical survey may be extended correspondingly.

(c) Intermediate surveys at intervals specified by the Administration but not exceeding thirty months, which shall be such as to ensure that the equipment and associated pump and piping systems, including oil discharge monitoring and control systems, oily-water separating equipment and oil filtering systems, fully comply with the applicable requirements of this Annex and are in good working order. Such intermediate surveys shall be endorsed on the International Oil Pollution Prevention Certificate (1973) issued under Regulation 5 of this Annex.

(2) The Administration shall establish appropriate measures for ships which are not subject to the provisions of paragraph (1) of this Regulation in order to ensure that the applicable provisions of this Annex are complied with.

(3) Surveys of the ship as regards enforcement of the provisions of this Annex shall be carried out by officers of the Administration. The Administration may, however, entrust the surveys either to surveyors nominated for the purpose or to organizations recognized by it. In every case the Administration concerned fully guarantees the completeness and efficiency of the surveys.

(4) After any survey of the ship under this Regulation has been completed, no significant change shall be made in the structure, equipment, fittings, arrangements or material covered by the survey without the sanction of the Administration, except the direct replacement of such equipment or fittings.

Regulation 5. Issue of Certificate

(1) An International Oil Pollution Prevention Certificate (1973) shall be issued, after survey in accordance with the provisions of Regulation 4 of this Annex, to any oil tanker of 150 tons gross tonnage and above and any other ships of 400 tons gross tonnage and above which are engaged in voyages to ports or offshore terminals under the jurisdiction of other Parties to the Convention. In the case of existing ships this requirement shall apply twelve months after the date of entry into force of the present Convention.

(2) Such Certificate shall be issued either by the Administration or by any persons or organization duly authorized by it. In every case the Administration assumes full responsibility for the certificate.

Regulation 6. Issue of a Certificate by Another Government

(1) The Government of a Party to the Convention may, at the request of the Administration, cause a ship to be surveyed and, if satisfied that the provisions of this Annex are complied with, shall issue or authorize the issue of an International Oil Pollution Prevention Certificate (1973) to the ship in accordance with this Annex.

(2) A copy of the Certificate and a copy of the survey report shall be transmitted as soon as possible to the requesting Administration.

(3) A Certificate so issued shall contain a statement to the effect that it has been issued at the request of the Administration and it shall have the same force and receive the same recognition as the Certificate issued under Regulation 5 of this Annex.

(4) No International Oil Pollution Prevention Certificate (1973) shall be issued to a ship which is entitled to fly the flag of a State which is not a Party.

Regulation 7. Form of Certificate

The International Oil Pollution Prevention Certificate (1973) shall be drawn up in the official language or languages of the issuing country in the form corresponding to the model given in Appendix II to this Annex. If the language used is neither English nor French, the text shall include a translation into one of these languages.

Regulation 8. Duration of Certificate

(1) An International Oil Pollution Prevention Certificate (1973) shall be issued for a period specified by the Administration, which shall not exceed five years from the date of issue, except as provided in paragraphs (2), (3) and (4) of this Regulation.

(2) If a ship at the time when the Certificate expires is not in a port or offshore terminal under the jurisdiction of the Party to the Convention whose flag the ship is entitled to fly, the certificate may be extended by the Administration, but such extension shall be granted only for the purpose of allowing the ship to complete its voyage to the State whose flag the ship is entitled to fly or in which it is to be surveyed and then only in cases where it appears proper and reasonable to do so.

(3) No Certificate shall be thus extended for a period longer than five months and a ship to which such extension is granted shall not on its arrival in the State whose flag it is entitled to fly or the port in which it is to be surveyed, be entitled by virtue of such extension to leave that port or State without having obtained a new Certificate.

(4) A Certificate which has not been extended under the provisions of paragraph (2) of this Regulation may be extended by the Administration for a period of grace of up to one month from the date of expiry stated on it.

(5) A Certificate shall cease to be valid if significant alterations have taken place in the construction, equipment, fittings, arrangements, or material required without the sanction of the Administration, except the direct replacement of such equipment or fittings, or if intermediate surveys as specified by the Administration under Regulation 4 (1) *(c)* of this Annex are not carried out.

(6) A Certificate issued to a ship shall cease to be valid upon transfer of such a ship to the flag of another State, except as provided in paragraph (7) of this Regulation.

(7) Upon transfer of a ship to the flag of another Party, the Certificate shall remain in force for a period not exceeding five months provided that it would not have expired before the end of that period, or until the Administration issues a replacement Certificate, whichever is earlier. As soon as possible after the transfer has taken place the Government of the Party whose flag the ship was formerly entitled to fly shall transmit to the Administration a copy of the Certificate carried by the ship before the transfer and, if available, a copy of the relevant survey report.

Chapter II. Requirements for control of operational pollution

Regulation 9. Control of Discharge of Oil

(1) Subject to the provisions of Regulations 10 and 11 of this Annex and paragraph (2) of this Regulation, any discharge into the sea of oil or oily mixtures from ships to which this Annex applies shall be prohibited except when all the following conditions are satisfied:

(a) For an oil tanker, except as provided for in subparagraph *(b)* of this paragraph:

  (i) The tanker is not within a special area;

 (ii) The tanker is more than 50 nautical miles from the nearest land;

(iii) The tanker is proceeding en route;

 (iv) The instantaneous rate of discharge of oil content does not exceed 60 litres per nautical mile;

  (v) The total quantity of oil discharged into the sea does not exceed for existing tankers 1/15,000 of the total quantity of the particular cargo of which the residue formed a part, and for new tankers 1/30,000 of the total quantity of the particular cargo of which the residue formed a part; and

 (vi) The tanker has in operation, except as provided for in Regulation 15 (3) of this Annex, an oil discharge monitoring and control system and a slop tank arrangement as required by Regulation 15 of this Annex;

(b) From a ship of 400 tons gross tonnage and above other than an oil tanker and from machinery space bilges excluding cargo pump room bilges of an oil tanker unless mixed with oil cargo residue:

  (i) The ship is not within a special area;

 (ii) The ship is more than 12 nautical miles from the nearest land;

(iii) The ship is proceeding en route;

 (iv) The oil content of the effluent is less than 100 parts per million; and

  (v) The ship has in operation an oil discharge monitoring and control system, oily water separating equipment, oil filtering system or other installation as required by Regulation 16 of this Annex.

(2) In the case of a ship of less than 400 tons gross tonnage other than an oil tanker whilst outside the special area, the Administration shall ensure that it is equipped as far as practicable and reasonable with installations to ensure the storage of oil residues on board and their discharge to reception facilities or into the sea in compliance with the requirements of paragraph (1) *(b)* of this Regulation.

(3) Whenever visible traces of oil are observed on or below the surface of the water in the immediate vicinity of a ship or its wake, Governments of Parties to the Convention should, to the extent they are reasonably able to do so, promptly investigate the facts bearing on the issue of whether there has been a violation of the provisions of this Regulation or Regulation 10 of this Annex. The investigation should include, in particular, the wind and sea conditions, the track and speed of the ship, other possible sources of the visible traces in the vicinity, and any relevant oil discharge records.

(4) The provisions of paragraph (1) of this Regulation shall not apply to the discharge of clean or segregated ballast. The provisions of subparagraph (1) *(b)* of this Regulation shall not apply to the discharge of oily mixture which without dilution has an oil content not exceeding 15 parts per million.

(5) No discharge into the sea shall contain chemicals or other substances in quantities or concentrations which are hazardous to the marine environment or chemicals or other substances introduced for the purpose of circumventing the conditions of discharge specified in this Regulation.

(6) The oil residues which cannot be discharged into the sea in compliance with paragraphs (1), (2) and (4) of this Regulation shall be retained on board or discharged to reception facilities.

Regulation 10. Methods for the Prevention of Oil Pollution from Ships While Operating in Special Areas

(1) For the purpose of this Annex the special areas are the Mediterranean Sea area, the Baltic Sea area, the Black Sea area, the Red Sea area and the "Gulfs area" which are defined as follows:

(a) The Mediterranean Sea area means the Mediterranean Sea proper including the gulfs and seas therein with the boundary between the Mediterranean and the Black Sea constituted by the 41° N. parallel and bounded to the west by the Straits of Gilbratar at the meridian at 5° 36′ W.

(b) The Baltic Sea area means the Baltic Sea proper with the Gulf of Bothnia, the Gulf of Finland and the entrance to the Baltic Sea bounded by the parallel of the Skaw in the Skagerrak at 57° 44.8′ N.

(c) The Black Sea area means the Black Sea proper with the boundary between the Mediterranean and the Black Sea constituted by the parallel 41° N.

(d) The Red Sea area means the Red Sea proper including the Gulfs of Suez and Aqaba bounded at the south by the rhumb line between Ras si Ane (12° 8.5′ N., 45° 19.6′ E.) and Husn Murad (12° 40.4′ N., 43° 30.2′ E.).

(e) The "Gulfs area" means the sea area located north-west of the rhumb line between Ras al Hadd (22° 30′ N., 59° 48′ E.) and Ras Al Fasteh (25° 04′ N., 61° 25′ E.).

(2) *(a)* Subject to the provisions of Regulation 11 of this Annex, any discharge into the sea of oil or oily mixture from any oil tanker and any ship of 400 tons gross tonnage and above other than an oil tanker shall be prohibited, while in a special area.

(b) Such ships while in a special area shall retain on board all oil drainage and sludge, dirty ballast and tank washing waters and discharge them only to reception facilities.

(3) *(a)* Subject to the provisions of Regulation 11 of this Annex, any discharge into the sea of oil or oily mixture from a ship of less than 400 tons gross tonnage, other than an oil tanker, shall be prohibited while in a special area, except when the oil content of the effluent without dilution does not exceed 15 parts per million or alternatively when all of the following conditions are satisfied:

   (i) The ship is proceeding en route;

  (ii) The oil content of the effluent is less than 100 parts per million; and

 (iii) The discharge is made as far as practicable from the land, but in no case less than 12 nautical miles from the nearest land.

(b) No discharge into the sea shall contain chemicals or other substances in quantities or concentrations which are hazardous to the marine environment or chemicals or other substances introduced for the purpose of circumventing the conditions of discharge specified in this Regulation.

(c) The oil residues which cannot be discharged into the sea in compliance with subparagraph *(a)* of this paragraph shall be retained on board or discharged to reception facilities.

(4) The provisions of this Regulation shall not apply to the discharge of clean or segregated ballast.

(5) Nothing in this Regulation shall prohibit a ship on a voyage only part of which is in a special area from discharging outside the special area in accordance with Regulation 9 of this Annex.

(6) Whenever visible traces of oil are observed on or below the surface of the water in the immediate vicinity of a ship or its wake, the Governments of Parties to the Convention should, to the extent they are reasonably able to do so, promptly investigate the facts bearing on the issue of whether there has been a violation of the provisions of this Regulation or Regulation 9 of this Annex. The investigation should include, in particular, the wind and sea conditions, the track and speed of the ship, other possible sources of the visible traces in the vicinity, and any relevant oil discharge records.

(7) Reception facilities within special areas:

(a) Mediterranean Sea, Black Sea and Baltic Sea areas.

(i) The Government of each Party to the Convention, the coastline of which borders on any given special area, undertakes to ensure that not later than 1 January 1977 all oil loading terminals and repair ports within the special area are provided with facilities adequate for the reception and treatment of all the dirty ballast and tank washing water from oil tankers. In addition all ports within the special area shall be provided with adequate reception facilities for other residues and oily mixtures from all ships. Such facilities shall have adequate capacity to meet the needs of the ships using them without causing undue delay.

(ii) The Government of each Party having under its jurisdiction entrances to seawater courses with low depth contour which might require a reduction of draught by the discharge of ballast undertakes to ensure the provision of the facilities referred to in subparagraph *(a)* (i) of this paragraph but with the proviso that ships required to discharge slops or dirty ballast could be subject to some delay.

(iii) During the period between the entry into force of the present Convention (if earlier than 1 January 1977) and 1 January 1977 ships while navigating in the special areas shall comply with the requirements of Regulation 9 of this Annex. However the Governments of Parties the coastlines of which border any of the special areas under this subparagraph may establish a date *earlier than 1 January 1977 but after the date of entry into force of the present Convention,* from which the requirements of this Regulation in respect of the special areas in question shall take effect:

(1) If all the reception facilities required have been provided by the date so established; and

(2) Provided that the Parties concerned notify the Organization of the date so established at least six months in advance, for circulation to other parties.

(iv) After 1 January 1977, or the date established in accordance with subparagraph *(a)* (iii) of this paragraph if earlier, each Party shall notify the Organization for transmission to the Contracting Governments concerned of all cases where the facilities are alleged to be inadequate.

(b) Red Sea area and "Gulfs area"

(i) The Government of each Party the coastline of which borders on the special areas undertakes to ensure that as soon as possible all oil loading terminals and repair ports within these special areas are provided with facilities adequate for the reception and treatment of all the dirty ballast and tank washing water from tankers. In addition all ports within the special area shall be provided with adequate reception facilities for other residues and oily mixtures from all ships. Such facilities shall have adequate capacity to meet the needs of the ships using them without causing undue delay.

(ii) The Government of each Party having under its jurisdiction entrances to seawater courses with low depth contour which might require a reduction of draught by the discharge of ballast shall undertake to ensure the provision of the facilities referred to in subparagraph *(b)* (i) of this paragraph but with the proviso that ships required to discharge slops or dirty ballast could be subject to some delay.

   (iii) Each Party concerned shall notify the Organization of the measures taken pursuant to provisions of subparagraph *(b)* (i) and (ii) of this paragraph. Upon receipt of sufficient notifications the Organization shall establish a date from which the requirements of this Regulation in respect of the area in question shall take effect. The Organization shall notify all Parties of the date so established no less than twelve months in advance of that date.

   (iv) During the period between the entry into force of the present Convention and the date so established, ships while navigating in the special area shall comply with the requirements of Regulation 9 of this Annex.

   (v) After such date oil tankers loading in ports in these special areas where such facilities are not yet available shall also fully comply with the requirements of this Regulation. However, oil tankers entering these special areas for the purpose of loading shall make every effort to enter the area with only clean ballast on board.

   (vi) After the date on which the requirements for the special area in question take effect, each Party shall notify the Organization for transmission to the Parties concerned of all cases where the facilities are alleged to be inadequate.

   (vii) At least the reception facilities as prescribed in Regulation 12 of this Annex shall be provided by 1 January 1977 or one year after the date of entry into force of the present Convention, whichever occurs later.

Regulation 11. Exception

Regulations 9 and 10 of this Annex shall not apply to:

(a) The discharge into the sea of oil or oily mixture necessary for the purpose of securing the safety of a ship or saving life at sea; or

(b) The discharge into the sea of oil or oily mixture resulting from damage to a ship or its equipment;

   (i) Provided that all reasonable precautions have been taken after the occurrence of the damage or discovery of the discharge for the purpose of preventing or minimizing the discharge; and

   (ii) Except if the owner or the Master acted either with intent to cause damage, or recklessly and with knowledge that damage would probably result; or

(c) The discharge into the sea of substances containing oil, approved by the Administration, when being used for the purpose of combating specific pollution incidents in order to minimize the damage from pollution. Any such discharge shall be subject to the approval of any Government in whose jurisdiction it is contemplated the discharge will occur.

Regulation 12. Reception Facilities

(1) Subject to the provisions of Regulation 10 of this Annex, the Government of each Party undertakes to ensure the provision at oil loading terminals, repair ports, and in other ports in which ships have oily residues to discharge, of facilities for the reception of such residues and oily mixtures as remain from oil tankers and other ships adequate to meet the needs of the ships using them without causing undue delay to ships.

(2) Reception facilities in accordance with paragraph (1) of this Regulation shall be provided in:

(a) All ports and terminals in which crude oil is loaded into oil tankers where such tankers have immediately prior to arrival completed a ballast voyage of not more than 72 hours or not more than 1,200 nautical miles;

(b) All ports and terminals in which oil other than crude oil in bulk is loaded at an average quantity of more than 1,000 metric tons per day;

(c) All ports having ship repair yards or tank cleaning facilities;

(d) All ports and terminals which handle ships provided with the sludge tank(s) required by Regulation 17 of this Annex;

(e) All ports in respect of oily bilge waters and other residues, which cannot be discharged in accordance with Regulation 9 of this Annex; and

(f) All loading ports for bulk cargoes in respect of oil residues from combination carriers which cannot be discharged in accordance with Regulation 9 of this Annex.

(3) The capacity for the reception facilities shall be as follows:

(a) Crude oil loading terminals shall have sufficient reception facilities to receive oil and oily mixtures which cannot be discharged in accordance with the provisions of Regulation 9 (1) *(a)* of this Annex from all oil tankers on voyages as described in paragraph (2) *(a)* of this Regulation.

(b) Loading ports and terminals referred to in paragraph (2) *(b)* of this Regulation shall have sufficient reception facilities to receive oil and oily mixtures which cannot be discharged in accordance with the provisions of Regulation 9 (1) *(a)* of this Annex from oil tankers which load oil other than crude oil in bulk.

(c) All ports having ship repair yards or tank cleaning facilities shall have sufficient reception facilities to receive all residues and oily mixtures which remain on board for disposal from ships prior to entering such yards or facilities.

(d) All facilities provided in ports and terminals under paragraph (2) *(d)* of this Regulation shall be sufficient to receive all residues retained according to Regulation 17 of this Annex from all ships that may reasonably be expected to call at such ports and terminals.

(e) All facilities provided in ports and terminals under this Regulation shall be sufficient to receive oily bilge waters and other residues which cannot be discharged in accordance with Regulation 9 of this Annex.

(f) The facilities provided in loading ports for bulk cargoes shall take into account the special problems of combination carriers as appropriate.

(4) The reception facilities prescribed in paragraphs (2) and (3) of this Regulation shall be made available no later than one year from the date of entry into force of the present Convention or by 1 January 1977, whichever occurs later.

(5) Each Party shall notify the Organization for transmission to the Parties concerned of all cases where the facilities provided under this Regulation are alleged to be inadequate.

Regulation 13. Segregated Ballast Oil Tankers

(1) Every new oil tanker of 70,000 tons deadweight and above shall be provided with segregated ballast tanks and shall comply with the requirements of this Regulation.

(2) The capacity of the segregated ballast tanks shall be so determined that the ship may operate safely on ballast voyages without recourse to the use of oil tanks for water ballast except as provided for in paragraph (3) of this Regulation. In all cases, however, the capacity of segregated ballast tanks shall be at least such that in any ballast condition at any part of the voyage, including the conditions consisting of lightweight plus segregated ballast only, the ship's draughts and trim can meet each of the following requirements;

(a) The moulded draught amidships (dm) in metres (without taking into account any ship's deformation) shall not be less than:

$dm = 2.0 + 0.02 \ L,$

(b) The draughts at the forward and after perpendiculars shall correspond to those determined by the draught amidships (dm), as specified in subparagraph *(a)* of this paragraph, in association with the trim by the stern of not greater than 0.015 L, and

(c) In any case the draught at the after perpendicular shall not be less than that which is necessary to obtain full immersion of the propeller(s).

(3) In no case shall ballast water be carried in oil tanks except in weather conditions so severe that, in the opinion of the Master, it is necessary to carry additional ballast water in oil tanks for the safety of the ship. Such additional ballast water shall be processed and discharged in compliance with Regulation 9 and in accordance with the requirements of Regulation 15 of this Annex, and entry shall be made in the Oil Record Book referred to in Regulation 20 of this Annex.

(4) Any oil tanker which is not required to be provided with segregated ballast tanks in accordance with paragraph (1) of this Regulation may, however, be qualified as a segregated ballast tanker, provided that in the case of an oil tanker of 150 metres in length and above it fully complies with the requirements of paragraphs (2) and (3) of this Regulation and in the case of an oil tanker of less than 150 metres in length the segregated ballast conditions shall be to the satisfaction of the Administration.

Regulation 14. *Segregation of Oil and Water Ballast*

(1) Except as provided in paragraph (2) of this Regulation, in new ships of 4,000 tons gross tonnage and above other than oil tankers, and in new oil tankers of 150 tons gross tonnage and above, no ballast water shall be carried in any oil fuel tank.

(2) Where abnormal conditions or the need to carry large quantities of oil fuel render it necessary to carry ballast water which is not a clean ballast in any oil fuel tank, such ballast water shall be discharged to reception facilities or into the sea in compliance with Regulation 9 using the equipment specified in Regulation 16 (2) of this Annex, and an entry shall be made in the Oil Record Book to this effect.

(3) All other ships shall comply with the requirements of paragraph (1) of this Regulation as far as reasonable and practicable.

Regulation 15. *Retention of Oil on Board*

(1) Subject to the provisions of paragraphs (5) and (6) of this Regulation, oil tankers of 150 tons gross tonnage and above shall be provided with arrangements in accordance with the requirements of paragraphs (2) and (3) of this Regulation, provided that in the case of existing tankers the requirements for oil discharge monitoring and control systems and slop tank arrangements shall apply three years after the date of entry into force of the present Convention.

(2) *(a)* Adequate means shall be provided for cleaning the cargo tanks and transferring the dirty ballast residue and tank washings from the cargo tanks into a slop tank approved by the Administration. In existing oil tankers, any cargo tank may be designated as a slop tank.

(b) In this system arrangements shall be provided to transfer the oily waste into a slop tank or combination of slop tanks in such a way that any effluent discharged into the sea will be such as to comply with the provisions of Regulation 9 of this Annex.

(c) The arrangements of the slop tank or combination of slop tanks shall have a capacity necessary to retain the slops generated by tank washing, oil residues and dirty ballast residues but the total shall be not less than 3 per cent of the oil carrying capacity of the ship, except that, where segregated ballast tanks are provided in accordance with Regulation 13 of this Annex, or where arrangements such as eductors involving the use of water additional to the washing water are not fitted, the Administration may accept 2 per cent. New oil tankers over 70,000 tons deadweight shall be provided with at least two slop tanks.

(d) Slop tanks shall be so designed particularly in respect of the position of inlets, outlets, baffles or weirs where fitted, so as to avoid excessive turbulence and entrainment of oil or emulsion with the water.

(3) *(a)* An oil discharge monitoring and control system approved by the Administration shall be fitted. In considering the design of the oil content meter to be incorporated in the system, the Administration shall have regard to the specification recommended by the Organization.* The system shall be fitted with a recording device to provide a continuous record of the discharge in litres per nautical mile and total quantity discharged, or the oil content and rate of discharge. This record shall be identifiable as to time and date and shall be kept for at least three years. The oil discharge monitor and control system shall come into operation when there is any discharge of effluent into the sea and shall be such as will ensure that any discharge of oily mixture is automatically stopped when the instantaneous rate of discharge of oil exceeds that permitted by Regulation 9 (1) *(a)* of this Annex. Any failure of this monitoring and control system shall stop the discharge and be noted in the Oil Record Book. A manually operated alternative method shall be provided and may be used in the event of such failure, but the defective unit shall be made operable before the oil tanker commences its next ballast voyage unless it is proceeding to a repair port. Existing oil tankers shall comply with all of the provisions specified above except that the stopping of the discharge may be performed manually and the rate of discharge may be estimated from the pump characteristic.

(b) Effective oil/water interface detectors approved by the Administration shall be provided for a rapid and accurate determination of the oil/water interface in slop tanks and shall be available for use in other tanks where the separation of oil and water is effected and from which it is intended to discharge effluent direct to the sea.

(c) Instructions as to the operation of the system shall be in accordance with an operational manual approved by the Administration. They shall cover manual as well as automatic operations and shall be intended to ensure that at no time shall oil be discharged except in compliance with the conditions specified in Regulation 9 of this Annex.**

(4) The requirements of paragraphs (1), (2) and (3) of this Regulation shall not apply to oil tankers of less than 150 tons gross tonnage, for which the control of discharge of oil under Regulation 9 of this Annex shall be effected by the retention of oil on board with subsequent discharge of all contaminated washings to reception facilities. The total quantity of oil and water used for washing and returned to a storage tank shall be recorded in the Oil Record Book. This total quantity shall be discharged to reception facilities unless adequate arrangements are made to ensure that any effluent which is allowed to be discharged into the sea is effectively monitored to ensure that the provisions of Regulation 9 of this Annex are complied with.

(5) The Administration may waive the requirements of paragraphs (1), (2) and (3) of this Regulation for any oil tanker which engages exclusively on voyages both of 72 hours or less in duration and within 50 miles from the nearest land, provided that the oil tanker is not required to hold and does not hold an International Oil Pollution Prevention Certificate (1973). Any such waiver shall be subject to the requirement that the oil tanker shall retain on board all oily mixtures for subsequent discharge to reception facilities and to the determination by the Administration that facilities available to receive such oily mixtures are adequate.

---

* Reference is made to Recommendations on International Performance Specifications for Oily-water Separating Equipment and Oil Content Meters adopted by the Organization by Resolution A.233 (VII).

** Reference is made to "Clean Seas Guide for Oil Tankers", published by the International Chamber of Shipping and the Oil Companies International Marine Forum.

(6) Where in the view of the Organization equipment required by Regulation 9 (1) *(a)* (vi) of this Annex and specified in subparagraph (3) *(a)* of this Regulation is not obtainable for the monitoring of discharge of light refined products (white oils), the Administration may waive compliance with such requirement, provided that discharge shall be permitted only in compliance with procedures established by the Organization which shall satisfy the conditions of Regulation 9 (1) *(a)* of this Annex except the obligation to have an oil discharge monitoring and control system in operation. The Organization shall review the availability of equipment at intervals not exceeding twelve months.

(7) The requirements of paragraphs (1), (2) and (3) of this Regulation shall not apply to oil tankers carrying asphalt, for which the control of discharge of asphalt under Regulation 9 of this Annex shall be effected by the retention of asphalt residues on board with discharge of all contaminated washings to reception facilities.

Regulation 16. Oil Discharge Monitoring and Control System and Oily Water Separating Equipment

(1) Any ship of 400 tons gross tonnage and above shall be fitted with an oily water separating equipment or filtering system complying with the provisions of paragraph (6) of this Regulation. Any such ship which carries large quantities of oil fuel shall comply with paragraph (2) of this Regulation or paragraph (1) of Regulation 14.

(2) Any ship of 10,000 tons gross tonnage and above shall be fitted:

(a) In addition to the requirements of paragraph (1) of this Regulation with an oil discharge monitoring and control system complying with paragraph (5) of this Regulation; or

(b) As an alternative to the requirements of paragraph (1) and subparagraph (2)*(a)* of this Regulation, with an oily water separating equipment complying with paragraph (6) of this Regulation and an effective filtering system, complying with paragraph (7) of this Regulation.

(3) The Administration shall ensure that ships of less than 400 tons gross tonnage are equipped, as far as practicable, to retain on board oil or oily mixtures or discharge them in accordance with the requirements of Regulation 9 (1) *(b)* of this Annex.

(4) For existing ships the requirements of paragraphs (1), (2) and (3) of this Regulation shall apply three years after the date of entry into force of the present Convention.

(5) An oil discharge monitoring and control system shall be of a design approved by the Administration. In considering the design of the oil content meter to be incorporated into the system, the Administration shall have regard to the specification recommended by the Organization.* The system shall be fitted with a recording device to provide a continuous record of the oil content in parts per million. This record shall be identifiable as to time and date and shall be kept for at least three years. The monitoring and control system shall come into operation when there is any discharge of effluent into the sea and shall be such as will ensure that any discharge of oily mixture is automatically stopped when the oil content of effluent exceeds that permitted by Regulation 9 (1) *(b)* of this Annex. Any failure of this monitoring and control system shall stop the discharge and be noted in the Oil Record Book. The defective unit shall be made operable before the ship commences its next voyage unless it is proceeding to a repair port. Existing ships shall comply with all of the provisions specified above except that the stopping of the discharge may be performed manually.

---

* Reference is made to the Recommendation on International Performance Specifications for Oily-water Separating Equipment and Oil Content Meters adopted by the Organization by Resolution A.233 (VII).

(6) Oily water separating equipment or an oil filtering system shall be of a design approved by the Administration and shall be such as will ensure that any oily mixture discharged into the sea after passing through the separator or filtering systems shall have an oil content of not more than 100 parts per million. In considering the design of such equipment, the Administration shall have regard to the specification recommended by the Organization.*

(7) The oil filtering system referred to in paragraph (2) *(b)* of this Regulation shall be of a design approved by the Administration and shall be such that it will accept the discharge from the separating system and produce an effluent the oil content of which does not exceed 15 parts per million. It shall be provided with alarm arrangements to indicate when this level cannot be maintained.

Regulation 17. Tanks for Oil Residues (Sludge)

(1) Every ship of 400 tons gross tonnage and above shall be provided with a tank or tanks of adequate capacity, having regard to the type of machinery and length of voyage, to receive the oily residues (sludges) which cannot be dealt with otherwise in accordance with the requirements of this Annex, such as those resulting from the purification of fuel and lubricating oils and oil leakages in the machinery spaces.

(2) In new ships, such tanks shall be designed and constructed so as to facilitate their cleaning and the discharge of residues to reception facilities. Existing ships shall comply with this requirement as far as is reasonable and practicable.

Regulation 18. Pumping, Piping and Discharge Arrangements of Oil Tankers

(1) In every oil tanker, a discharge manifold for connexion to reception facilities for the discharge of dirty ballast water or oil contaminated water shall be located on the open deck on both sides of the ship.

(2) In every oil tanker, pipelines for the discharge to the sea of effluent which may be permitted under Regulation 9 of this Annex shall be led to the open deck or to the ship's side above the waterline in the deepest ballast condition. Different piping arrangements to permit operation in the manner permitted in subparagraphs (4) *(a)* and *(b)* of this Regulation may be accepted.

(3) In new oil tankers means shall be provided for stopping the discharge of effluent into the sea from a position on upper deck or above located so that the manifold in use referred to in paragraph (1) of this Regulation and the effluent from the pipelines referred to in paragraph (2) of this Regulation may be visually observed. Means for stopping the discharge need not be provided at the observation position if a positive communication system such as telephone or radio system is provided between the observation position and the discharge control position.

(4) All discharges shall take place above the waterline except as follows:

(a) Segregated ballast and clean ballast may be discharged below the waterline in ports or at offshore terminals.

(b) Existing ships which, without modification, are not capable of discharging segregated ballast above the waterline may discharge segregated ballast below the waterline provided that an examination of the tank immediately before the discharge has established that no contamination with oil has taken place.

---

* Reference is made to the Recommendation on International Performance Specifications for Oily-water Separating Equipment and Oil Content Meters adopted by the Organization by Resolution A.233 (VII).

Regulation 19. Standard Discharge Connexion

To enable pipes of reception facilities to be connected with the ship's discharge pipe line for residues from machinery bilges, both lines shall be fitted with a standard discharge connexion in accordance with the following table:

STANDARD DIMENSIONS OF FLANGES FOR DISCHARGE CONNEXIONS

Description	Dimension
Outside diameter	215 mm
Inner diameter	According to pipe outside diameter
Bolt circle diameter	183 mm
Slots in flange	6 holes 22 mm in diameter equidistantly placed on a bolt circle of the above diameter, slotted to the flange periphery. The slot width to be 22 mm
Flange thickness	20 mm
Bolts and nuts: quantity, diameter	6, each of 20 mm diameter and of suitable length

The flange is designed to accept pipes up to a maximum internal diameter of 125 mm and shall be of steel or other equivalent material having a flat face. This flange, together with a gasket of oilproof material, shall be suitable for a service pressure of 6 kg/cm².

Regulation 20. Oil Record Book

(1) Every oil tanker of 150 tons gross tonnage and above and every ship of 400 tons gross tonnage and above other than an oil tanker shall be provided with an Oil Record Book, whether as part of the ship's official log book or otherwise, in the form specified in Appendix III to this Annex.

(2) The Oil Record Book shall be completed on each occasion, on a tank-to-tank basis, whenever any of the following operations take place in the ship:

(a) *For oil tankers*

  (i) Loading of oil cargo;

  (ii) Internal transfer of oil cargo during voyage;

  (iii) Opening or closing before and after loading and unloading operations of valves or similar devices which inter-connect cargo tanks;

  (iv) Opening or closing of means of communication between cargo piping and seawater ballast piping;

  (v) Opening or closing of ship's side valves before, during and after loading and unloading operations;

  (vi) Unloading of oil cargo;

  (vii) Ballasting of cargo tanks;

  (viii) Cleaning of cargo tanks;

  (ix) Discharge of ballast except from segregated ballast tanks;

  (x) Discharge of water from slop tanks;

  (xi) Disposal of residues;

(xii) Discharge overboard of bilge water which has accumulated in machinery spaces whilst in port, and the routine discharge at sea of bilge water which has accumulated in machinery spaces.

(b) *For ships other than oil tankers*

(i) Ballasting or cleaning of fuel oil tanks or oil cargo spaces;

(ii) Discharge of ballast or cleaning water from tanks referred to under (i) of this subparagraph;

(iii) Disposal of residues;

(iv) Discharge overboard of bilge water which has accumulated in machinery spaces whilst in port, and the routine discharge at sea of bilge water which has accumulated in machinery spaces.

(3) In the event of such discharge of oil or oily mixture as is referred to in Regulation 11 of this Annex or in the event of accidental or other exceptional discharge of oil not excepted by that Regulation, a statement shall be made in the Oil Record Book of the circumstances of, and the reasons for, the discharge.

(4) Each operation described in paragraph (2) of this Regulation shall be fully recorded without delay in the Oil Record Book so that all the entries in the book appropriate to that operation are completed. Each section of the book shall be signed by the officer or officers in charge of the operations concerned and shall be countersigned by the Master of the ship. The entries in the Oil Record Book shall be in an official language of the State whose flag the ship is entitled to fly, and, for ships holding an International Oil Pollution Prevention Certificate (1973) in English or French. The entries in an official national language of the State whose flag the ship is entitled to fly shall prevail in case of a dispute or discrepancy.

(5) The Oil Record Book shall be kept in such a place as to be readily available for inspection at all reasonable times and, except in the case of unmanned ships under tow, shall be kept on board the ship. It shall be preserved for a period of three years after the last entry has been made.

(6) The competent authority of the Government of a Party to the Convention may inspect the Oil Record Book on board any ship to which this Annex applies while the ship is in its port or offshore terminals and may make a copy of any entry in that book and may require the Master of the ship to certify that the copy is a true copy of such entry. Any copy so made which has been certified by the Master of the ship as a true copy of an entry in the ship's Oil Record Book shall be made admissible in any judicial proceedings as evidence of the facts stated in the entry. The inspection of an Oil Record Book and the taking of a certified copy by the competent authority under this paragraph shall be performed as expeditiously as possible without causing the ship to be unduly delayed.

Regulation 21. Special Requirements for Drilling Rigs and other Platforms

Fixed and floating drilling rigs when engaged in the exploration, exploitation and associated offshore processing of sea-bed mineral resources and other platforms shall comply with the requirements of this Annex applicable to ships of 400 tons gross tonnage and above other than oil tankers, except that:

(a) They shall be equipped as far as practicable with the installations required in Regulations 16 and 17 of this Annex;

(b) They shall keep a record of all operations involving oil or oily mixture discharges, in a form approved by the Administration; and

(c) In any special area and subject to the provisions of Regulation 11 of this Annex, the discharge into the sea of oil or oily mixture shall be prohibited except when the oil content of the discharge without dilution does not exceed 15 parts per million.

*Chapter III.   Requirements for minimizing oil pollution from oil tankers
due to side and bottom damages*

Regulation 22.   Damage Assumptions

(1) For the purpose of calculating hypothetical oil outflow from oil tankers, three dimensions of the extent of damage of a parallelepiped on the side and bottom of the ship are assumed as follows. In the case of bottom damages two conditions are set forth to be applied individually to the stated portions of the oil tanker.

(a) *Side damage*

(i) Longitudinal extent (l_c): $\frac{1}{3} L^{\frac{2}{3}}$ or 14.5 metres,

whichever is less

(ii) Transverse extent (t_c): $\frac{B}{5}$ or 11.5 metres,

(inboard from the ship's side at right angles to the centreline at the level corresponding to the assigned summer freeboard)

whichever is less

(iii) Vertical extent (v_c): from the base line upwards without limit

(b) *Bottom damage*

	For 0.3L from the forward perpendicular of ship	Any other part of ship
(i) Longitudinal extent (l_s)	$\frac{L}{10}$	$\frac{L}{10}$ or 5 metres, whichever is less
(ii) Transverse extent (t_s)	$\frac{B}{6}$ or 10 metres, whichever is less but not less than 5 metres	5 metres
(iii) Vertical extent from the baseline (v_s):	$\frac{B}{15}$ or 6 metres, whichever is less	

(2) Wherever the symbols given in this Regulation appear in this Chapter, they have the meaning as defined in this Regulation.

Regulation 23.   Hypothetical Outflow of Oil

(1) The hypothetical outflow of oil in the case of side damage (O_c) and bottom damage (O_s) shall be calculated by the following formulae with respect to compartments

breached by damage to all conceivable locations along the length of the ship to the extent as defined in Regulation 22 of the Annex.

(a) for side damages:

$$O_c = \Sigma\, W_i\ +\ \Sigma\, K_i\, C_i \tag{I}$$

(b) for bottom damages:

$$O_s = \frac{1}{3}\, (\Sigma\, Z_i\, W_i\ +\ \Sigma\, Z_i\, C_i) \tag{II}$$

where: W_i = volume of a wing tank in cubic metres assumed to be breached by the damage as specified in Regulation 22 of this Annex; W_i for a segregated ballast tank may be taken equal to zero,

C_i = volume of a centre tank in cubic metres assumed to be breached by the damage as specified in Regulation 22 of this Annex; C_i for a segregated ballast tank may be taken equal to zero,

$K_i = 1 - \dfrac{b_i}{t_c}$; when b_i is equal to or greater than t_c, K_i shall be taken equal to zero,

$Z_i = 1 - \dfrac{h_i}{v_s}$; when h_i is equal to or greater than v_s, Z_i shall be taken equal to zero,

b_i = width of wing tank in metres under consideration measured inboard from the ship's side at right angles to the centreline at the level corresponding to the assigned summer freeboard.

h_i = minimum depth of the double bottom in metres under consideration; where no double bottom is fitted h_i shall be taken equal to zero,

Whenever symbols given in this paragraph appear in this Chapter, they have the meaning as defined in this Regulation.

(2) If a void space or segregated ballast tank of a length less than l_c as defined in Regulation 22 of this Annex is located between wing oil tanks, O_c in formula (I) may be calculated on the basis of volume W_i being the actual volume of one such tank (where they are of equal capacity) or the smaller of the two tanks (if they differ in capacity), adjacent to such space, multiplied by S_i as defined below and taking for all other wing tanks involved in such a collision the value of the actual full volume.

$$S_i = 1 - \frac{l_i}{l_c}$$

where: l_i = length in metres of void space or segregated ballast tank under consideration.

(3) *(a)* Credit shall only be given in respect of double bottom tanks which are either empty or carrying clean water when cargo is carried in the tanks above.

(b) Where the double bottom does not extend for the full length and width of the tank involved, the double bottom is considered non-existent and the volume of the tanks above the area of the bottom damage shall be included in formula (II) even if the tank is not considered breached because of the installation of such a partial double bottom.

(c) Suction wells may be neglected in the determination of the value h_i provided such wells are not excessive in area and extend below the tank for a minimum distance and in no case more than half the height of the double bottom. If the depth of such a well exceeds half the height of the double bottom, h_i shall be taken equal to the double bottom height minus the well height.

Piping serving such wells if installed within the double bottom shall be fitted with valves or other closing arrangements located at the point of connexion to the tank served to prevent oil outflow in the event of damage to the piping. Such piping shall be installed as high from the bottom shell as possible. These valves shall be kept closed at sea at any time when the tank contains oil cargo, except that they may be opened only for cargo transfer needed for the purpose of trimming of the ship.

(4) In the case where bottom damage simultaneously involves four centre tanks, the value of O_s may be calculated according to the formula

$$O_s = \frac{1}{4} \left(\Sigma Z_i W_i + \Sigma Z_i C_i \right) \qquad\qquad \text{(III)}$$

(5) An Administration may credit as reducing oil outflow in case of bottom damage, an installed cargo transfer system having an emergency high suction in each cargo oil tank, capable of tranferring from a breached tank or tanks to segregated ballast tanks or to available cargo tankage if it can be assured that such tanks will have sufficient ullage. Credit for such a system would be governed by ability to transfer in two hours of operation, oil equal to one half of the largest of the breached tanks involved and by availability of equivalent receiving capacity in ballast or cargo tanks. The credit shall be confined to permitting calculation of O_s according to formula (III). The pipes for such suctions shall be installed at least at a height not less than the vertical extent of the bottom damage v_s. The Administration shall supply the Organization with the information concerning the arrangements accepted by it, for circulation to other Parties to the Convention.

Regulation 24. Limitation of Size and Arrangement of Cargo Tanks

(1) Every new oil tanker shall comply with the provisions of this Regulation. Every existing oil tanker shall be required, within two years after the date of entry into force of the present Convention, to comply with the provisions of this Regulation if such a tanker falls into either of the following categories:

(a) A tanker, the delivery of which is after 1 January 1977; or

(b) A tanker to which both the following conditions apply:

(i) Delivery is not later than 1 January 1977; and

(ii) The building contract is placed after 1 January 1974, or in cases where no building contract has previously been placed, the keel is laid or the tanker is at a similar stage of construction after 30 June 1974.

(2) Cargo tanks of oil tankers shall be of such size and arrangements that the hypothetical outflow O_c or O_s calculated in accordance with the provisions of Regulation 23 of this Annex anywhere in the length of the ship does not exceed 30,000 cubic metres or $400^3 \sqrt{DW}$, whichever is the greater, but subject to a maximum of 40,000 cubic metres.

(3) The volume of any one wing cargo oil tank of an oil tanker shall not exceed seventy-five per cent of the limits of the hypothetical oil outflow referred to in paragraph (2) of this Regulation. The volume of any one centre cargo oil tank shall not exceed 50,000 cubic metres. However in segregated ballast oil tankers as defined in Regulation 13 of this Annex, the permitted volume of a wing cargo oil tank situated between two segregated ballast tanks, each exceeding l_c in length, may be increased to the maximum limit of hypothetical oil outflow provided that the width of the wing tanks exceeds t_c.

(4) The length of each cargo tank shall not exceed 10 metres or one of the following values, whichever is the greater:

(a) Where no longitudinal bulkhead is provided:

0.1L

(b) Where a longitudinal bulkhead is provided at the centreline only:

0.15L

(c) Where two or more longitudinal bulkheads are provided:

(i) for wing tanks:

0.2L

(ii) for centre tanks:

(1) if $\frac{b_i}{B}$ is equal to or greater than 1/5:

0.2L

(2) if $\frac{b_i}{B}$ is less than 1/5:

—where no centreline longitudinal bulkhead is provided:

$$(0.5\frac{b_i}{B} + 0.1)\,L$$

—where a centreline longitudinal bulkhead is provided:

$$(0.25\frac{b_i}{B} + 0.15)\,L$$

(5) In order not to exceed the volume limits established by paragraphs (2), (3) and (4) of this Regulation and irrespective of the accepted type of cargo transfer system installed, when such system interconnects two or more cargo tanks, valves or other similar closing devices shall be provided for separating the tanks from each other. These valves or devices shall be closed when the tanker is at sea.

(6) Lines of piping which run through cargo tanks in a position less than t_c from the ship's side or less than v_c from the ship's bottom shall be fitted with valves or similar closing devices at the point at which they open into any cargo tank. These valves shall be kept closed at sea at any time when the tanks contain cargo oil, except that they may be opened only for cargo transfer needed for the purpose of trimming of the ship.

Regulation 25. Subdivision and Stability

(1) Every new oil tanker shall comply with the subdivision and damage stability criteria as specified in paragraph (3) of this Regulation, after the assumed side or bottom damage as specified in paragraph (2) of this Regulation, for any operating draught reflecting actual partial or full load conditions consistent with trim and strength of the ship as well as specific gravities of the cargo. Such damage shall be applied to all conceivable locations along the length of the ship as follows:

(a) In tankers of more than 225 metres in length, anywhere in the ship's length;

(b) In tankers of more than 150 metres, but not exceeding 225 metres in length, anywhere in the ship's length except involving either after or forward bulkhead bounding the machinery space located aft. The machinery space shall be treated as a single floodable compartment;

(c) In tankers not exceeding 150 metres in length, anywhere in the ship's length between adjacent transverse bulkheads with the exception of the machinery space. For tankers of 100 metres or less in length where all requirements of paragraph (3) of this Regulation cannot be fulfilled without materially impairing the operational qualities of the ship, Administrations may allow relaxations from these requirements.

Ballast conditions where the tanker is not carrying oil in cargo tanks excluding any oily residues, shall not be considered.

(2) The following provisions regarding the extent and the character of the assumed damage shall apply:

(a) The extent of side or bottom damage shall be as specified in Regulation 22 of this Annex, except that the longitudinal extent of bottom damage within 0.3L from the forward perpendicular shall be the same as for side damage, as specified in Regulation 22 (1) *(a)* (i) of this Annex. If any damage of lesser extent results in a more severe condition such damage shall be assumed.

(b) Where the damage involving transverse bulkheads is envisaged as specified in subparagraphs (1) *(a)* and *(b)* of this Regulation, transverse watertight bulkheads shall be spaced at least at a distance equal to the longitudinal extent of assumed damage specified in subparagraph *(a)* of this paragraph in order to be considered effective. Where transverse bulkheads are spaced at a lesser distance, one or more of these bulkheads within such extent of damage shall be assumed as non-existent for the purpose of determining flooded compartments.

(c) Where the damage between adjacent transverse watertight bulkheads is envisaged as specified in subparagraph (1) *(c)* of this Regulation, no main transverse bulkhead or a transverse bulkhead bounding side tanks or double bottom tanks shall be assumed damaged, unless:

(i) The spacing of the adjacent bulkheads is less than the longitudinal extent of assumed damage specified in subparagraph *(a)* of this paragraph; or

(ii) There is a step or a recess in a transverse bulkhead of more than 3.05 metres in length, located within the extent of penetration of assumed damage. The step formed by the after peak bulkhead and after peak tank top shall not be regarded as a step for the purpose of this Regulation.

(d) If pipes, ducts or tunnels are situated within the assumed extent of damage, arrangements shall be made so that progressive flooding cannot thereby extend to compartments other than those assumed to be floodable for each case of damage.

(3) Oil tankers shall be regarded as complying with the damage stability criteria if the following requirements are met:

(a) The final waterline, taking into account sinkage, heel and trim, shall be below the lower edge of any opening through which progressive flooding may take place. Such openings shall include air pipes and those which are closed by means of weathertight doors or hatch covers and may exclude those openings closed by means of watertight manhole covers and flush scuttles, small watertight cargo tank hatch covers which maintain the high integrity of the deck, remotely operated watertight sliding doors, and side scuttles of the non-opening type.

(b) In the final stage of flooding, the angle of heel due to unsymmetrical flooding shall not exceed 25 degrees, provided that this angle may be increased up to 30 degrees if no deck edge immersion occurs.

(c) The stability in the final stage of flooding shall be investigated and may be regarded as sufficient if the righting lever curve has at least a range of 20 degrees beyond the position of equilibrium in association with a maximum residual righting lever of at least 0.1 metre. The Administration shall give consideration to the potential hazard presented by protected or unprotected openings which may become temporarily immersed within the range of residual stability.

(d) The Administration shall be satisfied that the stability is sufficient during intermediate stages of flooding.

(4) The requirements of paragraph (1) of this Regulation shall be confirmed by calculations which take into consideration the design characteristics of the ship, the arrangements, configuration and contents of the damaged compartments; and the

distribution, specific gravities and the free surface effect of liquids. The calculations shall be based on the following:

(a) Account shall be taken of any empty or partially filled tank, the specific gravity of cargoes carried, as well as any outflow of liquids from damaged compartments.

(b) The permeabilities are assumed as follows:

Spaces	Permeability
Appropriated to stores	0.60
Occupied by accommodation	0.95
Occupied by machinery	0.85
Voids	0.95
Intended for consumable liquids	0 or 0.95*
Intended for other liquids	0 to 0.95**

* Whichever results in the more severe requirements.
** The permeability of partially filled compartments shall be consistent with the amount of liquid carried.

(c) The buoyancy of any superstructure directly above the side damage shall be disregarded. The unflooded parts of superstructures beyond the extent of damage, however, may be taken into consideration provided that they are separated from the damaged space by watertight bulkheads and the requirements of subparagraph (3) *(a)* of this Regulation in respect of these intact spaces are complied with. Hinged watertight doors may be acceptable in watertight bulkheads in the superstructure.

(d) The free surface effect shall be calculated at an angle of heel of 5 degrees for each individual compartment. The Administration may require or allow the free surface corrections to be calculated at an angle of heel greater than 5 degrees for partially-filled tanks.

(e) In calculating the effect of free surfaces of consumable liquids it shall be assumed that, for each type of liquid at least one transverse pair or a single centreline tank has a free surface and the tank or combination of tanks to be taken into account shall be those where the effect of free surfaces is the greatest.

(5) The Master of every oil tanker and the person in charge of a non-self-propelled oil tanker to which this Annex applies shall be supplied in an approved form with:

(a) Information relative to loading and distribution of cargo necessary to ensure compliance with the provisions of this Regulation; and

(b) Data on the ability of the ship to comply with damage stability criteria as determined by this Regulation, including the effect of relaxations that may have been allowed under subparagraph (1) *(c)* of this Regulation.

ANNEX II. REGULATIONS FOR THE CONTROL OF POLLUTION BY NOXIOUS LIQUID SUBSTANCES IN BULK

Regulation 1. Definitions

For the purposes of this Annex:

(1) "Chemical tanker" means a ship constructed or adapted primarily to carry a cargo of noxious liquid substances in bulk and includes an "oil tanker" as defined in Annex I of the present Convention when carrying a cargo or part cargo of noxious liquid substances in bulk.

(2) "Clean ballast" means ballast carried in a tank which, since it was last used to carry a cargo containing a substance in Category A, B, C, or D has been thoroughly

cleaned and the residues resulting therefrom have been discharged and the tank emptied in accordance with the appropriate requirements of this Annex.

(3) "Segregated ballast" means ballast water introduced into a tank permanently allocated to the carriage of ballast or to the carriage of ballast or cargoes other than oil or noxious liquid substances as variously defined in the Annexes of the present Convention, and which is completely separated from the cargo and oil fuel system.

(4) "Nearest land" is as defined in Regulation 1 (9) of Annex I of the present Convention.

(5) "Liquid substances" are those having a vapour pressure not exceeding 2.8 kp/cm² at a temperature of 37.8° C.

(6) "Noxious liquid substance" means any substance designated in Appendix II to this Annex or provisionally assessed under the provisions of Regulation 3 (4) as falling into Category A, B, C or D.

(7) "Special area" means a sea area where for recognized technical reasons in relation to its oceanographic and ecological condition and to its peculiar transportation traffic the adoption of special mandatory methods for the prevention of sea pollution by noxious liquid substances is required.

Special areas shall be:

(a) The Baltic Sea Area, and

(b) The Black Sea Area.

(8) "Baltic Sea Area" is as defined in Regulation 10 of Annex I of the present Convention.

(9) "Black Sea Area" is as defined in Regulation 10 of Annex I of the present Convention.

Regulation 2. Application

(1) Unless expressly provided otherwise the provisions of this Annex shall apply to all ships carrying noxious liquid substances in bulk.

(2) Where a cargo subject to the provisions of Annex I of the present Convention is carried in a cargo space of a chemical tanker, the appropriate requirements of Annex I of the present Convention shall also apply.

(3) Regulation 13 of this Annex shall apply only to ships carrying substances which are categorized for discharge control purposes in Category A, B or C.

Regulation 3. Categorization and Listing of Noxious Liquid Substances

(1) For the purpose of the Regulations of this Annex, except Regulation 13, noxious liquid substances shall be divided into four categories as follows:

(a) Category A—Noxious liquid substances which if discharged into the sea from tank cleaning or deballasting operations would present a major hazard to either marine resources or human health or cause serious harm to amenities or other legitimate uses of the sea and therefore justify the application of stringent anti-pollution measures.

(b) Category B—Noxious liquid substances which if discharged into the sea from tank cleaning or deballasting operations would present a hazard to either marine resources or human health or cause harm to amenities or other legitimate uses of the sea and therefore justify the application of special anti-pollution measures.

(c) Category C—Noxious liquid substances which if discharged into the sea from tank cleaning or deballasting operations would present a minor hazard to either marine resources or human health or cause minor harm to amenities or other legitimate uses of the sea and therefore require special operational conditions.

(d) Category D—Noxious liquid substances which if discharged into the sea from tank cleaning or deballasting operations would present a recognizable hazard to either marine resources or human health or cause minimal harm to amenities or other legitimate uses of the sea and therefore require some attention in operational conditions.

(2) Guidelines for use in the categorization of noxious liquid substances are given in Appendix I to this Annex.

(3) The list of noxious liquid substances carried in bulk and presently categorized which are subject to the provisions of this Annex is set out in Appendix II to this Annex.

(4) Where it is proposed to carry a liquid substance in bulk which has not been categorized under paragraph (1) of this Regulation or evaluated as referred to in Regulation 4 (1) of this Annex, the Governments of Parties to the Convention involved in the proposed operation shall establish and agree on a provisional assessment for the proposed operation on the basis of the guidelines referred to in paragraph (2) of this Regulation. Until full agreement between the governments involved has been reached, the substance shall be carried under the the most severe conditions proposed. As soon as possible, but not later than ninety days after its first carriage, the Administration concerned shall notify the Organization and provide details of the substance and the provisional assessment for prompt circulation to all Parties for their information and consideration. The Government of each Party shall have a period of ninety days in which to forward its comments to the Organization, with a view to the assessment of the substance.

Regulation 4. Other Liquid Substances

(1) The substances listed in Appendix III to this Annex have been evaluated and found to fall outside the Categories A, B, C and D, as defined in Regulation 3 (1) of this Annex because they are presently considered to present no harm to human health, marine resources, amenities or other legitimate uses of the sea, when discharged into the sea from tank cleaning or deballasting operations.

(2) The discharge of bilge or ballast water or other residues or mixtures containing only substances listed in Appendix III to this Annex shall not be subject to any requirement of this Annex.

(3) The discharge into the sea of clean ballast or segregated ballast shall not be subject to any requirement of this Annex.

Regulation 5. Discharge of Noxious Liquid Substances

Categories A, B and C Substances outside Special Areas and Category D Substances in All Areas

Subject to the provisions of Regulation 6 of this Annex,

(1) The discharge into the sea of substances in Category A as defined in Regulation 3 (1) (a) of this Annex or of those provisionally assessed as such or ballast water, tank washings, or other residues or mixtures containing such substances shall be prohibited. If tanks containing such substances or mixtures are to be washed, the resulting residues shall be discharged to a reception facility until the concentration of the substance in the effluent to such facility is at or below the residual concentration prescribed for that substance in column III of Appendix II to this Annex and until the tank is empty. Provided that the residue then remaining in the tank is subsequently diluted by the addition of a volume of water of not less than 5 per cent of the total volume of the tank, it may be discharged into the sea when all the following conditions are also satisfied:

(a) The ship is proceeding en route at a speed of at least 7 knots in the case of self-propelled ships or at least 4 knots in the case of ships which are not self-propelled;

(b) The discharge is made below the waterline, taking into account the location of the sea water intakes; and *(c)* The discharge is made at a distance of not less than 12 nautical miles from the nearest land and in a depth of water of not less than 25 metres.

(2) The discharge into the sea of substances in Category B as defined in Regulation 3 (1) *(b)* of this Annex or of those provisionally assessed as such, or ballast water, tank washings, or other residues or mixtures containing such substances shall be prohibited except when all the following conditions are satisfied:

(a) The ship is proceeding en route at a speed of at least 7 knots in the case of self-propelled ships or at least 4 knots in the case of ships which are not self-propelled;

(b) The procedures and arrangements for discharge are approved by the Administration. Such procedures and arrangements shall be based upon standards developed by the Organization and shall ensure that the concentration and rate of discharge of the effluent is such that the concentration of the substance in the wake astern of the ship does not exceed 1 part per million;

(c) The maximum quantity of cargo discharged from each tank and its associated piping system does not exceed the maximum quantity approved in accordance with the procedures referred to in subparagraph *(b)* of this paragraph, which shall in no case exceed the greater of 1 cubic metre or 1/3,000 of the tank capacity in cubic metres;

(d) The discharge is made below the waterline, taking into account the location of the sea water intakes; and

(e) The discharge is made at a distance of not less than 12 nautical miles from the nearest land and in a depth of water of not less than 25 metres.

(3) The discharge into the sea of substances in Category C as defined in Regulation 3 (1) *(c)* of this Annex or of those provisionally assessed as such, or ballast water, tank washings, or other residues or mixtures containing such substances shall be prohibited except when all the following conditions are satisfied:

(a) The ship is proceeding en route at a speed of at least 7 knots in the case of self-propelled ships or at least 4 knots in the case of ships which are not self-propelled;

(b) The procedures and arrangements for discharge are approved by the Administration. Such procedures and arrangements shall be based upon standards developed by the Organization and shall ensure that the concentration and rate of discharge of the effluent is such that the concentration of the substance in the wake astern of the ship does not exceed 10 parts per million;

(c) The maximum quantity of cargo discharged from each tank and its associated piping system does not exceed the maximum quantity approved in accordance with the procedures referred to in subparagraph *(b)* of this paragraph, which shall in no case exceed the greater of 3 cubic metres or 1/1,000 of the tank capacity in cubic metres;

(d) The discharge is made below the waterline, taking into account the location of the sea water intakes; and

(e) The discharge is made at a distance of not less than 12 nautical miles from the nearest land and in a depth of water of not less than 25 metres.

(4) The discharge into the sea of substances in Category D as defined in Regulation 3 (1) *(d)* of this Annex, or those provisionally assessed as such, or ballast water, tank washings, or other residues or mixtures containing such substances shall be prohibited except when all the following conditions are satisfied:

(a) The ship is proceeding en route at a speed of at least 7 knots in the case of self-propelled ships or at least 4 knots in the case of ships which are not self-propelled;

(b) Such mixtures are of a concentration not greater than one part of the substance in ten parts of water; and

(c) The discharge is made at a distance of not less than 12 nautical miles from the nearest land.

(5) Ventilation procedures approved by the Administration may be used to remove cargo residues from a tank. Such procedures shall be based upon standards developed by the Organization. If subsequent washing of the tank is necessary, the discharge into the sea of the resulting tank washings shall be made in accordance with paragraph (1), (2), (3) or (4) of this Regulation, whichever is applicable.

(6) The discharge into the sea of substances which have not been categorized, provisionally assessed, or evaluated as referred to in Regulation 4 (1) of this Annex, or of ballast water, tank washings, or other residues or mixtures containing such substances shall be prohibited.

Categories A, B and C Substances within Special Areas

Subject to the provisions of Regulation 6 of this Annex,

(7) The discharge into the sea of substances in Category A as defined in Regulation 3 (1) *(a)* of this Annex, or of those provisionally assessed as such, or ballast water, tank washings, or other residues or mixtures containing such substances shall be prohibited. If tanks containing such substances or mixtures are to be washed the resulting residues shall be discharged to a reception facility which the States bordering the special area shall provide in accordance with Regulation 7 of this Annex until the concentration of the substance in the effluent to such facility is at or below the residual concentration prescribed for that substance in column IV of Appendix II to this Annex and until the tank is empty. Provided that the residue then remaining in the tank is subsequently diluted by the addition of a volume of water of not less than 5 per cent of the total volume of the tank, it may be discharged into the sea when all the following conditions are also satisfied:

(a) The ship is proceeding en route at a speed of at least 7 knots in the case of self-propelled ships or at least 4 knots in the case of ships which are not self-propelled;

(b) The discharge is made below the waterline, taking into account the location of the sea water intakes; and

(c) The discharge is made at a distance of not less than 12 nautical miles from the nearest land and in a depth of water of not less than 25 metres.

(8) The discharge into the sea of substances in Category B as defined in Regulation 3 (1) *(b)* of this Annex or of those provisionally assessed as such, or ballast water, tank washings, or other residues or mixtures containing such substances shall be prohibited except when all the following conditions are satisfied:

(a) The tank has been washed after unloading with a volume of water of not less than 0.5 per cent of the total volume of the tank, and the resulting residues have been discharged to a reception facility until the tank is empty;

(b) The ship is proceeding en route at a speed of at least 7 knots in the case of self-propelled ships or at least 4 knots in the case of ships which are not self-propelled;

(c) The procedures and arrangements for discharge and washings are approved by the Administration. Such procedures and arrangements shall be based upon standards developed by the Organization and shall ensure that the concentration and rate of discharge of the effluent is such that the concentration of the substance in the wake astern of the ship does not exceed 1 part per million;

(d) The discharge is made below the waterline, taking into account the location of the sea water intakes; and

(e) The discharge is made at a distance of not less than 12 nautical miles from the nearest land and in a depth of water of not less than 25 metres.

(9) The discharge into the sea of substances in Category C as defined in Regulation 3 (1) *(c)* of this Annex or of those provisionally assessed as such, or ballast water, tank

washings, or other residues or mixtures containing such substances shall be prohibited except when all the following conditions are satisfied:

(a) The ship is proceeding en route at a speed of at least 7 knots in the case of self-propelled ships or at least 4 knots in the case of ships which are not self-propelled;

(b) The procedures and arrangements for discharge are approved by the Administration. Such procedures and arrangements shall be based upon standards developed by the Organization and shall ensure that the concentration and rate of discharge of the effluent is such that the concentration of the substance in the wake astern of the ship does not exceed 1 part per million;

(c) The maximum quantity of cargo discharged from each tank and its associated piping system does not exceed the maximum quantity approved in accordance with the procedures referred to in subparagraph *(b)* of this paragraph which shall in no case exceed the greater of 1 cubic metre or 1/3,000 of the tank capacity in cubic metres;

(d) The discharge is made below the waterline, taking into account the location of the sea water intakes; and

(e) The discharge is made at a distance of not less than 12 nautical miles from the nearest land and in a depth of water of not less than 25 metres.

(10) Ventilation procedures approved by the Administration may be used to remove cargo residues from a tank. Such procedures shall be based upon standards developed by the Organization. If subsequent washing of the tank is necessary, the discharge into the sea of the resulting tank washings shall be made in accordance with paragraphs (7), (8), or (9) of this Regulation, whichever is applicable.

(11) The discharge into the sea of substances which have not been categorized, provisionally assessed or evaluated as referred to in Regulation 4 (1) of this Annex, or of ballast water, tank washings, or other residues or mixtures containing such substances shall be prohibited.

(12) Nothing in this Regulation shall prohibit a ship from retaining on board the residues from a Category B or C cargo and discharging such residues into the sea outside a special area in accordance with paragraph (2) or (3) of this Regulation, respectively.

(13) *(a)* The Governments of Parties to the Convention, the coastlines of which border on any given special area, shall collectively agree and establish a date by which time the requirement of Regulation 7 (1) of this Annex will be fulfilled and from which the requirements of paragraphs (7), (8), (9) and (10) of this Regulation in respect of that area shall take effect and notify the Organization of the date so established at least six months in advance of that date. The Organization shall then promptly notify all Parties of that date.

(b) If the date of entry into force of the present Convention is earlier than the date established in accordance with subparagraph *(a)* of this paragraph, the requirements of paragraphs (1), (2) and (3) of this Regulation shall apply during the interim period.

Regulation 6. Exception

Regulation 5 of this Annex shall not apply to:

(a) The discharge into the sea of noxious liquid substances or mixtures containing such substances necessary for the purpose of securing the safety of a ship or saving life at sea; or

(b) The discharge into the sea of noxious liquid substances or mixtures containing such substances resulting from damage to a ship or its equipment:

(i) Provided that all reasonable precautions have been taken after the occurrence of the damage or discovery of the discharge for the purpose of preventing or minimizing the discharge; and

(ii) Except if the owner or the Master acted either with intent to cause damage, or recklessly and with knowledge that damage would probably result; or

(c) The discharge into the sea of noxious liquid substances or mixtures containing such substances, approved by the Administration, when being used for the purpose of combating specific pollution incidents in order to minimize the damage from pollution. Any such discharge shall be subject to the approval of any Government in whose jurisdiction it is contemplated the discharge will occur.

Regulation 7. Reception Facilities

(1) The Government of each Party to the Convention undertakes to ensure the provision of reception facilities according to the needs of ships using its ports, terminals or repair ports as follows:

(a) Cargo loading and unloading ports and terminals shall have facilities adequate for reception without undue delay to ships of such residues and mixtures containing noxious liquid substances as would remain for disposal from ships carrying them as a consequence of the application of this Annex; and

(b) Ship repair ports undertaking repairs to chemical tankers shall have facilities adequate for the reception of residues and mixtures containing noxious liquid substances.

(2) The Government of each Party shall determine the types of facilities provided for the purpose of paragraph (1) of this Regulation at each cargo loading and unloading port, terminal and ship repair port in its territories and notify the Organization thereof.

(3) Each Party shall notify to the Organization, for transmission to the Parties concerned, of any case where facilities required under paragraph (1) of this Regulation are alleged to be inadequate.

Regulation 8. Measures of Control

(1) The Government of each Party to the Convention shall appoint or authorize surveyors for the purpose of implementing this Regulation.

Category A Substance in All Areas

(2) *(a)* If a tank is partially unloaded or unloaded but not cleaned, an appropriate entry shall be made in the Cargo Record Book.

(b) Until that tank is cleaned every subsequent pumping or transfer operation carried out in connexion with that tank shall also be entered in the Cargo Record Book.

(3) If the tank is to be washed:

(a) The effluent from the tank washing operation shall be discharged from the ship to a reception facility at least until the concentration of the substance in the discharge, as indicated by analyses of samples of the effluent taken by the surveyor, has fallen to the residual concentration specified for that substance in Appendix II to this Annex. When the required residual concentration has been achieved, remaining tank washings shall continue to be discharged to the reception facility until the tank is empty. Appropriate entries of these operations shall be made in the Cargo Record Book and certified by the surveyor;

(b) After diluting the residue then remaining in the tank with at least 5 per cent of the tank capacity of water, this mixture may be discharged into the sea in accordance with the provisions of subparagraphs (1) *(a)*, *(b)* and *(c)* or 7 *(a)*, *(b)* and *(c)*, whichever is applicable, of Regulation 5 of this Annex. Appropriate entries of these operations shall be made in the Cargo Record Book.

(4) Where the Government of the receiving Party is satisfied that it is impracticable to measure the concentration of the substance in the effluent without causing undue

delay to the ship, that Party may accept an alternative procedure as being equivalent to subparagraph (3) *(a)* provided that:

(a) A, precleaning procedure for that tank and that substance, based on standards developed by the Organization, is approved by the Administration and that Party is satisfied that such procedure will fulfil the requirements of paragraph (1) or (7), whichever is applicable, of Regulation 5 of this Annex with respect to the attainment of the prescribed residual concentrations;

(b) A surveyor duly authorized by that Party shall certify in the Cargo Record Book that:

(i) The tank, its pump and piping system have been emptied, and that the quantity of cargo remaining in the tank is at or below the quantity on which the approved precleaning procedure referred to in subparagraph (ii) of this paragraph has been based;

(ii) Precleaning has been carried out in accordance with the precleaning procedure approved by the Administration for that tank and that substance; and

(iii) The tank washings resulting from such precleaning have been discharged to a reception facility and the tank is empty;

(c) The discharge into the sea of any remaining residues shall be in accordance with the provisions of paragraph (3) *(b)* of this Regulation and an appropriate entry is made in the Cargo Record Book.

Category B Substances Outside Special Areas and Category C Substances in All Areas

(5) Subject to such surveillance and approval by the authorized or appointed surveyor as may be deemed necessary by the Government of the Party, the Master of a ship shall, with respect to a Category B substance outside special areas or a Category C substance in all areas, ensure compliance with the following:

(a) If a tank is partially unloaded or unloaded but not cleaned, an appropriate entry shall be made in the Cargo Record Book.

(b) If the tank is to be cleaned at sea:

(i) The cargo piping system serving that tank shall be drained and an appropriate entry made in the Cargo Record Book;

(ii) The quantity of substance remaining in the tank shall not exceed the maximum quantity which may be discharged into the sea for that substance under Regulation 5 (2) *(c)* of this Annex outside special areas in the case of Category B substances, or under Regulations 5 (3) *(c)* and 5 (9) *(c)* outside and within special areas respectively in the case of Category C substances. An appropriate entry shall be made in the Cargo Record Book;

(iii) Where it is intended to discharge the quantity of substance remaining into the sea the approved procedures shall be complied with, and the necessary dilution of the substance satisfactory for such a discharge shall be achieved. An appropriate entry shall be made in the Cargo Record Book; or

(iv) Where the tank washings are not discharged into the sea, if any internal transfer of tank washings takes place from that tank an appropriate entry shall be made in the Cargo Record Book; and

(v) Any subsequent discharge into the sea of such tank washings shall be made in accordance with the requirements of Regulation 5 of this Annex for the appropriate area and Category of substance involved.

(c) If the tank is to be cleaned in port:

(i) The tank washings shall be discharged to a reception facility and an appropriate entry shall be made in the Cargo Record Book; or

(ii) The tank washings shall be retained on board the ship and an appropriate entry shall be made in the Cargo Record Book indicating the location and disposition of the tank washings.

(d) If after unloading a Category C substance within a special area, any residues or tank washings are to be retained on board until the ship is outside the special area, the Master shall so indicate by an appropriate entry in the Cargo Record Book and in this case the procedures set out in Regulation 5 (3) of this Annex shall be applicable.

Category B Substances within Special Areas

(6) Subject to such surveillance and approval by the authorized or appointed surveyor as may be deemed necessary by the Government of the Party, the Master of a ship shall, with respect to a Category B substance within a special area, ensure compliance with the following:

(a) If a tank is partially unloaded or unloaded but not cleaned, an appropriate entry shall be made in the Cargo Record Book.

(b) Until that tank is cleaned every subsequent pumping or transfer operation carried out in connexion with that tank shall also be entered in the Cargo Record Book.

(c) If the tank is to be washed, the effluent from the tank washing operation, which shall contain a volume of water not less than 0.5 per cent of the total volume of the tank, shall be discharged from the ship to a reception facility until the tank, its pump and piping system are empty. An appropriate entry shall be made in the Cargo Record Book.

(d) If the tank is to be further cleaned and emptied at sea, the Master shall:

(i) Ensure that the approved procedures referred to in Regulation 5 (8) *(c)* of this Annex are complied with and that the appropriate entries are made in the Cargo Record Book; and

(ii) Ensure that any discharge into the sea is made in accordance with the requirements of Regulation 5 (8) of this Annex and an appropriate entry is made in the Cargo Record Book.

(e) If after unloading a Category B substance within a special area, any residues or tank washings are to be retained on board until the ship is outside the special area, the Master shall so indicate by an appropriate entry in the Cargo Record Book and in this case the procedures set out in Regulation 5 (2) of this Annex shall be applicable.

Category D Substances in All Areas

(7) The Master of a ship shall, with respect to a Category D substance, ensure compliance with the following:

(a) If a tank is partially unloaded or unloaded but not cleaned, an appropriate entry shall be made in the Cargo Record Book.

(b) If the tank is to be cleaned at sea:

(i) The cargo piping system serving that tank shall be drained and an appropriate entry made in the Cargo Record Book;

(ii) Where it is intended to discharge the quantity of substance remaining into the sea, the necessary dilution of the substance satisfactory for such a discharge shall be achieved. An appropriate entry shall be made in the Cargo Record Book;

(iii) Where the tank washings are not discharged into the sea, if any internal transfer of tank washings takes place from that tank an appropriate entry shall be made in the Cargo Record Book; and

(iv) Any subsequent discharge into the sea of such tank washings shall be made in accordance with the requirements of Regulation 5 (4) of this Annex.

(c) If the tank is to be cleaned in port:

(i) The tank washings shall be discharged to a reception facility and an appropriate entry shall be made in the Cargo Record Book; or

(ii) The tank washings shall be retained on board the ship and an appropriate entry shall be made in the Cargo Record Book indicating the location and disposition of the tank washings.

Discharge from a Slop Tank

(8) Any residues retained on board in a slop tank, including those from pump room bilges, which contain a Category A substance, or within a special area either a Category A or a Category B substance, shall be discharged to a reception facility in accordance with the provisions of Regulation 5 (1), (7) or (8) of this Annex, whichever is applicable. An appropriate entry shall be made in the Cargo Record Book.

(9) Any residues retained on board in a slop tank, including those from pump room bilges, which contain a quantity of a Category B substance outside a special area or a Category C substance in all areas, in excess of the aggregate of the maximum quantities specified in Regulation 5 (2) *(c)*, (3) *(c)* or (9) *(c)* of this Annex, whichever is applicable, shall be discharged to a reception facility. An appropriate entry shall be made in the Cargo Record Book.

Regulation 9. Cargo Record Book

(1) Every ship to which this Annex applies shall be provided with a Cargo Record Book, whether as part of the ship's official log book or otherwise, in the form specified in Appendix IV to this Annex.

(2) The Cargo Record Book shall be completed, on a tank-to-tank basis, whenever any of the following operations with respect to a noxious liquid substance take place in the ship:

(i) Loading of cargo;

(ii) Unloading of cargo;

(iii) Transfer of cargo;

(iv) Transfer of cargo, cargo residues or mixtures containing cargo to a slop tank;

(v) Cleaning of cargo tanks;

(vi) Transfer from slop tanks;

(vii) Ballasting of cargo tanks;

(viii) Transfer of dirty ballast water;

(ix) Discharge into the sea in accordance with Regulation 5 of this Annex.

(3) In the event of any discharge of the kind referred to in Article 7 of the present Convention and Regulation 6 of this Annex of any noxious liquid substance or mixture containing such substance, whether intentional or accidental, an entry shall be made in the Cargo Record Book stating the circumstances of, and the reason for, the discharge.

(4) When a surveyor appointed or authorized by the Government of the Party to the Convention to supervise any operations under this Annex has inspected a ship, then that surveyor shall make an appropriate entry in the Cargo Record Book.

(5) Each operation referred to in paragraphs (2) and (3) of this Regulation shall be fully recorded without delay in the Cargo Record Book so that all the entries in the Book appropriate to that operation are completed. Each entry shall be signed by the officer or officers in charge of the operation concerned and, when the ship is manned, each page shall be signed by the Master of the ship. The entries in the Cargo Record Book shall be in an official language of the State whose flag the ship is entitled to fly, and, for ships holding an International Pollution Prevention Certificate for the Carriage

of Noxious Liquid Substances in Bulk (1973) in English or French. The entries in an official national language of the State whose flag the ship is entitled to fly shall prevail in case of a dispute or discrepancy.

(6) The Cargo Record Book shall be kept in such a place as to be readily available for inspection and, except in the case of unmanned ships under tow, shall be kept on board the ship. It shall be retained for a period of two years after the last entry has been made.

(7) The competent authority of the Government of a Party may inspect the Cargo Record Book on board any ship to which this Annex applies while the ship is in its port, and may make a copy of any entry in that book and may require the Master of the ship to certify that the copy is a true copy of such entry. Any copy so made which has been certified by the Master of the ship as a true copy of an entry in the ship's Cargo Record Book shall be made admissible in any judicial proceedings as evidence of the facts stated in the entry. The inspection of a Cargo Record Book and the taking of a certified copy by the competent authority under this paragraph shall be performed as expeditiously as possible without causing the ship to be unduly delayed.

Regulation 10. Surveys

(1) Ships which are subject to the provisions of this Annex and which carry noxious liquid substances in bulk shall be surveyed as follows:

(a) An initial survey before a ship is put into service or before the certificate required by Regulation II of this Annex is issued for the first time, which shall include a complete inspection of its structure, equipment, fittings, arrangements and material insofar as the ship is covered by this Annex. The survey shall be such as to ensure full compliance with the applicable requirements of this Annex.

(b) Periodical surveys at intervals specified by the Administration which shall not exceed five years and which shall be such as to ensure that the structure, equipment, fittings, arrangements and material fully comply with the applicable requirements of this Annex. However, where the duration of the International Pollution Prevention Certificate for the Carriage of Noxious Liquid Substances in Bulk (1973) is extended as specified in Regulation 12 (2) or (4) of this Annex, the interval of the periodical survey may be extended correspondingly.

(c) Intermediate surveys at intervals specified by the Administration which shall not exceed thirty months and which shall be such as to ensure that the equipment and associated pumps and piping systems, fully comply with the applicable requirements of this Annex and are in good working order. The survey shall be endorsed on the International Pollution Prevention Certificate for the Carriage of Noxious Liquid Substances in Bulk (1973) issued under Regulation 11 of this Annex.

(2) Surveys of a ship with respect to the enforcement of the provisions of this Annex shall be carried out by officers of the Administration. The Administration may, however, entrust the surveys either to surveyors nominated for the purpose or to organizations recognized by it. In every case the Administration concerned shall fully guarantee the completeness and efficiency of the survey.

(3) After any survey of a ship under this Regulation has been completed, no significant change shall be made in the structure, equipment, fittings, arrangements or material, covered by the survey without the sanction of the Administration, except the direct replacement of such equipment and fittings for the purpose of repair or maintenance.

Regulation 11. Issue of Certificate

(1) An International Pollution Prevention Certificate for the Carriage of Noxious Liquid Substances in Bulk (1973) shall be issued to any ship carrying noxious liquid substances which is engaged in voyages to ports or offshore terminals under the

jurisdiction of other Parties to the Convention after survey of such ship in accordance with the provisions of Regulation 10 of this Annex.

(2) Such Certificate shall be issued either by the Administration or by a person or organization duly authorized by it. In every case the Administration shall assume full responsibility for the certificate.

(3) *(a)* The Government of a Party may, at the request of the Administration, cause a ship to be surveyed and if satisfied that the provisions of this Annex are complied with shall issue or authorize the issue of a Certificate to the ship in accordance with this Annex.

(b) A copy of the Certificate and a copy of the survey report shall be transmitted as soon as possible to the requesting Administration.

(c) A Certificate so issued shall contain a statement to the effect that it has been issued at the request of the Administration and shall have the same force and receive the same recognition as a certificate issued under paragraph (1) of this Regulation.

(d) No International Pollution Prevention Certificate for the Carriage of Noxious Liquid Substances in Bulk (1973) shall be issued to any ship which is entitled to fly the flag of a State which is not a Party.

(4) The Certificate shall be drawn up in an official language of the issuing country in a form corresponding to the model given in Appendix V to this Annex. If the language used is neither English nor French, the text shall include a translation into one of those languages.

Regulation 12. Duration of Certificate

(1) An International Pollution Prevention Certificate for the Carriage of Noxious Liquid Substances in Bulk (1973) shall be issued for a period specified by the Administration, which shall not exceed five years from the date of issue, except as provided in paragraphs (2) and (4) of this Regulation.

(2) If a ship at the time when the Certificate expires is not in a port or offshore terminal under the jurisdiction of the Party to the Convention whose flag the ship is entitled to fly, the Certificate may be extended by the Administration, but such extension shall be granted only for the purpose of allowing the ship to complete its voyage to the State whose flag the ship is entitled to fly or in which it is to be surveyed and then only in cases where it appears proper and reasonable to do so.

(3) No Certificate shall be thus extended for a period longer than five months and a ship to which such extension is granted shall not on its arrival in the State whose flag it is entitled to fly or the port in which it is to be surveyed, be entitled by virtue of such extension to leave that port or State without having obtained a new Certificate.

(4) A Certificate which has not been extended under the provisions of paragraph (2) of this Regulation may be extended by the Administration for a period of grace of up to one month from the date of expiry stated on it.

(5) A Certificate shall cease to be valid if significant alterations have taken place in the structure, equipment, fittings, arrangements and material required by this Annex without the sanction of the Administration, except the direct replacement of such equipment or fitting for the purpose of repair or maintenance or if intermediate surveys as specified by the Administration under Regulation 10 (1) *(c)* of this Annex are not carried out.

(6) A Certificate issued to a ship shall cease to be valid upon transfer of such a ship to the flag of another State, except as provided in paragraph (7) of this Regulation.

(7) Upon transfer of a ship to the flag of another Party, the Certificate shall remain in force for a period not exceeding five months provided that it would not have expired before the end of that period, or until the Administration issues a replacement

certificate, whichever is earlier. As soon as possible after the transfer has taken place the Government of the Party whose flag the ship was formerly entitled to fly shall transmit to the Administration a copy of the Certificate carried by the ship before the transfer and, if available, a copy of the relevant survey report.

Regulation 13. Requirements for Minimizing Accidental Pollution

(1) The design, construction, equipment and operation of ships carrying noxious liquid substances in bulk which are subject to the provisions of this Annex shall be such as to minimize the uncontrolled discharge into the sea of such substances.

(2) Pursuant to the provisions of paragraph (1) of this Regulation, the Government of each Party shall issue, or cause to be issued, detailed requirements on the design, construction, equipment and operation of such ships.

(3) In respect of chemical tankers, the requirements referred to in paragraph (2) of this Regulation shall contain at least all the provisions given in the Code for the Construction and Equipment of Ships carrying Dangerous Chemicals in Bulk adopted by the Assembly of the Organization in Resolution A.212 (VII) and as may be amended by the Organization, provided that the amendments to that Code are adopted and brought into force in accordance with the provisions of Article 17 of the present Convention for amendment procedures to an Appendix to an Annex.

ANNEX III. REGULATIONS FOR THE PREVENTION OF POLLUTION BY HARM-FUL SUBSTANCES CARRIED BY SEA IN PACKAGED FORMS, OR IN FREIGHT CONTAINERS, PORTABLE TANKS OR ROAD AND RAIL TANK WAGONS

Regulation 1. Application

(1) Unless expressly provided otherwise, the Regulations of this Annex apply to all ships carrying harmful substances in packaged forms, or in freight containers, portable tanks or road and rail tank wagons.

(2) Such carriage of harmful substances is prohibited except in accordance with the provisions of this Annex.

(3) To supplement the provisions of this Annex the Government of each Party to the Convention shall issue, or cause to be issued, detailed requirements on packaging, marking and labelling, documentation, stowage, quantity limitations, exceptions and notification, for preventing or minimizing pollution of the marine environment by harmful substances.

(4) For the purpose of this Annex, empty receptacles, freight containers, portable tanks and road and rail tank wagons which have been used previously for the carriage of harmful substances shall themselves be treated as harmful substances unless adequate precautions have been taken to ensure that they contain no residue that is hazardous to the marine environment.

Regulation 2. Packaging

Packagings, freight containers, portable tanks and road and rail tank wagons shall be adequate to minimize the hazard to the marine environment having regard to their specific contents.

Regulation 3. Marking and Labelling

Packages, whether shipped individually or in units or in freight containers, freight containers, portable tanks or road and rail tank wagons containing a harmful substance, shall be durably marked with the correct technical name (trade names shall not be used as the correct technical name), and further marked with a distinctive label or stencil of label, indicating that the contents are harmful. Such identification shall be supplemented where possible by any other means, for example by the use of the United Nations number.

Regulation 4. Documentation

(1) In all documents relating to the carriage of harmful substances by sea where such substances are named, the correct technical name of the substances shall be used (trade names shall not be used).

(2) The shipping documents supplied by the shipper shall include a certificate or declaration that the shipment offered for carriage is properly packed, marked and labelled and in proper condition for carriage to minimize the hazard to the marine environment.

(3) Each ship carrying harmful substances shall have a special list or manifest setting forth the harmful substances on board and the location thereof. A detailed stowage plan which sets out the location of all harmful substances on board may be used in place of such special list or manifest. Copies of such documents shall also be retained on shore by the owner of the ship or his representative until the harmful substances are unloaded.

(4) In a case where the ship carries a special list or manifest or a detailed stowage plan, required for the carriage of dangerous goods by the International Convention for the Safety of Life at Sea in force, the documents required for the purpose of this Annex may be combined with those for dangerous goods. Where documents are combined, a clear distinction shall be made between dangerous goods and other harmful substances.

Regulation 5. Stowage

Harmful substances shall be both properly stowed and secured so as to minimize the hazards to the marine environment without impairing the safety of ship and persons on board.

Regulation 6. Quantity Limitations

Certain harmful substances which are very hazardous to the marine environment may, for sound scientific and technical reasons, need to be prohibited for carriage or be limited as to the quantity which may be carried aboard any one ship. In limiting the quantity due consideration shall be given to size, construction and equipment of the ship as well as the packaging and the inherent nature of the substance.

Regulation 7. Exceptions

(1) Discharge by jettisoning of harmful substances carried in packaged forms, freight containers, portable tanks or road and rail tank wagons shall be prohibited except where necessary for the purpose of securing the safety of the ship or saving life at sea.

(2) Subject to the provisions of the present Convention, appropriate measures based on the physical, chemical and biological properties of harmful substances shall be taken to regulate the washing of leakages overboard provided that compliance with such measures would not impair the safety of the ship and persons on board.

Regulation 8. Notification

With respect to certain harmful substances, as may be designated by the Government of a party to the Convention, the master or owner of the ship or his representative shall notify the appropriate port authority of the intent to load or unload such substances at least 24 hours prior to such action.

ANNEX IV. REGULATIONS FOR THE PREVENTION OF POLLUTION BY SEWAGE FROM SHIPS

Regulation 1. Definitions

For the purposes of the present Annex:

(1) "New ship" means a ship:

(a) For which the building contract is placed, or in the absence of a building contract, the keel of which is laid, or which is at a similar stage of construction on or after the date of entry into force of this Annex; or

(b) The delivery of which is three years or more after the date of entry into force of this Annex.

(2) "Existing ship" means a ship which is not a new ship.

(3) "Sewage" means:

(a) Drainage and other wastes from any form of toilets, urinals, and WC scuppers;

(b) Drainage from medical premises (dispensary, sick bay, etc.) via wash basins, wash tubs and scuppers located in such premises;

(c) Drainage from spaces containing living animals; or

(d) Other waste waters when mixed with the drainages defined above.

(4) "Holding tank" means a tank used for the collection and storage of sewage.

(5) "Nearest land". The term "from the nearest land" means from the baseline from which the territorial sea of the territory in question is established in accordance with international law except that, for the purposes of the present Convention "from the nearest land" off the north-eastern coast of Australia shall mean from a line drawn from a point on the coast of Australia in

latitude 11° South, longitude 142° 08′ East to a point in latitude 10° 35′ South,
longtiude 141° 55′ East, thence to a point latitude 10° 00′ South,
longitude 142° 00′ East, thence to a point latitude 9° 10′ South,
longitude 143° 51′ East, thence to a point latitude 9° 00′ South,
longitude 144° 30′ East, thence to a point latitude 13° 00′ South,
longitude 144° 00′ East, thence to a point latitude 15° 00′ South,
longitude 146° 00′ East, thence to a point latitude 18° 00′ South,
longitude 147° 00′ East, thence to a point latitude 21° 00′ South,
longitude 153° 00′ East, thence to a point on the coast of Australia in latitude 24° 42′ South, longitude 153° 15′ East.

Regulation 2. Application

The provisions of this Annex shall apply to:

(a) (i) New ships of more than 200 tons gross tonnage;
   (ii) New ships of not more than 200 tons gross tonnage which are certified to carry more than 10 persons;
   (iii) New ships which do not have a measured gross tonnage and are certified to carry more than 10 persons; and

(b) (i) Existing ships of more than 200 tons gross tonnage, 10 years after the date of entry into force of this Annex;
   (ii) Existing ships of not more than 200 tons gross tonnage which are certified to carry more than 10 persons, 10 years after the date of entry into force of this Annex; and
   (iii) Existing ships which do not have a measured gross tonnage and are certified to carry more than 10 persons, 10 years after the date of entry into force of this Annex.

Regulation 3. Surveys

(1) Every ship which is required to comply with the provisions of this Annex and which is engaged in voyages to ports or offshore terminals under the jurisdiction of other Parties to the Convention shall be subject to the surveys specified below:

(a) An initial survey before the ship is put in service or before the certificate required under Regulation 4 of this Annex is issued for the first time, which shall include a survey of the ship which shall be such as to ensure:

   (i) When the ship is equipped with a sewage treatment plant the plant shall meet operational requirements based on standards and the test methods developed by the Organization;

   (ii) When the ship is fitted with a system to comminute and disinfect the sewage, such a system shall be of a type approved by the Administration;

   (iii) When the ship is equipped with a holding tank the capacity of such tank shall be to the satisfaction of the Administration for the retention of all sewage having regard to the operation of ths ship, the number of persons on board and other relevant factors. The holding tank shall have a means to indicate visually the amount of its contents; and

   (iv) That the ship is equipped with a pipeline leading to the exterior convenient for the discharge of sewage to a reception facility and that such a pipeline is fitted with a standard shore connexion in compliance with Regulation 11 of this Annex.

This survey shall be such as to ensure that the equipment, fittings, arrangements and material fully comply with the applicable requirements of this Annex.

(b) Periodical surveys at intervals specified by the Administration but not exceeding five years which shall be such as to ensure that the equipment, fittings, arrangements and material fully comply with the applicable requirements of this Annex. However, where the duration of the International Sewage Pollution Prevention Certificate (1973) is extended as specified in Regulation 7 (2) or (4) of this Annex, the interval of the periodical survey may be extended correspondingly.

(2) The Administration shall establish appropriate measures for ships which are not subject to the provisions of paragraph (1) of this Regulation in order to ensure that the provisions of this Annex are complied with.

(3) Surveys of the ship as regards enforcement of the provisions of this Annex shall be carried out by officers of the Administration. The Administration may, however, entrust the surveys either to surveyors nominated for the purpose or to organizations recognized by it. In every case the Administration concerned fully guarantees the completeness and efficiency of the surveys.

(4) After any survey of the ship under this Regulation has been completed, no significant change shall be made in the equipment, fittings, arrangements, or material covered by the survey without the approval of the Administration, except the direct replacement of such equipment or fittings.

Regulation 4. Issue of Certificate

(1) An International Sewage Pollution Prevention Certificate (1973) shall be issued, after survey in accordance with the provisions of Regulation 3 of this Annex, to any ship which is engaged in voyages to ports or offshore terminals under the jurisdiction of other Parties to the Convention.

(2) Such Certificate shall be issued either by the Administration or by any persons or organization duly authorized by it. In every case the Administration assumes full responsibility for the Certificate.

Regulation 5. Issue of a Certificate by Another Government

(1) The Government of a Party to the Convention may, at the request of the Administration, cause a ship to be surveyed and, if satisfied that the provisions of this Annex are complied with, shall issue or authorize the issue of an International Sewage Pollution Prevention Certificate (1973) to the ship in accordance with this Annex.

(2) A copy of the Certificate and a copy of the survey report shall be transmitted as early as possible to the Administration requesting the survey.

(3) A Certificate so issued shall contain a statement to the effect that it has been issued at the request of the Administration and it shall have the same force and receive the same recognition as the certificate issued under Regulation 4 of this Annex.

(4) No International Sewage Pollution Prevention Certificate (1973) shall be issued to a ship which is entitled to fly the flag of a State, which is not a Party.

Regulation 6. Form of Certificate

The International Sewage Pollution Prevention Certificate (1973) shall be drawn up in an official language of the issuing country in the form corresponding to the model given in Appendix to this Annex. If the language used is neither English nor French, the text shall include a translation into one of these languages.

Regulation 7. Duration of Certificate

(1) An International Sewage Pollution Prevention Certificate (1973) shall be issued for a period specified by the Administration, which shall not exceed five years from the date of issue, except as provided in paragraphs (2), (3) and (4) of this Regulation.

(2) If a ship at the time when the Certificate expires is not in a port or offshore terminal under the jurisdiction of the Party to the Convention whose flag the ship is entitled to fly, the Certificate may be extended by the Administration, but such extension shall be granted only for the purpose of allowing the ship to complete its voyage to the State whose flag the ship is entitled to fly or in which it is to be surveyed and then only in cases where it appears proper and reasonable to do so.

(3) No Certificate shall be thus extended for a period longer than five months and a ship to which such extension is granted shall not on its arrival in the State whose flag it is entitled to fly or the port in which it is to be surveyed, be entitled by virtue of such extension to leave that port or State without having obtained a new Certificate.

(4) A Certificate which has not been extended under the provisions of paragraph (2) of this Regulation may be extended by the Administration for a period of grace of up to one month from the date of expiry stated on it.

(5) A Certificate shall cease to be valid if significant alterations have taken place in the equipment, fittings, arrangement or material required without the approval of the Administration, except the direct replacement of such equipment or fittings.

(6) A Certificate issued to a ship shall cease to be valid upon transfer of such a ship to the flag of another State, except as provided in paragraph (7) of this Regulation.

(7) Upon transfer of a ship to the flag of another Party, the Certificate shall remain in force for a period not exceeding five months provided that it would not have expired before the end of that period, or until the Administration issues a replacement Certificate, whichever is earlier. As soon as possible after the transfer has taken place the Government of the Party whose flag the ship was formerly entitled to fly shall transmit to the Administration a copy of the Certificate carried by the ship before the transfer and, if available, a copy of the relevant survey report.

Regulation 8. Discharge of Sewage

(1) Subject to the provisions of Regulation 9 of this Annex, the discharge of sewage into the sea is prohibited, except when:

(a) The ship is discharging comminuted and disinfected sewage using a system approved by the Administration in accordance with Regulation 3 (1) *(a)* at a distance of more than four nautical miles from the nearest land, or sewage which is not comminuted or disinfected at a distance of more than 12 nautical miles from the nearest land, provided that in any case, the sewage that has been stored in holding tanks shall not be discharged instantaneously but at a moderate rate when the ship is en route and proceeding at not less than 4 knots; the rate of discharge shall be approved by the Administration based upon standards developed by the Organization; or

(b) The ship has in operation an approved sewage treatment plant which has been certified by the Administration to meet the operational requirements referred to in Regulation 3 (1) *(a)* (i) of this Annex, and

    (i) The test results of the plant are laid down in the ship's International Sewage Pollution Prevention Certificate (1973);

    (ii) Additionally, the effluent shall not produce visible floating solids in, nor cause discolouration of, the surrounding water; or

(c) The ship is situated in the waters under the jurisdiction of a State and is discharging sewage in accordance with such less severe requirements as may be imposed by such State.

(2) When the sewage is mixed with wastes or waste water having different discharge requirements, the more severe requirements shall apply.

Regulation 9. Exceptions

Regulation 8 of this Annex shall not apply to:

(a) The discharge of sewage from a ship necessary for the purpose of securing the safety of a ship and those on board or saving life at sea;

(b) The discharge of sewage resulting from damage to a ship or its equipment if all reasonable precautions have been taken before and after the occurrence of the damage, for the purpose of preventing or minimizing the discharge.

Regulation 10. Reception Facilities

(1) The Government of each Party to the Convention undertakes to ensure the provision of facilities at ports and terminals for the reception of sewage, without causing undue delay to ships, adequate to meet the needs of the ships using them.

(2) The Government of each Party shall notify the Organization for transmission to the Contracting Governments concerned all cases where the facilities provided under this Regulation are alleged to be inadequate.

Regulation 11. Standard Discharge Connection

To enable pipes of reception facilities to be connected with the ship's discharge pipeline, both lines shall be fitted with standard discharge connection in accordance with the following table:

STANDARD DIMENSIONS OF FLANGES FOR DISCHARGE CONNECTIONS

Description	Dimension
Outside diameter	210 mm
Inner diameter	According to pipe outside diameter
Bolt circle diameter	170 mm
Slots in flange	4 holes 18 mm in diameter equidistantly placed on a bolt circle of the above diameter, slotted to the flange periphery. The slot width to be 18 mm
Flange thickness	16 mm
Bolts and nuts: quantity and diameter	4, each of 16 mm in diameter and of suitable length

The flange is designed to accept pipes up to a maximum internal diameter of 100 mm and shall be of steel or other equivalent material having a flat face. This flange, together with a suitable gasket, shall be suitable for a service pressure of 6 kg/cm².

For ships having a moulded depth of 5 metres and less, the inner diameter of the discharge connection may be 38 millimetres.

ANNEX V. REGULATIONS FOR THE PREVENTION OF POLLUTION BY GARBAGE FROM SHIPS

Regulation 1. Definitions

For the purposes of this Annex:

(1) "Garbage" means all kinds of victual, domestic and operational waste excluding fresh fish and parts thereof, generated during the normal operation of the ship and liable to be disposed of continuously or periodically except those substances which are defined or listed in other Annexes to the present Convention.

(2) "Nearest land". The term "from the nearest land" means from the baseline from which the territorial sea of the territory in question is established in accordance with international law except that, for the purposes of the present Convention "from the nearest land" off the north-eastern coast of Australia shall mean from a line drawn from a point on the coast of Australia in

latitude 11° South, longitude 142° 08′ East to a point in latitude 10° 35′ South, longitude 141° 55′ East, thence to a point latitude 10° 00′ South, longitude 142° 00′ East, thence to a point latitude 9° 10′ South, longitude 143° 52′ East, thence to a point latitude 9° 00′ South, longitude 144° 30′ East, thence to a point latitude 13° 00′ South, longitude 144° 00′ East, thence to a point latitude 15° 00′ South, longitude 146° 00′ East, thence to a point latitude 18° 00′ South, longitude 147° 00′ East, thence to a point latitude 21° 00′ South, longitude 153° 00′ East, thence to a point on the coast of Australia in latitude 24° 42′ South, longitude 153° 15′ East.

(3) "Special area" means a sea area where for recognized technical reasons in relation to its oceanographical and ecological condition and to the particular character of its traffic the adoption of special mandatory methods for the prevention of sea pollution by garbage is required. Special areas shall include those listed in Regulation 5 of this Annex.

Regulation 2. Application

   The provisions of this Annex shall apply to all ships.

Regulation 3. Disposal of Garbage Outside Special Areas

   (1) Subject to the provisions of Regulations 4, 5 and 6 of this Annex:

   (a) The disposal into the sea of all plastics, including but not limited to synthetic ropes, synthetic fishing nets and plastic garbage bags is prohibited;

   (b) The disposal into the sea of the following garbage shall be made as far as practicable from the nearest land but in any case is prohibited if the distance from the nearest land is less than:

     (i) 25 nautical miles for dunnage, lining and packing materials which will float;

     (ii) 12 nautical miles for food wastes and all other garbage including paper products, rags, glass, metal, bottles, crockery and similar refuse;

   (c) Disposal into the sea of garbage specified in subparagraph *(b)* (ii) of this Regulation may be permitted when it is passed through a comminuter or grinder and made as far as practicable from the nearest land but in any case is prohibited if the distance from the nearest land is less than 3 nautical miles. Such comminuted or ground garbage shall be capable of passing through a screen with openings no greater than 25 millimetres.

   (2) When the garbage is mixed with other discharges having different disposal or discharge requirements the more severe requirements shall apply.

Regulation 4. Disposals from Drilling Rigs

   (1) Fixed or floating platforms engaged in the exploration, exploitation and associated offshore processing of sea-bed mineral resources, and all other ships when alongside such platforms or within 500 metres of such platforms, are forbidden to dispose of any materials regulated by this Annex, except as permitted by paragraph (2) of this Regulation.

   (2) The disposal into the sea of food wastes when passed through a comminuter or grinder from such fixed or floating drilling rigs located more than 12 nautical miles from land and all other ships when positioned as above. Such comminuted or ground food wastes shall be capable of passing through a screen with openings no greater than 25 millimetres.

Regulation 5. Disposal of Garbage within Special Areas

   (1) For the purpose of this Annex the special areas are the Mediterranean Sea area, the Baltic Sea area, the Black Sea area, the Red Sea area and the "Gulfs area" which are defined as follows:

   (a) The Mediterranean Sea area means the Mediterranean Sea proper including the gulfs and seas therein with the boundary between the Mediterranean and the Black Sea constituted by the 41° N. parallel and bounded to the west by the Straits of Gibraltar at the meridian of 5° 36′ W.

   (b) The Baltic Sea area means the Baltic Sea proper with the Gulf of Bothnia and the Gulf of Finland and the entrance to the Baltic Sea bounded by the parallel of the Skaw in the Skagerrak at 57° 44.8′ N.

   (c) The Black Sea area means the Black Sea proper with the boundary between the Mediterranean and the Black Sea constituted by the parallel 41° N.

(d) The Red Sea area means the Red Sea proper including the Gulfs of Suez and Aqaba bounded at the south by the rhumb line between Ras si Ane (12° 8.5′ N., 43° 19.6′ E.) and Husn Murad (12° 40.4′ N., 43° 30.2′ E.).

(e) The "Gulfs area" means the sea area located north-west of the rhumb line between Ras al Hadd (22° 30′ N., 59° 48′ E.) and Ras al Fasteh (25° 04′ N., 61° 25′ E.).

(2) Subject to the provisions of Regulation 6 of this Annex:

(a) Disposal into the sea of the following is prohibited:

(i) All plastics, including but not limited to synthetic ropes, synthetic fishing nets and plastic garbage bags;

(ii) All other garbage, including paper products, rags, glass, metal, bottles, crockery, dunnage, lining and packing materials;

(b) Disposal into the sea of food wastes shall be made as far as practicable from land, but in any case not less than 12 nautical miles from the nearest land.

(3) When the garbage is mixed with other discharges having different disposal or discharge requirements the more severe requirements shall apply.

(4) Reception facilities within special areas.

(a) The Government of each party to the Convention, the coast line of which borders a special area undertakes to ensure that as soon as possible in all ports within a special area, adequate reception facilities are provided in accordance with Regulation 7 of this Annex, taking into account the special needs of ships operating in these areas.

(b) The Government of each party concerned shall notify the Organization of the measures taken pursuant to subparagraph *(a)* of this Regulation. Upon receipt of sufficient notifications the Organization shall establish a date from which the requirements of this Regulation in respect of the area in question shall take effect. The Organization shall notify all parties of the date so established no less than twelve months in advance of that date.

(c) After date so established, ships calling also at ports in these special areas where such facilities are not yet available, shall fully comply with the requirements of this Regulation.

Regulation 6. Exception

Regulations 3, 4 and 5 of this Annex shall not apply to:

(a) The disposal of garbage from a ship necessary for the purpose of securing the safety of a ship, the health of its personnel, or saving life at sea;

(b) The escape of garbage resulting from damage to a ship or its equipment provided all reasonable precautions have been taken before and after the occurrence of the damage, for the purpose of preventing or minimizing the escape;

(c) The accidental loss of synthetic fishing nets or synthetic material incidental to the repair of such nets, provided that all reasonable precautions have been taken to prevent such loss.

Regulation 7. Reception Facilities

(1) The Government of each party to the Convention undertakes to ensure the provisions of facilities at ports and terminals for the reception of garbage, without causing undue delay to ships, and according to the needs of the ships using them.

(2) The Government of each party shall notify the Organization for transmission to the parties concerned of all cases where the facilities provided under this Regulation are alleged to be inadequate.

514

INTERNATIONAL CONVENTION FOR THE PREVENTION OF POLLUTION FROM SHIPS, 1973

Protocol I. Provisions Concerning Reports on Incidents Involving Harmful Substances

(in accordance with Article 8 of the Convention)

Article I. Duty to Report

(1) The Master of a ship involved in an incident referred to in Article III of this Protocol, or other person having charge of the ship, shall report the particulars of such incident without delay and to the fullest extent possible in accordance with the provisions of this Protocol.

(2) In the event of the ship referred to in paragraph (1) of this Article being abandoned, or in the event of a report from such ship being incomplete or unobtainable, the owner, charterer, manager or operator of the ship, or their agents shall, to the fullest extent possible assume the obligations placed upon the Master under the provisions of this Protocol.

Article II. Methods of Reporting

(1) Each report shall be made by radio whenever possible, but in any case by the fastest channels available at the time the report is made. Reports made by radio shall be given the highest possible priority.

(2) Reports shall be directed to the appropriate officer or agency specified in paragraph (3) of Article 8 of the Convention.

Article III. When to Make Reports

The report shall be made whenever an incident involves:

(a) A discharge other than as permitted under the present Convention; or

(b) A discharge permitted under the present Convention by virtue of the fact that:

(i) It is for the purpose of securing the safety of a ship or saving life at sea; or

(ii) It results from damage to the ship or its equipment; or

(c) A discharge of a harmful substance for the purpose of combating a specific pollution incident or for purposes of legitimate scientific research into pollution abatement or control; or

(d) The probability of a discharge referred to in subparagraphs *(a)*, *(b)* or *(c)* of this Article.

Article IV. Contents of Report

(1) Each report shall contain in general:

(a) Identity of ship;

(b) The time and date of the occurrence of the incident;

(c) The geographic position of the ship when the incident occurred;

(d) The wind and sea conditions prevailing at the time of the incident; and

(e) Relevant details respecting the condition of the ship.

(2) Each report shall contain, in particular:

(a) A clear indication or description of the harmful substances involved, including if possible the correct technical names of such substances (trade names should not be used in place of the correct technical names);

(b) A statement or estimate of the quantities, concentrations and likely conditions of harmful substances discharged or likely to be discharged into the sea; and where relevant

(c) A description of the packaging and identifying marks; and if possible

(d) The name of the consignor, consignee or manufacturer.

(3) Each report shall clearly indicate whether the harmful substance discharged or likely to be discharged is oil, a noxious liquid substance, a noxious solid substance or a noxious gaseous substance and whether such substance was or is carried in bulk or contained in packaged form, freight containers, portable tanks, or road and rail tank wagons.

(4) Each report shall be supplemented as necessary by any other relevant information requested by a recipient of the report or which the person sending the report deems appropriate.

Article V. Supplementary Report

Any person who is obliged under the provisions of this Protocol to send a report shall when possible

(a) Supplement the initial report, as necessary, with information concerning further development; and

(b) Comply as fully as possible with requests from affected States for additional information concerning the incident.

Protocol II. Arbitration
(in accordance with Article 10 of the Convention)

Article I

Arbitration procedure, unless the Parties to the dispute decide otherwise, shall be in accordance with the rules set out in this Protocol.

Article II

(1) An Arbitration Tribunal shall be established upon the request of one Party to the Convention addressed to another in application of Article 10 of the present Convention. The request for arbitration shall consist of a statement of the case together with any supporting documents.

(2) The requesting Party shall inform the Secretary-General of the Organization of the fact that it has applied for the establishment of a Tribunal, of the names of the Parties to the dispute, and of the Articles of the Convention or Regulations over which there is in its opinion disagreement concerning their interpretation or application. The Secretary-General shall transmit this information to all Parties.

Article III

The Tribunal shall consist of three members: one Arbitrator nominated by each Party to the dispute and a third Arbitrator who shall be nominated by agreement between the two first named, and shall act as its Chairman.

Article IV

(1) If, at the end of a period of sixty days from the nomination of the second Arbitrator, the Chairman of the Tribunal shall not have been nominated, the Secretary-General of the Organization upon request of either Party shall within a further period of sixty days proceed to such nomination, selecting from a list of qualified persons previously drawn up by the Council of the Organization.

(2) If, within a period of sixty days from the date of the receipt of the request, one of the Parties shall not have nominated the member of the Tribunal for whose designation it is responsible, the other Party may directly inform the Secretary-General of the Organization who shall nominate the Chairman of the Tribunal within a period of sixty days, selecting him from the list prescribed in paragraph (1) of the present Article.

(3) The Chairman of the Tribunal shall, upon nomination, request the Party which has not provided an Arbitrator, to do so in the same manner and under the same conditions. If the Party does not make the required nomination, the Chairman of the Tribunal shall request the Secretary-General of the Organization to make the nomination in the form and conditions prescribed in the preceding paragraph.

(4) The Chairman of the Tribunal, if nominated under the provisions of the present Article, shall not be or have been a national of one of the Parties concerned, except with the consent of the other Party.

(5) In the case of the decease or default of an Arbitrator for whose nomination one of the Parties is responsible, the said Party shall nominate a replacement within a period of sixty days from the date of decease or default. Should the said Party not make the nomination, the arbitration shall proceed under the remaining Arbitrators. In case of the decease or default of the Chairman of the Tribunal, a replacement shall be nominated in accordance with the provisions of Article III above, or in the absence of agreement between the members of the Tribunal within a period of sixty days of the decease or default, according to the provisions of the present Article.

Article V

The Tribunal may hear and determine counter-claims arising directly out of the subject matter of the dispute.

Article VI

Each Party shall be responsible for the remuneration of its Arbitrator and connected costs and for the costs entailed by the preparation of its own case. The remuneration of the Chairman of the Tribunal and of all general expenses incurred by the Arbitration shall be borne equally by the Parties. The Tribunal shall keep a record of all its expenses and shall furnish a final statement thereof.

Article VII

Any Party to the Convention which has an interest of a legal nature which may be affected by the decision in the case may, after giving written notice to the Parties which have originally initiated the procedure, join in the arbitration procedure with the consent of the Tribunal.

Article VIII

Any Arbitration Tribunal established under the provisions of the present Protocol shall decide its own rules of procedure.

Article IX

(1) Decisions of the Tribunal both as to its procedure and its place of meeting and as to any question laid before it, shall be taken by majority vote of its members; the absence or abstention of one of the members of the Tribunal for whose nomination the Parties were responsible shall not constitute an impediment to the Tribunal reaching a decision. In cases of equal voting, the vote of the Chairman shall be decisive.

(2) The Parties shall facilitate the work of the Tribunal and in particular, in accordance with their legislation, and using all means at their disposal:

(a) Provide the Tribunal with the necessary documents and information;

(b) Enable the Tribunal to enter their territory, to hear witnesses or experts, and to visit the scene.

(3) Absence or default of one Party shall not constitute an impediment to the procedure.

Article X

(1) The Tribunal shall render its award within a period of five months from the time it is established unless it decides, in the case of necessity, to extend the time limit for a further period not exceeding three months. The award of the Tribunal shall be accompanied by a statement of reasons. It shall be final and without appeal and shall be communicated to the Secretary-General of the Organization. The Parties shall immediately comply with the award.

(2) Any controversy which may arise between the Parties as regards interpretation or execution of the award may be submitted by either Party for judgement to the Tribunal which made the award, or, if it is not available to another Tribunal constituted for this purpose, in the same manner as the original Tribunal.

3. [CONVENTION ON THE PROTECTION OF THE ENVIRONMENT BETWEEN DENMARK, FINLAND, NORWAY AND SWEDEN, DONE AT STOCKHOLM ON 19 FEBRUARY 1974][1]

4. CONVENTION ON THE PROTECTION OF THE MARINE ENVIRON-MENT OF THE BALTIC SEA AREA, DONE AT HELSINKI ON 22 MARCH 1974[2]

The States Parties to this Convention,

Conscious of the indispensable economic, social and cultural values of the marine environment of the Baltic Sea Area and its living resources for the peoples of the Contracting Parties;

Bearing in mind the exceptional hydrographic and ecological charac-teristics of the Baltic Sea Area and the sensitivity of its living resources to changes in the environment;

Noting the rapid development of human activities at the Baltic Sea Area, the considerable population living within its catchment area and the highly urbanized and industrialized state of the Contracting Parties as well as their intensive agriculture and forestry;

Noting with deep concern the increasing pollution of the Baltic Sea Area, originating from many sources such as discharges through rivers, estuaries, outfalls and pipelines, dumping and normal operations of vessels as well as through airborne pollutants;

Conscious of the responsibility of the Contracting Parties to protect and enhance the values of the marine environment of the Baltic Sea Area for the benefit of their peoples;

Recognizing that the protection and enhancement of the marine environment of the Baltic Sea Area are tasks that cannot effectively be accomplished by national efforts only but that also close regional co-operation and other appropriate international measures aiming at fulfilling these tasks are urgently needed;

Noting that the relevant recent international conventions even after having entered into force for the respective Contracting Parties do not cover all special requirements to protect and enhance the marine environment of the Baltic Sea Area;

Noting the importance of scientific and technological co-operation in the protection and enhancement of the marine environment of the Baltic Sea Area, particularly between the Contracting Parties;

Desiring to develop further regional co-operation in the Baltic Sea Area, the possibilities and requirements of which were confirmed by the signing of

---

[1] *Supra* Division I, Subdivision A, 4.

[2] Signed by Denmark, Finland, German Democratic Republic, Federal Republic of Germany, Polish People's Republic, Sweden and the Union of Soviet Socialist Republics. English text provided by the Ministry of Foreign Affairs of Denmark in a note verbale of 20 December 1974.

the Convention on Fishing and Conservation of the Living Resources in the Baltic Sea and the Belts, Gdansk 1973;

Conscious of the importance of regional intergovernmental co-operation in the protection of the marine environment of the Baltic Sea Area as an integral part of the peaceful co-operation and mutual understanding between all European States;

Have agreed as follows:

Article 1. Convention Area

For the purposes of the present Convention "the Baltic Sea Area" shall be the Baltic Sea proper with the Gulf of Bothnia, the Gulf of Finland and the entrance to the Baltic Sea bounded by the parallel of the Skaw in the Skagerrak at 57° 44′ 8″ N. It does not include internal waters of the Contracting Parties.

Article 2. Definitions

For the purposes of the present Convention:

1. "Pollution" means introduction by man, directly or indirectly, of substances or energy into the marine environment, including estuaries, resulting in such deleterious effects as hazard to human health, harm to living resources and marine life, hindrance to legitimate uses of the sea including fishing, impairment of the quality for use of sea water, and reduction of amenities;

2. "Land-based pollution" means pollution of the sea caused by discharges from land reaching the sea waterborne, airborne or directly from the coast, including outfalls from pipelines;

3. *(a)* "Dumping" means:
   (i) Any deliberate disposal at sea of wastes or other matter from vessels, aircraft, platforms or other man-made structures at sea;
   (ii) Any deliberate disposal at sea of vessels, aircraft, platforms or other man-made structures at sea;

(b) "Dumping" does not include:
   (i) The disposal at sea of wastes or other matter incidental to, or derived from the normal operations of vessels, aircraft, platforms or other man-made structures at sea and their equipment, other than wastes or other matter transported by or to vessels, aircraft, platforms or other man-made structures at sea, operating for the purpose of disposal of such matter or derived from the treatment of such wastes or other matter on such vessels, aircraft, platforms or structures;
   (ii) Placement of matter for a purpose other than the mere disposal thereof, provided that such placement is not contrary to the aims of the present Convention;

4. "Vessels and aircraft" means waterborne or airborne craft of any type whatsoever. This expression includes hydrofoil boats, air-cushion vehicles, submersibles, floating craft whether self-propelled or not, and fixed or floating platforms;

5. "Oil" means petroleum in any form including crude oil, fuel oil, sludge, oil refuse and refined products;

6. "Harmful substance" means any hazardous, noxious, or other substance, which, if introduced into the sea, is liable to cause pollution;

7. "Incident" means an event involving the actual or probable discharge into the sea of a harmful substance, or effluents containing such a substance.

Article 3. Fundamental principles and obligations

1. The Contracting Parties shall individually or jointly take all appropriate legislative, administrative or other relevant measures in order to prevent and abate pollution and to protect and enhance the marine environment of the Baltic Sea Area.

2. The Contracting Parties shall use their best endeavours to ensure that the implementation of the present Convention shall not cause an increase in the pollution of sea areas outside the Baltic Sea Area.

Article 4. Application

1. The present Convention shall apply to the protection of the marine environment of the Baltic Sea Area which comprises the water-body and the sea-bed including their living resources and other forms of marine life.

2. Without prejudice to the sovereign rights in regard to their territorial sea, each Contracting Party shall implement the provisions of the present Convention within its territorial sea through its national authorities.

3. While the provisions of the present Convention do not apply to internal waters, which are under the sovereignty of each Contracting Party, the Contracting Parties undertake, without prejudice to their sovereign rights, to ensure that the purposes of the present Convention will be obtained in these waters.

4. The present Convention shall not apply to any warship, naval auxiliary, military aircraft or other ship and aircraft owned or operated by a State and used, for the time being, only on government non-commercial service.

However, each Contracting Party shall ensure, by the adoption of appropriate measures not impairing the operations or operational capabilities of such ships and aircraft owned or operated by it, that such ships and aircraft act in a manner consistent, so far as is reasonable and practicable, with the present Convention.

Article 5. Hazardous substances

The Contracting Parties undertake to counteract the introduction, whether airborne, waterborne or otherwise, into the Baltic Sea Area of hazardous substances as specified in Annex I of the present Convention.

Article 6. Principles and obligations concerning land-based pollution

1. The Contracting Parties shall take all appropriate measures to control and minimize land-based pollution of the marine environment of the Baltic Sea Area.

2. In particular, the Contracting Parties shall take all appropriate measures to control and strictly limit pollution by noxious substances and materials in accordance with Annex II of the present Convention. To this end they shall, *inter alia*, as appropriate co-operate in the development and adoption of specific programmes, guidelines, standards or regulations concerning discharges, environmental quality, and products containing such substances and materials and their use.

3. The substances and materials listed in Annex II of the present Convention shall not be introduced into the marine environment of the Baltic Sea Area in significant quantities without a prior special permit, which may be periodically reviewed, by the appropriate national authority.

4. The appropriate national authority will inform the Commission referred to in Article 12 of the present Convention of the quantity, quality and way of discharge if it considers that significant quantities of substances and materials listed in Annex II of the present Convention were discharged.

5. The Contracting Parties shall endeavour to establish and adopt common criteria for issuing permits for discharges.

6. To control and minimize pollution of the Baltic Sea Area by harmful substances the Contracting Parties shall, in addition to the provisions of Article 5 of the present Convention, aim at attaining the goals and applying the criteria enumerated in Annex III of the present Convention.

7. If the discharge from a watercourse, flowing through the territories of two or more Contracting Parties or forming a boundary between them, is liable to cause pollution of the marine environment of the Baltic Sea Area, the Contracting Parties concerned shall in common take appropriate measures in order to prevent and abate such pollution.

8. The Contracting Parties shall endeavour to use best practicable means in order to minimize the airborne pollution of the Baltic Sea Area by noxious substances.

Article 7. Prevention of pollution from ships

1. In order to protect the Baltic Sea Area from pollution by deliberate, negligent or accidental release of oil, harmful substances other than oil, and by the discharge of sewage and garbage from ships, the Contracting Parties shall take measures as set out in Annex IV of the present Convention.

2. The Contracting Parties shall develop and apply uniform requirements for the capacity and location of facilities for the reception of residues of oil, harmful substances other than oil, including sewage and garbage, taking into account *inter alia* the special needs of passenger ships and combination carriers.

Article 8. Pleasure craft

The Contracting Parties shall, in addition to implementing those provisions of the present Convention which can appropriately be applied to pleasure craft, take special measures in order to abate harmful effects on the marine environment of the Baltic Sea Area of pleasure craft activities. The measures shall *inter alia* deal with adequate reception facilities for wastes from pleasure craft.

Article 9. Prevention of dumping

1. The Contracting Parties shall, subject to Paragraphs 2 and 4 of this Article, prohibit dumping in the Baltic Sea Area.

2. Dumping of dredged spoils shall be subject to a prior special permit by the appropriate national authority in accordance with the provisions of Annex V of the present Convention.

3. Each Contracting Party undertakes to ensure compliance with the provisions of this Article by vessels and aircraft:

(a) Registered in its territory or flying its flag;

(b) Loading, within its territory or territorial sea, matter which is to be dumped; or

(c) Believed to be engaged in dumping within its territorial sea.

4. The provisions of this Article shall not apply when the safety of human life or of a vessel or aircraft at sea is threatened by the complete destruction or total loss of the vessel or aircraft, or in any case which constitutes a danger to human life, if dumping appears to be the only way of averting the threat and if there is every probability that the damage consequent upon such dumping will be less than would otherwise occur. Such dumping shall be so conducted as to minimize the likelihood of damage to human or marine life.

5. Dumping made under the provisions of Paragraph 4 of this Article shall be reported and dealt with in accordance with Annex VI of the present Convention and shall also be reported forthwith to the Commission referred to in Article 12 of the present Convention in accordance with the provisions of Regulation 4 of Annex V of the present Convention.

6. In case of dumping suspected to be in contravention of the provisions of this Article the Contracting Parties shall co-operate in investigating the matter in accordance with Regulation 2 of Annex IV of the present Convention.

Article 10. Exploration and exploitation of the sea-bed and its subsoil

Each Contracting Party shall take all appropriate measures in order to prevent pollution of the marine environment of the Baltic Sea Area resulting from exploration or exploitation of its part of the sea-bed and its subsoil or from any associated activities thereon. It shall also ensure that adequate equipment is at hand to start an immediate abatement of pollution in that area.

Article 11. Co-operation in combating marine pollution

The Contracting Parties shall take measures and co-operate as set out in Annex VI of the present Convention in order to eliminate or minimize pollution of the Baltic Sea Area by oil or other harmful substances.

Article 12. Institutional and organizational framework

1. The Baltic Marine Environment Protection Commission, hereinafter referred to as "the Commission", is hereby established for the purposes of the present Convention.

2. The chairmanship of the Commission shall be given to each Contracting Party in turn in alphabetical order of the names of the States in the English language.

The Chairman shall serve for a period of two years, and cannot during the period of his chairmanship serve as representative of his country.

Should the chairmanship fall vacant, the Contracting Party chairing the Commission shall nominate a successor to remain in office until the term of chairmanship of that Contracting Party expires.

3. Meetings of the Commission shall be held at least once a year upon convocation by the Chairman. Upon the request of a Contracting Party, provided it is endorsed by another Contracting Party, the Chairman shall, as soon as possible, summon an extraordinary meeting at such time and place as the Chairman determines, however, not later than ninety days from the date of the submission of the request.

4. The first meeting of the Commission shall be called by the Depositary Government and shall take place within a period of ninety days from the date following the entry into force of the present Convention.

5. Each Contracting Party shall have one vote in the Commission. Unless otherwise provided under the present Convention, the Commission shall take its decisions unanimously.

Article 13. The duties of the Commission

The duties of the Commission shall be:

(a) To keep the implementation of the present Convention under continuous observation;

(b) To make recommendations on measures relating to the purposes of the present Convention;

(c) To keep under review the contents of the present Convention including its Annexes and to recommend to the Contracting Parties such amendments to the present Convention including its Annexes as may be required including changes in the lists of substances and materials as well as the adoption of new Annexes;

(d) To define pollution control criteria, objectives for the reduction of pollution, and objectives concerning measures, particularly according to Annex III of the present Convention;

(e) To promote in close co-operation with appropriate governmental bodies, taking into consideration subparagraph *(f)* of this Article, additional measures to protect the marine environment of the Baltic Sea Area and for this purpose:

(i) To receive, process, summarize and disseminate from available sources relevant scientific, technological and statistical information; and

(ii) To promote scientific and technological research;

(f) To seek, when appropriate, the services of competent regional and other international organizations to collaborate in scientific and technological

research as well as other relevant activities pertinent to the objectives of the present Convention;

(g) To assume such other functions as may be appropriate under the terms of the present Convention.

Article 14. Administrative provisions for the Commission

1. The working language of the Commission shall be English.

2. The Commission shall adopt its Rules of Procedure.

3. The office of the Commission, hereafter referred to as the "Secretariat", shall be in Helsinki.

4. The Commission shall appoint an Executive Secretary and make provisions for the appointment of such other personnel as may be necessary, and determine the duties, terms and conditions of the Executive Secretary.

5. The Executive Secretary shall be the chief administrative official of the Commission and shall perform the functions that are necessary for the administration of the present Convention, the work of the Commission and other tasks entrusted to the Executive Secretary by the Commission and its Rules of Procedure.

Article 15. Financial provisions for the Commission

1. The Commission shall adopt its Financial Rules.

2. The Commission shall adopt an annual or biennial budget of proposed expenditures and budget estimates for the fiscal period following thereafter.

3. The total amount of the budget, including any supplementary budget adopted by the Commission, shall be contributed by the Contracting Parties in equal parts, unless the Commission unanimously decides otherwise.

4. Each Contracting Party shall pay the expenses related to the participation in the Commission of its representatives, experts and advisers.

Article 16. Scientific and technological co-operation

1. The Contracting Parties undertake directly, or when appropriate through competent regional or other international organizations, to co-operate in the fields of science, technology and other research, and to exchange data as well as other scientific information for the purposes of the present Convention.

2. Without prejudice to Paragraphs 1, 2 and 3 of Article 4 of the present Convention the Contracting Parties undertake directly, or when appropriate through competent regional or other international organizations, to promote studies, undertake, support or contribute to programmes aimed at developing ways and means for the assessment of the nature and extent of pollution, pathways, exposures, risks and remedies in the Baltic Sea Area, and particularly to develop alternative methods of treatment, disposal and elimination of such matter and substances that are likely to cause pollution of the marine environment of the Baltic Sea Area.

3. The Contracting Parties undertake directly, or when appropriate through competent regional or other international organizations, and, on the

basis of the information and data acquired pursuant to Paragraphs 1 and 2 of this Article, to co-operate in developing inter-comparable observation methods, in performing baseline studies and in establishing complementary or joint programmes for monitoring.

4. The organization and scope of work connected with the implementation of tasks referred to in the preceding Paragraphs should primarily be outlined by the Commission.

Article 17. Responsibility for damage

The Contracting Parties undertake, as soon as possible, jointly to develop and accept rules concerning responsibility for damage resulting from acts or omissions in contravention of the present Convention, including, *inter alia*, limits of responsibility, criteria and procedures for the determination of liability and available remedies.

Article 18. Settlement of disputes

1. In case of a dispute between Contracting Parties as to the interpretation or application of the present Convention, they should seek a solution by negotiation. If the Parties concerned cannot reach agreement they should seek the good offices of or jointly request the mediation by a third Contracting Party, a qualified international organization or a qualified person.

2. If the Parties concerned have not been able to resolve their dispute through negotiation or have been unable to agree on measures as described above, such disputes shall be, upon common agreement, submitted to an ad-hoc arbitration tribunal, to a permanent arbitration tribunal, or to the International Court of Justice.

Article 19. Safeguard of certain freedoms

Nothing in the present Convention shall be construed as infringing upon the freedom of navigation, fishing, marine scientific research and other legitimate uses of the high seas, as well as upon the right of innocent passage through the territorial sea.

Article 20. Status of Annexes

The Annexes attached to the present Convention form an integral part of the Convention.

Article 21. Relation to other Conventions

The provisions of the present Convention shall be without prejudice to the rights and obligations of the Contracting Parties under treaties concluded previously as well as under treaties which may be concluded in the future, furthering and developing the general principles of the Law of the Sea that the present Convention is based upon and in particular provisions concerning the prevention of pollution of the marine environment.

Article 22. Revision of the Convention

A conference for the purpose of a general revision of the present Convention may be convened with the consent of the Contracting Parties or at the request of the Commission.

Article 23.   Amendments to the Articles of the Convention

1.   Each Contracting Party may propose amendments to the Articles of the present Convention. Any such proposed amendment shall be submitted to the Depositary Government and communicated by it to all Contracting Parties, which shall inform the Depositary Government of either their acceptance or rejection of the amendment as soon as possible after the receipt of the communication.

The amendment shall enter into force ninety days after the Depositary Government has received notifications of acceptance of that amendment from all Contracting Parties.

2.   With the consent of the Contracting Parties or at the request of the Commission a conference may be convened for the purpose of amending the present Convention.

Article 24.   Amendments to the Annexes and the adoption of Annexes

1.   Any amendment to the Annexes proposed by a Contracting Party shall be communicated to the other Contracting Parties by the Depositary Government and considered in the Commission. If adopted by the Commission, the amendment shall be communicated to the Contracting Parties and recommended for acceptance.

2.   Such amendment shall be deemed to have been accepted at the end of a period determined by the Commission unless within that period any one of the Contracting Parties has objected to the amendment. The accepted amendment shall enter into force on a date determined by the Commission.

The period determined by the Commission shall be prolonged for an additional period of six months and the date of entry into force of the amendment postponed accordingly, if, in exceptional cases, any Contracting Party before the expiring of the period determined by the Commission informs the Depositary Government that, although it intends to accept the proposal, the constitutional requirements for such an acceptance are not yet fulfilled in its State.

3.   An Annex to the present Convention may be adopted in accordance with the provisions of this Article.

4.   The Depositary Government shall inform all Contracting Parties of any amendments or the adoption of a new Annex which enter into force under this Article and of the date on which such amendment or new Annex enters into force.

5.   Any objection under this Article shall be made by notification in writing to the Depositary Government which shall notify all Contracting Parties and the Executive Secretary of any such notification and the date of its receipt.

Article 25.   Reservations

1.   The provisions of the present Convention shall not be subject to reservations.

2. The provision of Paragraph 1 of this Article does not prevent a Contracting Party from suspending for a period not exceeding one year the application of an Annex of the present Convention or part thereof or an amendment thereto after the Annex in question or the amendment thereto has entered into force.

3. If after the entry into force of the present Convention a Contracting Party invokes the provisions of Paragraph 2 of this Article it shall inform the other Contracting Parties, at the time of the adoption by the Commission of an amendment to an Annex or a new Annex, of those provisions which will be suspended in accordance with Paragraph 2 of this Article.

Article 26. Signature, ratification, approval, and accession

1. The present Convention shall be open for signature in Helsinki on 22 March 1974 by the Baltic Sea States participating in the Diplomatic Conference on the Protection of the Marine Environment of the Baltic Sea Area, held in Helsinki from 18 to 22 March 1974. The present Convention shall be open for accession to any other State interested in fulfilling the aims and purposes of the present Convention, provided that this State is invited by all the Contracting Parties.

2. The present Convention shall be subject to ratification or approval by the States which have signed it.

3. The instruments of ratification, approval or accession shall be deposited with the Government of Finland, which will perform the duties of the Depositary Government.

Article 27. Entry into force

The present Convention shall enter into force two months after the deposit of the seventh instrument of ratification or approval.

Article 28. Withdrawal

1. At any time after the expiry of five years from the date of entry into force of the present Convention any Contracting Party may, by giving written notification to the Depositary Government, withdraw from the present Convention. The withdrawal shall take effect for such Contracting Party on the thirty-first day of December of the year which follows the year in which the Depositary Government was notified of the withdrawal.

2. In case of notification of withdrawal by a Contracting Party the Depositary Government shall convene a meeting of the Contracting Parties for the purpose of considering the effect of the withdrawal.

Article 29. Language

The present Convention has been drawn up in a single copy in the English language. Official translations into the Danish, Finnish, German, Polish, Russian, and Swedish languages shall be prepared and deposited with the signed original.

In witness whereof the undersigned Plenipotentiaries, being duly authorized thereto, have signed the present Convention.

Done at Helsinki, this twenty-second day of March one thousand nine hundred and seventy-four.

ANNEX I. HAZARDOUS SUBSTANCES

The protection of the Baltic Sea Area from pollution by the substances listed below can involve the use of appropriate technical means, prohibitions and regulations of the transport, trade, handling, application, and final deposition of products containing such substances.

1. DDT (1,1,1-trichloro-2,2-bis-(chlorophenyl)-ethane) and its derivatives DDE and DDD.
2. PCB's (polychlorinated biphenyls).

ANNEX II. NOXIOUS SUBSTANCES AND MATERIALS

The following substances and materials are listed for the purposes of Article 6 of the present Convention.

The list is valid for substances and materials introduced as waterborne into the marine environment. The Contracting Parties shall also endeavour to use best practicable means to prevent harmful substances and materials from being introduced as airborne into the Baltic Sea Area.

A. For urgent consideration

1. Mercury, cadmium, and their compounds.

B.

2. Antimony, arsenic, beryllium, chromium, copper, lead, molybdenum, nickel, selenium, tin, vanadium, zinc, and their compounds, as well as elemental phosphorus.
3. Phenols and their derivatives.
4. Phthalic acid and its derivatives.
5. Cyanides.
6. Persistent halogenated hydrocarbons.
7. Polycyclic aromatic hydrocarbons and their derivatives.
8. Persistent toxic organosilicic compounds.
9. Persistent pesticides, including organophosphoric and organostannic pesticides, herbicides, slimicides and chemicals used for the preservation of wood, timber, wood pulp, cellulose, paper, hides and textiles, not covered by the provisions of Annex I of the present Convention.
10. Radioactive materials.
11. Acids, alkalis and surface active agents in high concentrations or big quantities.
12. Oil and wastes of petrochemical and other industries containing lipid-soluble substances.
13. Substances having adverse effects on the taste and/or smell of products for human consumption from the sea, or effects on taste, smell, colour, transparency or other characteristics of the water seriously reducing its amenity values.
14. Materials and substances which may float, remain in suspension or sink, and which may seriously interfere with any legitimate use of the sea.
15. Lignin substances contained in industrial waste waters.
16. The chelators EDTA (ethylenedinitrilotetraacetic acid or ethylenediaminete-.traacetic acid) and DTPA (diethylenetriaminopentaacetic acid).

ANNEX III. GOALS, CRITERIA AND MEASURES CONCERNING THE PREVENTION OF LAND-BASED POLLUTION

In accordance with the provisions of Article 6 of the present Convention the Contracting Parties shall endeavour to attain the goals and apply the criteria and measures enumerated in this Annex in order to control and minimize land-based pollution of the marine environment of the Baltic Sea Area.

1. Municipal sewage shall be treated in an appropriate way so that the amount of organic matter does not cause harmful changes in the oxygen content of the Baltic Sea Area and the amount of nutrients does not cause harmful eutrophication of the Baltic Sea Area.

2. Municipal sewage shall also be treated in an appropriate way to ensure that the hygienic quality, and in particular epidemiological and toxicological safety, of the receiving sea area is maintained at a level which does not cause harm to human health, and in a way that under the given composition of the sewage no significant amount of such harmful substances as are listed in Annexes I and II of the present Convention is formed.

3. The polluting load of industrial wastes shall be minimized in an appropriate way in order to reduce the amount of harmful substances, organic matter and nutrients.

4. The means referred to in Paragraph 3 of this Annex shall in particular include minimization of production of wastes by processing techniques, re-circulation and re-use of processing water, developing of water economy and improvement of qualifications for water treatment. In the treatment of waste water mechanical, chemical, biological and other measures, according to the quality of the waste water, and as required to maintain or improve the quality of the recipient water, shall be applied.

5. The discharge of cooling water from nuclear power plants or other kinds of industries using large amounts of water shall be effected in a way which minimizes the pollution of the marine environment of the Baltic Sea Area.

6. The Commission will define pollution control criteria, objectives for reduction of pollution and objectives concerning measures, including processing techniques and waste treatment, to reduce pollution of the Baltic Sea Area.

ANNEX IV. PREVENTION OF POLLUTION FROM SHIPS

Regulation 1

The Contracting Parties shall as appropriate co-operate and assist each other in initiating action by the Inter-Governmental Maritime Consultative Organization to develop:

(a) International rules for navigation of deep draught ships in narrow and shallow waters in international waters of the Baltic Sea Area and in the entrances to the Baltic Sea for the prevention of collisions, strandings and groundings;

(b) An international radio reporting system for large ships en route within the Baltic Sea Area as well as for ships carrying a significant amount of a harmful substance.

Regulation 2

The Contracting Parties shall, without prejudice to Paragraph 4 of Article 4 of the present Convention, as appropriate assist each other in investigating violations of the existing legislation on anti-pollution measures, which have occurred or are suspected to have occurred within the Baltic Sea Area. This assistance may include but is not limited to inspection by the competent authorities of oil record books, cargo record books, log books and engine log books and taking oil samples for analytical identification purposes and in respect of the system of tagging oil residues.

Regulation 3. Definitions

For the purposes of this Annex:

1. "Ship" means a vessel of any type whatsoever operating in the marine environment and includes hydrofoil boats, air-cushion vehicles, submersibles, floating craft and fixed or floating platforms.

2. "Administration" means the Government of the State under whose authority the ship is operating. With respect to a ship entitled to fly a flag of any State, the Administration is the Government of that State. With respect to fixed or floating platforms engaged in exploration and exploitation of the sea-bed and subsoil thereof adjacent to the coast over which the coastal State exercises sovereign rights for the purposes of exploration and exploitation of their natural resources, the Administration is the Government of the coastal State concerned.

3. *(a)* "Discharge", in relation to harmful substances or effluents containing such substances, means any release howsoever caused from a ship and includes any escape, disposal, spilling, leaking, pumping, emitting or emptying;

(b) "Discharge" does not include:

  (i) Dumping within the meaning of the Convention on the Prevention of Marine Pollution by Dumping of Wastes and Other Matter done at London on 29 December 1972; or

  (ii) Release of harmful substances directly arising from the exploration, exploitation and associated off-shore processing of sea-bed mineral resources; or

  (iii) Release of harmful substances for purposes of legitimate scientific research into pollution abatement or control.

4. "Nearest land". The term "from the nearest land" means from the baseline from which the territorial sea of the territory in question is established in accordance with international law.

5. The term "jurisdiction" shall be interpreted in accordance with international law in force at the time of application or interpretation of this Annex.

Regulation 4. Oil

The Contracting Parties shall as soon as possible but not later than 1 January 1977 or on the date of entry into force of the present Convention, whichever occurs later, apply the provisions of Paragraphs A to D of this Regulation on methods for the prevention of pollution by oil from ships while operating in the Baltic Sea Area.

A. Definitions

For the purposes of this Regulation:

1. "Oil" means petroleum in any form including crude oil, fuel oil, sludge, oil refuse and refined products (other than petrochemicals which are subject to the provisions of Regulation 5 of this Annex) and, without limiting the generality of the foregoing, includes the substances listed in Appendix I to this Annex.

2. "Oily mixture" means a mixture with any oil content.

3. "Oil fuel" means any oil used as fuel in connection with the propulsion and auxiliary machinery of the ship in which such oil is carried.

4. "Oil tanker" means a ship constructed or adapted primarily to carry oil in bulk in its cargo spaces and includes combination carriers and any "chemical tanker" as defined in Regulation 5 of this Annex when it is carrying a cargo or part cargo of oil in bulk.

5. "Combination carrier" means a ship designed to carry either oil or solid cargoes in bulk.

6. "Clean ballast" means the ballast in a tank which since oil was last carried therein has been so cleaned that effluent therefrom if it were discharged from a ship which is stationary into clean calm water on a clear day would not produce visible traces of oil on the surface of the water or on adjoining shore lines or cause a sludge or emulsion to be deposited beneath the surface of the water or upon adjoining shore lines. If the ballast is discharged through an oil discharge monitoring and control system approved by the Administration, evidence based on such a system to the effect that the oil content of the effluent did not exceed 15 parts per million shall be determinative that the ballast was clean, notwithstanding the presence of visible traces.

7. "Segregated ballast" means the ballast water introduced into a tank which is completely separated from the cargo oil and oil fuel system and which is permanently allocated to the carriage of ballast or to the carriage of ballast or cargoes other than oil or noxious substances as variously defined in the Regulations of this Annex.

B. Control of Discharge of Oil

1. *(a)* Subject to the provisions of Paragraph C of this Regulation, any discharge into the sea of oil or oily mixtures from any oil tanker and any ship of 400 tons gross tonnage and above other than an oil tanker shall be prohibited, while in the Baltic Sea Area;

(b) Such ships while in the Baltic Sea Area shall retain on board all oil drainage and sludge, dirty ballast and tank washing waters and discharge them only to reception facilities.

2. *(a)* Subject to the provisions of Paragraph C of this Regulation, any discharge into the sea of oil or oily mixtures from a ship of less than 400 tons gross tonnage, other than an oil tanker, shall be prohibited while in the Baltic Sea Area, except when the oil content of the effluent without dilution does not exceed 15 parts per million or alternatively when all of the following conditions are satisfied:

(i) The ship is proceeding en route;

(ii) The oil content of the effluent is less than 100 parts per million; and

(iii) The discharge is made as far as practicable from the land, but in no case less than 12 nautical miles from the nearest land;

(b) No discharge into the sea shall contain chemicals or other substances in quantities or concentrations which are hazardous to the marine environment or chemicals or other substances introduced for the purpose of circumventing the conditions of discharge specified in this Regulation;

(c) The oil residues which cannot be discharged into the sea in compliance with Sub-Paragraph 2 *(a)* of this Paragraph shall be retained on board or discharged to reception facilities.

3. The provisions of this Paragraph shall not apply to the discharge of clean or segregated ballast.

4. Whenever visible traces of oil are observed on or below the surface of the water in the immediate vicinity of a ship or its wake, the Contracting Parties should, to the extent they are reasonably able to do so, promptly investigate the facts bearing on the issue of whether there has been a violation of the provisions of this Regulation. The investigation should include, in particular, the wind and sea conditions, the track and speed of the ship, other possible sources of the visible traces in the vicinity, and any relevant oil discharge records.

C. Exceptions

Paragraph B of this Regulation shall not apply to:

(a) The discharge into the sea of oil or oily mixtures necessary for the purpose of securing the safety of a ship or saving life at sea; or

(b) The discharge into the sea of oil or oily mixtures resulting from damage to a ship or its equipment:

    (i) Provided that all reasonable precautions have been taken after the occurrence of the damage or discovery of the discharge for the purpose of preventing or minimizing the discharge; and ·

    (ii) Except if the owner or the Master acted either with intent to cause damage, or recklessly and with knowledge that damage would probably result; or

(c) The discharge into the sea of substances containing oil, approved by the Administration, when being used for the purpose of combatting specific pollution incidents in order to minimize the damage from pollution. Any such discharge shall be subject to the approval of any Contracting Party in whose jurisdiction it is contemplated the discharge will occur.

D. Special Requirements for Drilling Rigs and other Platforms

Fixed and floating drilling rigs when engaged in the exploration, exploitation and associated offshore processing of sea-bed mineral resources and other platforms shall comply with the requirements of this Regulation applicable to ships of 400 tons gross tonnage and above other than oil tankers, except that:

(a) They shall keep a record of all operations involving oil or oily mixture discharges, in a form approve by the Administration; and

(b) Subject to the provisions of Paragraph C of this Regulation, the discharge into the sea of oil or oily mixtures shall be prohibited except when the oil content of the discharge without dilution does not exceed 15 parts per million.

E. Reception Facilities of the Baltic Sea Area

The Contracting Parties undertake to ensure that not later than 1 January 1977 all oil loading terminals and repair ports of the Baltic Sea Area are provided with facilities adequate for the reception and treatment of all the dirty ballast and tank washing waters from oil tankers. In addition all ports of the area shall be provided with adequate reception facilities for other residues and oily mixtures from all ships. Such facilities shall have adequate capacity to meet the needs of the ships using them without causing undue delay.

Regulation 5. Noxious liquid substances in bulk

The Contracting Parties shall as soon as possible, but not later than 1 January 1977 or at a date not later than one year after the date of the entry into force of the present Convention, whichever occurs later, decide upon a date from which the provisions of Paragraphs A to D of this Regulation on the discharge of noxious liquid substances in bulk from ships while operating in the Baltic Sea Area shall apply.

A. Definitions

For the purposes of this Regulation:

1. "Chemical tanker" means a ship constructed or adapted primarily to carry a cargo of noxious liquid substances in bulk and includes an "oil tanker" as defined in Regulation 4 of this Annex when carrying a cargo or part cargo of noxious liquid substances in bulk.

2. "Clean ballast" means ballast carried in a tank which, since it was last used to carry a cargo containing a substance in Category A, B, C, or D has been thoroughly cleaned and the residues resulting therefrom have been discharged and the tank emptied in accordance with the appropriate requirements of this Regulation.

3. "Segregated ballast" means ballast water introduced into a tank permanently allocated to the carriage of ballast or to the carriage of ballast or cargoes other than oil

or noxious liquid substances as variously defined in the Regulations of this Annex, and which is completely separated from the cargo and oil fuel system.

4. "Liquid substances" are those having a vapour pressure not exceeding 2.8 kg/cm^2 at a temperature 37.8° C.

5. "Noxious liquid substance" means any substance designated in Appendix III to this Annex or provisionally assessed under the provisions of Sub-Paragraph 4 of Paragraph B of this Regulation as falling into Category A, B, C, or D.

B. Categorization and Listing of Noxious Liquid Substances

1. For the purposes of this Regulation noxious liquid substances shall be divided into four categories as follows:

(a) Category A–noxious liquid substances which if discharged into the sea from tank cleaning or deballasting operations would present a major hazard to either marine resources or human health or cause serious harm to amenities or other legitimate uses of the sea and therefore justify the application of stringent anti-pollution measures;

(b) Category B–noxious liquid substances which if discharged into the sea from tank cleaning or deballasting operations would present a hazard to either marine resources or human health or cause harm to amenities or other legitimate uses of the sea and therefore justify the application of special anti-pollution measures;

(c) Category C–noxious liquid substances which if discharged into the sea from tank cleaning or deballasting operations would present a minor hazard to either marine resources or human health or cause minor harm to amenities or other legitimate uses of the sea and therefore require special operational conditions;

(d) Category D–noxious liquid substances which if discharged into the sea from tank cleaning or deballasting operations would present a recognizable hazard to either marine resources or human health or cause minimal harm to amenities or other legitimate uses of the sea and therefore require some attention in operational conditions.

2. Guidelines for use in the categorization of noxious liquid substances are given in Appendix II to this Annex.

3. The list of noxious liquid substances carried in bulk and presently categorized which are subject to the provisions of this Regulation is set out in Appendix III to this Annex.

4. Where it is proposed to carry a liquid substance in bulk which has not been categorized under Sub-Paragraph 1 of this Paragraph or evaluated as referred to in Sub-Paragraph 1 of Paragraph C of this Regulation the Contracting Parties involved in the proposed operation shall establish and agree on a provisional assessment for the proposed operation on the basis of the guidelines referred to in Sub-Paragraph 2 of this Paragraph. Until full agreement between the Governments involved has been reached, the substance shall be carried under the most severe conditions proposed.

C. Other Liquid Substances

1. The substances listed in Appendix IV to this Annex have been evaluated and found to fall outside the Categories A, B, C, and D, as defined in Sub-Paragraph 1 of Paragraph B of this Regulation because they are presently considered to present no harm to human health, marine resources, amenities or other legitimate uses of the sea, when discharged into the sea from tank cleaning or deballasting operations.

2. The discharge of bilge or ballast water or other residues or mixtures containing only substances listed in Appendix IV to this Annex shall not be subject to any requirement of this Regulation.

3. The discharge into the sea of clean ballast or segregated ballast shall not be subject to any requirement to this Regulation.

D. Discharge of Noxious Liquid Substances

Subject to the provisions of Paragraph E of this Regulation:

1. The discharge into the sea of substances in Category A as defined in Sub-Paragraph 1 *(a)* of Paragraph B of this Regulation, or of those provisionally assessed as such or ballast water, tank washings, or other residues or mixtures containing such substances shall be prohibited. If tanks containing such substances or mixtures are to be washed, the resulting residues shall be discharged to a reception facility which the Contracting Parties shall provide in accordance with Paragraph II of this Regulation, until the concentration of the substance in the effluent to such facility is at or below the residual concentration prescribed for that substance in column IV of Appendix III to this Annex and until the tank is empty. Provided that the residue then remaining in the tank is subsequently diluted by the addition of a volume of water of not less than 5 per cent of the total volume of the tank, it may be discharged into the sea when all the following conditions are also satisfied:

(a) The ship is proceeding en route at a speed of at least 7 knots in the case of self-propelled ships or at least 4 knots in the case of ships which are not self-propelled;

(b) The discharge is made below the waterline, taking into account the location of the seawater intakes; and

(c) The discharge is made at a distance of not less than 12 nautical miles from the nearest land and in a depth of water of not less than 25 metres.

2. The discharge into the sea of substances in Category B as defined in Sub-Paragraph 1 *(b)* of Paragraph B of this Regulation or of those provisionally assessed as such or ballast water, tank washings, or other residues or mixtures containing such substances shall be prohibited except when all the following conditions are satisfied:

(a) The tank has been washed after unloading with a volume of water of not less than 0.5 per cent of the total volume of the tank, and the resulting residues have been discharged to a reception facility until the tank is empty;

(b) The ship is proceeding en route at a speed of at least 7 knots in the case of self-propelled ships or at least 4 knots in the case of ships which are not self-propelled;

(c) The procedures and arrangements for discharge and washings are approved by the Administration and shall ensure that the concentration and rate of discharge of the effluent is such that the concentration of the substance in the wake astern of the ship does not exceed 1 part per million;

(d) The discharge is made below the waterline, taking into account the location of the seawater intakes; and

(e) The discharge is made at a distance of not less than 12 nautical miles from the nearest land and in a depth of water of not less than 25 metres.

3. The discharge into the sea of substances in Category C as defined in Sub-Paragraph 1 *(c)* of Paragraph B of this Regulation or of those provisionally assessed as such or ballast water, tank washings, or other residues or mixtures containing such substances shall be prohibited except when all the following conditions are satisfied:

(a) The ship is proceeding en route at a speed of at least 7 knots in the case of self-propelled ships or at least 4 knots in the case of ships which are not self-propelled;

(b) The procedures and arrangements for discharge are approved by the Administration and shall ensure that the concentration and rate of discharge of the effluent is such that the concentration of the substance in the wake astern of the ship does not exceed 1 part per million;

(c) The maximum quantity of cargo discharged from each tank and its associated piping system does not exceed the maximum quantity approved in accordance with the procedures referred to in Sub-Paragraph 3 *(b)* of this Paragraph which shall in no case exceed the greater of 1 cubic metre or 1/3.000 of the tank capacity in cubic metres;

(d) The discharge is made below the waterline, taking into account the location of the seawater intakes; and

(e) The discharge is made at a distance of not less than 12 nautical miles from the nearest land and in a depth of water of not less than 25 metres.

4. The discharge into the sea of substances in Category D as defined in Sub-Paragraph 1 *(d)* of Paragraph B of this Regulation, or of those provisionally assessed as such or ballast water, tank washings, or other residues or mixtures containing such substances shall be prohibited except when all the following conditions are satisfied:

(a) The ship is proceeding en route at a speed of at least 7 knots in the case of self-propelled ships or at least 4 knots in the case of ships which are not self-propelled;

(b) Such mixtures are of a concentration not greater than one part of the substance in ten parts of water; and

(c) The discharge is made at a distance of not less than 12 nautical miles from the nearest land.

5. Ventilation procedures approved by the Administration may be used to remove cargo residues from a tank. If subsequent washing of the tank is necessary, the discharge into the sea of the resulting tank washings shall be made in accordance with Sub-Paragraphs 1, 2, 3, or 4 of this Paragraph, whichever is applicable.

6. The discharge into the sea of substances which have not been categorized, provisionally assessed, or evaluated as referred to in Sub-Paragraph 1 of Paragraph C of this Regulation, or of ballast water, tank washings, or other residues or mixtures containing such substances shall be prohibited.

E. Exceptions

Paragraph D of this Regulation shall not apply to:

(a) The discharge into the sea of noxious liquid substances or mixtures containing such substances necessary for the purpose of securing the safety of a ship or saving life at sea; or

(b) The discharge into the sea of noxious liquid substances or mixtures containing such substances resulting from damage to a ship or its equipment:

(i) Provided that all reasonable precautions have been taken after the occurrence of the damage or discovery of the discharge for the purpose of preventing or minimizing the discharge; and

(ii) Except if the owner or the Master acted either with intent to cause damage, or recklessly and with knowledge that damage would probably result; or

(c) The discharge into the sea of noxious liquid substances or mixtures containing such substances, approved by the Administration, when being used for the purpose of combating specific pollution incidents in order to minimize the damage from pollution. Any such discharge shall be subject to the approval of any Contracting Party in whose jurisdiction it is contemplated the discharge will occur.

F. Measures of Control

1. The Contracting Parties shall appoint or authorize surveyors for the purpose of implementing this Paragraph.

Category A Substances

2. *(a)* If a tank is partially unloaded or unloaded but not cleaned, an appropriate entry shall be made in the Cargo Record Book;

(b) Until that tank is cleaned every subsequent pumping or transfer operation carried out in connexion with that tank shall also be entered in the Cargo Record Book.

3. If the tank is to be washed:

(a) The effluent from the tank washing operation shall be discharged from the ship to a reception facility at least until the concentration of the substance in the discharge, as indicated by analyses of samples of the effluent taken by the surveyor, has fallen to the residual concentration specified for that substance in Appendix III to this Annex. When the required residual concentration has been achieved, remaining tank washings shall continue to be discharged to the reception facility until the tank is empty. Appropriate entries of these operations shall be made in the Cargo Record Book and certified by the surveyor; and

(b) After diluting the residue then remaining in the tank with at least 5 per cent of the tank capacity of water, this mixture may be discharged into the sea in accordance with the provisions of Sub-Paragraphs 1 *(a)*, *(b)*, and *(c)* of Paragraph D of this Regulation. Appropriate entries of these operations shall be made in the Cargo Record Book.

4. Where the Government of the receiving Party is satisfied that it is impracticable to measure the concentration of the substance in the effluent without causing undue delay to the ship, that Party may accept an alternative procedure as being equivalent to Sub-Paragraph 3 *(a)* of this Paragraph provided that:

(a) A precleaning procedure for that tank and that substance is approved by the Administration and that Party is satisfied that such procedure will fulfil the requirements of Sub-Paragraph 1 of Paragraph D of this Regulation with respect to the attainment of the prescribed residual concentrations;

(b) A surveyor duly authorized by that Party shall certify in the Cargo Record Book that:

  (i) The tank, its pump and piping system have been emptied, and that the quantity of cargo remaining in the tank is at or below the quantity on which the approved precleaning procedure referred to in Sub-Paragraph (ii) of this Sub-Paragraph has been based;

  (ii) Precleaning has been carried out in accordance with the precleaning procedure approved by the Administration for that tank and that substance; and

  (iii) The tank washings resulting from such precleaning have been discharged to a reception facility and the tank is empty;

(c) The discharge into the sea of any remaining residues shall be in accordance with the provisions of Sub-Paragraph 3 *(b)* of this Paragraph and an appropriate entry is made in the Cargo Record Book.

Category B Substances

5. Subject to such surveillance and approval by the authorized or appointed surveyor as may be deemed necessary by the Contracting Party, the Master of a ship shall, with respect to a Category B substance, ensure compliance with the following:

(a) If a tank is partially unloaded or unloaded but not cleaned, an appropriate entry shall be made in the Cargo Record Book;

(b) Until that tank is cleaned every subsequent pumping or transfer operation carried out in connection with that tank shall also be entered in the Cargo Record Book;

(c) If the tank is to be washed, the effluent from the tank washing operation, which shall contain a volume of water not less than 0.5 per cent of the total volume of the tank, shall be discharged from the ship to a reception facility until the tank, its pump and piping system are empty. An appropriate entry shall be made in the Cargo Record Book;

(d) If the tank is to be further cleaned and emptied at sea, the Master shall:

(i) Ensure that the approved procedures referred to in Sub-Paragraph 2 *(c)* of Paragraph D of this Regulation are complied with and that the appropriate entries are made in the Cargo Record Book; and

(ii) Ensure that any discharge into the sea is made in accordance with the requirements of Sub-Paragraph 2 of Paragraph D of this Regulation and an appropriate entry is made in the Cargo Record Book;

(e) If after unloading a Category B substance, any residues of tank washings are to be retained on board until the ship is outside the Baltic Sea Area, the Master shall so indicate by an appropriate entry in the Cargo Record Book.

Category C Substances

6. Subject to such surveillance and approval by the authorized or appointed surveyor as may be deemed necessary by the Contracting Party, the Master of a ship shall, with respect to a Category C substance, ensure compliance with the following:

(a) If a tank is partially unloaded or unloaded but not cleaned, an appropriate entry shall be made in the Cargo Record Book;

(b) If the tank is to be cleaned at sea:

(i) The cargo piping system serving that tank shall be drained and an appropriate entry made in the Cargo Record Book;

(ii) The quantity of substance remaining in the tank shall not exceed the maximum quantity which may be discharged into the sea for that substance under Sub-Paragraph 3 *(c)* of Paragraph D of the Regulation. An appropriate entry shall be made in the Cargo Record Book;

(iii) Where it is intended to discharge the quantity of substance remaining into the sea the approved procedures shall be complied with, and the necessary dilution of the substance satisfactory for such a discharge shall be achieved. An appropriate entry shall be made in the Cargo Record Book; or

(iv) Where the tank washings are not discharged into the sea, if any internal transfer of tank washings takes place from that tank an appropriate entry shall be made in the Cargo Record Book; and

(v) Any subsequent discharge into the sea of such tank washings shall be made in accordance with the requirements of Sub-Paragraph 3 of Paragraph D of this Regulation;

(c) If the tank is to be cleaned in port:

(i) The tank washings shall be discharged to a reception facility and an appropriate entry shall be made in the Cargo Record Book; or

(ii) The tank washings shall be retained on board the ship and an appropriate entry shall be made in the Cargo Record Book indicating the location and disposition of the tank washings;

(d) If after unloading a Category C substance within the Baltic Sea Area, any residues or tank washings are to be retained on board until the ship is outside the area, the Master shall so indicate by an appropriate entry in the Cargo Record Book.

Category D Substances

7. The Master of a ship shall, with respect to a Category D substance, ensure compliance with the following:

(a) If a tank is partially unloaded or unloaded but not cleaned, an appropriate entry shall be made in the Cargo Record Book;

(b) If the tank is to be cleaned at sea:

  (i) The cargo piping system serving that tank shall be drained and an appropriate entry made in the Cargo Record Book;

  (ii) Where it is intended to discharge the quantity of substance remaining into the sea, the necessary dilution of the substance satisfactory for such a discharge shall be achieved. An appropriate entry shall be made in the Cargo Record Book;

  (iii) Where the tank washings are not discharged into the sea, if any internal transfer of tank washings takes place from that tank an appropriate entry shall be made in the Cargo Record Book; and

  (iv) Any subsequent discharge into the sea of such tank washings shall be made in accordance with the requirements of Sub-Paragraph 4 of Paragraph D of this Regulation;

(c) If the tank is to be cleaned in port:

  (i) The tank washings shall be discharged to a reception facility and an appropriate entry shall be made in the Cargo Record Book; or

  (ii) The tank washings shall be retained on board the ship and an appropriate entry shall be made in the Cargo Record Book indicating the location and disposition of the tank washings.

Discharge from a Slop Tank

8. Any residues retained on board in a slop tank, including those from pump room bilges, which contain a Category A or a Category B substance, shall be discharged to a reception facility in accordance with the provisions of Sub-Paragraph 1 or 2 of Paragraph D of this Regulation, whichever is applicable. An appropriate entry shall be made in the Cargo Record Book.

9. Any residues retained on board in a slop tank, including those from pump room bilges, which contain a Category C substance in excess of the aggregate of the maximum quantities specified in Sub-Paragraph 3 *(c)* of Paragraph D of this Regulation shall be discharged to a reception facility. An appropriate entry shall be made in the Cargo Record Book.

G. Cargo Record Book

1. Every ship to which this Regulation applies shall be provided with a Cargo Record Book, whether as part of the ship's official log book or otherwise, in the form specified in Appendix V to this Annex.

2. The Cargo Record Book shall be completed, on a tank-to-tank basis, whenever any of the following operations with respect to a noxious liquid substance takes place in the ship:

  (i) Loading of cargo;

  (ii) Unloading of cargo;

  (iii) Transfer of cargo;

  (iv) Transfer of cargo, cargo residues or mixtures containing cargo to a slop tank;

  (v) Cleaning of cargo tanks;

  (vi) Transfer from slop tanks;

  (vii) Ballasting of cargo tanks;

  (viii) Transfer of dirty ballast water;

  (ix) Discharge into the sea in accordance with Paragraph D of this Regulation.

3. In the event of any discharge of the kind referred to in Annex VI of the present Convention and Paragraph E of this Regulation of any noxious liquid substance or

mixture containing such substance, whether intentional or accidental, an entry shall be made in the Cargo Record Book stating the circumstances of, and the reason for, the discharge.

4. When a surveyor appointed or authorized by a Contracting Party to supervise any operations under this Regulation has inspected a ship, then that surveyor shall make an appropriate entry in the Cargo Record Book.

5. Each operation referred to in Sub-Paragraphs 2 and 3 of this Paragraph shall be fully recorded without delay in the Cargo Record Book so that all the entries in the Book appropriate to that operation are completed. Each entry shall be signed by the officer or officers in charge of the operation concerned and, when the ship is manned, each page shall be signed by the Master of the ship. The entries in the Cargo Record Book shall be in an official language of the State whose flag the ship is entitled to fly, and, except when the ship is engaged in domestic voyages, in English or French. The entries in an official national language of the State whose flag the ship is entitled to fly shall prevail in case of a dispute or discrepancy.

6. The Cargo Record Book shall be kept in such a place as to be readily available for inspection and, except in the case of unmanned ships under tow, shall be kept on board the ship. It shall be retained for a period of two years after the last entry has been made.

7. The competent authority of a Contracting Party may inspect the Cargo Record Book on board any ship to which this Regulation applies while the ship is in its port, and may make a copy of any entry in that Book and may require the Master of the ship to certify that the copy is a true copy of such entry. Any copy so made which has been certified by the Master of the ship as a true copy of an entry in the ship's Cargo Record Book shall be made admissible in any judicial proceedings as evidence of the facts stated in the entry. The inspection of a Cargo Record Book and the taking of a certified copy by the competent authority under this Paragraph shall be performed as expeditiously as possible without causing the ship to be unduly delayed.

H. Reception Facilities

1. The Contracting Parties undertake to ensure the provision of reception facilities according to the needs of ships using their ports, terminals or repair ports of the Baltic Sea Area as follows:

(a) Cargo loading and unloading ports and terminals shall have facilities adequate for reception without undue delay to ships of such residues and mixtures containing noxious liquid substances as would remain for disposal from ships carrying them as a consequence of the application of this Regulation; and

(b) Ship repair ports undertaking repairs to chemical tankers shall have facilities adequate for the reception of residues and mixtures containing noxious liquid substances.

2. Each Contracting Party shall determine the types of facilities provided for the purpose of Sub-Paragraph 1 of this Paragraph at its cargo loading and unloading ports, terminals and ship repair ports of the Baltic Sea Area.

Regulation 6. Harmful substances in packaged forms

A. The Contracting Parties shall as soon as possible apply suitable uniform rules for the carriage of harmful substances in packaged forms or in freight containers, portable tanks or road and rail tank wagons.

B. With respect to certain harmful substances, as may be designated by the Commission, the Master or owner of the ship or his representative shall notify the appropriate port authority of the intent to load or unload such substances at least 24 hours prior to such action.

C. A report of an incident involving harmful substances shall be made in accordance with the provisions of Annex VI of the present Convention.

Regulation 7. Sewage

The Contracting Parties shall apply the provisions of Paragraphs A to D of this Regulation on discharge of sewage from ships while operating in the Baltic Sea Area.

A. Definitions

For the purposes of this Regulation:

1. "New ship" means a ship:

(a) For which the building contract is placed, or in the absence of a building contract, the keel of which is laid, or which is at a similar stage of construction, on or after the date of entry into force of the present Convention; or

(b) The delivery of which is three years or more after the date of entry into force of the present Convention.

2. "Existing ship" means a ship which is not a new ship.

3. "Sewage" means:

(a) Drainage and other wastes from any form of toilets, urinals, and WC scuppers;

(b) Drainage from medical premises (dispensary, sick bay, etc.) via wash basins, wash tubs and scuppers located in such premises;

(c) Drainage from spaces containing living animals; or

(d) Other waste waters when mixed with the drainages defined above.

4. "Holding tank" means a tank used for the collection and storage of sewage.

B. Application

1. The provisions of this Regulation shall apply to:

(a) New ships certified to carry more than 100 persons from a date not later than 1 January 1977;

(b) Existing ships certified to carry more than 400 persons from a date not later than 1 January 1978; and

(c) Other ships, as specified in Sub-Paragraphs (i), (ii), and (iii), from dates decided by the Contracting Parties on recommendation by the Commission:

    (i) Ships of 200 tons gross tonnage and above;

    (ii) Ships of less than 200 tons gross tonnage which are certified to carry more than 10 persons;

    (iii) Ships which do not have a measured gross tonnage and are certified to carry more than 10 persons.

In the case of new such ships the date shall be not later than 1 January 1979. In the case of existing such ships the date shall be not later than ten years after the date decided for new ships.

2. A Contracting Party may, if it is satisfied that the application of the provisions of Sub-Paragraph 1 *(b)* of this Paragraph with respect to a certain ship would necessitate constructional alterations which would be unreasonable, exempt the ship from the application until a date not later than ten years after the date of entry into force of the present Convention.

C. Discharge of Sewage

1. Subject to the provisions of Paragraph D of this Regulation, the discharge of sewage into the sea is prohibited, except when:

(a) The ship is discharging comminuted and disinfected sewage using a system approved by the Administration at a distance of more than 4 nautical miles from the

nearest land, or sewage which is not comminuted or disinfected at a distance of more than 12 nautical miles from the nearest land, provided that in any case the sewage that has been stored in holding tanks shall not be discharged instantaneously but at a moderate rate when the ship is en route and proceeding at not less than 4 knots; or

(b) The ship has in operation a sewage treatment plant which has been approved by the Administration, and

(i) The test results of the plant are laid down in a document carried by the ship;

(ii) Additionally, the effluent shall not produce visible floating solids in, nor cause discoloration of the surrounding water; or

(c) The ship is situated in the waters under the jurisdiction of a State and is discharging sewage in accordance with such less stringent requirements as may be imposed by such State.

2. When the sewage is mixed with wastes or waste water having different discharge requirements, the more stringent requirements shall apply.

D. Exceptions

Paragraph C of this Regulation shall not apply to:

(a) The discharge of sewage from a ship necessary for the purpose of securing the safety of a ship and those on board or saving life at sea; or

(b) The discharge of sewage resulting from damage to a ship or its equipment if all reasonable precautions have been taken before and after the occurrence of the damage for the purpose of preventing or minimizing the discharge.

E. Reception Facilities

1. Each Contracting Party undertakes to ensure the provision of facilities at its ports and terminals of the Baltic Sea Area for the reception of sewage, without causing undue delay to ships, adequate to meet the needs of the ships using them.

2. To enable pipes of reception facilities to be connected with the ship's discharge pipeline, both lines shall be fitted with a standard discharge connection in accordance with the following table:

STANDARD DIMENSICNS OF FLANGES FOR DISCHARGE CONNECTIONS

Description	*Dimension*
Outside diameter	210 mm
Inner diameter	According to pipe outside diameter
Bolt circle diameter	170 mm
Slots in flange	4 holes 18 mm in diameter equidistantly placed on a bolt circle of the above diameter, slotted to the flange periphery. The slot width to be 18 mm
Flange thickness	16 mm
Bolts and nuts: quantity and diameter	4, each of 16 mm diameter and of suitable length

The flange is designed to accept pipes up to a maximum internal diameter of 100 mm and shall be of steel or other equivalent material having a flat face. This flange, together with a suitable gasket, shall be suitable for a service pressure of 6 kg/cm^2.

For ships having a moulded depth of 5 metres and less, the inner diameter of the discharge connection may be 38 millimetres.

Regulation 8. *Garbage*

The Contracting Parties shall as soon as possible but not later than 1 January 1976 or on the date of entry into force of the present Convention, whichever occurs later, apply the provisions of Paragraphs A to D of this Regulation on the disposal of garbage from ships while operating in the Baltic Sea Area.

A. Definition

For the purposes of this Regulation:

"Garbage" means all kinds of victual, domestic and operational waste excluding fresh fish and parts thereof, generated during the normal operation of the ship and liable to be disposed of continuously or periodically except those substances which are defined or listed in other Regulations of this Annex.

B. Disposal of Garbage

1. Subject to the provisions of Paragraphs C and D of this Regulation:

(a) Disposal into the sea of the following is prohibited:

(i) All plastics, including but not limited to synthetic ropes, synthetic fishing nets and plastic garbage bags; and

(ii) All other garbage, including paper products, rags, glass, metal bottles, crockery, dunnage, lining and packing materials;

(b) Disposal into the sea of food wastes shall be made as far as practicable from land, but in any case not less than 12 nautical miles from the nearest land.

2. When the garbage is mixed with other discharges having different disposal or discharge requirements the more stringent requirements shall apply.

C. Special Requirements for Fixed and Floating Platforms

1. Subject to the provisions of Sub-Paragraph 2 of this Paragraph, the disposal of any materials regulated by this Regulation is prohibited from fixed or floating platforms engaged in the exploration, exploitation and associated offshore processing of sea-bed mineral resources, and all other ships when alongside or within 500 metres of such platforms.

2. The disposal into the sea of food wastes may be permitted when they have passed through a comminuter or grinder from such fixed or floating platforms located more than 12 nautical miles from land and all other ships when alongside or within 500 metres of such platforms. Such comminuted or ground food wastes shall be capable of passing through a screen with openings no greater than 25 millimetres.

D. Exceptions

Paragraphs B and C of this Regulation shall not apply to:

(a) The disposal of garbage from a ship necessary for the purpose of securing the safety of a ship and those on board or saving life at sea; or

(b) The escape of garbage resulting from damage to a ship or its equipment provided all reasonable precautions have been taken before and after the occurrence of the damage, for the purpose of preventing or minimizing the escape; or

(c) The accidental loss of synthetic fishing nets or synthetic material incidental to the repair of such nets, provided that all reasonable precautions have been taken to prevent such loss.

E. Reception Facilities

Each Contracting Party undertakes to ensure the provision of facilities at its ports and terminals of the Baltic Sea Area for the reception of garbage, without causing undue delay to ships, and according to the needs of the ships using them.

ANNEX V. EXCEPTIONS FROM THE GENERAL PROHIBITION OF DUMPING OF WASTE AND OTHER MATTER IN THE BALTIC SEA AREA

Regulation 1

In accordance with Paragraph 2 of Article 9 of the present Convention the prohibition of dumping shall not apply to the disposal at sea of dredged spoils provided that:

1. They do not contain significant quantities and concentrations of substances to be defined by the Commission and listed in Annexes I and II of the present Convention; and

2. The dumping is carried out under a prior special permit given by the appropriate national authority, either

(a) Within the area of the territorial sea of the Contracting Party; or

(b) Outside the area of the territorial sea, whenever necessary, after prior consultations in the Commission.

When issuing such permits the Contracting Party shall comply with the provisions in Regulation 3 of this Annex.

Regulation 2

1. The appropriate national authority referred to in Paragraph 2 of Article 9 of the present Convention shall:

(a) Issue special permits provided for in Regulation 1 of this Annex;

(b) Keep records of the nature and quantities of matter permitted to be dumped and the location, time and method of dumping;

(c) Collect available information concerning the nature and quantities of matter that has been dumped in the Baltic Area recently and up to the coming into force of the present Convention, provided that the dumped matter in question could be liable to contaminate water or organisms in the Baltic Sea Area, to be caught by fishing equipment, or otherwise to give rise to harm, and the location, time and method of such dumping.

2. The appropriate national authority shall issue special permits in accordance with Regulation 1 of this Annex in respect of matter intended for dumping in the Baltic Sea Area:

(a) Loaded in its territory;

(b) Loaded by a vessel or aircraft registered in its territory or flying its flag, when the loading occurs in the territory of a State not Party to the present Convention.

3. When issuing permits under Subparagraph 1 (a) above, the appropriate national authority shall comply with Regulation 3 of this Annex, together with such additional criteria, measures and requirements as they may consider relevant.

4. Each Contracting Party shall report to the Commission, and where appropriate to other Contracting Parties, the information specified in Subparagraph 1 (c) of Regulation 2 of this Annex. The procedure to be followed and the nature of such reports shall be determined by the Commission.

Regulation 3

When issuing special permits according to Regulation 1 of this Annex the appropriate national authority shall take into account:

1. Quantity of dredged spoils to be dumped.

2. The content of the matter referred to in Annexes I and II of the present Convention.

3. Location (e.g. co-ordinates of the dumping area, depth and distance from coast) and its relation to areas of special interest (e.g. amenity areas, spawning, nursery and fishing areas, etc.).

4. Water characteristics, if dumping is carried out outside the territorial sea, consisting of:

(a) Hydrographic properties (e.g. temperature, salinity, density, profile);

(b) Chemical properties (e.g. pH, dissolved oxygen, nutrients);

(c) Biological properties (e.g. primary production and benthic animals).

The data should include sufficient information on the annual mean levels and the seasonal variation of the properties mentioned in this Paragraph.

5. The existence and effects of other dumping which may have been carried out in the dumping area.

Regulation 4

Reports made in accordance with Paragraph 5 of Article 9 of the present Convention shall include the following information:

1. Location of dumping, characteristics of dumped material, and counter measures taken:

(a) Location (e.g. co-ordinates of the accidental dumping site, depth and distance from the coast);

(b) Method of deposit;

(c) Quantity and composition of dumped matter as well as its physical (e.g. solubility and density), chemical and biochemical (e.g. oxygen demand, nutrients), and biological properties (e.g. presence of viruses, bacteria, yeasts, parasites);

(d) Toxicity;

(e) Content of the substances referred to in Annexes I and II of the present Convention;

(f) Dispersal characteristics (e.g. effects of currents and wind, and horizontal transport and vertical mixing);

(g) Water characteristics (e.g. temperature, pH, redox conditions, salinity and stratification);

(h) Bottom characteristics (e.g. topography, geological characteristics and redox conditions);

(i) Counter measures taken and follow-up operations carried out or planned.

2. General considerations and conditions:

(a) Possible effects on amenities (e.g. floating or stranded material, turbidity, objectionable odour, discolouration and foaming);

(b) Possible effect on marine life, fish and shellfish culture, fish stocks and fisheries, seaweed harvesting and cultures; and

(c) Possible effects on other uses of the sea (e.g. impairment of water quality for industrial use, underwater corrosion of structures, interference with ship operations from floating materials, interference with fishing or navigation and protection of areas of special importance for scientific or conservation purposes).

ANNEX VI.   CO-OPERATION IN COMBATTING MARINE POLLUTION

Regulation 1

For the purposes of this Annex:

1. "Ship" means a vessel of any type whatsoever operating in the marine environment and includes hydrofoil boats, air-cushion vehicles, submersibles, floating craft and fixed or floating platforms.

2. "Administration" means the Government of the State under whose authority the ship is operating. With respect to a ship entitled to fly a flag of any State, the Administration is the Government of that State. With respect to fixed or floating platforms engaged in exploration and exploitation of the sea-bed and subsoil thereof adjacent to the coast over which the coastal State exercises sovereign rights for the purposes of exploration and exploitation of their natural resources, the Administration is the Government of the coastal State concerned.

3. *(a)* "Discharge", in relation to harmful substances or effluents containing such substances, means any release howsoever caused from a ship and includes any escape, disposal, spilling, leaking, pumping, emitting or emptying.

(b) "Discharge" does not include:

 (i) Dumping within the meaning of the Convention on the Prevention of Marine Pollution by Dumping of Wastes and Other Matter done at London on 29 December 1972; or

 (ii) Release of harmful substances directly arising from the exploration, exploitation and associated offshore processing of sea-bed mineral resources; or

 (iii) Release of harmful substances for purposes of legitimate scientific research into pollution abatement or control.

Regulation 2

The Contracting Parties undertake to maintain ability to combat spillages of oil and other harmful substances on the sea. This ability shall include adequate equipment, ships and manpower prepared for operations in coastal waters as well as on the high sea.

Regulation 3

The Contracting Parties shall, without prejudice to Paragraph 4 of Article 4 of the present Convention, develop and apply, individually or in co-operation, surveillance activities covering the Baltic Sea Area, in order to spot and monitor oil and other harmful substances released into the sea.

Regulation 4

In the case of loss overboard of harmful substances in packages, freight containers, portable tanks, or road and rail tank wagons, the Contracting Parties shall co-operate in the salvage and recovery of such packages, containers or tanks so as to minimize the danger to the environment.

Regulation 5

1. The Contracting Parties shall develop and apply a system for receiving, channeling and dispatching reports on significant spillages of oil or other harmful substances observed at sea, as well as any incident causing or likely to cause any kind of significant pollution.

2. The Contracting Parties shall request masters of ships and pilots of aircraft to report without delay in accordance with this system on significant spillages of oil or

other harmful substances observed at sea. Such reports should as far as possible contain the following data: time, position, wind and sea conditions, and kind, extent and probable source of the spill observed.

3. The master of a ship involved in an incident referred to in Paragraph 1 of this Regulation, or other person having charge of the ship, shall without delay and to the fullest extent possible report in accordance with this system and with the provisions of the Appendix to the present Annex.

4. Each Contracting Party undertakes to issue instructions to its maritime inspection vessels and aircraft and to other appropriate services, to report to its authorities any observation or incident referred to in Paragraph 1 of this Regulation. Such reports shall as far as possible contain the data referred to in Paragraphs 2 or 3 of this Regulation respectively, as well as possible indications on the spreading or drifting tendencies of the spill in question.

5. Whenever a Contracting Party is aware of a casualty or the presence of spillages of oil or other harmful substances in the Baltic Sea Area likely to constitute a serious threat to the marine environment of the Baltic Sea Area or the coast or related interests of any other Contracting Party, it shall without delay transmit all relevant information thereon to the Contracting Party which may be affected by the pollutant and, as regards ship casualty incidents, to the Administration of the ship involved.

Regulation 6

Each Contracting Party shall request masters of ships flying its flag to provide, in case of an incident, on request by the proper authorities, such detailed information about the ship and its cargo which is relevant to actions for preventing or combatting pollution of the sea, and to co-operate with these authorities.

Regulation 7

1. *(a)* The Contracting Parties shall as soon as possible agree bilaterally or multilaterally on those regions of the Baltic Sea Area in which they will take action for combatting or salvage activities whenever a significant spillage of oil or other harmful substances or any incidents causing or likely to cause pollution within the Baltic Sea Area have occurred or are likely to occur. Such agreements shall not prejudice any other agreements concluded between Contracting Parties concerning the same subject. The neighbouring States shall ensure the harmonization of the different agreements. The Contracting Parties shall inform each other about such agreements.

The Contracting Parties may ask the Commission for assistance to reach agreement, if needed.

(b) The Contracting Party within whose region a situation as described in Regulation 1 of this Annex occurs shall make the necessary assessments of the situation and take adequate action in order to avoid or minimize subsequent pollution effects and shall keep drifting parts of the spillage under observation until no further action is called for.

2. In the case that such a spillage is drifting or is likely to drift into a region, where another Contracting Party should take action for purposes as defined in Subparagraph 1 *(a)* of this Regulation, that Party shall without delay be informed of the situation and the actions that have been taken.

Regulation 8

A Contracting Party requiring assistance for combatting spillages of oil or other harmful substance at sea is entitled to call for assistance by other Contracting Parties, starting with those who seem likely also to be affected by the spillage. Contracting

Parties called upon for assistance in accordance with this Regulation shall use their best endeavours to bring such assistance.

Regulation 9

1. The Contracting Parties shall provide information to the other Contracting Parties and the Commission about

(a) Their national organization for dealing with spillages at sea of oil and other harmful substances;

(b) National regulations and other matters which have a direct bearing on combatting pollution at sea by oil and other harmful substances;

(c) The competent authority responsible for receiving and dispatching reports of pollution at sea by oil and other harmful substances;

(d) The competent authorities for dealing with questions concerning measures of mutual assistance, information and co-operation between the Contracting Parties according to this Annex;

(e) Actions taken in accordance with Regulation 8 of this Annex.

2. The Contracting Parties shall exchange information of research and development programs and results concerning ways in which pollution by oil and other harmful substances at sea may be dealt with and experiences in combatting such pollution.

Regulation 10

The authorities referred to in Subparagraph 1 *(d)* of Regulation 9 of this Annex shall establish direct contact and co-operate in operational matters.

5. CONVENTION FOR THE PREVENTION OF MARINE POLLUTION FROM LAND-BASED SOURCES, DONE AT PARIS ON 4 JUNE 1974[1]

The Contracting Parties:

Recognizing that the marine environment and the fauna and flora which it supports are of vital importance to all nations;

Mindful that the ecological equilibrium and the legitimate uses of the sea are increasingly threatened by pollution;

Considering the recommendations of the United Nations Conference on the Human Environment, held in Stockholm in June 1972;[2]

Recognizing that concerted action at national, regional and global levels is essential to prevent and combat marine pollution;

Convinced that international action to control the pollution of the sea from land-based sources can and should be taken without delay, as part of progressive and coherent measures to protect the marine environment from pollution, whatever its origin, including current efforts to combat the pollution of international waterways;

---

[1] English text provided by the Permanent Representative of the United Kingdom to the United Nations in a note verbale of 12 December 1974 as well as by the Ministry of Foreign Affairs of Denmark in a note verbale of 20 December 1974.

[2] Report of the United Nations Conference on the Human Environment. Document A/CONF.48/14.

Considering that the common interests of States concerned with the same marine area should induce them to co-operate at regional or sub-regional levels.

Recalling the Convention for the Prevention of Marine Pollution by Dumping from Ships and Aircraft concluded in Oslo on 15 February 1972;[1]

Have agreed as follows:

Article 1

1. The Contracting Parties pledge themselves to take all possible steps to prevent pollution of the sea, by which is meant the introduction by man, directly or indirectly, of substances or energy into the marine environment (including estuaries) resulting in such deleterious effects as hazards to human health, harm to living resources and to marine ecosystems, damage to amenities or interference with other legitimate uses of the sea.

2. The Contracting Parties shall adopt individually and jointly measures to combat marine pollution from land-based sources in accordance with the provisions of the present Convention and shall harmonize their policies in this regard.

Article 2

The present Convention shall apply to the maritime area within the following limits:

(a) Those parts of the Atlantic and Arctic Oceans and the dependent seas which lie north of 36° north latitude and between 42° west longitude and 51° east longitude, but excluding:

(i) The Baltic Sea and belts lying to the south and east of lines drawn from Hasenore Head to Gniben Point, from Korshage to Spodsbjerg and from Gilbjerg Head to Kullen, and

(ii) The Mediterranean Sea and its dependent seas as far as the point of intersection of the parallel of 36° north latitude and the meridian of 5° 36' west longitude;

(b) That part of the Atlantic Ocean north of 59° north latitude and between 44° west longitude and 42° west longitude.

Article 3

For the purpose of the present Convention:

(a) "Maritime area" means: the high seas, the territorial seas of Contracting Parties and water on the landward side of the base lines from which the breadth of the territorial sea is measured and extending in the case of watercourses, unless otherwise decided under article 16 *(c)* of the present Convention, up to the freshwater limit;

(b) "Freshwater limit" means: the place in the watercourse where, at low tide and in a period of low freshwater flow, there is an appreciable increase in salinity due to the presence of seawater;

---

[1] Reproduced in ST/LEG/SER.B/16, pp. 457-463.

(c) "Pollution from land-based sources" means: the pollution of the maritime area

    (i) Through watercourses;

    (ii) From the coast, including introduction through underwater or other pipelines;

    (iii) From man-made structures placed under the jurisdiction of a Contracting Party within the limits of the area to which the present Convention applies.

Article 4

1. The Contracting Parties undertake:

(a) To eliminate, if necessary by stages, pollution of the maritime area from land-based sources by substances listed in Part I of Annex A to the present Convention;

(b) To limit strictly pollution of the maritime area from land-based sources by substances listed in Part II of Annex A to the present Convention.

2. In order to carry out the undertakings in paragraph 1 of this Article, the Contracting Parties, jointly or individually as appropriate, shall implement programmes and measures:

(a) For the elimination, as a matter of urgency, of pollution of the maritime area from land-based sources by substances listed in Part I of Annex A to the present Convention;

(b) For the reduction or, as appropriate, elimination of pollution of the maritime area from land-based sources by substances listed in Part II of Annex A to the present Convention. These substances shall be discharged only after approval has been granted by the appropriate authorities within each contracting State. Such approval shall be periodically reviewed.

3. The programmes and measures adopted under paragraph 2 of this article shall include, as appropriate, specific regulations or standards governing the quality of the environment, discharges into the maritime area, such discharges into watercourses as affect the maritime area, and the composition and use of substances and products. These programmes and measures shall take into account the latest technical developments.

The programmes shall contain time-limits for their completion.

4. The Contracting Parties may, furthermore, jointly or individually as appropriate, implement programmes or measures to forestall, reduce or eliminate pollution of the maritime area from land-based sources by a substance not then listed in Annex A to the present Convention, if scientific evidence has established that a serious hazard may be created in the maritime area by that substance and if urgent action is necessary.

Article 5

1. The Contracting Parties undertake to adopt measures to forestall and, as appropriate, eliminate pollution of the maritime area from land-based sources by radioactive substances referred to in Part III of Annex A of the present Convention.

2. Without prejudice to their obligations under other treaties and conventions, in implementing this undertaking the Contracting Parties shall:

(a) Take full account of the recommendations of the appropriate international organizations and agencies;

(b) Take account of the monitoring procedures recommended by these international organizations and agencies;

(c) Co-ordinate their monitoring and study of radioactive substances in accordance with Articles 10 and 11 of the present Convention.

Article 6

1. With a view to preserving and enhancing the quality of the marine environment, the Contracting Parties, without prejudice to the provisions of Article 4, shall endeavour:

(a) To reduce existing pollution from land-based sources;

(b) To forestall any new pollution from land-based sources, including that which derives from new substances.

2. In implementing this undertaking, the Contracting Parties shall take account of:

(a) The nature and quantities of the pollutants under consideration;

(b) The level of existing pollution;

(c) The quality and absorptive capacity of the receiving waters of the maritime area;

(d) The need for an integrated planning policy consistent with the requirement of environmental protection.

Article 7

The Contracting Parties agree to apply the measures they adopt in such a way as to avoid increasing pollution:

— In the seas outside the area to which the present Convention applies;

— In the maritime area covered by the present Convention originating otherwise than from land-based sources.

Article 8

No provision of the present Convention shall be interpreted as preventing the Contracting Parties from taking more stringent measures to combat marine pollution from land-based sources.

Article 9

1. When pollution from land-based sources originating from the territory of a Contracting Party by substances not listed in Part I of Annex A of the present Convention is likely to prejudice the interests of one or more of the other Parties to the present Convention, the Contracting Parties concerned undertake to enter into consultation, at the request of any one of them, with a view to negotiating a co-operation agreement.

2. At the request of any Contracting Party concerned, the Commission referred to in Article 15 of the present Convention shall consider the question and may make recommendations with a view to reaching a satisfactory solution.

3. The special agreements specified in paragraph 1 of this Article may, among other things, define the areas to which they shall apply, the quality objectives to be achieved, and the methods for achieving these objectives including methods for the application of appropriate standards and the scientific and technical information to be collected.

4. The Contracting Parties signatory to these special agreements shall, through the medium of the Commission, inform the other Contracting Parties of their purport and of the progress made in putting them into effect.

Article 10

The Contracting Parties agree to establish complementary or joint programmes of scientific and technical research, including research into the best methods of eliminating or replacing noxious substances so as to reduce marine pollution from land-based sources, and to transmit to each other the information so obtained. In doing so they shall have regard to the work carried out, in these fields, by the appropriate international organizations and agencies.

Article 11

The Contracting Parties agree to set up progressively and to operate within the area covered by the present Convention a permanent monitoring system allowing:

— The earliest possible assessment of the existing level of marine pollution;

— The assessment of the effectiveness of measures for the reduction of marine pollution from land-based sources taken under the terms of the present Convention.

For this purpose the Contracting Parties shall lay down the ways and means of pursuing individually or jointly systematic and *ad hoc* monitoring programmes. These programmes shall take into account the deployment of research vessels and other facilities in the monitoring area.

The programmes shall take into account similar programmes pursued in accordance with conventions already in force and by the appropriate international organizations and agencies.

Article 12

1. Each Contracting Party undertakes to ensure compliance with the provisions of this Convention and to take in its territory appropriate measures to prevent and punish conduct in contravention of the provisions of the present Convention.

2. The Contracting Parties shall inform the Commission of the legislative and administrative measures they have taken to implement the provisions of the preceding paragraph.

Article 13

The Contracting Parties undertake to assist one another as appropriate to prevent incidents which may result in pollution from land-based sources, to minimize and eliminate the consequences of such incidents, and to exchange information to that end.

Article 14

1. The provisions of the present Convention may not be invoked against a Contracting Party to the extent that the latter is prevented, as a result of pollution having its origin in the territory of a non-Contracting State, from ensuring their full application.

2. However, the said Contracting Party shall endeavour to co-operate with the non-Contracting State so as to make possible the full application of the present Convention.

Article 15

A Commission composed of representatives of each of the Contracting Parties is hereby established. The Commission shall meet at regular intervals and at any time when due to special circumstances it is so decided in accordance with its rules of procedure.

Article 16

It shall be the duty of the Commission:

(a) To exercise overall supervision over the implementation of the present Convention;

(b) To review generally the condition of the seas within the area to which the present Convention applies, the effectiveness of the control measures being adopted and the need for any additional or different measures;

(c) To fix, if necessary, on the proposal of the Contracting Party or Parties bordering on the same watercourse and following a standard procedure, the limit to which the maritime area shall extend in that watercourse;

(d) To draw up, in accordance with Article 4 of the present Convention, programmes and measures for the elimination or reduction of pollution from land-based sources;

(e) To make recommendations in accordance with the provisions of Article 9;

(f) To receive and review information and distribute it to the Contracting Parties in accordance with the provisions of Articles 11, 12 and 17 of the present Convention;

(g) To make, in accordance with Article 18, recommendations regarding any amendment to the lists of substances included in Annex A to the present Convention;

(h) To discharge such other functions, as may be appropriate, under the terms of the present Convention.

Article 17

The Contracting Parties, in accordance with a standard procedure, shall transmit to the Commission:

(a) The results of monitoring pursuant to Article 11;

(b) The most detailed information available on the substances listed in the Annexes to the present Convention and liable to find their way into the maritime area.

The Contracting Parties shall endeavour to improve progressively techniques for gathering such information which can contribute to the revision of the pollution reduction programmes drawn up in accordance with Article 4 of the present Convention.

Article 18

1. The Commission shall draw up its own Rules of Procedure which shall be adopted by unanimous vote.

2. The Commission shall draw up its own Financial Regulations which shall be adopted by unanimous vote.

3. The Commission shall adopt, by unanimous vote, programmes and measures for the reduction or elimination of pollution from land-based sources as provided for in Article 4, programmes for scientific research and monitoring as provided for in Articles 10 and 11, and decisions under Article 16 *(c)*.

The programmes and measures shall commence for and be applied by all Contracting Parties two hundred days after their adoption, unless the Commission specifies another date.

Should unanimity not be attainable, the Commission may nonetheless adopt a programme or measures by a three quarters majority vote of its members. The programmes or measures shall commence for those Contracting Parties which voted for them two hundred days after their adoption, unless the Commission specifies another date, and for any other Contracting Party after it has explicitly accepted the programme or measures, which it may do at any time.

4. The Commission may adopt recommendations for amendments to Annex A to the present Convention by a three quarters majority vote of its members and shall submit them for the approval of the Governments of the Contracting Parties. Any Government of a Contracting Party that is unable to approve an amendment shall notify the depositary Government in writing within a period of two hundred days after the adoption of the Recommendation of amendment in the Commission. Should no such notification be

received, the amendment shall enter into force for all Contracting Parties two hundred and thirty days after the vote in the Commission. The depositary Government shall notify the Contracting Parties as soon as possible of the receipt of any notification.

Article 19

Within the area of its competence, the European Economic Community is entitled to a number of votes equal to the number of its member States which are Contracting Parties to the present Convention.

The European Economic Community shall not exercise its right to vote in cases where its member States exercise theirs and conversely.

Article 20

The depositary Government shall convene the first meeting of the Commission as soon as possible after the coming into force of the present Convention.

Article 21

Any dispute between Contracting Parties relating to the interpretation or application of the present Convention, which cannot be settled otherwise by the Parties concerned, for instance by means of inquiry or conciliation within the Commission, shall, at the request of any of those Parties, be submitted to arbitration under the conditions laid down in Annex B to the present Convention.

Article 22

The present Convention shall be open for signature at Paris, from 4 June 1974 to 30 June 1975, by the States invited to the Diplomatic Conference on the Convention for the prevention of Marine Pollution from Land-Based Sources, held at Paris, and by the European Economic Community.

Article 23

The present Convention shall be subject to ratification, acceptance or approval. The instruments of ratification, acceptance or approval shall be deposited with the Government of the French Republic.

Article 24

1. After 30 June 1975, the present Convention shall be open for accession by States referred to in Article 22 and by the European Economic Community.

2. The present Convention shall also be open for accession from the same date by any other Contracting Party to the Convention for the Prevention of Marine Pollution by Dumping from Ships and Aircraft, opened for signature at Oslo on 15 February 1972.

3. From the date of its entry into force, the present Convention shall be open for accession by any State not referred to in Article 22, located upstream on watercourses crossing the territory of one or more Contracting Parties to the present Convention and reaching the maritime area defined in Article 2.

4. The Contracting Parties may unanimously invite other States to accede to the present Convention. In that case the maritime area in Article 2 may, if necessary, be amended in accordance with Article 27 of the present Convention.

5. The instruments of accession shall be deposited with the Government of the French Republic

Article 25

1. The present Convention shall come into force on the thirtieth day following the date of deposit of the seventh instrument of ratification, acceptance, approval or accession.

2. For each Party ratifying, accepting or approving the present Convention or acceding to it after the deposit of the seventh instrument of ratification, acceptance, approval or accession, the present Convention shall enter into force on the thirtieth day after the date of deposit by that Party of its instrument of ratification, acceptance, approval or accession.

Article 26

At any time after the expiry of two years from the date of coming into force of the present Convention in relation to any Contracting Party such Party may withdraw from the Convention by notice in writing to the depositary Government. Such notice shall take effect one year after the date on which it is received.

Article 27

1. The depositary Government shall, at the request of the Commission on a decision taken by a two-thirds majority of its members, call a Conference for the purpose of revising or amending the present Convention.

2. Upon accession by a State as provided for in paragraphs 2, 3 and 4 of Article 24, the maritime area in Article 2 may be amended upon a proposal by the Commission adopted by a unanimous vote. These amendments shall enter into force after unanimous approval by the Contracting Parties.

Article 28

The depositary Government shall inform the Contracting Parties and those referred to in Article 22:

(a) Of signatures to the present Convention, of the deposit of instruments of ratification, acceptance, approval or accession, and of notices of withdrawal in accordance with Articles 22, 23, 24 and 26;

(b) Of the date on which the present Convention comes into force in accordance with Article 25;

(c) Of the receipt of notifications of approval or objection, and of the entry into force of amendments to the present Convention and its Annexes, in accordance with Articles 18 and 27.

Article 29

The original of the present Convention of which the French and English texts shall be equally authentic, shall be deposited with the Government of the French Republic which shall send certified copies thereof to the Contracting Parties and the States referred to in Article 22 and shall deposit a certified copy with the Secretary-General of the United Nations for registration and publication in accordance with Article 102 of the United Nations Charter.

ANNEX A

The allocation of substances to Parts I, II and III below takes account of the following criteria:

(a) Persistence;

(b) Toxicity or other noxious properties;

(c) Tendency to bio-accumulation;

These criteria are not necessarily of equal importance for a particular substance or group of substances, and other factors, such as the location and quantities of the discharge, may need to be considered.

Part I

The following substances are included in this Part

(i) Because they are not readily degradable or rendered harmless by natural processes; and

(ii) Because they may either

(a) Give rise to dangerous accumulation of harmful material in the food chain; or

(b) Endanger the welfare of living organisms causing undesirable changes in the marine ecosystems; or

(c) Interfere seriously with the harvesting of sea foods or with other legitimate uses of the sea; and

(iii) Because it is considered that pollution by these substances necessitates urgent action:

1. Organohalogen compounds and substances which may form such compounds in the marine environment, excluding those which are biologically harmless, or which are rapidly converted in the sea into substances which are biologically harmless.

2. Mercury and mercury compounds.

3. Cadmium and cadmium compounds.

4. Persistent synthetic materials which may float, remain in suspension or sink, and which may seriously interfere with any legitimate use of the sea.

5. Persistent oils and hydrocarbons of petroleum origin.

Part II

The following substances are included in this Part because, although exhibiting similar characteristics to the substances in Part I and requiring strict control, they seem less noxious or are more readily rendered harmless by natural processes:

1. Organic compounds of phosphorus, silicon, and tin and substances which may form such compounds in the marine environment, excluding those which are biologically harmless, or which are rapidly converted in the sea into substances which are biologically harmless.

2. Elemental phosphorus.

3. Non-persistent oils and hydrocarbons of petroleum origin.

4. The following elements and their compounds:

Arsenic	Lead
Chromium	Nickel
Copper	Zinc

5. Substances which have been agreed by the Commission as having a deleterious effect on the taste and/or smell of products derived from the marine environment for human consumption.

Part III

The following substances are included in this Part because, although they display characteristics similar to those of substances listed in Part I and should be subject to stringent controls with the aim of preventing and, as appropriate, eliminating the pollution which they cause, they are already the subject of research, recommendations and, in some cases, measures under the auspices of several international organizations and institutions; those substances are subject to the provisions of Article 5:

Radioactive substances, including wastes.

ANNEX B

Article 1

Unless the parties to the dispute decide otherwise, the arbitration procedure shall be in accordance with the provisions of this Annex.

Article 2

1. At the request addressed by one Contracting Party to another Contracting Party in accordance with Article 21 of the Convention, an arbitral tribunal shall be constituted. The request for arbitration shall state the subject matter of the application including in particular the Articles of the Convention, the interpretation or application of which is in dispute.

2. The claimant shall inform the Commission that he has requested the setting up of an arbitral tribunal, stating the name of the other party to the dispute and the Articles of the Convention the interpretation or application of which is in his opinion in dispute. The Commission shall forward the information thus received to all Contracting Parties to the Convention.

Article 3

The arbitral tribunal shall consist of three members: each of the parties to the dispute shall appoint an arbitrator; the two arbitrators so appointed shall designate by common agreement the third arbitrator who shall be the chairman of the tribunal. The latter shall not be a national of one of the parties to the dispute, nor have his usual place of residence in the territory of one of these parties, nor be employed by any of them, nor have dealt with the case in any other capacity.

Article 4

1. If the chairman of the arbitral tribunal has not been designated within two months of the appointment of the second arbitrator, the Secretary-General of the United Nations shall, at the request of either party, designate him within a further two months' period.

2. If one of the parties to the dispute does not appoint an arbitrator within two months of receipt of the request, the other party may inform the Secretary-General of the United Nations who shall designate the chairman of the arbitral tribunal within a further two months' period. Upon designation, the chairman of the arbitral tribunal shall request the party which has not appointed an arbitrator to do so within two months. After such period, he shall inform the Secretary-General of the United Nations who shall make this appointment within a further two months' period.

Article 5

1. The arbitral tribunal shall decide according to the rules of international law and, in particular, those of this Convention.

2. Any arbitral tribunal constituted under the provisions of this Annex shall draw up its own rules of procedure.

Article 6

1. The decisions of the arbitral tribunal, both on procedure and on substance, shall be taken by majority voting of its members.

2. The tribunal may take all appropriate measures in order to establish the facts. It may, at the request of one of the parties, recommend essential interim measures of protection.

3. If two or more arbitral tribunals constituted under the provisions of this Annex are seized of requests with identical or similar subjects, they may inform themselves of the procedures for establishing the facts and take them into account as far as possible.

4. The parties to the dispute shall provide all facilities necessary for the effective conduct of the proceedings.

5. The absence or default of a party to the dispute shall not constitute an impediment to the proceedings.

Article 7

1. The award of the arbitral tribunal shall be accompanied by a statement of reasons. It shall be final and binding upon the parties to the dispute.

2. Any dispute which may arise between the parties concerning the interpretation or execution of the award may be submitted by either party to the arbitral tribunal which made the award or, if the latter cannot be seized thereof, to another arbitral tribunal constituted for this purpose in the same manner as the first.

Article 8

The European Economic Community, like any Contracting Party to the present Convention, has the right to appear as applicant or respondent before the arbitral tribunal.

Subdivision B. Bilateral Treaties

1. [AGREEMENT BETWEEN DENMARK AND SWEDEN ON PRO-
   TECTION OF THE SOUND (ORESUND) AGAINST POLLUTION,
   SIGNED AT COPENHAGEN ON 5 APRIL 1974][1]

---

[1] *Supra* Division I, Subdivision B, 6.

FISHING AND CONSERVATION OF THE LIVING RESOURCES OF THE SEA

Subdivision A. MULTILATERAL TREATIES

1. [PROTOCOL OF ACCESSION TO THE SANTIAGO DECLARATION ON THE "MARITIME ZONE", DONE AT QUITO ON 6 OCTOBER 1955][1]

2. PROTOCOL ON AMENDMENT OF THE AGREEMENT OF 20 DECEMBER 1962 CONCERNING THE PROTECTION OF THE SALMON POPULATION IN THE BALTIC SEA, DONE AT STOCKHOLM ON 21 JANUARY 1972[2]

The Contracting Parties to the Agreement concerning the protection of the salmon population in the Baltic Sea, signed at Stockholm on 20 December 1962, hereinafter termed "the Agreement", have, in accordance with the recommendation of 6 March 1969 of the Standing Committee set up under article 10 of the Agreement, agreed as follows:

Article I

Article 5, paragraph 1, of the Agreement shall read as follows:

"The Contracting Parties shall not permit the use of floating trawls for salmon fishing. Similarly the Contracting Parties shall not permit, for the purposes of salmon fishing by drift net or hook and line, the use of gear having measurements other than those prescribed below."

Article II

The following provisions shall be inserted in the Agreement as article 5 *(a):*

"The Contracting Parties shall not permit salmon fishing by drift net or hook and line to be carried on, in international waters the area to which the Agreement applies, between 1 June and 25 August (both dates

---

[1] *Supra* Division I, Subdivision A, 1.

[2] Signed by Denmark, Poland, Federal Republic of Germany and Sweden. Danish German and Swedish texts provided by the Ministry of Foreign Affairs of Denmark in a note verbale of 4 January 1974. Translation by the Secretariat of the United Nations. For the entry into force, see article V (2).

inclusive) or, anywhere in the area to which the Agreement applies, between 20 December and 10 January (both dates inclusive).

"Each Contracting Party shall issue regulations making it unlawful to land within those periods, salmon caught in said areas by drift net or hook and line."

Article III

The following paragraph shall be added to article 6 of the Agreement:

"Paragraph 1 shall not apply to salmon caught with stationary gear inside the Swedish baseline north of the parallel of 60° latitude."

Article IV

(1) Article 10, second paragraph, second sentence, shall read as follows:

"The Committee shall also, on the basis of available information, discuss the desirability of amendments and additions to the Agreement and shall if necessary submit appropriate proposals to the depositary Government."

(2) The following provisions shall be inserted in the Agreement as article 10 *(a)*:

"The depositary Government shall forward to the Contracting Parties for consideration every proposal received under article 10, second paragraph. The Contracting Parties shall notify the depositary Government of their acceptance of the proposal and the depositary Government shall notify the Contracting Governments of every acceptance reported to it, stating the date of receipt of the acceptance.

"The proposal shall enter into force for all Contracting Parties four months after the date by which the depositary Government is in possession of notices of acceptance from all Contracting Parties."

Article V

(1) This Protocol shall be submitted to each Contracting Party to the Agreement for signature and ratification.

(2) This Protocol shall enter into force on the date by which all Contracting Parties to the Agreement have deposited instruments of ratification with the Government of the Kingdom of Sweden.

(3) Any State acceding to the Agreement after this Protocol has been submitted for signature shall at the same time accede also to this Protocol.

(4) The Government of the Kingdom of Sweden shall notify all Governments which have signed or acceded to the Agreement of the deposit of all instruments of ratification and of the date on which this Protocol enters into force.

3. AGREEMENT BETWEEN THE GOVERNMENTS OF THE UNION OF SOVIET SOCIALIST REPUBLICS, ICELAND AND NORWAY CONCERNING THE REGULATION OF FISHING OF THE ATLANTIC-SCANDiNAVIAN HERRING, DONE AT OSLO ON 6 MARCH 1973[1]

The Governments of the Union of Soviet Socialist Republics, Iceland and Norway, considering it necessary to regulate fishing of the Atlantic-Scandinavian herring with a view to conserving stocks of that fish,

Have agreed as follows:

Article 1

Fishing of the mature portion of stocks of Norwegian spring-spawning herring shall be prohibited in statistical regions I, II and Vb of the International Council for the Exploration of the Sea from the time of the entry into force of this Agreement.

This prohibition shall not extend to fishing connected with scientific research being conducted by fisheries institutions for the purpose of estimating stocks and migration.

Article 2

Each of the Contracting Parties shall undertake to limit its fishing of small herring and fat herring in statistical regions I and II of the International Council for the Exploration of the Sea to not more than 26 per cent of the amount which, according to available statistics, was caught by the Party concerned in 1969.

Article 3

The Contracting Parties shall take the necessary measures for the practical implementation of the provisions of articles 1 and 2 of this Agreement and shall inform each other of the measures taken.

Article 4

The competent organizations of the Contracting Parties shall send each other monthly data concerning fishing, as soon as the total catch exceeds 100 tons.

Article 5

This Agreement shall enter into force on the date of its signature by all three Parties and shall remain in force until 31 December 1973.

---

[1] Entered into force on 6 March 1973 in accordance with article 5. Russian text provided by the Permanent Representative of Norway to the United Nations in a note verbale of 21 January 1974. Translation by the Secretariat of the United Nations.

4. ARRANGEMENT BETWEEN JAPAN, NORWAY AND THE UNION OF SOVIET SOCIALIST REPUBLICS FOR THE REGULATION OF ANTARCTIC PELAGIC WHALING, DONE AT TOKYO ON 6 SEPTEMBER 1973[1]

The Governments of Japan, of the Kingdom of Norway and of the Union of Soviet Socialist Republics, being Parties to the International Convention for the Regulation of Whaling,[2] signed at Washington on 2 December 1946 (hereafter referred to as "the Convention"):

Have agreed upon the following arrangements:

Article 1

For the purpose of the present Arrangement, the term "season" shall mean the season during which the taking of baleen whales in the Antarctic is permitted under paragraph 7 *(a)* of the Schedule to the Convention.

Article 2

The total annual catches of fin whales and sei and Bryde's whales combined, authorized under the Convention to be taken in waters south of 40° South Latitude by pelagic expeditions, shall be allocated among the countries of the signatory Governments in the following manner:

Japan	867 fin whales
Norway	100 sei and Bryde's whales combined
Union of Soviet Socialist Republics	583 fin whales 1,768 sei and Bryde's whales combined

Article 3

The allocations mentioned in article 2 are not transferable as between one country and another.

Article 4

If a factory ship under the jurisdiction of a Government which is not a Party to the present Arrangement should engage in Antarctic pelagic whaling and that Government is or becomes a Party to the Convention, the present Arrangement shall be terminated.

Article 5

The present Arrangement shall enter into force on the day upon which it is signed by the Governments referred to in the preamble.

---

[1] English text, which is authentic, provided by the Permanent Representative of Norway to the United Nations in a note verbale of 21 January 1974.

[2] United Nations, *Treaty Series*, vol. 161, p. 72. The Convention as amended in 1956 is reproduced in ST/LEG/SER.B/15, pp. 827-831.

Article 6

The present Arrangement shall be operative until the end of 1973/74 season.

5. CONVENTION ON FISHING AND CONSERVATION OF THE LIVING RESOURCES IN THE BALTIC SEA AND THE BELTS, DONE AT GDANSK ON 13 SEPTEMBER 1973[1]

The States Parties to this Convention

Bearing in mind that maximum and stable productivity of the living resources of the Baltic Sea and the Belts is of great importance to the States of the Baltic Sea basin;

Recognizing their joint responsibility for the conservation of the living resources and their national exploitation;

Being convinced that the conservation of the living resources of the Baltic Sea and the Belts calls for closer and more expanded co-operation in this region,

have agreed as follows:

Article I

The Contracting States shall:

Co-operate closely with a view to preserving and increasing the living resources of the Baltic Sea and the Belts and obtaining the optimum yield, and, in particular to expanding and co-ordinating studies towards these ends;

Prepare and put into effect organizational and technical projects on conservation and growth of the living resources, including measures of artificial reproduction of valuable fish species and/or contribute financially to such measures, on a just and equitable basis, as well as take other steps towards rational and effective exploitation of the living resources.

Article II

1. The area to which this Convention applies, hereinafter referred to as "the Convention area", shall be all waters of the Baltic Sea and the Belts, excluding internal waters, bounded in the west by a line as from Hasenore Head to Gniben Point, from Korshage to Spodsbierg and from Gilbierg Head to the Kullen.

2. This Convention shall apply to all fish species and other living marine resources in the Convention area.

---

[1] Signed by Denmark, Finland, German Democratic Republic, Federal Republic of Germany, Polish People's Republic, Sweden and the Union of Soviet Socialist Republics. English text, which is authentic, transmitted by the Deputy Minister for Foreign Affairs of the Polish People's Republic with a letter dated 15 October 1973 addressed to the Chairman of the First Committee (GAOR, twenty-eighth session, agenda item 40, document A/C.1/1035—mimeographed).

Article III

Nothing in this Convention shall be deemed to affect the rights, claims or views of any Contracting State in regard to the limits of territorial waters and to the extent of jurisdiction over fisheries, according to international law.

Article IV

For the purpose of this Convention the term "vessel" means any vessel or boat employed in catching or treating fish or other living marine organisms and which is registered or owned in the territory of, or which flies the flag of, any Contracting State.

Article V

1. An International Baltic Sea Fishery Commission, hereinafter referred to as "the Commission", is hereby established for the purposes of this Convention.

2. Each Contracting State may appoint not more than two representatives as members of the Commission and such experts and advisers to assist them as that State may determine.

3. The Commission shall elect a Chairman and a Vice-Chairman from amongst its members who shall serve for a period of four years and who shall be eligible for re-election, but not for two consecutive terms of office.

The Chairman and the Vice-Chairman shall be elected from the representatives of different Contracting States.

4. A member of the Commission elected as its Chairman shall forthwith cease to act as a representative of a State and shall not vote. The State concerned shall have the right to appoint another representative to serve in the Chairman's place.

Article VI

1. The Office of the Commission shall be in Warsaw.

2. The Commission shall appoint its Secretary and as it may require appropriate staff to assist him.

3. The Commission shall adopt its rules of procedure and other provisions which the Commission shall consider necessary for its work.

Article VII

1. The Commission shall adopt its financial rules.

2. The Commission shall adopt a two years budget of proposed expenditures and budget estimates for the fiscal period following thereafter.

3. The total amount of the budget including any supplementary budget shall be contributed by the Contracting States in equal parts.

4. Each Contracting State shall pay the expenses related to the participation in the Commission of its representatives, experts and advisers.

Article VIII

1. Except where the Commission decides otherwise, it shall hold its sessions every two years in Warsaw at such time as it shall deem suitable. Upon the request of a representative of a Contracting State in the Commission, provided it is endorsed by a representative of another Contracting State, the Chairman of the Commission shall, as soon as possible, summon an extraordinary session at such time and place as he determines, however not later than three months from the date of the submission of the request.

2. The first session of the Commission shall be called by the Depositary Government of this Convention and shall take place within a period of ninety days from the date following the entry into force of this Convention.

3. Each Contracting State shall have one vote in the Commission. Decisions and recommendations of the Commission shall be taken by a two-thirds majority of votes of the Contracting States, present and voting at the meeting.

4. English shall be the working language of the Commission. The languages of the Signatory States are the official languages of the Commission. Only recommendations, decisions and resolutions of the Commission shall be made in these languages.

At meetings of the Commission any Contracting State has the right to have all the proceedings translated into its own language. All the costs related to such translations shall be borne by that State.

Article IX

1. It shall be the duty of the Commission:

(a) To keep under review the living resources and the fisheries in the Convention area by collecting, aggregating, analysing and disseminating statistical data, for example concerning catch, fishing effort, and other information;

(b) To work out proposals with regard to co-ordination of scientific research in the Convention area;

(c) To prepare and submit recommendations based as far as practicable on results of the scientific research and concerning measures referred to in Article X for consideration of the Contracting States.

2. In implementing its functions, the Commission shall, when appropriate, seek the services of the International Council for the Exploration of the Sea (ICES) and of other international technical and scientific organizations and shall make use of information provided by the official bodies of the Contracting States.

3. To perform its functions the Commission may set up working groups or other subsidiary bodies and determine their composition and terms of reference.

Article X

Measures relating to the purposes of this Convention which the Commission may consider and in regard of which it may make recommendations to the Contracting States are:

(a) Any measures for the regulation of fishing gear, appliances and catching methods;

(b) Any measures regulating the size limits of fish that may be retained on board vessels or landed, exposed or offered for sale;

(c) Any measures establishing closed seasons;

(d) Any measures establishing closed areas;

(e) Any measures improving and increasing the living marine resources, including artificial reproduction and transplantation of fish and other organisms;

(f) Any measures regulating and/or allocating between the Contracting States the amount of total catch or the amount of fishing effort according to objects, kinds, regions and fishing periods;

(g) Any measures of control over the implementation of recommendations binding on the Contracting States;

(h) Any other measures related to the conservation and rational exploitation of the living marine resources.

Article XI

1. Subject to the provisions of this Article, the Contracting States undertake to give effect to any recommendation made by the Commission under Article X of this Convention from the date determined by the Commission, which shall not be before the period for objection provided for in this Article has elapsed.

2. Any Contracting State may within ninety days from the date of notification of a recommendation object to it and in that event shall not be under obligation to give effect to that recommendation.

A Contracting State may also at any time withdraw its objection and give effect to a recommendation.

In the event of an objection being made within the ninety-days period, any other Contracting State may similarly object at any time within a further period of sixty days.

3. If objections to a recommendation are made by three or more Contracting States, the other Contracting States shall be relieved forthwith of any obligation to give effect to that recommendation.

4. The Commission shall notify each Contracting State immediately upon receipt of each objection or withdrawal.

Article XII

1. Each Contracting State shall take in regard to its nationals and its vessels appropriate measures to ensure the application of the provisions of

this Convention and of the recommendations of the Commission which have become binding for the Contracting State and in case of their infringement shall take appropriate action.

2. Without prejudice to the sovereign rights of the Contracting States in regard to their territorial sea and to the rights in their fishing zones, each Contracting State shall implement recommendations of the Commission binding on that State through its national authorities, within its territorial sea and in the waters under its fisheries jurisdiction.

3. Each Contracting State shall furnish to the Commission at such time and in such form as may be required by the Commission, the available statistical data and information referred to in Article IX paragraph 1 *(a)*, as well as information on all actions taken by it in accordance with paragraphs 1 and 2 of this Article.

Article XIII

The Commission shall draw the attention of any State which is not a party to this Convention to such fishing operations, undertaken by its nationals or vessels in the Convention area, which might affect negatively the activities of the Commission or the implementation of the purposes of this Convention.

Article XIV

The provisions of this Convention shall not apply to operations conducted solely for the purpose of scientific investigations by vessels authorized by a Contracting State for that purpose, or to fish and other marine organisms taken in the course of such operations. Catch so taken shall not be sold, exposed or offered for sale.

Article XV

1. The Commission shall co-operate with other international organizations having related objectives.

2. The Commission may extend an invitation to any international organization concerned or to the Government of any State, not a party to this Convention, to participate as an observer in the sessions of the Commission or meetings of its subsidiary bodies.

Article XVI

1. Each Contracting State may propose amendments to this Convention. Any such proposed amendment shall be submitted to the Depositary Government and communicated by it to all Contracting States, which shall inform the Depositary Government about either their acceptance or rejection of the amendment as soon as possible after the receipt of the communication.

The amendment shall enter into force ninety days after the Depositary Government has received notifications of acceptance of that amendment from all Contracting States.

2. Each State which shall become a party to this Convention after the entry into force of an amendment in accordance with the provisions of paragraph 1 of this Article, is obliged to apply the Convention as amended.

Article XVII

1. This Convention shall be subject to ratification or approval by the Signatory States. Instruments of ratification or instruments of approval shall be deposited with the Government of the Polish People's Republic which shall perform the functions of the Depositary Government.

2. This Convention shall be open for accession to any State interested in preservation and rational exploitation of living resources in the Baltic Sea and the Belts, provided that this State is invited by the Contracting States. Instruments of accession shall be deposited with the Depositary Government.

Article XVIII

1. This Convention shall enter into force on the ninetieth day following the date of the deposit of the fourth instrument of ratification or approval.

2. After entry into force of this Convention in accordance with paragraph 1 of this Article, the Convention shall enter into force for any other State, the Government of which has deposited an instrument of ratification, approval or accession. on the thirtieth day following the date of deposit of such instrument with the Depositary Government.

Article XIX

At any time after the expiration of five years from the date of entry into force of this Convention any Contracting State may, by giving written notice to the Depositary Government, withdraw from this Convention.

The withdrawal shall take effect for such Contracting State on the thirty-first of December of the year which follows the year in which the Depositary Government was notified of the withdrawal.

Article XX

1. The Depositary Government shall inform all Signatory and Acceding States:

(a) Of signatures of this Convention and deposit of each instrument of ratification, approval or accession, as well as of submitted declarations;

(b) Of the date of entry into force of this Convention;

(c) Of proposals relating to amendments to the Convention, notifications of acceptance and of the entry into force of such amendments;

(d) Of notifications of withdrawal.

2. The original of this Convention shall be deposited with the Government of the Polish People's Republic, which shall transmit certified copies thereof to the Government of all Signatory States and of all States which accede to this Convention.

3. The Depositary Government shall register this Convention with the Secretariat of the United Nations.

In witness whereof the undersigned Plenipotentiaries, being duly authorized thereto, have signed this Convention.

Done at Gdansk this thirteenth day of September, one thousand nine hundred and seventy three, in a single copy drawn up in the Danish, Finnish, German, Polish, Russian, Swedish and English languages, each text being equally authentic.

6. ARRANGEMENT RELATING TO FISHERIES IN WATERS SURROUNDING THE FAROE ISLANDS, DONE AT COPENHAGEN ON 18 DECEMBER 1973[1]

The Parties to this Arrangement,

Realizing that the scientific evidence available calls for immediate measures for the purpose of conservation of fish stocks in the Faroe Area (ICES Statistical Division V_b);

Considering the exceptional dependence of the Faroese economy on fisheries; and

Recognizing that the Faroe Islands should enjoy preference in waters surrounding the Faroe Islands;

Have agreed as follows:

Article 1

The fishing for the demersal species cod and haddock in the ICES Statistical Division V_b shall be limited annually as prescribed in the catch limitation scheme annexed hereto (Annex I),[2] which shall be an integral part of the present Arrangement.

Article 2

1. Contracting Parties directing their fisheries in the area solely towards demersal species other than those covered by article 1 shall not conduct their demersal fisheries in a way significantly different from those of the years 1968 to 1972.

Their annual catches from trawl fisheries shall not exceed by more than 10 per cent the highest figure they have respectively achieved in those years as recorded by the International Council for the Exploration of the Sea.

2. The annual catches of Parties to whom paragraph 1 applies and whose fleets fish solely by line and gill-nets in the area, shall not exceed by more than 25 per cent the highest figure achieved over the years 1968 to 1972 as recorded by the International Council for the Exploration of the Sea.

---

[1] United Nations, *Treaty Series*, vol. 925, No. I-13185. Entered into force on 1 January 1974 in accordance with article 6. Parties to the Arrangement are: Belgium, Denmark, France, the Federal Republic of Germany, Norway, Poland and the United Kingdom.

[2] Annex I is not reproduced in this volume.

3. Contracting Parties which have not habitually exercised fishing in the area shall limit their annual catches of demersal species mentioned in paragraph 1 to a maximum of 2,000 tons each.

Article 3

1. The sub-areas identified on the chart and accompanying description annexed hereto (Annexes II and III)[1] shall be closed for trawl fishing by vessels of all the Contracting Parties annually during the following months:

sub-area 1: 15 February to 15 May

sub-area 2: 1 June to 30 November

sub-area 3: 1 April to 30 June and 1 October to 31 December

sub-area 4: 1 December to 31 March and 1 May to 31 May

sub-area 5: 1 March to 31 March.

2. The maximum allowable size in terms of Gross Register Tons of trawlers fishing within the sub-areas mentioned in paragraph 1 shall not exceed the size habitually used before the end of the year 1973.

Article 4

Notwithstanding the provisions in article 3 small Faroese vessels may continue trawl fishing in the sub-areas mentioned in article 3.1 for the following annual quantities of demersal stocks:

In sub-area 2: 1,250 tons

In sub-area 3: 1,250 tons

In sub-area 4: 500 tons.

These quotas form part of the total Faroese quota according to the catch limitation scheme annexed hereto.

Article 5

Nothing in the present Arrangement shall be deemed to prejudice the views of any Contracting Party as to the delimitation and limits in international law of territorial waters, adjacent zones or jurisdiction in fishery matters.

Article 6

1. The present Arrangement shall enter into force on 1 January 1974.

2. Any Contracting Party may request a review of the Arrangement.

3. Any Contracting Party may withdraw from the Arrangement by means of a notice in writing addressed to the depositary Government who will notify the other Contracting Parties. Any such denunciation shall take effect six months after the date on which such notice is given.

. . .

---

[1] The annexes are not reproduced in this volume.

Subdivision B.   Bilateral Treaties

1.   AGREEMENT BETWEEN BRAZIL AND THE NETHERLANDS CONCERNING SHRIMP, DONE AT BRASILIA ON 13 DECEMBER 1972[1]

The Parties to this Agreement

Note the position of the Government of the Federative Republic of Brazil,

That it considers its territorial sea to extend to a distance of 200 nautical miles from Brazil's coast,

That the exploitation of crustaceans and other living resources, which are closely dependent on the sea-bed under the Brazilian territorial sea, is reserved to Brazilian fishing vessels,

And

That exceptions to this provision can only be granted through international agreements,

Note also the position of the Government of the Kingdom of the Netherlands that it does not consider itself obligated under international law to recognize territorial sea claims of more than 3 nautical miles nor fisheries jurisdiction of more than 12 nautical miles, beyond which zone of jurisdiction all nations have the right to fish freely, and that it does not consider that all crustaceans are living organisms belonging to sedentary species as defined in the 1958 Geneva Convention on the Continental Shelf, and further,

Recognizing that the difference in the respective juridical positions of the Parties has given rise to certain problems relating to the conduct of shrimp fisheries,

Considering the tradition of both Parties for resolving international differences by having recourse to negotiations,

Believing that their common interests as coastal states in the conservation of shrimp resources should be effectively safeguarded and their diverging interests regarding shrimping reconciled, and that therefore it is desirable to arrive at an interim solution for the conduct of shrimp fisheries without prejudicing either Party's legal position concerning the extent of territorial seas or fisheries jurisdiction under international law,

Concluding that, while general international solutions to issues of maritime jurisdiction are being sought, it is desirable to conclude the following interim Agreement,

---

[1] United Nations, *Treaty Series,* vol. 903, No. I.12891. In force on 1 January 1973 until 1 January 1974 in accordance with article XIV. Extended to 30 June and 31 December 1974 by exchanges of Notes effected, respectively, 31 December 1973 and 24 June 1974 (TIAS 7770 and 7862).

574

Have agreed as follows:

Article I

This Agreement will by no means establish any precedent as to the contents of any subsequent agreement.

Article II

Nothing contained in this Agreement shall be interpreted as prejudicing the position of either Party regarding the matter of territorial seas or fisheries jurisdiction under international law.

Article III

This Agreement shall apply to the fishery for shrimp:

(a) Of the species Penacus (M) duorarum notialis, Penacus brasiliensis and Penacus (M) aztecus subtilis;

(b) In an area having the isobath of thirty (30) metres as the south-west limit and the latitude 1° north as the southern limit and 47° 30' west longitude as the eastern limit;

(c) During a season limited to the period from 1 March to 30 November. However, shrimp fishing in that part of the above-mentioned area south-east of a bearing of 240° from Ponta do Céu radio-beacon shall be limited to the period 1 March to 1 July;

(d) By twenty (20) Surinam vessels flying the Kingdom of the Netherlands flag.

Article IV

Taking into account their common interests in the conservation of shrimp resources, the Parties agree that in the conduct of shrimping activities destructive practices in general should be prevented, in particular the following:

(a) The use of gear and equipment known to have destructive effects on the stocks, including electric equipment for fishing purposes;

(b) The use of chemical, toxic or explosive substances in or near the fishing areas;

(c) The discharge of oil and organic waste;

(d) Fishing in spawning and breeding areas.

Article V

1. Information on catch and effort and biological data relating to shrimp fisheries in the area defined in Article III shall be collected and exchanged by the Parties.

2. Each vessel fishing under this Agreement shall maintain a fishing log, according to the model provided for in the Annex.[1] Such fishing logs shall be

---

[1] Not reproduced in this volume.

delivered quarterly to the appropriate Party which shall use the data therein contained, and other information it obtains about the area defined in Article III, to prepare reports which shall be transmitted periodically to the other Party as appropriate.

3. Duly appointed organizations from both Parties shall meet in due time to exchange scientific data, publications and knowledge acquired on the shrimp fisheries in the area defined in Article III.

Article VI

1. The Party which under Article VII has the responsibility for enforcing observance of the terms of this Agreement by vessels of the other Party's flag shall receive from the latter Party the information necessary for identification and other enforcement functions, including the name of the vessel, copies of the documents of the vessel (registry certificate, up-to-date seaworthiness certificates, insurance certificate) port of registry, port where operations are usually based, general description and photograph in profile, radio frequencies by which communication may be established, main engine horsepower and speed, length (which shall not exceed eighty-five feet) and fishing methods and gear employed.

2. Such information shall be assembled and organized by the flag Government and communications relating to such information shall be carried out each year through diplomatic channels.

3. The Party which receives such information shall verify whether it is complete and in good order, and shall inform the other Party about the vessels found to comply with the requirements of paragraph 1 of this Article, as well as about those which would for some reason, require further consultation among the Parties.

4. Each of these vessels found in order shall receive and display an identification sign as provided for in the Annex.[1]

Article VII

The Parties agree that for the implementation in a specific shrimping area of measures pertinent to the attainment of objectives as those pursued in a bilateral agreement such as the present one, enforcement by one of the Parties is needed. They further agreed that, despite the difference in their respective legal positions as to the extent of territorial waters and fisheries jurisdiction, and without prejudice to said positions, it shall be incumbent on the Government of the Federative Republic of Brazil to ensure the proper conduct of shrimp fisheries in the area defined in Article III.

Article VIII

1. A duly authorized official of the Government of the Federative Republic of Brazil, in exercising the responsibility described in Article VII may, if he has reasonable cause to believe that any provision of this

---

[1] Not reproduced in this volume.

Agreement has been infringed, board and search a shrimp fishing vessel. Such action shall not unduly hinder fishing operations. When, after boarding or boarding and searching a vessel, the official continues to have reasonable cause to believe that any provision of this Agreement has been infringed, he may seize and detain such vessel. In the case of boarding or seizure and detention of a Surinam vessel, the Government of the Federative Republic of Brazil shall promptly inform the Government of the Kingdom of the Netherlands of its action.

2. After compliance with the provision of item *(c)* of Article XI, a Surinam vessel seized and detained under the terms of this Agreement shall, as soon as practicable, be delivered to an authorized official of the Kingdom of the Netherlands at the nearest Brazilian port to the place of seizure, or any other place which is mutually acceptable to the competent authorities of both Parties. The Government of the Federative Republic of Brazil shall, after delivering such vessel to an authorized official of the Kingdom of the Netherlands, provide a certified copy of the full report of the infringement and the circumstances of the seizure and detention.

3. If the nature of the infringement warrants it, and after carrying out the provision of Article XIII, vessels may also suffer forfeiture of that part of the catch determined to be taken illegally and forfeiture of the fishing gear.

4. In the case of vessels delivered to an authorized official of the Kingdom of the Netherlands under paragraph 2 of this Article, the Government of the Federative Republic of Brazil will be informed of the institution and disposition of any case by the Kingdom of the Netherlands.

Article IX

The vessels mentioned in Article III shall land the catch in Surinam, trans-shipment being permitted only between said vessels.

Article X

The Parties shall examine the possibilities of co-operating in the development of their fishing industries; the expansion of the international trade of fishery products; the improvement of storage, transportation and marketing of fishery products; and the encouragement of joint ventures between the fishing industries of the two Parties.

Article XI

In connexion with the enforcement arrangements specified in Article VII, including any unusual incurred in carrying out under the terms of paragraph 1 of Article VIII, the seizure and detention of a Surinam vessel registered in accordance with paragraph 1 of Article VI, the Government of the Federative Republic of Brazil will be compensated in the following amounts:

(a) US$ 100.00 (one hundred USA dollars) per vessel for each month of operation in the 1972 season, this amount being calculated from a date one month following the date on which the information on the vessel is

considered complete and in good order, according to paragraph 3 of Article VI;

(b) US$ 900.00 (nine hundred USA dollars) per vessel for the 1973 season;

(c) US$ 100.00 (one hundred USA dollars) for each day a vessel is detained by Brazilian enforcement authorities, pursuant to the terms of paragraph 1 of Article VIII.

Article XII

At the request of either Party, both Parties shall, within one month, conduct consultations for a review of the operation of this Agreement or of its provisions.

Article XIII

Problems concerning the interpretation and implementation of this Agreement shall be resolved through diplomatic channels.

Article XIV

This Agreement shall enter into force on 1 January 1973 and shall remain in force until 1 January 1974, unless the Parties agree to extend it.

2. EXCHANGE OF NOTES BETWEEN THE GOVERNMENT OF CANADA AND THE GOVERNMENT OF THE STATE OF SPAIN CONCERNING FISHERIES RELATIONS BETWEEN THE TWO COUNTRIES, DONE AT OTTAWA ON 18 DECEMBER 1972[1]

I

Canadian note

Ottawa, 18 December 1972

No. FLA-672

Excellency,

I have the honour to refer to the negotiations which have taken place between representatives of our Governments concerning the amendments of 26 June 1970, to the Territorial Sea and Fishing Zones Act of Canada,[2] and the designation, by Order in Council P.C. 1971-366 of 25 February 1971,[3] of certain areas of the sea adjacent to the coast of Canada as fishing zones of Canada. In accordance with the understanding reached in these negotiations the Canadian Government proposes the following:

---

[1] United Nations, *Treaty Series,* vol. 869, No. 12480. Entered into force on 18 December 1972.

[2] The Act as amended is reproduced in part in ST/LEG/SER.B/16, pp. 4-6.

[3] The Order is reproduced in part *Ibid.*, pp. 286-288.

1. The Government of Canada and the Government of the Spanish State will examine jointly the possibility of entering into an agreement providing for bilateral co-operation with respect to their future fishery relations on such matters as: conservation and management of the living resources of the sea; exchanges of scientific information between Governments and the provision of scientific and technical information to the fishermen of both countries; exchanges of technical personnel; studies of the economic and social aspects of the fishing of both countries relevant to possible future economic co-operation on fishery matters; arrangements to ensure co-operation in orderly methods of fishing; collaboration on problems of contamination of fisheries; joint oceanographic research; and the creation of a joint *ad hoc* commission to carry out such functions including settlement of disputes as may contribute to future fisheries co-operation between the two countries.

2. Spanish fishing vessels may continue to fish for cod by trawl until 30 November 1978, in those areas of the outer nine miles of the territorial sea of Canada where such vessels have fished during the period of five years immediately preceding 31 December 1970, subject to the provisions of subparagraphs 4, 5 and 7. These areas are illustrated on the charts marked as Annexes A and B[1] to this Note. The territorial sea on the Atlantic coast of Canada is measured from baselines as determined by the provisions of Annex C to this Note.

3. Spanish fishing vessels may continue to fish in the Gulf of St. Lawrence for cod by trawl in the months of January to July inclusive until 31 July 1976, in the area illustrated on the attached chart marked as Annex A to this Note, subject to the provisions of subparagraphs 4 and 5.

4. Spanish fishing vessels operating in the area referred to in subparagraphs 2 and 3 shall be subject, without discrimination in form or fact, to the same laws and regulations as Canadian fishing vessels. The Canadian authorities shall inform the Spanish authorities, within one month of the coming into force of the present agreement, of the fishing laws and regulations applicable to the said areas.

5. If at any time before 31 May 1978, the Canadian Government considers that there has been a substantial change in the intensity, character or pattern of the fishing activities carried out by Spanish vessels in any of the areas referred to in subparagraphs 2 and 3, the Canadian Government may raise the matter with the Spanish Government and both Governments shall review the situation jointly.

6. The Canadian Government undertakes to review in good faith at the request of the Government of the Spanish State the provisions of this exchange of Notes prior to the expiration of the periods referred to in subparagraphs 2 and 3, including the consideration of a continuance of the Spanish fishing effort in the areas covered by the present Agreement, on the basis of a licence or licences to be determined by the Canadian Government taking into account the nature, extent and social and economic characteristics of the Spanish fishing effort, and the conservation requirements of fishery resources.

---

[1] The annexes are not reproduced in this volume.

7. The Canadian authorities will give the Spanish authorities advance notice of particular areas and periods during which concentrations of gear of inshore fishermen may occur in those areas of the outer nine miles of the territorial sea of Canada where Spanish trawlers have fished during the period of five years immediately preceding 31 December 1970. The Spanish authorities will transmit any such information to Spanish trawlers likely to fish in such areas and will request such vessels, before actually fishing, to establish communication, as appropriate, with the Regional Fisheries Office of the Canadian Government in Halifax, Nova Scotia, or St. John's, Newfoundland, to obtain current information about the local situation for the purpose of enabling vessels the better to avoid damage to gear. The Spanish Government will not object to action by the Canadian authorities in cases of emergency to direct Spanish fishing vessels clear of gear concentrations, provided that Canadian and other fishing vessels of a similar size and class are subject to the same directions.

8. The present exchange of Notes does not in any way prejudice the position of either Government regarding the status of the waters mentioned herein.

If the foregoing proposals are acceptable to your Government I have the honour to propose that this Note, together with its Annexes, in English and French, and Your Excellency's reply in Spanish, shall constitute an agreement between the Government of Canada and the Government of the Spanish State, the English, French and Spanish versions of which shall be equally authentic. This Agreement shall enter into force on the date of your reply.

Accept, Excellency, the renewed assurances of my highest consideration.

The Secretary of State
for External Affairs

His Excellency Juan José Rovira,
Ambassador of Spain,
Ottawa

II

Spanish note

Embassy of Spain
Ottawa, 18 December 1972

Sir,

. I have the honour to acknowledge receipt of your Note of today's date, of which the Spanish translation reads as follows:

[See English version under note I.]

I have the honour to confirm the agreement of the Spanish Government to the foregoing.

Accept, Sir, the testimony of my highest consideration.

Juan José Rovira
Ambassador of Spain

The Honourable Mitchell Sharp
Minister of External Affairs
Ottawa

3. [AGREEMENT BETWEEN AUSTRALIA AND INDONESIA CONCERNING CERTAIN BOUNDARIES BETWEEN PAPUA NEW GUINEA AND INDONESIA, DONE AT CANBERRA ON 26 JANUARY 1973, ARTICLE 7][1]

4. AGREEMENT BETWEEN CANADA AND THE UNITED STATES OF AMERICA ON RECIPROCAL FISHING PRIVILEGES IN CERTAIN AREAS OFF THEIR COASTS, DONE AT OTTAWA ON 15 JUNE 1973[2]

The Government of Canada and the Government of the United States of America,

Considering that both Governments have established exclusive fishery zones;

Recognizing that fishermen of the two countries have traditionally fished for the same species in certain areas now encompassed within the exclusive fishery zones;

Deeming it desirable to establish the terms and conditions under which nationals and vessels of each of the two countries may conduct, on a reciprocal basis, commercial fishing operations within certain areas off their coasts; and

Having in mind the mutuality of interest on the part of the two countries in the conservation and rational exploitation of certain living marine resources off their coasts;

Have agreed as follows:

1. For the purposes of this Agreement,

(a) The reciprocal fishing area of the United States of America shall be the fishing zone established in 1966 south of 63° north latitude;

(b) The reciprocal fishing area of Canada shall be as follows:

(i) In those "Areas" listed in Order-in-Council P.C. 1967-2025, and Order-in-Council P.C. 1969-1109, issued by the Government of

---

[1] *Supra* Division II, Subdivision B, 7.

[2] United Nations, Treaty Series, vol. 916, No. I-13078. In force on 16 June 1973 until 24 April 1974 in accordance with article 8. Text provided by the Permanent Representative of Canada to the United Nations in a note verbale of 8 January 1975.

Canada on 8 November 1967, and 11 June 1969, respectively, those waters extending 9 miles seaward of the territorial sea of Canada as it existed in 1966;

(ii) In those areas not listed in the Orders-in-Council cited above, those waters south of 63° north latitude which are contiguous to and extend from three to twelve miles from the coast of Canada, with the exception of bays where they cease to exceed 24 miles in breadth.

Nothing in this Agreement shall affect waters other than those referred to in this paragraph

2. Nationals and vessels of each country may continue to fish within the reciprocal fishing area of the other country, except that there shall be no such fishing for the following:

(a) Any species of clam, scallop, crab, shrimp, lobster or herring;

(b) Any salmon other than salmon taken by trolling off the Pacific coasts of the United States and Canada west of a line joining Bonilla Point and Tatoosh Island; north of a line projected due west from Carroll Island (latitude 48° 00.3' North, longitude 124° 43.3' West) and south of a line projected from Bonilla Point to the intersection of the outer limits of the reciprocal fishing areas of the United States and Canada (latitude 48° 29.7' North, longitude 125° 00.7' West);

(c) Any black cod other than:

(i) A catch not to exceed 30,000 pounds annually taken by longline or pot gear off the west coast of Alaska between lines projected southwest (225° true) from Cape Ommaney and Cape Bingham respectively during the open seasons specified for fishing for black cod in the adjacent territorial sea; and

(ii) A catch not to exceed 15,000 pounds off the west coast of Vancouver Island between lines projected southwest (225° true) from Estevan Point and Cape Scott respectively;

(d) Any tuna other than a catch not to exceed 500 tons annually taken south and west of a line projected due east from Chatham Light on Cape Cod. Not more than two Canadian vessels exceeding 150 feet in overall length may take tuna within the area described, and only at such times and in the same general area as that in which United States tuna vessels exceeding 150 feet in overall length are fishing.

Subject to its domestic legislation, each Government will continue to permit transfers of herring between nationals and vessels of the two countries within the reciprocal fishing areas. The Governments agree that the principal purpose of this provision is to enable the continuation of transfers of herring intended for purposes other than reduction.

3. Nationals and vessels of either country will not initiate fisheries within the reciprocal fishing area of the other country for species which are fully utilized by fishermen of the latter country. If fishermen of either country wish to initiate a fishery within any part of the reciprocal fishing area of the other country for species not fully utilized, their Government will first consult with the other Government and reach an understanding concerning conditions for such a fishery.

4. Regulations established by one country pertaining to the taking or possession of fish within its reciprocal fishing area shall apply equally to the nationals and vessels of both countries operating within such area; in areas of the reciprocal fishing area of Canada in which Canadian domestic regulations at present prohibit trawl fishing by vessels exceeding 65 feet in length, such fishing by United States vessels exceeding 65 feet is also prohibited. These regulations shall be enforced by the Government which issued them. Should either Government consider it necessary to alter such fishery regulations, that Government shall notify the other Government of such proposed changes 60 days in advance of their application. Should such changes in fishery regulations require major changes in fishing gear, an adequate period of time, up to one year, will be afforded the nationals and vessels of the other country to adapt to such changes prior to their application.

5. The two Governments recognize the desirability of co-ordinating their regulations for certain salmon fisheries and agree as follows:

(a) The appropriate fishery management authorities of the two countries shall consult frequently with a view to co-ordinating the regulatory measures to be applied by them to the fisheries for coho and chum salmon in British Columbia Statistical Area 20 and Statistical Areas 1 and 2 of the Washington State Department of Fisheries;

(b) With respect to the chinook salmon fishery in the portion of Washington State Statistical Area 1 bounded on the north by the international boundary, on the east by the low-water line bordering the western and southern shores of Point Roberts peninsula, on the south by a line projected from Lily Point to Georgina Point on Mayne Island between Lily Point and its point of intersection with the boundary line, and, on the west by the international boundary and with respect to the chinook salmon fishery in British Columbia Statistical Area 29, the appropriate fisheries officials of the two countries shall consult for the purpose of co-ordinating regulations regarding the open fishing days for the two specified areas. The Canadian officials, when designating the open fishing days for the specified Canadian area, shall give appropriate weight to the needs and interests expressed by the United States officials. The United States officials shall, to the extent consistent with the needs of the United States fishery, designate the same open fishing days for the specified United States areas as are designated for the specified Canadian area and shall, in any case, designate the same number of open fishing days as designated for the specified Canadian area;

(c) With respect to the chum salmon fishery in the section of Washington State Statistical Area 1 westward of Point Roberts peninsula, bounded on the north by the international boundary, on the east by the low-water line of Point Roberts peninsula, and by a line projected from Iverson Dock (Point Roberts) to Turning Point No. 1 of the boundary line in latitude 49° 00′ 08.87″ North and longitude 123° 19′ 17.18″ West, and with respect to the chum salmon fishery in British Columbia Statistical Area 29, the appropriate fisheries officials of the two countries shall consult for the purpose of co-ordinating regulations regarding the open fishing days for the two specified areas. The following provisions shall be applicable from a date agreed by the appropriate fisheries officials of the two countries, which date shall be no earlier than the fifth and no later than the fifteenth of October:

(i) The Canadian officials, when designating the open fishing days for the specified Canadian area, shall give appropriate weight to the needs and interests expressed by the United States officials;

(ii) The United States officials shall designate the same open fishing days for the specific United States area as are set for the specified Canadian area.

6. The two Governments recognize the importance of maintaining the fishery resources in their reciprocal fishing areas at appropriate levels. Both Governments agree to continue and expand co-operation in both national and joint research programmes on species of common interest off their coasts. The appropriate agencies of the two Governments will arrange for exchanges and periodic joint reviews of scientific information.

7. Nothing in this Agreement shall prejudice the claims or views of either of the parties concerning internal waters, territorial waters, or jurisdiction over fisheries or the resources of the continental shelf; further, nothing in this Agreement shall affect either bilateral or multilateral agreements to which either Government is a party.

8. This Agreement shall enter into force on 16 June 1973, and shall remain in force until 24 April 1974. Representatives of the two Governments shall consult prior to expiration of the period of validity of this Agreement with a view to possible amendment and/or extension. However, if the Government of Canada gives notice to the Government of the United States of America of intent to extend its surflines off the west coast of Vancouver Island, and/or extends the troll season for salmon off the west coast of Vancouver Island, the Government of the United States of America may give notice of termination of the Agreement, which termination shall take effect 60 days after the giving of such notice.

5. (i) AGREEMENT CONCERNING THE GRANTING OF THE RIGHT TO FISHING VESSELS OF THE FEDERAL REPUBLIC OF GERMANY TO FISH IN THE MARINE FISHERY ZONE OF THE POLISH PEOPLE'S REPUBLIC, DONE AT WARSAW ON 14 DECEMBER 1973[1]

The Government of the Federal Republic of Germany and the Government of the Polish People's Republic,

Having regard to the Act of 12 February 1970 of the Polish People's Republic concerning the establishment of a maritime fishery zone off the coast of the Polish People's Republic, and

Desirous of developing and strengthening mutual relations and co-operation,

[1] Text provided by the Permanent Representative of the Federal Republic of Germany to the United Nations in a note verbale dated 4 March 1975. Translation by the Secretariat of the United Nations.

Have agreed as follows:

Article 1

(1) Fishing vessels of the Federal Republic of Germany shall be entitled to fish, to the extent indicated in paragraph (2) of this article, in the maritime fishery zone of the Polish People's Republic but outside of the territorial sea of the Polish People's Republic. The seaward boundary of the maritime fishery zone of the Polish People's Republic runs at a distance of 12 nautical miles measured from the baseline of the territorial sea of the Polish People's Republic. The said baseline runs from a point with the co-ordinates 54° 27′ 33″ N. and 19° 38′ 34″ E. to the point 54° 35′ 36″ N. and 18° 48′ 36″ E., thence continuing in a westerly direction along the coast of the Polish People's Republic to a point with the co-ordinates 53° 55′ 45″ N. and 14° 13′ 41″ E.

(2) The right to fish within the maritime fishery zone of the Polish People's Republic in accordance with paragraph (1) of this article shall be valid

(a) Until 31 December 1973 in the area between 3 and 6 nautical miles measured from the baseline of the territorial sea of the Polish People's Republic, and

(b) For an indefinite period in the area between 6 and 12 nautical miles measured from the baseline of the territorial sea of the Polish People's Republic.

(3) The areas mentioned in paragraphs (1) and (2) are indicated more precisely on the annexed official maritime charts Nos. 201 and 202 of the Polish People's Republic[1] which form an integral part of this Agreement.

Article 2

The regulations of the Polish People's Republic concerning maritime fishery and the protection of national frontiers are to be published early enough to enable fishermen to observe them.

Article 3

Pursuant to the Four-Power Agreement of 3 September 1971, this Agreement is extended to cover Berlin (West) in accordance with the established procedures.

Article 4

The Agreement is concluded for an indefinite period. It may be denounced by either Contracting Party by notice in writing and shall in such case become invalid 12 months after the date of receipt of the notice of denunciation.

---

[1] The charts are not reproduced in this volume.

585

Article 5

This Agreement shall enter into force on the date on which the two Governments have notified each other through an exchange of notes that the legal requirements for its entry into force have been fulfilled.

Done at Warsaw on 14 December 1973, in duplicate in the German and Polish languages, both texts being equally authentic.

(ii) EXCHANGES OF LETTERS

I

The Deputy Prime Minister and
  Minister of Shipping of the
  Polish People's Republic

Warsaw, 14 December 1973

Sir,

I have the honour to state that, from the date of the signature of the Agreement between the Government of the Polish People's Republic and the Government of the Federal Republic of Germany concerning the granting of the right to fishing vessels of the Federal Republic of Germany to fish in the marine fishery zone of the Polish People's Republic, the fishing vessels of the Federal Republic of Germany may make use of the right to fish in the area for the period stipulated in article 1, paragraph 2 *(a)*, of the above-mentioned Agreement.

Accept, Sir, the assurances of my highest consideration.

H.E. Dr. Hans Helmuth Ruete
Ambassador
  of the Federal Republic of Germany

II

The Ambassador
  of the Federal Republic of Germany

Warsaw, 14 December 1973

Sir,

I have the honour to acknowledge receipt of your letter of today's date, which reads as follows:

[See note I.]

Accept, Sir, the assurances of my highest consideration.

H.E. Mr. Kazimierz Olszewski
Deputy Prime Minister and
  Minister of Shipping
  of the Polish People's Republic

III

The Ambassador
of the Federal Republic of Germany

Warsaw, 14 December 1973

Sir,

On behalf of the Government of the Federal Republic of Germany, I wish to state that the Government of the Federal Republic of Germany undertakes, in the event of the establishment of a marine fishery zone (contiguous marine fishery zone), to enter forthwith into negotiations with the Government of the Polish People's Republic with a view to granting to fishermen from the Polish People's Republic, on the basis of reciprocity, the same rights as those granted to fishermen from the Federal Republic of Germany in the marine fishery zone of the Polish People's Republic.

Accept, Sir, the assurances of my highest consideration.

H.E. Mr. Kazimierz Olszewski
Deputy Prime Minister and
  Minister of Shipping
  of the Polish People's Republic

IV

The Deputy Prime Minister and
  Minister of Shipping of the
  Polish People's Republic

Warsaw, 14 December 1973

Sir,

I have the honour to acknowledge receipt of your letter of today's date, which reads as follows:

[See note III.]

Accept, Sir, the assurances of my highest consideration.

H.E. Dr. Hans Helmuth Ruete
Ambassador
  of the Federal Republic of Germany

———————